PENGUIN

CANADIAN LITERATURE
IN ENGLISH Texts and Contexts

VOLUME I

Cynthia Sugars
University of Ottawa

Laura Moss
University of British Columbia

PEARSON
Longman

Toronto

Library and Archives Canada Cataloguing in Publication

Canadian literature in English : texts and contexts/edited by Cynthia Sugars, Laura Moss.

Includes bibliographical references and index.
ISBN 978-0-321-31362-1

1. Canadian literature (English).   I. Sugars, Cynthia Conchita, 1963–
II. Moss, Laura F. E. (Laura Frances Errington), 1969–

PS8231.C36 2008   C810.8   C2008-900022-6

ISBN-13: 978-0-321-31362-1
ISBN-10: 0-321-31362-3

Vice President, Editorial Director: Gary Bennett
Acquisitions Editor: Christopher Helsby
Marketing Manager: Sally Aspinall
Supervising Developmental Editor: Suzanne Schaan
Production Editor: Richard di Santo
Copy Editor: Martha Breen
Proofreaders: Barbara Czarnecki, Anne Holloway
Production Coordinator: Janis Raisen
Composition: Integra
Photo research: Gaeby Abrahams, Sandy Cooke, Amanda McCormick
Art Director: Julia Hall
Interior Design: Gail Ferreira Ng-A-Kien
Cover Design: Michelle Bellemare
Cover Image: Veer Incorporated

For permission to reproduce copyrighted material, the publisher gratefully acknowledges the copyright holders listed on page 570, which is considered an extension of this copyright page.

14 V092 15

contents

"Hey, what are you doing?"
she said, and he said
"I'm just standing here
being a Canadian"
and she said "Wow
is that really feasible?"
and he said "Yes
but it requires plenty of imagination."
    —Lionel Kearns, "Public Poem for Manitoulin Island Canada Day"

This anthology has its origins at a conference in Hamilton, Ontario. Both of us happened to be staying at the same bed-and-breakfast, and one early morning over breakfast we started to grumble about having to make up course packs that held all the material we needed to teach our classes in Canadian literature. This led to an egg-and-cereal-induced revelation of our fantasies of the ideal Canadian literature anthology. We had both, separately, been thinking of compiling an anthology that would be more appropriate for the type of teaching we actually do than the Canadian literature collections already available. As we continued chatting, we realized that we shared a similar vision for this, as yet, "imaginary" text. The anthology, we agreed, would include visual materials and contextual pieces alongside important writings by canonical and non-canonical, literary and "non-literary" Canadian authors. It would include the kinds of contextual information we regularly bring to class on overheads or include in course packs. It would take into account the history of the settlement of Canada, while also representing a diversity of voices. It would provide a good sense of the debates surrounding the growth of Canadian literature, including a recognition of the ways this literature was inevitably linked to shifting notions of national identity. Moreover, it would provide substantial cultural–historical commentary on each period and its authors. And it would be fun! We wanted to dispel the myth of the humourless Canadian writer. Destiny had spoken. By the end of the conference, we had decided to co-edit a new anthology of Canadian literature.

Over the past four years we have tried to create something that resembles our vision. It has not been easy. Along the way we have struggled with issues of balance, representation, artistic merit, historical import, and space. Inevitably, we have had to make compromises and omit materials that we would very much like to have included. We have had to wrestle with some difficult questions. For example, how do we address the Eurocentrism of the explorers or the paternalism of settlers without taking an entirely "presentist" approach? How do we respectfully acknowledge the devastation wrought in the invasion of the land that is now Canada and the displacement of original inhabitants of that land? Further, how does one reconcile Duncan Campbell Scott's often beautiful poetry with his imposition of restrictive laws against Native peoples as part of his work in the Department of Indian Affairs, or Nellie McClung's ground-breaking feminism with her support of the sterilization of the "feeble-minded"? We have tried to provide enough contextual discussion to aid in an understanding of these and other questions. In many instances, of course, writers were echoing the ideas of their time. Fleshing out some of the issues surrounding the production and reception of literary works ultimately enhances readers' understanding of them in a way that censoring the authors' writings or ignoring some of the problematic issues surrounding the production of literature does not. We have tried to represent the predominant voices and concerns of each period and to represent voices that were marginalized in those periods. The non-mainstream inclusions are necessarily fewer in the earlier sections because these writers did not have equal access to political power, print, and a broad readership. To represent it otherwise would present a false and revisionist picture of Canadian literary history.

Deciding where to "begin" an anthology of Canadian literature was particularly difficult. Beginning with the period of European exploration is admittedly problematic, since such a perspective seems to take the arrival of Europeans as the starting point of North American culture, which of course it was not. It was also important not to relegate writing by Aboriginal peoples to a moment that is somehow outside of history or culture. We have attempted throughout this anthology to represent the active role indigenous people have played, and continue to play, in shaping the development of modern-day Canada and Canadian writing. While this anthology begins at the historical moment of European contact because of its representation of Canadian literature written in English, we have begun with a prefacing story by contemporary Mohawk writer and teacher Brian Maracle, "The First Words" (2004). This story, alongside an historical map of the traditional Aboriginal territories in North America prior to European invasion, opens the collection not only by retelling one story of the creation of "Turtle Island" (North America), but also by invoking the ceremonial "first words" that preface any instance of storytelling.

In order to facilitate readability, within each section authors are ordered chronologically by year of birth. While some authors' lives span two or even three sections, we have placed them in the section where they had their earliest impact. Under each author's name, poems and short stories are generally arranged chronologically according to first book publication, unless otherwise noted; the date appears in square brackets following each item. When we want to signal the first magazine publication of a poem for chronological purposes, two dates are provided separated by a comma: the first represents the magazine publication date; the second is the first book publication date. However, within the selections from a given book, the order in the book has not necessarily been duplicated. This offered us a little more flexibility to provide logical groupings of poems. Where possible, non-fictional prose pieces have been dated according to the first newspaper or magazine publication (since many of these were not collected into a book in the author's lifetime). Poems and stories are gathered separately under each author's name; in other words, we do not break up the poems with a short story simply because the publication date of the story falls somewhere amidst the poem dates.

A note on language: we have used the terms "First Nations," "Aboriginal" peoples, and "Native" peoples interchangeably in this text to refer to indigenous people in Canada. As several Aboriginal scholars note, these descriptors are capitalized in order to acknowledge that they refer to nations. In the excerpts, we have retained historically specific terms used by the authors such as "Indian," "Esquimaux," and "squaw," even though these are now considered derogatory and/or outdated. Finally, we have retained the term "Ojibway" instead of substituting it with the more contemporary term "Anishinaabe" to remain consistent with historical usage. We have also chosen to capitalize the terms "Black" and "White" when used with reference to "race" categories in order to signal the constructedness of both labels.

This anthology of Canadian literature has six main aims:

1. To provide a chronological survey of English-Canadian poetry, short fiction, pamphlets, nonfiction, and essays, ranging from the sixteenth century to the present. The range of works included in this anthology attests to the richness of the history of Canadian literature. Because we are attempting to cover a large span of time and space, we have had to construct some parameters to limit the inclusions. We have chosen not to include any excerpts from novels or plays on the assumption that they will be assigned as additional texts in most Canadian literature courses. We do, however, include selections from travellers' journals and emigrant guides. The one exception to this rule is Nellie McClung's "The Play" which is taken from her novel *Purple Springs* (1921); based on an actual play entitled "The Women's Parliament" that McClung and other suffragists performed in Winnipeg in 1914, this chapter stands on its own as an important historical and literary document. For practical reasons of space restriction, this is an anthology of Canadian literature written in English, so we do not include literary works in translation. Thus, we do not include stories originally told/written in First Nations languages or Inuktitut, or works originally written in French, or, for example, Icelandic, or Ukrainian. Further, courses in French- and English-Canadian literature tend to be separate in most university literature programs, a division that informs our restriction to the literary history of English-Canadian writing. The only exceptions to the "no translations rule" are the pieces included at the beginning of the anthology by Jacques Cartier, Samuel de Champlain, and the Jesuit missionaries, and the three texts by Inuit witnesses of the Franklin expedition. It is

impossible to paint an historical picture of the early European encounter with North America without some of the early French explorers, since otherwise the anthology would effectively begin *in medias res* (even more than it now does, with the explorers' written accounts superceding the oral stories of First Nations peoples and the Inuit). Cartier, Champlain, and the Jesuits were among the first Europeans to land on the shores of North America and have had a foundational influence on English Canada, not only in terms of the mapping and European settlement of North America, but also in a symbolic/cultural sense. They have become iconographic symbols of the European presence in Canada, and, in a sense, are part of English Canada's (as well as French Canada's) cultural–historical inheritance. We debated how best to represent First Nations and Inuit voices in Volume I of this anthology. To present oral narratives at the beginning of a collection of Canadian writing in English would suggest a formative influence on the subsequent development of Canadian literature that would not be historically accurate. Nevertheless, we are hopeful that the extensive representation of Aboriginal authors in the two volumes of this anthology will go a long way to expanding the Canadian literary and teaching canon to include more Native literature. In the two volumes, we have gathered works into seven sections: I. Narratives of Encounter; II. Narratives of Emigration, Settlement, and Invasion; III. Post-Confederation Period; IV. Turn of the Century; V. Modernism; VI. Contemporary Canada, 1960–1985; and VII. Contemporary Canada, 1985–present.

2. To include contextual materials to accompany the wide range of literary texts, including materials that might be used in classroom teaching, such as political speeches, government documents, maps, photographs, paintings, newspaper articles, cartoons, autobiographical statements, songs, popular culture texts, and essays. Again, because of space restrictions in a project of this scope, we could not include as many of these items as we would have liked. However, we have tried to provide enough of this material to create a reasonable portrait of the important intellectual debates and socio-cultural concerns of each period.

3. To provide extensive historical introductions to each section that present an overview of the period as well as a contextualizing discussion of specific authors and texts included in the anthology. The introductions include information about literary, political, cultural, and social history, print culture, and the "history of the book." We have tried to trace the intellectual and aesthetic debates over the various periods. These are complemented by biographical and literary header-notes for each author. Our hope is that these materials will be of use as background reading as well as constituting distinct teaching documents in themselves.

4. To chart the central debates surrounding the formation of Canadian national literary and cultural traditions, particularly debates about the links between literary production and national identity. In other words, this is a book in part about the consolidation and often contentious definition of Canadian literature

and art. This was an issue that was introduced by the early nineteenth-century writers from as diverse perspectives as Thomas Chandler Haliburton and Susanna Moodie. It was widely debated in the post-Confederation period alongside discussions of Canada's political future and independent status; persisted into the twentieth century, when the question of the "maturity" of Canadian literature gained ascendance in the '20s and '30s; continued into the '40s and '50s in the debates about the "colonial," the "native," and the "cosmopolitan" types of writing in Canada; and found fresh impetus during the period of ardent cultural nationalism of the 1960s and '70s. While Canadian cultural nationalism in a literary sense began as a means of distinguishing a specifically Canadian artistic ethos in a new land, its entrenchment by the 1970s meant that it needed to be updated to reflect the realities of contemporary Canadian demographics and artistic production. The endeavour to articulate a unified national identity that dominated the 1960s and '70s (formed around ideas of endurance, survival, isolation, and victimization) was displaced in the '90s and 2000s by concerns over who is included and excluded in such a conception of the nation.

In all of these discussions, three questions have been raised: What, if anything, is distinctive about Canadian literature (and, by extension, how does one define the qualifier "Canadian")? What is the connection between literature and nation? How does Canadian literature fit within an international literary context? These questions continue into the present day, when nation-based designations have become increasingly questioned in the context of diasporic migration, global culture, and transnationalism. Yet, as the historical snapshot of the debates included here reveals, transnationalism is not a new phenomenon, as many of the earlier writers knew only too well. Moreover, the difficulty—or impossibility, or undesirability, according to various points of view—of extracting an overarching Canadian national identity from a mix of highly disparate peoples (in terms of literary histories, languages, race, ethnicity, religion, geography, or political allegiance) was present in the formulation of the BNA Act in 1867 and continued into the debates surrounding Canada's official multiculturalism policy in the 1970s and '80s, as well as in the debates around cultural and institutional citizenship in recent years. Tracing these central debates over the past several hundred years reminds us that the issues we consider vital today are not necessarily new, even if they are differently formulated.

5. To gather works that make intertextual reference to one another. Such intertextuality articulates the authors' notions of community and literary history, as well as showing them to be writing from within a literary tradition or writing back to it. For example, John Franklin's disastrous expedition of 1821 is taken up in the twentieth century by Rudy Wiebe's essay "Exercising Reflection" and Margaret Atwood's short story "The Age of Lead." Duncan Campbell Scott's poems about Native peoples are given a new twist when placed beside Armand Garnet Ruffo's poem about Scott. Similarly, Morley Callaghan's "Loppy Phelan's

Double Shoot" and Ruffo's "Grey Owl" poems look back to the earlier selections by Grey Owl (Archibald Belaney), while Susanna Moodie's account of her settlement in the backwoods finds subsequent treatment in Atwood's poetry sequence *The Journals of Susanna Moodie*. The intellectual in-fighting both within a period and between periods is another kind of intertextuality. It shows the lack of unanimity on central issues among the public figures of a given period. Nellie McClung's "Speaking of Women," for instance, is a direct response to Stephen Leacock's essay of the previous year, "The Woman Question." Battles between poetic movements also fall into this category. Most famous of these is F.R. Scott's parody of the previous generation of Canadian writers in his poem "The Canadian Authors Meet," but this rejection of poetic predecessors is also evident in A.J.M. Smith's "Rejected Preface" to *The New Provinces* (1936). Similarly, the Kootenay School of poets were responding to the TISH poets of the 1960s, who were reworking the modernists, who were rejecting the Confederation poets, who were rethinking the Romantics before them. And yet all are working within a continuing tradition of poetry in Canada.

Intertextuality is also sometimes thematic; there are numerous works that develop similar subject matter. For example, the role of the CPR in Canadian history and culture is given extended treatment in Sara Jeannette Duncan's *A Social Departure* and E.J. Pratt's long poem, "Towards the Last Spike," and is later explored in such poems and songs as F.R. Scott's "All the Spikes But the Last," and Gordon Lightfoot's "Canadian Railroad Trilogy." Similarly, the environment (nature, animals, weather, ecology) plays a large and dynamic role in many of the works in this anthology. How can one begin to list the many evocative and often metaphysical stories and poems that treat the Canadian winter? Pieces include Anna Jameson's discovery of winter cold, Frederick Philip Grove's "Dawn and Diamonds," Margaret Avison's "Snow," P.K. Page's "Stories of Snow," and Patrick Lane's beautiful collection of poems, *Winter*.

6. To be representative of different regions, ethnicities, histories, and gender identities. In keeping with the changing demographics of Canada, we have tried to reflect the increasingly multicultural presence in the country's literatures (as well as the vibrant debates around topics such as racism, citizenship, institutions, and belonging). We have included a substantial representation of writing by Aboriginal authors across the sections of this anthology. This is the case more in the second volume than the first. Still, in Volume I we have included selections from the Indian Act to read beside Scott's poetry and George Copway's conversion narrative. Pauline Johnson and George Henry illustrate different sides of the performative elements of indigeneity and cultivation. Brant's letter concerning land claims can be read alongside the impassioned speech of Deskaheh over a

century later on land rights. In Volume II we have included poetry, fiction, and essays by a wide range of indigenous writers, storytellers, and public intellectuals. The voices of other under-represented Canadians are also present here in a variety of genres: for example, in Volume I, we have included a selection from the memoir of Boston King, a Black Loyalist, and a selection from Mary Ann Shadd's emigration pamphlet promoting Canada West to fugitive slaves. In Volume II, we have included works by "African Canadian" and "Africadian" writers as well as writers of the African, Asian, and South Asian diasporas. Further, Edith Maude Eaton's (Sui Sin Far's) "A Plea for the Chinaman," published in the *Montreal Daily Star* in 1896, is included alongside the more canonical writers of the Confederation period, and can be read in tandem with the excerpt from the Chinese Immigration Act of 1885, as well as with subsequent works such as F.R. Scott's "All the Spikes but the Last," Robert Kroetsch's "Elegy for Wong Toy," Madeleine Thien's "Simple Recipes," and excerpts from Fred Wah's biotext *Diamond Grill*. We have included historical documents that stand also as cultural documents, signifying important moments in Canadian life that have been "written back to" by poets, playwrights, and fiction writers since the events themselves: the photograph of the *Komagata Maru*, for example, stands as a reminder of the history of racism in Canada. In Volume II we include a series of texts relating to Newfoundland's contentious entry into Confederation. In Volume II we also include a cluster of documents outlining the development and responses to the Canadian policy of multiculturalism; these include excerpts from the Multiculturalism Act of 1985/88 and subsequent discussions of Canadian multiculturalism by several prominent cultural theorists. Finally, in both volumes we have attempted to show the evolving debates around gender concerns—"the man and woman question," as Jessie Sime's narrator terms it in *Sister Woman*. These debates range in topic from discussions of education and the changing role of women and men in the home and the community to issues of public citizenship, voting rights, and equality in the workplace. Important texts by Agnes Maule Machar, Sara Jeannette Duncan, Emily Murphy, Nellie McClung, and L.M. Montgomery all participate in the debates about education, maternalism, and the "New Woman" in Canadian society.

* * *

Lionel Kearns, in the poem provided as the epigraph above, suggests that "being a Canadian . . . requires plenty of imagination." So what is this "thing" called Canada, and how have Canadian writers chosen to imagine it over the centuries? Margaret Atwood defined it as a "shared set of circumstances," though undoubtedly a set of circumstances that is continually changing. As Geoff Pevere and Grieg Dymond put it in their 1996 study of Canadian popular culture, *Mondo Canuck*, "to be Canadian . . . is to exist in a state of constant becoming" (viii). This anthology explores this "becoming" from many perspectives. There is certainly no single, recognizable way of "writing" about Canada. According to Jacques Cartier, perhaps the first European explorer of what is today known as the St. Lawrence Seaway, Canada was the "land God gave to Cain." Two and a half centuries later, George Cartwright echoed these words when he wrote that people might be drawn to the conclusion "that this country was the last which God made, and that he had no other view than to throw together there, the refuse of his materials, as of no use to mankind" (341–42). Voltaire's famous lines about Canada in his satire *Candide* in 1759 dismiss the country as "a few acres of snow" (*quelques arpents de neige*), a sentiment that has been echoed down through the centuries, from Frances Brooke's complaint in her novel *The History of Emily Montague* (1769) that in Canada "the faculties of the mind are benumbed for half the year" to Gilles Vigneault's well-known celebration of the Canadian climate, "Mon pays, . . . c'est l'hiver" (1965). Northrop Frye's point that "the colonial position of Canada is [. . .] a frostbite at the roots of the Canadian imagination" (134) is countered in the dust jacket copy for *The Blasted Pine* (1957), an anthology of poems selected by Smith and Scott, noting how consistently and with what ferocity Canadian poets have employed strategies of irony and self-mockery: "almost as soon as Canadian poets appeared they were sounding a disrespectful note—a loud raspberry which echoes rudely down the corridors of history to our own day." Working well within this vein, Earle Birney wrote a number of biting and satirical poems, including "Up Her Canada" and "I Accuse Us," an anti-Vietnam war poem that rages at Canadian self-congratulation.

Ray Smith's 1969 collection of short stories, *Cape Breton is the Thought-Control Centre of Canada*, contains a surprising description of North America as "a large island to the west of the continent of Cape Breton" (72). In one short line, Smith manages to shake up received assumptions about the geography of Canada. In their very complexity these different historical threads, many of which contradict one another, exemplify the epigraph, taken from John Berger, to Michael Ondaatje's 1987 novel *In the Skin of a Lion*, "Never again will a single story be told as though it were the only one." Hopefully this anthology provides enough snapshots of times and places to achieve a sense of how many stories have been imagined within Canada.

* * *

We wish to thank many people for contributing ideas and suggestions to this anthology. Legions of people have commented on the project from conception to actualization. Because of the scope of this project, we have sought a great deal of expert advice along the way. A few instances of academic generosity stand out in each volume. We would like to thank John Steckley for letting us read his unpublished essay on "The Huron Carol" and for permission to use his translation of the song, Janice Fiamengo for the idea of including different versions of A.J.M. Smith's "The Lonely Land," and Roy Miki for suggesting specific letters from his edited book of Muriel Kitigawa's letters, *This Is My Own*. We'd also like to acknowledge the spirit of academic community exemplified by Carole Gerson and Gwendolyn Davies who shared with us their recent discovery that the marriage poem "Advice to Mrs. Mowat," included in their edited anthology *Canadian Poetry: From the Beginnings Through the First World War* (1994), was not so much the work of its attributed author, Anne Hecht, as her adaptation of a circulating text. We also appreciate the generosity of the following people who deserve our sincere thanks for their comments and opinions: Jennifer Andrews, Albert Braz, Robert J. Brown, Diana Brydon, Rob Budde, Alison Calder, Warren Cariou, Mridula Chakraborty, Mary Chapman, Sally Chivers, Carrie Dawson, Gwendolyn Davies, Glenn Deer, Jennifer Delisle, Debra Dudek, Marta Dvorak, John Eustace, Margery Fee, Janice Fiamengo, Carole Gerson, Susan Gingell, Terry Goldie, Sherrill Grace, Lisa Grekul, Beverley Haun, the late Gabi Helms, Erin Hurley, Douglas Ivison, Gillian Jerome, Brian Johnson, Chelva Kanaganayakam, Patrick Langston, Larissa Lai, Virginia Lavin, Gerald Lynch, Karen Macfarlane, Ian McLeish, Travis Mason, Kevin McNeilly, Roy Miki, Leslie Monkman, John Moss, Nima Naghibi, Bill New, Susie O'Brien, Tunji Osinubi, Pam Perkins, Donna Pennee, Michael Peterman, Laurie Ricou, Wendy Robbins, Duffy Roberts, Stephen Slemon, John Steckley, Janice Stewart, Brenda Vellino, Tracy Ware, and Jim Zucchero. We would also like to thank the members of the audience for our presentation at the August 2007 Association for Commonwealth Literature and Language Studies conference in Vancouver for their enthusiastic and extremely helpful input on the contents and structure of the anthology in its final stages.

We are indebted to the numerous peer reviewers who formally commented on the project proposal and/or Volume I at various stages along the way; they included Alison Calder, University of Manitoba; Sally Chivers, Trent University; Carrie Dawson, Dalhousie University; Cecily Devereux, University of Alberta; Renée Hulan, Saint Mary's University; Brian Johnson, Carleton University; Mary Beth Knechtel, Langara College; Kevin McNeilly, University of British Columbia; Seymour Mayne, University of Ottawa; Daniel O'Leary, Concordia University; Sam Solecki, University of Toronto; Tracy Ware, Queen's University; Susan Wasserman, Douglas College, and others who prefer to remain anonymous. We are grateful for the detailed work of our research assistants: at UBC, Kristin McHale, Terri Tomsky, Kathryn Grafton, Travis Mason, and especially Maryann Martin; at the University of Ottawa, Jessica Langston and Kathleen Patchell. We would also like to thank our editors at Pearson Education Canada, Jessica Mosher, Patty Riediger, Richard di Santo, and especially Suzanne Schaan, for their commitment to our vision of the book from start to finish, and the indefatigable Martha Uniacke Breen for her humour and polish.

Laura would like to note her indebtedness to her colleagues in the Department of English and the Faculty of Arts at the University of British Columbia as well as the University of New South Wales, Australia, where she spent an enjoyable six months as a Visiting Academic Fellow (2007) while working on Volume I of this book. Cynthia would like to express her gratitude to the Department of English and Faculty of Arts at the University of Ottawa.

Above all, we thank our families for their love and support throughout this process. Our six children (all currently under the age of 8) have provided fun, grounding, and balance in our lives as we have worked on this project, although we have been told more than once that our computer time is up. Laura's Simon, Owen, and Charlie, and Cynthia's Neve, Abbey, and Morgan have been part of this project from the beginning (though, admittedly, not present at the B&B in Hamilton). They have enjoyed the piles of recycled paper, listened to bedtime stories of emigration tales and prairie realism, reveled in the poems of Dennis Lee, helped to collate photocopies, and feigned interest when asked their thoughts on images of trains and horses. Charlie and Morgan, born within weeks of each other and a year into this project, will forever be our Canlit anthology babies. We'd most like to thank our husbands, Fred Cutler and Paul Keen, for providing boundless critical insights, advice, coffee, lunches, dinners, hugs, glasses of wine, pep talks, laughs, encouragement, feminist support, commiseration, mango smoothies, love, and, of course, an unfailing, and often ironic, enthusiasm for all things Canadian.

The creation of this anthology has been a truly collaborative project and has been one of the most rewarding, and tiring, academic experiences either of us has ever had. We have also helped each other over crises at home and at work and have forged a solid friendship out of it all. Over the course of hundreds and hundreds of email messages (with a record of 81 in one day), we have created this anthology together. We are both responsible for its strengths and its weaknesses. That we have chosen to list Volume I as edited by Cynthia Sugars and Laura Moss and Volume II as edited by Laura Moss and Cynthia Sugars is meant to reflect the collaborative nature of this venture.

Dedication:

To our families:
PAUL, NEVE, ABBEY, and MORGAN
FRED, SIMON, OWEN, and CHARLIE

Brian Maracle is a Mohawk writer and activist who worked as a journalist for the *Globe and Mail* and was the host of the CBC Radio program *Our Native Land*. He is the author of *Crazywater: Native Voices on Addiction and Recovery* (1993) and *Back on the Rez: Finding the Way Home* (1996), a memoir about corruption in the management of Native affairs in Canada and the author's search for his Aboriginal roots.

Maracle grew up as an urban "non-status" Indian, but now lives on the Six Nations Grand River Reserve in Brantford, where he teaches Mohawk language and culture. "The First Words" is an account of "*the* defining moment" in Iroquoian history, "the event that defined us as a people without reference to others [i.e., Europeans]." His story uses an innovative mixture of a traditional mythic creation story followed by the author/narrator's commentary on the story you have heard, placing it in a contemporary Native context. It is an appropriate beginning to an anthology of Canadian literature and culture, not only because it acknowledges the presence of Aboriginal communities in North America before the arrival of Europeans, but also because the thanks for Creation, as Maracle states, is the traditional way of opening any gathering or storytelling occasion. In two senses, then, these are "the words that come before all others."

The First Words

When I was invited to write about a "defining moment" in our people's history, I considered and immediately rejected obvious dates of great historical significance like 1492, when Columbus was discovered. And 1527, when Pizarro unleashed the holocaust of epidemics that eventually wiped out fifty million people. I rejected recent Canadian dates like 1982, when "aboriginal and treaty rights" were enshrined in the Constitution.

I also rejected significant events in the history of my own people, the Rotinonhsyón:ni—the people of the Six Nations Iroquois Confederacy. The people here in my home community of Grand River have long memories and a strong sense of history, and many would nominate 1779 as a defining moment. That's when George Washington burned our villages to the ground, thus earning him the Iroquois name that he and all the subsequent presidents of the United States are known by: Ranatakáryas, the Town Destroyer. Many would say a defining moment was 1784, when we were forced to move from New York State to the Grand River Territory. Others would say one was 1799, when the Seneca chief Skanyatarí:yo had a vision that led to the establishment of the longhouse "religion" that has kept our language and culture alive in the face of five hundred years of pressure to assimilate. And still others would choose 1924, when the Canadian government outlawed the traditional chiefs and—at gunpoint—installed an elected band council, creating a rift that has plagued our community to this day.

All of these were pivotal moments in our history, it's true. But all of them involve our interactions with so-called "white people." They were not about *us*. Most of them involve things that happened *to* us. They have helped determine where and how we live but they have not determined how we think or what we believe. The event that determined those things, that determined our true nature, the event that defined us as a people without reference to others, occurred a very long time ago.

But it wasn't, as some might think, the founding of the Iroquois Confederacy. Even though that event predates European contact and certainly was a defining moment in our history, it is not about our true self. We created the Confederacy as a reaction to a crisis we were facing. At that time the nations of the Iroquois were warring with one another in an endless and devastating cycle of blood feuds. So, we are told, the Creator sent a messenger to the earth who persuaded our ancestors to stop all the killing and accept a life of peace. This man, known in English as the Peacemaker, also brought with him a set of laws that laid out how the nations would work together in a confederacy based on consensus. When he had finished, the Peacemaker had restored the world to a life of peace and harmony, the way it was at the time of Creation.

And it was *that* time—the moment of Creation—that was *the* defining moment in our history. That was when our character as a people was determined. That was when we were given the gift of speech and, with it, a unique way of looking at and understanding the world. That was when we were given the sacred responsibilities that shape our lives. That was the moment that shaped how we think and what we believe.

*

The woman took a quick breath, opened her eyes, sat up, and looked around. She was sitting on a riverbank, surrounded by flowers and an abundance of plant life. Every variety of bird and animal stood, perched, or floated nearby, watching her. She was young, she was beautiful, and she was naked.

Hundreds of pairs of eyes silently watched her as she struggled to absorb everything in sight. Everything—*everything*—was entirely new to her and she was overwhelmed by the beauty and the wonder of it all. Every one of the creatures and plant forms, she noticed, was so different from every other and, as she looked down at herself, so different from her as well.

And then she noticed that one pair of eyes watched her with greater interest and intensity than all the others. They belonged to a creature whose life form was much like her own. She sensed a kinship with this being whose body glowed softly from within.

"Ónhka ní:se?" she asked at last. "Who are you?"

"Konya'tíson ní:'i," the being replied. "I am the one who made you."

"Ónhka ni:'i?" she asked. "Who am I?"

"Sónkwe ní:se," came the reply. "You are a human being."

"Oh ní:yoht takya'tíson?" she asked. "How did you make me?"

"Enkonna'tónhahse," the being replied. "I'll show you."

With a few quick movements, the glowing being reached down, scooped up a handful of clay from the riverbank, and shaped it into the doll-like form of a man. The being then laid the doll-like figure on the riverbank next to the woman and gently blew into its mouth. Instantly, the clay doll was transformed into a human being. Hair grew out of its head, skin covered its body, and facial features appeared. The man took a quick breath, opened his eyes, sat up, and looked around.

Like the woman, the man sat silently at first, awestruck and struggling to comprehend everything before him. The woman and the glowing being waited, saying nothing. Finally, the man began focusing his attention on the woman. He noticed that he did not have the breasts or the shape of the woman. Instead, he had the same muscles and form as the glowing figure. In spite of his physical resemblance to the glowing man he felt a greater kinship with the woman. And it was to her he spoke.

"Ónhka ní:se?' he asked. "Who are you?"

"Kónkwe . . . tenon . . . tenónkwe," she replied hesitantly. "I . . . we . . . we're human beings."

"Ónhka ne raónha?" the man asked. "Who is he?"

"Shonkwaya'tíson," she answered. "He is the one who made us."

"Ka' nítewe's?" he then asked. "Where are we? What is this place?"

The woman, not knowing what to say, looked to the glowing being.

"Tsyatahonhsí:yohst, keniyén:'a," he said. "Listen well, my children." He then settled himself on the ground before them and continued. "Enkenikaratónhahse. I will now tell you the story of this place and how you've come to be here. It's a long story and you must listen well."

The man and woman quickly nodded agreement and the glowing man began.

"È:neken tsyatkáhtho," he said. "Look up, into the sky."

The man and woman then tilted their heads back and scanned the sky.

"You see the flying creatures, the clouds and the sun, do you not?" he asked.

"Hén:'en," the humans responded. "Yes. We see all those things and it is all so beautiful."

"It is not within your power to see beyond the deepest part of the sky," the glowing man continued, "but I want you to know there is another world above this one, a sky-world. It is a special and beautiful place, just like here. And there are beings who live in the sky-world. They look much like you and me. And one day you and I, and many others, will all live together there."

The human beings did not know how to respond and sat there, silent, and the glowing manlike being continued.

"In the sky-world, there are manlike beings and womanlike beings. After they live together for a time, the womanlike being will bear a child. This, too, will happen to you one day."

The man and the woman looked at each other, bewildered, but said nothing.

"Many, many days ago, there was a womanlike being in the sky-world whose stomach grew bigger and bigger, a sign that she would soon bear a child.

"But one day the woman became sick. She was barely able to walk. She said to her elder brother, 'We must go to the shining tree. It is there I will find the medicine I need to make myself well again.' So the two of them journeyed to the centre of the sky-world where the shining tree stood.

"This tree is a giant tree," the glowing-being said. "Its limbs are heavy with blossoms, fruit, and nuts of every kind. It glows from within with the light of a sun that never sets.

"At the base of the tree grow the medicine plants that the beings of the sky-world use to make themselves well. When the woman and her brother arrived at the shining tree, the brother began digging the medicine roots and the woman began gathering the medicine leaves and flowers. Soon the woman had made and taken her medicine and was resting by the edge of the hole that her brother had dug.

"She looked into the hole but could not see its bottom. So she leaned over further and fell into the hole. She grabbed at the plants and roots at the edge of the hole but she could not stop her fall. She fell through the hole in the sky-world.

"Her brother reached out for her when he saw her begin to fall. He tried but he could not catch her. He looked down into the hole and saw her falling away into the blackness. He then went to the shining tree. He ate the fruit that hung from its limbs, and he began to glow from inside his body, just like the tree. He went back, lay down, and looked down into the hole, and his glowing face lit up the sky with the brightest of all light. He saw his sister falling further and further away.

"When his sister looked down, she saw nothing but water—water every-where—as far as the eye could see. She fell and she fell."

The human beings, even though they had no knowledge of falling or death, grew fearful. Shonkwaya'tíson then stopped his storytelling and pointed with his chin to the birds that were flying overhead. "Shé:ken ken ne thí:ken?" he asked. "Do you see them?"

"Hén:'en. Otsi'ten'okón:'a nen né:'e," the human beings replied. "Yes. They are flying beings."

"Well," Shonkwaya'tíson continued, "the flying beings were there at that time, and they saw the woman falling and went to help her. A great flock of many different flying beings flew very close together and made a bed with their wings. They caught her and stopped her fall. But they soon grew tired. They wanted to rest but there was no place to put her down, so they called to the water creatures for help.

"All the creatures that inhabit the waters came to the surface to help the woman who had fallen out of the sky. One of them, A'nó:wara—the shell crea-ture—rose from the waters and told the woman that she could rest on its shell. So the flying creatures placed the woman on A'nó:wara's back.

"The woman looked all around and saw only the hard, bare shell, the water, the sky, the flying beings, and the water creatures. She looked at her hands and noticed that many seeds and roots had stuck to her fingers when she fell through the hole in the sky-world. This made her think of her family and her home in the sky-world, and she became sad and lonely. She knew that the flying beings could not carry her back to the sky-world. They were too small, she was too big, and it was too far away. She knew she would have to live here, on the hard, bare shell of A'nó:wara.

"But, the woman thought, if only she had some earth, she could plant the seeds and roots that had stuck to her fingers and she could create a new life for herself on the shell creature's back. So she called the flying beings and the water creatures together. She asked them if they knew where to find some earth. 'There is earth at the bottom of the water,' they said."

Shonkwaya'tíson then told the humans to look at one of the water creatures floating nearby, a fat and furry one with a broad flat tail and long front teeth. "Tsyanì:to was the first to try. It dove for the bottom, and the woman and the other creatures waited and waited but Tsyanì:to never returned."

Shonkwaya'tíson then pointed to a long-bodied, short-limbed creature floating on its back nearby. "Tawí:ne was the next to try. It dove for the bottom and, like before, the woman and the other creatures waited a very long time but Tawí:ne never returned.

"The next creature to try," Shonkwaya'tíson said, "was that one—Anókyen," pointing to a round, brown furry creature that had burrowed into the riverbank. Its long, thin tail had no hair and it was the smallest of all the water creatures.

"Anókyen dove for the bottom, and the woman and the others waited. And waited. After a very long time, Anókyen finally rose to the surface. It was dead but it had a small piece of earth in its paws.

"The woman took the earth and placed it on the middle of the shell creature's back. After she planted the seeds and roots she had brought from the sky-world, she began to walk around the edge of the shell creature's back. As she walked, the earth on the shell began to grow. The more she walked, the more the earth grew. Soon the earth had completely covered over the shell creature's back. Finally, the time came when the woman gave birth to the child she was carrying, a daughter. The daughter grew up quickly, and she and her mother continued to walk around the edge of the earth and make it grow even more.

"One day, after she was fully grown, the daughter was lying down, asleep. As she slept, the wind from the west blew over her body. The west wind left two arrows resting on her stomach, one of them straight and sharp, the other bent and blunt. Her mother soon came and found her, woke her up, and showed her the two arrows. 'This is a sign,' the mother told her, 'that soon you will have children—twins.'

"Time passed and the daughter's stomach grew bigger and bigger. She was carrying twin boys. One was right-handed and had a good mind. The other was left-handed and had an evil mind. When the time came for them to be born, they began to argue about how they should leave her body.

"They could feel their mother's body pushing them outside. But the left-handed twin wanted to go out through his mother's side. The right-handed twin argued with his brother, trying to get him to follow him as he left. But the left-handed twin wouldn't listen and he tore his way out through his mother's side, and this killed her.

"So then the woman who fell from the sky buried her daughter and her body became one with the earth. From the head of her grave grew Ó:nenhste, Ohsahè:ta, and Onon'òn:sera."

Shonkwaya'tíson pointed at the plant life growing nearby. "There they are," he said. He pointed to the thin stalk that was taller than the human beings, its long leaves filled with tender kernels. He pointed as well to the vine of pointed leaves that twined up around the tall stalk bearing long, thin pods filled with seeds. He then pointed to the big-leafed vine that surrounded the stalk, shading its large gourds.

"These three sister beings are the foods you will use above all others to keep you alive. And those there," he said, pointing to a cluster of many different green growing things, "are Onónhkwa. They carry the medicines that you can use to make yourself well when you are sick, just as the sky-woman did before she entered this world.

"And one of the medicines," he added, "is that one, Niyohontéhsha, the one with a heart-shaped red fruit. It is sweet to eat and its juice is sweet to drink. Remember it well because a time will come when the plant life you see around you will stop growing and the earth will be covered by a cold white blanket for a long time. A wind from the south will bring warmth back to the land and the plant beings will grow again. Remember Niyohontéhsha, because it will be the first of the life-sustainers to appear when the cold time is over, and it will be a sign that more foods will come.

"And that there," Shonkwaya'tíson said, pointing to a broad-leafed plant with many small seed pods, "is Oyèn:kwa. It grew from where the heart of the daughter was buried. Its leaves are a messenger. You will need them one day to send your messages to me, because soon I will journey to the sky-world. You will put your thoughts into the dried leaves and put the leaves into the fire, and the smoke from the fire will carry your words to me."

The human beings sat there trying to absorb and understand it all, still saying nothing, so Shonkwaya'tíson continued.

"The woman who fell from the sky was sad and angry over her daughter's death and she called her grandsons to her. She named the right-handed twin Tharonhyawá:kon. She named the left-handed twin Thawíhskaron.

"The grandmother then asked the twins which one had killed her daughter. The left-handed one lied and said it was Tharonhyawá:kon who had killed their mother. He tricked his grandmother into believing him, so he became the twin she liked best. The grandmother then became angry with the right-handed twin, and she made him leave their lodge and live in the forest."

The thought of the woman sending her grandson away shocked the human beings.

"A great wrong was done to that boy that day," the glowing man-being said. Pausing slightly, he added, "And that boy was me."

The man and the woman were stunned. They looked at each other and looked at the glowing man-being, mouths open, struggling to comprehend everything that they had been told. Finally the woman said, "So you are the right-handed twin. You are Tharonhyawá:kon."

"Yes," he replied, "I am the right-handed twin. I am Tharonhyawá:kon. It was my grandmother who made me live in the forest. She was the one who fell out of the hole in the sky-world. It is her elder brother who brightens the sky during the day. It is my twin brother who ripped his way out of my mother's side and killed her. And it is my mother whose flesh we are resting on."

The man and woman were still speechless, so Shonkwaya'tíson—Tharonhyawá:kon—continued.

"When my grandmother pushed me out of her lodge and into the forest that day, the same wind that had blown over my mother's body—the west wind—my father—came up and swirled around me. He protected me from harm and whispered instructions that helped me find shelter in the forest. He helped me live and be strong. When I was fully grown, my father told me that I must make the earth ready for human beings—for you.

"And so then I began my work of creation."

Pointing to the long-legged, antlered animals standing nearby, he said, "I went across the earth and made Ohskennón:ton and Ska'nyónhsa." Pointing to the long-eared animals hopping nearby he said, "And I made Tehahonhtané:ken and Kwayén:'a. I made all these creatures so that their flesh will give you strength and their skins and fur will keep you warm.

"But when I had finished, my twin brother, Thawíhskaron, came along behind me and made other creatures to eat the creatures I had made." And here Shonkwaya'tíson pointed to Okwáho and Kén:reks—large, snarling, long-tailed creatures with big teeth and long claws that crouched nearby.

"I went across the land," Shonkwaya'tíson continued, "and laid down the waters. These are the waters you will use to sustain yourselves when you are thirsty. These are the waters you will use to travel about on this earth. I made these waters flow in two directions so that it would be easy for you to make your way.

"But again," he said, "my twin brother came along behind me and worked to undo what I had made. He spoiled some of the waters, making them undrinkable. He placed rocks in some of the waterways and made them flow in just one direction so that it will be hard and dangerous for you to travel.

"I then went to the waters and made Kéntsyonk." Pointing to the swimming creatures drifting in the river, Shonkwaya'tíson said, "I filled the waters with Kéntsyonk so that you could use their flesh to make you strong.

"And again," he said, "my twin brother came along after and undid what I had done. He made more creatures to eat the Kéntsyonk I made for you.

"I made many more foods grow from the earth. I made small crawling and flying creatures to help them grow. And again my brother came along after and spoiled what I had made. He made more crawling creatures to eat the foods

I had made. He made growing things that will sicken you if you eat them. He made growing things that sicken the foods I had made. He made crawling creatures to eat the foods I had made. And he made crawling, flying, biting creatures to sicken you and all the creatures I had made.

"Everything I tried to make, he tried to spoil. Even those things I had no hand in doing, he tried to undo." Looking up at the sun, which was now approaching the horizon, Shonkwaya'tíson said, "With some of his power he made the sun fall from the sky every day.

"Thawíhskaron then told me that since he had the power to move the sun, he would be the master of everything on earth. He demanded that I go to the underworld while the sun was in the sky but I refused. We argued for a long time, and finally we decided to settle it with a contest. Whoever won the contest would go to the underworld.

"We began by playing Kayentowá:nen." The man and woman exchanged quizzical glances and Shonkwaya'tíson explained. "It is a game played with a large wooden bowl holding stones that are blackened on one side. I tossed the bowl and tried to get all the dark sides of the stones to land face up but I couldn't. Then my brother tried and he couldn't. We played the game for many days but no one won.

"So then we played Tehonttsihkwá:'eks." Again the man and woman looked confused and Shonkwaya'tíson explained. "We each took a long stick, bent the end and laced it back together so that it would hold a small round stone. We then used these sticks and the stone and struggled against each other. I tried to move the stone past my brother and couldn't. He tried to move the stone past me and he couldn't. We battled for many days but no one won.

"And then we began to fight. I grabbed my brother and pushed him to the ground. He grabbed me and pulled me down. He tried to hold me down but I broke free. I tried to hold him down but he broke free. Neither one of us was stronger than the other. One moment I was on top, the next moment he was. We fought for many days.

"All the creatures that Thawíhskaron and I had created had long stopped what they were doing and had come to watch us fight. After we had been fighting for many days I saw one of them, Ohskennón:ton, the long-legged, sharp-antlered one, lower its head to the ground and drop its antlers. I picked them up and used them to push my brother back. Their power helped me push my brother over the edge of the earth."

At this, Tharonhyawá:kon sat quietly for several moments before continuing. "My brother still lives in the underworld. He is there right now and he wants to come back and spoil more things on earth. But now that I have created you," he said, looking squarely at the man and woman, "he wants to come back and create mischief and trouble for you."

The human beings exchanged worried glances.

"Do not be afraid," he said, "I will watch over you and protect you. I have asked my grandfather—the husband of the woman who fell from the sky—to come down from his home in the sky-world to help you. He is Rawé:ras and he lives with the west wind. From time to time he will come with the west wind and bring the rains that will replenish the waters on earth that will sustain you. He will use his loud voice and his bright fire spears to keep my brother in the underworld. So now the only time my brother can leave the world below is at night. And because the sun is no longer in the sky, he has no power when he is here on earth. He can only prowl about.

"When I pushed my brother over the edge of the world, my grandmother became very sad. She liked my brother very much, she missed him greatly, and she died soon after. So I put her head in the sky so that she would watch over the earth during the night and watch over her grandson when he comes up from the world below to move about.

"There was still one more thing that happened here on earth before I created you," Shonkwaya'tíson added. "I was walking through the forest one day when I met a manlike being. He said he was very powerful and could do many special things. He said that he had created all the swimming creatures, walking creatures, foods, and rivers on earth. I told him that it was not true, that I had created those things. So he challenged me to see who had the greater power. 'The one whose power is greater is the one who is telling the truth,' he said. I then told him to look in the distance, for there, far away, stood a great mountain. I challenged this being to use his power to move the mountain as far as he could. He stood there looking at the mountain, gathered all his powers, and made the mountain move closer. He turned to me, smiled and said, 'It's true, you see. I have great power for I have moved a mountain.'

"'It's my turn,' I told him. And I looked at the mountain, I looked *hard* at the mountain, and made it fly to where we were standing. It flew across the valley with a great roar and a rush of wind. This startled the being and he turned to see what had caused it. He turned so fast that he smashed his face on the side of the flying mountain just as it came to rest at his feet. When he turned back around, his face had been pushed to the side; his nose was bent and his lips were twisted.

"The deformed being then said to me, 'Truly, it is you who has the greater power and it was you who created all the good things on earth.' I then told him of my plan to create you, the human beings, and he agreed to use his powers to help you. So if a time comes when you become sick, you may burn the dried leaves of Oyèn:kwa and call on him for help. He will come to you and you will know him by his twisted mouth and broken nose. He will help you and make you well again.

"And then everything was in place for me to make you."

"Oh ní:yoht takya'tíson?" the man asked. "How did you make me?"

"Enyesahró:ri," he answered. "She will tell you. And together you will tell your children everything I have told you."

The man and woman looked at each other and nodded.

"Yes, you will have children. Many children. And," he said, nodding at the sun which was now settling into the horizon, "you will have much to tell them because there is still more I must tell you before I leave.

"You now know how you've come to be here and how this earth and everything on it was created. You should know that this land and all of its wonders I made just for you. I have given you the knowledge of how to use all the many forms of life on earth to sustain yourselves. I have given you the knowledge of how to build your lodges, where to find and how to make the things you will need. Everything you will need to know is already within you.

"Before I leave this earth I will make more human beings. You will meet them. In time you and they will have children. Together your children and their children will have more children. And it is my wish that you will all live together and love one another. It is also my wish that you respect the earth and all the blessings that I have laid for you.

"Now consider this. I have given you life, this land, the knowledge of survival, and the ability to speak with one another, with the medicine beings, and with me. It is my wish that you will be grateful for all of these things; that you will give me your thanks every day; that you will celebrate the earth's blessings at mid-winter, at harvest time, and at other times throughout the year; and lastly, that you will pass on my words to your children and their children until the end of time. This is what I ask of you."

The first human beings sat silent for several moments as they considered the burden to be borne for the magnitude of Creation. Finally, they spoke together. "Tó:kenhske ki wáhi, eh nenyakení:yere tsi niyenhén:we." "Truly, we will do these things of which you spoke forever."

Their promise made, Shonkwaya'tíson stood up and gathered himself to leave. It was dark now. His body, which had softly glimmered during the day, was now glowing warmly and lighting everything around him.

"My work here on earth is nearly complete. I will soon journey to the sky-world."

The humans looked dismayed but Shonkwaya'tíson went on. "Your days here on earth are numbered and when you have reached their end, you will do as I do. You will walk the path of stars that lead to the sky-world, where we will meet one another again."

The man and woman stood holding each other as the Creator moved away, his glow fading into the distance, his grandmother's face shining brightly in the southern sky.

To most people, the story I have just told is just that—a story. Quaint and colourful, yes, but just a story. But it is far more than that to the people who have been telling it since Shonkwaya'tíson told it to the first human beings.

For starters, when Shonkwaya'tíson told the first human beings the story of their creation, it wasn't in English. He told it to them in *His* language—the language He gave them when He gave them the gift of speech. And beginning with the first human beings, our people have handed down the story of our creation in the Creator's language ever since. Only in the most recent generation has the story been widely shared in English.

And when Shonkwaya'tíson gave us our language, He gave us a unique way of looking at the world around us—*His* way. He made it clumsy for us to express things that involve negative concepts. For example, we don't have a word in our language for "zero," "empty," or "failure." We *can* say them but only by saying, "It isn't something," "It doesn't have something in it," or "Something did not succeed."

He did not make us obsessed with objects. If He had, He would have given us the need and the ability to separate, categorize, and classify everything on earth by giving them all different names, just as Western society through the English language does. He could have given us this obsession, but He didn't.

One thing He did give us through our language, though, is an obsession with people. We have many more ways of describing exactly who is doing what than English has. For example, although there is only one word for "we" in English, there are four in our language, depending on the number of people involved in the "we" and whether "we" includes the person being spoken to. As a result, we are much more precise and much less ambiguous than we are in English when we are talking about people—which is to say, nearly all the time.

From these few observations about our language, outsiders can gain a few insights into our traditional values and way of thinking—the way our Creator wants us to think. We know from the language that our Creator has given us that we should not think "negatively"; that we should not be obsessed with objects; and that we should be more concerned with people and relationships. Pretty good advice, don't you think?

One telling aspect of the Creation Story is that all the nations of the Iroquois tell the story the same way. Many details vary from one version to another but the major elements are all the same: a woman fell through a hole in the sky-world and came to rest on a turtle's back. She gave birth to a daughter, who died giving birth to twin boys. After creating the features of the earth, the twins battled for control. The right-handed twin won and created the first human beings with a handful of clay.

Those first human beings we call *onkwehón:we*, the real, first, original persons. Today we say that an *onkwehón:we* is someone who speaks the language of the Creator, who still carries the unique way of thinking and looking at life that stems from our language. More important, an *onkwehón:we* is someone who still honours the instructions of the Creator—who loves people and respects the earth and who gives thanks to Him.

The Creation Story gives all *onkwehón:we* a shared way of thinking and looking at the world. But it does even more than that.

It specifically tells us that the *onkwehón:we* did not arrive here on what we now call Turtle Island by walking over some land bridge from Asia.

It explains why we call the earth our mother, the moon our grandmother, the sun our elder brother, and the thunder our grandfather.

It explains why we spend so much time giving thanks in our longhouses and in our daily get-togethers.

It gives us comfort, security, and a sense of purpose.

It tells us that the only things we were given were the knowledge of how to survive on this land, the gift of speech, and the responsibility to give thanks, and that therefore things like Aboriginal rights, tax exemptions, college tuition, and free prescriptions did not come from the Creator.

It tells us that the many social, economic, and political problems we now face are a distant second in importance to the overriding imperative that we honour our obligations stemming from the time of Creation.

Clearly, the Creation Story is more than just a story. We take its teachings to be the guiding light in how we conduct our lives. We honour our obligations, every day, all across Iroquoia, from Quebec to Wisconsin. In most of our schools and in every gathering of *onkwehón:we*, someone will stand and recite, in the Creator's language, the Ohén:ton Karihwatéhkwen—the words that come before all others. Known as the Opening Address or the Thanksgiving Address, this ritual gives thanks for all the blessings of Creation.

A short version may be just a few dozen words. A long, formal version may last forty-five minutes. But no matter who recites it and which language he uses (the speaker is traditionally a man), all of the speeches follow the same general pattern.

"Ó:nen sewatahonhsí:yohst kentyóhkwa," the speaker will begin. "Listen well, everyone who is now here assembled.

"It is my duty to recite the words of thanksgiving that come before all others. It is Shonkwaya'tíson's intention that whenever we gather together, we give thanks for all the blessings of Creation as our first order of business.

"So first of all, let us put our minds together as one and give greetings to all the peoples of the earth. And let us give thanks for all the people here gathered, that we have all arrived here safely, that we are all at peace and of a good mind. Let us remember those who could not be here because they are sick, and let us pray that they quickly regain their health. Let us remember as well and thank those who help us to keep our language and traditions alive.

"E'tho niyohtónhak nonkwa'nikòn:ra," the speaker will then say. "So let all of our minds come together as one on this matter." When the speaker finishes expressing this hope, the men in the crowd will respond on cue with a chorus of "Nyeah!" signifying that they are in agreement with what has just been said.

"And now let us give thanks to our mother the earth," the speaker will continue, "for all the blessings that she continues to provide for us. And let us give thanks to her for supporting our feet so lovingly as we walk about on the earth.

"E'tho niyohtónhak nonkwa'nikòn:ra," the speaker will add. "Nyeah!" the men will respond.

The speaker will then give similarly detailed thanks to all the elements of creation, beginning with the earth and reaching to the stars. He will give thanks to all the waters of the earth; the fish life that inhabits them; the insects; the medicine plants; the fruits, especially the strawberries; the food plants, especially corn, beans, and squash; the animals, especially the deer; the trees, especially the maple; the birds, especially the eagle; the four winds; the thunderers that bring the rains; the sun; the moon; the stars; Handsome Lake; and four special sky-beings who watch over human beings on earth.

Lastly, the speaker will tell the people to turn their faces to the sky-world where the Creator resides. "Let us put together our kindest and most loving words," he will say, "and throw them skyward to give Him our thanks for everything He has provided for us on this earth.

"E'tho niyohtónhak nonkwa'nikòn:ra," he will add. "Nyeah!" the men will respond.

Only when this sometimes lengthy ritual is finished can a meeting, or anything else, be started. And at the end of the meeting, before everyone goes home, a man will stand up and once again recite the verses of the Ohén:ton Karihwatéhkwen; the speaker reciting the reasons for being grateful and urging everyone to come to one mind, the men chorusing agreement.

The Thanksgiving Address, which constitutes the first words and the last words spoken at all of our gatherings, is a beautiful and impressive reminder of the abiding and loving relationship we are to have with one another and with all the works of Creation, and it reminds us that our relationship with the earth and our obligations to the Creator are more important than the day-to-day affairs of human beings.

"Nyeah!"

[2004]

SECTION I

Narratives of Encounter

Introduction: Who/What/Where Is Here?

> What is it, Canada? A country as big as a continent stretching from the Atlantic Ocean to the Pacific. . . . It's also just a word, six letters trying to hold all the granite, the grain, the timber, the fish scales, and the fur together. A word with a shifty meaning, a name for a shifting place.
> —Aimée Laberge, *Where the River Narrows* (48)

IN THE BEGINNING, Canada was where no land was supposed to be. Or at least, this was the perspective of the early European explorers who first encountered what came to be called the "New World." The designation "New World" is itself telling, for of course the world of North America was anything but "new." Aboriginal peoples had inhabited the area for centuries before the first Europeans appeared off the coast of Newfoundland in search of rich fishing grounds. A variety of distinct cultural and linguistic groups had long occupied their traditional territories, and trade among Aboriginal communities was already well established (Figure I-1). What is more, the trade route associated with the early *voyageurs*, from the St. Lawrence seaway to the Great Lakes, had been an Aboriginal trading route long before the first Europeans arrived. "[We] have lived here since the world began," is Arthur J. Ray's memorable phrase for Native people's perspective of their habitation of the land. To put things in a global perspective, there were extensive Aboriginal societies and civilizations well before the period that Europeans associate with the grandeur of ancient Egypt. Indeed, the earliest known inhabitants of North America predate the early Egyptians and Mesopotamians, and hence, even in the fifteenth century, represented long-rooted civilizations. The notion that Canada was a vast, empty landscape that lay waiting to be colonized, in the view put forth by various European writers in the seventeenth, eighteenth, and nineteenth centuries, is a gross misrepresentation. As any reading of early explorers' journals will attest, the land was securely inhabited. Further, Europeans would not have been able to explore and settle the land without the help of the Aboriginal peoples they encountered; Aboriginal people taught the Europeans survival and hunting skills, showed them their river trade routes and portages, gave them medicinal aid (especially in the treatment of scurvy), and in some cases, actively rescued them from certain death. European explorers as distinct as Jacques Cartier and John Franklin, both included in this anthology, tell harrowing tales of being saved in the nick of time by the Aboriginal people who befriended them. For instance, the leader of the Yellowknife people, Akaitcho, who aided Franklin in his disastrous expedition across the barrens in the early 1800s, saw himself as a host welcoming the White people into his land. "[A] Copper Indian can never permit white men to suffer from want of food on his lands, without flying to their aid," Akaitcho announced to the company, following his people's rescue of Franklin and his remaining handful of men.

The European "discovery" of the New World is itself a misnomer, since of course the land was intimately known by Aboriginal peoples, and many of these individuals helped the Europeans in their pursuits. This was especially true in the case of Jacques Cartier, Samuel de Champlain, and Samuel Hearne, as the excerpts provided here demonstrate. They all depended on Aboriginal guides to lead them through "unknown" territory—which, thereafter, would be memorialized as that explorer's "discovery" and become the basis of his claim to fame. Victor Hopwood, in his introduction to the *Travels* of David Thompson, qualifies this well when he says, "Discovery in our usage means that the discoverer brought the so-called unknown territory into the written record of European civilization" (8). This is signalled by Brian Maracle's identification of 1492 as the year that "Columbus was discovered" rather than the year Columbus discovered America (see the opening selection in this anthology). Nevertheless, in terms of Europeans' sense of geography and Christian predestination, North America was defined by an aspect of "newness," or what literary historian Stephen Greenblatt terms, in *Marvelous Possessions*, a sense of "wonder." Perhaps it is not surprising that European pictorial representations of the allegorical figure of "America" (comparable to portrayals of the classical figure of "Britannia") reveal a combined sense of attraction and fear toward the unknown. From the Renaissance well into the nineteenth century, allegorical portrayals of "America" depicted an exotic, partially clad "Indian" maiden adorned with feathers, spears, and arrows and, in some cases, carrying human remains for a cannibalistic feast (Figure I-3). The encounter between Europeans and Native North Americans was, for both, a startling and unsettling discovery.

Mapping the New World: The Allure of Trade

The outermost edges of the North American continent were already well known before what we think of as the "Age of Discovery" in the sixteenth century. This is especially true of the rich fishing grounds off Newfoundland and Cape

Breton, which had long been visited by Viking, Portuguese, French, and Basque fishermen.[1] Archeological evidence reveals conclusively that as early as 1000 AD, the Vikings established a settlement in L'Anse aux Meadows in Newfoundland. In the fifteenth century, European explorers travelled across the Atlantic in search of a route to the Eastern Indies (China, Japan, India), the realm of silk, spices, tea, and other riches. When Christopher Columbus chanced upon America in 1492, he maintained that he had reached the outermost territory of Asia. In 1497, the Italian navigator Giovanni Caboto (anglicized as John Cabot) sought to outdo Columbus's discovery by finding a shorter, more northerly route to Asia. Sailing under orders of the English king, Henry VII, he crossed the Atlantic and encountered a "new isle" which he claimed for England; it thereafter became known as "Terra Nova" or Newfoundland, though Cabot believed that he had reached the northern portion of Asia.[2] This theory remained predominant for some time, even though the Italian explorer Amerigo Vespucci postulated in 1502 that a separate continent lay in the way (Figure I-2). Vespucci was one of the first to recognize the "New World" for what it was. The immense land mass "America" was named after him.

The "discovery" of North America, in effect, was a disappointment. How was one to get around the obstruction and proceed to the real destination, the Eastern Indies? For some years after the discovery of North America, the goal was to find a passage through the continent (whose vast westward extent could not yet be imagined [Figure I-2]) that would lead directly to the Pacific Ocean. In 1534–35, Jacques Cartier took up the quest for the Orient, but he was stalled in his journey along the St. Lawrence by treacherous rapids, extreme weather, and scurvy. Samuel de Champlain continued the search in the early 1600s, convinced that the "southern sea" lay just beyond the Great Lakes and could be reached via the St. Lawrence. In 1610, Henry Hudson explored the eastern interior of Hudson Bay in the hope that what he was actually mapping was the western coast of the continent of North America. When it was discovered that the ship was caught inside a vast inland sea, his crew mutinied and set him adrift in a lifeboat, after which Hudson was never seen again. Quests for the fabled "Northwest Passage" took hold of the imaginations of numerous explorers in the centuries that followed, from Samuel Hearne in the late 1700s to Sir John Franklin in the mid-1800s. Alexander Mackenzie, spurred on by rumours of an inland passage through the Rocky Mountains, travelled down the Mackenzie River, thinking he had found the

---

[1] Recent, contentious theories, such as those of Gavin Menzies and Paul Chiasson, suggest that Chinese sailors had already traversed the globe before the age of Columbus and may have established settlements on Cape Breton Island (on the East Coast) and in the Queen Charlotte Islands (on the West), while a legend also exists about an Irish monk, Brendan of Clonfert, having reached the shores of Newfoundland or Nova Scotia in the sixth century (Hannon 29–32).

[2] It is not known for certain where in Atlantic Canada Cabot landed in June 1497, though the island we call Newfoundland acquired the name he gave to his discovery. Cabot described the great cod stocks that, he claimed, were so thick that they slowed down his ship, which suggests that he may have been near Cape Bonavista on the east coast of Newfoundland. Cabot's discovery marked the beginning of the European cod fishery in Canada.

route to the west. When the river veered northward and emptied into the Arctic Ocean, Mackenzie is said to have christened it "River Disappointment."

Combined with these various quests for a westward passage was another objective: a monopoly over the North American fur trade. It did not take long for Europeans to realize that they had in fact encountered a world that teemed with riches: the prolific fishing stocks of the eastern seaboard, and the profusion of fur-bearing animals throughout the continent. What began as an obstacle was soon transformed into a treasure trove, as the rush for "brown gold" (beaver pelts) became a prime motivator in the continued mapping and exploration of Canada. Indeed, the fur trade is considered by many to be the definitive event of Canada's past and was intricately linked first to the rivalry, and eventually the coexistence, of the French and English in North America. Canadian economist and historian Harold Innis's seminal 1930 study, *The Fur Trade in Canada*, argues that the fur trade was the founding event in the formation of the nation, and, moreover, that Canada evolved naturally along the pathways of its great river systems. Canada "emerged not in spite of geography, but because of it," Innis is often quoted as saying.

The fur trade became integrally linked to the long-standing European rivalry between England and France when, in the seventeenth and eighteenth centuries, the clash of these European empires was extended to North American territory. Initially, the French held most of the eastern territory in what we now think of as Canada, including all of "Acadia" (the present Maritime provinces— P.E.I. was originally known by the French name Île Saint-Jean, and Cape Breton as Île Royale), the St. Lawrence region, the area around the Great Lakes, parts of Hudson Bay, and a good deal of inland territory extending as far south as Louisiana to the mouth of the Mississippi (Figure I-6). Champlain's primary intent in choosing the location of what is now Quebec City as the central settle- ment of New France was to establish a French-held trading post that would con- trol the route to the interior fur markets. Hence, the establishment of a post at the location "where the river narrows" (the translation of the Mi'kmaq word *guébeg*—now *Quebec*) was strategic. The French controlled the North American fur trade for the next century, enlisting the aid of their Aboriginal allies to pro- cure animal pelts and fight on their side in their ongoing war with the English. The Jesuit missions of the mid- to late 1600s had as their goal the conversion of the eastern Huron peoples to Christianity, but they were also there to provide for the spiritual needs of the French settlers and *voyageurs*, whom they perceived as in need of religious instruction. In 1713, following the Treaty of Utrecht, France was forced to concede British ownership of the Hudson Bay region, Nova Scotia (which included present-day New Brunswick), and French territory in Newfoundland. The Seven Years War (1756–1763) was the deciding factor in the future of Canada, when the British and French fought for control over the northern territory of New France. The Fall of Quebec in 1759, after the momen- tous battle on the Plains of Abraham, and the capture of Montreal the following year finally left the entire territory in the hands of the British.

The Hudson's Bay Company had been established by the British in 1670, inspired by the vision of two independent French *coureurs de bois*, Pierre Esprit Radisson and Médard Chouart des Groseilliers, who suggested to Prince Rupert, cousin of King Charles II, that the North American fur trade could be better run via Hudson Bay than via the St. Lawrence. By the eighteenth century, the company had secured its operations through its establishment of a series of bayside posts on the western shore of Hudson Bay, where its ships would anchor to deliver and receive trade goods. Even after the territory fell into British hands after 1759, the company continued to endure competition from rival trading companies, which eventually amalgamated to form the powerful North West Company in 1783/1784.[3] The narratives of Samuel Hearne, David Thompson, Alexander Mackenzie, and others tell the tale of rival fur-trading companies vying for control over the inland fur market: while the Hudson's Bay Company controlled Hudson Bay as its link to the trade market, the North West Company used the St. Lawrence as its entry into inland trade. Indeed, Mackenzie's opposition to Lord Selkirk's establishment of the Red River Colony on the western prairies (in what is now southern Manitoba) was based on the fact that the colony interfered with the North West Company's trading routes and hunting grounds.

Exploration Narratives: From Field Journal to Adventure Story

Exploration and travel narratives were extremely popular in Europe from the sixteenth century onward. While many of these written accounts began as journals or reports composed for the directors of a fur-trading company or for the royal sponsor in England or France, in many cases the writers revised their accounts for commercial publication. The popularity of these narratives drew on a passion for exotic depictions of what was for Europeans a "new" and unfamiliar world. Many of these travel narratives included elaborate maps and illustrations, as well as detailed descriptions of North American Aboriginal peoples, who appeared as exotic to Europeans as did the peoples of China and India. "It comes as no surprise," writes contemporary literary historian I.S. MacLaren, "that what is now Canada looks both curious and remote in these books" ("English" 43).

Exploration adventures appeared in multi-volume editions, magazines, and encyclopedias. Several early explorers printed their accounts in compendia such as Richard Hakluyt's *Principall Navigations* (1589; 1598–1600) and Samuel Purchas's *Purchas His Pilgrimes* (1625), the latter of which contained Cartier's third voyage. The *Jesuit Relations* of the 1600s was, in effect, a periodical that

---

[3] The dating of the founding of the North West Company is tricky, in part because the company developed in stages. As early as 1776 the name was used to describe an amalgamation of Montreal fur traders, and it was later employed by another merger in 1779 (including the partnerships of Simon McTavish and James McGill, of McGill University fame). The organization acquired official status in 1783/1784. Although the company made extensive use of the French *voyageurs*, it was managed by Highland Scots, who took over the French trading territory following the accession of New France to Britain in 1763. Alexander Mackenzie was a major figure in the organization, as was David Thompson, who joined in 1797.

collected the Jesuit reports regularly submitted to Paris from New France, and was an important influence on many of the cartographers of the period (Morantz 34). In other instances, exploration narratives were published under the individual explorer's name, though this did not mean that the final product was not a collaborative one. Publishers were keenly aware of the need to cater to the interests and demands of the European reading audience, which led to a similarity of themes, tropes, and stereotypes in narratives about North America. These included an emphasis on the following topics: the formidable and unforgiving Arctic landscape, the fabled Northwest Passage, the lone hero/explorer (who actually was rarely alone), exotic but "uncivilized" Aboriginal peoples, superstitious and gullible French Canadians (in the case of English explorers describing the French *voyageurs*), and the sublime nature of the immense wilderness. In some cases, passages were inserted into texts to make them more exciting, as, for example, in the case of James Cook's account of his interactions with the Nootka people on the West Coast; a ghostwriter inserted passages about cannibalistic feasts that were not present in Cook's original notes (MacLaren, "English" 36). Likewise, Samuel Hearne's published account of the "Esquimaux" massacre differs greatly from his less melodramatic representation of the event in the transcriptions of his journals.[4]

Three background contexts for understanding exploration narratives are important. The first is the documentary, scientific undertaking that explorers were expected to complete. The period of the eighteenth century, when most of the explorations were conducted, has been described as the Age of Reason, when rational inquiry and systematic recording were considered of prime value in the pursuit of knowledge. Explorers of this period were sponsored by royal commissions or were company employees. In either case, they were expected to keep detailed documents and records of their findings, and were in turn expected to eliminate their own personalities from their accounts. Their records often took the form of extended logbooks or field notes, which were subsequently transposed into longer journal entries. Often these journals were written under conditions of extreme duress. In his journal entry of 18 September 1821, for example, Franklin states that the first priority after setting up camp was to thaw their shoes, following which "each person then wrote his notes of the daily occurrences"; even after the men were weak and starving and had discarded all but the bare essentials, each officer carried his journal to the end of his journey. Since the explorers were venturing into territory that was yet uncharted by Europeans, they saw their task as a communicative one: to transmit details about the new territory and its peoples. Their mission was to make the "strange" comprehensible. This became even more compelling in the eighteenth century, when encyclopedic and systematized taxonomies were considered of primary value. Nevertheless, what explorers soon discovered was the impossibility of this

4 Hearne, as was conventional in his day, uses the term "Esquimaux" throughout his narrative (a derogatory term that means "eater of raw flesh"). Today the people of the High Arctic are known as the "Inuit."

task. More often than not, they struggled with the incongruity between a purely factual account and their subjective responses to what were often disturbing and confusing experiences. At times, their narratives fluctuate from one to the other, as is evident in Samuel Hearne's formulaic account of his emotional response as a "man of feeling" to the Esquimaux massacre in 1771, or in David Thompson's reflective and often romanticized descriptions of his experiences.

The second context is the tradition of adventure and travel tales, which even in the 1500s had become very popular. These were tales of solitary heroes embarking on quests and enduring extreme trials; they were also tales of exotic lands, and strange new peoples and customs. Works such as Cartier's *Voyages* (1545–1600), Champlain's *Voyages* (1603–1632), and the *Jesuit Relations* (1632–1678/1679) were published serially and had huge audiences in France and England. William Shakespeare's imaginary island in *The Tempest* (1611), with its demonized Aboriginal inhabitant Caliban, is clearly responding to the accounts of the "discovery" of the New World that were prevalent during the Elizabethan and Jacobean Ages. So immensely popular were these discovery narratives that the novels of the eighteenth and nineteenth centuries began to mimic them, as one sees, for instance, in such texts as Daniel Defoe's *Robinson Crusoe* (1719), Jonathan Swift's *Gulliver's Travels* (1726), Mary Shelley's *Frankenstein* (1810), and Edgar Allan Poe's *The Narrative of Arthur Gordon Pym* (1850). The explorers composing their journals would have been fully aware of this tradition of writing, as were the publishers who later printed their narratives in book form. As a result, explorers' journals were substantially revised after the fact in order to make them more appealing to European reading audiences. Journals were often provided with more evident plotlines and were rendered stylistically complex through the use of literary features such as metaphors, suspense, definable characters, literary quotations, and flashbacks.

The third context to consider is that of commerce and imperialism, specifically in terms of British and French economic and territorial expansion. Early exploration narratives are clearly an expression of this. Indeed, most explorations had an economic imperative, not solely a selfless love of adventure, although some of these "heroes" have become mythologized as such (see, for example, Thomas D'Arcy McGee's figuration of Cartier in his 1858 poem "Jacques Cartier," or John Newlove's 1968 poem "Samuel Hearne in Wintertime"). In most cases the writers were commissioned to provide factual and useful information about the New World, particularly facts about resources and trade routes. The Hudson's Bay Company, founded in 1670 under the glamorous title "Company of Adventurers of England trading into Hudson's Bay," is the longest-running commercial enterprise in the history of the world. When rival fur traders began to pose a threat to the Hudson's Bay Company's success, the company had to look toward interior expansion in order to compete with independent traders and the North West Company (1783–84). Surveying and map-making, for both companies, became crucial to this enterprise. Henry Kelsey and Samuel Hearne, for example, were conducting inland reconnaissance for the Hudson's Bay Company, while

Thompson undertook similar assignments, first for the Hudson's Bay Company, and later for the North West Company.

As Sir Walter Raleigh said: "He who controls trade controls . . . the world." Likewise, he who controls the world controls the ways that world is documented and remembered. Written narratives by explorers and traders in effect determined the ways readers would imagine and assess the places and peoples they described. As Alan Morantz observes, exploration narratives and maps were "the prime means by which images of the New World were fixed in the minds of Europeans . . . [and they] served as subtle and overt symbols of possession" (52). Even more striking is Canadian critic Margaret Turner's contention that "[t]he first voyages west by Europeans expressed an interest not in finding a new world . . . but in finding a *known* world" (3). Many explorers brought to their experience of the New World their own firmly established assumptions about civilization, cosmography, language, humanity, and religion. Explorers set out with predetermined convictions about what they would encounter. In some cases, the observations and events they recorded served to confirm what they already believed; in other instances, their presuppositions were unravelled, requiring radical intellectual shifts.

Descriptions of Aboriginal peoples and customs are particularly contentious in this regard. Often, published works were used to legitimate European conquest of the New World. In order to achieve this end, Native peoples had to be represented as lawless and barbaric, and therefore in need of civilizing. While the English followed the Spanish usage in referring to the Aboriginal peoples of Canada as "Indians," a tradition started by Columbus in his assumption that he had encountered the "Indies" of the East, the French at this time used the descriptive term *sauvages*, which carried the meaning of "wild" rather than the more pejorative "savage"; nevertheless, the term *savage* tends to be used in most English translations of Cartier's and Champlain's works. This is not to say that the French did not, like the English, regard the Native peoples as "savage"; indeed, Cartier's assessment of the Native cultures he encounters confirms in his own mind the need for the "civilizing" and Christianizing mission that he is undertaking.

Moreover, the mapping and "discovery" of the land, and the publication of writings about it, were seen as a way of staking claims on a territory. Cartier and Champlain laid claim to the territories they explored in the name of France. A famous scene from the narrative of Cartier's first voyage describes his construction of a thirty-foot-high cross that was set up at the entrance to Gaspé Harbour, to the awestruck view of the Native inhabitants, "under the crossbar of which we fixed a shield with three *fleurs-de-lys* in relief, and above it a wooden board, engraved in large Gothic characters, where was written, LONG LIVE THE KING OF FRANCE" (26). In 1690, Henry Kelsey declared that in order to claim the western prairies for the Hudson's Bay Company, he set up a monument, "[c]ut out on it the date of year," and "added to it my master['s] name." Upon reaching the mouth of the Coppermine River in July 1771, Hearne records in his journals that he "erected a mark, and took possession of the coast, on behalf of the Hudson's Bay Company" (106). The notion that Aboriginal peoples might have had prior claim to the land simply does not arise, since it was outside the purview of securely established conceptions of divine intention and European superiority. This presumptuousness in some instances led to disputes between European explorers and Aboriginal peoples. When Cartier insults Donnacona by not seeking his permission, as ally and host, to traverse the territory of Stadacona, Donnacona attempts to thwart his progress up the St. Lawrence.

Contact Zones: Rendering the Strange Familiar

The story of European exploration and settlement of North America is initially a story of a clash of two worlds, and multiple world views. Even as European explorers sought to impose their own presuppositions and beliefs on the land and peoples they encountered, they experienced an increasing disjunction between their idea of themselves (and of the "Old World") and their experiences in the New World. As a result, first-person accounts written by early explorers reveal a certain psychic confusion brought about by the conflict between their traditional notions of the naturalness of Western values and the "truth" of European experience, and the realities of the new land. Such confusion often prompted an aggressive imposition of European belief systems. The existence of a world (and people) where none was expected to be was itself unsettling, especially since many Europeans of the fifteenth century had been taught to believe that they were central to an unfolding divine plan. Cartier, therefore, saw it as his mission to bring Christianity to the New World peoples, just as the Roman Empire had transmitted the Christian faith to the pagan Europeans. In this, he saw himself to be contributing to a divine, and natural, global design. Moreover, the climate, people, and ecology of northern North America (from the harshness of its winters, to the cultures and traditions of its peoples, to its unique flora and fauna) necessitated a reordering of old ways of thinking, and the development of a new vocabulary to describe the Europeans' experiences. Cartier, for instance, upon sighting walrus swimming in the Gulf of St. Lawrence, did not have a word to describe the creatures: "Round about this island are many great beasts, like large oxen, which have two tusks in their jaw like elephant's tusks and swim about in the water" (14). When spotting more of the animals at the mouth of the St. Lawrence, he describes them as "fish in appearance like horses which go on land at night but in the daytime remain in the water" (46). Many early accounts refer to them as "sea-horses" or "sea-cows." Likewise, Mackenzie did not yet have an English word for "moose," and so uses the French term *orignal* (itself from a Mi'kmaq word) throughout his journals. Many explorers made mistakes in their classifications of animals and plants. When the Hudson's Bay Company was granted its charter in 1670, the company was assigned an official coat of arms. The early crest depicts a shield of beaver held up by what are supposed to be two moose, but since the English heralds did not know what a moose looked like, they drew the emblem as two deer with enormous antlers. Subsequent designs altered the insignia to its present-day (and more accurate) depiction (Figure I-7).

Uncertainties over terminology extended to the naming of the land itself. Literary critic Northrop Frye famously claimed that the essential Canadian question is not "Who am I?" but "Where is here?" ("Conclusion" 220), thereby highlighting a foundational obsession with exile and place in the Canadian literary tradition. However, the question "Where is here?" is one that would only be posed by someone who feels ill at ease, or lost, in the landscape. In other words, it is not a question that would be posed by one of the early, and very much "at home," Aboriginal people of the continent. An anecdote related by Frye has it that when an Inuit man leading a southern traveller was told by the man that they were lost, the Inuit man "looked at him thoughtfully and said, 'We are not lost, we are here'" ("Haunted" 27). This story turns non-Native assumptions about the "strangeness" of the landscape inside out, while also highlighting the land's familiarity to those who live in the Arctic.

The imposition of "foreign" names on the landscape is evident in many explorers' accounts, beginning as early as Cartier's naming of the various spots he visits in terms of his experiences there. His naming of Chaleur Bay, for instance, commemorates the "warmth" with which the Iroquois people there greeted him, while the present name of the city of Montreal originates in Cartier's renaming of the mountain at the centre of the established Iroquois village, Hochelaga, to memorialize French royalty—hence "Mont Réal" or, in English, "Mount Royal."[5] The lake where the important battle between the Hurons and their enemies occurred, in which Champlain takes part, is, in Champlain's account, immodestly designated Lake Champlain in honour of himself as the people's "saviour." Sometimes, these renamings appear ludicrous and inappropriate, as, for instance, when Franklin "names" the various bays and cliffs along the Arctic coastline after the officers on his expedition (an act that acquires an element of pathos when Franklin's inability to survive in that landscape becomes so painfully apparent). This is evident, as well, when Hearne names the point at the mouth of the Coppermine River "Bloody Fall" after the Esquimaux massacre he witnesses, an appellation that is subsequently conserved by Franklin when he visits the place.

In many instances, of course, the Aboriginal names of things and places were retained, or sometimes creatively reconfigured. Canadian English abounds with words that have an Aboriginal origin—words such as *chipmunk, chinook, toboggan, kayak, raccoon,* and *skunk*— not to mention the fact that the now often-parodied "symbol" of Canada, maple syrup, has its origin in eastern Aboriginal cultures (see Catharine Parr Traill's recipe for making maple sugar in Section II).

---

[5] In sixteenth-century French, *réal* and *royal* had the same meaning, and both variations of "Mont Réal" and "Mont Royal" have been identified. In the early 1600s, Champlain and the Jesuits referred to the area as the island of "Mont-réal." By the late 1600s, "Montreal" replaced "Hochelaga" as the name of the community established there, so that the island, the mountain, and the city all came to be designated by the same name (Rayburn 163–64).

Nevertheless, it is true that European languages and cultures assumed priority over the Aboriginal cultures they encountered and were influenced by. Thomas King's satirical rendering of an Aboriginal "Garden of Eden" in his 1993 novel *Green Grass, Running Water* has the figure of Adam (or "Ahdamn," as he is called in the book) imposing ridiculous names on the animals in the garden, as a way of highlighting the fact that Aboriginal peoples' world was very much a known— and already "named"—space, as dramatized by the story of Creation in Brian Maracle's "The First Words." Also poignant is Duncan Campbell Scott's 1905 poem, "Indian Place-Names" (see Section III), which invokes the many Aboriginal names that linger in the Canadian landscape (names such as *Toronto, Winnipeg,* and *Quebec*), but in so doing conjures the loss of the living cultures and languages that were suppressed by the coming of Europeans.

Most notable among examples of Europeans adopting Aboriginal words is the naming of Canada itself. Various suggestions for the origin of the word "Canada" have been put forward. The most widely accepted explanation is that it is an Iroquois word, *kanata,* meaning village or town. When Cartier returned for the second time to Canada in 1535 with his two Iroquois captives, the Native men were said to have pointed up the St. Lawrence River, saying: "That is the way to Canada" (roughly the area in the vicinity of Quebec City). Following this, Cartier consistently refers to the area as "Canada" and to the St. Lawrence River as the "rivière de Canada." Another account suggests that "Canada" derives from the Spanish or Portuguese phrase *aca nada* or *ca nada,* meaning "there is nothing," by which such explorers referred to the fact that no gold was to be found there. As early as 1536, a couple of years after Cartier's first voyage, maps appeared with the name "Canada" labelled on the territory he had travelled. In his 1613 *Voyages,* Champlain uses the term *Canadian* to refer to St. Lawrence Native peoples, as opposed to the French colonizers. Gradually, however, from the 1550s to the late 1700s, "Canada" was used to describe the territory of New France. Hence one finds the use of the term "Canadians" in English explorers' narratives to refer specifically to French Canadians, and more specifically, to the *voyageurs* who played such a key role in the early fur trade (see, for example, the account by Franklin). This has echoes, in both English and French literary contexts, in the use of the terms *Canadiens* or *Canadians* to refer to French-Canadians (as in Frances Brooke's 1769 novel *The History of Emily Montague,* Philippe Aubert de Gaspé's 1863 historical novel about French-Canadians, *Les Anciens Canadiens,* or more recently, in the naming of the Montreal hockey team "Les Canadiens"). The label "Canada" did not apply officially to British territory until some time after the British conquest of New France (1759), when in 1791, the combined territory of "Québec" was divided into Upper and Lower Canada. This was in order to separate the primarily French-speaking area of Lower Canada from the area given to the United Empire Loyalists, who had fought on the side of the British in the American War of Independence and were rewarded with land grants in Upper Canada and New Brunswick (see Section II). In 1841, Upper and Lower

Canada were joined once again into a single province called Canada. At the time of Confederation in 1867, the British North America Act declared "Canada" the name of the new dominion (see Section III).

The Beginnings of a Distinct Culture

One sense in which the explorers might be said to have encountered a "new world" in North America is in the emerging hybrid "culture" that came into existence following Native and European contact. As literary critic Germaine Warkentin observes, exploration texts "testify in written form to moments of cultural crisis, and to the emergence of new cultures from such crises" (xi). The mixing of British, French, and Aboriginal peoples in the first few centuries following the arrival of Cartier laid the foundations of a nascent society and culture, initiated perhaps by an experience of "cultural crisis," but which was consolidated in the fur trade and continued to transform and develop thereafter. Although the stereotype of the Arctic explorer has long been that of the solitary hero, the opposite was in fact the case. Complex networks and communities arose as a result of the fur trade. Explorers travelled in groups, often in the company of communities of Aboriginal people. This is evident, for example, in the narratives by Hearne, Thompson, and Franklin. Traders, like Thompson, moved from one trading post to another, and joined communities of traders and Native people in each location. Thompson was often accompanied in his travels by his wife and children. Some of the trading posts had small libraries, and settlements such as that of Port Royal (in the French territory of Acadia, present-day Nova Scotia) engaged in amateur theatricals. *Le Théâtre de Neptune*, a play written by Marc Lescarbot in the early 1600s, is heralded as "the first theatrical performance in North America" (Blais 31), and represents a new hybrid textual form through its inclusion of speeches in French and Mi'kmaq (32). As Warkentin attests, "[B]etween 1660 and 1860 the men and women of the fur trade, native and European, developed in that enigmatic space on the map what can only be called a culture: a world of shared social, linguistic, and eventually historical experience" (xiii).

The narratives included here provide a glimpse of people trying to make sense of themselves as a newly emergent community. Hearne, for example, invokes the experience of fellow traders like himself, thereby signalling his awareness of a new community in the making. "The relation of such uncommon hardships may perhaps gain little credit in Europe," he states, "while those who are conversant with the history of Hudson's Bay, and who are thoroughly acquainted with the distress which the natives of the country about it frequently endure, may consider them as no more than the common occurrences of an Indian life" (22). Likewise, explorers would often refer to the work or experiences of their predecessors. Champlain refers to the early settlement of Cartier and in turn set up the first missionaries in New France, which eventually led to the establishment of the

Jesuit missions; Thompson, for a time, worked under Hearne; Franklin asserts his indebtedness to Hearne and Mackenzie. A shared culture was coming into being, defined by historical precedents and practical realities that were not present in Britain and France. The explorers and traders, in other words, were linked in their experience of a common world, marked by a mingling of languages, peoples, and cultures. For the Europeans, this included exposure to new traditions, new foods, new wildlife, and new landscapes, all of which in a very short time ceased to be "new" and became regarded as familiar and natural. On the Pacific Coast, a trade language known as Chinook emerged that highlights this cultural synthesis, for it was a composite language made up of a mixture of Salish, Nootka, French, and English. Likewise, Aboriginal communities were altered by their interactions with Europeans, not only by acquiring new technologies or being converted to Christianity, but also by using the fur trade as a way of involving Europeans in their own trading alliances and rivalries with other Aboriginal groups.

Nevertheless, different individuals responded to the worlds they were inhabiting in very different ways. Although many traders experienced a changing conception of themselves as a result of their adaptation to new landscapes and encounters with diverse Aboriginal cultures, they did not all respond to Native peoples in the same way. It has become standard to highlight European condescension and aggression toward Aboriginal peoples in North America, and there is some justification in this reading. However, it is also true that some explorers came to respect the Aboriginal peoples they encountered, albeit still within a Eurocentric world view. This is particularly evident when contrasting Champlain's account with Cartier's, or Thompson's with Hearne's. Cartier's high-handed and authoritative manner leads the Iroquois people to suspect him of duplicity, which he in turn uses against them when he becomes fearful of their betrayal of him should they discover that most of his men have succumbed to scurvy. Ironically, it is Dom Agaya, one of the men he kidnapped at the conclusion of his first voyage, who saves Cartier and his men by showing them the cure for the disease. Nevertheless, Cartier uses their supposed treachery to excuse his subsequent abduction of their leader, Donnacona. Champlain, by contrast, immerses himself in the immediate concerns of his Aboriginal allies, and risks his life engaging in their wars. Certainly his interests are motivated to some extent by his desire to win their support as his allies, but his participation in their social world leads them to trust and admire him.

Similarly, Hearne's inability to truly respect the Aboriginal people he encounters, despite the fact that he is utterly dependent on them to lead him to the mouth of the Coppermine River, means that they are less than thoroughly helpful (a point about which he repeatedly complains). Indeed, on his first journey in 1769, he was abandoned by his Aboriginal guide and had to make his own way back to Prince of Wales's Fort. Hearne dismisses the Native men's religious beliefs as "silly notions," unlike Thompson who takes an intense interest in the imaginative world of Aboriginal peoples (and who eventually had a family with a Native woman). Cartwright stands as an odd figure in this respect. His arrogance toward the Labrador Inuit is countered by his obvious admiration (and perhaps hint of envy) of their lives. His desire to be admired by them when he takes them to London comes across as pathetic: he becomes the needy one, and his world appears tarnished in contrast to theirs. As a reader, one cannot help but feel his horrified realization of what he has done to these people when they succumb to smallpox at the outset of the return journey to Labrador.

For many early writers, the experience of Canada was of a world turned upside down. For some, the return to Europe required a second adjustment, and some, such as Thompson, chose to live out their lives in Canada rather than return to a world to which they no longer belonged. "The real experience of discovery," writes Warkentin, "was when Europeans who had thought their society perfect and complete suddenly encountered the unrecognizable 'other'. . . and were forced to reinterpret *themselves* in the light cast by this 'new world'" (xxi). Canadian culture, as we think of it today, with its roots in colonial history and its clash of different peoples, begins here.

Reimagining Discovery: Canadian Literature's Fascination with the Exploration Period

Numerous critics have suggested that the tradition of exploration literature has been fundamental in its influence on later generations of Canadian writers, in part because the contradictions and ambivalences that are so prevalent in early responses to North America have a counterpart in subsequent expressions of the conflicted nature of Canadian identity and experience. It is certainly true that a sense of "incomplete belonging" in Canada continued into the colonial and settlement period (consider Susanna Moodie's contradictory statements about the new world she found herself in), and perhaps even into the decades following Confederation, when so many Canadian writers and thinkers were struggling with what it meant to be Canadian. This conflicted response to the circumstance of being Canadian, what some critics have described almost as a sense of colonial inferiority, persisted into the modernist period of the early twentieth century, with its impassioned debates about the definition and status of Canadian art and literature, and flourished in the Canadian nationalist movement of the 1960s and '70s, when so many Canadians were fervently caught up in debates about Canadian cultural identity.

Margaret Atwood's discussion of "the search for the fabled Canadian identity" in *Strange Things* (8), her 1995 study of the Canadian North, overtly aligns the unsettledness associated with the Canadian "state of mind" with the exploration period (indeed, with the "fabled" Northwest Passage). A central "image-cluster" of Canadian literature, as Atwood puts it (*Strange* 7), is an obsession with the alien nature and menace of the Canadian landscape, a phenomenon that is present in early exploration narratives, though particularly in the written and visual renditions of the Franklin disaster in the late nineteenth century (see Figure I-10). It persists in Susanna Moodie's fear of the wilderness in *Roughing It in the Bush* (1852), Robert Service's figurations of the "spell" and curse of the Yukon (1907), E.J. Pratt's poetic rendering of the Laurentian Shield as a vengeful prehistoric lizard in "Towards the Last Spike" (1952), Earle Birney's renditions of a hostile nature in such poems as "Bushed" and "David" (1952, 1942), and Atwood's poetic sequence *The Journals of Susanna Moodie* (1970), which construes Moodie as an emblem of Canadians' "schizophrenic" response to their placement "here." As William Lyon Mackenzie King famously put it in 1936, Canada is a country with "too much geography."

Frye has been influential in suggesting links between Canadians' tormented relationship with an often threatening landscape (and, by extension, the land's Aboriginal inhabitants) and the experiences of the early adventurers. "[E]very-thing that is heroic and romantic in the Canadian tradition," he maintains, emerges from this history: "The traveller from Europe edges into [Canada] like a tiny Jonah entering an inconceivably large whale. . . . [T]o enter Canada is a matter of being silently swallowed by an alien continent" (217–18, 217). In 1972, Atwood phrased this in terms of the obsession with "survival" in Canadian liter-ature. According to historian Victor Hopwood, it is exploration writings that rep-resent the beginning of an indigenous tradition in English-speaking Canada, since the Old World myths and folk legends that had been transplanted to the New World did not originate there: "The proto-form of our still largely unwrit-ten foundation literature is of necessity the record of our explorers, fur traders, and pioneers" (19).

Nevertheless, rooting Canadian literature and identity in the experience of early explorers or settlers has its shortcomings. Such unifying versions of Canadian identity have come under attack in recent years for being too exclu-sionary and, indeed, politically suspect. On the one hand, such a perspective takes the arrival of Europeans as the starting point of North American culture, which of course it was not. This is the gist of King's critique of Canadian post-colonial theory in relation to Aboriginal cultures in his 1990 essay "Godzilla vs. Post-Colonial." Bruce Trigger's important historical study, *Natives and Newcomers: Canada's "Heroic Age" Reconsidered* (1985), and Arthur J. Ray's *I Have Lived Here Since the World Began* (1996) go some way to rectifying the Eurocentric bias in many historical accounts of first contact by emphasizing the active role Aboriginal peoples had in shaping the development of modern-day Canada. In addition, it has been argued by such theorists as Anne McClintock that the figuration of New World landscapes as menacing and smothering, as is evident in Frye's description of the "alien" land "swallowing" the lone explorer (217), is an inherently imperialist and patriarchal one, in which the landscape is often figured as a female Other set to consume the male explorer. One sees this in Figure I-3, in which Vespucci is depicted "discovering" a female America, as well as in Figure I-10, in which the "jaws" of the Arctic landscape appear to be about to devour the Franklin search party. Further, by gendering the continent as female, these maps highlight the notion that the land is a "virginal" space, ready to be tamed, controlled, and overtaken.

The feminization of the new space makes it easier to justify conquest in a patriarchal system such as the European one of the time. The female body of America becomes the object of male desire in the commercial gaze, and thus becomes an obvious metaphor for desired colonial domination. In his novel *Kiss of the Fur Queen* (1999), Tomson Highway critiques the emphasis on exploration narratives in the study of Canadian history by highlighting the sexual nature of colonial "penetration" and conquest.

Another important critique of the emphasis on discovery and first contact in discussions of Canadian literature and identity has been raised by such theorists as Terry Goldie and Leslie Monkman, both of whom have examined the ways non-Native Canadians have for generations sought to become native or "indigenized" to Canada in order to overcome their "separation of belonging" from it (Goldie, *Fear* 12). In many cases, this belonging is accomplished by appropriating Native customs and traditions, while at the same time supporting the erasure of Native peoples. As Goldie puts it: "The white Canadian looks at the Indian. The Indian is Other and therefore alien. But the Indian is indigenous and therefore cannot be alien. So the Canadian must be alien. But how can the Canadian be alien within Canada?" (12). If the desire to "go Native" has long been a European-Canadian obsession, as in the notorious case of Archie Belaney/Grey Owl in the 1930s (see Volume II), it does not seem to apply to subsequent immigrants to Canada, nor to Canadian Aboriginal peoples themselves.

It is not surprising, then, that in recent decades many Aboriginal authors have tried to provide an alternative perspective on the "discovery" of North America. For example, Basil Johnston's short story "The Prophecy" (1990) and Jeannette Armstrong's poem "History Lesson" (1991), both included in Volume II of this anthology, consider the arrival of Europeans from a Native perspective. In Johnston's story, an Ojibwa elder predicts the coming of the White man to a group of bemused listeners; Armstrong's poem takes a critical look at the violence of the fur trade and the age of "discovery" as it affected Native peoples. Similarly, King's short story "A Coyote Columbus Story" (1993) is a tongue-in-cheek account in which the trickster figure, Coyote, mischievously conjures Christopher Columbus into existence. King's novel *Green Grass, Running Water* (1993) and Daniel David Moses's play *Brébeuf's Ghost* (2000) create a comparable "defamiliarizing," revisionary effect.

In addition, many non-Native writers have turned to the exploration period for its evocative potential as subject matter for contemporary poetry, drama, and fiction. In some instances, these writers have mythologized the explorers as emblematic "heroes," as is the case in such works as Thomas D'Arcy McGee's poem "Jacques Cartier" (1858), Wilfred Campbell's "The Discoverers" (1905), Marjorie Pickthall's "Père Lalemant" (1913), Bliss Carman's "David Thompson" (1922), E.J. Pratt's "Brébeuf and His Brethren" (1940), Gwendolyn MacEwen's play about Franklin, *Terror and Erebus* (1965), John Newlove's poem "Samuel Hearne in Wintertime" (1968), and Stan Rogers's 1981 song "Northwest Passage" (the latter two are both included in Volume II).

In other instances, writers have revisited the exploration period with a critical eye, in part by critiquing the violence and disruption of the imperialist encounter, but more interestingly, by grappling with the moral ambiguity of the period. This concern is evident in a host of contemporary literary texts, including Don Gutteridge's poem sequence about Samuel Hearne, *The Quest for North: Coppermine* (1973); George Bowering's self-reflexive, postmodern novel about George Vancouver's exploration of the Canadian West Coast, *Burning Water* (1980); Jon Whyte's long poem, *Homage, Henry Kelsey* (1981), which fuses the voice of the poet with that of the explorer; Brian Moore's *Black Robe* (1985), a novel about the Jesuit missionaries' encounters with Aboriginal peoples in seventeenth-century New France; Brian Fawcett's short story "The Secret Journal of Alexander Mackenzie" (1985), which attempts to fill in the gaps in Mackenzie's 1793 Pacific journals by inventing some missing entries; Mordecai Richler's *Solomon Gursky Was Here* (1989), a satirical novel which places a Jewish stowaway aboard the famous 1845 Franklin expedition; Margaret Atwood's short story "The Age of Lead" (1991), in which a young woman aligns her experience in the twentieth century with the fate of Franklin's poisoned crew (see Volume II); John Steffler's *The Afterlife of George Cartwright* (1992), a novel in which the ghost of Cartwright is doing penance for his arrogance toward the Inuit of Labrador; Audrey Thomas's novel *Isobel Gunn* (1999), loosely based on the historical case of a Scottish woman who disguises herself as a man and joins the Hudson's Bay Company; Fred Stenson's novel about the early days of the Hudson's Bay Company, *The Trade* (2000); Michael Crummey's *River Thieves* (2001), a novel about the extermination of the Beothuk peoples in nineteenth-century Newfoundland; Douglas Glover's *Elle* (2003), a Governor General's Award-winning novel about a French woman who is marooned on an island in the St. Lawrence during Cartier's third voyage; and a recent Gothic novel about Franklin, Dan Simmons's *The Terror* (2007), in which something is stalking the men and killing them off one by one. Rudy Wiebe's 1989 essay, "Exercising Reflection," and his 1994 novel *A Discovery of Strangers* offer a critical reconsideration of Franklin's disastrous first voyage partly from the perspective of the Aboriginal peoples and Canadian *voyageurs* on the expedition (texts that might be read alongside the Inuit testimony concerning encounters with members of Franklin's crew on his final expedition). In many cases, the more recent works represent attempts to consider the history of exploration from the perspective of those who were left without a voice in the historical record. The Aboriginal peoples who were so affected by European imperialism, yet who were seldom given an independent voice in the explorers' narratives, are prominent in these accounts, as are women and minority figures who would also have been present.

According to Leslie Monkman, the focus of many contemporary poems and fictions about the exploration period has been the disconnection between European discourse and the North American continent and its peoples ("Visions" 81), the impossibility of putting the New World into Old

World words. In each of these texts, it is the human element that remains of prime interest: the moral dilemma of those involved in an ever-expanding quest for "progress," or those who are affected by such a mission, who find themselves immersed in altogether new (perhaps disturbing, perhaps enthralling) circumstances they did not expect. The pull between human ambition and humane decency, and the failure of the one in the thrall of the other, lies at the centre of many of these fictions. As MacEwen puts it in *Terror and Erebus*, her play about Franklin,

> The earth insists
> There is but one geography, but then
> There is another still—
> The complex, crushed geography of men. (42)

An ambivalent relationship with the "crushed geography of men," and women, persists well into the settlement phase of Canadian literature and beyond.

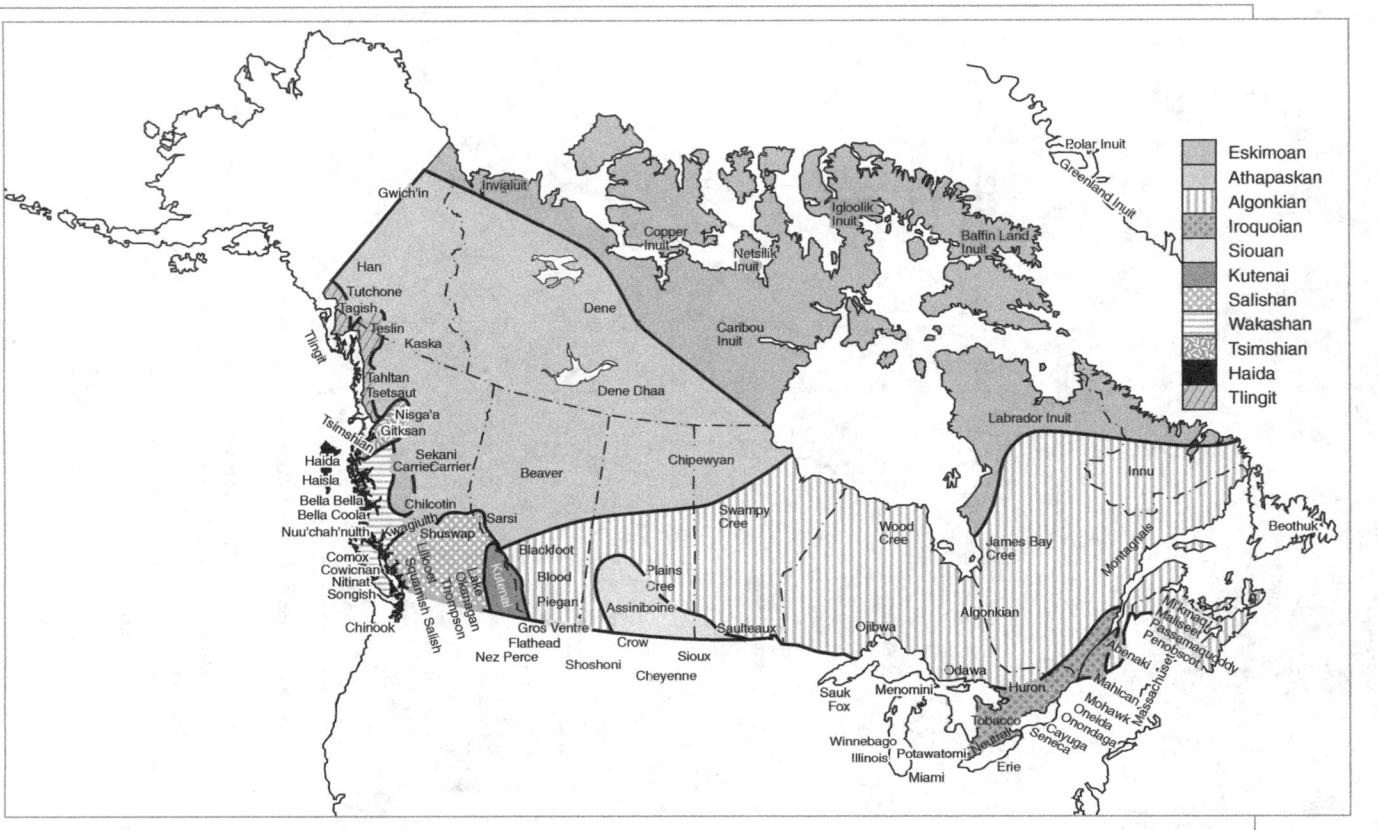

FIGURE I-1 Map of Native Canada Prior to European Contact

Source: Courtesy of Carolyn King, Cartographic Office, York University.

FIGURE I-2 *World Map* (woodcut, detail, c.1532), Hans Holbein the Younger
(1497–1543)

Entitled *Typus Cosmographia Universalis*, and based on Amerigo Vespucci's postulation of
the existence of a North American continent. The outlines of the eastern coast of North
America are visible, with Newfoundland labelled Terra Cortesia. The illustrations in the upper
and lower left-hand corners illustrate the strangeness of the New World as a place of
grotesque animals and cannibals.

Source: The Granger Collection, New York.

AMERICA.

Americen Americus retexit, & *Semel vocauit inde semper excitam .*

FIGURE I-3 "Amerigo Vespucci Discovering America" (engraving, c.1575/1580), Jan van der Straet (1523–1605)

The illustration shows the conventional allegorical depiction of "America" as a Native woman. It depicts scenes of cannibalism in the background, including a severed leg roasting on a spit, and "America" herself is shown to be surprised by the European explorer, Vespucci, while she lazily lounges in a hammock. The contrast between the clothed, rational European (who holds two imperial objects: a staff with a Christian banner and an astrolabe) and the naked, violent Aboriginal woman (whose spear is leaning against a tree) reveals many of the assumptions Europeans brought to the new worlds they were encountering.

Source: Library of Congress.

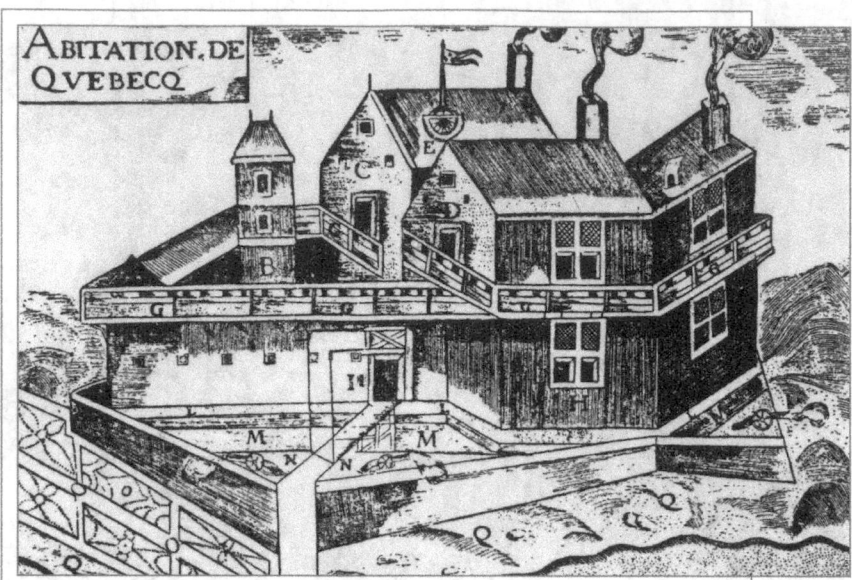

FIGURE I-4 "The Fort at Québec" (engraving, *Voyages* 1613), Samuel de Champlain (1570–1635)

Source: Rischgitz/Betty Images.

FIGURE I-5 "Battle with the Iroquois" (engraving, *Voyages* 1613), Samuel de Champlain (1570–1635)

Champlain's illustration of himself engaged in battle with the Iroquois, which depicts many of the details included in his written account. Certain elements, such as the nudity of the warriors and the palm trees in the background, do not accord with Champlain's narrative but reflect European stereotypes of Aboriginal peoples at the time.

Source: The New York Public Library/Art Resource, NY.

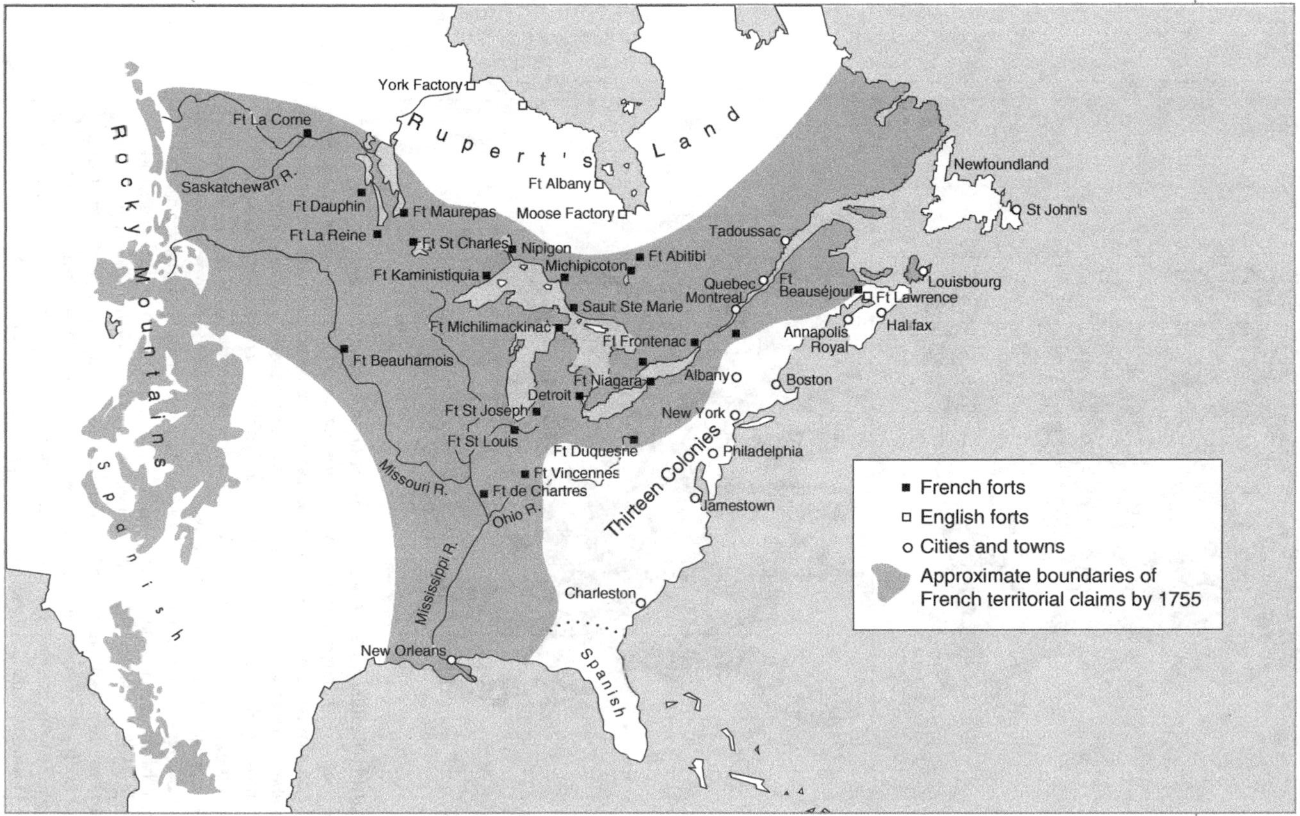

FIGURE I-6 Map of New France in 1759

Source: Conrad/Finkel, *History of the Canadian Peoples*, Vol. 1, Fourth Edition, p.141. Reprinted with permission of Pearson Education Canada.

FIGURE I-7 Hudson's Bay Company Coat of Arms, 1756 and 1962

The Hudson's Bay Company armourial emblem was first used in 1671, one year after the found-ing of the company. Early versions of the coat of arms reveal the fact that the New World was still perceived as a strange place by Europeans. The emblem represents what are supposed to be two moose (the heralds called them "elk") supporting a shield upon which are pictured four beaver separated by a red cross of St. George (the traditional emblem of England). The original beaver, pictured above, are curious long-legged creatures, while the moose more accurately resemble English deer. This discrepancy was due to the fact that the English heralds had never seen either animal (indeed, the word "moose" is an Aboriginal word). In subsequent centuries the coat of arms was adapted to depict the animals with more accuracy. The Latin phrase *"pro pelle cutem"* has often been translated as "a skin for a skin," a curious motto suggesting that animal skins (*pellis*) such as those of the beaver and fox depicted here, were acquired at the cost of many human lives or "skins" *(cutis)*. A more accurate translation is "for the sake of the pelt, the skin," meaning that the skin (*cutis*) was taken in order to get the downy underfur (*pellis*), which was the source of the beaver felt that was used in making hats.

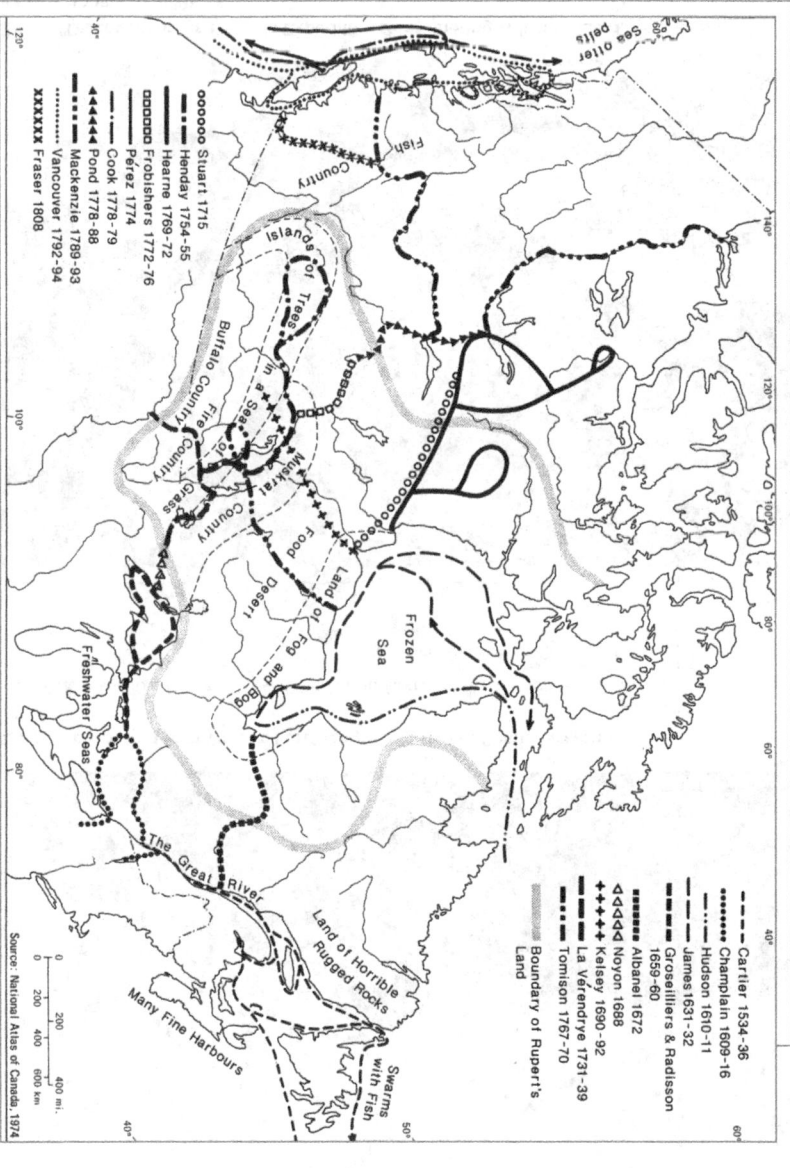

FIGURE I-8 Routes of Explorers, 1534 to 1808

This map charts the journeys of Cartier, Champlain, Hearne, and other European explorers.

Source: Courtesy of Carolyn King, Cartographic Office, York University.

Legend (left):
- ○○○○○○ Stuart 1715
- ● ● ● ● Henday 1754–55
- Hearne 1769–72
- □□□□□ Frobishers 1772–76
- – · – · – Pérez 1774
- – ·· – ·· Cook 1778–79
- ▲▲▲▲ Pond 1778–88
- ▲▲▲▲▲ Mackenzie 1789–93
- ········· Vancouver 1792–94
- XXXXXX Fraser 1808

Legend (right):
- – · – · Cartier 1534–36
- ● ● ● ● Champlain 1609–16
- ····· Hudson 1610–11
- – · – · James 1631–32
- Groseilliers & Radisson 1659–60
- ■■■■■ Albanel 1672
- △△△△ Noyon 1688
- ++++++ Kelsey 1690–92
- +++ La Vérendrye 1731–39
- Tomison 1767–70
- Boundary of Rupert's Land

Map labels: Sea otter pelts, Fish Country, Islands of Trees, Buffalo Country, Grease Country, Musk... Sea of..., Food Country, Land of Little Sticks, Land of Fog and Bog, Desert, Frozen Sea, Freshwater Seas, The Great River, Land of Horrible Rugged Rocks, Swarms with Fish, Many Fine Harbours

Coordinates: 120°, 100°, 80°, 60°, 40°, 140°, 120°, 100°, 80°, 60°, 50°, 40°

Scale: 0 200 400 600 km / 0 200 400 mi.

Source: National Atlas of Canada 1974.

FIGURE I-9 **"View of Prince of Wales's Fort" (engraving, 1777), Samuel Hearne (1745–1792)**

Published in *A Journey from Prince of Wales's Fort in Hudson's Bay to the Northern Ocean*.

Source: Library and Archives Canada/C-00681.

FIGURE I-10 **"Discovery of the Franklin Expedition Boat on King William's Land by Lieutenant Hobson" (1859)**

This engraving, produced for the 29 October 1859 issue of *Harper's Weekly*, accompanied an article on the Franklin expedition following the findings of Francis Leopold McClintock's search party. The article and illustration reveal the lurid fascination with the Canadian North in Britain at the time. The North was often depicted in threatening terms, and the fate of Franklin's crew, who seemed to have been swallowed up by the landscape, assumed iconographic proportions.

Source: Provided courtesy of HarpWeek.

Little is known about Jacques Cartier, the man born in the city of St. Malo, France, who became one of North America's celebrated navigators and explorers. No original manuscripts exist for *The Voyages of Jacques Cartier, 1534, 1535–36, 1541*, and some scholars have disputed the authenticity of the published versions. Nevertheless, Cartier's three published volumes of *Voyages* have held a firm place in Canadian literary history because they document the French discovery of the St. Lawrence seaway, providing the first account of a European impression of the St. Lawrence region of North America and its inhabitants. His journals provide generous detail about the geography of the area, its flora and fauna, and the ethnography of the St. Lawrence Iroquois peoples of Stadacona (present-day Quebec City) and Hochelaga (Montreal, named after the mountain Cartier himself christened Mount Royal).

Like later explorers of North America who journeyed in search of the fabled Northwest Passage, Cartier's primary goal was to seek a route to Asia through the North American continent. In his journals, Cartier continually asks the Native peoples if they know how to navigate through the landmass; he questions them about sources of gold and other riches. Alongside this, however, he had another mission: to contribute to the spread of Catholicism across the globe. As he puts it in his voyage of 1535–36, "I . . . am of opinion that it pleases God in His divine goodness that all human beings inhabiting the surface of the globe, just as they have sight and knowledge of the sun, . . . are to have in time to come knowledge of and belief in our holy faith."

Altogether, Cartier made three voyages to North America between 1534 and 1541. His first voyage, in 1534, took him to Newfoundland and New Brunswick, at which time he missed the entrance to the St. Lawrence River. This voyage concluded with Cartier's kidnapping of two Iroquois men off the Gaspé coast, Dom Agaya and Taignoagny, the sons of Donnacona, the chief of Stadacona. Returning to Canada in 1535 with his two prisoners, Cartier allowed the men to guide him up the St. Lawrence toward their home. A few days later, when Cartier had some doubts about this plan, "the two savages assured [him] that this was the way to the mouth of the great river . . . and the route towards Canada." Thus began the European "discovery" and settlement of the St. Lawrence region.

Cartier's second voyage is his most famous one. It provides an account of meeting Donnacona and his people, his journey up the St. Lawrence to the Native settlements of Stadacona and Hochelaga, the extreme suffering he and his men endured as a result of scurvy (which was relieved only through the intervention of Native people), and his eventual betrayal and kidnapping of Donnacona and his sons. He hoped that Donnacona's account of the riches of the fabled Kingdom of the Saguenay would help him convince the French king to finance a settlement on the St. Lawrence. Some years later, languishing in France, the ten Native people Cartier had brought with him died. When Cartier returned to Stadacona in 1541 to establish a French colony at Cap Rouge, he had to admit to the new leader of the people, Agona, that Donnacona was dead. About the others, he lied, and told Agona that they had become "great Lords, and were married, and would not return back into their country." The new colony was a failure, largely because of increasing hostility with the Stadaconians, and Cartier abandoned it in 1542, returning to France, where he died in 1557.

Cartier's *Voyages* must be read for what it is: an interpretation of what he encountered. The American literary critic Stephen Greenblatt describes the ways Cartier and other early explorers "discovered" in the New World what they already expected to be there. To be sure, many of these accounts represent an attempt to render the unfamiliar familiar, either by interpreting events through a European lens, or by renaming the places and things they encountered. This attempt was only partially successful, as the men's experiences in the New World continued to mystify them and defy their expectations. Such is the case, for example, in Cartier's discovery of the strange animals of the St.Lawrence region. He describes a fish that "is very similar to a grey-hound about the body and head and is as white as snow," thus describing what we today know as a beluga whale. Cartier's response to the Native peoples he encounters also demonstrates a degree of hesitation and suspicion. The second voyage describes a series of miscommunications between Cartier and Donnacona's people. Indeed, Cartier became suspicious of their motives toward him and came to feel increasingly vulnerable in their presence, so much so that, in the winter of 1535–36, he was reluctant to ask the Native people for help when his men became gravely ill with scurvy. Instead, he barricaded his people within their fort and resorted to a series of ploys to mask the diminution in his ranks. While he felt that the Native people could be easily conquered and converted to Catholicism, a factor that he thought would aid in future French settlement of the region, he also unhesitatingly regarded them as barbaric and uncivilized, and therefore in need of the intervention of European colonization. For this reason, he had no qualms in forcibly kidnapping Native people and bringing them back to France, a practice that had become common in Europeans' dealings with Aboriginal peoples in South America.

It is difficult today to conceive of the pure wonder, astonishment, and courage that prevailed on both sides in these early instances of contact and discovery between Native peoples and Europeans. Both peoples were forced to reassess their prior sense of their place in the world. Both were inevitably unsettled, even traumatized, by the discovery. Both sought to learn about the other, and both, inevitably, felt betrayed. Cartier's *Voyages* endure as important documents of this revolutionary moment of the meeting between disparate worlds.

From The Voyages of Jacques Cartier

Cartier's First Encounter with Native Peoples in Chaleur Bay (First Voyage, 1534)

On Thursday the eighth of the said month [July] as the wind was favourable for getting under way with our ships, we fitted up our longboats to go and explore this [Chaleur] bay. [. . .] While making our way along the [north] shore, we caught sight of the savages on the side of a lagoon and low beach, who were making many fires that smoked. We rowed over to the spot, and finding there was an entrance from the sea into the lagoon, we placed our longboats on one side of the entrance. The savages came over in one of their canoes and brought us some strips of cooked seal, which they placed on bits of wood and then withdrew, making signs to us that they were making us a present of them. We sent two men on shore with hatchets, knives, beads, and other wares, at which they showed great pleasure. And at once they came over in a crowd in their canoes to the side where we were, bringing skins and whatever else they possessed, in order to obtain some of our wares. They numbered, both men, women and children, more than 300 persons. [. . .] I am more than ever of the opinion that these people would be easy to convert to our holy faith. They call a hatchet in their language, *cochy*, and a knife, *bacan*. We named this bay, Chaleur Bay. [. . .]

Capture of Donnacona's Sons (First Voyage, 1534)

On the twenty-fourth of the said month [July], we had a cross made thirty feet high, which was put together in the presence of a number of savages on the point at the entrance to this harbour, under the crossbar of which we fixed a shield with three *fleurs-de-lys* in relief, and above it a wooden board, engraved in large Gothic characters, where was written, LONG LIVE THE KING OF FRANCE. We erected this cross on the point in their presence and they watched it being put together and set up. And when it had been raised in the air, we all knelt down with our hands joined, worshipping it before them; and made signs to them, looking up and pointing towards heaven, that by means of this we had our redemption, at which they showed many marks of admiration, at the same time turning and looking at the cross.

When we had returned to our ships, the captain, dressed in an old black bear-skin, arrived in a canoe with three of his sons and his brother; but they did not come so close to the ships as they had usually done. And pointing to the cross he made us a long harangue, making the sign of the cross with two of his fingers; and then he pointed to the land all around about, as if he wished to say that all this region belonged to him, and that we ought not to have set up this cross without his permission. And when he had finished his harangue, we held up an axe to him, pretending we would barter it for his skin. To this he nodded assent and little by little drew near the side of our vessel, thinking he would have the axe. But one of our men, who was in our dinghy, caught hold of his canoe, and at once two or three more stepped down into it and made them come on board our vessel, at which they were greatly astonished. When they had come on board, they were assured by the captain that no harm would befall them, while at the same time every sign of affection was shown to them; and they were made to eat and to drink and to be of good cheer. And then we explained to them by signs that the cross had been set up to serve as a landmark and guidepost on coming into the harbour, and that we would soon come back and would bring them iron wares and other goods; and that we wished to take two of his sons away with us and afterwards would bring them back again to that harbour. And we dressed up his two sons in shirts and ribbons and in red caps, and put a little brass chain round the neck of each, at which they were greatly pleased; and they proceeded to hand over their old rags to those who were going back on shore. To each of these three, whom we sent back, we also gave a hatchet and two knives at which they showed great pleasure. When they had returned on shore, they told the others what had happened. About noon on that day, six canoes came off to the ships, in each of which were five or six men who had come to say goodbye to the two we had detained, and to bring them some fish. These made signs to us that they would not pull down the cross, delivering at the same time several harangues which we did not understand. [. . .]

Meeting with Donnacona's People (Second Voyage, 1535)

On the morrow [8 September], the lord of Canada,[1] named Donnacona (but as leader they call him *Agouhanna*), came to our ships accompanied by many people in twelve canoes. He then sent back ten of these and came alongside our ships with only two canoes carrying sixteen men. And when he was opposite to the smallest of our three ships, this *Agouhanna* began to make a speech and to harangue us, moving his body and his limbs in a marvellous manner, as is their custom when showing joy and contentment. And when he came opposite to the Captain's vessel,[2] on board of which were Taignoagny and Dom Agaya, the leader spoke to them and they to him, telling him what they had seen in France, and the good treatment meted out to them there. [. . .] We thought this river [St. Charles] a suitable place in which to lay up our ships in safety. We named it 'Ste Croix,' as we arrived there that day. Near this spot lives a people of which this Donnacona is leader, and he himself resides there. The village is called Stadacona [Quebec City]. [. . .]

On the following day, we set sail with our ships to bring them to the spot called Ste Croix, where we arrived the next day, the fourteenth of the month. And Donnacona, Taignoagny, and Dom Agaya came to meet us with twenty-five canoes filled with people who were coming from the direction whence we had set out and were making towards Stadacona, which is their home. And all came over towards our ships, showing many signs of joy, except the two men we had brought with us, to wit, Taignoagny and Dom Agaya, who were altogether changed in their attitude and goodwill, and refused to come on board our ships, although many times begged to do so. At this we began somewhat to distrust them. [. . .] Taignoagny began to make a speech and to say to the Captain, that Donnacona was vexed that the Captain and his people carried so many weapons

---

[1] Earlier in the account of his second voyage, Cartier refers to the moment when Donnacona's two sons, upon sighting the coast of Anticosti Island at the mouth of the St. Lawrence, pointed upriver as the route leading to their village, "Canada." The label was gradually expanded to refer to the area under Chief Donnacona's jurisdiction near Stadacona (Quebec City), and then later to the territory along the St. Lawrence roughly between Grosse-Île and Trois-Rivières.

[2] In many of the journals, Cartier is referred to in the third person. The references to the "Captain" throughout these segments of the journals are therefore to Cartier himself.

when they on their side carried none. To this the Captain replied that for all Donnacona's grief, he would not cease to carry them since such was the custom in France as Taignoagny well knew. But for all this the Captain and Donnacona were most friendly towards each other. [. . .]

On the morrow, the sixteenth of that month, we placed our two largest vessels inside the harbour and river. [. . .] And Taignoagny told the Captain that Donnacona was annoyed because he [Cartier] intended to go to Hochelaga [Montreal],[3] and was most unwilling that Taignoagny should accompany him, as he had promised to do; for the river was not worth exploring. To this the Captain made reply, that notwithstanding this he would use his efforts to reach there; for he had orders from the king his master to push on as far as possible. [. . .]

Visit to Hochelaga (Montreal) (Second Voyage, 1535)

On the next day, the eighteenth of the month, they devised a great ruse to prevent us still from going to Hochelaga. They dressed up three men as devils, arraying them in black and white dog-skins, with horns as long as one's arm and their faces coloured black as coal, and unknown to us put them into a canoe. They themselves then came towards our ships in a crowd as usual but remained some two hours in the wood without appearing, awaiting the moment when the tide would bring down the above-mentioned canoe. At that hour they all came out of the wood and showed themselves in front of our ships but without coming so near as they were in the habit of doing. And Taignoagny proceeded to greet the Captain, who asked him if he wished the ship's boat. Taignoagny answered that he did not wish it for the moment but that presently he would come on board the ships. Soon after arrived the canoe in which were the three men dressed as devils, with long horns on their heads. And as they drew near, the one in the middle made a wonderful harangue, but they passed by our ships without once turning their faces towards us, and proceeded to head for the shore and to run their canoe on land. Donnacona and his people at once seized the canoe and the three men, who had let themselves fall to the bottom of it like dead men, and carried them, canoe and men, into the wood which was distant a stone's throw from our ships; and not a soul remained in sight but all retired into the wood. And there in the wood they began a preaching and a speechifying that could be heard from our ships, which lasted about half an hour. After that, Taignoagny and Dom Agaya came out of the wood, walking in our direction, with their hands joined and their caps under their arms, pretending to be much astonished. And Taignoagny began to speak and repeated three times, 'Jesus,' 'Jesus,' 'Jesus,' lifting his eyes towards heaven. Then Dom Agaya called out 'Jesus,' 'Maria,' 'Jacques Cartier,' looking up to heaven as the other had done. The Captain, seeing their grimaces and gesticulations, began to ask them what was the

[3] According to Bruce Trigger, Cartier had offended Iroquois custom by announcing a visit to Hochelaga before he had obtained the chief's permission to travel through Stadacona territory.

matter, and what new event had happened? They replied that there was bad news, adding that indeed it was far from good. The Captain again asked them what was the trouble? They answered that their god, Cudouagny by name, had made an announcement at Hochelaga, and that the three above-mentioned men had come in his name to tell them the tidings, which were that there would be so much ice and snow that all would perish. At this we all began to laugh and to tell them that their god Cudouagny was a mere fool who did not know what he was saying; and that they should tell his messengers as much; and that Jesus would keep them safe from the cold if they would trust in him. [. . .] *[The next day, Cartier departed for Hochelaga.]*

[O]n reaching Hochelaga, there came to meet us more than a thousand persons, men, women, and children, who gave us as good a welcome as ever father gave to his son, making great signs of joy; for the men danced in one ring, the women in another, and the children also apart by themselves. After this they brought us quantities of fish, and of their bread which is made of corn, throwing so much of it into our longboats that it seemed to rain bread. Seeing this the Captain, accompanied by several of his men, went on shore; and no sooner had he landed than they all crowded about him and about the others, giving them a wonderful reception. And the women brought their babies in their arms to have the Captain and his companions touch them, while all held a merry-making which lasted more than half an hour. Seeing their generosity and friendliness, the Captain had the women all sit down in a row and gave them some tin beads and other trifles; and to some of the men he gave knives. [. . .]

At daybreak the next day, the Captain, having put on his armour, had his men marshalled for the purpose of paying a visit to the village and home of these people, and to a mountain which lies near the town. The Captain was accompanied by the gentlemen and by twenty sailors, the remainder having been left behind to guard the longboats. And he took three men of the village as guides to conduct them thither. [. . .] When this was done we marched on, and about half a league thence found that the land began to be cultivated. It was fine land with large fields covered with the corn of the country, which resembles Brazil millet, and is about as large or larger than a pea. They live on this as we do on wheat. And in the middle of these fields is situated and stands the village of Hochelaga, near and adjacent to a mountain, the slopes of which are fertile and are cultivated, and from the top of which one can see for a long distance. We named this mountain 'Mount Royal.' [. . .]

There are some fifty houses in this village, each about fifty or more paces in length, and twelve or fifteen in width, built completely of wood and covered in and bordered up with large pieces of the bark and rind of trees, as broad as a table, which are well and cunningly lashed after their manner. And inside these houses are many rooms and chambers; and in the middle is a large space without a floor, where they light their fire and live together in common. Afterwards the men retire to the above-mentioned quarters with their wives and children. And, furthermore, there are lofts in the upper part of their houses, where they store the corn of which they make their bread. [. . .]

This whole people gives itself to manual labour and to fishing merely to obtain the necessities of life; for they place no value upon the goods of this world, both because they are unacquainted with them and because they do not move from home and are not nomads like those of Canada and of the Saguenay, notwithstanding that the Canadians and some eight or nine other peoples along this river are subjects of theirs. [. . .]

As we drew near to their village, great numbers of the inhabitants came out to meet us and gave us a hearty welcome, according to the custom of the country. [. . .] [T]he ruler and leader of this country, whom in their language they call *Agouhanna*, was carried in, seated on a large deer-skin, by nine or ten men, who came and set him down upon the mats near the Captain, making signs to us that this was their ruler and leader. This *Agouhanna*, who was some fifty years of age, was in no way better dressed than the others except that he wore about his head for a crown a sort of red band made of hedgehog's skin. This leader was completely paralyzed and deprived of the use of his limbs. When he had saluted the Captain and his men, by making signs which clearly meant that they were very welcome, he showed his arms and legs to the Captain motioning to him to be good enough to touch them, as if he thereby expected to be cured and healed. On this the Captain set about rubbing his arms and legs with his hands. Thereupon this *Agouhanna* took the band of cloth he was wearing as a crown and presented it to the Captain. And at once many sick persons, some blind, others with but one eye, others lame or impotent and others again so extremely old that their eyelids hung down to their cheeks, were brought in and set down or laid out near the Captain, in order that he might lay his hands upon them, so that one would have thought Christ had come down to earth to heal them.

Seeing the suffering of these people and their faith, the Captain read aloud the Gospel of St John, namely, 'In the beginning,' etc., making the sign of the cross over the poor sick people, praying God to give them knowledge of our holy faith and of our Saviour's passion, and grace to obtain baptism and redemption. Then the Captain took a prayer-book and read out, word for word, the Passion of our Lord, that all who were present could hear it, during which all these poor people maintained great silence and were wonderfully attentive, looking up to heaven and going through the same ceremonies they saw us do. After this the Captain had all the men range themselves on one side, the women on another, and the children on another, and to the headmen he gave hatchets, to the others, knives, and to the women, beads and other small trinkets. He then made the children scramble for little rings and tin *agnus Dei*,[4] which afforded them great amusement. The Captain next ordered the trumpets and other musical instruments to be sounded, whereat the people were much delighted. We then took leave of them and proceeded to set out upon our return. [. . .]

---

[4] Latin, Lamb of God. These refer to representations of Jesus as a lamb bearing a cross or a Christian banner, meant to signify Christ's sacrifice (like a lamb at an altar) to redeem the sins of humankind.

Attack of Scurvy (Second Voyage, 1535–36)

In the month of December we received warning that the pestilence had broken out among the people of Stadacona to such an extent that already, by their own confession, more than fifty persons were dead. Upon this we forbade them to come either to the fort or about us. But notwithstanding we had driven them away, the sickness broke out among us accompanied by most marvellous and extraordinary symptoms; for some lost all their strength, their legs became swollen and inflamed, while the sinews contracted and turned as black as coal. In other cases the legs were found blotched with purple-coloured blood. Then the disease would mount to the hips, thighs, shoulders, arms, and neck. And all had their mouths so tainted that the gums rotted away down to the roots of the teeth, which nearly all fell out. The disease spread among the three ships to such an extent that, in the middle of February [1536], of the 110 men forming our company, there were not ten in good health so that no one could aid the other, which was a grievous sight considering the place where we were. For the people of the country who used to come daily to the fort saw few of us about. And not only were eight men dead already but there were more than fifty whose case seemed hopeless. [. . .]

After this the disease increased daily to such an extent that at one time, out of the three vessels, there were not three men in good health, so that on board one of the ships there was no one to go down under the quarter-deck to draw water for himself and the rest. And already several had died, whom from sheer weakness we had to bury beneath the snow; for at that season the ground was frozen and we could not dig into it, so feeble and helpless were we. We were also in great dread of the people of the country, lest they should become aware of our plight and helplessness. And to hide the sickness, our Captain, whom God kept continually in good health, whenever they came near the fort, would go out and meet them with two or three men, either sick or well, whom he ordered to follow him outside. When these were beyond the enclosure, he would pretend to try to beat them, and vociferating and throwing sticks at them, would drive them back on board the ships, indicating to the savages by signs that he was making all his men work below the decks, some at calking, others at baking bread and at other tasks; and that it would not do to have them come and loaf outside. This they believed. And the Captain had the sick men hammer and make a noise inside the ships with sticks and stones, pretending that they were calking. [. . .]

From the middle of November [1535] until the fifteenth of April [1536], we lay frozen up in the ice, which was more than two fathoms in thickness, while on shore there were more than four feet of snow, so that it was higher than the bulwarks of our ships. This lasted until the date mentioned above, with the result that all our beverages froze in their casks. And all about the decks of the ships, below hatches and above, there was ice to the depth of four finger breadths. And the whole river [St. Lawrence] was frozen where the water was fresh up to beyond Hochelaga. During this period there died to the number of twenty-five of the best and most able seamen we had, who all succumbed to the aforesaid malady.

And at that time there was little hope of saving more than forty others, while the whole of the rest were ill, except three or four. But God in His divine grace had pity upon us and sent us knowledge of a remedy which cured and healed all. [...]

One day our Captain, seeing the disease so general and his men so stricken down by it, on going outside the fort to walk up and down on the ice, caught sight of a band of people approaching from Stadacona, and among them was Dom Agaya whom he had seen ten or twelve days previous to this, extremely ill with the very disease his own men were suffering from; for one of his legs about the knee had swollen to the size of a two-year-old baby, and the sinews had become contracted. His teeth had gone bad and decayed, and the gums had rotted and become tainted. The Captain, seeing Dom Agaya well and in good health, was delighted, hoping to learn what had healed him in order to cure his own men. And when they had come near the fort, the Captain inquired of him what had cured him of his sickness. Dom Agaya replied that he had been healed by the juice of the leaves of a tree [white cedar] and the dregs of these, and that this was the only way to cure sickness. Upon this the Captain asked him if there was not some of it thereabouts, and to show it to him that he might heal his servant who had caught the disease when staying in Donnacona's house at Canada, being unwilling that he should know how many sailors were ill. Thereupon Dom Agaya sent two women with our Captain to gather some of it; and they brought back nine or ten branches. They showed us how to grind the bark and the leaves and to boil the whole in water. Of this one should drink every two days, and place the dregs on the legs where they were swollen and affected. According to them this tree cured every kind of disease. They call it in their language *Annedda*.

The Captain at once ordered a drink to be prepared for the sick men but none of them would taste it. At length one or two thought they would risk a trial. As soon as they had drunk it they felt better, which must clearly be ascribed to miraculous causes; for after drinking it two or three times they recovered health and strength and were cured of all the diseases they had ever had. And some of the sailors who had been suffering for five or six years from the French pox were by this medicine cured completely. When this became known, there was such a press for the medicine that they almost killed each other to have it first; so that in less than eight days a whole tree as large and as tall as any I ever saw was used up, and produced such a result that had all the doctors of Louvain and Montpellier been there, with all the drugs of Alexandria, they could not have done so much in a year as did this tree in eight days; for it benefited us so much that all who were willing to use it recovered health and strength, thanks be to God. [...]

Kidnapping of Donnacona (Second Voyage, 1536)

On 21 April, Dom Agaya came on board our vessels with several fine-looking, powerful men whom we had not been in the habit of seeing, and told us that Donnacona would be back on the following day and would bring with him a quantity of deer's meat and other venison. And the next day, the twenty-second of the month,

Donnacona did arrive at Stadacona accompanied — why or for what purpose we did not know — by a great number of men. [. . .] The Captain, being informed how on their return they had brought back so many people, and how Dom Agaya, on coming to tell us of this, had been unwilling to cross the river lying between us and Stadacona [the St. Charles], and had refused to come over, a thing he was not in the habit of doing, became suspicious of treason, as did the rest of us. [. . .]

The Captain, on being informed of the large number of people at Stadacona, though unaware of their purpose, yet determined to outwit them and to seize their leader [Donnacona], Taignoagny, Dom Agaya, and the headmen. And moreover he had quite made up his mind to take Donnacona to France, that he might relate and tell to the king all he had seen in the west of the wonders of the world; for he assured us that he had been to the land of the Saguenay[5] where there are immense quantities of gold, rubies, and other rich things, and that the men there are white as in France and go clothed in woollens. [. . .]

Taignoagny and Dom Agaya debated together for more than an hour before they would cross, but in the end they did so and came and spoke to the Captain. And Taignoagny begged the Captain to consent to seize [Agona, a rival leader] and carry him off to France. This the Captain refused, saying that the king [Francis I], his master, had forbidden him to carry off to France any man or woman but only two or three boys to learn the language; but that he would willingly take him to Newfoundland and set him upon an island. The Captain spoke thus in order to calm their fears and to induce Donnacona, who still kept on the other side of the river, to cross over. Taignoagny was much pleased at these words, which made him hope he should never go back to France, and he promised the Captain to return on the following day, which was Holy Cross Day and to bring with him Donnacona and all the people of Stadacona. . . .

On 3 May, which was the festival of the Holy Cross, the Captain in celebration of this solemn feast had a beautiful cross erected some thirty-five feet high, under the cross-bar of which was attached an escutcheon, embossed with the arms of France, whereupon was printed in Roman characters: LONG LIVE FRANCIS I. BY GOD'S GRACE KING OF FRANCE. And that day about noon several persons arrived from Stadacona, both men, women, and children, who told us that Donnacona with Taignoagny, Dom Agaya, and the rest of their party were on their way, which pleased us, as we were in hopes of being able to capture them. They arrived about two o'clock in the afternoon; and as soon as they came opposite to our ships the Captain went and greeted Donnacona, who likewise was friendly enough but kept his eye constantly

[5] The Native peoples told Cartier about the "Kingdom of the Saguenay," which was rumoured to abound in gold and other treasures and to be populated by a fair-skinned people. There is some ambiguity about the location of this mysterious kingdom. At times, it appears to refer to the area along today's Saguenay River, which branches off from the St. Lawrence at Tadoussac; at other points, it refers to an area to the northwest of Hochelaga (Montreal), beyond the Ottawa River. The kingdom was said to be situated on a sea, possibly Hudson Bay. Despite repeated attempts, Cartier never did reach the fabled land.

fixed on the wood and was wonderfully uneasy. [. . .] Soon after the leader [Donnacona] entered the fort in company with the Captain, whereupon Taignoagny immediately rushed in to make him go out again. Seeing there was no other chance, our Captain proceeded to call to his men to seize them. At this they rushed forth and laid hands upon the leader and the others whose capture had been decided upon. The Canadians, beholding this, began to flee and to scamper off like sheep before wolves, some across the river, others into the wood, each seeking his own safety. When the above-mentioned had been captured and the rest had all disappeared, Donnacona and his companions were placed in safe custody.

[1534, 1535–36[6]]

---

[6] The dating of the publication of Cartier's *Voyages* is difficult because the first published texts (as opposed to the various manuscript versions that circulated) were translations. For example, the account of the first voyage was initially published in Italian in 1565, well before the first published French version of 1598. The second voyage was published in French anonymously before the first in 1545. For this reason, in the case of Cartier only, we are providing the dates of the voyages themselves rather than the date of first publication. This text of Cartier's *Voyages* is based on Henry Percival Biggar's 1924 English translation. The authorship of the *Voyages* is also in question. They may have been based on Cartier's logbooks, but shaped into narrative form by someone else.

SAMUEL DE CHAMPLAIN ■ (1570–1635)

Samuel de Champlain is often called the "Father of New France," as it was Champlain who, in 1608, founded the settlement of Quebec, which he dreamed would become the centre of the fur-trading and religious colony of New France. Nor was he wrong: today, Quebec City is the oldest continually inhabited European settlement in North America. Before settling on the site of Quebec, Champlain had begun to travel and map the St. Lawrence region, following and extending the path of Cartier laid down almost a century before. He made his first voyage to Canada in 1603 and published his account of his experiences that same year, under the title *Des Sauvages*. This work contains his initial impressions of the St. Lawrence region and of the Montagnais and Algonquin peoples he encountered. He made a second voyage to North America in 1604, acting as an unofficial geographer on the expedition led by Pierre de Monts and establishing a settlement in Acadia. This mission ended abruptly in 1607, when the group's trading privileges were revoked and the colonists were ordered back to France. His third journey in April 1608 has now become his most famous, because it was during this time that Champlain established the colony at Quebec, as he announces in the opening excerpt provided here (see Figure I-4). The second volume of his published *Voyages* (1613) covers the period from 1604 to 1612, and contains his account of the settlement of Quebec and his involvement in the Algonquin-Iroquois wars in the region. During these travels, Champlain thoroughly mapped the area of New France, providing information on routes that would be consulted for the next two centuries.

The French traders and settlers promised the Algonquin, Montagnais, and Huron peoples that they would help them in their wars against their enemies in exchange for their cooperation in their cause: to explore, map, and colonize eastern Canada in the name of the King of France, and to establish a trading monopoly. Together with the third volume of his *Voyages* (1619), these books provide an account of Champlain's participation in battles alongside his allies against the Iroquois (in two separate battles, Champlain was wounded by Iroquoian arrows). According to Bruce Trigger, the battle in the summer of 1609 (described in the excerpt included here and shown in Figure I-5) is the "first recorded encounter of the Iroquois with European firearms." To commemorate the victory, Champlain named the location of this conflict Lake Champlain (in present-day New York and Vermont). This and other accounts of his encounters with Aboriginal peoples reveal a sharp contrast between Champlain's relations with Native peoples and Cartier's. Champlain was considered a trusted friend, and according to his Algonquin and Huron acquaintances, he had proved his courage and allegiance. In contrast to some others like Cartwright, he was lenient in his judgment of "infractions" committed by Aboriginal people, because he felt it necessary to preserve the peace. Nor was Champlain as suspicious as Cartier. In fact, most of Champlain's problems arose from the competition and jealousy of other French traders, who he felt wanted him "to run a thousand risks in discovering nations and countries in order that they may keep the profits and the others the hardships." The complex trading alliances among Aboriginal communities, however, added to his difficulties,

since certain Native groups were reluctant to give up their role as middlemen and allow Champlain to make direct contact with their trading partners.

It is interesting to note the difficulty early explorers had in distinguishing their perception of the violence of the Aboriginal peoples they encountered from their own participation in aggressive campaigns. Also noteworthy is what is at times a certain disingenuousness in the Europeans' dealings with Native peoples. Champlain is very quick to assure the Algonquins that the Basque traders they encounter merely want "to obtain possession of the Indians' goods," even though Champlain's mission is hardly dissimilar. Likewise, Champlain is not above lying to his Native acquaintances about his true objectives. In his journey into the interior in search of the fabled "northern sea" (Hudson Bay), Champlain tells the Native people that he is there to offer his services in their war plans, rather than revealing his true motives. "[I]t was very necessary to assist them," he states in a later journal, "both to engage them the more to love us, and also to provide the means of furthering my enterprises and explorations which apparently could not be carried out without their help." In his dedication to the King in his published *Voyages* of 1619, he condemns those traders who are "urged on by the lust of gain," and asserts his own motive as that of "enlarg[ing] the bounds of charity towards [God's] unfortunate creatures."

Notwithstanding these and many other contradictions, Champlain's accounts provide some of the most detailed and comprehensive historical descriptions of the region and its inhabitants that are available to us today. Increasingly, Champlain dreamed of reaching the Pacific via the St. Lawrence seaway; for this purpose he travelled up the Ottawa River to Lake Ontario and Lake Huron, mapping out the trade route that was to be used by French fur traders for the next few centuries (it has been called the "original Trans-Canada Highway"). This transcontinental journey was accomplished two centuries later by Alexander Mackenzie, but not along the course Champlain had anticipated. His genius as a cartographer and artist is also noteworthy. In *Des Sauvages* Champlain predicted that Hudson Bay was an inland gulf rather than a sea, long before Henry Hudson's deception on this score led to his tragic demise in the freezing waters of the bay (with his son, he was cast adrift in a lifeboat by his mutinous crew); unfortunately for Champlain, Hudson charted the bay before Champlain was able to do it himself and claim it for France. The maps and illustrations Champlain included with his published accounts are also remarkable for their detail and their artistry.

After more than ten journeys to North America, in the early 1630s Champlain set himself the task of revising his narrative of the settlement of New France, rewriting his earlier journals and republishing them in a new version in 1632. In 1633, less than two years before his death, he returned to Quebec as the official governor of New France. He died there on Christmas Eve, 1635, and was buried in the Catholic chapel he had constructed a few years before. An astrolabe that is attributed to Champlain, which he is presumed to have lost sometime in his 1613 travels in the Ottawa region, was found in 1867 (near Cobden, Ontario), and is today on display in the Canadian Museum of Civilization in Gatineau, Quebec.

From Voyages

Settlement of Quebec (1608)

From the island of Orleans to Quebec is one league, and I arrived there on July the third. On arrival I looked for a place suitable for our settlement, but I could not find any more suitable or better situated than the point of Quebec,[1] so called by the natives, which was covered with nut-trees. I at once employed a part of our workmen in cutting them down to make a site for our settlement, another part in sawing planks, another in digging the cellar and making ditches, and another in going to Tadoussac with the pinnace to fetch our effects. [. . .]

I continued the construction of our quarters, which contained three main buildings of two stories. Each one was three fathoms long and two and a half wide. The storehouse was six long and three wide, with a fine cellar six feet high. All the way round our buildings I had a gallery made, outside the second story, which was a very convenient thing. There were also ditches fifteen feet wide and six deep, and outside these I made several salients [angled fortifications] which enclosed a part of the buildings, and there we put our cannon. In front of the building there is an open space four fathoms wide and six or seven long, which

[1] Quebec is an Algonquian word designating the place where the St. Lawrence River narrows.

abuts upon the river's bank. Round about the buildings are very good gardens, and an open place on the north side of a hundred, or a hundred and twenty, yards long and fifty or sixty wide [see Figure I-4]. Nearer Quebec there is a little river [St. Charles], which comes from a lake in the interior, distant six or seven leagues from our settlement. I consider that in this river, which is north a quarter north-west of our settlement, was the place where Jacques Cartier passed the winter; since at a league's distance up this river are still the remains as of a chimney, whose foundation we discovered, and to all appearance what seem to have been ditches about his house, which was small. [. . .]

Whilst the carpenters, sawyers, and other workmen were busy at our quarters, I set all the rest to work clearing the land about our settlement in order to make gardens in which to sow grains and seed, for the purpose of seeing how the whole thing would succeed, particularly since the soil seemed to be very good.

Meanwhile many of the natives had encamped near us, who used to fish for eels, which begin to come up about September 15 and finish on October 15. [. . .] All these tribes suffer so much from hunger that sometimes they are obliged to live on certain shell-fish, and to eat their dogs and the skins with which they clothe themselves against the cold. I consider that, if anyone were to show them how to live, and how to till the soil, and other things, they would learn very well; for there are many of them who have good judgment, and reply pointedly to the questions put to them. But they have bad points: they are revengeful and awful liars, people whom one must not trust too far, but rather judiciously, and with force in one's hand. They promise readily, but perform badly. They are people, the majority of whom, so far as I have been able to see, respect no law, but have plenty of false beliefs. I asked them what sort of ceremonies they used in praying to their God. They told me that they had no other than this, that each one prayed to God in his heart, just as it suited him. [. . .]

War Against the Iroquois (1609)

Still continuing our journey I met with some two or three hundred Indians who were encamped near a small island called St. Eloi, a league and a half from St. Mary. We approached to investigate and found that they were tribes of Indians called Ochateguins [Hurons] and Algonquins, who were on their way to Quebec to help us to explore the country of the Iroquois, with whom they are in mortal conflict, and they spare nothing belonging to these enemies.[2]

[. . .] [T]hey now besought me to return to our settlement, for them to see our houses, and that three days later we should all set off on the war-path together. [. . .] After listening to their speech, I made answer, that to please them I was glad to go back to our settlement for their greater satisfaction, and that they could see that I had no other intention than to make war; for we had with us only arms

[2] In the years intervening between Cartier's and Champlain's sojourns in Canada, the Iroquois settlements along the St. Lawrence at Stadacona and Hochelaga had vanished.

and not merchandise for barter, as they had been led to understand, and that my only desire was to perform what I had promised them. [...]

Now as we began to get within two or three days' journey of the home of their enemy, we proceeded only by night, and during the day we rested. Nevertheless, they kept up their usual superstitious ceremonies in order to know what was to happen to them in their undertakings, and often would come and ask me whether I had had dreams and had seen their enemies. I would tell them that I had not, but nevertheless continued to inspire them with courage and good hope. [...]

Evening having come, we embarked in our canoes in order to proceed on our way, and as we were paddling along very quietly, and without making any noise, about ten o'clock at night on the twenty-ninth of the month, at the extremity of a cape which projects into the lake on the west side, we met the Iroquois on the war-path. Both they and we began to utter loud shouts and each got his arms ready. We drew out into the lake and the Iroquois landed and arranged all their canoes near one another. Then they began to fell trees with the poor axes which they sometimes win in war, or with stone axes; and they barricaded themselves well.

Our Indians all night long also kept their canoes close to one another and tied to poles in order not to get separated, but to fight all together in case of need. We were on the water within bowshot of their barricades. And when they were armed, and everything in order, they sent two canoes which they had separated from the rest, to learn from their enemies whether they wished to fight, and these replied that they had no other desire, but that for the moment nothing could be seen and that it was necessary to wait for daylight in order to distinguish one another. They said that as soon as the sun should rise, they would attack us, and to this our Indians agreed. [...] After we were armed with light weapons, we took, each of us, an arquebus[3] and went ashore. I saw the enemy come out of their barricade to the number of two hundred, in appearance strong, robust men. They came slowly to meet us with a gravity and calm which I admired; and at their head were three chiefs. Our Indians likewise advanced in similar order, and told me that those who had the three big plumes were the chiefs, and that there were only these three, whom you could recognize by these plumes, which were larger than those of their companions; and I was to do what I could to kill them. I promised them to do all in my power, and told them that I was very sorry they could not understand me, so that I might direct their method of attacking the enemy, all of whom undoubtedly we should thus defeat; but that there was no help for it, and that I was very glad to show them, as soon as the engagement began, the courage and readiness which were in me.

As soon as we landed, our Indians began to run some two hundred yards towards their enemies, who stood firm and had not yet noticed my white companions who went off into the woods with some Indians. Our Indians began to call to me with loud cries; and to make way for me they divided into two groups,

---

[3] An arquebus was an early type of portable firearm.

and put me ahead some twenty yards, and I marched on until I was within some thirty yards of the enemy, who as soon as they caught sight of me halted and gazed at me and I at them. When I saw them make a move to draw their bows upon us, I took aim with my arquebus and shot straight at one of the three chiefs, and with this shot two fell to the ground and one of their companions was wounded who died thereof a little later. I had put four bullets into my arquebus. As soon as our people saw this shot so favourable for them, they began to shout so loudly that one could not have heard it thunder, and meanwhile the arrows flew thick on both sides [see Figure I-5]. The Iroquois were much astonished that two men should have been killed so quickly, although they were provided with shields made of cotton thread woven together and wood, which were proof against their arrows. This frightened them greatly. As I was reloading my arquebus, one of my companions fired a shot from within the woods, which astonished them again so much that, seeing their chiefs dead, they lost courage and took to flight, abandoning the field and their fort, and fleeing into the depth of the forest, whither I pursued them and laid low still more of them. [. . .]

After we had gained the victory, our Indians wasted time in taking a large quantity of Indian corn and meal belonging to the enemy, as well as their shields, which they had left behind, the better to run. Having feasted, danced, and sung, we three hours later set off for home with the prisoners. The place where this attack took place is in 43° and some minutes of latitude, and was named Lake Champlain. [. . .]

[1613]

THE JESUIT RELATIONS ■ (1632–1678/79)

The Jesuit Relations, written by different contributors over the years 1632 to 1678/79, are the most significant documentary texts of the seventeenth century to outline the contact of Europeans with Native North Americans. The Jesuit order, or Society of Jesus, was founded in 1534. It was expressly devoted to education, which is apparent in many of the goals outlined for the mission in New France (indeed, the Jesuit mission contains the germ of the first residential schools for North American Aboriginal people). The first Jesuit mission in New France was established in Acadia in 1611, and in Quebec and "Huronia" in 1632, though the Jesuit presence was but a small part of the larger French presence in eastern North America. A series of missionary reports published in French during the seventeenth century to spread word about the North American missions, *The Jesuit Relations* were reports sent from the missions to the superior in Quebec City, who compiled and edited the letters from the field, and sent them on to Paris to be published. Although the reports were made from 1611 into the late 1700s, the published documents, amounting to more than 70 volumes, were primarily written between 1632 and 1678. For a brief period, between 1629 and 1632, the English occupied New France and the Jesuits were expelled. They returned in 1632, led by Paul Le Jeune.

The Jesuit accounts are both adventure narratives and ethnographic accounts of Native cultures. The accounts provided by Father Jean de Brébeuf in 1636 are particularly known for their extensive detail of Huron culture. While *The Jesuit Relations* were immensely popular and eagerly anticipated in France, some dissenting readers mocked their extravagance. Today, these accounts may appear shockingly intolerant of Native beliefs, particularly in the terminology that is used to describe the peoples they encountered (barbarian, primitive, savage, infidel, etc.). Yet it is also important to note that the Jesuits immersed themselves in Native life (learning Native languages and cultural traditions) and consulted with Native peoples in the writing of their accounts and their mapping of the north-eastern interior. Even as they denigrated the pagan nature of their subjects, they also celebrated the Native peoples' humanity, bravery, and generosity. In some instances, Native peoples were considered more God-fearing than the French-Canadian settlers and fur traders, who the Jesuits felt had become cor-rupted by greed and excessive liberality.

The Jesuit mission took place during the long-standing wars among Native nations. The Jesuits established them-selves within the existing Native alliance system, allying themselves with the Hurons, Montagnais, and Algonquins in the north against the five nations of the Iroquois Confederacy (Mohawk, Onondaga, Oneida, Cayuga, and Seneca) in the south. The Dutch traders in the south had already allied themselves with the Iroquois and were using them to help them in their land expansion. Many of the Jesuit documents take on the tone of a crusade against infidels, or "barbarians," as the Iroquois enemy were described. For many Jesuits, the posting to New France was considered a sacrifice or trial under-taken for the glory of God. Indeed, a num-ber of the Jesuit priests were killed in the Iroquois invasions. Two accounts, in par-ticular, stand out: the torture and captivity of Father Jogues in 1642, who lived to survive his ordeal and write about it (form-ing part of Father L'Alemant's *Relation* of 1647), and the martyrdom of Father Brébeuf in 1649, who was canonized as a saint in 1930, making him the first bona fide saint of the New World. Shortly after Father Brébeuf's murder, the main Jesuit headquarters, Ste. Marie Among the Hurons, which by that time was sheltering some 9000 Hurons, had to be abandoned due to Iroquois attacks. Today, the remains of some of the Jesuit martyrs, including the skull of Father Brébeuf, are held in the Martyrs' Shrine Church in Midland, Ontario (close to the location of the original Ste. Marie mission).

From The Jesuit Relations

Relation of What Occurred Among the Hurons (1635)

Jean de Brébeuf

I cannot better express the fashion of the Huron dwellings than to compare them to bowers or garden arbors,—some of which, in place of branches and vegetation, are covered with cedar bark, some others with large pieces of ash, elm, fir, or spruce bark. [. . .]

There are no different stories; there is no cellar, no chamber, no garret. It has neither window nor chimney, only a miserable hole in the top of the cabin, left to permit the smoke to escape. This is the way they built our cabin for us. [. . .]

As to the interior, we have suited ourselves; so that, even if it does not amount to much, the Savages never weary of coming to see it, and seeing it, to admire it. We have divided it into three parts. The first compartment, nearest the door, serves as an ante-chamber, as a storm door, and as a storeroom for our provisions, in the fashion of the Savages. The second is that in which we live, and is our kitchen, our carpenter shop, our mill, or place for grinding wheat, our Refectory, our parlor and our bedroom. On both sides, in the fashion of the Hurons, are two benches which they call *Endicha*, on which are boxes to hold our clothes and other little conveniences; but below, in the place where the Hurons keep their wood, we have contrived some little bunks to sleep in, and to store away some of our clothing from the thieving hands of the Hurons. They sleep beside the fire, but still they and we have only the earth for bedstead; for mattress and pillows, some bark or boughs covered with a rush mat; for sheets and coverings, our clothes and some skins do duty.

The third part of our cabin is also divided into two parts by means of a bit of carpentry which gives it a fairly good appearance, and which is admired here for its novelty. In the one is our little Chapel, in which we celebrate every day holy Mass, and we retire there daily to pray to God. It is true that the almost continual noise they make usually hinders us, and compels us to go outside to say our prayers. In the other part we put our utensils. [. . .] As to the clock, a thousand things are said of it. They all think it is some living thing, for they cannot imagine how it sounds of itself; and when it is going to strike, they look to see if we are all there, and if some one has not hidden, in order to shake it.

They think it hears, especially when, for a joke, one of our Frenchmen calls out at the last stroke of the hammer, "That's enough," and then it immediately becomes silent. They call it the Captain of the day. When it strikes they say it is speaking; and they ask when they come to see us how many times the Captain has already spoken. They ask us about its food; they remain for a whole hour, and sometimes several, in order to be able to hear it speak. They used to ask at first what it said. We told them two things that they have remembered very well; one, that when it sounded four o'clock of the afternoon, during winter, it was saying, "Go out, go away that we may close the door," for immediately they arose, and went out. The other, that at midday it said, *yo eiouahaoua*, that is, "Come, put on the kettle;" and this speech is better remembered than the other, for some of these spongers never fail to come at that hour, to get a share of our Sagamité.[1] They eat at all hours, when they have the wherewithal, but usually they have only two meals a day, in the morning and in the evening; consequently they are very glad during the day to take a share with us.

[1] Cree, *kisamitew*: A type of hot drink or broth.

Speaking of their expressions of admiration, I might here set down several on the subject of the loadstone, into which they looked to see if there was some paste; and of a glass with eleven facets, which represented a single object many times, of a little phial in which a flea appears as large as a beetle; of the prism, of the joiner's tools; but above all, of the writing; for they could not conceive how, what one of us, being in the village, had said to them, and put down at the same time in writing, another, who meantime was in a house far away, could say readily on seeing the writing. I believe they have made a hundred trials of it. All this serves to gain their affections, and to render them more docile when we introduce the admirable and incomprehensible mysteries of our Faith; for the belief they have in our intelligence and capacity causes them to accept without reply what we say to them.

[1635]

What the Hurons Think About Their Origin (1636)

Jean de Brébeuf

It is astonishing to see so much blindness in regard to the things of Heaven, in a people who do not lack judgment and knowledge in reference to those of earth. This is what their vices and brutality have merited from God. There are some indications, as can be seen in certain details in their fables, that in the past they had some knowledge of the true God that was more than merely natural. [. . .] Since they were unwilling to acknowledge God in their habits and actions, they have lost the thought of him and have become worse than beasts in his sight for the lack of respect they display.

To begin with fundamental beliefs, most of them take pride in deriving their origin from heaven. Their conviction is based on the following fable, which passes among them for the truth.

They recognize as head of their nation a certain woman whom they call Aataentsic, who fell from heaven, they say, into their midst.[2] For they think the heavens existed long before this wonder occurred, but they cannot tell you when or how its great bodies were drawn from the abysses of nothingness. They even suppose that above the vault of heaven there was, and still is, a land like this one, with woods, lakes, rivers, and fields, as there are here on earth, and with peoples who inhabit them. There is some disagreement as to the manner in which this fortunate fall occurred. Some say that one day, as she was working in her field, she perceived a bear. Her dog began to pursue it, and then she herself went after it. The bear, seeing himself closely pressed and seeking only to escape the teeth of the dog, fell by accident into a hole. The dog followed him. Aataentsic approached this precipice and, finding neither the bear nor the dog in view, despaired and threw herself into the hole after them. However, her fall happened

[2] See the story of Sky Woman and the Creation of Turtle Island in Brian Maracle's story "The First Words," which opens this anthology.

to be more favorable than she had expected. For she fell down into the waters of the earth without being hurt, even though she was pregnant. After this, the waters dried up little by little, and the earth appeared and became habitable.

Others attribute this fall to another cause, which seems to have something to do with Adam, though the story is predominantly falsehood. They say that the husband of Aataentsic, being very sick, dreamed that it was necessary to cut down a certain tree from which the people who dwelt in Heaven obtained their food. Eating the fruit of this tree, he believed, would cure him immediately. Aataentsic, knowing the desire of her husband, took his ax and went off to accomplish the task. She had no sooner dealt the first blow than the tree at once melted, almost under her feet, and fell to the earth. She was so astonished that, after carrying the news to her husband, she returned and threw herself after it. As she fell, the Turtle happened to raise its head above water and perceived her. Not knowing what to do at the sight of this astonishing wonder, she called together the other aquatic animals to get their advice. They immediately assembled, and she showed them what she had seen, asking what they thought she should do. The majority voted to refer the matter to the beaver, who, as a courtesy, left it to the Turtle's judgment. The latter finally concluded that they should all promptly set to work, dive to the bottom of the water, bring up soil to her, and put it on her back. No sooner said than done, and the woman fell very gently on this island. She was pregnant when she fell, and after a time she gave birth to a daughter, who almost immediately became pregnant herself. (If you ask them how this could happen, you will make them very uncomfortable. "The fact is," they tell you, "that she was pregnant." Some throw the blame upon some strangers who landed on this island. Try, I pray you, to make this agree with what they say: that before Aataentsic fell from the sky there were no men on earth!) Be that as it may, she brought forth two boys, Tawiscaron and Iouskeha, who, when they grew up, quarreled with one another. (Does this not relate in some way to the murder of Abel?) They came to blows, but with very different weapons. Iouskeha had the horns of a stag; Tawiscaron used only some wild rose hips, in the belief that, as soon as he struck his brother with them, [his brother] would fall dead at his feet. But it happened quite differently than he had expected, and instead Iouskeha struck him so hard in the side that he bled profusely. This poor wretch immediately fled, and from his blood, which was sprinkled across the land, certain stones sprang up, like those we employ in France to strike a gun, which the Indians call even today Tawiscara, from the name of this unfortunate man. His brother pursued him and killed him. This is what most of the Hurons believe concerning the origin of these nations. [. . .]

All that we do is to bear witness to them that we feel compassion for their gross ignorance. We take the occasion, if they seem capable of understanding, to explain some of our mysteries, showing them how fully they conform to reason. They listen very willingly and are well satisfied with this.

[1636]

"The Huron Carol" is often described as Canada's first Christmas hymn. Father Jean de Brébeuf, one of the Jesuit missionaries sent to New France in the 1600s, composed the words to "The Huron Carol" ("Jesous Ahatonhia") in the Huron language in Quebec around 1643, while recovering from an injury. Brébeuf set the song to the music of a sixteenth-century French carol, "Une Jeune Pucelle." His aim was to teach the Hurons about the birth of Jesus Christ by using references to their own culture. A "translation" of the song was written by Jesse Edgar Middleton in 1926. This version, which is the one that is most popular today, is notable for its haunting quality, though its sentimentalized text may be more in keeping with twentieth-century stereotypes of Native cultures than with the Jesuits' knowledge of Huron people in the seventeenth century. More recently, John Steckley, named Teondecheron by the Wyandot of Kansas, produced a literal translation of the Huron original that more closely communicates Brébeuf's version. Both versions are provided here. "The Huron Carol" has become a popular Christmas hymn in Canada, even if the original version was used in the widespread goal of converting Native peoples to Christianity. The song has recently been included in the Hymn Books of the Canadian Anglican and United Churches. Aboriginal singer/actor Tom Jackson has become well known for his annual Christmas benefit concert, which features "The Huron Carol" as part of its repertoire. It is also included on Bruce Cockburn's 1993 Christmas album, where he sings the song in Huron.

The Huron Carol

Jesse Edgar Middleton (inspired by Jean de Brébeuf)

'Twas in the moon of winter-time, when all the birds had fled,
That mighty Gitchi Manitou sent angel choirs instead;
Before their light the stars grew dim,
And wond'ring hunters heard the hymn:
Jesus your King is born, Jesus is born, *in excelsis gloria.*

Within a lodge of broken bark the tender Babe was found,
A ragged robe of rabbit skin enwrapped his beauty round;
But as the hunter braves drew nigh,
The angel song rang loud and high.
Jesus your King is born, Jesus is born, *in excelsis gloria.*   10

The earliest moon of winter-time is not so round and fair
As was the ring of glory on the helpless Infant there.
The chiefs from far before him knelt

With gifts of fox and beaver pelt.
Jesus your King is born, Jesus is born, *in excelsis gloria*.   20

O children of the forest free,
O sons of Manitou,
The Holy Child of earth and heaven is born today for you.
Come kneel before the radiant Boy,
Who brings you beauty, peace, and joy.
Jesus your King is born, Jesus is born, *in excelsis gloria*.

[1643/1926]

Jesus, He Is Born

Jean de Brébeuf/John Steckley (Teondecheron)

Have courage, you who are humans. Jesus, he is born
Behold, the spirit who had us as prisoners, domestic animals, has fled.
Do not listen to it, as it corrupts our minds, the spirit of our thoughts.
Jesus, he is born.

They are spirits, coming with a message for us, the sky people.
They are coming to say, "Be on top of life rejoice!
Mary has just given birth, come on, rejoice."
Jesus, he is born.

Three have left for such a place, they are Elders.
A star that has just appeared over the horizon leads them there.   10
He will seize the path, a star that leads them there.
Jesus, he is born.

As they arrived there, where he was born, Jesus,
The star was at the point of stopping, he was not far past it.
Having found someone for them, he says, "Come here."
Jesus, he is born.

Behold, they have arrived there and have seen Jesus,
They praised a name many times saying "Hurray, he is good in nature."
They greeted him with respect, greasing his scalp many times, saying "Hurray!"
Jesus, he is born.   20

We will give to him praise, honour for his name."
Let us show reverence for him, as he comes to be compassionate with us.
It is providential that you love us, and think "I should make them part of my family."
Jesus, he is born.

[1643/1984]

The journals of George Cartwright give us a unique picture of early Canadian settlement in the late eighteenth century. Born in Marnham, England, into an aristocratic family, Cartwright was obliged to make his own living when the family's fortunes declined. He sought his fortune overseas in Labrador, making his first voyage there in 1766 with his brother John.

Cartwright determined to begin a settlement and trading operation on the Labrador coast, which he did between 1770 and 1786. In his early years, Cartwright lived very close to an Inuit community, and his accounts of his relations with the Inuit are of particular interest. In 1772, Cartwright took an Inuit family to England to show them to the King and to help raise funds to continue his work in North America. Cartwright's account of this Inuit delegation sets his journals apart from those of Cartier and Champlain, who likewise took Aboriginal people to France but did not write about the Native peoples' response to Europe. In scenes that are at once poignant and humorous, the Inuit remain unimpressed by all of England's riches. Tragically, on the journey home, all of the family but one died from smallpox. Cartwright's aim to impress the Inuit people in Labrador with the rightness of English sovereignty through these people's reports of the Old World was foiled. Years later, on 28 March 1779, Cartwright received news of the large-scale death of the Inuit, who he assumed had contracted smallpox from the one survivor of his European voyage.

Cartwright's *Journal of Transactions and Events, during a Residence of Nearly Sixteen Years on the Coast of Labrador* (1792) stands apart from other travel narratives in this anthology because his account was initially written for his own personal perusal, and hence contains intimate and domestic details of his day-to-day life in Labrador. From the endless accounts of his hunting expeditions, to his dealings with the English and Newfoundland people in his settlement, to his contacts with Native peoples, Cartwright's observations have an honesty, and at times arrogance, that distinguish them from the more determined missions of his contemporaries in North America. Indeed, he repeatedly refers to the people in his settlement as his "family," at once an affectionate and proprietorial term that acquires additional resonance when in a late journal of 26 May 1779 he reveals that his housekeeper, Mrs. Selby, is in fact his mistress.

In his preface to the published journal, Cartwright apologizes for his "inability to entertain the reader with the Style and Language of some late writers." Nevertheless, his journal is compelling and instructive, particularly in his conflicted attitude toward the Inuit family he befriends, whom he genuinely admires but cannot help viewing through his utilitarian ethos. While he admires the Inuit for their generosity and integrity, a stance that is fairly unusual among European accounts of the Inuit of this period, he nevertheless considers them British property. The tragedy of his journey to London with the group, which he followed by a second journey in 1773 accompanied by a young Inuit boy (whom he had inoculated against smallpox and who subsequently died from the inoculation), demonstrates a reluctance to comprehend the real atrocity of the imperialist mission in Canada. Cartwright continued his Labrador venture until 1786, first working for the merchant company Noble and Pinson, and then striking out on his own or with various partners. However, he was never able to fully recoup his losses after his post was attacked in 1778 by American privateers, who stole and destroyed his property. In 1784, back in England, Cartwright was forced to file for bankruptcy. With his brother, he inherited a share of the family estate, and resided in England from 1787 until his death, at the age of 80, in 1819. Notwithstanding the severity of his losses, and his overall disappointment in his Labrador enterprise, Cartwright appears to have genuinely loved Labrador. In his later years in England, Cartwright was dubbed "Old Labrador" by his acquaintances and family, attesting to his heartfelt ties with the place.

From Journal of Transactions and Events

Contact with the Labrador Inuit (1771–72)

Tuesday, July 9, 1771. Early this morning I went to Cape Charles, and there pitched my tent upon the continent, directly opposite the Indian Camp; having a tickle[1] between us, not more than eighty yards wide. The instant that I was ready to open shop, I sent my people home, with injunctions not to come near me until I sent them an order in writing for that purpose; or, unless they had any business with me, which could not be deferred till my return. My tent was soon filled with Indians, and we carried on a very brisk trade till two o'clock in the afternoon. [. . .]

Wednes., July 10, 1771. [. . .] Very little more than the mere necessaries of life (which, a little reflection will convince everyone, are few indeed) will satisfy an Indian;[2] for he has no stimulus to industry. When he has killed food he has generally procured clothing also; therefore he will work no longer. [. . .] Yet I have not a doubt, but commerce will, in progress of time, have the same effect on these people, that it ever has had on other nations: it will introduce luxury, which will increase their wants, and urge them to much more industry than they at present possess. They will then purchase traps, learn to build deathfalls, and contrive other devices to kill furs, at such times as a successful seal-chase shall give them leisure to pay proper attention to that branch of trade.

[. . . B]eing informed by one of their people, that a principal man amongst them, had stolen a skein of thread; I immediately sent to the chief a peremptory order to bring the thread to my tent, which he accordingly complied with. Having reproved him in a very angry tone for his behaviour, I gave him a few strokes. He instantly made resistance, when catching him in my arms, I gave him a cross-buttock (a method of throwing unknown to them) and pitched him with great force headlong out of my tent. I then appealed to the rest for the justice of

[1] A tickle is a small passage of water between a continent and an island or between islands.

[2] Cartwright uses the terms "Indian" and "Esquimau" (i.e., Inuk) interchangeably throughout his journals.

my cause, who not only applauded me for the action, but seemed to have a high opinion both of my lenity and strength. The man went immediately to his tent, and returned with a beautiful seal-skin as a present to me; but I would by no means accept of it, making him and the rest understand, that I did not quarrel with him, that he should make me a present to be reconciled; but because he had been guilty of a dishonest action; and that as he now seemed to be sensible of his crime, I was perfectly satisfied. I told them, that I would never steal anything from them, and as I would not suffer any of my people to plunder them, so neither would I suffer them to rob me with impunity: and I moreover assured them; that nothing should ever induce me to take away their lives. By words and signs together, I made them fully comprehend my meaning, which had the desired effect; for we were afterwards not only upon the most friendly terms; but I seemed likewise to have established an authority over them. [. . .]

Journey to England with an Inuit Family (1772)

Thursday, October 29, 1772. [. . .] It was this day determined, that Attuiock, Ickcongoque, his youngest wife; Ickeuna, her daughter; (a child under four years of age) Tooklavinia, Attuiock's youngest brother; and Caubvick his wife, should accompany me to England. Another brother, with his wife, are already gone to England with Perkins and Coghlan's head-man;[3] and their other two brothers, Nawadlock and Scheidley, with their families, and Attuiock's other three wives, with the rest of their children, are to winter at my sealing-post at Stage Cove. I gave them very particular injunctions for their behaviour, and they promised obedience.

Friday, October 30, 1772. [. . .] The rest of the Indians being gone to Charles Harbour, those who are to go to England with me are accommodated in Mr. Pinson's house. On going into the room where they slept, I observed Attuiock performing a ceremony, which, for its singularity, I shall take the liberty to relate. His wife was laid upon the floor, with her hands by her sides: Attuiock sat on the right side of his wife, so far back, as to have her head opposite to his knees. He had placed a loose strap under her head, which came over her forehead. In this strap he put the end of a strong stick, which he held in his hands across his knees. With great gravity, and in a low, doleful cadence, he sung a song, frequently laying a strong emphasis on some particular word which I did not understand; at the same time, by the help of a lever, he raised her head as high as the length of her neck would permit, and then let it bump down again upon the floor, keeping time to the tune. As I supposed it was a religious rite, (he being a priest) I silently observed what was going foreward. At length, the old gentleman fixing his eyes on me, pointed to his wife, with an important look, and said, "It is very good, very good." "That may be," replied I, "but pray what is it good for?" "My wife has got the head-ach," answered the priest. Not willing to affront him, I got out of the room as fast as possible, that I might indulge myself in a hearty laugh, at the curious Esquimau method of curing that complaint. [. . .]

[3] Thomas Perkins and Jeremiah Coghlan were English merchants with whom Cartwright had set up a business partnership.

Sunday, November 8, 1772. At day-break we put to sea, and set sail for Ireland. We found a very great sea in the streights, and by night were two leagues to the eastward of the island of Belle Isle. [. . .]

Sunday, November 22, 1772. The Indians grew extremely uneasy to-day, and insisted that we had lost ourselves and should never more see land. I then examined the log book, and shewed them upon the chart where we were; adding, that we should make the land of Ireland, near Cape Clear, to-morrow; but they gave very little credit to what I said. [. . .]

Monday, December 14, 1772. I went down the river this morning, met the vessel in the Pool, and brought the women on shore. They were greatly astonished at the number of shipping which they saw in the river; for they did not suppose that there were so many in the whole world: but I was exceedingly disappointed to observe them pass through London Bridge without taking much notice of it. I soon discovered that they took it for a natural rock which extended across the river. They laughed at me when I told them it was the work of men; nor could I make them believe it, till we came to Blackfriars Bridge, which I caused them to examine with more attention; shewing them the joints, and pointing out the marks of the chizzels upon the stones. They no sooner comprehended by what means such a structure could be erected, than they expressed their wonder with astonishing significancy of countenance.

On landing at Westminster Bridge, we were immediately surrounded by a great concourse of people; attracted not only by the uncommon appearance of the Indians who were in their seal-skin dresses, but also by a beautiful eagle, and an Esquimau dog; which had much the resemblance of a wolf, and a remarkable wildness of look. I put them all into coaches, with as much expedition as possible, and drove off to the lodgings which I had prepared in Leicester Street. [. . .]

Being willing, as far as lay in my power, to comply with the incessant applications of my friends for a sight of the Indians; and finding it impossible either to have any rest, or time to transact business, I appropriated two days a week to that purpose, viz., Tuesdays and Fridays. On those days, not only my house was filled, even to an inconvenience, but the street was so much crowded with carriages and people, that my residence was a great nuisance to the neighbourhood.

As their skin dresses had a dirty appearance and an offensive smell, I provided a quantity of broad-cloth, flannel, and beads, together with whatever else was necessary; and the women now having leisure to work, and being excellent taylors, soon clothed them all anew; preserving their own fashion in the cut of their garments.

I once took the men to the opera when their Majesties were there, and we chanced to sit near Mr. Coleman, the manager of Covent Garden Theatre, who politely invited all the Indians and myself to a play at his house. He fixed on Cymbeline, and they were greatly delighted with the representation. But their pride was most highly gratified, at being received with a thundering applause by the audience on entering the box. The men soon observed to their wives, that they were placed in the King's box, and received in the same manner as their

Majesties were at the opera; which added considerably to the pleasure which they felt from the *tout ensemble*. Never did I observe so young a child pay such unremitting attention to the whole representation, as little Ickeuna; no sooner did the swords begin to clash, in the fighting scene between Posthumus and Iachimo, but she set up a most feeling scream.

About a fortnight after our arrival in town, having provided great-coats, boots, and hats for the men, in order that they might pass through the streets unobserved, I took Attuiock with me and walked beyond the Tower. We there took [a] boat, rowed up the river, and landed at Westminster Bridge; from whence we walked to Hyde Park Corner, and then home again. I was in great expectation, that he would begin to relate the wonders which he had seen, the instant he entered the room; but I found myself greatly disappointed. He immediately sat down by the fire side, placed both his hands on his knees, leaned his head forward, fixed his eyes on the ground in a stupid stare; and continued in that posture for a considerable time. At length, tossing up his head, and fixing his eyes on the ceiling, he broke out in the following soliloquy; "Oh! I am tired; here are too many houses; too much smoke; too many people; Labrador is very good; seals are plentiful there; I wish I was back again." By which I could plainly perceive, that the multiplicity, and variety of objects had confounded his ideas. [. . .]

Although they had often passed St. Paul's without betraying any great aston-ishment, or at least not so much as all Europeans do at the first sight of one of those stupendous islands of ice, which are daily to be seen near the east coast of their own country, yet when I took them to the top of it, and convinced them that it was built by the hands of men (a circumstance which had not entered their heads before, for they had supposed it a natural production) they were quite lost in amazement. The people below, they compared to mice; and insisted, that it must at least be as high as Cape Charles, which is a mountain of considerable altitude. Upon my asking them how they should describe it to their countrymen on their return, they replied, with a look of the utmost expression, they should neither mention it, nor many other things which they had seen, lest they should be called liars, from the seeming impossibility of such astonishing facts. [. . .]

And it was a great treat to me, both then and at all other times, to observe their different emotions, much more forcibly expressed in their countenances, than is possible to be done by those, whose feelings are not equally genuine. Civilized nations imperceptibly contract an artificial expression of countenance, to help out their languid feelings; for knowledge, by a communication with the world and books, enlightens our ideas so much, that they are not so liable to be taken by surprise, as the uninformed mind of the savage, who never had the least hint given him, that certain things are in existence; consequently, they break upon him as unexpectedly, and forcibly, as the sun would do upon a man who was born deaf and blind, in case he should suddenly be brought to sight on a clear day. [. . .]

After my return to town, by his Majesty's permission, I took them to Court; where their dresses and behaviour made them greatly taken notice of. They were also at the houses of several of the nobility and people of fashion; and I omitted nothing, which came within the compass of my pocket, to make their stay in England agreeable, or to impress them with ideas of our riches and strength. The latter I thought highly necessary, as they had often, when in Labrador, spoken of our numbers with great contempt, and told me they were so numerous, that they could cut off all the English with great ease, if they thought proper to collect themselves together; an opinion which could not fail to produce in me very unpleasant reflections. But they had not been long in London before they confessed to me, that the Esquimaux were but as one, compared to that of the English. [. . .]

Smallpox and the Return to Labrador (1773)

Saturday, May 8, 1773. Having now completed all my business in town, and the wind being fair, at two o'clock this afternoon we made sail down the river; the Esquimaux well pleased in the expectation of soon seeing their native country, their relations and friends again; and I very happy in the prospect of carrying them back, apparently in perfect health. [. . .]

Thursday, May 13, 1773. The pleasing prospects which I so lately had before me were of very short duration; for this evening as Caubvick was going to bed, she complained of great sickness at her stomach, had a very bad night, and daily grew worse. On my arrival at Lymmington on the thirteenth, and consulting a surgeon there, (for my own, I found, was utterly ignorant of her complaint) he declared her malady to be the small-pox: which had nearly the same effect on me, as if he had pronounced my sentence of death. As it was vain to expect that the rest should escape the infection, medicines were immediately given to prepare them for it. [. . .]

At two o'clock in the morning of the twenty-ninth, we weighed again, and proceeded down the channel with a fair wind and pleasant weather; still in hopes of arriving in sufficient time for my business; but at ten o'clock, so dreadful a stench pervaded the whole vessel, all the Indians being now ill, that three of the ship's crew now were seized with a fever, and we had reason to expect, that a pestilential disorder would soon attack us all. I therefore ordered captain Monday to carry the vessel into Plymouth, although I foresaw that measure would prove an immense loss to me, by the ruin of my voyage, and we came to an anchor in Catwater the next afternoon at two o'clock. I went on shore immediately, and made a personal application to Earl Cornwallis, Admiral Spry, and the Mayor of Plymouth, for an house to put the Indians in, but could not succeed.

Monday, May 31, 1773. Ickeuna died this morning, Caubvick had a violent fever on her, and the rest were extremely ill. In the evening I bargained for a house at Stonehouse, for two guineas and a half per week. At four o'clock the next morning we weighed and removed the vessel to Stonehouse Pool. I got the Indians on shore immediately, and Ickcongoque died that night. [. . .]

Thursday, June 10, 1773. I left London on my return to Plymouth at six o'clock this morning, and arrived at Stonehouse on Saturday evening. I was now informed that both the men died in the night of the third Instant, and that Caubvick had been given over, but was at length in a fair way of recovery, though reduced to a skeleton, and troubled with a great many large boils. She recovered so very slowly, that it was not until the fourth of July that I durst venture to remove her, when I once more embarked with her and all the rest of my family (except my maid whom I had discharged for bad behaviour) to proceed on my intended voyage. [. . .]

Caubvick's hair falling off, and being matted with the small-pox, I had much difficulty to prevail on her to permit me to cut it off, and shave her head. Notwithstanding I assured her that the smell of the hair would communicate the infection to the rest of her country folks on her return, yet I was not able to prevail on her to consent to its being thrown overboard. She angrily snatched it from me, locked it up in one of her trunks, and never would permit me to get sight of it afterwards; flying into a violent passion of anger and grief whenever I mentioned the subject, which I did almost every day, in hopes of succeeding at last. [. . .]

Tuesday, August 31, 1773. About noon almost the whole of the three southern-most tribes of Esquimaux, amounting to five hundred souls or thereabouts, arrived from Chateau in twenty-two old English and French boats [. . .] but the wind did not suit them to come hither till this morning.

I placed myself upon a rock near the water-side, and Caubvick sat down a few paces behind me. We waited for the landing of the Indians with feelings very different from theirs; who were hurrying along with tumultuous joy at the thoughts of immediately meeting their relations and friends again. As the shore would not permit them to land out of their boats, they brought them to their anchors at a distance off, and the men came in their kyacks, each bringing two other persons, lying flat on their faces; one behind and the other before, on the top of the skin covering. On drawing near the shore, and perceiving only Caubvick and myself, their joy abated, and their countenances assumed a different aspect. Being landed, they fixed their eyes on Caubvick and me, in profound, gloomy silence. At length, with great perturbation and in faltering accents, they enquired, separately, what was become of the rest; and, were no sooner given to understand, by a silent, sorrowful shake of my head, that they were no more, than they instantly set up such a yell, as I had never before heard. Many of them, but particularly the women, snatched up stones, and beat themselves on the head and face till they became shocking spectacles. [. . .] In short, the violent, frantic expressions of grief were such, as far exceeded my imagination; and I could not help participating with them so far, as to shed tears most plentifully. They no sooner observed my emotion, than, mistaking it for the apprehensions which I was under for fear of their resentment, they instantly seemed to forget their own feelings, to relieve those of mine. They pressed round me, clasped my hands, and said and did all in their power to convince me, that they did not entertain any suspicion of my conduct towards their departed friends. As soon as the first violent transports of grief began to subside, I related the melancholy tale, and explained to them, as well as I could, the disorder by which they were carried off; and pointed to Caubvick, who bore very strong, as well as recent, marks of it. They often looked very attentively at her, but, during the whole time, they never spoke one word to her, nor she to them. As soon as I had brought the afflicting story to a conclusion, they assured me of their belief of every particular, and renewed their declarations of friendship.

[1792]

By the time Samuel Hearne undertook his exploration work for the Hudson's Bay Company, trading relations between Aboriginal peoples and Europeans in eastern Canada were well established. Hearne, born in England in 1745, has been celebrated as the first European to reach the Arctic Ocean by land. He was also the founder of Cumberland House in 1774, the Hudson's Bay Company's first inland post and the oldest permanent settlement in what is now Saskatchewan. Unlike other explorers before him, Hearne lived and travelled as his Native companions did, sharing their eating habits and nomadic lifestyle, acquiring their survival methods, and enduring their hardships. His journals are noted for their detailed accounts of these journeys and his endurance of extreme adversity — labour, cold, near-starvation, mosquitoes, physical pain, and violence. His method of exploration travel inspired subsequent explorers to imitate his technique, while his narrative style exerted a strong influence on the next generation of explorers' writings, including those of Mackenzie and Thompson. However, according to Ken McGoogan, Hearne's fame extends even beyond this. In his biography of Hearne, McGoogan tells how the explorer had become infamous in England for his recitations of his North American voyages. In 1791, Hearne was scheduled to appear at the Christ Church Hospital in London. Samuel Taylor Coleridge, who was in attendance, "found himself swept away" by Hearne's impassioned account. According to McGoogan, Hearne became one of the models for Coleridge's guilt-ridden and glittering-eyed sailor in his haunting poem "The Rime of the Ancient Mariner" (James Cook and Thomas James have also been identified as key influences on Coleridge's poem).

In the context of Canadian literary history, Hearne's writings are important for another reason. Although he lacked a formal education (he joined the Royal Navy in 1756 at the age of eleven), his writings have outlasted many other accounts of northern travel from the same period, and are notable for their immediacy and detail. This is not to say that Hearne's accounts are free of prejudice or fabrication. While they provide geographical and ethnographic descriptions of the regions and people he encountered, Hearne's empirical approach prevents him from trying to understand the Aboriginal people he travels with. Throughout, he assumes them to be his intellectual and moral inferiors. His description of his "emotional" response to the massacre of the Esquimaux (today known as "Inuit") at the end of this excerpt does not necessarily indicate a new, more sensitive perspective toward the Aboriginal people, but makes use of highly formulaic language that is in keeping with the conventions of the period.

Hearne's narrative should be read in the context of the imperialist enterprise of which it forms a part. As an employee following orders, his job was to aid in the Hudson's Bay Company's commercial expansion. More than this, the journals served to justify the British cause in claiming the land and its peoples as British property. To achieve this end, the Native people had to be portrayed as barbaric and in need of civilization. In a telling moment toward the end of his narrative, Hearne refers to the ingratitude of the Native people toward the Company's generosity (a theme that recurs throughout his journals); they should, he argues, "have sense enough to set a proper value on the favours and indulgences which are granted to them while they remain at the Company's Factories, or elsewhere within their territories." The phrase "or elsewhere within their territories" suggests that in Hearne's (and the Company's) mind there was no question of who had a right to this land, even though Hearne, as we see from these excerpts, was intimately dependent on the Natives for his survival there. Hearne's journals, then, must be read with a combined admiration for his achievement, and a certain skepticism concerning some of his observations. His narrative is indubitably a combination of fact and fiction.

Hearne first joined the Hudson's Bay Company in 1766 as a seaman and worked in the area of what is now Churchill, Manitoba, on the western coast of Hudson Bay. In 1769, he was selected for a special company mission: by travelling on foot across the northern barrens, he was to gain a knowledge of the northern country and chart a route to the rumoured Coppermine River, which was said to abound in furs and precious metals, and discern whether this river was navigable. His orders expressly commanded him to "take possession of [the river] on behalf of the Hudson's Bay Company." In the process, he was to see if he could locate a Northwest Passage that would lead through the continent. Hearne set out from Prince of Wales's Fort (today, Churchill, Manitoba) on three separate voyages (see his drawing of the fort in Figure I-9). The first two journeys, in 1769 and 1770, ended in failure, largely because of the mutinous behaviour of Hearne's Aboriginal guides. Part way through the first voyage, in 1769, Hearne was abandoned by his guides and had to make his way back to the fort alone. On the second journey, not only was he forced to wander aimlessly for more than eight months with his guide Conneequeese, but he accidentally broke his quadrant, which made any further charting of the route impossible. The third voyage, undertaken under the leadership of his guide Matonabbee and his people, proved more successful. Hearne and his company reached the Coppermine River, only to discover it to be unnavigable. The stores of copper and other riches that were said to abound there proved to have been exaggerated. Nevertheless, as Hearne recounts in his journal of 18 July 1771, "For the sake of form, . . . I erected a mark, and took possession of the coast on behalf of the Hudson's Bay Company." After a voyage that lasted eighteen months and twenty-three days, Hearne returned to Prince of Wales's Fort in June 1772, disappointed yet confident in having carried out his mission.

For years afterward, Hearne's journal, despite its geographical inaccuracies, remained the primary sourcebook for much of Canada's northern area. John Franklin made use of the text in his subsequent journey, in 1820–21, from Great Slave Lake to the Polar Sea. I.S. MacLaren speculates that because Franklin was likely using the smaller octavo edition of Hearne's narrative, which contained a different map of Hearne's journey across the barrens than the first edition, it could have contributed to Franklin's losing his way (and the accompanying loss of lives). In his journal, Franklin notes the location of the famous Esquimaux massacre, Bloody Fall, which he identifies by the scattering of human skulls and bones still marking the spot. Nevertheless, Hearne's main intention in publishing his journal was to entertain and edify reading audiences in England. As he writes in his introduction to the book, it was intended "for the amusement of candid and indulgent readers, who may perhaps feel themselves in some measure gratified by having the face of a country brought to their view which has hitherto been entirely unknown to every European except myself."

Like most explorers' narratives of the time, Hearne's journals, published as *A Journey from Prince of Wales's Fort in Hudson's Bay to the Northern Ocean* (1795), were substantially revised for publication. As Hearne himself admits in his preface to the book, "I have been enabled to rectify some inaccuracies that had, by trusting too much to memory, crept into [it]." While none of the original manuscripts of his journals survive, there do exist transcribed manuscripts which, when compared with Hearne's published text, reveal the extent to which he expanded his account for publication. Many of the more detailed, meditative, and retrospective passages were added long after the journeys took place. More

interestingly, it has been suggested that Hearne's famous account of the massacre of the Esquimaux might have been substantially altered to make it more horrific and dramatic, which would have been in keeping with the Gothic literary style that had become popular in his day. In Hearne's field notes about the event, the young girl who twines around a spear "like an eel," one of the most memorable similes in Hearne's published narrative, is entirely absent, as is his account of his emotionally distraught response to the scene. It is also possible that Hearne omitted details of the extensive raids on the part of both groups (Chipewyan and Inuit) in order to make the massacre seem unprovoked and utterly vicious.

It is widely accepted that Hearne made substantial revisions to his original field notes after he became chief of Prince of Wales's Fort in 1776. The story has it that when the fort fell to the French in 1782, the French commander, Comte de la Pérouse, returned Hearne's journals to him and insisted that he publish them. Subsequent revisions were made once Hearne had returned to London. Sadly, the fort itself, which plays such a prominent part in Hearne's account and in the history of the Hudson's Bay Company overall, was all but destroyed by French gunfire. It is said that Hearne's guide Matonabbee, of whom we hear so much in the excerpts included here, hanged himself in despair upon learning of the fate of the company's station. When Hearne returned to Hudson Bay in 1783, he attempted to build a smaller version of the fort near the former site, but the desperate circumstances of his Aboriginal allies, who had been depleted by smallpox and starvation, compounded by escalated competition from French traders, led Hearne to resign in 1787 and return to England. His narrative, published in 1795 three years after his death, remains one of the classics of Canadian exploration literature.

From A Journey from Prince of Wales's Fort in Hudson's Bay to the Northern Ocean

Orders and Instructions from the Hudson's Bay Company (1769)

MR. Samuel Hearne,

Sir,

Whereas the Honourable Hudson's Bay Company have been informed by the report from Indians, that there is a great probability of considerable advantages to be expected from a better knowledge of their country by us, than what hitherto has been obtained; and as it is the Company's earnest desire to embrace every circumstance that may tend to the benefit of the said Company, or the Nation at large, they have requested you to conduct this Expedition; and as you have readily consented to undertake the present Journey, you are hereby desired to proceed as soon as possible, [. . .] and six or eight of the best Northern Indians[1] we can procure, with a small part of their families, are to conduct you, provide for you, and assist you and your companions in every thing that lays in their power, having particular orders so to do.

2dly, Whereas you and your companions are well fitted-out with every thing we think necessary, as also a sample of light trading goods; these you are to dispose of by way of presents (and not by way of trade) to such far-off Indians as you may meet with, and to smoke your Calimut of Peace[2] with their leaders, in order to establish a friendship with them. You are also to persuade them as much as possible from going to war with each other, to encourage them to exert themselves in procuring furrs and other articles for trade, and to assure them of good payment for them at the Company's Factory. [. . .]

3dly, The Indians who are now appointed your guides, are to conduct you to the borders of the Athapuscow Indians country,[3] where Captain Matonabbee is to meet you in the Spring of one thousand seven hundred and seventy, in order to conduct you to a river represented by the Indians to abound with copper ore, animals of the furr kind, &c., and which is said to be so far to the Northward, that in the middle of the Summer the Sun does not set, and is supposed by the Indians to empty itself into some ocean. This river, which is called by the Northern Indians Neetha-san-san-dazey, or the Far Off Metal River, you are, if possible, to trace to the mouth, and there determine the latitude and longitude as near as you can; but more particularly so if you find it navigable, and that a settlement can be made there with any degree of safety, or benefit to the Company. [. . .]

[1] In general, "Northern Indians" throughout refers to the Chipewyan (part of the Athapaskan family), while "Southern Indians" designates the Cree (the Algonquin family).

[2] A ceremonial peace-pipe used by many Native groups and adopted by European traders in their negotiations with Native peoples.

[3] Northern region around Lake Athabaska and the Athabaska River.

And if the said river be likely to be of any utility, take possession of it on behalf of the Hudson's Bay Company, by cutting your name on some of the rocks, as also the date of the year, month, &c.[4] [. . .]

4thly, Another material point which is recommended you, is to find out, if you can, either by your own travels, or by information from the Indians, whether there is a passage through this continent.[5] It will be very useful to clear up this point, if possible, in order to prevent farther doubts from arising hereafter respecting a passage out of Hudson's Bay into the Western Ocean, as hath lately been represented by the American Traveller.[6] The particulars of those remarks you are to insert in your Journal, to be remitted home to the Company. [. . .]

It will be pleasing to hear by the first opportunity, in what latitude and longitude you meet the Leader Matonabbee, and how far he thinks it is to the Coppermine River, as also the probable time it may take before you can return. But in case any thing should prevent the said Leader from joining you, according to expectation, you are then to procure the best Indians you can for your guides, and either add to, or diminish, your number, as you may from time to time think most necessary for the good of the expedition.

So I conclude, wishing you and your companions a continuance of health, together with a prosperous Journey, and a happy return in safety. Amen.

MOSES NORTON, Governor.

Dated at Prince of Wales's Fort, Churchill River, Hudson's Bay, North America, November 6th, 1769.

Hardships Endured While Travelling (Second Expedition, 1770)

Every thing being in readiness for our departure, on the twenty-third of February I began my second journey accompanied by three Northern Indians and two of the home-guard (Southern Indians) [. . .] [M]y part of the luggage consisted of the

---

[4] [Hearne's note:] I was not provided with instruments for cutting on stone; but for form-sake, I cut my name, date of the year, &c., on a piece of board that had been one of the Indian's targets, and placed it in a heap of stones on a small eminence near the entrance of the river, on the South side.

[5] [Hearne's note:] The Continent of America is much wider than many people imagine, particularly Robson, who thought that the Pacific Ocean was but a few days journey from the West coast of Hudson's Bay. This, however, is so far from being the case, that when I was at my greatest Western distance, upward of five hundred miles from Prince of Wales's Fort, the natives, my guides, well knew that many tribes of Indians lay to the West of us, and they knew no end to the land in that direction; nor have I met with any Indians, either Northern or Southern, that ever had seen the sea to the Westward. It is, indeed, well known to the intelligent and well-informed part of the Company's servants, that an extensive and numerous tribe of Indians, called E-arch-e-thinnews, whose country lies far West of any of the Company's or Canadian settlements, must have traffic with the Spaniards on the West side of the Continent; because some of the Indians who formerly traded to York Fort, when at war with those people, frequently found saddles, bridles, muskets, and many other articles, in their possession; which were undoubtedly of Spanish manufactory. I have seen several Indians who have been so far West as to cross the top of that immense chain of mountains which run from North to South of the continent of America. Beyond those mountains all rivers run to the Westward. [. . .]

[6] Reference to Alexander Cluny's *The American Traveller* (London, 1769).

following articles, viz. the quadrant and its stand, a trunk containing books, papers, &c., a land-compass, and a large bag containing all my wearing apparel; also a hatchet, knives, files, &c., besides several small articles, intended for presents to the natives. The aukwardness of my load, added to its great weight, which was upward of sixty pounds, and the excessive heat of the weather, rendered walking the most laborious task I had ever encountered; and what considerably increased the hardship, was the badness of the road, and the coarseness of our lodging, being, on account of the want of proper tents, exposed to the utmost severity of the weather. The tent we had with us was not only too large, and unfit for barren ground service, where no poles were to be got, but we had been obliged to cut it up for shoes, and each person carried his own share. Indeed my guide behaved both negligently and ungenerously on this occasion; as he never made me, or my Southern Indians, acquainted with the nature of pitching tents on the barren grounds; which had he done, we could easily have procured a set of poles before we left the woods. He took care, however, to procure a set for himself and his wife; and when the tent was divided, though he made shift to get a piece large enough to serve him for a complete little tent, he never asked me or my Southern Indians to put our heads into it.

Beside the inconvenience of being exposed to the open air, night and day, in all weathers, we experienced real distress from the want of victuals. When provisions were procured, it often happened that we could not make a fire, so that we were obliged to eat the meat quite raw; which at first, in the article of fish particularly, was as little relished by my Southern companions as myself. [. . .]

From the twentieth to the twenty-third [of June] we walked every day near twenty miles, without any other subsistence than a pipe of tobacco, and a drink of water when we pleased. [. . .]

Early in the morning of the twenty-third, we set out as usual, but had not walked above seven or eight miles before we saw three musk-oxen grazing by the side of a small lake. The Indians immediately went in pursuit of them; and as some of them were expert hunters, they soon killed the whole of them. This was no doubt very fortunate; but, to our great mortification, before we could get one of them skinned, such a fall of rain came on, as to put it quite out of our power to make a fire; which, even in the finest weather, could only be made of moss, as we were near an hundred miles from any woods. This was poor comfort for people who had not broke their fast for four or five days. Necessity, however, has no law; and having been before initiated into the method of eating raw meat, we were the better prepared for this repast: but this was by no means so well relished, either by me or the Southern Indians, as either raw venison or raw fish had been: for the flesh of the musk-ox is not only coarse and tough, but smells and tastes so strong of musk as to make it very disagreeable when raw, though it is tolerable eating when properly cooked. The weather continued so remarkably bad, accompanied with constant heavy rain, snow, and sleet, and our necessities were so great by the time the weather permitted us to make a fire, that we had nearly eat to the amount of one buffalo quite raw. [. . .]

None of our natural wants, if we except thirst, are so distressing, or hard to endure, as hunger; and in wandering situations, like that which I now experienced, the hardship is greatly aggravated by the uncertainty with respect to its duration, and the means most proper to be used to remove it, as well as by the labour and fatigue we must necessarily undergo for that purpose, and the disappointments which too frequently frustrate our best concerted plans and most strenuous exertions: it not only enfeebles the body, but depresses the spirits, in spite of every effort to prevent it. Besides, for want of action, the stomach so far loses its digestive powers, that after long fasting it resumes its office with pain and reluctance. During this journey I have too frequently experienced the dreadful effects of this calamity, and more than once been reduced to so low a state by hunger and fatigue, that when Providence threw any thing in my way, my stomach has scarcely been able to retain more than two or three ounces, without producing the most oppressive pain. Another disagreeable circumstance of long fasting is, the extreme difficulty and pain attending the natural evacuations for the first time; and which is so dreadful, that of it none but those who have experienced can have an adequate idea.

To record in detail each day's fare since the commencement of this journey, would be little more than a dull repetition of the same occurrences. A sufficient idea of it may be given in a few words, by observing that it may justly be said to have been either all feasting, or all famine; sometimes we had too much, seldom just enough, frequently too little, and often none at all. [. . .] On those pressing occasions I have frequently seen the Indians examine their wardrobe, which consisted chiefly of skin-clothing, and consider what part could best be spared; sometimes a piece of an old, half-rotten deer skin, and at others a pair of old shoes, were sacrificed to alleviate extreme hunger. The relation of such uncommon hardships may perhaps gain little credit in Europe; while those who are conversant with the history of Hudson's Bay, and who are thoroughly acquainted with the distress which the natives of the country about it frequently endure, may consider them as no more than the common occurrences of an Indian life. [. . .]

Effect of Trade on the Natives (Third Expedition, 1771)

[March 1771.] It is undoubtedly the duty of every one of the Company's servants to encourage a spirit of industry among the natives, and to use every means in their power to induce them to procure furrs and other commodities for trade, by assuring them of a ready purchase and good payment for every thing they bring to the Factory: and I can truly say, that this has ever been the grand object of my attention. But I must at the same time confess, that such conduct is by no means for the real benefit of the poor Indians; it being well known that those who have the least intercourse with the Factories, are by far the happiest. As their whole aim is to procure a comfortable subsistence, they take the most prudent methods to accomplish it; and by always following the lead of the deer, are seldom exposed to the griping [sic] hand of famine, so frequently felt by those who are called the annual traders. It is true, that there are few of the Indians, whose manner of life I have just described, but have once in their lives at least visited Prince of Wales's Fort; and the hardships and dangers which most of them experienced on those occasions, have left such a lasting impression on their minds that nothing can induce them to repeat their visits: nor is it, in fact, the interest of the Company that people of this easy turn, and who require only as much iron-work at a time as can be purchased with three or four beaver skins, and that only once in two or three years, should be invited to the Factories; because what they beg and steal while there, is worth, in the way of trade, three times the quantity of furrs which they bring. For this reason, it is much more for the interest of the Company that the annual traders should buy up all those small quantities of furrs, and bring them in their own name, than that a parcel of beggars should be encouraged to come to the Factory with scarcely as many furrs as will pay for the victuals they eat while they are on the plantation. [. . .]

Massacre of the Esquimaux (Third Expedition, 1771)

[May 1771.] [. . .] It should have been observed, that during our stay at Clowey [near Great Slave Lake] a great number of Indians entered into a combination with those of my party to accompany us to the Copper-mine River; and with no other intent than to murder the Esquimaux, who are understood by the Copper Indians to frequent that river in considerable numbers. [. . .]

When I was acquainted with the intentions of my companions, and saw the warlike preparations that were carrying on, I endeavoured as much as possible to persuade them from putting their inhuman design into execution; but so far were my intreaties from having the wished-for effect, that it was concluded I was actuated by cowardice; and they told me, with great marks of derision, that I was afraid of the Esquimaux. As I knew my personal safety depended in a great measure on the favourable opinion they entertained of me in this respect, I was obliged to change my tone, and replied, that I did not care if they rendered the name and race of the Esquimaux extinct; adding at the same time, that though I was no enemy to the Esquimaux, and did not see the necessity of attacking them without cause, yet if I should find it necessary to do it, for the protection of any one of my company, my own safety out of the question, so far from being afraid of a poor defenceless Esquimaux, whom I despised more than feared, nothing should be wanting on my part to protect all who were with me. This declaration was received with great satisfaction; and I never afterwards ventured to interfere with any of their war-plans. Indeed, when I came to consider seriously, I saw evidently that it was the highest folly for an individual like me, and in my situation, to attempt to turn the current of a national prejudice which had subsisted between those two nations from the earliest periods, or at least as long as they had been acquainted with the existence of each other. [. . .]

[June 1771.] As soon as the fine weather began, we set out and walked about seven or eight miles to the Northward, when we came to a branch of the Conge-ca-tha-wha-chaga River; on the North side of which we found several Copper Indians, who were assembled, according to annual custom, to kill deer as they cross the river in their little canoes. [. . .]

Whether it was from real motives of hospitality, or from the great advantages which they expected to reap by my discoveries, I know not; but I must confess that their civility far exceeded what I could expect from so uncivilized a tribe, and I was exceedingly sorry that I had nothing of value to offer them. However, such articles as I had, I distributed among them, and they were thankfully received by them. Though they have some European commodities among them, which they purchase from the Northern Indians, the same articles from the hands of an Englishman were more prized. As I was the first whom they had ever seen, and in all probability might be the last, it was curious to see how they flocked about me, and expressed as much desire to examine me from top to toe, as an European Naturalist would a non-descript animal. They, however, found and pronounced me to be a perfect human being, except in the colour of my hair and eyes: the former, they said, was like the stained hair of a buffaloe's tail, and the latter, being light, were like those of a gull. The whiteness of my skin also was, in their opinion, no ornament, as they said it resembled meat which had been sodden in water till all the blood was extracted. On the whole, I was viewed as so great a curiosity in this part of the world, that during my stay there, whenever I combed my head, some or other of them never failed to ask for the hairs that came off, which they carefully wrapped up, saying, "When I see you again, you shall again see your hair." [. . .]

[July 1771.] We had scarcely arrived at the Copper-mine River when [. . .] I was not a little surprised to find the river differ so much from the description which the Indians had given of it at the Factory; for, instead of being so large as to be navigable for shipping, as it had been represented by them, it was at that part scarcely navigable for an Indian canoe, being no more than one hundred and eighty yards wide, every where full of shoals, and no less than three falls were in sight at first view. [. . .]

Soon after our arrival at the river-side, three Indians were sent off as spies, in order to see if any Esquimaux were inhabiting the river-side between us and the sea. After walking about three-quarters of a mile by the side of the river, we put up, when most of the Indians went a hunting, and killed several musk-oxen and some deer. They were employed all the remainder of the day and night in splitting and drying the meat by the fire. As we were not then in want of provisions, and as deer and other animals were so plentiful, that each day's journey might have provided for itself, I was at a loss to account for this unusual economy of my companions; but was soon informed, that those preparations were made with a view to have victuals enough ready-cooked to serve us to the river's mouth, without being obliged to kill any in our way, as the report of the guns, and the smoke of the fires, would be liable to alarm the natives, if any should be near at hand, and give them an opportunity of escaping. [. . .]

Early in the morning of the sixteenth, the weather being fine and pleasant, I again proceeded with my survey, and continued it for ten miles farther down the river; but still found it the same as before, being every where full of falls and shoals. At this time (it being about noon) the three men who had been sent as spies met us on their return, and informed my companions that five tents of Esquimaux were on the west side of the river. The situation, they said, was very convenient for surprising them; and, according to their account, I judged it to be about twelve miles from the place we met the spies. When the Indians received this intelligence, no farther attendance or attention was paid to my survey, but their whole thoughts were immediately engaged in planning the best method of attack, and how they might steal on the poor Esquimaux the ensuing night, and kill them all while asleep. To accomplish this bloody design more effectually, the Indians thought it necessary to cross the river as soon as possible; and, by the account of the spies, it appeared that no part was more convenient for the purpose than that where we had met them, it being there very smooth, and at a considerable distance from any fall. Accordingly, after the Indians had put all their guns, spears, targets, &c. in good order, we crossed the river, which took up some time.

When we arrived on the West side of the river, each painted the front of his target or shield; some with the figure of the Sun, others with that of the Moon, several with different kinds of birds and beasts of prey, and many with the images of imaginary beings, which, according to their silly notions, are the inhabitants of the different elements, Earth, Sea, Air, &c.

On enquiring the reason of their doing so, I learned that each man painted his shield with the image of that being on which he relied most for success in the intended engagement. Some were contented with a single representation; while others, doubtful, as I suppose, of the quality and power of any single being, had their shields covered to the very margin with a group of hieroglyphics, quite unintelligible to every one except the painter. Indeed, from the hurry in which this business was necessarily done, the want of every colour but red and black, and the deficiency of skill in the artist, most of those paintings had more the appearance of a number of accidental blotches, than "of any thing that is on the earth, or in the water under the earth";[7] and though some few of them conveyed a tolerable idea of the thing intended, yet even these were many degrees worse than our country sign-paintings in England. [. . .]

Never was reciprocity of interest more generally regarded among a number of people, than it was on the present occasion by my crew, for not one was a moment in want of any thing that another could spare; and if ever the spirit of disinterested friendship expanded the heart of a Northern Indian, it was here exhibited in the most extensive meaning of the word. Property of every kind that could be of general use now ceased to be private, and every one who had any thing which came under that description, seemed proud of an opportunity of giving it, or lending it to those who had none, or were most in want of it.

[7] Cf. Revelations 5:13.

The number of my crew was so much greater than that which five tents could contain, and the warlike manner in which they were equipped so greatly superior to what could be expected of the poor Esquimaux, that no less than a total massacre of every one of them was likely to be the case, unless Providence should work a miracle for their deliverance.

The land was so situated that we walked under cover of the rocks and hills till we were within two hundred yards of the tents. There we lay in ambush for some time, watching the motions of the Esquimaux; and here the Indians would have advised me to stay till the fight was over, but to this I could by no means consent; for I considered that when the Esquimaux came to be surprised, they would try every way to escape, and if they found me alone, not knowing me from an enemy, they would probably proceed to violence against me when no person was near to assist. For this reason I determined to accompany them, telling them at the same time, that I would not have any hand in the murder they were about to commit, unless I found it necessary for my own safety. [. . .]

While we lay in ambush, the Indians performed the last ceremonies which were thought necessary before the engagement. These chiefly consisted in painting their faces; some all black, some all red, and others with a mixture of the two; and to prevent their hair from blowing into their eyes, it was either tied before and behind, and on both sides, or else cut short all round. The next thing they considered was to make themselves as light as possible for running; which they did, by pulling off their stockings, and either cutting off the sleeves of their jackets, or rolling them up close to their armpits; and though the muskettoes at that time were so numerous as to surpass all credibility, yet some of the Indians actually pulled off their jackets and entered the lists quite naked, except their breech-cloths and shoes. Fearing I might have occasion to run with the rest, I thought it also advisable to pull off my stockings and cap, and to tie my hair as close up as possible.

By the time the Indians had made themselves thus completely frightful, it was near one o'clock in the morning of the seventeenth; when finding all the Esquimaux quiet in their tents, they rushed forth from their ambuscade, and fell on the poor unsuspecting creatures, unperceived till close at the very eves of their tents, when they soon began the bloody massacre, while I stood neuter in the rear.

In a few seconds the horrible scene commenced; it was shocking beyond description; the poor unhappy victims were surprised in the midst of their sleep, and had neither time nor power to make any resistance; men, women, and children, in all upward of twenty, ran out of their tents stark naked, and endeavoured to make their escape; but the Indians having possession of all the landside, to no place could they fly for shelter. One alternative only remained, that of jumping into the river; but, as none of them attempted it, they all fell a sacrifice to Indian barbarity!

The shrieks and groans of the poor expiring wretches were truly dreadful; and my horror was much increased at seeing a young girl, seemingly about eighteen years of age, killed so near me, that when the first spear was stuck into her side she fell down at my feet, and twisted round my legs, so that it was with difficulty that I could disengage myself from her dying grasps. As two Indian men pursued this unfortunate victim, I solicited very hard for her life; but the murderers made no reply till they had stuck both their spears through her body, and transfixed her to the ground. They then looked me sternly in the face, and began to ridicule me, by asking if I wanted an Esquimaux wife; and paid not the smallest regard to the shrieks and agony of the poor wretch, who was twining round their spears like an eel! Indeed, after receiving much abusive language from them on the occasion, I was at length obliged to desire that they would be more expeditious in dispatching their victim out of her misery, otherwise I should be obliged, out of pity, to assist in the friendly office of putting an end to the existence of a fellow-creature who was so cruelly wounded. On this request being made, one of the Indians hastily drew his spear from the place where it was first lodged, and pierced it through her breast near the heart. The love of life, however, even in this most miserable state, was so predominant, that though this might justly be called the most merciful act that could be done for the poor creature, it seemed to be unwelcome, for though much exhausted by pain and loss of blood, she made several efforts to ward off the friendly blow. My situation and the terror of my mind at beholding this butchery, cannot easily be conceived, much less described; though I summed up all the fortitude I was master of on the occasion, it was with difficulty that I could refrain from tears; and I am confident that my features must have feelingly expressed how sincerely I was affected at the barbarous scene I then witnessed; even at this hour I cannot reflect on the transactions of that horrid day without shedding tears.

[1795]

DAVID THOMPSON ■ (1770–1857)

David Thompson is widely celebrated as the foremost cartographer of the Canadian Northwest. He was born in London in 1770, and at the age of seven was placed in a charity school for poor children. He grew up to become one of the greatest scientific geographers of the period, and produced detailed maps covering nearly 4 million square miles of the vast area in the Northwest between Lake Superior and the Pacific Ocean. At the age of fourteen, Thompson was apprenticed to the Hudson's Bay Company, and travelled to North America in 1784, never to return to England. For the first year, he served at Prince of Wales's Fort under the leadership of Samuel Hearne. One of his assignments was to help Hearne in the enormous task of transcribing his journals. In December 1788, while posted at an inland fort on the Saskatchewan River, he broke his leg while hauling a sled of wood and was forced to recuperate at Cumberland House for more than a year. As Thompson himself wrote, this occurrence "turned out to be the best thing that ever happened to me," for while convalescing he studied mathematics and astronomy under the tutelage of Philip Turnor, who was already established as an expert cartographer and had been brought to the fort as a surveyor.

The story of David Thompson is the story of rival trading companies vying for control over the Canadian Northwest. Before 1774, the Hudson's Bay Company had limited its trading enterprise to various posts along the western shore of Hudson Bay, while the French traders controlled the St. Lawrence River for access to the interior. Native traders and hunters were expected to bring their furs to the Hudson's Bay Company's forts, and the furs would subsequently be loaded onto ships, which had arrived from England toward the end of the summer and anchored in the bay. The Hudson's Bay Company was being pressured to extend its operations inland because of increasing competition from the "Nor'Westers" (later the North West Company traders), who ventured into the interior and established trading posts there. The well-known tales of the *voyageurs* and *coureurs de bois* form part of the history of the activities of the rival North West Company. It was not until 1774, under the guidance of Samuel Hearne, that the first inland Hudson's Bay Company trading post, Cumberland House, was established on the Saskatchewan River.

Although Thompson began his career as a clerk and surveyor for the Hudson's Bay Company, he became increasingly disaffected with the company's limitations in exploring the vast interior of the country. It may be for this reason that he eventually switched his allegiance to the North West Company in 1797 and became one of its chief surveyors (and a partner in the company in 1804), travelling with canoe brigades and living with numerous Aboriginal communities in his travels across the continent (for his explorations eventually took him beyond the Rocky Mountains). In 1797, he began mapping the Canadian/American boundary in the West, charting the major rivers between Lake Superior and Lake Winnipeg (in 1817, he would be hired by the boundary commission to conduct a similar US border survey in Upper Canada). The North West Company allowed Thompson to fulfill his dream of becoming a great map-maker. During his exploration of the Athabaska region in 1798 and 1799, Thompson met Charlotte Small, the Métis daughter of a retired NWC partner, with whom he entered into a lifelong and loving marriage (altogether, the couple had 13 children). His most significant expedition took place in 1807, when Thompson, travelling with a group of eight men as well as his wife and children, mapped a route through the Rocky Mountains to the Columbia River and surveyed the territories of the Kootenay peoples west of the Rockies. In 1812, he returned to Montreal, where he retired from active trading and set to work preparing his map of Canada for the North West Company. He also at this time had his "country marriage" to his wife renewed in a Presbyterian church. During the latter part of his life, Thompson drifted into financial decline, in part because an agent in the NWC went bankrupt and Thompson lost a good portion of his life savings. To make ends meet, he took small jobs as a street surveyor in Montreal, and later was forced to pawn his astronomical instruments. In 1845, he and his wife moved in with one of their daughters in the nearby town of Longueuil, Quebec. During this period, Thompson set to work revising his *Narrative* for publication, but his dwindling eyesight made the task difficult, and by 1851 he was totally blind. When he died in 1857, the *Narrative* remained unfinished.

Both Hearne's and Thompson's accounts are notable for their vividness and immediacy, but there is little question that Thompson is the more skilful writer and more expansive thinker. His narrative of his experiences is rife with philosophical meditations, inset vignettes, detailed stories of individuals he encountered, vivid dialogue, and astute observations about the havoc wreaked by the coming of the Europeans on the increasingly dependent Aboriginal peoples. Thompson's greater empathy toward Aboriginal peoples was in part connected to his marriage to a Métis woman. As Thompson admits in an early draft of his *Narrative*, "My lovely wife [being] of the blood of [the Nahathaways] . . . gives me a great advantage." His comments on the damaging effects of liquor, the loss of Native traditions, the depletion of the beaver and other animals, and the spread of smallpox are a testament to his awareness of his complicity in the increasing destitution to which he was witness. Thompson was also morally self-righteous, abstemious, and devoutly Christian. Part of his antipathy toward Samuel Hearne, in addition to what might be seen as jealousy of the older man's success as a writer, stemmed from the latter's self-proclaimed atheism. Within five pages of the beginning of his narrative,

Thompson includes a diatribe against Hearne's "cowardice" and recalls an instance when Hearne proclaimed "Voltaire's Dictionary" to be his bible.

Thompson began the revisions to his *Narrative* after settling in Montreal in 1812. By the 1840s, the main body of it was under way, though the entire manuscript, *Narrative of His Explorations in Western America 1784–1812*, was not published until 1916, well after his death, under the editorship of Joseph Burr Tyrrell. The book succeeded in memorializing Thompson's impressive achievements and consolidating his reputation. Like Hearne's, Thompson's final narrative was written long after the events occurred and therefore contains errors and frequent omissions. Indeed, the first two chapters of his *Narrative* were written entirely from memory. Because he composed his book with an eye to publication, it was reformulated less as a series of journal entries than as a kind of adventure story. In his narrative, he tells how as a youth in London he was entranced with the tales of other lands, including such works as *The Arabian Nights*, *Robinson Crusoe*, and *Gulliver's Travels*. There is no doubt that he wanted to place his work in the company of similar illustrious adventure stories of the Canadian North: Cartier's, Champlain's, Hearne's, Mackenzie's, and others'. Thompson had travelled across the continent, from Hudson Bay to the Pacific; he had worked for both fur-trading companies; his experiences in the Canadian Northwest spanned more than a quarter of a century. Nevertheless, in his final years, blind and poor, Thompson became convinced that the world had forgotten him, little realizing the fame that awaited him in the twentieth and twenty-first centuries.

From Narrative of His Explorations in Western America, 1784-1812

The Fur Trade (1786)[1]

The fur traders from Canada for several years past had so far extended their trading posts through the interior country as almost to cut off the trade from the Factories. The whole of the furs collected at Churchill barely loaded the ships long boat. The Hudson's Bay [Company] therefore found it necessary to make trading houses in a few different places, and as the Kisiskatchewan [Saskatchewan] is the great leading river of the country, these trading houses were situated on its [banks] or the branches which flow into it. This inland trade was still in its infancy. The company had only two houses, Cumberland House built by Mr. Samuel Hearne and Hudson House about 300 miles above it. [. . .]

It was now thought proper to make a trading house about 200 miles higher up the River, leave Hudson House for the present and instead to build a house about 40 miles to the southward, on the right bank of the Bow River, the great South Branch of the Kisiskatchewan; the latter to be under the charge of Mr. Mitchel Oman, a native of the Isle of Orkney. He had no education, but a fine looking manly powerful man of a tenacious memory and high moral qualities, and much respected by the Indians and whose language he had acquired. I was appointed to be his clerk and embarked with him. [. . .] On the evening of the third day up the River we came opposite to where houses were building for the furr trade and next morning crossed over and placed ourselves eighty yards above them. These houses were on account of two companies from Canada [i.e., Montreal]; one of them of the firm of McTavish and company; under the charge of a Scotch gentleman of the name of Thorburn. The other was of the firm of Gregory and company under the care of a french gentleman.[2] [. . .] Mr. Thorburn had been some time in the naval service, and had the frank manners of an english gentleman. He was about 35 years of age and had seen much of the world; he was glad to see us and have the pleasure of speaking english. From him during winter we obtained information on the fur trade of Canada. He remarked to us that at the cession of Canada to England [1763] the furr trade with all its influence over the Indians was wholly in the hands of the French. The British merchants soon acquired a share of it, and at length the whole of it, but by means of french traders to whom they furnished the goods for the trade. Some of these were good

---

[1] Thompson's writing is inconsistent in spelling and punctuation. We have chosen not to standardize these elements in order to retain the flavour of his prose. There are different published versions of Thompson's narrative because he died before he finished revising his journals for publication. The first published edition, based on Thompson's incomplete 700-page handwritten draft, was edited by J.B. Tyrrell in 1916. This version is taken from Richard Glover's 1962 edition.

[2] The firm of McTavish and Co. was that of the North West Company, which had been officially founded by 1784. Gregory and Co. was a powerful rival organization that had not been included in the NWC merger. In 1786, the time of which he is writing in this account, Thompson had not yet joined the North West Company.

characters men of integrity. Where this was the case the furr trade gave a decent profit to both the Indian trader and the merchant, but it was too frequently otherwise. With a slight education, if any, and no books, when in their wintering houses they passed their time in card playing, gambling and dancing; which brought on disputes, quarrels and all respect was lost. Goods beyond the extent of their wages were taken by the men to pay their gambling dedts [sic], and every festival of the church of Rome was an excuse to get drunk; the fisheries on which they depended for provisions for their support were neglected and starvation stared them in the face; there was little left to trade furrs and they returned to the merchant in beggary and distress, and instead of a cargo of furrs recounted their miseries and sufferings brought on themselves by their own folly and dissipation. To remedy this sad state of the trade, the merchants had formed two companies, which this winter would unite and form only one company [the North West Company], and as fast as could conveniently be done, place at the head of each trading house men of British origen of sober and steady habits on whom they could rely and this system was now in operation.[3] [. . .]

Nahathaway Customs and Beliefs (1792–1806)

Of all the several distinct Tribes of Natives on the east side of the mountains, the Nahathaway Indians appear to deserve the most consideration; under different names the great families of this race occupy a great extent of country, and however separated and unknown to each other, they have the same opinions on religion, on morals, and their customs and manners differ very little. They are the only Natives that have some remains of ancient times from tradition. In the following account I have carefully avoided as their national opinions all they have learned from white men, and my knowledge was collected from old men, whom with my own age extend backwards to upwards of one hundred years ago, and I must remark, that what other people may write as the creed of these natives, I have always found it very difficult to learn their real opinion on what may be termed religious subjects. Asking them questions on this head, is to no purpose, they will give the answer best adapted to avoid other questions, and please the enquirer. My knowledge has been gained when living and travelling with them and in times of distress and danger in their prayers to invisible powers, and their view of a future state of themselves and others, and like most of mankind, those in youth and in the prime of life think only of the present but declining manhood, and escapes from danger turn their thoughts on futurity. [. . .]

A Missionary has never been among them, and my knowledge of their language has not enabled me to do more than teach the unity of God, and a future state of rewards and punishments; hell fire they do not believe, for they do not think it possible that any thing can resist the continued action of fire: It is doubtful if their language in its present simple state can clearly express the

---

[3] See note 3 in the introduction to this section. The merger of McTavish and Gregory occurred in 1787, still under the name of the North West Company.

doctrines of Christianity in their full force. They believe in the self existence of the Keeche Keeche Manito (The Great, Great Spirit) they appear to derive their belief from tradition, and [believe] that the visible world, with all its inhabitants must have been made by some powerful being: but have not the same idea of his constant omnipresence, omniscience and omnipotence that we have, but [think] that he is so when he pleases, he is the master of life, and all things are at his disposal; he is always kind to the human race, and hates to see the blood of mankind on the ground, and sends heavy rain to wash it away. He leaves the human race to their own conduct, but has placed all other living creatures under the care of Manitos (or inferior Angels) all of whom are responsible to Him; but all this belief is obscure and confused, especially on the Manitos, the guardians and guides of every genus of Birds and Beasts; each Manito has a separate command and care, as one has the Bison, another the Deer; and thus the whole animal creation is divided amongst them. On this account the Indians, as much as possible, neither say, nor do anything to offend them, and the religious hunter, at the death of each animal, says, or does, something, as thanks to the Manito of the species for being permitted to kill it. [. . .]

They believe in the immortality of the soul, and that death is only a change of existence which takes place directly after death. The good find themselves in a happy country, where they rejoin their friends and relations, the Sun is always bright, and the animals plenty; and most of them carry this belief so far, that they believe whatever creatures the great Spirit has made must continue to exist somewhere, and under some form; But this fine belief is dark and uncertain. [. . .] It wanted the sure and sacred promise of the Heavenly Redeemer of mankind, who brought life and immortality to light. [. . .]

It may now [be well to] say something of myself, and of the character the Natives and the french Canadians entertained of me, they were almost my only companions.[4] My instruments for practical astronomy [. . .] I was in the constant practice of using in clear weather for observations on the Sun, Moon, Planets and Stars; to determine the positions of the Rivers, Lakes, Mountains and other parts of the country I surveyed from Hudson Bay to the Pacific Ocean. Both Canadians[5] and Indians often inquired of me why I observed the Sun, and sometimes the Moon, in the day time, and passed whole nights with my instruments looking at the Moon and Stars. I told them it was to determine the distance and direction from the place I observed to other places; neither the Canadians nor the Indians believed me; for both argued that if what I said was truth, I ought to look to the ground, and over it; and not to the Stars. Their opinions were, that I was looking into futurity and seeing every body, and what they were doing; how to raise the wind; but did not believe I could calm it, this they argued from seeing me obliged to wait the calming of the wind on the great Lakes, to which the Indians added that I knew where the Deer were, and

[4] By this point in his narrative, Thompson had joined the North West Company.
[5] Thompson uses the terms "Canadians" and "French Canadians" interchangeably.

other superstitious opinions. During my life I have always been careful not to pretend to any knowledge of futurity, and [said] that I knew nothing beyond the present hour; neither argument, nor ridicule had any effect, and I had to leave them to their own opinions and yet inadvertingly on my part, several things happened to confirm their opinions[.] One fine evening in February two Indians came to the house to trade; the Moon rose bright and clear with the planet Jupiter a few degrees on its east side; and the Canadians as usual predicted that Indians would come to trade in the direction of this star. To show them the folly of such predictions, I told them the same bright star, the next night, would be as far from the Moon on its west side; this of course took place from the Moon's motion in her orbit; and is the common occurrence of almost every month, and yet all parties were persuaded I had done it by some occult power to falsify the predictions of the canadians. Mankind are fond of the marvelous, it seems to heighten their character by relating they have seen such things. I had always admired the tact of the Indian in being able to guide himself through the darkest pine forests to exactly the place he intended to go, his keen, constant attention on every thing; the removal of the smallest stone, the bent or broken twig; a slight mark on the ground, all spoke plain language to him. I was anxious to acquire this knowledge, and often being in company with them, sometimes for several months, I paid attention to what they pointed out to me, and became almost equal to some of them; which became of great use to me: The North West Company of Furr Traders, from their Depot in Lake Superior sent off Brigades of Canoes loaded with about three Tons weight of Merchandise, Provisions and Baggage; those for the most distant trading Posts are sent off first; with an allowance of two days time between each Brigade to prevent incumbrances on the Carrying Places; I was in my first year in the third Brigade of six Canoes each and having nothing to do but sketch off my survey and make Observations, I was noticing how far we gained, or lost ground on the Brigade before us, by the fires they made, and other marks, as we were equally manned with five men to each canoe: In order to prevent the winter coming on us, before we reached our distant winter quarters the Men had to work very hard from daylight to sunset, or later, and at night slept on the ground, constantly worried by Musketoes; and had no time to look about them; I found we gained very little on them; at the end of fifteen days we had to arrive at Lake Winipeg, (that is the Sea Lake from its size) and for more than two days it had been blowing a north west gale, which did not allow the Brigade before us to proceed; and I told the Guide, that early the next morning we should see them; these Guides have charge of conducting the march and are all proud of coming up to the canoes ahead of them, and by dawn of day we entered the Lake now calm, and as the day came on us, saw the Brigade that were before us, only one Mile ahead of us. The Guide and the men shouted with joy, and when we came up to them told them of my wonderful predictions, and that I had pointed out every place they had slept at, and all by looking at the Stars; one party seemed delighted in being credulous, the other in exageration; such are ignorant men, who never give themselves a moment's reflection. The fact is Jean Baptiste will not think, he is not paid for it; when he has a minute's respite he smokes his pipe, his constant companion and all goes well; he will go through hardships, but requires a belly full, at least once a day, good Tobacco to smoke, a warm Blanket, and a kind Master who will take his share of hard times and be the first in danger. Naval and Military Men are not fit to command them in distant countries, neither do they place confidence in one of themselves as a leader; they always prefer an Englishman, but they ought always to be kept in constant employment however light it may be. [. . .]

Writers on the North American Indians always write as comparing them, with themselves who are all men of education, and of course [the Indians] lose by comparison; this is not fair; let them be compared with those who are uneducated in Europe, yet even in this comparison the Indian has the disadvantage in not having the light of Christianity. Of course his moral character has not the firmness of christian morality, but in practice he is fully equal to those of his class in Europe; living without law, they are a law to themselves. The Indian is said to be a creature of apathy, when he appears to be so, he is in an assumed character to conceal what is passing in his mind; as he has nothing of the almost infinite diversity of things which interest and amuse the civilised man; his passions, desires and affections are strong, however appeared subdued, and engage the whole man; the law of retaliation, which is fully allowed, makes the life of man respected; and in general he abhors the sheding [sic] of blood, and should sad necessity compel him to it, which is sometimes the case, he is held to be an unfortunate man; but he who has committed wilful murder is held in abhorrence, as one with whom the life of no person is in safety, and possessed with an evil spirit. [. . .]

Although the climate and country of which I am writing is far better than that of Hudson's Bay, yet the climate is severe in Winter the Thermometer often from thirty to forty degrees below Zero. The month of December is the coldest; the long absence of the Sun gives full effect to the action of the cold. [. . .] In one of the calms of this month Tapahpahtum, a good hunter came to us for some provisions and fish hooks, he said his three wives and his children had had very little to eat for nearly a whole Moon adding you may be sure that we suffer hunger when I come to beg fish, and get hooks for my women to angle with. He took away about thirty pounds of fish, which he had to carry about twenty miles to his tent. I felt for him, for nothing but sad necessity can compel a Nahathaway hunter to carry away fish, and angle for them, this is too mean for a hunter; meat he carries with pleasure, but fish is degradation. The calm still continued; and two days after Tapahpahtum came in the evening; he looked somewhat wild; he was a powerful man of strong passions; as usual I gave him a bit of Tobacco, he sat down and smoked, inhaling the smoke as if he would have drawn the tobacco through the pipe stem; then saying, now I have smoked, I may speak; I do not come to you for fish, I hope never to disgrace myself again; I now come for a wind which you must give me; in the mood he was in to argue with him was of no use, and I said, why did you not bring one of your women with you, she would have taken some fish to the tent; "My women are too weak, they snare a hare, or two every day, barely enough to keep them alive. I am come for a wind which you must give me"; "You know as well as I do that the Great Spirit alone is master of the Winds; you must apply to him, and not to me"; "Ah, that is always your way of talking to us, when you will not hear us, then you talk to us of the Great Spirit. I want a Wind, I must have it, now think on it, and dream, how I am to get it." I lent him an old Bison Robe to sleep on; which was all we could spare. The next day was calm; he sat on the floor in a despondent mood, at times smoking his pipe; and saying to me, "Be kind to me, be kind to me, give me a Wind that we may live." I told him the Good Spirit alone could cause the wind to blow, and my French Canadians were as foolish as the poor Indian; saying to one another, it would be a good thing, and well done, if he got a wind; we should get meat to eat. The night was very fine and clear, I passed most of it observing the Moon and Stars as usual; the small meteors were very numerous, which indicated a Gale of Wind; the morning rose fine, and before the appearance of the Sun, tho' calm with us, the tops of the tall Pines were waving, all foretelling a heavy gale, which usually follows a long calm; all this was plain to every one; Very early Tapahpahtum said; Be kind and give me a strong wind; vexed with him, I told him to go, and take care that the trees did not fall upon him; he shouted "I have got it"; sprang from the floor, snatched his gun, whipt on his Snow Shoes, and dashed away at five miles an hour; the gale from North East came on as usual with snow and high drift, and lasted three days; for the two first days we could not visit the nets, which sometimes happens; the third day the drift ceased, but the nets had been too long in the water without being washed, and we had to take them up. On this gale of wind, a common occurence, I learnt my men were more strangely foolish than the Indians; something better than two months after this gale, I sent three of the men with letters to an other trading house and to bring some articles I wanted; here these men related how I had raised a storm of wind for the Indian, but had made it so strong that for two days they got no fish from the nets, adding, they thought I would take better care another time. In these distant solitudes, Men's minds seem to partake of the wildness of the country they live in. Four days after Tapahpahtum with one of his women came, he had killed three Moose Deer, of which he gave us one, for which I paid him; He was now in his calm senses: and I reasoned with him on the folly of looking to any one, to get what the Good Spirit alone could give, and that it made us all liable to his anger. He said [...] I came to you, in hopes that you had power over the winds; for we all believe the Great Spirit speaks to you in the night, when you are looking at the Moon and Stars, and tells you of what we know nothing. [...]

[1916]

John Franklin has acquired an almost legendary status in the narrative of Canadian exploration. No other explorer contributed as much to the charting of the Arctic coastline. However, it is the story of his ill-fated last journey, begun in 1845, that has caught the imagination of subsequent generations. As he endeavoured to chart the Northwest Passage by travelling through the Arctic Ocean, Franklin's ships, the *Terror* and *Erebus*, became trapped in the polar ice and he and his entire crew of 129 men perished. In the ten years following his disappearance, numerous search parties were sent to uncover the fate of the Franklin expedition, a number of which were financed by Franklin's grieving widow. British explorer John Rae, who began searching for Franklin in 1848 with John Richardson (the doctor on Franklin's first northern expedition), created a public scandal in Britain in 1854 when he offered testimony, based on his interviews with Inuit people who had encountered some of the ship's crew, stating that Franklin's men had resorted to cannibalism. In 1859, Francis Leopold McClintock's expedition discovered a cairn on King William Island containing a record of Franklin's death on 11 June 1847. Subsequent investigations in the 1980s, initiated by forensic scientist Owen Beattie, revealed that the crew had been slowly poisoned by the lead casings of the canned provisions they had brought for the journey (see Figure VI-8 accompanying Margaret Atwood's "The Age of Lead" in Volume II). With more than two years' supply of food, the crew gradually succumbed to lead poisoning, which affected their judgment in the final months of their ordeal. However, while the remains of some crew members have been found,

Franklin's grave, and the ships themselves, have never been located. As a result, the story of the Franklin expedition has become one of the most memorable and compelling mysteries of Canadian and British history.

At the time, Franklin's fate inspired a plethora of narrative and visual treatments of the expedition's demise in the Canadian North. Newspaper accounts provided extended, dramatic narratives about the findings of the various search parties, and were often accompanied by lurid illustrations (see Figure I-10). These, and the hundreds of fictional treatments of the Franklin saga, sold in great numbers throughout Britain and Canada. Algernon Charles Swinburne ("The Death of Sir John Franklin") and Alfred, Lord Tennyson ("No Earthly Pole") produced poetic treatments of the event (as did Canadian poet Wilfrid Campbell in his 1893 poem "Unabsolved"), and Joseph Conrad's *Heart of Darkness* (1902) is thought to have been partly inspired by his enthusiasm for the Franklin story.

While the ill-fated third expedition is the most famous of Franklin's voyages, he had already led two previous expeditions into the Canadian Arctic. Franklin joined the British navy at the age of fourteen, and later formed part of an expedition to map the coast of Australia in 1802. In the early 1800s the British Admiralty renewed its interest in mapping a northwest passage through North America. In 1819, two expeditions were established: one led by William Edward Parry from Baffin Bay; the other, to proceed overland from Hudson Bay, to be led by Franklin. Prior to this, only two British explorers had reached the Arctic coast overland: Samuel Hearne and Alexander Mackenzie. On the first expedition, which lasted from 1819 to 1822, Franklin set out to travel to the mouth of the Coppermine River and chart the Arctic coastline in an easterly direction. Franklin undertook assiduous preparations for the journey. In his introduction to his *Narrative of a Journey to the Shores of the Polar Sea in the Years 1819, 20, 21, and 22* (1823), he tells of meeting with Alexander Mackenzie in England in order to benefit from the veteran explorer's advice. In July 1820, Franklin established an agreement with the Yellowknife/Dene (Copper Indian) leader, Akaitcho, for his help in guiding and providing food for the expedition. Travelling with a troop of French Canadian voyageurs, Métis interpreters, and Dene hunters, Franklin reached the spot near the mouth of the Coppermine made famous in Hearne's account, describing the scene in his journal of 15 June 1821: "Several human skulls which bore the marks of violence, and many bones were strewed about the ground near to the encampment, and as the spot exactly answers the description given by Mr. Hearne, of the place where the Chipewyans who accompanied him perpetrated the dreadful massacre on the Esquimaux, we had no doubt of this being the place. . . . We have, therefore, preserved the appellation of Bloody Fall, which he bestowed upon it." Upon reaching this spot, the Native people wisely turned back to rejoin their families and pursue their traditional hunting patterns. Franklin, however, insisted on remaining to trace the Arctic coastline to the east, naming many of the coves and inlets after fellow explorers and acquaintances. However, his return journey inland was a disaster. He lost more than ten men, and it appears that one of the men, under duress, resorted to cannibalism and murder (a situation which also appears to have occurred toward the end of his last expedition).

Some commentators have been critical of Franklin's judgment on this expedition, for it was clear, early on, that the men had insufficient rations to carry them through the return journey. In many respects, Franklin's published narrative was an attempt to explain the failures of the expedition and preserve his reputation, while at the same time praising those whom he considered most loyal to him. He was not without arrogance and high-handedness toward his men, particularly toward the French Canadians who were doing most of the heavy labour (each voyageur carried a pack of up to ninety pounds, not to mention tents and canoes). Throughout the narrative, he frequently accuses the French *voyageurs* of selfish and immoral behaviour and complains about their constant demands for food; Franklin even goes so far as to suspect them of vandalizing the canoes and fishing nets in an attempt to force the expedition to turn back. In his 1989 contemplation on the Franklin expedition in *Playing Dead*, Rudy Wiebe considers the expedition from the perspective of the *voyageurs,* nine of whom died. These men, asserts Wiebe, "on a quest whose purpose none of them could fathom, nevertheless made possible the journey and all the honours Franklin and Richardson and Back were to receive later." Certainly a degree of hubris and invincibility informs all explorers' endeavours, an element that Margaret Atwood picks up on in her 1991 short story about Franklin's last expedition, "The Age of Lead" (see Volume II). Rudy Wiebe's 1994 novel based on Franklin's first Arctic journey, *A Discovery of Strangers*, highlights the mixture of audacity and idealism that characterized the expedition. It is important to consider the enterprise from both viewpoints. On the one hand, through sheer perseverance, Franklin and his men were able to achieve undreamed-of results; Franklin's concluding sentence of the narrative of his first journey observes that altogether, the men travelled 5500 miles. On the other hand, it was only through the timely intervention of their Aboriginal allies that the remaining members of the expedition were saved. Following their rescue, Franklin expressed regret that Akaitcho's people had not received their promised reward, which was in part due to the fact that the rival trading companies had united in 1821 and the promissory notes provided to the Native peoples had been annulled. Akaitcho's speech in response to this disappointment is evidence of his benevolent disposition toward the British: "[Y]ou are poor, the traders appear to be poor, I and my party are poor likewise. . . . I do not regret having supplied you with provisions, for a Copper Indian can never permit white men to suffer from want of food on his lands, without flying to their aid."

Franklin's second journey, begun in 1825, had as its goal to reach the mouth of the Mackenzie River and chart the Arctic coastline in both westerly and easterly directions. Following imperial orders, Franklin turned back before he had completed the task, but in the interim his crew mapped over 1000 miles.

Franklin's narratives are somewhat different in style from other exploration accounts of this and earlier periods. His texts are extremely polished, with clear chapter divisions, excerpts from his fellow officers' journals, expressions of regret for the men lost, and direct addresses to the reader. In the published account of his first journey, he includes illustrations that were produced by two of the expedition members, George Back and Robert Hood (the latter of whom died on the return journey across the barrens). Notwithstanding his apology for his "defective style" in his introduction to the narrative of his first journey, his account is highly literate and gripping. Apologies of this sort had become requisite fare in explorers' accounts, for many of them felt embarrassed to be setting themselves before the public as reputable authors. Indeed, reviewers of the time could be rather snide about the nature of these published records, despite their enormous popularity with the British reading public. Isaac D'Israeli wrote disparagingly in 1791, "Every captain, who can write his own logbook, has of late obtruded his discoveries of every ten yards of land he has happened to observe, and worked up into pathos his account of storms and provisions." To be sure, the market had become glutted with such accounts. However, Franklin's harrowing ordeal, in his first and subsequent journeys, has left a lasting trace on the Canadian imagination. If one of the explorers included in this anthology can be said to have achieved mythic status in contemporary Canadian culture, it is John Franklin.

From Narrative of a Journey to the Shores of the Polar Sea, 1819-1822

[1820.] [. . .] We encamped for the night on a rocky island, and by eight A.M. on the following morning [July 29], arrived at Fort Providence, which is situated twenty-one miles from the entrance of the bay. The post is exclusively occupied by the North-West Company, the Hudson's Bay Company having no settlement to the northward of Great Slave Lake.[1] We found Mr. Wentzel[2] and our interpreter Jean Baptiste Adam here, with one of the Indian guides. [. . .]

As we were informed that external appearances made lasting impressions on the Indians, we prepared for the interview by decorating ourselves in uniform, and suspending a medal round each of our necks. Our tents had been previously pitched, and over one of them a silken union flag was hoisted. Soon after noon, on July 30th, several Indian canoes were seen advancing in a regular line, and on their approach, the chief was discovered in the headmost, which was paddled by two men. On landing at the fort, the chief assumed a very grave aspect. [. . .] He was rejoiced, he said to see such great chiefs on his lands, his tribe were poor, but they loved white men who had been their benefactors; and he hoped that our visit would be productive of much good to them. [. . .]

In reply to this speech, which I understood had been prepared for many days, I endeavoured to explain the objects of our mission in a manner best calculated to ensure his exertions in our service. With this view, I told him that we were sent out by the greatest chief in the world, who was the sovereign also of the trading companies in the country; that he was the friend of peace, and had the interest of every nation at heart. Having learned that his children in the north, were much in want of articles of merchandise, in consequence of the extreme length and difficulty of the present route; he had sent us to search for a passage by the sea, which if found, would enable large vessels to transport great quantities of goods more easily to their lands. That we had not come for the purpose of traffic, but solely to make discoveries for their benefit, as well as that of every other people. That we had been directed to inquire into the nature of all the productions of the countries we might pass through, and particularly respecting their inhabitants. That we desired the assistance of the Indians in guiding us, and providing us with food. [. . .] I also communicated to him that owing to the distance we had travelled, we had now few more stores than were necessary for the use of our own party, a part of these, however, should be forthwith presented to him; on his return he and his party should be remunerated with cloth, ammunition, tobacco, and some useful iron materials, besides having their debts to the North-West Company discharged.

The chief, whose name is Akaitcho or Big-foot, replied by a renewal of his assurances, that he and his party would attend us to the end of our journey, and that they would do their utmost to provide us with the means of subsistence. [. . .]

[1] Franklin was aligned with neither company but was working for the British Admiralty. He had been told that he could depend on help from both companies, but because of the trade warfare between the two and the general shortage of men and supplies, he received scant help from either.

[2] Willard Ferdinand Wentzel, a trader with the North West Company at Fort Providence who initially formed part of Franklin's party.

*[The expedition embarked overland from Fort Providence, on Great Slave Lake,
on 2 August 1820. Forced to stop because of the depletion of their supplies, they
constructed a base camp at Winter Lake which they named Fort Enterprise.
A party led by George Back was sent back to Fort Providence and other posts for
supplies. In July 1821, Franklin's party eventually reached the Arctic Ocean and
the site of Samuel Hearne's "Bloody Fall" near the mouth of the Coppermine
River. At this point, Mr. Wentzel and the Native hunters turned back, with the
promise to deposit provisions at Fort Enterprise. Franklin and nineteen men
continued their mapping of the polar coast. However, the success of the
expedition was marred by the disastrous return journey across the barrens
to Fort Enterprise, in the course of which Franklin lost ten of his men.]*

[1821. August 15] [. . .] [O]ur people, who had hitherto displayed in following us
through dangers and difficulties no less novel than appalling to them, a courage
beyond our expectation, now felt serious apprehensions for their safety, which
so possessed their minds that they were not restrained even by the presence of
their officers from expressing them. Their fears, we imagined, had been principally excited by the interpreters, St. Germain[3] and Adam, who from the outset
had foreboded every calamity; and we now strongly suspected that their recent
want of success in their hunting excursions, had proceeded from an intentional
relaxation in their efforts to kill deer, in order that the want of provision might
compel us to put a period to our voyage.

I must now mention that many concurrent circumstances had caused me,
during the few last days, to meditate on the approach of this painful necessity.
The strong breezes we had encountered for some days, led me to fear that the
season was breaking up, and severe weather would soon ensue, which we could
not sustain in a country destitute of fuel. Our stock of provision was now
reduced to a quantity of pemmican only sufficient for three days' consumption,
and the prospect of increasing it was not encouraging, for though rein-deer
were seen, they could not be easily approached on the level shores we were now
coasting, besides it was to be apprehended they would soon migrate to the
south. [. . .] and it was equally obvious that as our distance from any of the trading establishments would increase as we proceeded, the hazardous traverse
across the barren grounds, which we should have to make, if compelled to aban-
don the canoes upon any part of the coast, would become greater.

I this evening communicated to the officers my sentiments on these points,
as well as respecting our return, and was happy to find that their opinions coincided with my own. [. . .] I announced my determination of returning after four
days' examination, unless, indeed, we should previously meet the Esquimaux,

---

[3] Pierre St. Germain, a Métis translator on the expedition. Both Jean Baptiste Adam and
St. Germain were disgruntled because they had asked to be discharged from the expedition
once the Native guides and hunters had departed at Bloody Fall in July 1821. They argued that
their services as translators were no longer needed. Franklin refused their request and held
them to their contract because he wanted to keep them on as hunters.

and be enabled to make some arrangement for passing the winter with them. This communication was joyfully received by the men, and we hoped that the industry of our hunters being once more excited, we should be able to add to our stock of provision. [. . .] *[Shortly afterwards, realizing that they were in a desperate state and facing starvation, Franklin ordered the party to turn back.]*

[September 4] Having walked twelve miles and a half, we encamped at seven P.M., and distributed our last piece of pemmican, and a little arrow-root for supper, which afforded but a scanty meal. This evening was warm, but dark clouds overspread the sky. Our men now began to find their burdens very oppressive, and were much fatigued by this day's march, but did not complain. [. . .] As we had nothing to eat, and were destitute of the means of making a fire, we remained in our beds all the day; but the covering of our blankets was insufficient to prevent us from feeling the severity of the frost, and suffering inconvenience from the drifting of the snow into our tents. [. . .]

[September 25] The bounty of Providence was most seasonably manifested to us next morning, in our killing five small deer out of a herd, which came in sight as we were on the point of starting. This unexpected supply reanimated the drooping spirits of our men, and filled every heart with gratitude.

The voyagers instantly petitioned for a day's rest, which we were most reluctant to grant, being aware of the importance of every moment at this critical period of our journey. But they so earnestly and strongly pleaded their recent sufferings, and their conviction, that the quiet enjoyment of two substantial meals, after eight days' famine, would enable them to proceed next day more vigorously, that we could not resist their entreaties. [. . .] We all suffered much inconvenience from eating animal food after our long abstinence, but particularly those men who indulged themselves beyond moderation. We learned, in the evening that the Canadians,[4] with their usual thoughtlessness, had consumed above a third of their portions of meat. [. . .]

October 4.— [. . .] That no time might be lost in procuring relief, I immediately despatched Mr. Back[5] with St. Germain, Solomon Belanger, and Beauparlant, to search for the Indians, directing him to go to Fort Enterprise, where we expected they would be, or where, at least, a note from Mr. Wentzel would be found to direct us in our search for them. If St. Germain should kill any animals on his way, a portion of the meat was to be put up securely for us, and conspicuous marks placed over it. [. . .]

[October 5] The want of *tripe de roche*[6] caused us to go supperless to bed. Showers of snow fell frequently during the night. The breeze was light next

---

[4] Franklin uses the term "Canadians" to refer to the French-Canadian *voyageurs*.

[5] George Back, officer and artist on Franklin's expedition. He would eventually take part in planning the massive search campaign to find Franklin's remains in the mid-1800s. According to Back's journal, Gabriel Beauparlant, a *voyageur* who was part of this group, died on October 17th.

[6] *Tripe de roche* is a brownish-black rock lichen that grows in the Far North. As the men became more desperate for food, they depended on it as their only food source, and had to scrape the small patches of it from the rocks. The lichen was extremely hard to digest and contributed to stomach and bowel ailments, further weakening some of the men.

morning, the weather cold and clear. We were all on foot by day-break, but from the frozen state of our tents and bed clothes, it was long before the bundles could be made, and as usual, the men lingered over a small fire they had kindled, so that it was eight o'clock before we started. Our advance from the depth of the snow was slow, and about noon coming to a spot where there was some *tripe de roche*, we stopped to collect it, and breakfasted. Mr. Hood,[7] who was now very feeble, and Dr. Richardson, who attached himself to him, walked together at a gentle pace in the rear of the party. I kept with the foremost men, to cause them to halt occasionally, until the stragglers came up. Resuming our march after breakfast, we followed the track of Mr. Back's party, and encamped early, as all of us were much fatigued, particularly Crédit, who having to-day carried the men's tent, it being his turn to do so, was so exhausted, that when he reached the encampment he was unable to stand. The *tripe de roche* disagreed with this man and with Vaillant, in consequence of which, they were the first whose strength totally failed.[8] We had a small quantity of this weed in the evening, and the rest of our supper was made up of scraps of roasted leather. The distance walked to-day was six miles. As Crédit was very weak in the morning, his load was reduced to little more than his personal luggage, consisting of his blanket, shoes, and gun. Previous to setting out, the whole party ate the remains of their old shoes, and whatever scraps of leather they had, to strengthen their stomachs for the fatigue of the day's journey. We left the encampment at nine, and pursued our route over a range of bleak hills. [. . .] Those in advance made as usual frequent halts, yet being unable from the severity of the weather to remain long still, they were obliged to move on before the rear could come up, and the party, of course, straggled very much.

About noon Samandré coming up, informed us that Crédit and Vaillant could advance no further. Some willows being discovered in a valley near to us, I proposed to halt the party there, whilst Dr. Richardson went back to visit them. I hoped too, that when the sufferers received the information of a fire being kindled at so short a distance, they would be cheered, and use their utmost efforts to reach it, but this proved a vain hope. The Doctor found Vaillant about a mile and a half in the rear, much exhausted with cold and fatigue. Having encouraged him to advance to the fire, after repeated solicitations he made the attempt, but fell down amongst the deep snow at every step. Leaving him in this situation, the Doctor went about half a mile farther back, to the spot where Crédit was said to have halted, and the track being nearly obliterated by the snow drift, it became unsafe for him to go further. Returning he passed Vaillant, who having moved

---

[7] Robert Hood, officer and artist on the expedition. He was murdered by Michel Teroahauté, an Iroquois *voyageur*, on October 20th. The latter was subsequently executed by the expedition's physician and naturalist, John Richardson, who feared for the safety of the rest of the party.

[8] Mathew Pelonquin (Crédit) and Registe Vaillant were two French-Canadian *voyageurs* on the expedition. From this account, it appears that they both died on October 6th.

only a few yards in his absence, had fallen down, was unable to rise, and could scarcely answer his questions. Being unable to afford him any effectual assistance, he hastened on to inform us of his situation. When J.B. Belanger had heard the melancholy account, he went immediately to aid Vaillant, and bring up his burden. Respecting Crédit, we were informed by Samandré, that he had stopped a short distance behind Vaillant, but that his intention was to return to the encampment of the preceding evening.

When Belanger came back with Vaillant's load, he informed us that he had found him lying on his back, benumbed with cold, and incapable of being roused. The stoutest men of the party were now earnestly entreated to bring him to the fire, but they declared themselves unequal to the task; and, on the contrary, urged me to allow them to throw down their loads, and proceed to Fort Enterprise with the utmost speed. A compliance with their desire would have caused the loss of the whole party, for the men were totally ignorant of the course to be taken, and none of the officers, who could have directed the march, were sufficiently strong to keep up at the pace they would then walk; besides, even supposing them to have found their way, the strongest men would certainly have deserted the weak. Something, however, was absolutely necessary to be done, to relieve them as much as possible from their burdens, and the officers consulted on the subject. Mr. Hood and Dr. Richardson proposed to remain behind, with a single attendant, at the first place where sufficient wood and *tripe de roche* should be found for ten days' consumption; and that I should proceed as expeditiously as possible with the men to the house, and thence send them immediate relief. They strongly urged that this arrangement would contribute to the safety of the rest of the party, by relieving them from the burden of the tent, and several other articles; and that they might afford aid to Crédit, if he should unexpectedly come up. I was distressed beyond description at the thought of leaving them in such a dangerous situation, and for a long time combated their proposal; but they strenuously urged, that this step afforded the only chance of safety for the party, and I reluctantly acceded to it. The ammunition, of which we had a small barrel, was also to be left with them, and it was hoped that this deposit would be a strong inducement for the Indians to venture across the barren grounds to their aid. We communicated this resolution to the men, who were cheered at the slightest prospect of alleviation of their present miseries, and they promised with great appearance of earnestness to return to those officers, upon the first supply of food.

The party then moved on; Vaillant's blanket and other necessaries were left in the track, at the request of the Canadians, without any hope, however, of his being able to reach them. After marching until dusk without seeing a favourable place for encamping, night compelled us to take shelter under the lee of a hill, amongst some willows, with which, after many attempts, we at length made a fire. It was not sufficient, however, to warm the whole party, much less to thaw our shoes; and the weather not permitting the gathering of *tripe de roche*, we had nothing to cook.

The painful retrospection of the melancholy events of the day banished sleep, and we shuddered as we contemplated the dreadful effects of this bitterly cold night on our two companions, if still living. Some faint hopes were entertained of Crédit's surviving the storm, as he was provided with a good blanket, and had leather to eat.

[October 7] The weather was mild next morning. We left the encampment at nine, and a little before noon came to a pretty extensive thicket of small willows, near which there appeared a supply of *tripe de roche* on the face of the rocks. At this place Dr. Richardson and Mr. Hood determined to remain, with John Hepburn,[9] who volunteered to stop with them. The tent was securely pitched, a few willows collected, and the ammunition and all other articles were deposited, except each man's clothing, one tent, a sufficiency of ammunition for the journey, and the officers' journals. I had only one blanket, which was carried for me, and two pair of shoes. The offer was now made for any of the men, who felt themselves too weak to proceed, to remain with the officers, but none of them accepted it. Michel alone felt some inclination to do so. After we had united in thanksgiving and prayers to Almighty God, I separated from my companions, deeply afflicted that a train of melancholy circumstances should have demanded of me the severe trial of parting from friends in such a condition, who had become endeared to me by their constant kindness, and co-operation, and a participation of numerous sufferings. This trial I could not have been induced to undergo, but for the reasons they had so strongly urged the day before, to which my own judgment assented, and for the sanguine hope I felt of either finding a supply of provision at Fort Enterprise, or meeting the Indians in the immediate vicinity of that place, according to my arrangements with Mr. Wentzel and Akaitcho. [. . .]

Greatly as Mr. Hood was exhausted, and, indeed, incapable as he must have proved, of encountering the fatigue of our very next day's journey, so that I felt his resolution to be prudent, I was sensible that his determination to remain, was mainly prompted by the disinterested and generous wish to remove impediments to the progress of the rest of the party. Dr. Richardson and Hepburn, who were both in a state of strength to keep pace with the men, beside this motive which they shared with him, were influenced in their resolution to remain; the former by the desire which had distinguished his character, throughout the expedition, of devoting himself to the succour of the weak, and the latter by the zealous attachment he had ever shewn towards his officers. [. . .]

Descending afterwards into a more level country, we found the snow very deep, and the labour of wading through it so fatigued the whole party, that we were compelled to encamp, after a march of four miles and a half. Belanger[10] and Michel

9 John Hepburn, a seaman who had served with Franklin previously and remained intensely loyal to the captain. Like Richardson, he took part in the search parties to find Franklin's remains after he went missing during his third expedition.

10 Jean Baptiste Belanger, one of the French-Canadian *voyageurs* on the expedition. Franklin later speculated that Michel had murdered Belanger and Perrault, and John Richardson's account of the expedition suggests that Michel may have been feeding himself on their remains. Neither man was ever found.

were left far behind, and when they arrived at the encampment appeared quite exhausted. The former, bursting into tears, declared his inability to proceed with the party, and begged me to let him go back next morning to the tent, and shortly afterwards Michel made the same request. I was in hopes they might recover a little strength by the night's rest and therefore deferred giving any permission until the morning. The sudden failure in the strength of these men cast a gloom over the rest, which I tried in vain to remove, by repeated assurances that the distance to Fort Enterprise was short, and that we should, in all probability, reach it in four days. Not being able to find any *tripe de roche*, we drank an infusion of the Labrador tea plant, *(ledum palustre)*, and ate a few morsels of burnt leather for supper. We were unable to raise the tent, and found its weight too great to carry it on; we, therefore, cut it up, and took a part of the canvass for a cover. [. . .] In the morning Belanger and Michel renewed their request to be permitted to go back to the tent, assuring me they were still weaker than on the preceding evening, and less capable of going forward; and they urged, that the stopping at a place where there was a supply of *tripe de roche* was their only chance of preserving life; under these circumstances, I could not do otherwise than yield to their desire. I wrote a note to Dr. Richardson and Mr. Hood, informing them of the pines we had passed, and recommending their removing thither. Having found that Michel was carrying a considerable quantity of ammunition, I desired him to divide it among my party, leaving him only ten balls and a little shot, to kill any animals he might meet on his way to the tent. This man was very particular in his inquiries respecting the direction of the house, and the course we meant to pursue. [. . .][11]

Scarcely were these arrangements finished, before Perrault and Fontano[12] were seized with a fit of dizziness, and betrayed other symptoms of extreme debility. Some tea was quickly prepared for them, and after drinking it, and eating a few morsels of burnt leather, they recovered, and expressed their desire to go forward. [. . .] Belanger and Michel were left at the encampment, and proposed to start shortly afterwards. By the time we had gone about two hundred yards, Perrault became again dizzy, and desired us to halt, which we did, until he, recovering, proposed to march on. Ten minutes more had hardly elapsed before he again desired us to stop, and, bursting into tears, declared he was totally exhausted, and unable to accompany us further. As the encampment was not more than a quarter of a mile distant, we proposed that he should return to it, and rejoin Belanger and Michel, whom we knew to be still there, from perceiving the smoke of a fresh fire; and because they had not made any preparation for starting when we left them. He readily acquiesced in the proposition, and having taken a friendly leave of each of us, and enjoined us to make all the haste we could in sending relief, he turned back, keeping his gun and ammunition. [. . .]

---

[11] Franklin, composing much of this after the events occurred, hints at Michel's treachery.

[12] Ignace Perrault and Vincenza Fontano, two *voyageurs* who died during the expedition. That same day, both turned back to rejoin Belanger and Michel Teroahauté. Richardson and Franklin suspected that Perrault was cannibalized by Michel.

The labour we experienced in wading through the deep snow induced us to cross a moderate sized lake, which lay in our track, but we found this operation far more harassing. As the surface of the ice was perfectly smooth, we slipt at almost every step, and were frequently blown down by the wind with such force as to shake our whole frames.

Poor Fontano was completely exhausted by the labour of making this traverse, and we made a halt until his strength was recruited, by which time the party was benumbed with cold. Proceeding again, he got on tolerably well for a little time, but being again seized with faintness and dizziness, he fell often, and at length exclaimed that he could go no further. We immediately stopped, and endeavoured to encourage him to persevere, until we should find some willows, to encamp; he insisted, however, that he could not march any longer through this deep snow; and said, that if he should even reach our encampment this evening, he must be left there, provided *tripe de roche* could not be procured to recruit his strength. The poor man was overwhelmed with grief, and seemed desirous to remain at that spot. We were about two miles from the place where the other men had been left, and as the track to it was beaten, we proposed to him to return thither, as we thought it probable he would find the men still there: at any rate, he would be able to get fuel to keep him warm during the night; and, on the next day, he could follow their track to the officers' tent; and, should the path be covered by the snow, the pines we had passed yesterday would guide him, as they were yet in view.

I cannot describe my anguish on the occasion of separating from another companion under circumstances so distressing. There was, however, no alternative. The extreme debility of the rest of the party, put the carrying him quite out of the question, as he himself admitted; and it was evident that the frequent delays he must occasion if he accompanied us, and did not gain strength, must have endangered the lives of the whole. [. . .] After some hesitation he determined on returning, and set out, having bid each of us farewell in the tenderest manner. We watched him with inexpressible anxiety for some time. [. . .]

The party was now reduced to five persons, Adam, Peltier, Benoit, Samandré, and myself.[13] Continuing the journey, we came, after an hour's walk, to some willows, and encamped under the shelter of a rock, having walked in the whole four miles and a half. We made an attempt to gather some *tripe de roche*, but could not, owing to the severity of the weather. Our supper, therefore, consisted of tea and a few morsels of leather. [. . .]

[*October 11*] Next morning [. . .] our minds were agitated between hope and fear, and, contrary to the custom we had kept up, of supporting our spirits by conversation, we went silently forward.

---

[13] Jean Baptiste Adam was one of the expedition's interpreters. The other three are names of some of the French-Canadian *voyageurs*. Joseph Peltier and François Samandré died in November at Fort Enterprise.

At length we reached Fort Enterprise, and to our infinite disappointment and grief found it a perfectly desolate habitation. There was no deposit of provision, no trace of the Indians, no letter from Mr. Wentzel to point out where the Indians might be found. It would be impossible for me to describe our sensations after entering this miserable abode, and discovering how we had been neglected: the whole party shed tears, not so much for our own fate, as for that of our friends in the rear, whose lives depended entirely on our sending immediate relief from this place.

I found a note, however, from Mr. Back, stating that he had reached the house two days ago, and was going in search of the Indians, at a part where St. Germain deemed it probable they might be found. If he was unsuccessful, he purposed walking to Fort Providence, and sending succour from thence. But he doubted whether either he or his party could perform the journey to that place in their present debilitated state. [. . .]

[Finding no food supplies at Fort Enterprise, the men lived for weeks on boiled tripe de roche and discarded animal bones, becoming so weakened that they were unable to hunt when a herd of deer appeared in the vicinity; they were also forced to burn sections of the house for fuel. On October 29, following the death of Hood, Richardson and Hepburn, who had been left behind on October 7, rejoined their companions at Fort Enterprise.]

November 7.— Adam had passed a restless night, being disquieted by gloomy apprehensions of approaching death, which we tried in vain to dispel. He was so low in the morning as to be scarcely able to speak. I remained in bed by his side to cheer him as much as possible. The Doctor and Hepburn went to cut wood. They had hardly begun their labour, when they were amazed at hearing the report of a musket. They could scarcely believe that there was really any one near, until they heard a shout, and immediately espied three Indians close to the house. Adam and I heard the latter noise, and I was fearful that a part of the house had fallen upon one of my companions, a disaster which had in fact been thought not unlikely. My alarm was only momentary, Dr. Richardson came in to communicate the joyful intelligence that relief had arrived. He and myself immediately addressed thanksgiving to the throne of mercy for this deliverance, but poor Adam was in so low a state that he could scarcely comprehend the information. When the Indians entered, he attempted to rise but sank down again. But for this seasonable interposition of Providence, his existence must have terminated in a few hours, and that of the rest probably in not many days.

The Indians had left Akaitcho's encampment on the 5th November, having been sent by Mr. Back with all possible expedition, after he had arrived at their tents. They brought but a small supply of provision that they might travel quickly. It consisted of dried deer's meat, some fat, and a few tongues. Dr. Richardson, Hepburn, and I, eagerly devoured the food, which they imprudently presented to us, in too great abundance, and in consequence we suffered dreadfully from indigestion, and had no rest the whole night. Adam being unable to feed himself was more judiciously treated by them, and suffered less; his spirits revived hourly. The circumstance of our eating more food than was proper in our present condition, was another striking proof of the debility of our minds. [. . .]

November 8.— The Indians this morning requested us to remove to an encampment on the banks of the river, as they were unwilling to remain in the house in which the bodies of our deceased companions were lying exposed to view. We agreed to remove, but the day proved too stormy, and Dr. Richardson and Hepburn having dragged the bodies to a short distance, and covered them with snow, the objections of the Indians to remain in the house were removed, and they began to clear our room of the accumulation of dirt and fragments of pounded bones. The improved state of our apartment, and the large and cheerful fires they kept up, produced in us a sensation of comfort to which we had long been strangers. In the evening they brought in a pile of dried wood, which was lying on the river-side, and on which we had often cast a wishful eye, being unable to drag it up the bank. The Indians set about every thing with an activity that amazed us. Indeed, contrasted with our emaciated figures and extreme debility, their frames appeared to us gigantic, and their strength supernatural. These kind creatures next turned their attention to our personal appearance, and prevailed upon us to shave and wash ourselves. [. . .]

[*November 15*] As it was of consequence to get amongst the rein-deer before our present supply should fail, we made preparations for quitting Fort Enterprise the next day; and, accordingly, at an early hour, on the 16th, having united in thanksgiving and prayer, the whole party left the house after breakfast. Our feelings on quitting the Fort, where we had formerly enjoyed much comfort, if not happiness, and, latterly, experienced a degree of misery scarcely to be paralleled, may be more easily conceived than described. The Indians treated us with the utmost tenderness, gave us their snow-shoes, and walked without themselves, keeping by our sides, that they might lift us when we fell. We descended Winter River, and, about noon, crossed the head of Round-Rock Lake, distant about three miles from the house, where we were obliged to halt, as Dr. Richardson was unable to proceed. The swellings in his limbs rendered him by much the weakest of the party. The Indians prepared our encampment, cooked for us, and fed us as if we had been children; evincing humanity that would have done honour to the most civilized people. The night was mild, and fatigue made us sleep soundly.

From this period to the 26th of November we gradually continued to improve, under the kindness and attention of our Indians. On this day we arrived in safety at the abode of our chief and companion, Akaitcho.

[1823]

According to literary historian David Woodman, "the lore of the doomed Franklin expedition has been told almost exclusively from the point of view of the European culture that sent it forth. Yet the stories have always held a great fascination for the Inuit of the central Arctic as well. The tales of the dead explorers and their ships were told and retold during the long winter nights." Stories of meeting with the White "kabloonas" have been passed down within Inuit communities and have become part of a living culture. Embedded in the past as these tales are, they nevertheless add important pieces to the puzzle of the fate of Franklin's last expedition. Although for many years the accounts of Inuit people were disregarded, more recently scholars have been trying to unravel the reports given by Inuit men and women about their encounters with some of Franklin's crew members. The Inuit reports are notable for their detail, and comparisons between early recorded testimonies and those passed down orally to later descendants show a remarkable consistency. Woodman's book *Unravelling the Franklin Mystery: Inuit Testimony* (1991) provides an important investigation into the information that local people have contributed to the Franklin mystery. Prior to this, such figures as the American explorer Charles Francis Hall (in his expeditions from 1860–1873) and the Greenlander anthropologist Knud Rasmussen (Fifth Thule Expedition, 1921–1924) had spoken with Inuit people and recorded their recollections of encounters with survivors of the Franklin expedition.

Until recently, most historians have ignored the Inuit testimony and relied primarily on the information deposited in the cairn left by Captain James Fitzjames, commander of the *Erebus*, on King William Island. The note stated that the 105 remaining men were abandoning the ships in April 1848. It would appear, however, that the group did not stay together, for Inuit accounts record encounters with much smaller groups of White men. Some accounts also suggest that some of Franklin's men returned to the ship after the 1848 abandonment. Central in many of these accounts is a figure named "Aglooka" (presumed to be either Captain Fitzjames or Captain Francis Crozier), who is mentioned in the account by Tuk-ke-ta and Ow-wer. In total, it would appear that the Inuit encountered various members of the Franklin expedition for at least two years, suggesting that at least a handful of men managed to survive for substantially longer than the official record suggests. Mordecai Richler's 1989 novel *Solomon Gursky Was Here* takes the Inuit testimony into account in his fictional treatment of a stowaway aboard the Franklin expedition who gets adopted by an Inuit community (and in turn leaves a trail of "relics" that subsequent Canadian researchers find and attempt to explain).

Notable in Inuit accounts about the Franklin expedition is the absence of surprise or horror. What Europeans considered a shocking "tragedy" was for the Inuit a reasonable result of inadequate preparation in the environment. Many of these accounts show more interest in the technology and objects of the

Europeans than in the events being described; this is particularly evident in Qaqortingneq's account of finding one of the expedition's ships, as well as in Tooktoocheer's mention of the children having taken many of the objects from the abandoned lifeboat as playthings.

One reason why Inuit accounts may have been discounted for so long is that they did not represent an orderly scene of stoic British men, but rather a series of lost stragglers suffering from illness and starvation, some of whom engaged in cannibalism.

Discovery of an Abandoned Ship

Testimony by Qaqortingneq given to Knud Rasmussen, 1921

Two brothers were out hunting seal to the northwest of Qeqertaq (King William's Land). It was in the spring, at the time when the snow melts about the breathing holes of the seal. They caught sight of something far out on the ice; a great black mass of something, that could not be any animal they knew. They studied it and made out at last that it was a great ship. Running home at once, they told their fellows, and on the following day all went out to see. They saw no men about the ship; it was deserted; and they therefore decided to take from it all they could find for themselves. But none of them had ever before met with white men, and they had no knowledge as to the use of all the things they found.

One man, seeing a boat that hung out over the side of the ship, cried: "Here is a fine big trough that will do for meat! I will have this!" He had never seen a boat before, and did not know what it was. And he cut the ropes that held it up, and the boat crashed down endways on to the ice and was smashed.

They found guns, also, on the ship, and not knowing what was the right use of these things, they broke away the barrels and used the metal for harpoon heads. So ignorant were they indeed, in the matter of guns and belonging to guns, that on finding some percussion caps, such as were used in those days, they took them for tiny thimbles, and really believed that there were dwarfs among the white folk, little people who could use percussion caps for thimbles.

At first they were afraid to go down into the lower part of the ship, but after a while they grew bolder, and ventured also into the houses underneath. Here they found many dead men, lying in the sleeping places there; all dead. And at last they went down also into a great dark space in the middle of the ship. It was quite dark down there and they could not see. But they soon found tools and set to work and cut a window in the side. But here those foolish ones, knowing nothing of the white men's things, cut a hole in the side of the ship below the water line, so that the water came pouring in, and the ship sank. It sank to the bottom with all the costly things; nearly all that they had found was lost again at once.

But in the same year, later on in the spring, three men were on their way from Qeqertaq to the southward, going to hunt caribou calves. And they found a boat with the dead bodies of six men. There were knives and guns in the boat, and much food also, so the men must have died of disease. [. . .]

And that is all I know about your white men who once came to our land, and perished; whom our fathers met but could not help to live.

[1927]

Meeting with "Aglooka" on the Ice

Testimony by Tuk-ke-ta and Ow-wer given to Charles Francis Hall, May 1869
Tuk-ke-ta and Ow-wer now tell that they with Too-shoo-art-thar-u *[sic]* and Mong-er [. . .] were on the west shore of Kikituk [King William Island] with their families sealing, & this a long time ago. They were getting ready to move—the time in the morning & the sun high—when Tuk-ke-ta saw something in the distance on the smooth ice that looked white & thought it was a bear. The company had got all ready to start travelling on the land. Soon as Tuk-ke-ta saw this something white, he told his companions of it, when all waited, hoping it was a bear. As they watched, the white object grew larger, for it was coming down towards them. They saw the white thing moving along in the direction of the coast, turning in a kind of circling way just as the little bay turned. At length they began to see many black objects moving along with what they had first espied as white in the distance. The object that they 1st had seen as white proved to be a sail raised on the boat & as this got nearer saw this sail shake in the wind. On seeing what they did, the object grew plainer and they thought of white men and began to be afraid.

As the company of men (strangers)[1] & what they were drawing got quite near, 2 men came on ahead of all & were walking on the ice & were getting near where the Innuits were standing looking out, which was on the land, the 2 men (Koblunas) came walking up to where they were. Too-shoo-art-thar-u and Ow-wer started to meet them, walking there on the ice. When they came to a crack in the ice, they stopped for the two white men to come up. Then the 2 white men came close to Ow-wer and Too-shoo-art-thar-u. One had a gun which he carried in his arms. The crack in the ice separated the meeting natives. The man that carried the gun stopped behind—a little back, while the other man came as close up to Ow-wer & Too-shoo-art-thar-u as the crack in the ice would allow him. The man that came up to the crack had nothing in his

[1] The parenthetical insertions and translations throughout this document are Hall's. The man referred to as "Aglooka" is generally thought to have been Captain Crozier or Captain Fitzjames, both of whom were officers on Franklin's expedition. The men had deserted the stranded ships in April 1848; Franklin had died the year before.

hands or on his shoulder. As he stopped, he cried out "C'hi-mo".[2] The first man that came up then spoke to the man a little behind, when he laid the gun down and came up at once along side the 1st man.

The 1st man then showed that he had an oo-loo when he stooped down beside the ice crack which divided the white men from the Innuits & began cutting the ice with a peculiar kind of circling motion with the oo-loo (Civilization mincing-knife or Innuit women's knife). This peculiar motion now showed by Ow-wer with his oo-loo on the snow floor of the igloo. At the same time, or rather right after this man had made these "chippings" or "scratchings" (as you call it) on the ice, he put his hand up to his mouth and lowered it all the way down his neck and breast, as if to say he wanted to get something to eat. Then the two white men moved along the one side, till they found a place where they could pass over to the 2 Innuits—Ow-wer & Too-shoo-art-thar-u. On the 2 Kabloonas (white men) getting to them, the 1st man, who was Aglooka, spoke to them, saying, "Man-nik-too-me", at the same time stroking 1st one & then the other down the breast, and also shook hands with each, repeating "Man-nik-too-me" several times. [. . .]

Aglooka pointed with his hand to the southward & eastward & at the same time repeating the word I-wil-ik. The Innuits could not understand whether he wanted them to show him the way there or that he was going there. He then made a motion to the northward & spoke the word oo-me-en, making them to understand there were 2 ships in that direction; which had, as they supposed, been crushed in the ice. As Aglooka pointed to the N., drawing his hand & arm from that direction he slowly moved his body in a falling direction and all at once dropped his head side ways into his hand, at the same time making a kind of combination of whirring, buzzing & wind blowing noise. This the pantomimic representation of ships being crushed in the ice. [. . .]

[1991]

Finding of a Lifeboat with Skeletons

Testimony by Tooktoocheer given to Lieutenant Frederick Schwatka, 1879
[Tooktoocheer] said she had never seen any of Franklin's men alive, but saw six skeletons on the main-land and an adjacent island . . . [her son] Ogzeuckjeuwock took up the thread of the narrative here. In answer to a question which we asked his mother, he said he saw books at the boat place in a tin case, about two feet long and a foot square, which was fastened, and they broke it open. The case was full. Written and printed books were shown him, and he said they were like the printed ones. Among the books he found what was probably the needle of a compass or other magnetic instrument because he said when it touched any iron it stuck fast. The boat was right side up, and the tin

[2]"Chimo" is a word of greeting in Inuktitut.

case in the boat. Outside the boat he saw a number of skulls. He forgot how many, but said there were more than four. He also saw bones from legs and arms that appeared to have been sawed off. Inside the boat was a box filled with bones; the box was about the same size as the one with books in it . . . In the boat he saw canvas and four sticks (a tent or sail), saw a number of watches, open-faced; a few were gold, but most were silver. They are all lost now. They were given to the children to play with, and have been broken up and lost . . . His reason for thinking that they had been eating each other was because the bones were cut with a knife or saw. They found one big saw and one small one in the boat; also a large red tin case of smoking tobacco and some pipes. There was no cairn there. The bones are now covered up with sand and sea-weed, as they were lying just at high-water mark. Some of the books were taken home for the children to play with, and finally torn and lost . . .

[1881]

ANONYMOUS ■ (mid-/late 1800s)

After Sir John Franklin's ship and crew went missing in the Canadian Arctic during their 1845 search for the Northwest Passage, numerous search parties were assembled to discover their fate. Once the British Admiralty had given up on the quest, Franklin's widow launched a further series of search parties, which she funded from her own private inheritance and from public funds that she had raised for the mission. One of the expeditions Lady Franklin financed was undertaken by Francis McClintock in 1857. In 1859, his search party discovered a message left in a cairn on King William Island, which revealed that the two ships had been abandoned and that Franklin had died twelve years earlier in 1847. The disappearance of the Franklin expedition caught the public imagination, as did the story of the grieving widow, and a popular ballad was written about the event. Numerous versions of this ballad exist, including one that mentions the crew resorting to cannibalism; the following is the best-known version. A more recent counterpart to this ballad is Stan Rogers's renowned 1981 song "Northwest Passage," included in Volume II.

Lady Franklin's Lament

It was homeward bound one night on the deep
Swinging in my hammock I fell asleep
I dreamed a dream and I thought it true
Concerning Franklin and his gallant crew.

With a hundred seamen he sailed away
To the frozen ocean in the month of May
To seek that passage around the pole
Where we poor sailors do sometimes go.

Through cruel hardship his men did go
His ship on mountains of ice was drove   10
Where the Eskimo in his skin canoe
Was the only one who ever came through.

In Baffin Bay where the Whale fish blow
The fate of Franklin no man may know
The fate of Franklin no tongue can tell
Lord Franklin along with his sailors do dwell.

And now my burden it gives me pain
For my long lost Franklin I'd cross the main
Ten thousand pounds would I freely give
To know on earth that my Franklin do live.   20

[mid-/late 1800s]

Narratives of Emigration, Settlement, and Invasion

Introduction: Canada as Home

He would impress upon the Emigrant, with all the force his words can impart, the absolute necessity of sobriety, industry, and resolute determination to overcome temporary obstacles: then he will find in Canada a home which, for substantial comfort, could not be excelled.
— John Miller Grant, *To Emigrants: Canada: Its Advantages to Settlers*

You will not have long to wait until you find yourself in a much improved condition to that you left, unless the latter was a very good one. Grumblers, complainers, cranks, and slanderers are not invited.
— *Pamphlet Descriptive of Manitoba, Showing Her Attractions for Agriculturalists, Stock Raisers, Dairymen, and All Who Desire Comfortable Homes and Prosperity*, issued by the Provincial Government of Manitoba

WHILE SAMUEL HEARNE, Alexander Mackenzie, and David Thompson were exploring the regions of Canada unsettled by Europeans, a lively culture already established in the East was producing a variety of narratives mixing adventure and social commentary. The explorers were searching for a way to make the experience of the unknown familiar and reassuring. In the early narratives of settlement in Canada, one finds a further elaboration of this experience of dislocation, but with a difference: now, for the first time, writers began to express an awareness that a revised way of thinking and "being" was needed in order to really belong in this new place. In other words, they had to *forge* a sense of belonging; it did not come automatically. The exoticism of the New World prevalent in the explorer narratives is replaced in the literature of the late eighteenth and early nineteenth centuries by images of domestication. These narratives tend to be either artistic renditions of life in the colonies, or practical guides to such a life. Since many of the explorers were venturing into territory that had yet to be charted, they saw their mission as a communicative one: to transfer details about the new territory and its peoples. Now the mission of writers was to communicate different kinds of information about British North America, as both a viable place to live and a valuable place to fight for. Geography also played an important part in determining what kinds of narratives were composed in the pre-Confederation period. The West was still the frontier of exploration (it is therefore largely unrepresented in this section), the areas that later became known as Upper and Lower Canada were increasingly places of settlement, and the Maritime colonies were by this period well-established communities with distinctive historical, cultural, and political traditions. Early writers located their stories and tales in Canada and worked at integrating Canadian geography, climate, and people into their literature.

This section showcases the transition from representing British North America either in scientific terms or as an exotic location full of wild animals, sublime landscapes, and "savage" peoples, to depicting it as a place that was open and ready for settlement, and finally, to portraying it as a place with a unique history and society. This pattern can be traced in Oliver Goldsmith's poem "The Rising Village" (1825, 1834). The poem delineates the evolution of a community from its beginnings, with a lonely settler mapping his position in the wilderness, to an aspirant village with a few key buildings, to a burgeoning town. Goldsmith's poem, like many others of the time, is a guardedly optimistic portrait of Canada. It begins on a note of sadness about the decline of Britain and ends with hope for the future of the colony.

The literature from such established cities as Quebec and Halifax paints a dramatically different vision of North America from either the exploration narratives or early settler accounts. It is interesting to compare the accounts of encounter and exploration with the sketches of the Nova Scotian satirists (Thomas Chandler Haliburton and Thomas McCulloch), on the one hand, and on the other, those of the figure of the "lady traveller," the Englishwoman who explored the New World, helped to propagate colonial ideas, and challenged conventional ideas of femininity. Elizabeth Simcoe is perhaps the most well known early woman traveller to document her tours around the colony. During the five years that Simcoe lived in Canada, she wrote a series of diaries and produced many important watercolour sketches that document both the rugged beauty of the landscape and the quotidian life of an early gentlewoman. The diaries that were written as letters home to her family and friends tell of her adventures and misadventures in the colonies. From her privileged position as the wife of John Graves Simcoe (the first lieutenant governor of Upper Canada, 1791–96), Simcoe was able to travel to many corners of Upper and Lower Canada that might have been inaccessible to other visitors to the colonies. Her diaries were published as *The Diary of Mrs. John Graves Simcoe* in 1911.

Anna Jameson's *Winter Studies and Summer Rambles* (1838) is another example of the work of a "lady traveller." Jameson disparagingly likens Toronto to a "fourth- or fifth-rate provincial town with the pretensions of a capital city." In turn, her account of the city stands in marked contrast to the emergent society depicted in the Upper Canadian settlement narratives of Susanna Moodie and her sister Catharine Parr Traill. Much of the work of Moodie and Traill was written in the form of guidebooks for potential emigrants to British North America. To address the concerns of emigrants about the voyage over and the life to expect upon arrival, British officials, private individuals, and organizations (such as the Society for Promoting Christian Knowledge) began to publish guides in the early 1800s. Some guides encouraged potential emigrants (Traill), while other guides braced newcomers for their arrival (Moodie). The literature of the period is thus a mixture of many genres: satires, travel and adventure stories, and emigrant guides.

It is also important to be aware of the sequence in which different parts of Canada were settled and the various names that were appended to the territory we now know as "Canada" (see the maps from 1791 and 1849 in Figures II-1, and II-2). After the 1759 conquest of New France by the British, the territory spanning today's Quebec and Ontario was known as "Quebec," with Nova Scotia (later divided in 1784 to form Nova Scotia and New Brunswick), Prince Edward Island, and Newfoundland constituting separate colonies. However, most of the authors included in this section are writing after this period, when the label "Canada" began to be used for both English and French territories. In 1791, Quebec was divided into Upper and Lower Canada. In 1840, the two areas were joined into a territory known as "Canada." The term "Canada" is used for the sake of convenience throughout this section, with the understanding that the label referred to very distinct configurations depending on the period in question.

The Audience Back "Home"

While the American War of Independence (1775–83) inspired American writers to distance themselves and their works from British literature, those who wrote about Canada at this time hailed predominantly from Britain and brought their sensibilities and training with them. Many of these authors were explicitly writing to an audience back "home." Even if born in Canada, most writers regarded their central audience to be where the centre of culture was: England.

Goldsmith's "The Rising Village" (1825, 1834) is an excellent example of a poem that traces the growth of a community in the New World, but still addresses an audience in the old one. So, writing with the expectations of a British audience in mind, poets such as Goldsmith used the language of British poetry to shape the landscapes in front of them. Much early nineteenth-century poetry in Canada was imitative of the sentimental poetry being written in Britain, but the language that evolved to suit the needs of European poetry did not fit the Canadian landscape. William Wordsworth's poetic glorification of the common-place set out in his preface to the *Lyrical Ballads* in 1802, for instance, was ill equipped to convey the experience of a settler in British North America. Wordsworth wrote that the "aim" of the *Lyrical Ballads* was "to choose incidents and situations from common life" and to use a "selection of language really spoken by men," for which the source is "humble and rustic life" (7). He wrote of the need to have the "spontaneous overflow of powerful feeling" come out in verses "recollected in tranquility" (8). Such tranquility fit uncomfortably with the actual settler experience—whether in Halifax or Peterborough. The humble and rustic life of Wordsworth's Lake District was not the settler life of British North America. It took several years for the language of poetry composition in Canada to reflect more comfortably the environment in which it was written. Poets such as Charles G.D. Roberts and Bliss Carman, writing at the end of the century, were more successful at adapting their poetry to the Canadian context than the early poets, in part because there was an audience for their work by that time in Canada as well as abroad.

Because the primary audience was elsewhere at the beginning of the nineteenth century, much of the writing in this section exhibits a sense of social responsibility and contains a clear didactic intent: either to promote Canadian settlement or to deter compatriots from emigration. There were also practical considerations that made the British, and later American, audiences more accessible than Canadian ones, even for writers in Canada. In a letter to her publisher in London, Moodie herself jokes that she read the reviews of her work before she saw copies of the books because of the delay getting packages through the post. She also had to rely primarily on gifts of books from friends and relatives in England because they were too expensive for her to purchase in Canada. A dearth of publishers and printers in Canada made it difficult to produce texts; the long distances between readers made distribution challenging; the lack of lending libraries made accessibility of texts difficult; the publication of works in England and the United States made them expensive in Canada; and a smaller literate public in the new colony meant there were fewer people able to read the work even when it was accessible.

Writing and reading were sometimes considered to be luxuries for settlers. However, at the same time, literary societies flourished. They were a popular form of cultural, educational, and social organization, particularly as the nineteenth century went on. Such societies appealed to both settlers and Canadian-born women and men as venues for "self-improvement" through reading, study, and intellectual exchange. In *Come, Bright Improvement! The Literary Societies of Nineteenth-Century Ontario* (2002), literary historian Heather Murray discusses over three hundred literary societies that existed around the province of Ontario from the 1820s until 1900. A forerunner to today's book clubs, such societies provided a lively social and intellectual forum where people could gather and discuss books, cultural affairs, and current events. Following the proliferation of such societies in the United States and Britain, they emerged in Canada as a part of the "civilized" life of the colony. Their existence reinforced the prevailing notion that a settler could be remade in the new land. The literary society meetings included discussion of a wide range of genres such as fiction, non-fictional prose essays, autobiography, history, and travel writing. According to Murray, literary study was not confined to textual interpretation, but included the rhetorical arts of composition and oratory. So a meeting of a literary society might include discussion of an assigned text; reading of members' essays on the text; presentation of creative works by members; recitation of poetic selections; performance of dramatic scenes; formal debate; and a recital of instrumental or vocal music. The societies were central to community formation in emergent areas of the colony. Following on the principle of self-improvement, Murray notes how many groups formed literary societies of their own. She gives examples of groups of workers (mechanics' institutes), women, Black fugitives, and members of religious denominations such as Quakers and Methodists who formed societies dedicated to adult education.

Still, in spite of the proliferation of literary societies, writing conditions in early Canada were far from ideal. For example, Moodie conserved her paper by writing horizontally on a sheet and then turning it ninety degrees and writing horizontally again (Figure II-8). Sometimes she would turn it again and overlay a third layer. Traill's writing was curtailed for several years because she could not afford staples such as food and clothing for her family, let alone ink and paper. Paradoxically, though, both Moodie and Traill turned to the pen as a respectable source of income for them as gentlewomen fallen on hard times. Writing at night by the light of "sluts" (twisted rags dipped in lard and stuck in a bottle), Moodie wrote portraits of settler life for *The Literary Garland*. Canada presented a space in which women's roles were being reassessed, in terms of both gender and class politics, and in which women could write, edit, publish, and earn a living in the socially acceptable role of "authoress." Moodie, Traill, and Jameson, among others, published using their own names. This was not the case with all women of their class writing in England at the time, even though Agnes Strickland, the sister of Moodie and Traill, published her *Lives of the Queens of England, from the Norman Conquest* (12 vols., 1840–49) and *Lives of the Queens of Scotland and English Princesses* (8 vols., 1850–59) under her own name. Jane Austen, whose novel *Pride and Prejudice* was published when Moodie was ten, wrote anonymously. Charlotte and Emily Brontë (authors of *Jane Eyre* and *Wuthering Heights* respectively), whose main works were published in the 1840s, when Moodie and Traill were carving out a living in the Canadian backwoods, wrote using the pseudonyms of Currer and Ellis Bell. Also in England, Mary Anne Evans published her famous novels *Middlemarch* and *Adam Bede* under the name George Eliot in the following decades. Since economic hardship, or what Moodie calls "stern necessity," drove most emigrants to leave Britain, it is important to note that writing provided both economic and psychological relief, particularly when it concerned the act of emigration. The increase in emigration meant that there was virtually an insatiable curiosity among British audiences for narratives about emigration. As Moodie puts it in her 1852 introduction to *Roughing It in the Bush*, a "Canada mania pervaded the middle ranks of British society." A receptive audience was willing to pay for books on Canada and, as a result, London publishers such as Richard Bentley were willing to invest in such works. It made good economic sense to write for a British reading public and to write what the market demanded: stories of hardship and prosperity; stories of adventure and gradual acclimatization; stories of survival and hope.

Over the course of the period, however, writers as diverse as Moodie, William Lyon Mackenzie, Joseph Howe, Thomas McCulloch, and Mary Ann Shadd composed stories and articles for a growing local reading public, as they founded, edited, and wrote in newspapers for local distribution. Most new communities established a printing press and a newspaper so that settlers could communicate with each other at relatively little cost and across the immense distances between neighbours. Print culture historian Janet Friskney also notes the rise in denominational newspapers and periodicals, especially after 1840. The newspaper, and later the magazine, was a vital part of the growth of local "imagined communities," to use cultural theorist Benedict Anderson's term. Well aware that such newspapers helped to create a sense of community among the readership, writers often used them as vehicles for political ideas. Although they were small-scale operations, the newspapers were able to garner enough support for some vital political issues to irritate the colonial governments and provoke the settlers. Often partisan, the newspaper editors kept like-minded settlers in touch with each other—whether in terms of fomenting rebellion, as Mackenzie did in the *Colonial Advocate*; advocating political reforms such as freedom of the press and responsible government, as Howe did in *The Novascotian*; educating their readership, as Shadd did in the *Provincial Freeman*; or trying to grow a local literary culture, as Moodie and others did in *The Literary Garland* and *The Albion* (published out of New York for emigrants from Britain in North America).

The local newspapers were also places where satire became popular and a new form of Canadian humour was born. Immensely popular in England, the sketches of McCulloch and Haliburton were first published in newspapers meant for consumption by local audiences. Although Traill's settler guide, *The Backwoods of Canada*, and Haliburton's *The Clockmaker* were published in the same year (1836), they read as though they are from different worlds—and in a sense, they are. Haliburton's work, unlike Traill's, concerns not emigration but rather the foibles of a well-settled part of Nova Scotia. His main character, Sam Slick, is the satirical figure of a "Yankee" con man, duping the gullible "Bluenoses" (Nova Scotians). Although Haliburton's work met with an appreciative audience in Britain, it was initially composed for an audience closer to home. Haliburton followed in the tradition of eighteenth-century satirists like Jonathan Swift, Henry Fielding, and Laurence Sterne, but he situated his work squarely in the geography of Nova Scotia. He uses local place names and language that suits the geography as he has his picaresque hero comment on social stability, social progress, slavery, economic development, and new forms of democracy. The coarse, ribald, caustic "Yankee" embodies some of the clashes in ideology between the United States and British North America. By publishing the sketches in a newspaper first (*The Novascotian*), Haliburton could also gauge public support of his characters as he provided a running commentary on the pressing issues of the day.

The Literary Garland, published in Montreal from December 1838 to December 1851, is notable as an important vehicle for many literary authors from this period who were writing for a local audience and working on creating a Canadian voice. Moodie, for instance, published in all its thirteen issues. *The Literary Garland* was the first successful literary periodical in either Upper or Lower Canada. Much of that success can be attributed to its emphasis on original compositions and its appeal to readers beyond the boundaries of the Canadas. It was one of the first Canadian publications to be written for both a Canadian and international audience. This is another key point: while those writing about Canada desired a local readership, they also wanted to compete on a global scale and to be read internationally.

It is useful to place the works included in this anthology in an international literary context and in the context of the major political events of the day in Canada, in order to understand what kinds of influences the writers might have had and the kinds of issues to which they might have been responding. Three years before Samuel Hearne reached the Arctic Ocean (1771), Frances Brooke published what has been called the first Canadian novel: *The History of Emily Montague* (1769). Governor John Graves Simcoe's wife, Elizabeth Simcoe, began her diary of life in Canada in 1791, the year before Captain Galiano and Captain Vancouver charted the Pacific coast (1792) and two years before Alexander Mackenzie reached the Pacific by an overland route (1793). The first novel by a native-born Canadian published in what is now Canada, Julia Catherine Beckwith Hart's *St. Ursula's Convent or the Nun of Canada* (1824), appeared shortly after McCulloch's *The Letters of Mephibosheth Stepsure* were published in the Halifax *Acadian Recorder* (1821–23), a year after John Franklin's *Narrative of a Journey to the Shores of the Polar Sea* (1823), and a year before "The Rising Village" (1825). The rebellions in Upper and Lower Canada (1837–38) followed the release of *The Backwoods of Canada* (1836) and *The Clockmaker* (1836). The celebrated works of Traill and Haliburton were published the same year Anna Jameson shot the falls at Sault Ste. Marie in a canoe (1836), and a year before Victoria became queen (1837). George Copway's *Life, History and Travels of Kah-ge-ga-gah-bowh* (1847) came out at the same time as the Moodies edited *The Victoria Magazine* (1847–48) and responsible government was instituted in Nova Scotia and the United Canadas. That year also marked one of the banner years in the literature of Victorian England, with the publication of Anne Brontë's *Agnes Grey* (1847), Charlotte Brontë's *Jane Eyre* (1847), Emily Brontë's *Wuthering Heights* (1847), Charles Dickens's *Dombey and Son* (in serial form, 1847–48), William Makepeace Thackeray's *Vanity Fair* (1847), as well as the American publication of *Evangeline, A Tale of Acadie* by Henry Wadsworth Longfellow. James Douglas became the governor of Vancouver Island (1850) the year before the Fugitive Slave Act (1851) was passed in the United States, and two years before Mary Ann Shadd founded the *Provincial Freeman* (1852) and Harriet Beecher Stowe's novel *Uncle Tom's Cabin* (1852) became available. Moodie published *Roughing It in the Bush* (1852) a year after Herman Melville's *Moby-Dick* (1851), and two years before Henry David Thoreau's *Walden* (1854). Moodie and many other writers of this generation were writing during the height of the search for Franklin's lost northern expedition in the 1850s. The late eighteenth- and early nineteenth-century authors in Canada were often well aware of the politics, culture, and ideas in the world around them.

A Brief History of Settlement

While the literary focus of this section is on the late eighteenth and early nineteenth centuries, it is useful to contextualize such writing by providing a brief overview of some of the major historical events leading up to and affecting the patterns of settlement. It is also interesting to see the developing relationships between the British, French, American, and indigenous peoples that have repercussions even today in culture and in politics.

The French established the first permanent settlement at Île Sainte-Croix on the Atlantic coast in 1604. In 1605, the site was moved to Port-Royal on the Bay of Fundy, and then in 1608, to Quebec on the St. Lawrence River. Meanwhile, the French formed alliances with the two main Aboriginal groups of the area, the Mi'kmaq and the Maliseet. Together, the French settlements in northeastern North America were known as "Acadia." Over the next one hundred and fifty years, the French and the English fought over its possession. In 1713 France ceded Acadia to England in the Treaty of Utrecht. In 1755 Charles Lawrence, the lieutenant-governor of Nova Scotia, insisted that the Acadians take an unconditional oath of allegiance to the British Crown. When they refused, approximately ten thousand French Acadians were sent into exile. Although some returned in the next generation to settle the land that is present-day Nova Scotia, New Brunswick, and Prince Edward Island, most did not. Given the importance of controlling both the trade routes and the growing population, Britain and France continued to fight over the land adjacent to the St. Lawrence.

The English conquest of New France culminated in the 13 September 1759 Battle of the Plains of Abraham, where General James Wolfe defeated Louis Joseph, Marquis de Montcalm, on a plateau overlooking the river where Quebec City stands. Benjamin West's painting *The Death of General Wolfe*

[Figure II-3] commemorates this decisive battle by romanticizing the fall of General Wolfe. Literary historian Pam Perkins notes how the fall of Quebec was viewed, at least by some, in terms of religious triumph: "According to Samuel Langdon, a New England minister who thought it self-evident that France was a tool of the Antichrist, Britain had been granted a miraculous opportunity to slow down the work of Satan by spreading Protestantism, good government, and the English language all across the new world" (153). The Treaty of Paris, signed on 7 February 1763, transferred all of France's North American territories, with the exceptions of New Orleans and St. Pierre and Miquelon, to Britain. The French were not the only ones incensed by their defeat. When Native allies of the French (such as the Delaware, Seneca, Chippewa, Miami, Potawotomi, and Huron) learned that they were expected to transfer their loyalty to George III of Britain, they were outraged because they assumed that the British were more interested in expansive settlement than the French, that British traders were not as fair as the French in their trading, and that the British were difficult allies. The result was Chief Pontiac's rebellion against the British forces. John Richardson's novel *Wacousta* (1832) is set in the midst of Pontiac's war of the 1760s. Richardson turns the insurgence into a Gothic tale of mistaken identity, savagery, and romance. In actuality, it was an uprising that demonstrated the power of the indigenous forces.

The Treaty of Paris was followed by a Royal Proclamation, issued on 7 October 1763, clarifying the position of Britain with regard to the newly renamed Province of Quebec and to western expansion. Its primary aim was to transform the French colony into a British one through the establishment of British institutions and laws with a view to assimilation. However, assimilation was not forthcoming: Quebec attracted only a trickle of English-speaking immigrants (though, of the few who were there, a powerful minority of English merchants had enormous influence). When it became clear that Quebec was unlikely to become anglicized, the Quebec Act of 1774 reversed the policies set out in the Royal Proclamation and reinstated French civil law, the seigneurial system of landholding, and the right of the Roman Catholic Church to collect the tithe. Perkins notes that "the hardcore Protestantism of Langdon and his like-minded compatriots explains some of the deep outrage that greeted the British decision, in 1774, to allow Quebec to retain its religion and civil law and, after 1792, to establish representative government" (153). From then on, Canada consisted of two nations beside the First Nations. Certainly there was a hierarchy of nations: French was to be subservient to English, and the Aboriginal nations subservient to both, but they still existed in parallel, both linguistically and culturally. The literary works to come out of the period around the fall of Quebec capitalized on the coexistence of the French and the British, alongside their indigenous allies, to paint a romanticized portrait of the meeting of nations in a colony. For instance, Brooke's *The History of Emily Montague* highlights the cultural palimpsest of Quebec society, with the French Canadiens coexisting with the English as well as the Huron and the Iroquois.

Meanwhile, as British power was being eroded in Quebec, a growing sense of nationalism led the Thirteen Colonies in New England to demand greater self-government. Britain's attempt to tax the colonies led to open rebellion with the first armed clash of the American Revolution at Lexington, Massachusetts, in 1775. During the War of Independence, many Americans, including farmers, crafts-men, landowners, and government workers, remained loyal to the British Crown. After Britain's defeat in America, roughly 80,000 United Empire Loyalists (UELs) chose to, or were forced to, depart with the British garrisons. The most attractive location because of proximity, availability of land, continuity of British rule, and predominance of Protestantism was the remaining British North American colonies: Nova Scotia (which at that time still included New Brunswick), Prince Edward Island, and Quebec. Subsequently, as part of an accommodation to the English-speaking Loyalists, the Constitutional Act of 1791 amended the Quebec Act to set aside an upriver portion of Quebec, to be known as Upper Canada, where the Loyalists could settle, leaving the French the downriver part to be named Lower Canada. New Brunswick and Upper Canada were settled by large populations of exiled UELs. Each colony was administered separately, each with its own institutions of representative government. The current Ontario motto on the provincial coat of arms, "Loyal she began, loyal she remains" ("*Ut Incepit Fidelis Sic Permanent*"), commemorates this history. In recognition of the costs of remaining loyal to the Crown, the Loyalists were granted tax exemptions and issued provisions, medicine, clothing, tools, and seeds, and most importantly, were provided with free land. Some former military officers received a stipend of half-pay for life; some received land grants in compensation for losses sustained during the revolution. Although most Loyalists were subsistence farmers, there were also Loyalists who were part of the "Family Compact" (William Lyon Mackenzie's favoured term for the elite governing clique linked by family ties) and Loyalists who fought for democracy. The Loyalists joined the early settlers to become an integral part of Canadian society.

A notable group of Loyalists to arrive in Canada after the American Revolution was the Black Loyalists. In 1779, Sir Henry Clinton, commander-in-chief of the British military in America, issued the Phillipsburg Proclamation. The proclamation promised not only freedom but full security to "all Negroes" who escaped to British lines. This military tactic was designed to help bolster foundering British numbers and to dampen the American economy by with-drawing a valuable part of its workforce. Following the war, those men and women who had served the British sailed from New York to Nova Scotia. Some of those who arrived in Nova Scotia were former slaves who chose to fight with the British and were thereafter given certificates of freedom; others were ser-vants of Loyalist army officers required to accompany them to Nova Scotia. In total, over 3,000 free African Americans loyal to the Crown moved to Nova Scotia. The *Book of Negroes* (1783) is regarded as the first large-scale public docu-mentation of Black people in North America. It is a 156-page handwritten ledger that lists the names, ages, places of origin, and descriptions of the Black Loyalists who were granted permission to leave New York for resettlement in Nova Scotia if they could prove service to the British Crown (Nova Scotia Museum). Alongside the 3,000 freed slaves, an estimated 2,500 Black slaves were brought to serve their White Loyalist slave-holding "owners" as domestic workers, labourers, and farmhands (see Hill). The influx in 1783 contributed greatly to the approximately 10,000 Black people who came to Nova Scotia between 1749 and 1816. Most African descendants brought to Nova Scotia between 1749 and 1782 were slaves of English or American settlers. Following the arrival of the Black Loyalists, there was a further wave of refugees who left America for Canada following the War of 1812. The War of 1812, like the War of Independence, provided enslaved African Americans with the opportunity to fight for Britain and escape slavery. In April 1814, British military authorities offered Americans who deserted to the British side the opportunity of entering into British military service or going as free settlers to one of the British colonies. Several thousand slaves took up this offer. Still, slavery was legal in parts of British North America until the British parliament's Slavery Abolition Act of 1833 put a stop to slavery in all parts of the British Empire.

Birchtown, where Boston King (a Loyalist, escaped slave, carpenter, and Methodist preacher named in the original *Book of Negroes*, along with his wife, Violet) settled in 1783, was among the largest and most influential of the settlements of Black Loyalists (Nova Scotia Museum). Although they had freedom, the Black Loyalists were not treated equally with the White Loyalists by the government. Land promised to them was difficult to obtain. When it was obtained, it was smaller and less fertile than that granted the other Loyalists, and was often located in a remote part of the region. Many of the skilled workers—carpenters, sawyers, barbers, seamstresses, midwives, and coopers—had a difficult time finding employment. They were given fewer provisions to assist with farming and establishing a community. Many such emigrants to Canada died of hunger in the first years because of inadequate resources. Others failed to prosper because of their lack of proper tools and the bleakness of the land. Almost a decade after first settling, because of the general frustration at their treatment by the government, many Black Loyalists chose to emigrate to Freetown, Sierra Leone, in West Africa, where they had been offered free passage and land upon arrival. Some people chose to stay in Nova Scotia, but their communities were devastated. Literary historian and poet George Elliott Clarke makes a case for Susannah Smith, a Black Loyalist, as being the first African-Canadian woman writer, citing her letter of 12 May 1792 to the superintendent of the Sierra Leone colony requesting soap as a key document in what Clarke calls "Africadian" literary history. Boston King's narrative account of his life from 1794 is also a central document in helping to map out the history of Nova Scotia. The excerpt included here illustrates some of the hardships he endured as a settler in Nova Scotia. In 2007, Canadian writer Lawrence Hill published a novel entitled *The Book of Negroes* that follows the story of a woman's life after she is captured from her family in Africa, enslaved in America, and transported to Nova Scotia in search of freedom in 1783, and, finally, emigrates to Sierra Leone. Both King's historic account and Hill's contemporary novel remind readers that Canada was not always a haven for slaves along the Underground Railroad, as Mary Ann Shadd's emigrant pamphlet (1852) published sixty years later suggests, but rather a place firmly implicated in the slave trade and differential treatment based on race.

Other than King, several writers in this section have Loyalist connections. Oliver Goldsmith, whose continued allegiance to Britain is clearly evident in "The Rising Village," was the son of an Irish Loyalist. In addition, knowing that Haliburton was the grandson of Loyalists helps one understand his conservative politics and critical depiction of both Nova Scotians and "Yankees" in *The Clockmaker*. Haliburton's Sam Slick criticizes democratic ideals, saying, "[T]here is no tyranny on airth equal to the tyranny of the majority." Conversely, the views of Joseph Howe, the son of a loyal Massachusetts newspaper editor, were fundamental to the rise of responsible government and freedom of speech in Nova Scotia.

In the years following the initial influx of UELs, in an effort to boost settlement, the first lieutenant governor of Upper Canada, Colonel John Graves Simcoe, appealed to any formerly British subjects south of the border who had fought on the side of the Americans in the War of Independence and offered them free land. These "late Loyalists" poured in from the American frontier and settled in the fertile land of what is now southwestern Ontario. Their regained allegiance to the Crown seems to have been driven more by the economic expediency of free land than by ideological commitment. Many of the "Yankee" settlers depicted by Moodie in *Roughing It in the Bush* appear to have been of this group. Indeed, some of these settlers held on to their republican beliefs and helped foment rebellion two decades later. The Loyalists arrived in two waves: the first wave emigrated in the 1780s, the second between 1791 and 1812. By 1811, almost 90,000 people had settled in Upper Canada. A few decades later, between 1829 and 1860, a subsequent wave of British emigrants arrived in even greater numbers.

There was another significant influx of settlers attracted to Upper Canada after the American War of Independence. According to the Mennonite Society of Canada, the Swiss Mennonite families who had settled in Pennsylvania in search of religious tolerance, pacifism, and freedom chose to relocate to Upper Canada. Attracted by available, inexpensive land, the first few Swiss Mennonite families left Pennsylvania following the "Trail of the Conestoga" in covered wagons, to settle on the Niagara Peninsula and along the Grand River. From 1785 to 1825, approximately 2,000 more Mennonites from Pennsylvania crossed the Niagara River. In the next twenty-five years they were joined by 1000 Amish moving directly from France and Germany to Waterloo County. Subsequent waves of (Russian) Mennonites moved to Manitoba and further west in the 1880s, in the 1920s, and in the 1940s. The Mennonite settlers were pacifists who sought to live in peace apart from the other settlers. It is from these Mennonites that contemporary writers such as Rudy Wiebe, Armin Wiebe, Patrick Friesen, Di Brandt, and Miriam Toews are descended.

As with the War of Independence, the War of 1812 led to increased immigration by Mennonites as well as a second wave of British Loyalists. The War of 1812–1814 formally began on 18 June 1812, with the American declaration of war against British North America and the invasion of Britain's North American colonies. However, the local British forces, Canadian volunteers, and Native allies were able to hold off the attacks and defend their borders, despite the fact that, with most of the British forces engaged in the Napoleonic Wars at the time of the attack, British North America had minimal troops to defend against the much larger military force of the United States. The war is said to have united the French-speaking and English-speaking colonies against a common enemy, and created a sense of nationalistic pride at having successfully repulsed the invaders.

By the late 1820s, in the wake of some of the ideals being fought over in the War of 1812 and the subsequent growth of the colonies, men such as William Lyon Mackenzie of Upper Canada, Joseph Howe in Nova Scotia, and Louis-Joseph Papineau in Lower Canada supported the right of the colonies to self-government. In Lower Canada, four years of crop failure led to a very real threat of starvation for many settlers. A profound economic crisis in Upper Canada also gave rise to discontent. Further, the anti-elitism which had spread during the French Revolution and the American Revolution was also growing in British North America. Since 1791, the inhabitants of the colonies were able to elect representatives to the local Houses of Assembly; the problem was that the assemblies adopted laws but had little political power. Instead, a governor appointed by Parliament in London, England, and his appointed councillors governed each colony. In 1833, Mackenzie, a journalist originally from Scotland, denounced the leaders of Upper Canada in his newspaper the *Colonial Advocate* as a "few shrewd, crafty, covetous men." In his view, a colonial mindset was holding back the intellectual and social progress of the colonies. In this, he echoes the opinions of Haliburton, though the two thinkers represent opposite sides of the political spectrum.

In 1837, Mackenzie led a rebellion in Upper Canada against the governor in favour of a republican state. It failed, in part, because of the governor's support by recent emigrants such as John Moodie, the husband of the author of *Roughing It in the Bush*. In opposition to the influence of the "late Loyalists" and the reformers, the "influx of British Emigrants" sided with the government ruled from England. An editorial in the St. Thomas *Liberal*, from 4 April 1833, railed against the government's tactics: "From the moment an Irishman or Englishman sets foot upon our soil, his ears are stunned by the cry of Treason and Rebellion which is constantly kept up to deceive the ignorant and unwary." The editor further argues that new settlers were taught to view the American settlers with suspicion, and to call them "Yankees" and "Republicans" as a reproach. This helps explain Susanna Moodie's virulent dislike of her "Yankee" neighbours in *Roughing It*. In the 1830s, one was either pro-American or pro-British. Though she became more sympathetic to the reformers in later life, at this point Moodie was unquestionably pro-British.

Historians argue that one reason for the rebellions in both Upper and Lower Canada was the sudden influx of thousands of settlers fleeing financial misfortune in Britain and France and seeking prosperity in the colonies. Such a rapidly expanding population was more volatile than the more stable settled population in eastern Canada. What manifested as rebellions in Upper and Lower Canada came out in heated newspaper debates in Nova Scotia. There was also no unanimity on political issues among new settlers: some wanted reform; some wanted to keep the status quo; some were loyal to the Crown; some were provoked by republican ideals; some feared they would lose their social positions; some enjoyed the social and class mobility of the new colonies; and some were working too hard at settlement to engage in politics.

Following the failed rebellions, John George Lambton ("Radical Jack"), the first Earl of Durham, was appointed Governor-in-Chief and Lord High Commissioner of British North America. His primary mission was to make recommendations about the future government of the British North American colonies, particularly about how to avoid further rebellions. Lord Durham's subsequent report, entitled *Report on the Affairs of British North America* (1839), advocated the union of Lower Canada with Upper Canada, in order to preserve Canadian loyalty to Great Britain, to address the risk of the annexation of Canada by the United States, and most importantly, to create an English majority to assist in his goal of the assimilation of the French. As a result, following the Act of Union of 1840, the two provinces were united to form the province of "Canada," establishing a shared government and legislature.

In cultural terms Durham's report is most notorious for its derisive comments about French Canadians. Durham is said to have acted upon the advice of a merchant who stated: "Lower Canada must be English, at the expense, if necessary, of not being British." Durham based the problems in Lower Canada on a struggle "between races" in epistemologies, institutions, traditions, social classes, and political life. Durham wrote of the Canadiens: "[T]here can hardly be conceived a nationality more destitute of all that can invigorate and elevate a people" (294). According to Durham, they had no history, no literature, and therefore no future. Defending the Canadiens against Durham's argument, the French-Canadian poet and historian François-Xavier Garneau wrote his *Histoire du Canada depuis sa découverte jusqu'à nos jours* (1845). "Lord Durham," commented Upper Canadian Lieutenant-Governor Sir George Arthur at the time of the report, "has thrown a firebrand amongst the People" (207). Such a firebrand contributed to developing French-Canadian nationalism and English-Canadian reform.

In a letter to Susanna Moodie on 24 May 1839, John Moodie makes clear his support of Durham's report and the reform agenda of Robert Baldwin and his supporters. Yet Moodie's support of political reform did not compromise his loyalty to Britain and the British legacy in Canada. Instead, it shows the calming of the political situation. With the union of the Canadas in 1841, attention turned to forms of local responsible government.

Emigration Versus Immigration

In Canada today we generally speak of immigration or *coming to* Canada. In the late eighteenth and early nineteenth centuries, however, the emphasis was not so much on entering Canada but on leaving a country *for* Canada. "To emigrate" means to leave one's country in order to settle permanently in another, whereas "to immigrate" means to enter a country for the purpose of settling there. The shift in perspective from emigration to immigration, from leaving to arriving, is a shift that has come with the building of Canada as a nation. In the late eighteenth and early nineteenth centuries, although both terms were in use, the perspective in literature was still predominantly on departure rather than arrival. The Moodies and Traills, for instance, were essentially reluctant settlers, hailing from educated middle-class families that had suffered a decline in fortune. But there were many other reasons for emigration to British North America as well. Some settled as part of the infrastructure of trading and trapping; others were encouraged to settle in the New World by their governments as France and Britain fought to establish dominance in the region; other settlers moved to the North American colonies when their loyalty to the Crown was tested. Further, economic hardship brought about by the rapidly expanding population base in Britain forced many others to try their hands at settling in British North America, in part because they were lured by the promise of opportunity that came with owning, clearing, and farming their own land. Some of the new people had been impoverished as a result of crop failures and had no real choice. Still other emigrants fought religious persecution. By the mid-nineteenth century, there were emigrants from an increasing number of European locations as well as America and Britain. The majority of those writing about emigration in English, however, hailed from English, Irish, and Scottish families.

The report of the Select Committee on Emigration, struck in the British House of Commons in 1826 to "inquire into the expediency of encouraging emigration from the United Kingdom," establishes three general positions on why the government should promote emigration to its North American colonies:

> Firstly, the redundancy of the population, that is the excess of the demand beyond the supply of labour in certain districts of England, Scotland, and Ireland, and the distressing effects of this redundancy. Secondly, the capabilities of the British colonies to subsist and provide for this surplus population; and lastly, the beneficial tendency of emigration upon the colonies themselves, and upon national wealth, considering the colonies as integral parts of the nation at large. (Robeson 6)

The "nation" here, remember, is not Canada but Britain. The British government needed to market, promote, and sell Canada in order to solve problems at home and build a stronger empire. Further, the committee continues to argue for the necessity of land grants and public support of the emigrants: "[T]hey conceive that it is utterly erroneous to suppose that a redundant population of absolute paupers can be removed by casual and unassisted emigration" (qtd. in Robeson 7).

In the difficult times of the 1820s, at least one in ten Britons lived in a state of substantial economic hardship. For them, emigration offered both an escape from being "absolute paupers" and a possibility for the future of their families. The government also gave free grants of several hundred acres of land in Upper Canada to retired half-pay officers from the Napoleonic Wars, such as John Moodie and Thomas Traill, partly as reward and partly with the understanding that if there were another insurrection from America (a constant threat after the War of 1812), they would be on the ground ready to defend British interests. Indeed John Moodie's decision to defend the Crown following the Upper Canada Rebellion came in part from his loyalty to the government for granting him land.

However, the British government was inconsistent in its position on land grants. A few years after the 1826 report, the government changed its mind and decided that land grants were an unnecessary way of dealing with poverty. An 1832 pamphlet entitled *Information published by His Majesty's Commissioners for Emigration, respecting the British Colonies in North America*, laid out "such information as is likely to be useful to Persons who desire either to Emigrate, or to assist others to Emigrate, to the British Possessions in North America." Dispelling the rumours set out in part by its own past practices, and in part by the land speculators trying to make a profit on the expectations of eager emigrants, the government writes: "No pecuniary aid will be allowed by Government to Emigrants to the North American Colonies; nor after their arrival will they receive Grants of Land, or gifts of Tools, or a supply of Provisions" [caps *sic*]. They soften this rather harsh list of what is not offered with the statement that "no assistance of the extraordinary extent above described is allowed, because in Colonies where those who desire to work cannot fail to do well for themselves, none such is needed" (8). The government's message was echoed in the regular public lectures delivered by agents of the Canada Company, who received a bonus for every emigrant they recruited to Canada. John Moodie heard one such agent, William Catermole, speak in Norwich, England, of the fertile soil, water access, exemption from taxation, and commercial advantages of the colony. Catermole did not mention the density of forest to be cleared, the political unrest, the harsh winter, or the difficulties in movement between communities. Susanna Moodie, who was thoroughly disillusioned upon her arrival in Canada, refers to such hucksters as "speculators in the folly and credulity of [their] fellow men" (see excerpt below from the introduction to *Roughing It*). The message from the agents and from the government was clear: if you work hard, you will prosper.

Several writers harnessed such a work ethic and used the same tone in their writing. The attitude that prosperity comes out of forbearance is illustrated well in Thomas McCulloch's *The Letters of Mephibosheth Stepsure* (1821–23). From a different perspective, in *The Backwoods of Canada*, Traill points to hard work as one of the necessary qualifications for a settler's wife: "A settler's wife should be active, industrious, cheerful, not above putting her hand to whatever is necessary to be done in her household, nor too proud to profit by the advice and experience of older portions of the community, from whom she may learn many excellent lessons of practical wisdom." She also identifies Canada in *Backwoods* as "a fine country for the poor labourer, who, after a few years of hard toil, can sit down in his own log-house . . . and see his children well settled in life as independent freeholders." Traill's writing is more practical and less didactic than McCulloch's satire, but it hinges on the same valuing of hard work above all else.

Precisely what appealed to some new settlers about Canada was the way in which birth ceased to be the primary indicator of social standing and was replaced by a work ethic, though admittedly, this criterion was ethnically biased in that it applied primarily to British emigrants. Alexander McLachlan, later in the century, writes about the social equalization that is possible in his poem "Young Canada Or Jack's as Good as His Master" (1874):

> Where none are slaves, that lordly knaves
> May idyll all the year;
> For rank and caste are of the past,—
> They'll never flourish here!
> And Jew and Turk if he'll but work,
> Need never fear disaster;
> He reaps the crop he sowed in hope,
> For Jack's as good's his master. (Gerson and Davies 95)

While some settlers, Moodie most vocally, were disturbed by the social and class mobility possible in the colony, others sought the liberating potential of this loosening of class distinctions. Indeed, Moodie herself was attracted to Canada for its egalitarianism, a characteristic of the newly formed society that enabled her and her husband to forge a future for their poverty-stricken family. While Moodie supported the rejection of landed wealth and bloodline as a marker of social status, she remained committed to a revised notion of class distinction based on manners and education—hence her swift dismissal of the Irish servants and "Yankees" whom she considered her social inferiors. Aboriginal people, by comparison, are praised for their quiet gentility (for example, she allows them to share supper at her table—a privilege she does not extend to her Irish servants). Nevertheless, even Moodie's notion of "Canadian" class divisions had to be revised in the face of her experiences in Canada. The new society that was emerging combined British etiquette and culture with American egalitarianism. These qualities would come to characterize "Canadian" society for the generations that followed.

Much of the writing of this period comes with a dual sense of nostalgia for Britain and hope for the future in the new land. The emigrant guides give practical advice on how to survive and prosper, but they also wax eloquent about what is being given up in leaving Britain. While McLachlan titles one poem "I Winna Gae Hame," he also writes about the economic uncertainty of that home and the inevitability of movement away from such a place. Although McLachlan's poetry presents a tentative optimism about emigration, others were not so confident. Moodie uses her writing as a forum for warning emigrants to Canada about the hardships they will face. With a great deal less bitterness, Traill writes that she was motivated to compose *The Backwoods of Canada* in order to "afford every possible information to the wives and daughters of emigrants of the higher class who contemplate seeking a home amid our Canadian wilds" (see her "Introduction" in this section). Mary Ann Shadd intended her emigrants' guide to attract escaped slaves and free men and women to Canada from the United States after the Fugitive Slave Act was passed in 1851. Her guide is less focused on survival and prosperity in the bush and more on establishing a community in freedom and safety. Shadd writes in the most optimistic terms of the education system, the land, and the people. For Shadd, emigration to Canada and integration once in Canada are the only viable options.

In his autobiography, George Copway details the effects of the arrival of British settlers on his people. While Copway writes with respect about the traditions of the "Ojibwa," he is also explicit in linking the future of his people with education and Christianity. A strong advocate of conversion, Copway promoted himself as the "noble Christian convert" who lectured on what he saw as lost (complex systems of communication, skills such as hunting and fishing, and modes of governance) and gained (civility, education, and the word of God) by the influx of immigrants to British North America. Further, the early settlers, and the Christian converts in particular, saw the spread of Christianity and civilization as their moral duty. Copway and Boston King use their own life stories as extended examples to promote the merits of Christianity and conversion. This agenda gave them a reason to consider their own stories worthy of transcription and for publishers to think them worthy of publication.

Christian values underscored many emigrant accounts as well. During this period the Anglican Church held the same official position as it did in Great Britain. The strong sense of moral duty evinced in the emigrant narratives goes hand-in-hand with the role religion played in the British justification of settlement and colonial rule. The moral imperative behind the spread of Christianity is also irrefutably linked with the "civilizing mission" of the colonizers in their relationships with indigenous peoples. Usually, one of the first structures that a local population erected was a church that could provide a place of worship for the community. Most towns, even small ones, had a Catholic church and at least one Protestant church (or several denominations depending on the size of the community and the mixture of religions in the area). The church was an important link to "Home," civilization, and morality. The church leaders were also important figures in establishing the values and setting the morals of a new region. In "God's Peculiar Peoples," for instance, historian S.F. Wise argues that sermons preached from the pulpits of Upper Canada were key instruments in creating an Upper Canadian mindset. Wise notes in particular that these sermons were often anti-American in tone and that they helped encourage a sense of local loyalty to the Anglican Church. Janet Friskney argues that churches "used print to define, debate, advance, and defend their spiritual positions, as well as their political and social status in society, for Christianity in the colonies was fraught with sectarian differences" (143). Although the innumerable religious pamphlets that were published during this period "addressed different aspects of Christian faith, practice, and politics in the northeastern part of North America, collectively they represented the intersection of the power of the word with the power of the Word, print being a chosen servant in the mission of communicating the Christian message" (Friskney 144). Beyond the Christian pamphlets themselves, many of the emigrant writers were listening to the religious debates and were engaging with them in their own works. Still, in spite of sectarian differences, establishing a firmly Christian community was viewed as key to the success of the colony. The majority of emigrant writers, whether criticizing emigration or championing it, share a commitment to the value of a Christian presence in the New World.

Settler/Invader Attitudes

Contemporary scholars note that in British and American emigration narratives it is rare to find settlers grappling with the ethical or moral issues surrounding colonization: displacement of indigenous peoples, imposition of new institutional and cultural structures, disregard for belief systems and replacement with new ones, or exploitation of natural resources. While it is now common to call Canada a "settler/ invader" colony in recognition of the government's dishonest negotiations on treaties, generations of failed promises, and the ultimate displacement from their land of the First Nations people and the Inuit, the concept of settlement as invasion was non-existent for the emigrants under consideration here. While many writers speak of the relations with the "Indians," few question their own right of settlement on the land that was formerly Native territory. The settlers believed that Canada was open and ready for settlement, an empty space (*terra nullius*), even as the government and traders negotiated with the first peoples and relied on their expertise in times of peace and war. This contradiction was possible because of the settlers' sense of entitlement to the land—as Britons and as Christians. It did not occur to them to question their own presence on the land or to fathom the extent to which they themselves were displacing tens of thousands of people. Indeed, through the process of treaty making and the practice of giving presents in return for loyalty to the King (or the Queen after 1837), the majority of settlers saw themselves as benevolent in allowing the Native peoples to have land at all. Anna Jameson is one of the few commentators to note the inconsistencies of the government in the gift-giving ceremony she witnesses, yet she relies on the well-worn tropes of travel writers about some of the indigenous people she encounters, in describing both her fascination and repulsion at their customs. It is interesting to read her account beside Duncan Campbell Scott's 1906 autobiographical essay, "The Last of the Indian Treaties" (see Section III), which provides an illuminating view of the hierarchical bias of such ceremonial exchanges. Literary critic Diana Brydon writes about how Canada needs to be "reconceptualized as a contact zone" in order to address the legacy of colonial settlement and invasion (62). Indeed, reading these emigrants' accounts helps us to reconsider the results of the contact between cultures and communities.

Of course, the indigenous people were not silent in the matter of settlement on their land. Many leaders attempted to negotiate with the King's government. Arguing his people's right to land in 1831, Mi'kmaq leader Chief Louis Francis Algimou presented a succinct history of relations with the colonial forces, in a speech to the Legislative Assembly in Prince Edward Island:

> *Fathers: Before the white men crossed the great waters, our Woods offered us food and clothes in plenty—the waters gave us fish—and the woods game— our fathers were hardy, brave and free—we knew no want—we were the only owners of the Land. Fathers: when the French came to us they asked for land to set up their Wigwam. We gave it freely—in return they taught us new arts— protected and cherished us—sent holy men amongst our fathers—who taught us Christianity—who made books for us—and taught us to read them—that was good and we were grateful. Fathers: When your fathers came and drove away our French Fathers—we were left alone—our people were sorry, but they were brave—they raised the war cry—and took up the tomahawk against your fathers.—Then your fathers spoke to us—they said, put up the axe—we will protect you —we will become your Fathers. Our fathers and your fathers had long talks around the Council fire—the hatchets were buried and we became friends. Fathers: They promised to leave us some of our land—but they did not—they drove us from place to place like wild beasts—that was not just. . . . Fathers, our tribe in Nova Scotia, Canada, New Brunswick and Cape Breton, have land on which their families are happy.—We ask of you, Fathers, to give us part of that land once our fathers'—wherein we may live, and our children also—else, Fathers, you may soon see not one drop of Indian blood in this Island, once our own—where is now our land?—we have none. Fathers, we are poor—do not forsake us—remember the promises your fathers made to ours.* (qtd. in Whitehead 207–08)

Similar sentiments had prevailed a generation before in Joseph Brant's fight for land and recognition. Brant was a tireless advocate for Native rights, securing land for the Six Nations Confederacy (a union of Iroquois nations that included the Seneca, Cayuga, Oneida, Onondaga, Mohawk, and Tuscarora) in recognition of their loyalty during the American War of Independence. During the war, Brant had travelled to England to present Iroquois grievances about encroachments on their lands to Lord George Germain, secretary of state for the American colonies. He argued: "Indeed it is very hard when we have let the King's subjects have so much land for so little value, they should want to cheat us in this manner of the small spots we have left for our women and children to live on. We are tired out in making complaints & getting no redress" (qtd. in O'Callaghan 671). In response, Germain promised "every support England could render them" if they remained loyal to the King in the time of the American rebellion. Brant subsequently became renowned for leading the Iroquois forces in several battles as allies of the British. Britain failed to keep its side of the bargain, though, and ignored the needs of its Six Nations allies as it ceded their territory to the United States following the war. Under pressure from Brant, British General Sir Frederick Haldimand arranged for a grant of land on the Grand River in Ontario for "Mohawk Indians" and "others of the Six Nations who have lost their settlements within the Territory of the American States or wish to retire from them to the British" (Treaty 106). Brant further relied on British fears of "Indian" alliances with Americans or with the French to preserve the Grand River land from encroachment. This is the settlement that is so eloquently defended, one hundred and thirty years later, by Chief Deskaheh in his radio speech of 1925 (see Section IV), as well as in Pauline Johnson's 1894 interview in the London *Gazette* (see Section III). Treaty No. 106 is the document to which Deskaheh attempts to hold the Canadian government accountable.

While indigenous leaders saw themselves as negotiating in good faith with equals, the British were more opportunistic on their side and approached the "Indians" as an obstacle rather than as equal partners. According to historian Barbara Graymount, Brant in particular failed to understand the nature of British imperialism and to comprehend the fact that the British would not permit two sovereignties to exist in Upper Canada. Brant was not alone in trusting the British government and then being disappointed in its decision not to act on its promises. This was standard in the opportunistic treatment of the Native allies, whose support was vital in winning wars against both the French and the Americans.

Until 1830, the administration of Indian affairs was conducted through a branch of the military called the British Indian Department. When Native peoples were no longer considered necessary allies, the British government shifted from treating them as allies in battle to treating them more like children, assuming guardianship over the people and taking control of the administration of the land and its resources. Paternalistic attitudes to First Nations peoples prevailed from that point forth. The government presented itself as protecting the people and their lands from abuse only until they could make decisions for themselves, but the 1857 Civilization of Indian Tribes Act expressly made assimilation its goal. It was declared that "Indians" who were "sufficiently advanced education wise or capable of managing their own affairs" would be enfranchised. Full, unconditional franchise for indigenous peoples did not materialize until 1960.

The paternalistic attitude of the government is evident in the narratives of the day. While some of the emigrant guides (Jameson, Moodie, and Traill) give practical advice on how to listen and learn from the experience of indigenous people, some of the works of fiction and poetry (Goldsmith, Haliburton, Richardson) depict indigenous people as a dangerous and ever-lurking threat.

Literary critic and cultural theorist Edward Said writes in *Culture and Imperialism* that the effect of "stories was to enhance in the popular mind the innate inferiority of the Other, and so validate the inevitability, indeed the virtue, of a European imperium over the savage world" (7). Since the main audience of the emigrants' narratives and settlers' tales was in Britain, the representation of Native peoples is important. If they are depicted as either savage or noble but dying out, then they become easier to overlook (morally and ethically) in the zeal for emigration.

According to the Australian critic Alan Lawson, in order to "put the settler in the cultural and discursive place of the indigene whose physical space has already been invaded" (32), and in order to help legitimize the settler's presence in the new world, settler narratives often depict indigenous characters either as members of a dying race or as carrying the potential for the contamination of European culture and morals. Lawson outlines three specific tropes that predominate in settler narratives. First, there is the trope of "going native." This is manifested in an affinity with the land, animals, and the environment; a taking on of a kind of savagery; or, conversely, a kind of transcendent wisdom and nobility. This desire of settlers to acquire qualities of Aboriginal peoples has been described by literary theorist Terry Goldie as an attempt to "indigenize," or as a process of "indigenization." The process enables settlers to convince themselves that they belong in the new locale, and thereby compensates for the discomfort that might otherwise be associated with the geographical and cultural displacement of large groups of people. While the process of "indigenization" sometimes begins with solidarity or affiliation with the "cultural other," it often ends in a state of insanity or derangement. As such, it acts as a warning against a rejection of European cultural values that might come with association with Native peoples. The second trope is one of presenting the Native people as part of a vanishing or dying race. As such, the authors write of the people's inability to adapt to settler culture and governance. This approach relies heavily on the notion that in a time before contact, before history, Indians were a noble race, but that this race cannot exist in the changing world. It places the indigenous person firmly in the past rather than as a figure being affected by colonialism in the present. The third trope is one of "incorporation" or of the lost child, where a child separated from his family is raised by the "Indians," or wolves, or the land. This trope functions as a cautionary tale for women and children who might think of straying "out of place" (reinforcing fears of miscegenation, headhunting, cannibalism, infanticide, and sexual deviance). Traill's *Canadian Crusoes* (1852) and Frederick Marryat's *Settlers in Canada* (1844) are two popular novels that exemplify these tropes. In Canada, these tropes begin in the eighteenth century and are sustained well into the twentieth. We see elements of them in this period, but they also resurface in the works of writers such as Duncan Campbell Scott, Grey Owl/Archie Belaney, and Earle Birney. Recently, Native writers such as Thomas King, Beth Brant, Eden Robinson, and Tomson Highway have published reworkings of these pervasive myths, and have shown them to be destructive.

Indeed, many contemporary writers have undertaken rewritings of the history of settlement from non-traditional perspectives. Bernice Morgan's *Random Passage* (1992) retells the story of settlement in Newfoundland and the disappearance of the Beothuk people; the characters in Jane Urquhart's *Away* (1997) flee the Irish famine of the 1840s for settlement in Canada; George Elliott Clarke's *Beatrice Chancy* (2001) conveys the story of a slave woman in the Annapolis Valley of Nova Scotia in the nineteenth century; and Merilyn Simonds's *The Holding* (2004) relates the stories of two women who live a century and a half apart on the same parcel of land: a Scottish woman who emigrates in 1859 and a Canadian woman going "back to the land" in the 1990s. Some writers go so far as to integrate real historical figures into their work. For example, appearances are made by fictionalized representations of Traill and Moodie in Atwood's *The Journals of Susanna Moodie* (1970) and *Alias Grace* (1997), Margaret Laurence's *The Diviners* (1974), and Timothy Findley's *Headhunter* (1993).

One finds something of a contradiction in early writing about Canadian society. On the one hand, settlers sought to make themselves feel or appear "native" to Canada by defining themselves as part of a newly emergent society and identifying with Aboriginal myths as a way of contributing to the uniqueness of that society. Think, for example, of how proud Anna Jameson and Susanna Moodie are at their newly acquired canoeing skills, an accomplishment that women of their time would never have been able to achieve in England. On the other hand, many of these early writers looked to England as the mother country and source of their identity. Critics have argued that settlers were in fact caught between divergent worlds and fit completely in neither. Settlers identified both as British imperialists and as Canadian colonials, but the more they felt themselves to be members of an emerging and increasingly long-standing New World society, the more distanced they felt from their European roots. However, they could not completely identify with the "locals" of the place either; they needed to believe that the Native peoples were not as morally advanced as they were, in order to justify appropriating and settling their land.

If one sees the beginnings of a definable "Canadian" culture being forged during this period, it is also an identity marked by crisis and ambivalence. This is the gist of Margaret Atwood's rewriting of Moodie's story in her 1970 sequence of poems, *The Journals of Susanna Moodie*. Moodie, critics have argued, is the archetypal Canadian settler: caught between Old World and New, uncertain of how to fit in, yet reluctant to pull herself away. By the end of her writing life, Moodie had grown to love her new home. If she was not entirely resigned to her life in Canada, she at least recognized that England was not the norm against which everything should be compared. The most momentous political event for Canada in the nineteenth century, the achievement of independent status as a nation in 1867, occurred during Moodie's and Traill's lifetimes. The quest for an identifiable Canadian identity and literature, distinct from Britain and the United States, continued into the next century.

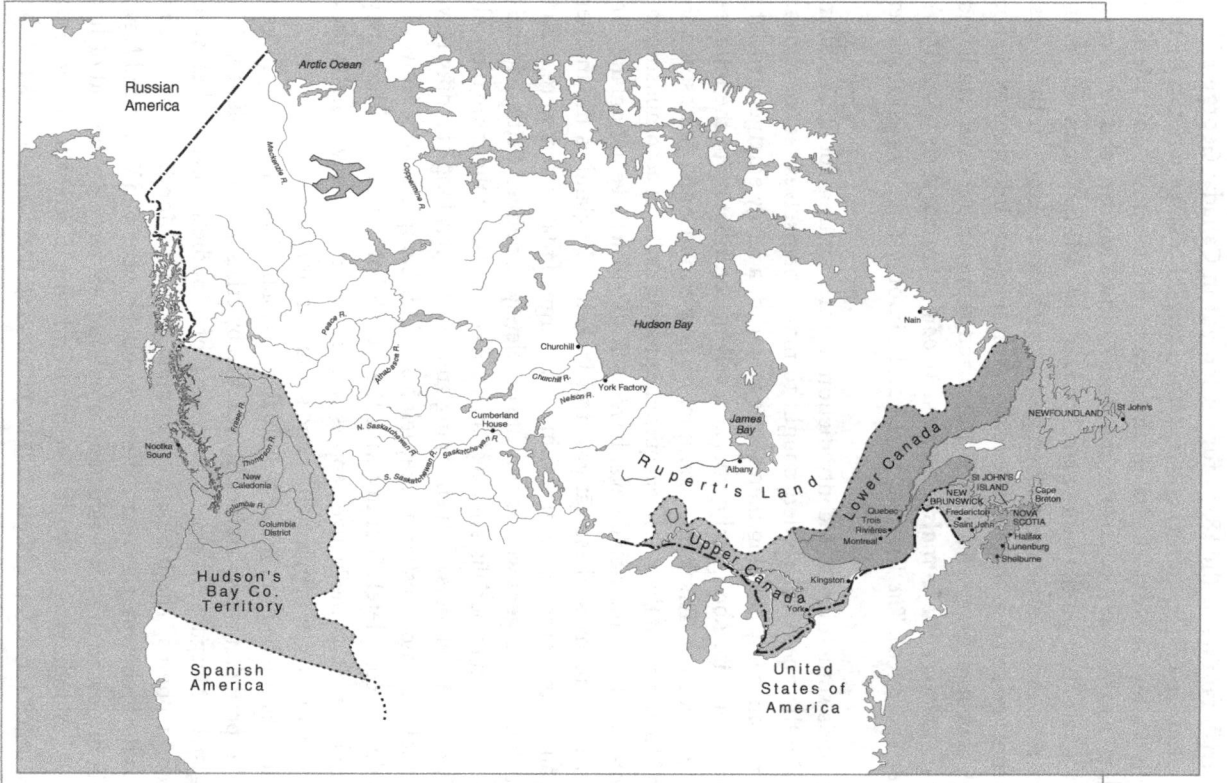

FIGURE II-1 British North America in 1791, Following the Constitutional Act

Source: Conrad/Finkel, *History of the Canadian Peoples*, Vol.1, Fourth Edition, p.187. Reprinted with permission of Pearson Education Canada.

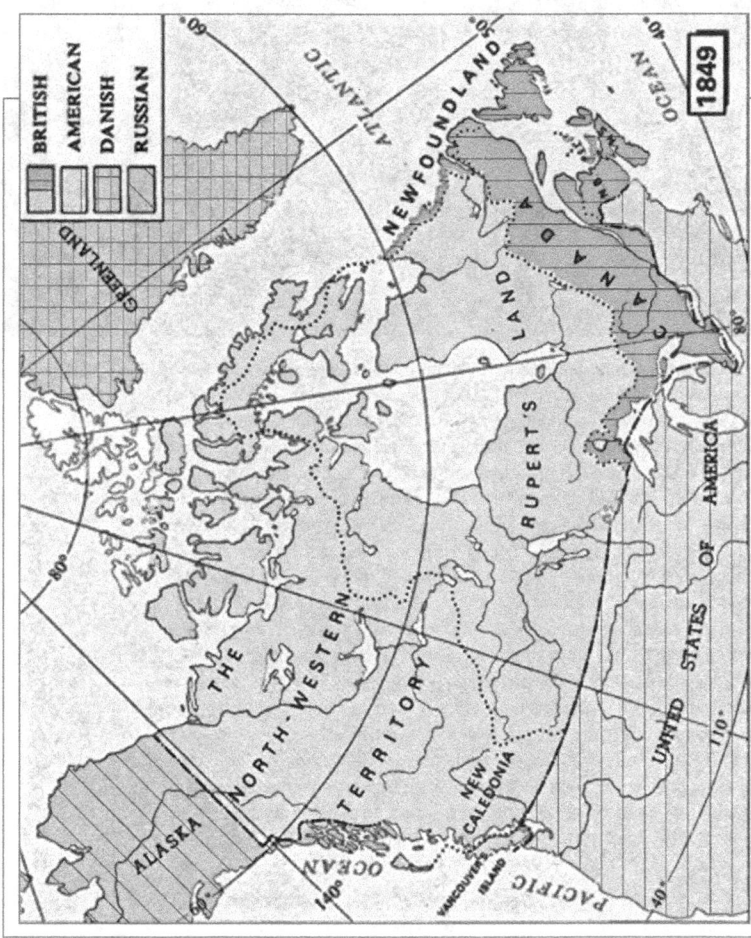

FIGURE II-2 Map of Canada, Following the 1840 Act of Union, Which Joined Upper and Lower Canada (1849)

Source: Original map data provided by The Atlas of Canada http://atlas.gc.ca. ©2006. Produced under license from Her Majesty the Queen in Right of Canada, with permission of Natural Resources Canada.

FIGURE II-3 *The Death of General Wolfe* **(oil painting, 1770), Benjamin West (1738–1820)**
Benjamin West's painting of the English general's last gasp on 13 September 1759, at the
moment of his victory over the French in the Battle of the Plains of Abraham, has become the
accepted visual record of the conquest of Canada and an archetypal image of patriotic heroism. The painting has been called "probably the most famous of all historical paintings" in
Canada, but it has also recently been shown to be a historically inaccurate depiction of the
events of the battle. Although the figures in the scene are real military figures who were
instrumental in the British campaign at Quebec, critics argue that it is most unlikely that all
were present at the moment of Wolfe's death. Indeed, for the later engraved version of the
painting, the printer asked the officers for payment of one hundred pounds each for the
privilege of being depicted at the scene. It is also probable that the Iroquois man kneeling
at Wolfe's side would not have been so positioned. Given that West was one of the first
painters to record a recent historical scene in contemporary dress rather than placing his figures in Greek or Roman costume, as was the tradition, it is ironic that he depicted the scene
with such historical inaccuracy. The painter, known as the "American Raphael," depicts the
fall of Wolfe in the highly romanticized terms of contemporary classicism. The painting was
so much admired when it was shown in England that King George III commissioned a copy
of the original to be painted for himself. Reportedly, the painting became the single most
reproduced work of art in eighteenth-century England, with the creation of an engraved
version of the scene from which thousands of prints were made.

Source: Benjamin West, 1738–1820, *The Death of General Wolfe*, 1770, oil on canvas, 152.6 × 214.5 cm.
National Gallery of Canada, Ottawa. Transfer from the Canadian War Memorials, 1921 (Gift of the 2nd Duke
of Westminster, Eaton Hall, Cheshire, 1918).

FIGURE II-4 "The Emigrant's Welcome to Canada"

This critical cartoon, which first appeared In the British magazine *Punch* around 1820, spoofs many of the myths that were being circulated in England to entice prospective settlers to Canada. Here, the poor settler is ill-equipped to cope with the reality of the world he has entered. On his back he carries such useless articles as silk stockings and dancing shoes; the "apartment to let" is a bear's den; the publicity tracts lie discarded on the snow; and the geese mock the immigrant for his gullibility.

Source: Library and Archives Canada/R9266-3510.

HERE   AND   THERE

Or, emigration a remedy

FIGURE II-5 "Here and There: Or, emigration a remedy"

This cartoon, which appeared in the British magazine *Punch* on 15 July 1848, contrasts a poor family in Ireland during the 1840s famine and a prosperous family in the New World.

Source: Charles and Cynthia Hou, *Great Canadian Political Cartoons, 1820 to 1914* (Vancouver: Moody's Lookout, 1997)

FIGURE II-6 Catharine Parr Traill
Miniature portrait of Catharine Parr Traill as a young woman.

Source: Library and Archives Canada/NL–15557.

FIGURE II-7 Susanna Moodie
Miniature watercolour portrait of Susanna Moodie as a young woman.

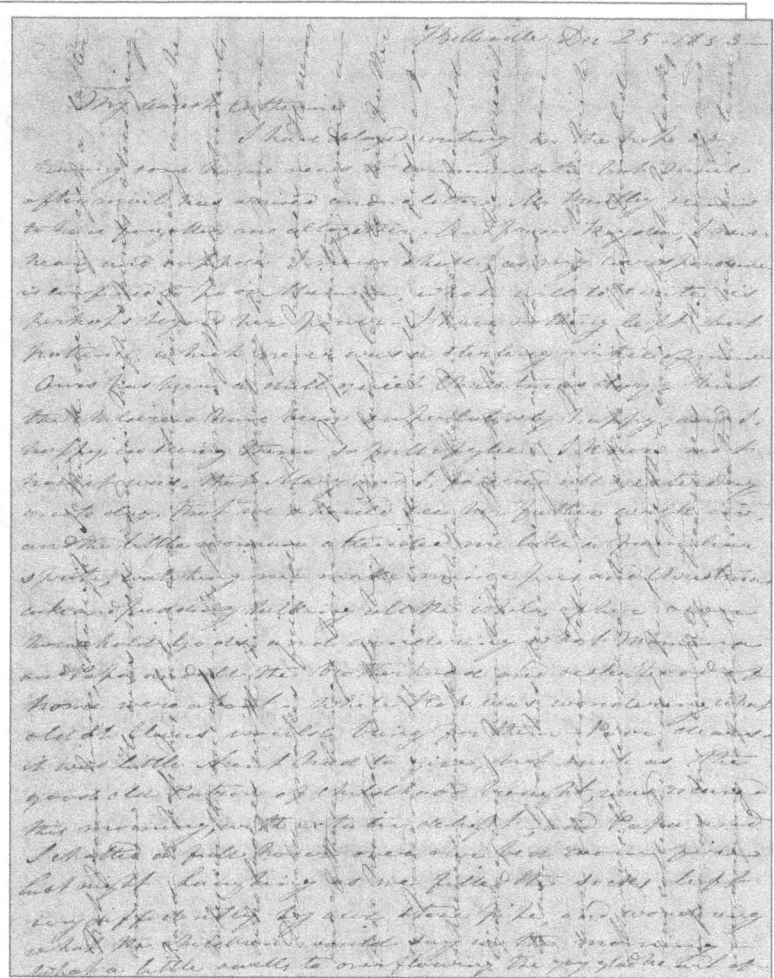

FIGURE II-8 A Cross-written Letter from Susanna Moodie to Catharine Parr Traill
A cross-written letter from Susanna Moodie to Catharine Parr Traill that was inscribed
horizontally and then vertically to economize on paper.

Source: Library and Archives Canada/e000000527.

FIGURE II-9 *The Phantom Hunter* **(oil painting, 1888), William Blair Bruce (1859–1906)**
This painting, now hanging in the Art Gallery of Hamilton, was inspired by Charles Dawson
Shanly's 1859 poem "The Walker of the Snow" (see pages 238–239). The painting, like the
poem, represents the "snow walker" as a ghostly figure who leaves no footprints. As in
Shanly's poem, the status of the "ghost" is ambiguous: is it real or a figment of the hunter's
imagination? The painting seems to favour a psychological (as opposed to a supernatural)
interpretation of the hunter's story, and yet it also allows for the possibility that the ghostly
form is emerging from the body of the dying man. Is the snow walker a kind of incubus who
feeds on the souls of wayward travellers, or has the teller of the story himself been transformed into "the walker of the snow"? The painting is part of the traditional nineteenth-century iconography of the North as a monstrous and deadly space, one in which humans are
either killed or rendered insane. It thus echoes the many pictorial and poetic renditions of
Sir John Franklin's tragic 1845 expedition, in which Franklin's crew is depicted as having
been consumed by an unforgiving Arctic landscape. The snowbanks in the background are
apparently based on the landscape behind Bruce's family home in Hamilton, Ontario.

Source: William Blair Bruce (Canadian 1859–1906), *The Phantom Hunter*, 1888, oil on canvas. Art
Gallery of Hamilton, Bruce Memorial, 1914.

Bridesmaid Anne Hecht likely read this dedicatory poem aloud from the birch bark it was written on at the wedding ceremony of eighteen-year-old Hetty (a nickname for Mehetible) Calef and Captain David Mowat in Saint John, New Brunswick, 1786. The address is a version of a poem that seems to have circulated in England, America, and the British North American colonies. Recently, literary historians Gwen Davies and Carole Gerson have identified phrases of the poem in verses addressed to Clementina Cruikshank in Philadelphia in 1768 (originally quoted in Karin A. Wulf's *Not All Wives: Women of Colonial Philadelphia*). Much of the poem was published earlier in *The London Magazine, or, Gentlemen's Monthly Intelligencer* (1735). Its enduring popularity is confirmed by the fact that it was included in Joseph Addison's *Interesting Anecdotes, Memoirs, Allegories, Essays, and Poetical Fragments, Tending to Amuse the Fancy and Inculcate Morality* (London, 1797). The poem is available in variant forms in a number of locations. The individual versions situate the poem in a particular place and in reference to a particular couple. The range of variants of this poem indicates the extent to which print culture was a transatlantic phenomenon, especially in relation to social poetry that could be adapted to specific environments. It is unclear from which specific source Anne Hecht borrowed the poem, but it is clear that it was relevant in the colonial setting of Loyalist New Brunswick. The poem clearly situates early "Canadian" literary activity in the larger colonial world.

The poem is an excellent example of the marriage poem convention. Aside from the irony (recognized by the speaker in the final lines of the poem) of an unmarried woman giving advice on marriage, this poem neatly illustrates some of the social norms of the eighteenth century. It shows the onus placed upon the woman to be responsible for the health, success, and happiness of her husband, her family, and, analogously, her community. In the late eighteenth century in New Brunswick, as in much of the rest of the Western world, the institution of marriage was seen as key to achieving "bliss." It was also, in a rapidly expanding colony, fundamental to the growth of the community. In a place where social and political institutions were nascent, the institution of marriage was vital to help ensure stability and order. Part of the stable, well-ordered world view came in the form of the patriarchal views on the role of women expressed in this poem. Marriage was a duty for women, a place where they should be virtuous, self-sacrificing, and supportive. The rhetoric of female domesticity in this poem is in keeping with the colonial rhetoric of domesticating the new colonial lands. Just as Hetty's future as a mother and ruler of her own domain is necessary to "fix" the empire of her husband's heart, it is also vital as a way to "fix" the empire itself.

Advice to Mrs. Mowat

Poem written to Mehetible Calef, on her Marriage to Captain David Mowat, composed by her Bridesmaid, Anne Hecht, in the Year 1786.

Dear Hetty—
  Since the single state
You've left to choose yourself a mate,
Since metamorphosed to a wife,
And bliss or woe insured for life,
A friendly muse the way should show
To gain the bliss and miss the woe.
But first of all I must suppose
You've with mature reflection chose.
And thus premised I think you may
Here find to married bliss the way.   10
Small is the province of a wife
And narrow is her sphere in life,
Within that sphere to walk aright
Should be her principal delight.
To grace the home with prudent care
And properly to spend and spare,
To make her husband bless the day
He gave his liberty away,
To train the tender infant's mind,
These are the tasks to wives assigned.   20
Then never think domestic care
Beneath the notice of the fair.
But matters every day inspect
That naught be wasted by neglect.
Be frugal (plenty round you seen)
And always keep the golden mean.
Let decent neatness round you shine
Be always clean but seldom fine.
If once fair decency be fled
Love soon deserts the genial bed.   .30
Not nice your house, though neat and clean
In all things there's a proper mean.
Some of our sex mistake in this;
Too anxious some—some too remiss.
The early days of married life
Are oft o'er cast with childish strife.
Then let it be your chiefest care
To keep that hour bright and fair;
Then is the time, by gentlest art
To fix his empire in your heart.   40
For should it by neglect expire
No art again can light the fire.
To charm his reason dress your mind

Till love shall be with friendship joined.
Raised on that basis t'will endure
From time and death itself secure.
Be sure you ne'er for power contend
Or try with tears to gain your end.
Sometimes the tears that dim your eyes
From pride and obstancy arise.   50
Heaven gave to man unquestioned sway.
Then Heaven and man at once obey.
Let sullen looks your brow ne'er cloud
Be always cheerful, never loud.
Let trifles never discompose
Your temper, features or repose.
Abroad for happiness ne'er roam
True happiness resides at home.
Still make your partner easy there
Man finds abroad sufficient care.   60
If every thing at home be right
He'll always enter with delight.
Your presence he'll prefer to all,
That cheats the world does pleasure call.
With cheerful chat his cares beguile
And always greet him with a smile,
Never with woe his thoughts engage
Nor ever meet his rage with rage.
With all our sex's softening art
Recall lost reason to his heart.   70
Thus calm the tempest in his breast
And sweetly soothe his soul to rest.
Be sure you ne'er arraign his sense,
Few husbands pardon that offence,
T'will discord raise, disgust it breeds
And hatred certainly succeeds.
Then shun, O shun that hated self,
Still think him wiser than yourself.
And if you otherwise believe
Ne'er let him such a thought perceive.   80
When cares invade your partner's heart
Bear you a sympathetic part.
. . . .
From morn till noon, from noon till night
To see him pleased your chief delight.
And now, methinks, I hear you cry;
Shall she presume—Oh vanity!

To lay down rules for wedded life
Who never was herself a wife?
I've done nor longer will presume
To trespass on time that's not your own.   90

[1786]

JOSEPH BRANT (THAYENDANEGEA) ■ (1742–1807)

Born in the Ohio Valley, Mohawk leader and British military officer Joseph Brant (Thayendanegea) is remembered for his role as a statesman, a negotiator, a warrior, and a leader. He is one of the best-known First Nations leaders of the nineteenth century as the chief of the Iroquois Confederacy of the Six Nations (Mohawks, Senecas, Oneidas, Cayugas, Onondagas, and Tuscaroras). He led a group of Iroquois to settle on the banks of the Grand River in 1784 following the American War of Independence.

Brant was educated at Moor's Indian Charity School in Connecticut. He then acted as an interpreter for both Sir William Johnson (the superintendent for northern Indian affairs, who was married to Brant's sister Molly) and his successor in the British Indian Department Guy Johnson. A committed Anglican, Brant also aided missionaries in teaching Christianity to his people, and helped translate religious materials (such as the Gospel of Mark) into the Mohawk language. According to historian James Paxton, Brant "accommodated colonization by attempting to create a coherent world from the diversity of the Mohawk Valley that fitted Europeans and their practices into a worldview rooted in Mohawk culture and values." Brant travelled to England in 1775–76 with Johnson to present grievances about encroachments on Mohawk lands during the American Revolution. In England, Brant was feted by leading figures in the arts, letters, and government. He even had his portrait painted by the

foremost portrait artist of the day, George Romney, and was presented to King George III to be inducted into the brotherhood of Freemasons. Lord George Germain, the secretary of state for the American colonies, promised Brant that after the dispute with the King's rebellious colonies had been settled, Brant and his people could be assured "of every support England could render them." Germain's promise satisfied Brant and convinced him that the welfare of his people lay in an alliance with the King rather than retaining a position of neutrality.

On his return from England, Brant urged the Iroquois to fight on the side of the British. In 1777–78, Brant led a group of Mohawk and non-Mohawk Loyalists on a series of raids in Pennsylvania and New York. He was made "captain of the Northern Confederate Indians" in appreciation of his "astonishing activity and success" in the King's service, and continued to fight with the British until the end of the war. But in negotiating the Treaty of Paris of 1782, which ended the American Revolution, Britain ignored Germain's promise of support to its allies and transferred sovereignty over all British-claimed land as far west as the Mississippi River to the Americans, even though most of the territory was occupied by the American Indians, who had not relinquished it to the British. When Brant learned the treaty terms, he angrily exclaimed that England had "sold the Indians to Congress." Under pressure from Brant, the governor general of Canada, Sir Frederick Haldimand, arranged for a grant of approximately two million acres of land on the Grand River, in what was soon to be known as Upper Canada, for "Mohawk Indians" and "others of the Six Nations who have lost their settlements within the Territory of the American States or wish to retire from them to the British." Another smaller settlement of Mohawk Loyalists was established on the Bay of Quinte on Lake Ontario, by John and Joseph Deserontyon, at the same time (now Deseronto).

Through the terms of the Haldimand Treaty (No. 106) of 25 October 1784, the Mohawk Loyalists were granted land six miles on either side of the Grand River from its source to its mouth. By 1788 Brant had helped to establish a village at the crossing point on the river ("Brant's Ford"). The 1785 census shows a total of 1,843 people in the community (including more than four hundred Mohawk people, several hundred Cayugas and Onondagas, and smaller groups of Senecas, Tuscaroras, Delawares, Nanticokes, Tutelos, Creeks, and Cherokees). Committed to establishing a Christian community on the banks of the Grand River, Brant helped secure a school, a schoolmaster, and a church, and by 1789 he had also translated a primer and the liturgy of the Church of England into the Mohawk language. Treaty No. 106 is the settlement that was so eloquently defended one hundred and thirty years later by Chief Deskaheh in his radio speech of 1925 (see Section

IV), as well as in Pauline Johnson's 1894 interview in the London *Gazette* (see Section III).

Problems arose when Governor John Graves Simcoe claimed that a mistake had been made in the original grant in that the northern portion (of the Grand River) had never been bought from the Mississaugas and the King could not grant what he had not bought. Further trouble ensued when Brant negotiated land leases and sales to finance a transition (controversial among his people) to European-style farming. He had understood that the land was freely given on the same basis as land given to other Loyalists, to do with as they saw fit. However, the government officials believed that land sales should be limited and the Crown should approve all transactions. Brant rejected what he considered to be interference in his affairs and continued to lease and sell land. He eventually won the right to lease the land, but his victory was a hollow one, since it resulted in the loss of much of the original grant. The letter included here concerns Brant's claims to the full grant of land. For the remainder of his life, until his death in 1807, Brant was determined to secure full Indian sovereignty over the Grand River land. By 1841, when the land was surrendered to the Crown to be established as a reserve, only a small portion of the original grant remained. The parcel of land currently contested in Caledonia is a remnant of the original grant given to the Six Nations.

Letter to Capt. Green

Grand River, Dec. 10, 1798

Sir,

Our former acquaintance encourages me to take the freedom of writing you; but knowing the multiplicity of business you have on your hands, I would not trouble you with this, did not the particular situation of our affairs seem to require it, thinking it necessary for me candidly to acquaint my friends with the feelings of my mind.

I presume that you are well acquainted with the long difficulties we had concerning the lands on this river—these difficulties we had not the least idea of when we first settled here, looking on them as granted us to be indisputably our own, otherwise we would never have accepted the lands, yet afterwards it seemed a little odd to us that the writings Gov. Haldimand gave us after our settling on the lands, was not so compleat as the strong assurances and promises he had made us at first, but this made no great impression on our minds, still confiding in the goodness of his Majesty's intentions, and in the weight we caputed our former services would have with him—Had it not been for this confidence and affection we bore the Kings we still had opportunities left after the war, in providing for ourselves in the free and independent manner natural to Indians, unhappily for us we have been made acquainted too late with the first real intentions of Ministry; that is, that they never intended us to have it in our power to alienate any part of the lands; and here we have even been prohibited from taking tenants on them, it having been represented as inconsistent for us, being but King's allies, to have King's subjects as tenants, consequently I suppose their real meaning was, we should in a manner be but tenants ourselves, as for me I see no difference in it any farther than that we are as yet rent free—they seemingly intending to forbid us any other use of the lands than that of sitting down or walking on them. It plainly appears by this that their motives can be no other than to tie us down in such a manner, as to have us entirely at their disposal for whatever services they may in future want from us, and that in case we should be worried out, and obliged to move the lands would then fall to them with our improvements of labour.

Sir, I hope I shall not tire your patience, in making a few remarks on what I suppose may naturally be the thoughts of Government on our conduct— With respect to myself they might say he has half pay and yet talks so much on these matters, it is very true I enjoy that bounty of his Majesty, so many worthless fellows like me do, that have never risked their property or anything else in his causes but am I for this entirely to forsake the interests of my people? that put their dependence on me besides my family which is very numerous cannot be benefitted by my half pay when I am no more; which at my time of life I have reason to look on as a period not so very distant. I think it therefore incumbent on me to secure what they must look to for a future support. With respect to the Nation they may also say, that they have received their losses, for instance our hunting grounds that were very extensive, besides several other tracts of land were never mentioned—The Miller, blacksmith, and School-master, that is allowed us by government may also be spoken of—we are indeed very thankful for it; but we look upon this as all temporary and the continuance of it to be uncertain—it may likewise be said they receive annual presents what do they want more, we gratefully thank his Majesty, for his bounty in this respect; but I am sorry to have to observe that this goes very little ways in clothing the poor and helpless—and the country is so much changed that hunting is of very little account to the young and robust.

I beg [leave] to say a few words more on this subject, the movements of Gov. Simcoe in attempting to curtail our lands to one half of the River; and recollecting our deed from Gov. Haldimand to be unequal to his first promises caused us to make such a large sale at once that the matter might come to a point and we might know whether the land was ours or not—the next reason was, that the lands all round us being given away to different people, some of them, those that had even been engaged in war against us, we found it necessary to sell some land, that we might have an income, the hunting being entirely destroyed.—We now learn that the ministry never intended we should alienate the lands, alleging that by doing so, disaffected people might be introduced into the country that might injure government—the people we have sold the lands to are loyalist & we expect, that as other people settled in the province, they will become subjects to His Majesty, the same as if Gov. Simcoe had himself curtailed the land and given it to them, as he has done with the adjacent lands.

I am sorry for having taken up so much of your time with so tedious a letter but I assure my present disagreeable situation, affects my feelings so much, that I cannot avoid expressing it rather fully especially as I think this shall be the last time I will trouble you on the subject.

Capt. Green
Sir I am
Your most obed^t and
Humb. Servt.
Jos. Brant

[1798]

BOSTON KING ■ (1760–unknown)

Boston King was an escaped slave, a carpenter, a "Black Loyalist," and a Methodist preacher. King's memoir illustrates some of the trials of the Black Loyalists as slaves, as servants of British army officers, as settlers in Nova Scotia, and as emigrants to Freetown, Sierra Leone. First published in 1798 in the *Methodist Magazine,* his work entitled *Memoirs of the Life of Boston King, a Black Preacher: Written by Himself, during his residence at Kingswood School* provides a wealth of information on life as a slave in the late eighteenth century. It also tells, in great detail, of one man's Christianity. On the way, King highlights the consequences of the American War of Independence for slaves, their escape to Nova Scotia, their harsh treatment there, and finally their move to Sierra Leone.

Born on a plantation in South Carolina in 1760, King is listed in the compendium of facts on the Black Loyalists, *The Book of Negroes: Loyalist Refugees from New York in 1783,* as "23, stout fellow. Formerly the property of Richard Waring of Charlestown South Carolina; left him 4 years ago. GBC." GBC stands for the certificate of freedom given by General Birch under the 1779 Phillipsburg Proclamation that promised not only freedom but full security to any slave who sought refuge in the British army during the war. King outlines the details of the proclamation as it affected him in the account of his life excerpted here. Arriving in Nova Scotia in 1783, King and his wife, Violet, were among the first settlers of Birchtown, a settlement of predominantly Black Loyalists near Shelburne. In Birchtown, King converted to Methodism and became a preacher, travelling around the province working as a carpenter and preaching the word of God.

Nova Scotia did not provide settlers such as King with the prosperity they sought. Following several years of harsh life in Nova Scotia, including the famine of 1789, during which the British government failed to fulfill all its promises to the Loyalists, some settlers were ready for a change. John Clarkson, an agent of the Sierra Leone Company, recruited heavily in Nova Scotia. He writes of the settlers in Birchtown: "[T]hey were unanimous in the desire for embarking for Africa, telling me their labour was lost upon the land in this country and their utmost efforts would barely keep them in existence—being now sunk to the lowest wretchedness they had made up their minds for quitting this country." Over a thousand people decided to leave Nova Scotia for Sierra Leone in 1792. Among them were King, his family, and his congregation. Interestingly, the year after the Black Loyalists departed for Sierra Leone (1792), the Upper Canada Parliament abolished the practice of bringing slaves into the colony (1793). It was not until 1833, however, that the British Parliament's Slavery Abolition Act put a stop to slavery in all parts of the British Empire.

From Memoirs of the Life of Boston King

It is by no means an agreeable task to write an account of my life, yet my gratitude to Almighty God, who considered my affliction, and looked upon me in my low estate, who delivered me from the hand of the oppressor, and established my goings, impels me to acknowledge his goodness. And the importunity of many respectable friends, whom I highly esteem, have induced me to set down, as they occurred to my memory, a few of the most striking incidents I have met with in my pilgrimage. I am well aware of my inability for such an undertaking, having only a slight acquaintance with the language in which I write, and being obliged to snatch a few hours, now and then, from pursuits which to me, perhaps, are more profitable. However, such as it is, I present it to the Friends of Religion and Humanity, hoping that it will be of some use to mankind.

I was born in the Province of South Carolina, 28 miles from Charles Town. My father was stolen away from Africa when he was young. I have reason to believe that he lived in the fear and love of God. He attended to that true Light which lighteth every man that cometh into the world. He lost no opportunity of hearing the Gospel, and never omitted praying with his family every night. He likewise read to them, and to as many as were inclined to hear. On the Lord's Day he rose very early, and met his family; after which he worked in the field till about three in the afternoon, and then went into the woods and read till sunset: The slaves being obliged to work on the Lord's Day to procure such things as were not allowed by their masters. He was beloved by his master, and had the charge of the plantation as a driver for many years.

In his old age he was employed as a mill-cutter. Those who knew him say that they never heard him swear an oath, but on the contrary, he reproved all who spoke improper words in his hearing. To the utmost of his power he endeavoured to make his family happy, and his death was a very great loss to us all. My mother was employed chiefly in attending upon those who were sick, having some knowledge of the virtue of herbs, which she learned from the Indians. She likewise had the care of making the people's clothes, and on these accounts was indulged with many privileges which the rest of the slaves were not.

When I was six years old I waited in the house upon my master. In my 9th year I was put to mind the cattle. [. . .] When 16 years old, I was bound apprentice to a trade. After being in the shop about two years, I had the charge of my master's tools, which being very good, were often used by the men, if I happened to be out of the way. When this was the case, or any of them were lost, or misplaced, my master beat me severely, striking me upon my head, or any other part without mercy.

One time in the holy-days, my master and the men being from home, and the care of the house devolving upon me and the younger apprentices, the house was broke open, and robbed of many valuable articles, thro' the negligence of the apprentice who had then the charge of it. When I came home in the evening, and saw what had happened, my consternation was inconceivable, as all that we had in the world could not make good the loss. The week following, when the master came to town, I was beat in a most unmercial manner, so that I was not able to do any thing for a fortnight. [. . . *Several years pass.]* To escape his cruelty, I determined to go to Charles Town, and throw myself into the hands of the English. They received me readily, and I began to feel the happiness of liberty, of which I knew nothing before, altho' I was most grieved at first, to be obliged to leave my friends, and remain among strangers. In this situation I was seized with the small pox, and suffered great hardships; for all the Blacks affected with that disease were ordered to be carried a mile from camp, lest the soldiers should be infected, and disabled from marching. This was a grievous circumstance to me and many others.

[. . .] About which time [1783], the horrors and devastation of war happily terminated and peace was restored between America and Great Britain, which diffused universal joy among all parties, except us, who had escaped from slavery and taken refuge in the English army; for a rumour prevailed at New York, that all the slaves, in number 2000, were to be delivered up to their masters, altho' some of them had been three or four years among the English.

This dreadful rumour filled us all with inexpressible anguish and terror, especially when we saw our old masters coming from Virginia, North Carolina, and other parts, and seizing upon their slaves in the streets of New York, or even dragging them out of their beds. Many of the slaves had very cruel masters, so that the thoughts of returning home with them embittered life to us. For some days we lost our appetite for food, and sleep departed from our eyes.

The English had compassion upon us in the day of distress, and issued out a Proclamation, importing that all slaves should be free, who had taken refuge in the British lines, and claimed the sanction and privileges of the Proclamation respecting the security and protection of the Negroes. In consequence of this, each of us received a certificate from the commanding officer at New York, which dispelled all our fears, and filled us with joy and gratitude. Soon after, ships were fitted out, and furnished with every necessary for conveying us to Nova Scotia. We arrived at Birchtown in the month of August where we all safely landed. Every family had a lot of land, and we exerted all our strength in order to build comfortable huts before the cold weather set in.

That winter, the work of religion began to revive among us; and many were convinced of the sinfulness of sin, and turned from the error of their ways. It pleased the Lord to awaken my wife under the preaching of Mr. Wilkinson; she was struck to the ground, and cried out for mercy; she continued in great distress for near two hours, when they sent for me. At first I was much displeased, and refused to go; but presently my mind relented, and I went to the house, and was struck with astonishment at the sight of her agony. In about six days after, the Lord spoke peace to her soul: she was filled with divine consolation, and walked in the light of God's countenance about nine months. But being unacquainted with the corruptions of her own heart, she again gave place to bad tempers, and fell into great darkness and distress. Indeed, I never saw any person, either before or since, so overwhelmed with anguish of spirit on account of backsliding, as she was. The trouble of her soul brought affliction upon her body, which confined her to bed a year and a half.

However, the Lord was pleased to sanctify her afflictions, and to deliver her from all her fears. He brought her out of the horrible pit, and set her soul at perfect liberty. The joy and happiness which she now experienced, were too great to be concealed, and she was enabled to testify of the goodness and loving-kindness of the Lord, with such liveliness and power, that many were convinced by her testimony, and sincerely sought the Lord. As she was the first person at Birchtown that experienced deliverance from evil tempers, and exhorted and urged others to seek and enjoy the same blessing, she was not a little opposed by some of our Black brethren. But these trials she endured with the meekness and patience becoming a Christian; and when Mr. Freeborn Garrettson came to Birchtown to regulate the society and form them into classes, he encouraged her to hold fast her confidence, and cleave to the Lord with her whole heart.

Soon after my wife's conversion, the Lord strove powerfully with me. I felt myself a miserable wretched sinner, so that I could not rest night or day. I went to Mr. Brown, one evening, and told him my case. He received me with great kindness and affection, and entreated me to seek the Lord with all my heart. The more he spoke to me, the more my distress increased; and when he went to prayer, I found myself burdened with a load of guilt too heavy for me to bear. On my return home, I had to pass thro' a little wood, where I intended to fall down on my knees and pray for mercy; but every time I attempted, I was so terrified, that I thought my hair stood upright, and that the earth moved beneath my feet. I hastened home in great fear and horror, and yet hoped that the Lord would bless me as well as my neighbours. [. . .]

In the year 1787, I found my mind drawn out to commiserate my poor brethren in Africa; and especially when I considered that we who had the happiness of being brought up in a Christian land, where the Gospel is preached, were notwithstanding our great privileges, involved in gross darkness and wickedness; I thought, what a wretched condition then must those poor creatures be in, who never heard the Name of God or of Christ; nor had any instruction afforded them with respect to a future judgment. As I had not the least prospect at that time of ever seeing Africa, I contented myself with pitying and praying for the poor benighted inhabitants of that country which gave birth to my forefathers. I laboured in Birchtown and Shelwin two years, and the word was blessed to the conversion of many, most of whom continued steadfast in the good way to the heavenly kingdom.

About this time, the country was visited with a dreadful famine, which not only prevailed at Birchtown, but likewise at Chebucto, Annapolis, Digby and other places. Many of the poor people were compelled to sell their best gowns for five pounds of flour, in order to support life. When they had parted with all their clothes, even to their blankets, several of them fell down dead in the streets, thro' hunger. Some killed and eat their dogs and cats, and poverty and distress prevailed on every side, so that to my great grief I was obliged to leave Birchtown, because I could get no employment.

I travelled from place to place, to procure the necessaries of life, but in vain. At last I came to Shelwin on the 20th of January. After walking from one street to the other, I met with Capt. Selex, and he engaged me to make him a chest. I rejoiced at the offer, and returning home, set about it immediately. I worked all night, and by eight o'clock next morning finished the chest, which I carried to the Captain's house, thro' the snow which was three feet deep. But to my great disappointment he rejected it. However he gave me directions to make another. On my way home, being pinched with hunger and cold, I fell down several times, thro' weakness, and expected to die upon the spot. But even in this situation, I found my mind resigned to the divine will, and rejoiced in the midst of tribulation; for the Lord delivered me from all murmurings and discontent, altho' I had but one pint of Indian meal left for the support of myself and wife.

Having finished another chest, I took it to my employer the next day; but being afraid he would serve me as he had done before, I took a saw along with me in order to sell it. On the way, I prayed that the Lord would give me a prosperous journey, and was answered to the joy of my heart, for Capt. Selex paid me for the chest in Indian corn, and the other chest I sold for 2s. 6d. and the saw for 3s. 9d. altho' it cost me a guinea; yet I was exceeding thankful to procure a reprieve from the dreadful anguish of perishing by famine. O what a wonderful deliverance did God work for me that day! And he taught me to live by faith, and to put my trust in him, more than I ever had done before.

While I was admiring the goodness of God, and praising him for the help he afforded me in the day of trouble, a gentleman sent for me, and engaged me to make three flat-bottomed boats for the salmon-fishery, at 1£ each. The gentleman advanced two baskets of Indian corn, and found nails and tar for the boats. I was enabled to finish the work by the time appointed, and he paid me honestly. Thus did the kind hand of Providence interpose in my preservation, which appeared still greater, upon viewing the wretched circumstances of many of my Black brethren at the time, who were obliged to sell themselves to the merchants, some for two or three years; and others for five or six years. The circumstances of the white inhabitants were likewise very distressing, owing to their great imprudence in building large houses, and striving to exceed one another in this piece of vanity. When their money was almost expended, they began to build small fishing vessels, but alas, it was too late to repair their error. Had they been wise enough at first to have turned their attention to the fishery, instead of fine houses, the place would soon have been in a flourishing condition; whereas it was reduced in a short time to a heap of ruins, and its inhabitants were compelled to flee to other parts of the continent for sustenance.

Next winter, the same gentleman employed me to build him some more boats. When they were finished he engaged me to go with him to Chebucto, to build a house, to which place he intended to remove his family. He agreed to give me 2£ per month, and a barrel of mackerel, and another of herrings, for my winter's provision. I was glad to embrace this offer, altho' it gave me much pain to leave the people of God. On the 20th of April I left my wife and friends and sailed for Chebucto. When we arrived at that place, my employer had not all the men necessary for the fishing voyage; he therefore solicited me to go with him. [. . .] He answered, that he could purchase a house for less money than build one, and that if I would go with him to Bayshallow, I should greatly oblige him; to which I at length consented. [. . .] On the 11th of August we sailed for home; and my master thanked me for my fidelity and diligence, and said, "I believe if you had not been with me, I should not have made half a voyage this season." On the 16th, we arrived at Chebucto, and unloaded the vessels. When this business was finished, we prepared for the herring fishery in Pope's Harbour, at which place we arrived on the 27th of August, and began to set the nets and watch for the herrings. One day as we were attending our net at the mouth of the harbour, we dropped one of the oars, and could not recover it; and having a strong west wind, it drove us out to sea. Our alarm was very great, but the kind hand of Providence interposed and saved us; for when we were driven about two miles from our station, the people on shore saw our danger, and immediately sent two boats to our assistance, which came up with us about sun-set, and brought us safe into the harbour.

October 24, we left Pope's Harbour, and came to Halifax, where we were paid off, each man receiving 15£ for his wages; and my master gave me two barrels of fish agreeable to his promise. When I returned home, I was enabled to clothe my wife and myself, and my winter's store consisted of one barrel of flour, three bushels of corn, nine gallons of treacle, 20 bushels of potatoes which my wife had set in my absence, and the two barrels of fish; so that this was the best Winter I ever saw in Birchtown.

[1794]

When *The Letters of Mephibosheth Stepsure* were published in the *Acadian Recorder* in Halifax (1821–23), they were met by an audience receptive to Thomas McCulloch's new brand of social satire. According to Northrop Frye, "McCulloch is the founder of genuine Canadian humour: that is, of the humour which is based on a vision of society and is not merely a series of wisecracks on a single theme." McCulloch's deeply conservative vision is set forth in a gently sarcastic and highly moralistic manner of social criticism.

By 1821, McCulloch was well suited to write such a commentary on his community. He and his family arrived in Pictou, Nova Scotia, from Scotland in November 1803 en route to Prince Edward Island. Apparently, impressed by his collection of books and his evident erudition, the townspeople enticed McCulloch to winter in Pictou, arguing that it was already late in the season and the trip to P.E.I. would be treacherous. The townspeople turned out to be right about McCulloch's knowledge. He was educated at Glasgow University, where he took a course in medicine and in the arts. He was then ordained as a Presbyterian minister in Ayrshire and offered his services as a missionary to the colonies. McCulloch ended up staying in Pictou for decades. His training as a minister and in medicine was useful in the young settlement. In the early years he is said to have walked many miles making medical and spiritual calls for the community of recent immigrants.

From his arrival in Pictou, McCulloch disagreed with the religious influences in Nova Scotia. As a Presbyterian theologian, he pulled no punches. The titles of his works signal the virulence of his ideas, particularly against "Popery" (Catholicism): *Popery Condemned by Scripture and the Fathers* (1808); *Popery Condemned Again* (1810); *The Nature and Uses of a Liberal Education* (1819); and *Calvinism: The Doctrine of the Scriptures* (1849). As an educator and an educational reformer, he founded a theological college and in 1838 became the first president of Dalhousie College (which became Dalhousie University). As a social reformer, he started a newspaper in Pictou called the *Colonial Patriot* (1827). Nominated to the Senate of Canada in 1867, he resigned in 1871 to become a judge of the Supreme Court of Canada.

During his career as a minister and educator, McCulloch also put his political and social ideas into the form of popular satire. In literary circles, he is best known for writing a series of letters to the newspaper with observations about Nova Scotians from a fictional country correspondent named Mephibosheth Stepsure. The first sixteen letters appeared in the *Acadian Recorder* between Saturday, 22 December 1821 and Saturday, 11 May 1822; a second series of six responses appeared from 4 January to 29 March 1823. As a testament to their enduring popularity, they were published in book form as

The Letters of Mephibosheth Stepsure in 1862 and remain in print today. The letters are those of a self-righteous and frugal farmer who comments on the laziness and wasted industry of his neighbours. Through portraits of local citizens like the bankrupt merchants, or the publicans Tipple and Soakem and the gamesters Trump and Cribbage, McCulloch's lessons are simple: stay close to home, don't drink, attend to the soul, avoid ignorance, and work hard. In letter XVI, McCulloch focuses on two of his favourite targets of satire: vanity and laziness.

As W. H. New notes, "[A]lthough Stepsure (not McCulloch) may seem to a modern reader something of a pious fraud, his didactic function was clear in the 1820s. McCulloch was arguing through satiric fiction a case for reforming governmental and economic structures." McCulloch wanted a more industrious, well-educated, tolerant (in his Presbyterian terms) community. He tried to achieve this through his religious tracts, his educational acts, and his fictional letters. He greatly influenced future generations of satirists, including Thomas Chandler Haliburton, Stephen Leacock (whose character Dean Drone in *Sunshine Sketches of a Little Town* recalls Parson Drone here), and Robertson Davies (especially Davies's satirical newspaper column written by his fictional persona Samuel Marchbanks).

From The Letters of Mephibosheth Stepsure

Letter XVI

Gentlemen,—

Since I began to write my own life, a variety of events has occurred in our town: some of a pleasing and others of an afflicting kind. But the greater part of them it is not necessary to mention, for your readers would care about them just as little as our people care about the society which Saunders and a few others have begun, in order to improve the agriculture of the town. I shall therefore send you only a few brief notices, to show you how we are getting on; and first of all I may observe, that, for anything I can see, Mr. Catchem, poor gentleman, is likely to be ruined. I do not mean that he neglect his duty: but nobody will employ him: creditors now say that it is of no use either to sell property or put debtors in jail.

On the other hand, our townsmen who have been allowed to go at large, have, I assure you, been active in no ordinary degree. Between travelling to Mr. Gawpus' store, (which by the bye is now pretty well emptied,) attending the courts, looking into Tipple's occasionally, visiting each other to deplore the badness of the times, and going about their ordinary business, such as hanging all day about the mill or the blacksmith's shop, they have been very seldom at home. You must not, however, imagine that our people want industry. On the contrary, they rarely go abroad without making great bargains, and in the meantime, at home, they suffer no loss; for, except during spring, haying time, and harvest, they have nothing to do upon their farms. Indeed I may say, that, in having winter and misfortune together, we have been extremely lucky, for during that season of the year our people can not only talk about their troubles at leisure, but also do a great deal to make them sit lightly. Winter is the time of good cheer, which, you may depend upon it, we have not been neglecting; and good eating and thinking, you know, are a great comfort to persons who have hard times to bewail.

Nor have the youth of our town been less actively employed. But, as I have lately explained the nature of their education, it is not very necessary to detail what they have been doing. I must remark, however, that they, as well as the old people, have been experiencing hard times and misfortunes. Miss Sippit's tea party and frolic have not passed off with all the éclat which the young lady expected. Never had a meeting of our young folks excited such high expectations, and never before was there a meeting attended with so many serious disasters. Old Stot's son Hodge, in particular, poor fellow, is not likely to get over it soon. To record calamities, is a disagreeable task; but, in the present case, it is an act of justice to our town which ought not to be omitted. It will show you that we have society as elegant and refined as any other part of the Province, and, I am sure it will convince all your readers that when the children of farmers become ladies and gentlemen, they have a great deal to do and suffer, and deserve a great deal of praise.

I formerly stated that Miss Sippit, being relieved from the disagreeable necessity of preparing for death, had resolved to redeem her lost time, and celebrate her recovery by a tea party and frolic. This, of course, required a great deal of preparation and bustling about, such as borrowing a little flour here, and a little butter there; for, though we are a very genteel township, and before company make an elegant appearance, it would be foolish to suppose that our country gentlemen in general possess every thing requisite for the entertainment of a large party. Indeed I may say that the preparation extended to almost the whole town. Near every house, the fences indicated that our young gentlemen were getting their ruffled shirts in order; and the ladies, their gown or some other part of dress, for the joyful occasion.

At last the expected evening arrived, when our youngsters and Mrs. McCackle, who had been appointed mistress of ceremonies, convened in Sippit's. In commendation of this lady, I must observe that a better choice for conducting the business in genteel style, could not have been made. With the exception of Mr. Peter Longshanks, I question if there be another who knows half so much about the manner in which young people should behave in company. Under her direction, therefore, every thing was conducted with due decorum. Indeed it was the general opinion that our young ladies had never sitten so erectly nor displayed such a ladylike appearance before. The gentlemen, too, exerted themselves mightily to find out the best positions for their legs and arms, which, I assure you, is not easily discovered by a young country gentleman when he gets into a company where he thinks everybody looking at him. Upon the whole, however, Mrs. McCackle was very well pleased, and declared that as how they were the most graceful assembly she had ever beheld, and indeed how could it be otherwise? for all our young people and all their finery were there.

Having never myself been in such polite company, I must, of course, be ignorant of the general modes of proceeding, and therefore I shall not attempt to describe them. I understand, however, that it is the ordinary custom for the gentlemen to go about taking care of the ladies. In conformity with this order of things, Mrs. McCackle had requested old Stot's son Hodge to have the goodness to be so kind as to hand round the fried pork to the ladies. Hodge was upon the alert in an instant, and, as politeness required, determined to present it with an elegant bow, which, in our town, consists in pushing out the right foot and then bringing it back with a scrape upon the ground, at the same time bending the body forward with suitable solemnity. Now, it unfortunately happened that the young gentleman's shoes, which he had sent to the mending, were not ready in time; but in order to be at the frolic, he had put on a new pair of his father's, which the old man had carefully fortified with an abundant supply of hobnails, and scarcely had the poor fellow entered upon his bow, when a shriek from Miss Sippit admonished him that he had begun his scrape at her shin, and was subjecting her satin slipper to an unmerciful visitation. In such a case, it was natural for him to draw back his foot as fast and as far as possible; but, in his haste, it escaped him that where the head goes one way and the feet another, there is always a violation of the order of nature, and before he was aware, he had placed the fried pork, melted and unmelted, in the young lady's lap, and was himself fast following. Emergency, however, will, at times, produce wonderful exertion. One powerful effort relieved him from the apparent danger. But no man can think of two things at once; and, of course, he who is falling forward does not consider that there may be danger behind. Hodge only thought of getting back from the young lady, but in his haste to retreat, forgetting to take his legs with him, he unfortunately overturned the tea table and its contents upon Mrs. McCackle's new poplin. Whether this unusual combination of accidents had produced a sudden convulsion of nature, or whether Hodge had been dining upon cabbage, which you know, are a windysome kind of food, I cannot tell; but the poor fellow, in falling, made a lengthy apology, which scandalized the whole assembly of young ladies amazingly; and, indeed, no wonder; for such a speaker was never introduced into any genteel company, and much less allowed to lift up his voice.

Hodge is a stout-hearted fellow, and can bear with perfect equanimity any ordinary trial, such as losses upon a bargain or getting himself capiased; but here was an accumulation of sore adversities—adversities, too, which brought with them the loss of character. One spring placed the door between him and the rest of our young ladies and gentlemen, and since that time he has never been seen by any of them.

When matters in Sippit's were restored to a little order, the young people agreed to get on with the frolicking, and, accordingly Driddle was called; but the old man, having been obliged to fill himself with tea instead of grog, was seized with the belly ache very badly. Here was a real disappointment, for you may depend upon it that a fiddler with the belly ache has got other concerns to mind than either music or dancing. As Miss Sippit's piano was out of order, all hope seemed to be gone, when young Kickit recollected that he had seen Mrs. McCackle sing and dance at the same time. He therefore proposed that she should officiate in the place of old Driddle, and as a compliment to the old lady he insisted that he should open the ball with her. Mrs. McCackle, from the recollection of her damaged poplin, was not in a very tuneful mood; still she was willing to gratify the young folks, and no less willing to display her own talents. To it, accordingly, they went; and an elegant couple they must have been, I assure you. Kickit is one of our tallest young fellows, with legs like rafters, and as nimble as Peter Longshanks. Mrs. McCackle, too, is a handsome figure, only, not being a native of our town, she is a little differently formed. Nature, in the construction of the upper part of her frame, had forgotten that legs are an indispensable appendage, and, afterward, in order that the whole might be of a reasonable longitude, she was necessitated to add such extremities as suited the case.

Of the exhibition of this uncommon couple, you must not expect me to give you an account, for I am not very far seen in the dancing myself, and besides I was not there. I can only say, that in the opinion of our young people, between singing, and turning, and wheeling, and shuffling, and leaping, and skipping, it was truly enchanting. But just when delight was wound up to rapture, Kickit's foot, in one of his high leaps, thought of taking a look into Mrs. McCackle's pocket, and afterward, like every other violent possessor, positively refused to renounce its claims. Now, it would be unreasonable to expect that any lady would either sing or dance with a gentleman's foot in her pocket. I must, however, do young Kickit the justice to say, that he was still, if possible, more ready than ever to gratify the delighted spectators. Having parted, with one foot, he was even anxious to make the other do the business of two; and the more eager Mrs. McCackle became to withdraw from the enchanting scene, the more earnest he was upon the dance, and hopped around the old lady with surprising diligence, till at last a wrong step, from the want of the music, brought them both to the floor.

After a specimen of such superior style, none of the youngsters was willing to exhibit. They therefore agreed to disperse; but scarcely had they left Mr. Sippit's, when the violent rain of last week overtook them, and subjected the gumflowers and other finery of the town to a sweeping destruction.

Our young ladies and gentlemen, you see, are, as well as their parents, meeting with hard times. Still, great as their misfortunes and disappointments are, it is well for them that they are not in the hands of my neighbour Scantocreesh. Saunders declares that if his foot had been in old Stot's shoe instead of kicking Miss Sippit's shins and tearing her slipper, he would have broken the leg of the brazen-faced limmer. The old vagabond Driddle, he says, with his fiddling and drinking and corrupting the youth, deserves to be fed upon tea all the days of his life; and as for the rest of the ne'er-to-do wells, instead of letting them off with the loss of their trumpery, he would have applied a cudgel to their back and sent them home with their buttocks bare; and then, instead of junketing about the town, they would be glad to stay home and wear homespun, like other decent folk.

I now inform you that I have arrived at the end of the first book of the chronicles of our town; and, for a number of reasons, winter must return before I enter upon the second. In the first place, I have resolved to make the ensuing summer the busiest of my life. The exertions of you Halifax gentlemen to promote the agriculture of the Province, have suggested to me a great many improvements, which my present system of farming needs. These I have resolved to make; and when my neighbours are lamenting the badness of the times, and executing the present determination to raise nothing upon their farms till the prices rise, I will banish all discouraging thoughts by working a little harder; and if better times come, or if bad times continue, my good crop will be in readiness to meet them.

Secondly, I have got myself a great deal of ill will from many of the neighbours, who say that I have made them and our whole town a laughing stock to the rest of the Province. Old Grub, in particular, is very anxious about the mending of the trowsers. He says that the high dignity of his office ought to have been treated with greater reverence; and that, as clouting the covering of his nether extremities was no part of his magisterial duty, I had no right to meddle with it. He says also that things in our town are coming to a fine pass, when even the lame despise dignities; and he hopes to see the day, that, when worthy gentlemen are sitting upon the bench to maintain the honour of the town, Mephibosheth, and others like him, will be sitting in the stocks, as a warning to revilers.

That the worthy gentleman should be offended, has grieved me sorely. In vindication of myself I must say that the story of the trowsers was told expressly for the purpose of showing his care to maintain the high dignity of his office; for this honourable member of the bench does not always mend his trowsers in bed. But the truth is, that some of our young ladies happening to pass his house, and resolving to pop in and see what old Squire Grub was doing, the worthy gentleman descried them coming, and buried the unseemly parts of his frame among the blankets, which was, surely, more becoming the high dignity of his office than if they had found him in his ordinary way, as my neighbour Saunders expresses it. Indeed, he is, in many respects, as I may by and bye show you, a pattern of industry and economy, worthy of imitation.

Our reverend old parson, too, is not altogether satisfied. He says that, touching the matter of the swine, I have allowed my waggery to overrun my judgment: that albeit he did nourish and maintain a few of those unclean beasts for the sustenance of himself and his household, it was not for edification to hold up his labours among them as a spectacle to the world, and much less to place them before his public ministrations. Now, I positively assert that Mr. Drone is not even related to the Tulliber family. He does not feed pigs for sale—he has no delight in feeding them, and, in dividing his labours would, if possible, place the people of our town before them. But when our folks starve him, necessity has no law; pigs must be reared, and, of course, the feeding of the town limited to the remnants and husks of his time.

In the third place, I have got a character to maintain, and must take care not to lose it, as persons who are perpetually writing very generally do. Trudge, the pedlar of our town, is just come from Halifax with a large assortment of notions and news. Among other things he tells me that when he and Tug the truckman were taking a glass of grog together, they were both of opinion that my letters were a very clever thing; and farther, that a number of their friends were going to use their influence with government to get me a pension. This, you may be sure, was very gratifying to me; for every decent man likes to be respected by respectable persons, such as Trudge and his acquaintance Tug. At the same time I must confess that when Trudge told me the news, I had some misgivings about its truth, both because pedlars are privileged talkers, and also because when he was speaking about the pension, he was persuading my spouse to purchase a great bargain of a shawl, which would cost her only ten dollars. On this account, when my old woman was telling him that the first ten dollars of the pension should go for a shawl, I resolved not to believe all that he had said till I should learn the truth of it from some other quarter. Still I was very anxious to believe. You may judge, then, how much I was gratified when Saunders came running over with the Chronicle, and, in the speech of that worthy, clever-spoken, sensible gentlemen, the Honourable the Attorney General, pointed out to me the following words: "Turn where you will, folly and extravagance stare you in the face. That Gentleman, Mephibosheth Stepsure, had given us a picture of ourselves, which, he was sorry to say, was too true; but he did not approve of its being hung up in the newspapers for all the world to look at. But he should be obliged to him if he would go to every door in the province, and sound his reproofs in their ears. For his own part, he was surprised to see our extravagance in dress. The east and the west—the north and the south—the whole world was ransacked, to collect the rags which were to be thrown upon a young woman's back."

Who would have believed that lame Boshy would ever be called a Gentleman at a public meeting of the grandees of the Province? To say nothing of my own feelings, my old woman is wonderfully pleased, and says that honour will not be brought to shame by meeting with Mephibosheth Stepsure: that I am not like Puff and others of our poor gentry, who wear five coats and nothing in their pockets but an account from Mr. Ledger or a summons to the court. On the contrary, that having arrived at great respectability, I have something which will help to maintain the dignity of my character. Even I, myself, too, am beginning to think myself possessed of more dignity than I was formerly aware of; and I have a kind of notion that when I get myself seated in style, with a table before me covered with a green cloth reaching down to the floor, so as to keep my feet out of the way, I shall make a very respectable looking gentleman. My spouse seems to think that now when I am become somebody, reading the Chronicles of our town at every man's door would confer upon me more notoriety than honour, and, upon the whole, I am rather inclined to shift the business, for I am no great hand at the running; and, you know, it would be necessary to get away very nimbly from every door as soon as they were read. Old Trot, when he is going after the news, could do it very well; but the poor man is getting feeble, and could neither run very fast nor stand much beating.

Could the clever-spoken, sensible gentleman, the Honorable the Attorney General, be induced to comply with the plan of my neighbour Saunders, it would do the business completely. Saunders is delighted with his speech. He declares that it is as good as one of parson Drone's best sermons, and that the decent gentleman understands the ne'er-to-do-wells of our town better than they understand themselves. But to put the speech in the papers, he thinks, will do them no good, as they never read anything from one end of the year to the other, except, perhaps, an advertisement at the store or the blacksmith's shop. Could the worthy gentleman, however, be induced to come to our town, and say the same things over again, by advertising a cattle show or a town meeting at Tipple's, our people will turn out to a man; or, he says, that, though it be no credit to a decent farmer to be a constable, he and the rest of the hard-working, homespun neighbours, will get themselves sworn in to catch the villains and force them to the meeting; and as he will then be clothed with authority and have the law upon his side, his staff of office shall be faithfully used to command attention and to apply the doctrine. He thinks, also, that, as our females will of course be there to see that their husbands get full justice when the doctrine is applied, it would not be amiss to tender them a word of exhortation too; not that he wished to have any hand in the application, but he thinks that when their husbands are receiving instructions about industry, a few hints upon the subject of economy might be useful to themselves. Nothing, he says, has prevented our town from being one of the wealthiest places in the world but want of industry and want of economy.

But, as the execution of Saunders' plan is rather to be desired than expected, there is still another scheme which would be equally successful. Were every person who could stand an examination upon the Chronicles, to be made a magistrate or a militia officer, the most of our people would soon have them by heart.

Gentlemen, after telling you so many truths about the people of our town, I must now beg leave to say a few words to your readers. Some of them, I have been told, are a good-humoured, laughing sort of folks; and others are just as crusty and angry at the Chronicles of our town. To the former I would observe, that they have a right to laugh at themselves as much as they please, and when they get their laugh out to reform as fast as they can; but when they meet with their angry neighbours they should remember that laughing is a very serious thing, and ought to be tempered with a great deal of gravity, for no man in a passion likes to be laughed at. As for your crusty readers, they have just as good a right to be angry, and far more reason. I would advise them, therefore, to make themselves more angry still, which they may easily do, by telling everybody their complaints and receiving the consolation which their case deserves; and when they have thus learned that everybody is laughing at them, instead of continuing their displeasure against the exposure of folly, they might transfer their rage to the fools who needed to be exposed. For my own part, I am sorry that the

Chronicles have affronted them; very sorry, indeed, that their neighbours should be laughing at them; for I must say that all your readers would be a very decent sort of folks if they had only good management. They are not willing to be like lame Meph, whom everybody despised—nor like lame Boshy, whom nobody cared about; but, before they have well fixed themselves upon a wood lot, and raised a few potatoes, they wish to be like

Mephibosheth Stepsure, Gent.

[1862]

OLIVER GOLDSMITH ■ (1794–1861)

Oliver Goldsmith's poem "The Rising Village" (1825, 1834) is one of the most anthologized long poems in Canadian writing. Born in the village of St. Andrews, New Brunswick, on 6 July 1794, the author of "The Rising Village" was the third son of Henry Goldsmith, an Irish-born Loyalist, and the grandnephew of the renowned Irish poet Oliver Goldsmith (1728–74). The older Goldsmith was the author of the nostalgic pastoral poem "The Deserted Village" (1770), the comedy *She Stoops to Conquer* (1773), and the celebrated novel *The Vicar of Wakefield* (1766). "The Rising Village" is a direct response to "The Deserted Village" and mimics its predecessor in structure and form (both, for instance, are written in heroic couplets). The latter poem concludes with its destitute English villagers leaving for the New World; "The Rising Village" shows what became of these emigrants once they settled in North America.

In the dedication, Goldsmith places "The Rising Village" in the context of the earlier treatment of emigration:

The celebrated Author of the "Deserted Village" has pathetically displayed the anguish of his Countrymen, on being forced, from various causes, to quit their native plains, endeared to them by so many delightful recollections; and to seek refuge in regions at that time unknown, or but little heard of. . . . In the "Rising Village" I have endeavoured to describe the sufferings which the early settlers experienced, the difficulties which they surmounted, the rise and progress of a young country, and the prospects which promise happiness to its future possessors.

By shifting the setting from the fictional village of Auburn in England (or, it has been argued, Ireland) to Acadia (Nova Scotia), Goldsmith has also altered the tone from a reluctant pessimism to a guarded optimism. The older Goldsmith writes: "Ill fares the land, to hast'ning ills a prey, / Where wealth accumulates, and men decay." The later poem celebrates the challenges of developing the new land, but also advocates commercial and cultural progress in the name of British expansion. By the end of the poem, wealth accumulates and men can prosper in peace.

Goldsmith starkly contrasts "Britannia's" majestic palaces, bustling crowds, and bountiful harvests with the solitude of the "lonely settler" in the "desert woods" and "desert land." In its description of a growing Nova Scotian village, the poem supplies both a history of local agriculture and an allegory of settlement of the colony. A pastoral narrative in heroic couplets, the poem describes the important stages of almost fifty years of growth in the village, including imagined battles with "Indians," the establishment of the community's church, the evolution of commerce from the wandering peddler to the well-stocked shops, the development of education, and the maturation of the village. It provides a portrait of the colonial world that also carries with it some of the prejudices of the time, particularly with respect to the sublimely terrifying landscape and fearful "savages" perceived to be lurking in the woods. The poem applies Christian values to the settlement of the new land and details civilization's increased control over the wilderness. The embedded tale of Flora and Albert serves as an allegorical warning about the future of the newly deflowered land if treated with disrespect and abandoned. Compare the warning in the marriage poem "Advice to Mrs. Mowat" with the severity of the consequences of the "ruin" of Flora. Without her virtue, she is forever damaged.

"The Rising Village" was originally published in England in 1825, but was republished in Saint John, N.B. with some revisions in 1834. It clearly echoes Thomas McCulloch's defence of the need for moral virtues within a potentially chaotic society-in-formation. In this respect, Goldsmith's outlook on the British North American colonies serves as a precursor to the sentiments of Susanna Moodie's observations about the licentious but nevertheless egalitarian society that was being constituted in Canada. Curiously, while Goldsmith's poem ends on a note of loyalty to the new land and a call for its success, it also concludes by acknowledging the debt of the New World to Britain: "For wealth, for freedom, happiness, and ease, / Thy grateful thanks to Britain's care are due." In spite of the poet's place of birth, he is undoubtedly writing for a British audience as a colonial gentleman advocating the imperialist order. Tame the wild land and peoples; impose order, religion, commerce, education, and good governance; be mindful of your predecessors; and the colony will prosper in peace.

The Rising Village

Thou dear companion of my early years,[1]
Partner of all my boyish hopes and fears,
To whom I oft addressed the youthful strain,
And sought no other praise than thine to gain;
Who oft hast bid me emulate his fame[2]
Whose genius formed the glory of our name:
Say, when thou canst, in manhood's ripened age,

[1] The poem is dedicated to Henry Goldsmith, Esq., the poet's brother (1786–1845), who was a barrister-at-law and the collector of customs at the town of Annapolis Royal, Nova Scotia.

[2] Goldsmith refers to the fame of the older Oliver Goldsmith, the author of "The Deserted Village."

With judgment scan the more aspiring page,
Wilt thou accept this tribute of my lay,
By far too small thy fondness to repay? 10
Say, dearest Brother, wilt thou now excuse
This bolder flight of my advent'rous muse?

If, then, adown your cheek a tear should flow
For Auburn's Village, and its speechless woe;
If, while you weep, you think the "lowly train"
Their early joys can never more regain,
Come, turn with me where happier prospects rise,
Beneath the sternness of Acadian skies.
And thou, dear spirit! whose harmonious lay
Didst lovely Auburn's[3] piercing woes display, 20
Do thou to thy fond relative impart
Some portion of thy sweet poetic art;
Like thine, Oh! let my verse as gently flow,
While truth and virtue in my numbers glow:
And guide my pen with thy bewitching hand,
To paint the Rising Village of the land.

How chaste and splendid are the scenes that lie
Beneath the circle of Britannia's sky!
What charming prospects there arrest the view,
How bright, how varied, and how boundless too! 30
Cities and plains extending far and wide,
The merchant's glory, and the farmer's pride.
Majestic palaces in pomp display
The wealth and splendour of the regal sway;
While the low hamlet and the shepherd's cot,
In peace and freedom mark the peasant's lot.
There nature's vernal bloom adorns the field,
And Autumn's fruits their rich luxuriance yield.
There men, in busy crowds, with men combine,
That arts may flourish, and fair science shine; 40
And thence, to distant climes their labours send,
As o'er the world their widening views extend.
Compar'd with scenes like these, how lone and drear
Did once Acadia's woods and wilds appear;
Where wandering savages, and beasts of prey,
Displayed, by turns, the fury of their sway.
What noble courage must their hearts have fired,
How great the ardour which their souls inspired,

---

[3] Auburn is the name of the fictional village in "The Deserted Village."

Who leaving far behind their native plain,
Have sought a home beyond the Western main;   50
And braved the perils of the stormy seas,
In search of wealth, of freedom, and of ease!
Oh! none can tell but they who sadly share
The bosom's anguish, and its wild despair,
What dire distress awaits the hardy bands,
That venture first on bleak and desert lands.
How great the pain, the danger, and the toil,
Which mark the first rude culture of the soil.
When, looking round, the lonely settler sees
His home amid a wilderness of trees;   60
How sinks his heart in those deep solitudes,
Where not a voice upon his ear intrudes;
Where solemn silence all the waste pervades,
Heightening the horror of its gloomy shades;
Save where the sturdy woodman's strokes resound,
That strew the fallen forest on the ground.
See! from their heights the lofty pines descend,
And crackling, down their pond'rous lengths extend.
Soon from their boughs the curling flames arise,
Mount into air, and redden all the skies;   70
And, where the forest once its foliage spread,
The golden corn triumphant waves its head.[4]

How blest did nature's ruggedness appear
The only source of trouble or of fear;
How happy, did no hardship meet his view,
No other care his anxious steps pursue;
But, while his labour gains a short repose,
And hope presents a solace for his woes,
New ills arise, new fears his peace annoy,
And other dangers all his hopes destroy.   80
Behold the savage tribes in wildest strain,
Approach with death and terror in their train;
No longer silence o'er the forest reigns,
No longer stillness now her power retains;
But hideous yells announce the murderous band,
Whose bloody footsteps desolate the land;

[4] Goldsmith's note: "The process of clearing land, though simple, is attended with a great deal
of labour. The trees are all felled, so as to lie in the same direction; and after the fire has passed
over them in that state, whatever may be left is collected into heaps, and reduced to ashes. The
grain is then sown between the stumps of the trees, which remain, until the lapse of time, from
seven to fifteen years, reduces them to decay."

He hears them oft in sternest mood maintain,
Their right to rule the mountain and the plain;
He hears them doom the white man's instant death,
Shrinks from the sentence, while he gasps for breath,   90
Then, rousing with one effort all his might,
Darts from his hut, and saves himself by flight.
Yet, what a refuge! Here a host of foes,
On every side, his trembling steps oppose;
Here savage beasts around his cottage howl,
As through the gloomy wood they nightly prowl,
Till morning comes, and then is heard no more
The shouts of man, or beast's appalling roar;
The wandering Indian turns another way,
And brutes avoid the first approach of day.   100
Yet, tho' these threat'ning dangers round him roll,
Perplex his thoughts, and agitate his soul,
By patient firmness and industrious toil,
He still retains possession of the soil;
Around his dwelling scattered huts extend,
Whilst every hut affords another friend.
And now, behold! his bold aggressors fly,
To seek their prey beneath some other sky;
Resign the haunts they can maintain no more,
And safety in far distant wilds explore.   110
His perils vanished, and his fears o'ercome,
Sweet hope portrays a happy peaceful home.
On every side fair prospects charm his eyes,
And future joys in every thought arise.
His humble cot, built from the neighbouring trees,
Affords protection from each chilling breeze;
His rising crops, with rich luxuriance crowned,
In waving softness shed their freshness round;
By nature nourished, by her bounty blest,
He looks to Heaven, and lulls his cares to rest.   120

The arts of culture now extend their sway,
And many a charm of rural life display.
Where once the pine upreared its lofty head,
The settlers' humble cottages are spread;
Where the broad firs once sheltered from the storm,
By slow degrees a neighbourhood they form;
And, as its bounds, each circling year, increase
In social life, prosperity, and peace,
New prospects rise, new objects too appear,

To add more comfort to its lowly sphere.   130
Where some rude sign or post the spot betrays,
The tavern first its useful front displays.
Here, oft the weary traveller at the close
Of evening, finds a snug and safe repose.
The passing stranger here, a welcome guest,
From all his toil enjoys a peaceful rest;
Unless the host, solicitous to please,
With care officious mar his hope of ease,
With flippant questions to no end confined,
Exhaust his patience, and perplex his mind.   140

Yet, let no one condemn with thoughtless haste,
The hardy settler of the dreary waste,
Who, far removed from every busy throng,
And social pleasures that to life belong,
Whene'er a stranger comes within his reach,
Will sigh to learn whatever he can teach.
To this, must be ascribed in great degree,
That ceaseless, idle curiosity,
Which over all the Western world prevails,
And every breast, or more or less, assails;   150
Till, by indulgence, so o'erpowering grown,
It seeks to know all business but its own.
Here, oft when winter's dreary terrors reign,
And cold, and snow, and storm, pervade the plain,
Around the birch-wood blaze the settlers draw,
"To tell of all they felt, and all they saw."
When, thus in peace are met a happy few,
Sweet are the social pleasures that ensue.
What lively joy each honest bosom feels,
As o'er the past events his memory steals,   160
And to the listeners paints the dire distress,
That marked his progress in the wilderness;
The danger, trouble, hardship, toil, and strife,
Which chased each effort of his struggling life.
In some lone spot of consecrated ground,
Whose silence spreads a holy gloom around,
The village church in unadorned array,
Now lifts its turret to the opening day.
How sweet to see the villagers repair
In groups to pay their adoration there;   170
To view, in homespun dress, each sacred morn,
The old and young its hallowed seats adorn,

While, grateful for each blessing God has given,
In pious strains, they waft their thanks to Heaven.
Oh, heaven-born faith! sure solace of our woes,
How lost is he who ne'er thy influence knows,
How cold the heart thy charity ne'er fires,
How dead the soul thy spirit ne'er inspires!
When troubles vex and agitate the mind,
By gracious Heaven for wisest ends designed,   180
When dangers threaten, or when fears invade,
Man flies to thee for comfort and for aid;
The soul, impelled by thy all-powerful laws,
Seeks safety, only, in a Great First Cause!
If, then, amid the busy scene of life,
Its joy and pleasure, care, distrust, and strife;
Man, to his God for help and succour fly,
And on his mighty power to save, rely;
If, then, his thoughts can force him to confess
His errors, wants, and utter helplessness;   190
How strong must be those feelings which impart
A sense of all his weakness to the heart,
Where not a friend in solitude is nigh,
His home the wild, his canopy the sky;
And, far removed from every human arm,
His God alone can shelter him from harm.

While now the Rising Village claims a name,
Its limits still increase, and still its fame.
The wandering Pedlar, who undaunted traced
His lonely footsteps o'er the silent waste;   200
Who traversed once the cold and snow-clad plain,
Reckless of danger, trouble, or of pain,
To find a market for his little wares,
The source of all his hopes, and all his cares,
Established here, his settled home maintains,
And soon a merchant's higher title gains.
Around his store, on spacious shelves arrayed,
Behold his great and various stock in trade.
Here, nails and blankets, side by side, are seen,
There, horses' collars, and a large tureen;   210
Buttons and tumblers, fish-hooks, spoons and knives,
Shawls for young damsels, flannel for old wives;
Woolcards and stockings, hats for men and boys,
Mill-saws and fenders, silks, and children's toys;
All useful things, and joined with many more,
Compose the well-assorted country store.

The half-bred Doctor next then settles down,
And hopes the village soon will prove a town.
No rival here disputes his doubtful skill,
He cures, by chance, or ends each human ill;   220
By turns he physics, or his patient bleeds,
Uncertain in what case each best succeeds.
And if, from friends untimely snatched away,
Some beauty fall a victim to decay;
If some fine youth, his parents' fond delight,
Be early hurried to the shades of night,
Death bears the blame, 'tis his envenomed dart
That strikes the suffering mortal to the heart.

Beneath the shelter of a log-built shed
The country school-house next erects its head.   230
No "man severe," with learning's bright display,
Here leads the opening blossoms into day;
No master here, in every art refined,
Through fields of science guides the aspiring mind;
But some poor wanderer of the human race,
Unequal to the task, supplies his place,
Whose greatest source of knowledge or of skill
Consists in reading, and in writing ill;
Whose efforts can no higher merit claim,
Than spreading Dilworth's[5] great scholastic fame.   240
No modest youths surround his awful chair,
His frowns to deprecate, or smiles to share,
But all the terrors of his lawful sway
The proud despise, the fearless disobey;
The rugged urchins spurn at all control,
Which cramps the movements of the free-born soul,
Till, in their own conceit so wise they've grown,
They think their knowledge far exceeds his own.

As thus the village each successive year
Presents new prospects, and extends its sphere,   250
While all around its smiling charms expand,
And rural beauties decorate the land.
The humble tenants, who were taught to know,
By years of suffering, all the weight of woe;
Who felt each hardship nature could endure,
Such pains as time alone could ease or cure,
Relieved from want, in sportive pleasures find

[5] Thomas Dilworth was an eighteenth-century schoolmaster who produced textbooks including
Arithmetic and *A Spelling Book*.

A balm to soften and relax the mind;
And now, forgetful of their former care,
Enjoy each sport, and every pastime share.   260
Beneath some spreading tree's expanded shade
Here many a manly youth and gentle maid,
With festive dances or with sprightly song
The summer's evening hours in joy prolong,
And as the young their simple sports renew,
The aged witness, and approve them too.
And when the Summer's bloomy charms are fled,
When Autumn's fallen leaves around are spread,
When Winter rules the sad inverted year,
And ice and snow alternately appear,   270
Sports not less welcome lightly they essay,
To chase the long and tedious hours away.
Here, ranged in joyous groups around the fire,
Gambols and freaks[6] each honest heart inspire;
And if some venturous youth obtain a kiss,
The game's reward, and summit of its bliss,
Applauding shouts the victor's prize proclaim,
And every tongue augments his well-earned fame;
While all the modest fair one's blushes tell
Success had crowned his fondest hopes too well.   280
Dear humble sports, Oh! long may you impart
A guileless pleasure to the youthful heart,
Still may your joys from year to year increase,
And fill each breast with happiness and peace.

Yet, tho' these simple pleasures crown the year,
Relieve its cares, and every bosom cheer,
As life's gay scenes in quick succession rise,
To lure the heart and captivate the eyes;
Soon vice steals on, in thoughtless pleasure's train,
And spreads her miseries o'er the village plain.   290
Her baneful arts some happy home invade,
Some bashful lover, or some tender maid;
Until, at length, repressed by no control,
They sink, debase, and overwhelm the soul.
How many aching breasts now live to know
The shame, the anguish, misery and woe,
That heedless passions, by no laws confined,
Entail forever on the human mind.

[6] Games.

Oh, Virtue! that thy powerful charms could bind
Each rising impulse of the erring mind.   300
That every heart might own thy sovereign sway,
And every bosom fear to disobey;
No father's heart would then in anguish trace
The sad remembrance of a son's disgrace;
No mother's tears for some dear child undone
Would then in streams of poignant sorrow run,
Nor could my verse the hapless story tell
Of one poor maid who loved—and loved too well.

Among the youths that graced their native plain,
Albert was foremost of the village train;   310
The hand of nature had profusely shed
Her choicest blessings on his youthful head;
His heart seemed generous, noble, kind, and free,
Just bursting into manhood's energy.
Flora[7] was fair, and blooming as that flower
Which spreads its blossom to the April shower;
Her gentle manners and unstudied grace
Still added lustre to her beaming face,
While every look, by purity refined,
Displayed the lovelier beauties of her mind.   320

Sweet was the hour, and peaceful was the scene
When Albert first met Flora on the green;
Her modest looks, in youthful bloom displayed,
Then touched his heart, and there a conquest made.
Nor long he sighed, by love and rapture fired,
He soon declared the passion she inspired.
In silence, blushing sweetly, Flora heard
His vows of love and constancy preferred;
And, as his soft and tender suit he pressed,
The maid, at length, a mutual flame confessed.   330

Love now had shed, with visions light as air,
His golden prospects on this happy pair;
Those moments soon rolled rapidly away,
Those hours of joy and bliss that gently play
Around young hearts, ere yet they learn to know
Life's care or trouble, or to feel its woe.

---

[7] The Roman goddess of flowers and the spring (known by the Greek name Chloris).

The day was fixed, the bridal dress was made,
And time alone their happiness delayed,
The anxious moment that, in joy begun,
Would join their fond and faithful hearts in one.　340
'Twas now at evening's hour, about the time
When in Acadia's cold and northern clime
The setting sun, with pale and cheerless glow,
Extends his beams o'er trackless fields of snow,
That Flora felt her throbbing heart oppressed
By thoughts, till then, a stranger to her breast.
Albert had promised that his bosom's pride
That very morning should become his bride;
Yet morn had come and passed; and not one vow
Of his had e'er been broken until now.　350
But, hark! a hurried step advances near,
'Tis Albert's breaks upon her listening ear;
Albert's, ah, no! a ruder footstep bore,
With eager haste, a letter to the door;
Flora received it, and could scarce conceal
Her rapture, as she kissed her lover's seal.
Yet, anxious tears were gathered in her eye,
As on the note it rested wistfully;
Her trembling hands unclosed the folded page,
That soon she hoped would every fear assuage,　360
And while intently o'er the lines she ran,
In broken half breathed tones she thus began:

"Dear Flora, I have left my native plain,
And fate forbids that we shall meet again:
'Twere vain to tell, nor can I now impart
The sudden motive to this change of heart.
The vows so oft repeated to thine ear
As tales of cruel falsehood must appear.
Forgive the hand that deals this treacherous blow,
Forget the heart that can afflict this woe;　370
Farewell! and think no more of Albert's name,
His weakness pity, now involved in shame."

Ah! who can paint her features as, amazed,
In breathless agony, she stood and gazed!
Oh, Albert, cruel Albert! she exclaimed,
Albert was all her faltering accents named.
A deadly feeling seized upon her frame,
Her pulse throbb'd quick, her colour went and came;

A darting pain shot through her frenzied head,
And from that fatal hour her reason fled! 380

The sun had set; his lingering beams of light
From western hills had vanished into night.
The northern blast along the valley rolled,
Keen was that blast, and piercing was the cold,
When, urged by frenzy, and by love inspired,
For what but madness could her breast have fired!
Flora, with one slight mantle round her waved,
Forsook her home, and all the tempest braved.
Her lover's falsehood wrung her gentle breast,
His broken vows her tortured mind possessed; 390
Heedless of danger, on she bent her way
Through drifts of snow, where Albert's dwelling lay,
With frantic haste her tottering steps pursued
Amid the long night's darkness unsubdued;
Until, benumbed, her fair and fragile form
Yielded beneath the fury of the storm;
Exhausted nature could no further go,
And, senseless, down she sank amid the snow.

Now as the morn had streaked the eastern sky
With dawning light, a passing stranger's eye, 400
By chance directed, glanced upon the spot
Where lay the lovely sufferer: To his cot
The peasant bore her, and with anxious care
Tried every art, till hope became despair.
With kind solicitude his tender wife
Long vainly strove to call her back to life;
At length her gentle bosom throbs again,
Her torpid limbs their wonted power obtain;
The loitering current now begins to flow,
And hapless Flora wakes once more to woe: 410
But all their friendly efforts could not find
A balm to heal the anguish of her mind.

Come hither, wretch, and see what thou hast done,
Behold the heart thou hast so falsely won,
Behold it, wounded, broken, crushed and riven,
By thy unmanly arts to ruin driven;
Hear Flora calling on thy much loved name,
Which, e'en in madness, she forbears to blame.
Not all thy sighs and tears can now restore
One hour of pleasure that she knew before; 420
Not all thy prayers can now remove the pain,

That floats and revels o'er her maddened brain.
Oh, shame of manhood! that could thus betray
A maiden's hopes, and lead her heart away;
Oh, shame of manhood! that could blast her joy,
And one so fair, so lovely, could destroy.

Yet, think not oft such tales of real woe
Degrade the land, and round the village flow.
Here virtue's charms appear in bright array,
And all their pleasing influence display;   430
Here modest youths, impressed in beauty's train,
Or captive led by love's endearing chain,
And fairest girls whom vows have ne'er betrayed,
Vows that are broken oft as soon as made,
Unite their hopes, and join their lives in one,
In bliss pursue them, as at first begun.
Then, as life's current onward gently flows,
With scarce one fault to ruffle its repose,
With minds prepared, they sink in peace to rest,
To meet on high the spirits of the blest. [. . .]   440

[. . .] Happy Acadia![8] though around thy shore
Is heard the stormy wind's terrific roar;
Though round thee Winter binds his icy chain,
And his rude tempests sweep along thy plain,
Still Summer comes, and decorates thy land
With fruits and flowers from her luxuriant hand;
Still Autumn's gifts repay the labourer's toil
With richest products from thy fertile soil;
With bounteous store his varied wants supply,
And scarce the plants of other suns deny.   450
How pleasing, and how glowing with delight
Are now thy budding hopes! How sweetly bright
They rise to view! How full of joy appear
The expectations of each future year!
Not fifty Summers yet have blessed thy clime,
How short a period in the page of time!
Since savage tribes, with terror in their train,
Rushed o'er thy fields, and ravaged all thy plain.
But some few years have rolled in haste away
Since, through thy vales, the fearless beast of prey,   460
With dismal yell and loud appalling cry,

[8] Goldsmith's note: "Happy Acadia! The Provinces of Nova Scotia and New Brunswick now comprehend that part of British North America, which was formerly denominated Acadia, or L'Acadie, by the French, and Nova Scotia by the English."

Proclaimed his midnight reign of terror nigh.
And now how changed the scene! the first, afar,
Have fled to wilds beneath the northern star;
The last has learned to shun man's dreaded eye,
And, in his turn, to distant regions fly.
While the poor peasant, whose laborious care
Scarce from the soil could wring his scanty fare;
Now in the peaceful arts of culture skilled,
Sees his wide barn with ample treasures filled;   470
Now finds his dwelling, as the year goes round,
Beyond his hopes, with joy and plenty crowned.

Nor culture's arts, a nation's noblest friend,
Alone o'er Scotia's fields their power extend;
From all her shores, with every gentle gale,
Commerce expands her free and swelling sail;
And all the land, luxuriant, rich, and gay,
Exulting owns the splendour of their sway.
These are thy blessings, Scotia, and for these,
For wealth, for freedom, happiness, and ease,   480
Thy grateful thanks to Britain's care are due,
Her power protects, her smiles past hopes renew,
Her valour guards thee, and her councils guide,
Then, may thy parent ever be thy pride!

Happy Britannia![9] though thy history's page
In darkest ignorance shrouds thine infant age,
Though long thy childhood's years in error strayed,
And long in superstition's bands delayed;
Matur'd and strong, thou shin'st in manhood's prime,
The first and brightest star of Europe's clime.   490
The nurse of science, and the seat of arts,
The home of fairest forms and gentlest hearts;
The land of heroes, generous, free, and brave,
The noblest conquerors of the field and wave;
Thy flag, on every sea and shore unfurled,
Has spread thy glory, and thy thunder hurled.
When, o'er the earth, a tyrant would have thrown
His iron chain, and called the world his own,
Thine arm preserved it, in its darkest hour,
Destroyed his hopes, and crushed his dreaded power,   500
To sinking nations life and freedom gave,
'Twas thine to conquer, as 'twas thine to save.

[9] In the 1825 version of the poem, Goldsmith writes "O England! Although doubt around thee play's" instead of this line.

Then blest Acadia! ever may thy name,
Like hers, be graven on the rolls of fame;
May all thy sons, like hers, be brave and free,
Possessors of her laws and liberty;
Heirs of her splendour, science, power, and skill,
And through succeeding years her children still.
And as the sun, with gentle dawning ray,
From night's dull bosom wakes, and leads the day,   510
His course majestic keeps, till in the height
He glows one blaze of pure exhaustless light;
So may thy years increase, thy glories rise,
To be the wonder of the Western skies;
And bliss and peace encircle all thy shore,
Till empires rise and sink, on earth, no more.[10]

[1825, 1834]

[10] The final line of the 1825 poem is "Till sun, moon, and stars shall be no more."

ANNA BROWNELL JAMESON ■ (1794–1860)

Over the course of an adventurous life, Anna Brownell Jameson (née Murphy) was a traveller, a governess, a reluctant wife, and most importantly for Canadian readers, a writer. Born in Ireland and raised in England, Jameson was well connected to many important literary figures of her day. Her social network cut across literary, political, artistic, philanthropic, and feminist circles. Jameson was a friend of such notable figures as Lady Byron, Ottilie von Goethe, Harriet Martineau, Mary Russell Mitford, Robert Browning, and Elizabeth Barrett Browning.

By the time of her visit to Canada in 1836, the forty-year-old Jameson was already well travelled and well published. She had toured Europe for years, working as a governess for several prominent families, and had published works on a variety of topics. Her first major book, *The Diary of an Ennuyée* (1826), a fictitious account of her travels in Italy, was followed by an influential study of Shakespeare's female characters, *Characteristics of Women* (1832). During

a year-long visit to Toronto and environs, Jameson wrote her famous Canadian travel book, *Winter Studies and Summer Rambles in Canada* (1838). She journeyed to Toronto in an attempted reconciliation with her estranged husband, Robert Sympson Jameson, who was soon to become the first vice chancellor of the Court of Equity in the province.

Although Jameson only spent one year in Canada, the account of her travels remains valuable for the picture it provides of nineteenth-century sensibilities, genteel society, relations with First Nations peoples, and remote geographies. It provides a detailed description of the people she meets, their dress, customs, and personal histories, and the landscape she passes through. While *Winter Studies* details her rather contemptuous first impressions of Toronto, *Summer Rambles* describes her adventures travelling around Ontario by cart, steamer, and canoe. Setting herself up as an intrepid explorer and advocate for women's independence, Jameson writes: "[W]hile in Canada I was thrown into scenes and regions hitherto unde-scribed by any traveler and into relations with the Indian tribes such as few European women of refined and civilized habits have ever risked and none have recorded." She positions herself as a gen-tlewoman in search of adventure: "[T]he truth is that a woman of very delicate and fastidious habits must learn to endure some very disagreeable things, or she had best stay at home." The narrative voice dips between that of an adventurer and that of a proper gentlewoman. She is enthralled by the scenery and the people she meets, and yet is judgmental about their unseemly habits.

Jameson's accounts are multi-faceted. She is eloquent in her descrip-tions of southwestern Ontario. Describing the flora and fauna of Woodstock, for example, she writes that "no one who has a single atom of imagination can travel through the forest roads of Canada without being strongly impressed and excited." Like many settlers of the period, she describes the mosquito as her foe. Her greatest friends are the family of

Henry Rowe Schoolcraft (1793–1864), the ethnologist and author who was Indian agent at Michilimackinac. Jameson describes how she stays with the Schoolcrafts in Mackinaw and then travels to meet Mrs. Schoolcraft's family (the Johnstons) at Sault Ste. Marie. There, after she shows her daring and shoots the rapids (or rather, sits in a canoe while others paddle), she is given a Chippewa name, "Wah,sàh,ge,wah,nó,quà," meaning "the woman of the bright foam."

In the wide-ranging selections here from *Winter Studies and Summer Rambles*, Jameson is a disdainful society woman, an adventurer, a romanticist about nature, an ethnologist, and a storyteller. Her writing reveals a certain unpredictability in mood: the descriptions of Canada in 1836 range from high praise to sharp condemnation. For the contem-porary reader, it is particularly interesting to read her political comments on how the government breaks treaty rights with the "Indians," and to follow her path around a burgeoning Ontario.

From Winter Studies and Summer Rambles in Canada

Winter Studies in Canada

Dec. 20th, 1836

Toronto—such is now the sonorous name of this our sublime capital—was, thirty years ago, a wilderness, the haunt of the bear and deer, with a little, ugly, inefficient fort, which, however, could not be more ugly or inefficient than the present one. Ten years ago Toronto was a village, with one brick house and four or five hundred inhabitants; five years ago it became a city, containing about five thousand inhab-itants, and then bore the name of Little York; now it is Toronto, with an increasing trade, and a population of ten thousand people. So far I write as *per* book.

What Toronto may be in summer, I cannot tell; they say it is a pretty place. At present its appearance to me, a stranger, is most strangely mean and melan-choly. A little ill-built town on low land, at the bottom of a frozen bay, with one very ugly church, without tower or steeple; some government offices, built of staring red brick, in the most tasteless, vulgar style imaginable; three feet of snow all around; and the gray, sullen, wintry lake, and the dark gloom of the pine forest bounding the prospect; such seems Toronto to me now. [. . .]

Dec. 27.

With regard to the society, I can as yet say nothing, having seen nothing of it. All the official gentlemen have called, and all the ladies have properly and politely left their cards: so yesterday, in a sleigh, well wrapped up in furs and buffalo robes, I set out duly to return these visits. I learned something of the geography of the town—nothing of the people. Those whom I did see, looked somewhat formal and alarmed, but they may be very excellent people for all that. I returned trembling and shuddering, chilled outwardly and inwardly, for none of my fur defences prevailed against the frost and the current of icy air, through which we glided, or rather flew, along the smooth road.

The appearance of the town was much more cheerful than on my first landing, but still melancholy enough. There was little movement or animation; few people in the streets; some good shops and some brick houses, but the greater number of wood. The very different appearance of the town and bay in the summer season, the blueness of the water, the brightness of the verdure, the throng of vessels, the busy crowds along the piers, were often described to me, but without conveying to my mind any very definite or cheering picture. The very novelty of the scene before me, by strongly impressing my imagination, seemed to shut out all power of anticipation. [. . .]

Jan. 16.

This morning, before I was quite dressed, a singular visit was announced. I had expressed to my friend Mr. Hepburne a wish to see some of the aborigines of the country; he had the kindness to remember my request, and Colonel Givins, the principal Indian agent, had accordingly brought some Indians to visit us. Those to whom the appearance of these people is familiar and by no means interesting, were surprised by a curiosity which you will at least allow was very natural and *feminine*.

The party consisted of three—a chief named the White Deer, and two of his friends. The chief wore a blanket coat, and leggings, and a blanket hood with a peak from which depended a long black eagle plume; stout moccasins or shoes of undressed deer-skin completed his attire; he had about fifty strings of blue wampum round his neck. The other two were similarly dressed, with the exception of the wampum and the feathers. Before I went down I had thrown a chain of wampum round my neck, which seemed to please them. Chairs being presented, they sat down at once, (though, as Colonel Givins said, they would certainly have preferred the floor,) and answered with a grave and quiet dignity the compliments and questions addressed to them. Their deportment was taciturn and self-possessed, and their countenances melancholy; that of the chief was by far the most intelligent. They informed me that they were Chippewas from the neighborhood of Lake Huron; that the hunting season had been unsuccessful; that their tribe was suffering the extremity of hunger and cold; and that they had come to beg from their Great Father the Governor rations of food, and a supply of blankets for their women and children. They had walked over the snow, in their snow-shoes, from the lake, one hundred and eighty miles, and for the last forty-eight hours none of them had tasted food. A breakfast of cold meat, bread, and beer, was immediately ordered for them; and though they had certainly never beheld in their lives the arrangement of an European table, and were besides half famished, they sat down with unembarrassed tranquillity, and helped themselves to what they wished, with the utmost propriety—only, after one or two trials, using their own knives and fingers in preference to the table knife and fork. After they had eaten and drunk sufficiently, they were conducted to the government-house to receive from the governor presents of blankets, rifles, and provisions, and each, on parting, held out his hand to me, and the chief, with a grave earnestness, prayed for the blessing of the Great Spirit on me and my house. On the whole, the impression they left, though amusing and exciting from its mere novelty, was melancholy. The sort of desperate resignation in their swarthy countenances, their squalid, dingy habiliments, and their forlorn story, filled me with pity, and, I may add, disappointment; and all my previous impressions of the independent children of the forest are for the present disturbed.

These are the first specimens I have seen of that fated race, with which I hope to become better acquainted before I leave the country. Notwithstanding all I have heard and read, I have yet but a vague idea of the Indian character; and the very different aspect under which it has been represented by various travellers, as well as writers of fiction, adds to the difficulty of forming a correct estimate of the people. [. . .]

Toronto, February 7.
[. . .] It is a remarkable fact, with which you are probably acquainted, that when one growth of timber is cleared from the land, another of quite a different species springs up spontaneously in its place. Thus, the oak or the beech succeeds to the pine, and the pine to the oak or maple. This is not accounted for, at least I have found no one yet who can give me a reason for it. We passed by a forest lately consumed by fire, and I asked why, in clearing the woods, they did not leave groups of the finest trees, or even single trees, here and there, to embellish the country? But it seems that this is impossible—for the trees thus left standing, when deprived of the shelter and society to which they have been accustomed, uniformly perish—which, for mine own poor part, I thought very natural.

A Canadian settler *hates* a tree, regards it as his natural enemy, as something to be destroyed, eradicated, annihilated by all and any means. The idea of useful or ornamental is seldom associated here even with the most magnificent timber trees, such as among the Druids had been consecrated, and among the Greeks would have sheltered oracles and votive temples. The beautiful faith which assigned to every tree of the forest its guardian nymph, to every leafy grove its tutelary divinity, would find no votaries here. Alas! for the Dryads and Hamadryads of Canada!

There are two principal methods of killing trees in this country, besides the quick, unfailing destruction of the axe; the first by setting fire to them, which sometimes leaves the root uninjured to rot gradually and unseen, or be grubbed up at leisure, or, more generally, there remains a visible fragment of a charred and blackened stump, deformed and painful to look upon; the other method is slower, but even more effectual; a deep gash is cut through the bark into the stem, quite round the bole of the tree. This prevents the circulation of the vital juices, and by degrees the tree droops and dies. This is technically called *ringing* timber. Is not this like the two ways in which a woman's heart may be killed in this world of ours—by passion and by sorrow? But better far the swift fiery death than this "ringing," as they call it!

February 17.
"There is no *society* in Toronto," is what I hear repeated all around me—even by those who compose the only society we have. "But," you will say, "what could be expected in a remote town, which forty years ago was an uninhabited swamp, and twenty years ago only began to exist?" I really do not know what I expected, but I will tell you what I did *not* expect. I did not expect to find here in this new capital of a new country,[1] with the boundless forest within half a mile of us on almost every side—concentrated as it were the worst evils of our old and most artificial social system at home, with none of its *agrémens*, and none of its advantages. Toronto is like a fourth or fifth rate provincial town, with the pretensions of a capital city. We have here a petty colonial oligarchy, a self-constituted aristocracy, based upon nothing real, nor even upon any thing imaginary; and we have all the mutual jealousy and fear, and petty gossip, and mutual meddling and mean rivalship, which are common in a small society of which the members are well known to each other, a society composed, like all societies, of many heterogeneous particles; but as these circulate within very confined limits, there is no getting out of the way of what one most dislikes: we must necessarily hear, see, and passively endure much that annoys and disgusts any one accustomed to the independence of a large and liberal society, or the ease of continental life. It is curious enough to see how quickly a new fashion, or a new folly, is imported from the old country, and with what difficulty and delay a new idea finds its way into the heads of the people, or a new book into their hands. Yet, in the midst of all this, I cannot but see that good spirits and corrective principles are at work; that progress is making: though the march of intellect be not here in double quick time, as in Europe, it does not absolutely stand stock-still.

There reigns here a hateful factious spirit in political matters, but for the present no public or patriotic feeling, no recognition of general or generous

---

[1] Toronto was the capital of Upper Canada until the Act of Union 1840 amalgamated the provinces of Upper and Lower Canada into the Province of Canada and the capital moved to Kingston (1841–1843), Montreal (1844–49), Toronto and Quebec City (1849–1865), and finally to Ottawa (1866–).

principles of policy: as yet I have met with none of these. Canada is a colony, not a *country*; it is not yet identified with the dearest affections and associations, remembrances, and hopes of its inhabitants: it is to them an adopted, not a real mother. Their love, their pride, are not for poor Canada, but for high and happy England; but a few more generations must change all this. [. . .]

There is among all parties a general tone of complaint and discontent—a mutual distrust—a languor and supineness—the causes of which I cannot as yet understand. Even those who are enthusiastically British in heart and feeling, who sincerely believe that it is the true interest of the colony to remain under the control of the mother country, are as discontented as the rest: they bitterly denounce the ignorance of the colonial officials at home, with regard to the true interests of the country: they ascribe the want of capital for improvement on a large scale to no mistrust in the resources of the country, but to a want of confidence in the measures of the government, and the security of property.

February 18.
Toronto is, as a residence, worse and better than other small communities—*worse* in so much as it is remote from all the best advantages of a high state of civilization, while it is infected by all its evils, all its follies; and *better*, because, besides being a small place, it is a *young* place; and in spite of this affectation of looking back, instead of looking up, it must advance—it may become the thinking head and beating heart of a nation, great, wise, and happy; who knows? And there are moments when, considered under this point of view, it assumes an interest even to me; but at present it is in a false position, like that of a youth aping maturity; or rather like that of the little boy in Hogarth's picture, dressed in a long-flapped laced waistcoat, ruffles, and cocked-hat, crying for bread and butter.

May 19.
[. . .] This beautiful Lake Ontario!—my lake—for I begin to be in love with it, and look upon it as mine!—it changed its hues every moment, the shades of purple and green fleeting over it, now dark, now lustrous, now pale—like a dolphin dying; or, to use a more exact though less poetical comparison, dappled and varying like the back of a mackerel, with every now and then a streak of silver light dividing the shades of green: magnificent, tumultuous clouds came rolling round the horizon; and the little graceful schooners, falling into every beautiful attitude and catching every variety of light and shade, came curtseying into the bay: and flights of wild geese, and great black loons, were skimming, diving, sporting over the bosom of the lake; and beautiful little unknown birds, in gorgeous plumage of crimson and black, were fluttering about in the garden: all life, and light, and beauty were abroad—the resurrection of Nature! How beautiful it was! How dearly welcome to my senses—to my heart—this spring which comes at last—so long wished for, so long waited for!

Summer Rambles

The Island of Mackinaw

[July 25th]

[...] The next morning, at earliest dawn, I was wakened by an unusual noise and movement on board, and putting out my head to inquire the cause, was informed that we were arrived at the island of Mackinaw, and that the captain being most anxious to proceed on his voyage, only half an hour was allowed to make all my arrangements, take out my luggage, and so forth. I dressed in all haste and ran up to the deck, and there a scene burst at once upon my enchanted gaze, such as I never had imagined, such as I wish I could place before you in words,—but I despair, unless words were of light, and lustrous hues, and breathing music. However, here is the picture as well as I can paint it. We were lying in a tiny bay, crescent-shaped, of which the two horns or extremities were formed by long narrow promontories projecting into the lake. On the east, the whole sky was flushed with a deep amber glow, fleckered with softest shades of rose-colour—the same intense splendour being reflected in the lake; and upon the extremity of the point, between the glory above and the glory below, stood the little Missionary church, its light spire and belfry defined against the sky. On the opposite side of the heavens hung the moon, waxing paler and paler, and melting away, as it seemed, before the splendour of the rising day. Immediately in front rose the abrupt and picturesque heights of the island, robed in richest foliage, and crowned by the lines of the little fortress, snow-white, and gleaming in the morning light. At the base of these cliffs, all along the shore, immediately on the edge of the lake, which, transparent and unruffled, reflected every form as in a mirror, an encampment of Indian wigwams extended far as my eye could reach on either side. Even while I looked, the inmates were beginning to bestir themselves, and dusky figures were seen emerging into sight from their picturesque dormitories, and stood gazing on us with folded arms, or were busied about their canoes, of which some hundreds lay along the beach.

There was not a breath of air; and while heaven and earth were glowing with light, and colour, and life, an elysian stillness—a delicious balmy serenity wrapt and interfused the whole. O how passing lovely it was! how wondrously beautiful and strange! I cannot tell how long I may have stood, lost—absolutely lost, and fearing even to wink my eyes, lest the spell should dissolve, and all should vanish away like some air-wrought phantasy, some dream out of fairy land,—when the good Bishop of Michigan came up to me, and with a smiling benevolence waked me up out of my ecstatic trance; and reminding me that I had but two minutes left, seized upon some of my packages himself, and hurried me on to the little wooden pier just in time. We were then conducted to a little inn, or boardinghouse, kept by a very fat half-cast Indian woman, who spoke Indian, bad French, and worse English, and who was addressed as *Madame*. Here I was able to arrange my hasty toilette, and we, that is, General Brady, his aide-de-camp, the bishop, two Indian traders, myself, and some others, sat down to an excellent breakfast of white-fish, eggs, tea and coffee, for which the charge was twice what I should have given at the first hotel in the United States, and yet not unreasonable, considering that

European luxuries were placed before us in this remote spot. By the time breakfast was discussed it was past six o'clock, and taking my sketch-book in my hand, I sauntered forth alone to the beach till it should be a fitting hour to present myself at the door of the American agent, Mr. Schoolcraft.

The first object which caught my eye was the immense steamer gliding swiftly away towards the straits of Michilimackinac, already far, far to the west. Suddenly the thought of my extreme loneliness came over me—a momentary wonder and alarm to find myself so far from any human being who took the least interest about my fate. I had no letter to Mr. Schoolcraft, and if Mr. and Mrs. MacMurray had not passed this way, or had forgotten to mention me, what would be my reception? what should I do? Here I must stay for some days at least. All the accommodation that could be afforded by the half French, half Indian "Madame," had been already secured, and, without turning out the bishop, there was not even a room for me. These thoughts and many others, some natural doubts, and fears, came across my mind, but I cannot say that they remained there long, or that they had the effect of rendering me uneasy and anxious for more than half a minute. With a sense of enjoyment keen and unanticipative as that of a child—looking neither before nor after—I soon abandoned myself to the present, and all its delicious exciting novelty, leaving the future to take care of itself,—which I am more and more convinced is the truest wisdom, the most real philosophy, after all.

The sun had now risen in cloudless glory—all was life and movement. I strayed and loitered for full three hours along the shore, I hardly knew whither, sitting down occasionally under the shadow of a cliff or cedar fence to rest, and watching the operations of the Indian families. It were endless to tell you of each individual group or picture as successively presented before me. But there were some general features of the scene which struck me at once. There were more than one hundred wigwams, and round each of these lurked several ill-looking, half-starved, yelping dogs. The women were busied about their children, or making fires and cooking, or pounding Indian corn, in a primitive sort of mortar, formed of part of a tree hollowed out, with a heavy rude pestle which they moved up and down as if churning. The dress of the men was very various—the cotton shirt, blue or scarlet leggings, and deerskin moccasins and blanket coat, were most general; but many had no shirt nor vest, merely the cloth leggings, and a blanket thrown round them as drapery; the faces of several being most grotesquely painted. The dress of the women was more uniform; a cotton shirt, and cloth leggings and moccasins, and a dark blue blanket. Necklaces, silver armlets, silver earrings, and circular plates of silver fastened on the breast, were the usual ornaments of both sexes. There may be a general equality of rank among the Indians; but there is evidently all that inequality of condition which difference of character and intellect might naturally produce; there were rich wigwams and poor wigwams; whole families ragged, meagre, and squalid, and others gay with dress and ornaments, fat and well-favoured: on the whole, these were beings quite distinct from any Indians I had yet seen, and realised all my ideas of the wild and lordly savage. I remember I came upon a family group, consisting of a fine tall young man and two squaws; one had a child swaddled in one of their curious bark cradles, which she composedly hung up against the side of the wigwam. They were then busied launching a canoe, and in a moment it was dancing upon the rippling waves: one woman guided the canoe, the other paddled; the young man stood in the prow in a striking and graceful attitude, poising his fish-spear in his hand. When they were about a hundred yards from the shore, suddenly I saw the fish-spear darted down into the water, and disappear beneath it; as it sprang up again to the surface, it was rapidly seized, and a large fish was sticking to the prongs; the same process was repeated with unerring success, and then the canoe was paddled back to the land. The young man flung his spear into the bottom of the canoe, and, drawing his blanket round him, leapt on shore, and lounged away without troubling himself farther; the women drew up the canoe, kindled a fire, and suspended the fish over it, to be cooked *à la mode Indienne.* [. . .]

About ten o'clock I ventured to call on Mr. Schoolcraft, and was received by him with grave and quiet politeness. They were prepared, he said, for my arrival, and then he apologised for whatever might be deficient in my reception, and for the absence of his wife, by informing me that she was ill, and had not left her room for some days.

I leave you to imagine how much I was discomposed—how shocked to find myself an intruder under such circumstances. I said so, and begged that they would not think of me—that I could easily provide for myself—and so I could and would. I would have laid myself down in one of the Indian lodges rather than have been *de trop.* But Mr. Schoolcraft said, with much kindness, that they knew already of my arrival by one of my fellow-passengers—that a room was prepared for me, a servant already sent down for my goods, and Mrs. Schoolcraft, who was a little better that morning, hoped to see me. Here, then, I am installed for the next few days—and I know not how many more—so completely am I at the mercy of "fates, destinies, and such branches of learning!"

I am charmed with Mrs. Schoolcraft. When able to appear, she received me with true lady-like simplicity. The damp, tremulous hand, the soft, plaintive voice, the touching expression of her countenance, told too painfully of resigned and habitual suffering. Mrs. Schoolcraft's features are more decidedly Indian than those of her sister Mrs. MacMurray. Her accent is slightly foreign—her choice of language pure and remarkably elegant. In the course of an hour's talk, all my sympathies were enlisted in her behalf, and I thought that I perceived that she, on her part, was inclined to return these benignant feelings. I promised myself to repay her hospitality by all the attention and gratitude in my power. I am here a lonely stranger, thrown upon her sufferance; but she is good, gentle, and in most delicate health, and there are a thousand quiet ways in which woman may be kind and useful to her sister woman. Then she has two sweet children about eight or nine years old—no fear, you see, but that we shall soon be the best friends in the world! [. . .]

The scenes I at first described are of constant reiteration. Every morning when I leave my room and come out into the porch, I have to exchange *bo-jou!*

and shake hands with some twenty or thirty of my dingy, dusky, greasy, painted, blanketed, smiling friends: but to-day we have had some new scenes.

First, however, I forgot to tell you that yesterday afternoon there came in a numerous fleet of canoes, thirty or forty at least; and the wind blowing fresh from the west, each with its square blanket sail came scudding over the waters with astonishing velocity; it was a beautiful sight. Then there was the usual bustle, and wigwam building, fire-lighting, and cooking, all along the shore, which is now excessively crowded: and yelling, shouting, drinking and dancing at the whiskey-store—but all this I have formerly described to you.

I presume it was in consequence of these new arrivals that we had a grand *talk* or council after breakfast this morning, at which I was permitted to be present, or, as the French say, to *assist*.

There were fifty-four of their chiefs, or rather chief men, present, and not less than two hundred Indians round the house, their dark eager faces filling up the windows and doorways; but they were silent, quiet, and none but those first admitted attempted to enter. All as they came up took my hand: some I had seen before, and some were entire strangers, but there was no look of surprise, and all was ease and grave self-possession: a set of more perfect gentlemen, in manner, I never met with.

The council was convened to ask them if they would consent to receive goods instead of dollars in payment for the pensions due to them on the sale of their lands, and which, by the conditions of sale, were to be paid in money. So completely do the white men reckon on having everything their own way with the poor Indians, that a trader had contracted with the government to supply the goods which the Indians had not yet consented to receive, and was actually now on the island, having come with me in the steamer.

As the chiefs entered, they sat down on the floor. The principal person was a venerable old man with a bald head, who did not speak. The orator of the party wore a long gray blanket-coat, crimson sash, and black neckcloth, with leggings and moccasins. There was also a well-looking young man dressed in the European fashion, and in black; he was of mixed blood, French and Indian; he had been carried early to Europe by the Catholic priests, had been educated in the Propaganda College at Rome, and was lately come out to settle as a teacher and interpreter among his people. He was the only person besides Mr. Schoolcraft who was seated on a chair, and he watched the proceedings with great attention. On examining one by one the assembled chiefs, I remarked five or six who had good heads—well developed, intellectual, and benevolent. The old chief, and my friend the Rain, were conspicuous among them, and also an old man with a fine square head and lofty brow, like the picture of Red Jacket,[2] and a young man with a pleasing countenance, and two scalps hung as ornaments to his belt. Some faces were mild and vacant, some were stupid and coarse, but in none was there a trace of insolence or ferocity, or of that vile

---

[2] Chief Red Jacket (Sagoyewatha) (1750?–1830) was a Seneca leader with famed oratorical powers who lived in New York State.

expression I have seen in a depraved European of the lowest class. The worst physiognomy was that of a famous medicine-man—it was mean and cunning. Not only the countenances but the features differed; even the distinct characteristics of the Indian, the small deep-set eye, breadth of face and high cheek-bones, were not universal: there were among them regular features, oval faces, aquiline noses. One chief had a head and face which reminded me strongly of the Marquis Wellesley. All looked dirty, grave, and picturesque, and most of them, on taking their seats on the ground, pulled out their tobacco-pouches and lighted their wooden pipes.

The proposition made to them was evidently displeasing. The orator, after whispering with the chief, made a long and vehement speech in a loud emphatic voice, and at every pause the auditors exclaimed, "Hah!" in sign of approbation. I remarked that he sometimes made a jest, which called forth a general smile, even from the interpreter and Mr. Schoolcraft. Only a few sentences were translated: from which I understood that they all considered this offer as a violation of the treaty which their great father at Washington, the president, had made with them. They did not want goods,—they wanted the stipulated dollars. Many of their young men had procured goods from the traders on credit, and depended upon the money due to them to discharge their debts; and, in short, the refusal was distinct and decided. I am afraid, however, it will not avail them much. The mean, petty-trader style in which the American officials make (and *break*) their treaties with the Indians is shameful. I met with none who attempted to deny it or excuse it. Mr. Schoolcraft told me, that during the time he had been Indian agent (five-and-twenty years,) he had never known the Indians to violate a treaty or break a promise. He could not say the same of his government, and the present business appeared most distasteful to him; but he was obliged to obey the order from the head of his department. [. . .]

Shooting the Rapids

July 29

[. . .] George Johnston[3], on whose arm I was leaning, (and I had much ado to *reach* it,) gave me such a vivid idea of the delight of coming down the cataract in a canoe, that I am half resolved to attempt it. Terrific as it appears, yet in a good canoe, and with experienced guides, there is no absolute danger, and it must be a glorious sensation. [. . .]

The more I looked upon those glancing, dancing rapids, the more resolute I grew to venture myself in the midst of them. George Johnston went to seek a fit canoe and a dexterous steersman, and meantime I strolled away to pay a visit to Wayish,ky's family, and made a sketch of their lodge, while pretty Zah,gah,see, gah,qua[4] held the umbrella to shade me.

[3] Following her sojourn to Mackinaw Island, Jameson visited the Johnstons, the family of Mrs. Schoolcraft, at Sault Ste. Marie.

[4] Wayish,ky is Mrs. Johnston's brother and Zah,gah,see,gah,qua is Wayish,ky's daughter.

The canoe being ready, I went up to the top of the portage, and we launched into the river. It was a small fishing canoe about ten feet long, quite new, and light and elegant and buoyant as a bird on the waters. I reclined on a mat at the bottom, Indian fashion, (there are no seats in a genuine Indian canoe;) in a minute we were within the verge of the rapids, and down we went with a whirl and a splash!—the white surge leaping around me—over me. The Indian with astonishing dexterity kept the head of the canoe to the breakers, and somehow or other we danced through them. I could see, as I looked over the edge of the canoe, that the passage between the rocks was sometimes not more than two feet in width, and we had to turn sharp angles—a touch of which would have sent us to destruction—all this I could see through the transparent eddying waters, but I can truly say, I had not even a momentary sensation of fear, but rather of giddy, breathless, delicious excitement. I could even admire the beautiful attitude of a fisher, past whom we swept as we came to the bottom. The whole affair, from the moment I entered the canoe till I reached the landing place, occupied seven minutes, and the distance is about three quarters of a mile.

My Indians were enchanted, and when I reached *home*, my good friends were not less delighted at my exploit: they told me I was the first European female who had ever performed it, and assuredly I shall not be the last. I recommend it as an exercise before breakfast. Two glasses of champagne could not have made me more tipsy and more self-complacent! As for my Neengai,[5] she laughed, clapped her hands, and embraced me several times. I was declared duly initiated, and adopted into the family by the name of Wah,sàh,ge,wah,nó,quà. They had already called me among themselves, in reference to my complexion and my travelling propensities, O,daw,yaun,gee, *the fair changing moon*, or rather, *the fair moon which changes her place*; but now, in compliment to my successful achievement, Mrs. Johnston bestowed this new appellation, which I much prefer. It signifies *the bright foam*, or more properly, with the feminine adjunct *qua*, *the woman of the bright foam*; and by this name I am henceforth to be known among the Chippewas.

[1838]

[5] Jameson was asked to call Mrs. Schoolcraft's mother, Mrs. Johnston, "Neengai," meaning "mother," while Mrs. Johnston called Jameson "Nindannis," meaning "daughter."

THOMAS CHANDLER HALIBURTON ■ (1796–1865)

Remembered in literary circles as the creator of the "Yankee" con man Sam Slick, Thomas Chandler Haliburton was an accomplished lawyer, legislator, judge, and politician, as well as a writer. In his professional career he was a "liberal Tory," who established a law practice in Annapolis Royal, became a member of the Legislative Assembly arguing for close ties to Britain, and then became the chief justice of the Supreme Court of Nova Scotia. He published a wide range of books about maritime history and government, including *A General Description of Nova Scotia*

(1823); what many consider to be the first history of Nova Scotia, *An Historical and Statistical Account of Nova Scotia* (1829); and *The Rule and Misrule of the English in America* (1851). He also published several works of fiction—*The Letterbag of the Great Western* (1840) and *The Old Judge; or, Life in a Colony* (1849)—as well as two political tracts written in response to Lord Durham's appointment to the position of governor general. *The Bubbles of Canada* (1839) and *A Reply to the Report of the Earl of Durham* (1839) were written to denounce the Durham Report. The tracts express his opposition to several of Durham's recommendations, particularly his recommendations for dealing with the French. According to Haliburton, too many concessions had already been given to the Canadiens as conquered people. He also opposed Durham's suggestion of a federal union of the British North American provinces, on the ground that it would expedite the move of the British North American colonies toward further independence from Britain.

Born in Windsor, Nova Scotia, and therefore a "Bluenose," Haliburton wrote a series of satirical sketches that juxtaposed colonial Nova Scotia life with the progressive individualism of the American republic, in what has been designated British North America's first bestseller, *The Clockmaker; or, the Sayings and Doings of Samuel Slick, of Slickville* (1836). In these stories, a Nova Scotian squire accompanies the garrulous and entrepreneurial Sam Slick, an American clock salesman, on his sales circuit through the Nova Scotia countryside. The Sam Slick sketches were originally published in serial form, from September 1835 to February 1836, in Joseph Howe's Halifax newspaper, *The Novascotian*. Their immense popularity led Howe to collect the sketches into a book. However, Haliburton published simultaneous editions in Britain and America, including additional collections

of Sam Slick stories, and thereby eclipsed Howe's Canadian edition. Howe, who had shown such faith in Haliburton's work early on, was trumped by market forces and the precarious nature of colonial publishing, for there was no copyright protection in the colonies. He lived to regret his investment in the book as it gained more and more fame internationally.

With the publication of the Sam Slick sketches in England and America, Haliburton became one of the first Canadian writers to achieve "international fame in the world of letters," as a plaque erected to him in 1937 states. Over the course of twenty years, Haliburton published a total of eleven volumes starring Sam Slick, in Nova Scotia and later in England. In 1858, Haliburton's contributions to literature were recognized by Oxford University when he became the first colonial writer to be awarded an honorary degree in literature. Some critics call Haliburton the "father of American humour." Others call him the father of Canadian humour. (This is contested by those who give such an honour to Thomas McCulloch.) Known for his wit and his epigrammatic style, Haliburton is credited by R.E. Watters as the originator of many well-known phrases and sayings, including "There's many a true word said in jest," "conniption fit," "it's raining cats and dogs," "the early bird gets the worm," and "as quick as a wink." One of the first fiction writers to use colloquial dialect to indicate the cultural context of his stories, Haliburton was also an influence on the famous American writer Mark Twain.

Haliburton's humorous portraits of the brash "Yankee" clock trader Sam Slick illustrate the attitudes of Nova Scotians toward the republicanism of America. Through the voice of Sam Slick, he also criticizes the foibles of Nova Scotians, mainly their laziness and gullibility, as he describes Sam

Slick's travels around the province selling clocks. While it is ironic that Haliburton used an American to voice his opinion of Canadians, it is doubly ironic that the American Sam Slick, who is blessed with a keen wit, entrepreneurial skill, and unsnobbish manners, became a far more admired and popular character than the Nova Scotian squire with whom he travels. Indeed, it has been postulated that the popularity of Slick led to the sobriquet "Uncle Sam" to refer to the United States. One might say that Sam Slick and his Nova Scotian acquaintance, the squire, represent the reformist and conservative sides of Haliburton's own character.

Like McCulloch's *Letters of Mephibosheth Stepsure*, Haliburton's satirical sketches were written with the goal of promoting social and political change. The artist C.W. Jefferys, who illustrated later editions of Sam Slick, commented that "he was altogether a fine old reactionary who believed in pretty nearly everything that has been abolished or is now in process of demolition." It is indeed jarring for a contemporary reader to read some of the racist characterizations of ethnic minorities in the stories. While some criticize Haliburton's use of stereotypes, others read the Sam Slick sketches as a mirror of colonial society. His characters are still celebrated today: the town of Windsor, Nova Scotia, now holds "Sam Slick Days," a three-day festival in early August in honour of its venerable fictional citizen.

From The Clockmaker

The Trotting Horse

I was always well mounted. I am fond of a horse, and always piqued myself on having the fastest trotter in the Province. I have made no great progress in the world, I feel doubly, therefore, the pleasure of not being surpassed on the road. I never feel so well or so cheerful as on horseback, for there is something exhilarating in quick motion; and, old as I am, I feel a pleasure in making any person whom I meet on the way put his horse to the full gallop, to keep pace with my trotter. Poor Ethiope! you recollect him, how he was wont to lay back his ears on his arched neck, and push away from all competition. He is done, poor fellow! the spavin spoiled his speed, and he now roams at large upon 'my farm at Truro.' Mohawk never failed me till this summer.

I pride myself, (you may laugh at such childish weakness in a man of my age,) but still, I pride myself in taking the conceit out of coxcombs I meet on the road, and on the ease with which I can leave a fool behind, whose nonsense disturbs my solitary musings.

On my last journey to Fort Lawrence, as the beautiful view of Colchester had just opened upon me, and as I was contemplating its richness and exquisite scenery, a tall thin man, with hollow cheeks and bright twinkling black eyes, on a good bay horse, somewhat out of condition, overtook me; and drawing up, said, I say, stranger, I guess you started early this morning, didnt you? I did, sir, I replied. You did not come from Halifax, I presume, sir, did you? in a dialect too rich to be mistaken as genu*ine* Yankee. And which way may you be travelling?

asked my inquisitive companion. To Fort Lawrence. Ah! said he, so am I, it is *in my circuit.* The word *circuit* sounded so professional, I looked again at him, to ascertain whether I had ever seen him before, or whether I had met with one of those nameless, but innumerable limbs of the law, who now flourish in every district of the Province. There was a keenness about his eye, and an acuteness of expression, much in favour of the law; but the dress, and general bearing of the man, made against the supposition. His was not the coat of a man who can afford to wear an old coat, nor was it one of 'Tempest and More's,' that distinguish country lawyers from country boobies. His clothes were well made, and of good materials, but looked as if their owner had shrunk a little since they were made for him; they hung somewhat loose on him. A large brooch, and some superfluous seals and gold keys, which ornamented his outward man, looked 'New England' like. A visit to the States had, perhaps, I thought, turned this Colchester beau into a Yankee fop. Of what consequence was it to me who he was—in either case I had nothing to do with him, and I desired neither his acquaintance nor his company—still I could not but ask myself who can this man be? I am not aware, said I, that there is a court sitting at this time at Cumberland? Nor am I, said my friend. What then could he have to do with the circuit? It occurred to me he must be a Methodist preacher. I looked again, but his appearance again puzzled me. His attire might do—the colour might be suitable—the broad brim not out of place; but there was a want of that staidness of look, that seriousness of countenance, that expression, in short, so characteristic of the clergy.

I could not account for my idle curiosity—a curiosity which, in him, I had the moment before viewed both with suspicion and disgust; but so it was—I felt a desire to know who he could be who was neither lawyer nor preacher, and yet talked of his *circuit* with the gravity of both. How ridiculous, I thought to myself, is this; I will leave him. Turning towards him, I said, I feared I should be late for breakfast, and must therefore bid him good morning. Mohawk felt the pressure of my knees, and away we went at a slapping pace. I congratulated myself on conquering my own curiosity, and on avoiding that of my travelling companion. This, I said to myself, this is the value of a good horse; I patted his neck—I felt proud of him. Presently I heard the steps of the unknown's horse—the clatter increased. Ah, my friend, thought I, it won't do; you should be well mounted if you desire my company; I pushed Mohawk faster, faster, faster,—to his best. He outdid himself; he had never trotted so handsomely—so easily—so well.

I guess that is a pretty considerable smart horse, said the stranger, as he came beside me, and apparently reined in, to prevent his horse passing me; there is not, I reckon, so spry a one on *my circuit.*

Circuit, or no circuit, one thing was settled in my mind; he was a Yankee, and a very impertinent Yankee, too. I felt humbled, my pride was hurt, and Mohawk was beaten. To continue this trotting contest was humiliating; I yielded, therefore, before the victory was palpable, and pulled up.

Yes, continued he, a horse of pretty considerable good action, and a pretty fair trotter, too, I guess. Pride must have a fall—I confess mine was prostrate in the dust. These words cut me to the heart. What! is it come to this, poor Mohawk, that you, the admiration of all but the envious, the great Mohawk, the standard by which all other horses are measured—trots next to Mohawk, only yields to Mohawk, looks like Mohawk—that you are, after all, only a counterfeit, and pronounced by a straggling Yankee to be merely 'a pretty fair trotter!'

If he was trained, I guess that he might be made to do a little more. Excuse me, but if you divide your weight between the knee and the stirrup, rather most on the knee, and rise forward on the saddle, so as to leave a little daylight between you and it, I hope I may never ride *this circuit again*, if you don't get a mile more an hour out of him.

What! not enough, I mentally groaned, to have my horse beaten, but I must be told that I don't know how to ride him; and that, too, by a Yankee. Aye, there's the rub—a Yankee what? Perhaps a half-bred puppy, half yankee, half blue-nose. As there is no escape, I'll try to make out my riding master. *Your circuit*, said I, my looks expressing all the surprise they were capable of—your circuit, pray what may that be? Oh, said he, the eastern circuit—I am on the eastern circuit, sir. I have heard, said I, feeling that I now had a lawyer to deal with, that there is a great deal of business on this circuit—pray, are there many cases of importance? There is a pretty fair business to be done, at least there has been, said he, but the cases are of no great value—we don't make much out of them, we get them up very easy, but they don't bring much profit. What a beast, thought I, is this; and what a curse to a country, to have such an unfeeling pettifogging rascal practising in it—a horse jockey, too, what a finished character! I'll try him on that branch of his business.

That is a superior animal you are mounted on, said I—I seldom meet one that can keep pace with mine. Yes, said he coolly, a considerable fair traveller, and most particular good bottom. I hesitated: this man who talks with such unblushing effrontery of getting up cases, and making profit out of them, cannot be offended at the question—yes, I will put it to him. Do you feel an inclination to part with him? I never part with a horse, sir, that suits me, said he—I am fond of a horse—I don't like to ride in the dust after every one I meet, and I allow no man to pass me but when I choose. Is it possible, I thought, that he can know me? that he has heard of my foible, and is quizzing me, or have I this feeling in common with him. But, continued I, you might supply yourself again. Not on *this circuit*, I guess, said he, nor yet in Campbell's circuit. Campbell's circuit—pray, sir, what is that? That, said he, is the western—and Lampton rides the shore circuit; and as for the people on the shore, they know so little of horses, that Lampton tells me, a man from Aylesford once sold a hornless ox there, whose tail he had cut and nicked, for a horse of the Goliath breed. I should think, said I, that Mr. Lampton must have no lack of cases among such enlightened clients. Clients, sir! said my friend, Mr. Lampton is not a lawyer. I beg pardon, I thought you said he rode the *circuit*. We call it a circuit, said the stranger, who seemed by no means flattered by the mistake—we divide the Province, as in the Almanack, into circuits, in each of which we separately carry on our business of manufacturing and selling clocks. There are few, I guess, said the Clockmaker, who go upon *tick* as much as we do, who have so little use for lawyers; if attornies could wind a *man up again*, after he has been fairly *run down*, I guess they'd be a pretty harmless sort of folks.

This explanation restored my good humour, and as I could not quit my companion, and he did not feel disposed to leave me, I made up my mind to travel with him to Fort Lawrence, the limit of *his circuit*.

The Clockmaker

I had heard of Yankee clock pedlars, tin pedlars, and bible pedlars, especially of him who sold Polyglot Bibles (*all in English*) to the amount of sixteen thousand pounds. The house of every substantial farmer had three substantial ornaments, a wooden clock, a tin reflector, and a Polyglot Bible. How is it that an American can sell his wares, at whatever price he pleases, where a blue-nose would fail to make a sale at all? I will enquire of the Clockmaker the secret of his success.

What a pity it is, Mr. *Slick*, (for such was his name) what a pity it is, said I, that you, who are so successful in teaching these people the value of *clocks*, could not also teach them the value of *time*. I guess, said he, they have got that ring to grow on their horns yet, which every four year old has in our country. We reckon hours and minutes to be dollars and cents. They do nothin in these parts, but eat, drink, smoke, sleep, ride about, lounge at taverns, make speeches at temperance meetings, and talk about "*House of Assembly*."[1] If a man don't hoe his corn, and he don't get a crop, he says it is all owin to the Bank; and if he runs into debt and is sued, why he says lawyers are a cuss to the country. They are a most idle set of folks, I tell *you*.

But how is it, said I, that you manage to sell such an immense number of clocks, (which certainly cannot be called necessary articles) among a people with whom there seems to be so great a scarcity of money?

Mr. Slick paused, as if considering the propriety of answering the question, and looking me in the face, said, in a confidential tone, Why, I don't care if I do tell you, for the market is glutted, and I shall quit this circuit. It is done by a knowledge of *soft sawder* and *human natur*. But here is Deacon Flint's, said he, I have but one clock left, and I guess I will sell it to him.

At the gate of a most comfortable looking farm house stood Deacon Flint, a respectable old man, who had understood the value of time better than most of his neighbours, if one might judge from the appearance of every thing about him. After the usual salutation, an invitation to "alight" was accepted by Mr. Slick, who said, he wished to take leave of Mrs. Flint before he left Colchester.

[1] The House of Assembly in Nova Scotia is a unicameral legislature.

We had hardly entered the house, before the Clockmaker pointed to the view from the window, and, addressing himself to me, said, if I was to tell them in Connecticut, there was such a farm as this away down east here in Nova Scotia, they wouldn't believe me—why there aint such a location in all New England. The deacon has a hundred acres of dyke.—Seventy, said the deacon, only seventy. Well, seventy; but then there is your fine deep bottom, why I could run a ramrod into it.—Interval, we call it, said the Deacon, who, though evidently pleased at this eulogium, seemed to wish the experiment of the ramrod to be tried in the right place.—Well, interval if you please, (though Professor Eleazer Cumstick, in his work on Ohio, calls them bottoms,) is just as good as dyke. Then there is that water privilege, worth 3,000 or 4,000 dollars, twice as good as what Governor Cass paid 15,000 dollars for. I wonder, Deacon, you don't put up a carding mill on it: the same works would carry a turning lathe, a shingle machine, a circular saw, grind bark, and—Too old, said the Deacon, too old for all those speculations.—Old, repeated the Clockmaker, not you; why you are worth half a dozen of the young men we see, now a-days, you are young enough to have—here he said something in a lower tone of voice, which I did not distinctly hear; but whatever it was, the Deacon was pleased, he smiled, and said he did not think of such things now.

But your beasts, dear me, your beasts must be put in and have a feed; saying which, he went out to order them to be taken to the stable.

As the old gentleman closed the door after him, Mr. Slick drew near to me, and said in an under tone, Now that is what I call "*soft sawder.*" An Englishman would pass that man as a sheep passes a hog in a pastur, without lookin at him; or, said he, looking rather archly, if he was mounted on a pretty smart horse, I guess he'd trot away, *if he could.* Now I find—Here his lecture on "*soft sawder*" was cut short by the entrance of Mrs. Flint. Jist come to say good bye, Mrs. Flint.—What, have you sold all your clocks?—Yes, and very low, too, for money is scarce, and I wished to close the concarn; no, I am wrong in saying all, for I have jist one left. Neighbour Steel's wife asked to have the refusal of it, but I guess I won't sell it; I had but two of them, this one and the feller of it that I sold Governor Lincoln. General Green, the Secretary of State for Maine, said he'd give me 50 dollars for this here one—it has composition wheels and patent axles, it is a beautiful article—a real first chop—no mistake, genuine superfine, but I guess I'll take it back; and beside, Squire Hawk might think kinder harder that I didn't give him the offer. Dear me, said Mrs. Flint, I should like to see it; where is it? It is in a chist of mine over the way, at Tom Tape's store. I guess he can ship it on to Eastport. That's a good man, said Mrs. Flint, jist let's look at it.

Mr. Slick, willing to oblige, yielded to these entreaties, and soon produced the clock—a gawdy, highly varnished, trumpery looking affair. He placed it on the chimney-piece where its beauties were pointed out and duly appreciated by Mrs. Flint, whose admiration was about ending in a proposal, when Mr. Flint returned from giving his directions about the care of the horses. The Deacon praised the clock, he too thought it a handsome one; but the Deacon was a prudent man, he had a watch—he was sorry, but he had no occasion for a clock. I guess you're in the wrong furrow this time, Deacon, it an't for sale, said Mr. Slick; and if it was, I reckon neighbour Steel's wife would have it, for she gives me no peace about it. Mrs. Flint said, that Mr. Steel had enough to do, poor man, to pay his interest, without buying clocks for his wife. It's no concarn of mine, said Mr. Slick, so long as he pays me, what he has to do, but I guess I don't want to sell it, and besides it comes too high; that clock can't be made at Rhode Island under 40 dollars. Why it an't possible, said the Clockmaker, in apparent surprise, looking at his watch, why as I'm alive it is 4 o'clock, and if I hav'nt been two blessed hours here—how on airth shall I reach River Philip to-night? I'll tell you what, Mrs. Flint, I'll leave the clock in your care till I return on my way to the States—I'll set it a goin and put it to the right time.

As soon as this operation was performed, he delivered the key to the Deacon with a sort of serio-comic injunction to wind up the clock every Saturday night, which Mrs. Flint said she would take care should be done, and promised to remind her husband of it, in case he should chance to forget it.

That, said the Clockmaker, as soon as we were mounted, that I call *"human natur!"* Now that clock is sold for 40 dollars—it cost me jist 6 dollars and 50 cents. Mrs. Flint will never let Mrs. Steel have the refusal—nor will the Deacon larn, until I call for the clock, that having once indulged in the use of a superfluity, how difficult it is to give it up. We can do without any article of luxury we have never had, but when once obtained, it isnt *"in human natur"* to surrender it voluntarily. Of fifteen thousand sold by myself and partners in this Province, twelve thousand were left in this manner, and only ten clocks were ever returned—when we called for them they invariably bought them. We trust to *"soft sawder"* to get them into the house, and to *"human natur"* that they never come out of it.

[*1836*]

CATHARINE PARR TRAILL ■ (1802–1899)

In the popular imagination, Catharine Parr Traill (née Strickland) is a pioneer woman who struggled against the wilderness with a smile. Because of her characteristic optimism in the face of adversity, Margaret Laurence even goes so far as to call her "Saint Catharine" in her novel *The Diviners* (1974). However, Traill was far more complex than such a characterization suggests. While she writes, "[I]t has ever been my way to extract the sweet rather than the bitter in the cup of life," she is also the author of some of the most practical, well-grounded, rational advice of any settler writer. The daughter of a successful businessman who died leaving his family in a reduced financial state, Traill turned to her pen for needed income while still a teenager. Although she was the fifth of eight children in a literary family—seven of the children became published authors—Traill was the first to publish. The author of several children's books before she was married, Traill is best known for her books written in Canada on emigration and on natural history. Traill's writing about life in Canada spans over sixty years and several genres.

In 1832 Catharine and her Scottish husband, Lieutenant Thomas Traill, a retired veteran of the Napoleonic Wars, emigrated to Upper Canada to take up a land grant in Douro Township, near the Otonabee River close to Peterborough. British soldiers, at this time, were offered free land in the colonies. Proving that opposites attract, Thomas Traill once wrote: "I am not disposed to be sanguine about anything." Knowing that they had no chance of remaining gentry in Britain, they decided to emigrate to the promised prosperity of Canada. The Traills arrived within a week of Catharine's sister Susanna Moodie, who had moved to the same area, and seven years after Catharine's brother Samuel Strickland. The Traills, Moodies, and Stricklands had land adjacent or near to one another.

Faced with many hardships upon arrival in the Peterborough area, Traill once again turned to the income from her pen for survival. The mother of nine children, Traill was eminently practical in her writing. In *The Female Emigrant's Guide* (1854), she writes: "In cases of emergency, it is folly to fold one's hands and sit down to bewail in abject terror: it is better to be up and doing." In 1836, *The Backwoods of Canada: Being Letters from the Wife of an Emigrant Officer, Illustrative of the Domestic Economy of British North America* was published in London by the Society for the Diffusion of Useful Knowledge. It was indeed useful knowledge. Written as a series of letters to her mother and friends in England, *Backwoods* details the obstacles Traill and her family faced in their first two and a half years in Canada. The book tells of the challenges of emigration for women and children, and of the "domestic economy of the settler's life," as Traill writes in her introduction. It is a practical handbook for those Traill called "the wives and daughters of emigrants of the higher class of settlers." As such, it is a conduct book detailing everything a gentlewoman should know about what to expect and how to act upon finding herself in Canada. The book is meant to prepare women for settlement, because, as Traill writes, "this seems to be a complaint with all classes; the women are discontented and unhappy." Unlike Anna Jameson, who writes as a visitor to Canada, from the beginning Traill writes as a participant in Canadian life.

Originally published in England, *The Backwoods of Canada* was reissued at least eight times over the twenty years following its publication, but was not published in Canada until 1929. It is cited by many emigrants to Canada as a valuable practical resource. A recurring question in Traill's works, as well as in those of Moodie, is: Who is best suited to Canada? The answer for Traill seems to be the hard-working woman who is prepared to learn practical skills and who will rise to the challenges of a new geography. From the outset, we see a more appreciative view of the environment and a greater sense of awe at the inhabitants in the landscape compared with other writers of the time. Traill writes: "I must say, for all its roughness, I love Canada, and am as happy in my humble log-house as if it were a courtly hall or bower; habit reconciles us to many things that at first were distasteful." For Traill, "Canada is a land of hope; here everything is new; everything going forward; it is scarcely possible for arts, sciences, agriculture, manufactures to retrograde; they must keep advancing." And yet *The Backwoods of Canada* is not an emigration promotional pamphlet. Traill places long descriptions of the beauty of the land in sun and snow beside sketches of what she calls her family's "adventures and misadventures," including illness while travelling, enduring the extreme cold of February, suffering from the "ague," going hungry in the winter, and roasting in the heat of the summer.

Class is also an issue in the book, as Traill outlines interactions between settlers of different ethnic and social backgrounds. Like her sister, for instance, Traill seems to posit unquestioningly the inferiority of the Irish. However, unlike her sister, she tends to accept her dependence on her neighbours, regardless of their place of origin or their social standing. Further, by showing the extent of her own work and domestic labour, she demonstrates that the new settler cannot afford to retain strict class distinctions. Regardless of class positioning, an emigrant will not thrive unless she has a flexible approach to work and is willing to do the work that would be reserved for servants in England. For example, in her description of a house-raising bee, where others might focus on the work of the men building the house, Traill provides a full menu for the workers—including Canadian nectar (whiskey), salted pork, and rice pudding—and outlines her role organizing the food and drinks. Always sensible, Traill demonstrates that the settler cannot adhere to the class and social distinctions of England. Whereas Traill presents an optimistic narrative voice in light of such class fluidity, Moodie is harsher in her judgment of the people and the place. Moodie has more trouble transcending the class divides prominent in England, even though, over the course of their lives in Canada, both Moodie and Traill were in positions of deprivation and poverty. For several years, Traill could not afford food or clothing, let alone servants.

In spite of the fact that *The Backwoods of Canada* was well reviewed, quickly sold out its first printing of eleven thousand copies, and

went into several reprints in the next few years, Traill saw little profit. By this time, the family lived hand-to-mouth (with reports of the children sharing shoes or going barefoot in the winter, being sickly because of lack of proper nutrition and heat, and wearing threadbare hand-me-down clothing). Living off the sale of eggs and goose down at a local market, or simply off the generosity of others, Traill was unable to write for several years for want of ink, paper, or tallow to burn at night for light (she resorted to burning pine cones). In constant worry over her family's finances, Traill finally published "Forest Gleanings," thirteen sketches about life in the bush and the clearings. Relying on a favourite classic, *Robinson Crusoe*, her children's novel *Canadian Crusoes*, about two children lost in the Canadian woods, appeared to acclaim in 1853. Her next publication, *The Female Emigrant's Guide, and Hints on Canadian Housekeeping*, was issued in four instalments by the publisher Maclear in 1854 and 1855. It was brought together in a single volume as *The Canadian Settler's Guide* (1855) and subsequently published in numerous Canadian and British editions. Always practical, Traill included a chart detailing the "equivalent value of currency and cents from one copper to one dollar," along with instructions for baking and preserving fruit. The recipes from *The Backwoods of Canada* included here reveal the practicality of Traill's texts and show what the settler woman had available to her in her log kitchen.

Traill next turned her attention from emigration manuals to sketches of plant life. An ardent environmentalist, Traill was committed to cataloguing the specific animals and plants of Canada. Although she struggled to find a Canadian publisher for her naturalist writings, she eventually published *Canadian Wild Flowers* (1868) in collaboration with her niece Agnes FitzGibbon, who supplied artistic renderings of plants beside botanical essays by Traill. Years later, she published a larger selection of her work by subscription in *Studies of Plant Life in Canada* (1885). With these works she achieved fame as a distinguished naturalist. In recognition of the value of her work, she was awarded an island in the Otonabee River by the Canadian government. Her final work, *Pearls and Pebbles: Notes of an Old Naturalist*

(1894), published when she was ninety-two years old, shows her indefatigable dedication to nature in Canada.

Throughout her many works, Traill represented the "hardships and difficulties" of settlement life with a sense of wonder at the natural world and at the possibility of what she calls "female ingenuity," "expediency," and "high-spirited cheerfulness" in it. As someone who looked "firmly in the face" of the facts of emigration and life in early Canada and yet retained her optimism for the future of the country, Traill's iconic status is understandable.

From The Backwoods of Canada

Introduction

Among the numerous works on Canada that have been published within the last ten years, with emigration for their leading theme, there are few, if any, that give information regarding the domestic economy of a settler's life, sufficiently minute to prove a faithful guide to the person on whose responsibility the whole comfort of a family depends—the mistress, whose department it is "to haud the house in order."

Dr. Dunlop, it is true, has published a witty and spirited pamphlet, "The Backwoodsman," but it does not enter into the routine of feminine duties and employment, in a state of emigration.[1] Indeed, a woman's pen alone can describe half that is requisite to be told of the internal management of a domicile in the backwoods, in order to enable the outcoming female emigrant to form a proper judgment of the trials and arduous duties she has to encounter.

"Forewarned, forearmed," is a maxim of our forefathers, containing much matter in its pithy brevity; and, following its spirit, the writer of the following pages has endeavoured to afford every possible information to the wives and daughters of emigrants of the higher class who contemplate seeking a home amid our Canadian wilds. Truth has been conscientiously her object in the work,

---

[1] Dr. William Tiger Dunlop (1792–1848) was a soldier, doctor, journalist, land company agent (warden of the woods and forests for the Canada Company), farmer-settler, and Member of Parliament who played a key role around the settlement of the southeast shore of Lake Huron. His *Statistical Sketches of Upper Canada for the Use of Emigrants, by a Backwoodsman* (London, 1832) was very popular.

for it were cruel to write in flattering terms calculated to deceive emigrants into the belief that the land to which they are transferring their families, their capital, and their hopes, is a land flowing with milk and honey, where comforts and affluence may be obtained with little exertion. She prefers honestly representing facts in their real and true light, that the female part of the emigrant's family may be enabled to look them firmly in the face; to find a remedy in female ingenuity and expediency for some difficulties; and, by being properly prepared, encounter the rest with that high-spirited cheerfulness of which well-educated females often give extraordinary proofs. She likewise wishes to teach them to discard every thing exclusively pertaining to the artificial refinement of fashionable life in England; and to point out that, by devoting the money consumed in these incumbrances to articles of real use, which cannot be readily obtained in Canada, they may enjoy the pleasure of superintending a pleasant, well-ordered home. She is desirous of giving them the advantage of her three years' experience, that they may properly apply every part of their time, and learn to consider that every pound or pound's worth belonging to any member of an out-coming emigrant's family, ought to be sacredly considered as *capital*, which must make proper returns either as the means of bringing increase in the shape of income, or, what is still better, in healthful domestic comfort.

These exhalations in behalf of utility in preference to artificial personal refinement, are not so needless as the English public may consider. The emigrants to British America are no longer of the rank of life that formerly left the shores of the British Isles. It is not only the poor husbandmen and artisans, that move in vast bodies to the west, but it is the enterprising English capitalist, and the once affluent landholder, alarmed at the difficulties of establishing numerous families in independence, in a country where every profession is overstocked, that join the bands that Great Britain is pouring forth into these colonies! Of what vital importance is it that the female members of these most valuable colonists should obtain proper information regarding the important duties they are undertaking; that they should learn beforehand to brace their minds to the task, and thus avoid the repinings and discontent that is apt to follow unfounded expectations and fallacious hopes!

It is a fact not universally known to the public, that British officers and their families are usually denizens of the backwoods; and as great numbers of unattached officers of every rank have accepted grants of land in Canada, they are the pioneers of civilization in the wilderness, and their families, often of delicate nurture and honourable descent, are at once plunged into all the hardships attendant on the rough life of a bush-settler. The laws that regulate the grants of lands, which enforce a certain time of residence, and certain settlement duties to be performed, allow no claims to absentees when once the land is drawn. These laws wisely force a superiorly-educated man with resources of both property and intellect, to devote all his energies to a certain spot of uncleared land. It may easily be supposed that no persons would encounter these hardships who have not a young family to establish in the healthful ways of independence. This family renders the residence of such a head still more valuable to the colony; and the half-pay officer, by thus leading the advanced guard of civilization, and bringing into these rough districts gentle and well-educated females, who soften and improve all around them by *mental* refinements, is serving his country as much by founding peaceful villages and pleasant homesteads in the trackless wilds, as ever he did by personal courage, or military stratagem, in times of war.

It will be seen, in the course of this work, that the writer is as earnest in recommending ladies who belong to the higher class of settlers to cultivate all the mental resources of a superior education, as she is to induce them to discard all irrational and artificial wants and mere useless pursuits. She would willingly direct their attention to the natural history and botany of this new country, in which they will find a never-failing source of amusement and instruction, at once enlightening and elevating the mind, and serving to fill up the void left by the absence of those lighter feminine accomplishments, the practice of which are necessarily superseded by imperative domestic duties. To the person who is capable of looking abroad into the beauties of nature, and adoring the Creator through his glorious works, are opened stores of unmixed pleasure, which will not permit her to be dull or unhappy in the loneliest part of our Western Wilderness. The writer of these pages speaks from experience, and would be pleased to find that the simple sources from which she has herself drawn pleasure, have cheered the solitude of future female sojourners in the backwoods of Canada.

As a general remark to all sorts and conditions of settlers, she would observe, that the struggle up the hill of Independence is often a severe one, and it ought not to be made alone. It must be aided and encouraged by the example and assistance of an active and cheerful partner. Children should be taught to appreciate the devoted love that has induced their parents to overcome the natural reluctance felt by all persons to quit for ever the land of their forefathers, the scenes of their earliest and happiest days, and to become aliens and wanderers in a distant country,—to form new ties and new friends, and begin, as it were, life's toilsome march anew, that their children may be placed in a situation in which, by industry and activity, the substantial comforts of life may be permanently obtained, and a landed property handed down to them, and their children after them.

Young men soon become reconciled to this country, which offers to them that chief attraction to youth,—great personal liberty. Their employments are of a cheerful and healthy nature; and their amusements, such as hunting, shooting, fishing, and boating, are peculiarly fascinating. But in none of these can their sisters share. The hardships and difficulties of the settler's life, therefore, are felt peculiarly by the female part of the family. It is with a view of ameliorating these privations that the following pages have been written, to show how some difficulties may be best borne and others avoided. The simple truth, founded entirely on personal knowledge of the facts related, is the basis of the work; to have had recourse to fiction might have rendered it more acceptable to many readers, but would have made it less useful to that class for whom it is especially intended. For those who, without intending to share in the privations and dangers of an emigrant's life, have a rational curiosity to become acquainted with scenes and manners so different from those of a long-civilized country, it is hoped that this little work will afford some amusement, and inculcate some lessons not devoid of moral instruction.

Letter 15

September the 20th, 1834.
I promised when I parted from you before I left England to write as soon as I could give you any satisfactory account of our settlement in this country. I shall do my best to redeem that promise, and forward you a slight sketch of our proceedings, with such remarks on the natural features of the place in which we have fixed our abode, as I think likely to afford you interest or amusement. [. . .]

You will have heard, through my letters to my dear mother, of our safe arrival at Quebec, of my illness at Montreal, of all our adventures and misadventures during our journey up the country, till after much weary wandering we finally found a home and resting-place with a kind relative, whom it was our happiness to meet after a separation of many years.

As my husband was anxious to settle in the neighbourhood of one so nearly connected with me,[2] thinking it would rob the woods of some of the loneliness that most women complain so bitterly of, he purchased a lot of land on the shores of a beautiful lake, one of a chain of small lakes belonging to the Otanabee[3] river.

Here, then, we are established, having now some five-and-twenty acres cleared, and a nice house built. Our situation is very agreeable, and each day increases its value. When we first came up to live in the bush, with the exception of S——, here were but two or three settlers near us, and no roads cut out. The only road that was available for bringing up goods from the nearest town was on the opposite side of the water, which was obliged to be crossed in a log, (known by the expressive name of a dug-out), or birch-bark canoe; the former is nothing better than a large pine-log hollowed with the axe, so as to contain three or four persons; it is flat-bottomed, and very narrow, on which account it is much used on these shallow waters. The birch canoe is made of sheets of birch bark, ingeniously fashioned and sewn together by the Indians with the tough roots of the cedar, young pine, or larch (tamarack, as it is termed by the Indians); it is exceedingly light, so that it can be carried by two persons easily, or even by one. These

[2] Samuel Strickland, Traill's brother, had been a settler near the Otonabee River in Douro Township since 1825.

[3] The "Otanabee" River is now generally spelled "Otonabee" River.

then, were our ferry-boats, and very frail they are, and require great nicety in their management, they are worked in the water with paddles, either kneeling or standing. The squaws are very expert in the management of the canoes, and preserve their balance with admirable skill, standing up while they impel the little bark with great velocity through the water.

Very great is the change that a few years have effected in our situation. A number of highly respectable settlers have purchased land along the shores of these lakes, so that we no longer want society. The roads are now cut several miles above us, and though far from good can be travelled by waggons and sleighs, and are, at all events, better than none.

A village has started up where formerly a thick pine-wood covered the ground, we have now within a short distance of us an excellent saw-mill, a grist-mill, and store, with a large tavern and many good dwellings. A fine timber bridge, on stone piers, was erected last year to connect the opposite townships and lessen the distance to and from Peterborough; and though it was unfortunately swept away early last spring by the unusual rising of the Otanabee lakes, a new and more substantial one has risen upon the ruins of the former, through the activity of an enterprising young Scotchman, the founder of the village. [. . .]

Canada is the land of hope; here every thing is new; every thing going forward; it is scarcely possible for arts, sciences, agriculture, manufactures, to retrograde; they must keep advancing; though in some situations the progress may seem slow, in others they are proportionably rapid.

There is a constant excitement on the minds of emigrants, particularly in the partially settled townships, that greatly assists in keeping them from desponding. The arrival of some enterprising person gives a stimulus to those about him: a profitable speculation is started, and lo, the value of the land in the vicinity rises to double and treble what it was thought worth before; so that, without any design of befriending his neighbours, the schemes of one settler being carried into effect shall benefit a great number. We have already felt the beneficial effect of the access of respectable emigrants locating themselves in this township, as it has already increased the value of our own land in a three-fold degree.

All this, my dear friend, you will say is very well, and might afford subject for a wise discussion between grave men, but will hardly amuse us women; so pray turn to some other theme, and just tell me how you contrive to pass your time among the bears and wolves of Canada.

One lovely day last June I went by water to visit the bride of a young naval officer, who had purchased a very pretty lot of land some two miles higher up the lake; our party consisted of my husband, baby, and myself; we met a few pleasant friends, and enjoyed our excursion much. Dinner was laid out in the *stoup*, which, as you may not know what is meant by the word, I must tell you that it means a sort of wide verandah, supported on pillars, often of unbarked logs; the floor is either of earth, beaten hard, or plank; the roof covered with sheets of bark, or else shingled. These stoups are of Dutch origin, and were introduced, I have been told, by the first Dutch settlers in the states, since which they have found their way all over the colonies.

Wreathed with the scarlet creeper, a native plant of our woods and wilds, the wild vine, and also with the hop, which here grows luxuriantly, with no labour or attention to its culture, these stoups have a very rural appearance; in summer serving the purpose of an open ante-room, in which you can take your meals and enjoy the fanning breeze without being inconvenienced by the extreme heat of the noon-day sun.

The situation of the house was remarkably well chosen, just on the summit of a little elevated plain, the ground sloping with a steep descent to a little valley, at the bottom of which a bright rill of water divided the garden from the opposite corn-fields, which clothed a corresponding bank. In front of the stoup, where we dined, the garden was laid out with a smooth plot of grass, surrounded with borders of flowers, and separated from a ripening field of wheat by a light railed fence, over which the luxuriant hop-vine flung its tendrils and graceful blossoms. Now I must tell you the hop is cultivated for the purpose of making a barm for raising bread. As you take great interest in housewifery concerns, I shall send you a recipe for what we call hop-rising.

The Yankees use a fermentation of salt, flour, and warm water or milk; but though the *salt-rising* makes beautiful bread to look at, being far whiter and firmer than the hop-yeast bread, there is a peculiar flavour imparted to the flour that does not please every one's taste, and it is very difficult to get your salt-rising to work in very cold weather.

And now, having digressed while I gave you my recipes, I shall step back to my party within the stoup, which, I can assure you, was very pleasant, and most cordially disposed to enjoy the meeting. We had books and drawings, and good store of pretty Indian toys, the collection of many long voyages to distant shores, to look at and admire. Soon after sun-set we walked down through the woods to the landing at the lake shore, where we found our bark canoe ready to convey us home.

During our voyage, just at the head of the rapids, our attention was drawn to some small object in the water, moving very swiftly along; there were various opinions as to the swimmer, some thinking it to be a water-snake, others a squirrel, or a musk-rat; a few swift strokes of the paddles brought us up so as to intercept the passage of the little voyager; it proved to be a fine red squirrel, bound on a voyage of discovery from a neighbouring island. The little animal, with a courage and address that astonished his pursuers, instead of seeking safety in a different direction, sprung lightly on the point of the uplifted paddle, and from thence with a bound to the head of my astonished baby, and having gained my shoulder, leaped again into the water, and made direct for the shore, never having deviated a single point from the line he was swimming in when he first came in sight of our canoe. I was surprised and amused by the agility and courage displayed by this innocent creature; I could hardly have given credence to the circumstance, had I not been an eye-witness of its conduct, and moreover been wetted plentifully on my shoulder by the sprinkling of water from his coat. [. . .]

How my little friend Emily would delight in such a pet! Tell her if ever I should return to dear old England, I will try to procure one for her; but at present she must be contented with the stuffed specimens of the black, red, and striped squirrels which I enclose in my parcel. I wish I could offer you any present more valuable, but our arts and manufactures being entirely British, with the exception of the Indians' toys, I should find it a difficult matter to send you any thing worth your attention; therefore I am obliged to have recourse to the natural productions of our woods as tokens of remembrance to our friends *at home*, for it is ever thus we speak of the land of our birth.

You wish to know if I am happy and contented in my situation, or if my heart pines after my native land. I will answer you candidly, and say that, as far as regards matters of taste, early association, and all those holy ties of kindred, and old affections that make "home" in all countries, and among all nations in the world, a hallowed spot, I must ever give the preference to Britain.

On the other hand, a sense of the duties I have chosen, and a feeling of conformity to one's situation, lessen the regret I might be inclined to indulge in. Besides, there are new and delightful ties that bind me to Canada: I have enjoyed much domestic happiness since I came hither,—and is it not the birthplace of my dear child? Have I not here first tasted the rapturous delight arising from maternal feelings? When my eye rests on my smiling darling, or I feel his warm breath upon my cheek, I would not exchange the joy that fills my breast for any pleasure the world could offer me. "But this feeling is not confined to the solitude of your Canadian forests, my dear friend," you will say. I know it; but here there is nothing to interfere with your little nursling. You are not tempted by the pleasures of a gay world to forget your duties as a mother; there is nothing to supplant him in your heart; his presence endears every place; and you learn to love the spot that gave him birth, and to think with complacency upon the country, because it is *his* country; and in looking forward to his future welfare you naturally become doubly interested in the place that is one day to be his.

Perhaps I rather estimate the country by my own feelings; and when I find, by impartial survey of my present life, that I am to the full as happy, if not really happier, than I was in the old country, I cannot but value it.

Possibly, if I were to enter into a detail of the advantages I possess, they would appear of a very negative character in the eyes of persons revelling in all the splendour and luxury that wealth could procure, in a country in which nature and art are so eminently favourable towards what is usually termed the pleasures of life; but I never was a votary at the shrine of luxury or fashion. A round of company, a routine of pleasure, were to me sources of weariness, if not of disgust. "There's nothing in all this to satisfy the heart," says Schiller; and I admit the force of the sentiment.

I was too much inclined to spurn with impatience the fetters that etiquette and fashion are wont to impose on society, till they rob its followers of all freedom and independence of will; and they soon are obliged to live for a world that in secret they despise and loathe, for a world, too, that usually regards them with contempt, because they dare not act with an independence, which would be crushed directly it was displayed.

And I must freely confess to you that I do prize and enjoy my present liberty in this country exceedingly: in this we possess an advantage over you, and over those that inhabit the towns and villages in *this* country, where I see a ridiculous attempt to keep up an appearance that is quite foreign to the situation of those that practise it. Few, very few, are the emigrants that come to the colonies, unless it is with the view of realizing an independence for themselves or their children. Those that could afford to live in ease at home, believe me, would never expose themselves to the privations and disagreeable consequences of a settler's life in Canada: therefore, this is the natural inference we draw, that the emigrant has come hither under the desire and natural hope of bettering his condition, and benefiting a family that he had not the means of settling in life in the home country. It is foolish, then, to launch out in a style of life that everyone knows cannot be maintained; rather ought such persons to rejoice in the consciousness that they can, if they please, live according to their circumstances, without being the less regarded for the practice of prudence, economy, and industry.

Now, we *bush-settlers* are more independent: we do what we like; we dress as we find most suitable and most convenient, we are totally without the fear of any Mr. or Mrs. Grundy;[4] and having shaken off the trammels of Grundyism, we laugh at the absurdity of those who voluntarily forge afresh and hug their chains.

If our friends come to visit us unexpectedly we make them welcome to our humble homes, and give them the best we have; but if our fare be indifferent, we offer it with good will, and no apologies are made or expected: they would be out of place; as every one is aware of the disadvantages of a new settlement; and any excuses for want of variety, or the delicacies of the table, would be considered rather in the light of a tacit reproof to your guest for having unseasonably put your hospitality to the test.

Our society is mostly military or naval; so that we meet on equal grounds, and are, of course, well acquainted with the rules of good breeding and polite life; too much so to allow any deviation from those laws that good taste, good sense, and good feeling have established among persons of our class.

Yet here it is considered by no means derogatory to the wife of an officer or gentleman to assist in the work of the house, or to perform its entire

---

[4] Mrs. Grundy is a character in Thomas Morton's play *Speed the Plough* (produced 1798), who is, according to the *Oxford English Dictionary*, the personification of the "tyranny of social opinion in matters of conventional propriety." Grundyism refers to the principles of Mrs. Grundy, or conventionalism and prudery.

duties, if occasion requires it; to understand the mystery of soap, candle, and sugar-making; to make bread, butter, and cheese, or even to milk her own cows; to knit and spin, and prepare the wool for the loom. In these matters we bush-ladies have a wholesome disregard of what Mr. or Mrs. So-and-so thinks or says. We pride ourselves on conforming to circumstances, and as a British officer must needs be a gentleman and his wife a lady, perhaps we repose quietly on that incontestable proof of our gentility, and can afford to be useful without injuring it.

Our husbands adopt a similar line of conduct: the officer turns his sword into a ploughshare, and his lance into a sickle; and if he be seen ploughing among the stumps in his own field, or chopping trees on his own land, no one thinks less of his dignity, or considers him less of a gentleman, than when he appeared upon parade in all the pride of military etiquette, with sash, sword and epaulette. Surely this is as it should be in a country where independence is inseparable from industry; and for this I prize it.

Among many advantages we in this township possess, it is certainly no inconsiderable one that the lower or working class of settlers are well disposed, and quite free from the annoying Yankee manners that distinguish many of the earlier-settled townships. Our servants are as respectful, or nearly so, as those at home; nor are they admitted to our tables, or placed on an equality with us, excepting at "bees," and such kinds of public meetings; when they usually conduct themselves with a propriety that would afford an example to some that call themselves gentlemen, viz., young men who voluntarily throw aside those restraints that society expects from persons filling a respectable situation. [. . .]

I am rather interested in a young lad that has come out from England to learn Canadian farming. The poor boy had conceived the most romantic notions of a settler's life, partly from the favourable accounts he had read, and partly through the medium of a lively imagination, which had aided in the deception, and led him to suppose that his time would be chiefly spent in the fascinating amusements and adventures arising from hunting the forest in search of deer and other game, pigeon and duck-shooting, spearing fish by torchlight, and voyaging on the lakes in a birch-bark canoe in summer, skating in winter, or gliding over the frozen snow like a Laplander in his sledge, wrapped up to the eyes in furs, and travelling at the rate of twelve miles an hour to the sound of the harmonious peal of bells. What a felicitous life to captivate the mind of a boy of fourteen, just let loose from the irksome restraint of boarding-school!

How little did he dream of the drudgery inseparable from the duties of a lad of his age, in a country where the old and young, the master and the servant, are alike obliged to labour for a livelihood, without respect to former situation or rank!

Here the son of the gentleman becomes a hewer of wood and drawer of water; he learns to chop down trees, to pile brush-heaps, split rails for fences, attend the fires during the burning season, dressed in a coarse over-garment of hempen cloth, called a logging-shirt, with trousers to correspond, and a Yankee straw hat flapped over his eyes, and a handspike to assist him in rolling over the burning brands. To tend and drive oxen, plough, sow, plant Indian corn and pumpkins, and raise potatoe-hills, are among some of the young emigrant's accomplishments. His relaxations are but comparatively few, but they are seized with a relish and avidity that give them the greater charm.

You may imagine the disappointment felt by the poor lad on seeing his fair visions of amusement fade before the dull realities and distasteful details of a young settler's occupation in the backwoods.

Youth, however, is the best season for coming to this country; the mind soon bends itself to its situation, and becomes not only reconciled, but in time pleased with the change of life. There is a consolation, too, in seeing that he does no more than others of equal pretensions as to rank and education are obliged to submit to, if they would prosper, and perhaps he lives to bless the country which has robbed him of a portion of that absurd pride that made him look with contempt on those whose occupations were of humble nature. It were a thousand pities wilfully to deceive persons desirous of emigrating with false and flattering picture of the advantages to be met with in this country. Let the *pro* and *con*, be fairly stated, and let the reader use his best judgment unbiassed by prejudice or interest in a matter of such vital importance not only as regards himself, but the happiness and welfare of those over whose destinies Nature has made him the guardian. It is, however, far more difficult to write on the subject of emigration than most persons think: it embraces so wide a field that what would be perfectly correct as regards one part of the province would by no means prove so as regarded another. One district differs from another, and one township from another, according to its natural advantages; whether it be long settled or unsettled, possessing water privileges or not; the soil and even the climate will be different, according to situation and circumstances.

Much depends on the tempers, habits, and dispositions of the emigrants themselves. What suits one will not another; one family will flourish, and accumulate every comfort about their homesteads, while others languish in poverty and discontent. It would take volumes to discuss every argument for and against, and to point out exactly who are and who are not fit subjects for emigration.

Have you read Dr. Dunlop's spirited and witty "Backwoodsman?" If you have not, get it as soon as you can; it will amuse you. I think a Backwoodswoman might be written in the same spirit, setting forth a few pages, in the history of bush-ladies, as examples for our sex. Indeed, we need some wholesome admonitions on our duties and the folly of repining at following and sharing the fortunes of our spouses, whom we have vowed in happier hours to love "in riches and in poverty, in sickness and in health." Too many pronounce these words without heeding their importance, and without calculating the chances that may put their faithfulness to the severe test of quitting home, kindred, and country, to share the hard lot of a settler's life; for even this sacrifice renders it hard to be borne; but the truly attached wife will do this, and more also, if required by the husband of her choice.

But now it is time I say farewell: my dull letter, grown to a formidable packet, will tire you, and make you wish it at the bottom of the Atlantic.

Maple-Sugar[5]

This spring I have made maple-sugar of a much finer colour and grain than any I have yet seen and have been assured by many old settlers it was the best, or nearly the best, they had ever met with: which commendation induces me to give the plan I pursued in manufacturing it. The sap having been boiled down in the sugar-bush from about sixteen pailsful to two, I first passed it through a thin flannel bag, after the manner of a jelly-bag, to strain it from the first impurities which are great. I then passed the liquor through another thicker flannel into the iron pot, in which I purposed boiling down the sugar, and while yet cold, or at best but luke-warm, beat up the white of one egg to a froth, and spread it gently over the surface of the liquor, watching the pot carefully after the fire began to heat it, that I might not suffer the scum to boil into the sugar. A few minutes before it comes to a boil, the scum must be carefully removed with a skimmer, or ladle—the former is best. I consider that on the care taken to remove every particle of scum depends, in a great measure, the brightness and clearness of the sugar. The best rule I can give as to the sugaring-off, as it is termed, is to let the liquid continue at a fast boil: only be careful to keep it from coming over by keeping a little of the liquid in your stirring-ladle, and when it boils up to the top, or you see it rising too fast, throw in a little from time to time to keep it down; or if you boil on a cooking-stove, throwing open one or all of the doors will prevent boiling over. Those that sugar-off outside the house have a wooden crane fixed against a stump, the fire being lighted against the stump, and the kettle suspended on the crane: by this simple contrivance (for any bush-boy can fix a crane of the kind) the sugar need never rise over if common attention be paid to the boiling; but it does require constant watching: one idle glance may waste much of the precious fluid. I had only a small cooking-stove to boil my sugar on, the pots of which were thought too small, and not well shaped, so that at first my fears were that I must relinquish the trial; but I persevered, and experience convinces me a stove is an excellent furnace for the purpose as you can regulate the heat as you like.

One of the most anxious periods in the boiling I found to be when the liquor began first to assume a yellowish frothy appearance, and cast up so great

---

[5] For North American settlers, maple sugar became an important staple, not only because it was cheaper than imported cane sugar but because it was not produced by the slave trade. Settlers were encouraged to use only maple sugar as a protest against slavery, an abolitionist position that Traill and Moodie had already supported in England before emigrating.

a volume of steam from its surface as to obscure the contents of the pot; as it may then rise over almost unperceived by the most vigilant eye. As the liquor thickens into molasses, it becomes a fine yellow, and seems nothing but thick froth. When it is getting pretty well boiled down, the drops begin to fall clear and ropy from the ladle; and if you see little bright grainy-looking bubbles in it, drop some on a cold plate, and continue to stir or rub it till it is quite cold: if it is ready to granulate, you will find it gritty, and turn whitish or pale straw colour, and stiff. The sugar may then safely be poured off into a tin dish, pail, basin, or any other utensil. I tried two different methods after taking the sugar from the fire, but could find little difference in the look of the sugar, except that in one the quantity was broken up more completely; in the other the sugar remained in large lumps, but equally pure and sparkling. In the first I kept stirring the sugar till it began to cool and form a whitish thick substance, and the grains were well crystallized; in the other process—which I think preferable, as being the least troublesome—I waited till the mass was hardened into sugar, and then, piercing the crust in many places, I turned the mass into a cullender, and placed the cullender over a vessel to receive the molasses that drained from the sugar. In the course of the day or two, I frequently stirred the sugar, which thus became perfectly free from moisture, and had acquired a fine sparkling grain, tasting exactly like sugar-candy, free from any taste of the maple-sap, and fit for any purpose.

I observed that in general maple-sugar, as it is commonly made, is hard and compact, showing little grain, and weighing very heavy in proportion to its bulk. Exactly the reverse is the case with that I made, it being extremely light for its bulk, all the heavy molasses having been separated, instead of dried into the sugar. Had the present season been at all a favourable one, which it was not, we should have made a good quantity of excellent sugar.

Candles

Everyone makes their own candles (*i.e.*, if they have any materials to make them from). The great difficulty of making candles—and, as far as I see the only one, is procuring the tallow, which a bush-settler, until he begins to kill his own beef, sheep, and hogs, is rarely able to do, unless he buys; and a settler buys nothing that he can help. A cow, however, that is unprofitable, old, or unlikely to survive the severity of the coming winter, is often suffered to go dry during the summer, and get her own living, till she is fit to kill in the fall. Such an animal is often slaughtered very advantageously, especially if the settler have little fodder for his cattle. The beef is often excellent, and good store of candles and soap may be made from the inside fat. These candles, if made three parts beef and one part hogs'-lard, will burn better than any store-candles, and cost less than half price. The tallow is merely melted in a pot or pan convenient for the purpose, and having run the cotton wicks into the moulds (tin or pewter moulds for six candles cost three shillings at the stores, and last many years), a stick or skewer is passed through the loops of your wicks, at the upper part of the stand, which serve the purpose of drawing the candles and the ends tied below after the sticks have been put through the loops and the wicks drawn tight. The melted fat, not too hot, but in a fluid state, is then poured into the moulds till they are full; as the fat gets cold it shrinks, and leaves a hollow at the top of the mould: this requires filling up when quite cold. If the candles do not draw readily, plunge the mould for an instant into hot water, and the candles will come out easily. Many persons prefer making dip-candles for kitchen use; but for my own part I think the trouble quite as great, and give the preference, in point of neatness of look, to the moulds. It may be, my maid and I did not succeed so well in making the dips as the moulds. The universal use of petroleum or coal oil has almost superseded the tallow candle even far back in the bush, though probably among the poorest class of settlers the old candle or even pine knots may still be made use of—as avoiding any outlay of money.

[1836]

SUSANNA MOODIE ■ (1803–1885)

Susanna Moodie has often been regarded as the archetypal pioneer woman in Canada. Moodie's account of her first seven years in Canada, *Roughing It in the Bush, or, Life in Canada* (1852) is perhaps the best-known nineteenth-century work of Canadian literature. Like many celebrated works of literature, Moodie's text has elicited ambivalent responses since its publication. Some have viewed it as a valuable portrait of settlement, while others have read it as the words of a spoiled member of the English gentry. Moodie's work typifies what has become one of the enduring myths of Canadian literature: the settler as a victim of circumstance who must tolerate extreme hardship in order to survive. While Moodie clearly writes about enduring isolation, loneliness, privation, and adversity, she also writes about the sublime beauty of her adopted home and the pleasures of living there with her growing family.

Born twenty-three months after her sister Catharine Parr Traill, Susanna Moodie (née Strickland) grew up in Sussex, England, and emigrated to Upper Canada in 1832. Before her marriage and emigration, however, Moodie had already begun to establish her reputation as a poet (*Enthusiasm and Other Poems*, 1831) and a writer of stories for young adults (*Hugh Latimer: or, a Young Boy's Friendship*, 1828). A vocal opponent of slavery, she was also the "lady who wrote down the narratives of Mary Prince and Ashton Warner" that were published as *The History of Mary Prince* (1831) and *Negro Slavery Described by a Negro: Being the Narrative of Ashton Warner, a Native of St. Vincent's* (1831). Worried that her feminist politics (being a bluestocking) would be diluted by marriage, she wrote to a friend: "[M]y bluestockings, since I became a wife, have turned so pale that I think they will soon be quite white, or at least only tinged with a hue of London smoke." Still, by all accounts Moodie was passionate in her marriage to the like-minded writer John Wedderburn Dunbar Moodie, a friend of Thomas Traill and fellow-veteran of the Napoleonic Wars, and author of *A Narrative of the Campaign of 1814* (1831) and *Ten Years in South Africa* (1835). Together, with their baby daughter, they immigrated to Upper Canada in the summer of 1832.

In 1840, the Moodies moved to Belleville so he could take up an appointment as the sheriff of Victoria District (later Hastings County). Moodie's two major books were published while she lived in Belleville, as they follow the family's path in settlement. *Roughing It in the Bush* is a cautionary tale that details the hardships of settlement, while *Life in the Clearings versus the Bush* (1853) outlines life, people, and politics in the small town. While in Belleville, the Moodies also edited the *Victoria Magazine* (1847–48), and Moodie published sketches and essays in the *Literary Garland* out of Montreal, as well as in other literary venues in Canada, England, and America. In the years following the publication of *Life in the Clearings versus the Bush*, Moodie was prolific, publishing numerous works of fiction. But it is for *Roughing It in the Bush* that she is primarily remembered.

In all her writings Moodie makes it clear that financial circumstances, or "stern necessity," rather than choice, forced her family to emigrate to Canada. The Strickland family had suffered a severe decline in fortune after Moodie's father died leaving the family in serious debt. Struggling to maintain their social standing in England, Traill and Moodie, with the enthusiasm of their new husbands, soon realized that their only hope for financial security lay in the prospect of emigration to British North America. Neither had married wealthy men, so emigration offered the possibility of regaining the social and economic status that their family had lost. This would also, they hoped, ensure a financially

secure future for their children that would be impossible at home. Their reasons for emigration were, according to Moodie, that "not being overgifted with the good things of this world—the younger sons of old British families seldom are—[her husband] had, after mature deliberation, determined to try his fortunes in Canada, and settle upon a grant of 400 acres of land, ceded by the Government to officers upon half-pay." Encouraged by the portraits of fertile soil, genteel society, and easy prosperity being offered by agents of the Canada Company such as William Catermole, the Moodies reluctantly decided to leave British society for the possibilities of the future in Canada.

When the Moodies and their baby daughter, Katie, settled on land adjacent to Traill and to Moodie's brother Samuel Strickland, in Douro Township near Peterborough, they were not ready for the difficulties they met. For gentry fallen on hard times with no experience of manual labour, class mobility, or physical hardship, Canada was a rude awakening. Two decades after her arrival, Moodie published *Roughing It in the Bush*, an account of her early days of settlement. Unlike Traill, who sought to educate her gentlewomen readers on how to survive in the bush, Moodie saw her work as a cautionary tale warning potential settlers "not to take up grants and pitch their tents in the wilderness and by so doing, reduce themselves and their families to hopeless poverty." Moodie argues that the poor gentleman is unfit, by habits and education, to be a "hewer of the forest and a tillor of the soil." In *Roughing It*, she counters the propaganda put forth by hucksters trying to attract those "rich in hope and poor in purse," and scolds the people selling land and false hopes. Yet, perhaps because *Roughing It* is a retrospective, published years after Moodie's arrival in Canada and after Moodie became accustomed to the place, it is full of contradictory positions about the country and its people. On the one hand, Moodie celebrates the egalitarianism of the new society; on the other, she bemoans the audacity and licentiousness of the "Yankees" and the Irish people she encounters. This also applies to her initial view of the landscape. "A Visit to Grosse Isle" illustrates her romanticized notions of the landscape and Canada as a place of hope and prosperity, which are then exploded once she lands and witnesses the squalor of the cholera quarantine station. Similarly, *Roughing It* is a fascinating study in contrasts in which she subscribes to common stereotypes about "Indians" as *tabulae rasae* (blank slates) but is eloquent in noting her debt to them for their teachings and generosity. Her view of her predicament frequently oscillates between elation and despair. At one point, she writes that her feeling for Canada was "allied to that which the condemned criminal entertains for his cell—his only hope of escape being through the portals of the grave." Later, she offers the reverse opinion: "Canada! thou art a noble, free, and rising country . . . the offspring of Britain, thou must be great, and I will and do love thee, land of my adoption, and of my children's birth; and, oh, dearer still to a mother's heart—land of their graves!" Such ambivalence is partly responsible for Moodie's iconic status as an emblem of the divided nature of Canadian identity.

In the afterword to *The Journals of Susanna Moodie* (1970), a series of poems based on the works of Moodie composed well over a century after *Roughing It*, Margaret Atwood writes:

> If the national mental illness of the United States is megalomania, that of Canada is paranoid schizophrenia.

Mrs. Moodie is divided down the middle: she praises the Canadian landscape but accuses it of destroying her; she dislikes the people already in Canada but finds in people her only refuge from the land itself; she preaches progress and the march of civilization while brooding elegiacally on the destruction of the wilderness.

The longevity of Moodie's writing is rooted in this firmly doubled sense of Canadian society. Though Moodie's perspective changes in the course of her sojourn in the woods, she remains committed to lingering class distinctions. She sees the beginnings of a new, egalitarian, self-sufficient society in Canada (much as Haliburton had hoped for of his Nova Scotians), yet she cannot help but feel that a new hierarchy is the order of the day, one based on manners and education. Part of the ambivalence in *Roughing It* also comes from the fact that Moodie has combined genres with different readerly expectations: emigration manual, memoir, confessional, and sentimental tale. As a good nineteenth-century heroine of her own story, Moodie casts herself in this ambivalent role as tragic on one hand (with many shows of tears), and as a hearty survivor on the other.

Roughing It was met with mainly positive reviews in England. *The Atheneum* praised it for presenting the "dark side of the emigrant's life" without being "needlessly lachrymose." The review in *Blackwood's Edinburgh Magazine*, entitled "Forest Life in Canada" and excerpted here, asks its female readers to "behold one, gently nurtured as yourselves, cheerfully condescending to rudest toils, unrepiningly enduring hardships you never dreamed of." *The Observer*, however, did take exception to her disdainful treatment of the Irish. In Canada, Moodie received more mixed reviews. One reviewer went so far as to call her "an ape of the aristocracy. Too poor to lie on the sofa and too proud to work for her bread." Further, Moodie's older sister, Agnes Strickland, the most famous royal biographer of her day and friend at court, was outraged that Moodie had dedicated such a book to her. She found *Roughing It* to be an undignified account of living in squalor, working at jobs unbecoming a lady (making maple sugar, milking cows, digging gardens), and communing with servants, drunks, Americans, and other undesirables. Although Moodie is rightly accused by her critics of being a class snob, she does not hold a candle to her mortified sister. Agnes Strickland insisted that the dedication be removed from subsequent printings and commissioned her brother, Samuel Strickland, to write a corrective account of emigration. The next year he published his rather wooden memoir, with some heavy editing by Agnes Strickland, *Twenty-Seven Years in Canada West* (1853). Moodie herself decided to write *Life in the Clearings versus the Bush* in order to address some of the criticisms of *Roughing It*. The introduction to *Life in the Clearings* contains Moodie's response to her detractors. Tired of the negative reviews, in a letter to her publisher Richard Bentley on 8 October 1853, Moodie writes, "Alas, that one should have to work for money. But it cannot be helped, and I ought not to feel ashamed of turning the capacity God gave me to account, but ought rather to be grateful; still, it paralizes *[sic]* the mind having to tax it for daily supplies." Indeed, she continued to tax it for years to come, and established herself as one of the central figures in Canadian writing. Several Canadian writers have responded to Moodie's now iconic status in Canadian culture with contemporary re-envisionings of her stories and poems. Armand Garnet Ruffo's poem "Creating a Country" and Atwood's *The Journals of Susanna Moodie* are two examples in Volume II of this anthology.

From Roughing It in the Bush

Introduction

In most instances, emigration is a matter of necessity, not of choice; and this is more especially true of the emigration of persons of respectable connections, or of any station or position in the world. Few educated persons, accustomed to the refinements and luxuries of European society, ever willingly relinquish those advantages, and place themselves beyond the protective influence of the wise and revered institutions of their native land, without the pressure of some urgent cause. Emigration may, indeed, generally be regarded as an act of severe duty, performed at the expense of personal enjoyment, and accompanied by the sacrifice of those local attachments which stamp the scenes amid which our childhood grew, in imperishable characters upon the heart. Nor is it until adversity has pressed sorely upon the proud and wounded spirit of the well-educated sons and daughters of old but impoverished families, that they gird up the loins of the mind, and arm themselves with fortitude to meet and dare the heart-breaking conflict.

The ordinary motives for the emigration of such persons may be summed up in a few brief words;—the emigrant's hope of bettering his condition, and of escaping from the vulgar sarcasms too often hurled at the less wealthy by the purse-proud, commonplace people of the world. But there is a higher motive still, which has its origin in that love of independence which springs up spontaneously in the breasts of the high-souled children of a glorious land. They cannot labour in a menial capacity in the country where they were born and educated to command. They can trace no difference between themselves and the more fortunate individuals of a race whose blood warms their veins, and whose name they bear. The want of wealth alone places an impassable barrier between them and the more favoured offspring of the same parent stock and they go forth to make for themselves a new name and to find another country, to forget the past and to live in the future, to exult in the prospect of their children being free and the land of their adoption great.

The choice of the country to which they devote their talents and energies depends less upon their pecuniary means than upon the fancy of the emigrant or the popularity of a name. From the year 1826 to 1829, Australia and the Swan River were all the rage. No other portions of the habitable globe were deemed worthy of notice. These were the *El Dorados*[1] and lands of Goshen[2] to which all respectable emigrants eagerly flocked. Disappointment, as a matter of course, followed their high-raised expectations. Many of the most sanguine of these adventurers returned to their native shores in a worse condition than when they left them. In 1830, the great tide of emigration flowed westward. Canada became the great land-mark for the rich in hope and poor in purse. Public newspapers and private letters teemed with the unheard-of advantages to be derived from a settlement in this highly-favoured region.

Its salubrious climate, its fertile soil, commercial advantages, great water privileges, its proximity to the mother country, and last, not least, its almost total exemption from taxation—that bugbear which keeps honest John Bull[3] in a state of constant ferment—were the theme of every tongue, and lauded beyond all praise. The general interest, once excited, was industriously kept alive by pamphlets, published by interested parties, which prominently set forth all the *good* to be derived from a settlement in the Backwoods of Canada; while they carefully concealed the toil and hardship to be endured in order to secure these advantages. They told of lands yielding forty bushels to the acre, but they said nothing of the years when these lands, with the most careful cultivation, would barely return fifteen; when rust and smut, engendered by the vicinity of damp over-hanging woods, would blast the fruits of the poor emigrant's labour, and almost deprive him of bread. They talked of log houses to be raised in a single day, by the generous exertions of friends and neighbours, but they never

[1] The name of a fictitious city or country abounding in gold, believed by the Spanish and by Sir Walter Raleigh to exist upon the Amazon within the jurisdiction of the governor of Guiana (according to the *Oxford English Dictionary*). It has come to stand for a place of desire and dreams or, as Moodie says later, a land of milk and honey.

[2] A place of plenty or of light.

[3] John Bull is a personification of the English nation. It also refers to a typical Englishman.

ventured upon a picture of the disgusting scenes of riot and low debauchery exhibited during the raising, or upon a description of the dwellings when raised—dens of dirt and misery, which would, in many instances, be shamed by an English pig-sty. The necessaries of life were described as inestimably cheap; but they forgot to add that in remote bush settlements, often twenty miles from a market town, and some of them even that distance from the nearest dwelling, the necessaries of life, which would be deemed indispensable to the European, could not be procured at all, or, if obtained, could only be so by sending a man and team through a blazed forest road,—a process far too expensive for frequent repetition.

Oh, ye dealers in wild lands—ye speculators in the folly and credulity of your fellow men—what a mass of misery, and of misrepresentation productive of that misery, have ye not to answer for! You had your acres to sell, and what to you were the worn-down frames and broken hearts of the infatuated purchasers? The public believed the plausible statements you made with such earnestness, and men of all grades rushed to hear your hired orators declaim upon the blessings to be obtained by the clearers of the wilderness.

Men who had been hopeless of supporting their families in comfort and independence at home, thought that they had only to come out to Canada to make their fortunes; almost even to realise the story told in the nursery, of the sheep and oxen that ran about the streets, ready roasted, and with knives and forks upon their backs. They were made to believe that if it did not actually rain gold, that precious metal could be obtained, as is now stated of California and Australia, by stooping to pick it up.

The infection became general. A Canada mania pervaded the middle ranks of British society; thousands and tens of thousands, for the space of three or four years landed upon these shores. A large majority of the higher class were officers of the army and navy, with their families—a class perfectly unfitted by their previous habits and education for contending with the stern realities of emigrant life. The hand that has long held the sword, and been accustomed to receive implicit obedience from those under its control, is seldom adapted to wield the spade and guide the plough, or try its strength against the stubborn trees of the forest. Nor will such persons submit cheerfully to the saucy familiarity of servants, who, republicans in spirit, think themselves as good as their employers. Too many of these brave and honourable men were easy dupes to the designing land-speculators. Not having counted the cost, but only looked upon the bright side of the picture held up to their admiring gaze, they fell easily into the snares of their artful seducers.

To prove their zeal as colonists, they were induced to purchase large tracts of wild land in remote and unfavourable situations. This, while it impoverished and often proved the ruin of the unfortunate immigrant, possessed a double advantage to the seller. He obtained an exorbitant price for the land which he actually sold, while the residence of a respectable settler upon the spot greatly enhanced the value and price of all other lands in the neighbourhood.

It is not by such instruments as those I have just mentioned, that Providence works when it would reclaim the waste places of the earth, and make them subservient to the wants and happiness of its creatures. The Great Father of the souls and bodies of men knows the arm which wholesome labour from infancy has made strong, the nerves which have become iron by patient endurance, by exposure to weather, coarse fare, and rude shelter; and he chooses such, to send forth into the forest to hew out the rough paths for the advance of civilisation. These men become wealthy and prosperous, and form the bones and sinews of a great and rising country. Their labour is wealth, not exhaustion; its produce independence and content, not home-sickness and despair. What the Backwoods of Canada are to the industrious and ever-to-be-honoured sons of honest poverty, and what they are to the refined and accomplished gentleman, these simple sketches will endeavour to portray. They are drawn principally from my own experience, during a sojourn of nineteen years in the colony. [. . .]

A Visit to Grosse Isle

The dreadful cholera was depopulating Quebec and Montreal, when our ship cast anchor off Grosse Isle, on the 30th of August, 1832. [. . .]

By daybreak all was hurry and confusion on board the *Anne*.[4] I watched boat after boat depart for the island, full of people and goods, and envied them the glorious privilege of once more standing firmly on the earth, after two long months of rocking and rolling at sea. How ardently we anticipate pleasure, which often ends in positive pain! Such was my case when at last indulged in the gratification so eagerly desired. As cabin passengers, we were not included in the general order of purification, but were only obliged to send our servant, with the clothes and bedding we had used during the voyage, on shore, to be washed.

The ship was soon emptied of all her live cargo. My husband went off with the boats, to reconnoitre the island, and I was left alone with my baby, in the otherwise empty vessel. Even Oscar, the Captain's Scotch terrier, who had formed a devoted attachment to me during the voyage, forgot his allegiance, became possessed of the land mania, and was away with the rest. With the most intense desire to go on shore, I was doomed to look and long and envy every boatful of emigrants that glided past. [. . .]

As the sun rose above the horizon, all these matter-of-fact circumstances were gradually forgotten, and merged in the surpassing grandeur of the scene that rose majestically before me. The previous day had been dark and stormy; and a heavy fog had concealed the mountain chain, which forms the stupendous background to this sublime view, entirely from our sight. As the clouds rolled away from their grey, bald brows, and cast into denser shadow the vast forest belt that girdled them round, they loomed out like mighty giants—Titans of the earth, in all their rugged and awful beauty—a thrill of wonder and delight pervaded my mind. The spectacle floated dimly on my sight—my eyes were

[4] The Moodies boarded the *Anne* on July 1 at Leith, Scotland, and landed in a quarantine station at Grosse-Île on 30 August 1832.

blinded with tears—blinded with the excess of beauty. I turned to the right and to the left, I looked up and down the glorious river; never had I beheld so many striking objects blended into one mighty whole! Nature had lavished all her noblest features in producing that enchanting scene.

The rocky isle in front, with its neat farm-houses at the eastern point, and its high bluff at the western extremity, crowned with the telegraph—the middle space occupied by tents and sheds for the cholera patients, and its wooded shores dotted over with motley groups—added greatly to the picturesque effect of the land scene. Then the broad, glittering river, covered with boats darting to and fro, conveying passengers from twenty-five vessels, of various size and tonnage, which rode at anchor, with their flags flying from the mast-head, gave an air of life and interest to the whole. Turning to the south side of the St. Lawrence, I was not less struck with its low fertile shores, white houses, and neat churches, whose slender spires and bright tin roofs shone like silver as they caught the first rays of the sun. As far as the eye could reach, a line of white buildings extended along the bank; their background formed by the purple hue of the dense, interminable forest. It was a scene unlike any I had ever beheld, and to which Britain contains no parallel. Mackenzie, an old Scotch dragoon, who was one of our passengers, when he rose in the morning, and saw the parish of St. Thomas for the first time, exclaimed—"Weel, it beats a'! Can thae white clouts be a' houses? They look like claes hung out to drie!" There was some truth in this odd comparison, and for some minutes, I could scarcely convince myself that the white patches scattered so thickly over the opposite shore could be the dwellings of a busy, lively population.

"What sublime views of the north side of the river those *habitans* of St. Thomas must enjoy," thought I. Perhaps familiarity with the scene has rendered them indifferent to its astonishing beauty.

Eastward, the view down the St. Lawrence towards the Gulf, is the finest of all, scarcely surpassed by anything in the world. Your eye follows the long range of lofty mountains until their blue summits are blended and lost in the blue of the sky. Some of these, partially cleared round the base, are sprinkled over with neat cottages; and the green slopes that spread around them are covered with flocks and herds. The surface of the splendid river is diversified with islands of every size and shape, some in wood, others partially cleared, and adorned with orchards and white farm-houses. As the early sun streamed upon the most prominent of these, leaving the others in deep shade, the effect was strangely novel and imposing. In more remote regions, where the forest has never yet echoed to the woodman's axe, or received the impress of civilisation, the first approach to the shore inspires a melancholy awe, which becomes painful in its intensity. [. . .]

My day-dreams were dispelled by the return of the boat, which brought my husband and the captain from the island.

"No bread," said the latter, shaking his head; "you must be content to starve a little longer. Provision-ship not in till four o'clock." My husband smiled at the look of blank disappointment with which I received these unwelcome tidings,

"Never mind, I have news which will comfort you. The officer who commands the station sent a note to me by an orderly, inviting us to spend the afternoon with him. He promises to show us everything worthy of notice on the island. Captain —— claims acquaintance with me; but I have not the least recollection of him. Would you like to go?"

"Oh, by all means. I long to see the lovely island. It looks a perfect paradise at this distance."

The rough sailor-captain screwed his mouth on one side, and gave me one of his comical looks, but he said nothing until he assisted in placing me and the baby in the boat.

"Don't be too sanguine, Mrs. Moodie; many things look well at a distance which are bad enough when near."

I scarcely regarded the old sailor's warning, so eager was I to go on shore— to put my foot upon the soil of the new world for the first time. I was in no humour to listen to any depreciation of what seemed so beautiful.

It was four o'clock when we landed on the rocks, which the rays of an intensely scorching sun had rendered so hot that I could scarcely place my foot upon them. How the people without shoes bore it, I cannot imagine. Never shall I forget the extraordinary spectacle that met our sight the moment we passed the low range of bushes which formed a screen in front of the river. A crowd of many hundred Irish emigrants had been landed during the present and former day; and all this motley crew—men, women, and children, who were not confined by sickness to the sheds (which greatly resembled cattle-pens)—were employed in washing clothes, or spreading them out on the rocks and bushes to dry.

The men and boys were *in* the water, while the women, with their scanty garments tucked above their knees, were trampling their bedding in tubs, or in holes in the rocks, which the retiring tide had left half full of water. Those who did not possess washing-tubs, pails, or iron pots, or could not obtain access to a hole in the rocks, were running to and fro, screaming and scolding in no measured terms. The confusion of Babel[5] was among them. All talkers and no hearers— each shouting and yelling in his or her uncouth dialect, and all accompanying their vociferations with violent and extraordinary gestures, quite incomprehensible to the uninitiated. We were literally stunned by the strife of tongues. I shrank, with feelings almost akin to fear, from the hard-featured, sun-burnt harpies, as they elbowed rudely past me.

I had heard and read much of savages, and have since seen, during my long residence in the bush, somewhat of uncivilised life; but the Indian is one of Nature's gentlemen—he never says or does a rude or vulgar thing. The vicious, uneducated barbarians who form the surplus of over-populous European countries, are far behind the wild man in delicacy of feeling or natural courtesy. The

---

[5] A scene of confusion or a confused assembly of people. In the Bible, the builders of the Tower of Babel are punished for their hubris by being made to speak different languages, thus rendering communication impossible. The clashing dialects and curses that Moodie hears remind her of this scene.

people who covered the island appeared perfectly destitute of shame, or even of a sense of common decency. Many were almost naked, still more but partially clothed. We turned in disgust from the revolting scene, but were unable to leave the spot until the captain had satisfied a noisy group of his own people, who were demanding a supply of stores.

And here I must observe that our passengers, who were chiefly honest Scotch labourers and mechanics from the vicinity of Edinburgh, and who while on board ship had conducted themselves with the greatest propriety, and appeared the most quiet, orderly set of people in the world, no sooner set foot upon the island than they became infected by the same spirit of insubordination and misrule, and were just as insolent and noisy as the rest.

While our captain was vainly endeavouring to satisfy the unreasonable demands of his rebellious people, Moodie had discovered a woodland path that led to the back of the island. Sheltered by some hazel-bushes from the intense heat of the sun, we sat down by the cool, gushing river, out of sight, but, alas! not out of hearing of the noisy, riotous crowd. Could we have shut out the profane sounds which came to us on every breeze, how deeply should we have enjoyed an hour amid the tranquil beauties of that retired and lovely spot! [. . .]

Here, the shores of the island and mainland, receding from each other, formed a small cove, overhung with lofty trees, clothed from the base to the summit with wild vines, that hung in graceful festoons from the topmost branches to the water's edge. The dark shadows of the mountains, thrown upon the water, as they towered to the height of some thousand feet above us, gave to the surface of the river an ebon hue. The sunbeams, dancing through the thick, quivering foliage, fell in stars of gold, or long lines of dazzling brightness, upon the deep black waters, producing the most novel and beautiful effects. It was a scene over which the spirit of peace might brood in silent adoration; but how spoiled by the discordant yells of the filthy beings who were sullying the purity of the air and water with contaminating sights and sounds!

We were now joined by the sergeant, who very kindly brought us his capful of ripe plums and hazel-nuts, the growth of the island; a joyful present, but marred by a note from Captain ——, who had found that he had been mistaken in his supposed knowledge of us, and politely apologised for not being allowed by the health-officers to receive any emigrant beyond the bounds appointed for the performance of quarantine.

I was deeply disappointed, but my husband laughingly told me that I had seen enough of the island; and turning to the good-natured soldier, remarked, that "it could be no easy task to keep such wild savages in order."

"You may well say that, sir — but our night scenes far exceed those of the day. You would think they were incarnate devils; singing, drinking, dancing, shouting, and cutting antics that would surprise the leader of a circus. They have no shame — are under no restraint — nobody knows them here, and they think they can speak and act as they please; and they are such thieves that they rob one another of the little they possess. The healthy actually run the risk of taking the cholera by robbing the sick. If you have not hired one or two stout, honest fellows from among your fellow-passengers to guard your clothes while they are drying, you will never see half of them again. They are a sad set, sir, a sad set. We could, perhaps, manage the men; but the women, sir!—the women! Oh, sir!"

Anxious as we were to return to the ship, we were obliged to remain until sun-down in our retired nook. We were hungry, tired, and out of spirits; the mosquitoes swarmed in myriads around us, tormenting the poor baby, who, not at all pleased with her first visit to the new world, filled the air with cries; when the captain came to tell us, that the boat was ready. It was a welcome sound. Forcing our way once more through the still squabbling crowd, we gained the landing place. Here we encountered a boat, just landing a fresh cargo of lively savages from the Emerald Isle.[6] One fellow, of gigantic proportions, whose long, tattered great-coat just reached below the middle of his bare red legs, and, like charity, hid the defects of his other garments, or perhaps concealed his want of them, leaped upon the rocks, and flourishing aloft his shilelagh,[7] bounded and capered like a wild goat from his native mountains. "Whurrah! my boys!" he cried, "Shure we'll all be jontlemen!"

"Pull away, my lads!" exclaimed our captain, and in a few moments we were again on board. Thus ended my first day's experience of the land of all our hopes.

Our First Settlement

[. . .] The place we first occupied was purchased of Mr. C——, a merchant, who took it in payment of sundry large debts which the owner, a New England loyalist, had been unable to settle. Old Joe H——, the present occupant, had promised to quit it with his family, at the commencement of sleighing; and as the bargain was concluded in the month of September, and we were anxious to plough for fall wheat, it was necessary to be upon the spot. No house was to be found in the immediate neighbourhood, save a small dilapidated log tenement, on an adjoining farm (which was scarcely reclaimed from the bush) that had been some months without an owner. The merchant assured us that this could be made very comfortable until such time as it suited H—— to remove, and the owner was willing to let us have it for the *moderate* sum of four dollars a month.

Trusting to Mr. C——'s word, and being strangers in the land, we never took the precaution to examine this delightful summer residence before entering upon it, but thought ourselves very fortunate in obtaining a temporary home so near our own property, the distance not exceeding half-a-mile. The agreement was drawn up, and we were told that we could take possession whenever it suited us.

The few weeks that I had sojourned in the country had by no means prepossessed me in its favour. The home-sickness was sore upon me, and all my

---

[6] Ireland.

[7] An Irish shilelagh (or shilleagh) is a wooden club or cudgel (of blackthorn or oak traditionally).

solitary hours were spent in tears. My whole soul yielded itself up to a strong and overpowering grief. One simple word dwelt for ever in my heart, and swelled it to bursting—"Home!" I repeated it waking a thousand times a day, and my last prayer before I sank to sleep was still "Home! Oh, that I could return, if only to die at home!" And nightly I did return; my feet again trod the daisied meadows of England; the song of her birds was in my ears; I wept with delight to find myself once more wandering beneath the fragrant shade of her green hedge-rows; and I awoke to weep in earnest when I found it but a dream. But this is all digression, and has nothing to do with our unseen dwelling. The reader must bear with me in my fits of melancholy, and take me as I am.

It was the 22nd September that we left the Steam-boat Hotel, to take possession of our new abode. During the three weeks we had sojourned at ——, I had not seen a drop of rain, and I began to think that the fine weather would last for ever; but this eventful day arose in clouds. Moodie had hired a covered carriage to convey the baby, the servant-maid, and myself to the farm, as our driver prognosticated a wet day; while he followed with Tom Wilson and the teams that conveyed our luggage.

The scenery through which we were passing was so new to me, so unlike anything that I had ever beheld before, that in spite of its monotonous character, it won me from my melancholy, and I began to look about me with considerable interest. Not so my English servant, who declared that the woods were frightful to look upon; that it was a country only fit for wild beasts; that she hated it with all her heart and soul, and would go back as soon as she was able.

About a mile from the place of our destination the rain began to fall in torrents, and the air, which had been balmy as a spring morning, turned as chilly as that of a November day. Hannah shivered; the baby cried, and I drew my summer shawl as closely round as possible, to protect her from the sudden change in our hitherto delightful temperature. Just then, the carriage turned into a narrow, steep path, overhung with lofty woods, and after labouring up it with considerable difficulty, and at the risk of breaking our necks, it brought us at length to a rocky upland clearing, partially covered with a second growth of timber, and surrounded on all sides by the dark forest.

"I guess," quoth our Yankee driver, "that at the bottom of this 'ere swell, you'll find yourself *to hum*;" and plunging into a short path cut through the wood, he pointed to a miserable hut, at the bottom of a steep descent, and cracking his whip, exclaimed, "'Tis a smart location that. I wish you Britishers may enjoy it."

I gazed upon the place in perfect dismay, for I had never seen such a shed called a house before. "You must be mistaken; that is not a house, but a cattle-shed, or pig-sty."

The man turned his knowing, keen eye upon me, and smiled, half-humorously, half-maliciously, as he said,

"You were raised in the old country, I guess; you have much to learn, and more, perhaps, than you'll like to know, before the winter is over."

I was perfectly bewildered—I could only stare at the place, with my eyes swimming in tears; but as the horses plunged down into the broken hollow, my attention was drawn from my new residence to the perils which endangered life and limb at every step. The driver, however, was well used to such roads, and, steering us dexterously between the black stumps, at length drove up, not to the door, for there was none to the house, but to the open space from which that absent but very necessary appendage had been removed. Three young steers and two heifers, which the driver proceeded to drive out, were quietly reposing upon the floor. A few strokes of his whip, and a loud burst of gratuitous curses, soon effected an ejectment; and I dismounted, and took possession of this untenable tenement. Moodie was not yet in sight with the teams. I begged the man to stay until he arrived, as I felt terrified at being left alone in this wild, strange-looking place. He laughed, as well he might, at our fears, and said that he had a long way to go, and must be off; then, cracking his whip, and nodding to the girl, who was crying aloud, he went his way, and Hannah and myself were left standing in the middle of the dirty floor.

The prospect was indeed dreary. Without, pouring rain; within, a fireless hearth; a room with but one window, and that containing only one whole pane of glass; not an article of furniture to be seen, save an old painted pine-wood cradle, which had been left there by some freak of fortune. This, turned upon its side, served us for a seat, and there we impatiently awaited the arrival of Moodie, Wilson, and a man whom the former had hired that morning to assist on the farm. Where they were all to be stowed might have puzzled a more sagacious brain than mine. It is true there was a loft, but I could see no way of reaching it, for ladder there was none, so we amused ourselves, while waiting for the coming of our party, by abusing the place, the country, and our own dear selves for our folly in coming to it.

Now, when not only reconciled to Canada, but loving it, and feeling a deep interest in its present welfare, and the fair prospect of its future greatness, I often look back and laugh at the feelings with which I then regarded this noble country.

When things come to the worst, they generally mend. The males of our party no sooner arrived than they set about making things more comfortable. James, our servant, pulled up some of the decayed stumps, with which the small clearing that surrounded the shanty was thickly covered, and made a fire, and Hannah roused herself from the stupor of despair, and seized the corn-broom from the top of the loaded waggon, and began to sweep the house, raising such an intolerable cloud of dust that I was glad to throw my cloak over my head, and run out of doors, to avoid suffocation. Then commenced the awful bustle of unloading the two heavily-loaded waggons. The small space within the house was soon entirely blocked up with trunks and packages of all descriptions. There was scarcely room to move, without stumbling over some article of household stuff.

The rain poured in at the open door, beat in at the shattered window, and dropped upon our heads from the holes in the roof. The wind blew keenly through a thousand apertures in the log walls; and nothing could exceed the uncomfortableness of our situation. For a long time the box which contained a hammer and nails was not to be found. At length Hannah discovered it, tied up with some bedding which she was opening out in order to dry. I fortunately spied the door lying among some old boards at the back of the house, and Moodie immediately commenced fitting it to its place. This, once accomplished, was a great addition to our comfort. We then nailed a piece of white cloth entirely over the broken window, which, without diminishing the light, kept out the rain. James constructed a ladder out of the old bits of boards, and Tom Wilson assisted him in stowing the luggage away in the loft. [. . .] [W]e were all busily employed—even the poor baby, who was lying upon a pillow in the old cradle, trying the strength of her lungs, and not a little irritated that no one was at leisure to regard her laudable endeavours to make herself heard. [. . .]

Brian, the Still-Hunter

It was early day. I was alone in the old shanty, preparing breakfast, and now and then stirring the cradle with my foot, when a tall, thin, middle-aged man walked into the house, followed by two large, strong dogs.

Placing the rifle he had carried on his shoulder, in a corner of the room, he advanced to the hearth and without speaking, or seemingly looking at me, lighted his pipe, and commenced smoking. The dogs, after growling and snapping at the cat, who had not given the strangers a very courteous reception, sat down on the hearth-stone on either side of their taciturn master, eyeing him from time to time, as if long habit had made them understand all his motions. There was a great contrast between the dogs. The one was a brindled bulldog of the largest size, a most formidable and powerful brute; the other a staghound, tawny, deep-chested, and strong-limbed. I regarded the man and his hairy companions with silent curiosity.

He was between forty and fifty years of age; his head, nearly bald, was studded at the sides with strong, coarse, black curling hair. His features were high, his complexion brightly dark, and his eyes, in size, shape, and colour, greatly resembled the eyes of a hawk. The face itself was sorrowful and taciturn; and his thin, compressed lips looked as if they were not much accustomed to smile, or often to unclose to hold social communion with any one. He stood at the side of the huge hearth, silently smoking, his eyes bent on the fire, and now and then he patted the heads of his dogs, reproving their exuberant expressions of attachment, with—"Down, Music; down, Chance!"

"A cold, clear morning," said I, in order to attract his attention and draw him into conversation.

A nod, without raising his head, or withdrawing his eyes from the fire, was his only answer; and, turning from my unsociable guest, I took up the baby, who just then awoke, sat down on a low stool by the table, and began feeding her. During this operation, I once or twice caught the stranger's hawk-eye fixed upon me and the child, but word spoke he none; and presently, after whistling to his dogs, he resumed his gun, and strode out.

When Moodie and Monaghan came in to breakfast, I told them what a strange visitor I had had; and Moodie laughed at my vain attempt to induce him to talk.

"He is a strange being," I said; "I must find out who and what he is."

In the afternoon an old soldier, called Layton, who had served during the American war, and got a grant of land about a mile in the rear of our location, came in to trade for a cow. Now, this Layton was a perfect ruffian; a man whom no one liked, and whom all feared. He was a deep drinker, a great swearer, in short, a perfect reprobate; who never cultivated his land, but went jobbing about from farm to farm, trading horses and cattle, and cheating in a pettifogging way. Uncle Joe had employed him to sell Moodie a young heifer, and he had brought her over for him to look at. When he came in to be paid, I described the stranger of the morning; and as I knew that he was familiar with every one in the neighbourhood, I asked if he knew him.

"No one should know him better than myself," he said; "'tis old Brian B——, the still-hunter, and a near neighbour of your'n. A sour, morose, queer chap he is, and as mad as a March hare! He's from Lancashire, in England, and came to this country some twenty years ago, with his wife, who was a pretty young lass in those days, and slim enough then, though she's so awful fleshy now. He had lots of money, too, and he bought four hundred acres of land, just at the corner of the concession line, where it meets the main road. And excellent land it is; and a better farmer, while he stuck to his business, never went into the bush, for it was all bush here then. He was a dashing, handsome fellow, too, and did not hoard the money either; he loved his pipe and his pot too well; and at last he left off farming, and gave himself to them altogether. Many a jolly booze he and I have had, I can tell you. Brian was an awful passionate man, and, when the liquor was in, and the wit was out, as savage and as quarrelsome as a bear. At such times there was no one but Ned Layton dared go near him. We once had a pitched battle, in which I was conqueror; and ever arter he yielded a sort of sulky obedience to all I said to him. Arter being on the spree for a week or two, he would take fits of remorse, and return home to his wife; would fall down at her knees, and ask her forgiveness, and cry like a child. At other times he would hide himself up in the woods, and steal home at night, and get what he wanted out of the pantry, without speaking a word to any one. He went on with these pranks for some years, till he took a fit of the blue devils.

"'Come away, Ned, to the ——lake, with me,' said he; 'I am weary of my life, and I want a change.'

"'Shall we take the fishing-tackle?' says I. 'The black bass are in prime season, and F—— will lend us the old canoe. He's got some capital rum up from Kingston. We'll fish all day, and have a spree at night.'

"'It's not to fish I'm going,' says he.

"'To shoot, then? I've bought Rockwood's new rifle.'

"'It's neither to fish nor to shoot, Ned: it's a new game I'm going to try; so come along.'

"Well, to the —— lake we went. The day was very hot, and our path lay through the woods, and over those scorching plains, for eight long miles. I thought I should have dropped by the way; but during our long walk my companion never opened his lips. He strode on before me, at a half-run, never once turning his head.

"'The man must be the devil!' says I, 'and accustomed to a warmer place, or he must feel this. Hollo, Brian! Stop there! Do you mean to kill me?'

"'Take it easy,' says he; 'you'll see another day arter this—I've business on hand, and cannot wait.'

"Well, on we went, at the same awful rate, and it was mid-day when we got to the little tavern on the lake shore, kept by one F——, who had a boat for the convenience of strangers who came to visit the place. Here we got our dinner, and a glass of rum to wash it down. But Brian was moody, and to all my jokes he only returned a sort of grunt; and while I was talking with F——, he steps out, and a few minutes arter we saw him crossing the lake in the old canoe.

"'What's the matter with Brian?' says F——; 'all does not seem right with him, Ned. You had better take the boat, and look arter him.'

"'Pooh!' says I; 'he's often so, and grows so glum now-a-days that I will cut his acquaintance altogether if he does not improve.'

"'He drinks awful hard,' says F——; 'may be he's got a fit of the delirium-tremulous. There is no telling what he may be up to at this minute.'

"My mind misgave me too, so I e'en takes the oars, and pushes out, right upon Brian's track; and, by the Lord Harry! if I did not find him, upon my landing on the opposite shore, lying wallowing in his blood, with his throat cut. 'Is that you, Brian?' says I, giving him a kick with my foot, to see if he was alive or dead. 'What upon earth tempted you to play me and F—— such a dirty, mean trick, as to go and stick yourself like a pig, bringing such a discredit upon the house?—and you so far from home and those who should nurse you.'

"I was so mad with him, that (saving your presence, ma'am) I swore awfully, and called him names that would be ondacent to repeat here; but he only answered with groans and a horrid gurgling in his throat. 'It's choking you are,' said I; 'but you shan't have your own way, and die so easily either, if I can punish you by keeping you alive.' So I just turned him upon his stomach, with his head down the steep bank; but he still kept choking and growing black in the face."

Layton then detailed some particulars of his surgical practice which it is not necessary to repeat. He continued,

"I bound up his throat with my handkerchief, and took him neck and heels, and threw him into the bottom of the boat. Presently he came to himself a little, and sat up in the boat; and—would you believe it?—made several attempts to throw himself into the water. 'This will not do,' says I; 'you've done mischief enough already by cutting your weasand! If you dare to try that again, I will kill you with the oar.' I held it up to threaten him; he was scared, and lay down as quiet as a lamb. I put my foot upon his breast. 'Lie still now! or you'll catch it.' He looked piteously at me, he could not speak, but his eyes seemed to say, 'Have pity upon me, Ned; don't kill me.'

"Yes, ma'am; this man, who had just cut his throat, and twice arter that tried to drown himself, was afraid that I should knock him on the head and kill him. Ha! ha! I never shall forget the work that F—— and I had with him arter I got him up to the house.

"The doctor came, and sewed up his throat; and his wife—poor crittur!—came to nurse him. Bad as he was, she was mortal fond of him! He lay there, sick and unable to leave his bed, for three months, and did nothing but pray to God to forgive him, for he thought the devil would surely have him for cutting his own throat; and when he got about again, which is now twelve years ago, he left off drinking entirely, and wanders about the woods with his dogs, hunting. He seldom speaks to any one, and his wife's brother carries on the farm for the family. He is so shy of strangers that 'tis a wonder he came in here. The old wives are afraid of him; but you need not heed him—his troubles are to himself, he harms no one."

Layton departed, and left me brooding over the sad tale which he had told in such an absurd and jesting manner. It was evident from the account he had given of Brian's attempt at suicide, that the hapless hunter was not wholly answerable for his conduct—that he was a harmless maniac.

The next morning, at the very same hour, Brian again made his appearance; but instead of the rifle across his shoulder, a large stone jar occupied the place, suspended by a stout leather thong. Without saying a word, but with a truly benevolent smile, that flitted slowly over his stern features, and lighted them up, like a sunbeam breaking from beneath a stormy cloud, he advanced to the table, and unslinging the jar, set it down before me, and in a low and gruff, but by no means an unfriendly voice, said, "Milk, for the child," and vanished.

"How good it was of him! How kind!" I exclaimed, as I poured the precious gift of four quarts of pure new milk out into a deep pan. I had not asked him—had never said that the poor weanling wanted milk. It was the courtesy of a gentleman—of a man of benevolence and refinement.

For weeks did my strange, silent friend steal in, take up the empty jar, and supply its place with another replenished with milk. The baby knew his step, and would hold out her hands to him and cry "Milk!" and Brian would stoop down and kiss her, and his two great dogs lick her face.

"Have you any children, Mr. B——?"

"Yes, five; but none like this."

"My little girl is greatly indebted to you for your kindness."

"She's welcome, or she would not get it. You are strangers; but I like you all. You look kind, and I would like to know more about you."

Moodie shook hands with the old hunter, and assured him that we should always be glad to see him. After this invitation, Brian became a frequent guest. He would sit and listen with delight to Moodie while he described to him elephant-hunting at the Cape;[8] grasping his rifle in a determined manner, and whistling an encouraging air to his dogs. I asked him one evening what made him so fond of hunting.

""Tis the excitement," he said; "it drowns thought, and I love to be alone. I am sorry for the creatures, too, for they are free and happy; yet I am led by an instinct I cannot restrain to kill them. Sometimes the sight of their dying agonies recalls painful feelings; and then I lay aside the gun, and do not hunt for days. But 'tis fine to be alone with God in the great woods—to watch the sunbeams stealing through the thick branches, the blue sky breaking in upon you in patches, and to know that all is bright and shiny above you, in spite of the gloom that surrounds you."

After a long pause, he continued, with much solemn feeling in his look and tone.

"I lived a life of folly for years, for I was respectably born and educated, and had seen something of the world, perhaps more than was good, before I left home for the woods; and from the teaching I had received from kind relatives and parents I should have known how to have conducted myself better. But, madam, if we associate long with the depraved and ignorant, we learn to become even worse than they are. I felt deeply my degradation—felt that I had become the slave to low vice; and in order to emancipate myself from the hateful tyranny of evil passions, I did a very rash and foolish thing. I need not mention the manner in which I transgressed God's holy laws; all the neighbours know it, and must have told you long ago. I could have borne reproof, but they turned my sorrow into indecent jests, and, unable to bear their coarse ridicule, I made companions of my dogs and gun, and went forth into the wilderness. Hunting became a habit. I could no longer live without it, and it supplies the stimulant which I lost when I renounced the cursed whiskey bottle.

"I remember the first hunting excursion I took alone in the forest. How sad and gloomy I felt! I thought that there was no creature in the world so miserable as myself. I was tired and hungry, and I sat down upon a fallen tree to rest. All was still as death around me, and I was fast sinking to sleep, when my attention was aroused by a long, wild cry. My dog, for I had not Chance then, and he's no hunter, pricked up his ears, but instead of answering with a bark of defiance, he crouched down, trembling, at my feet. 'What does this mean?' I cried, and I cocked my rifle and sprang upon the log. The sound came nearer upon the wind. It was like the deep baying of a pack of hounds in full cry. Presently a noble deer rushed past me, and fast upon his

---

[8] Cape of Good Hope. John Moodie published his book *Ten Years in South Africa, Including a Particular Description of the Wild Sports* based on his own travels in 1835.

trail—I see them now, like so many black devils—swept by a pack of ten or fifteen large, fierce wolves, with fiery eyes and bristling hair, and paws that seemed hardly to touch the ground in their eager haste. I thought not of danger, for, with their prey in view, I was safe; but I felt every nerve within me tremble for the fate of the poor deer. The wolves gained upon him at every bound. A close thicket intercepted his path, and, rendered desperate, he turned at bay. His nostrils were dilated, and his eyes seemed to send forth long streams of light. It was wonderful to witness the courage of the beast. How bravely he repelled the attacks of his deadly enemies, how gallantly he tossed them to the right and left, and spurned them from beneath his hoofs; yet all his struggles were useless, and he was quickly overcome and torn to pieces by his ravenous foes. At that moment he seemed more unfortunate even than myself, for I could not see in what manner he had deserved his fate. All his speed and energy, his courage and fortitude, had been exerted in vain. I had tried to destroy myself; but he, with every effort vigorously made for self-preservation, was doomed to meet the fate he dreaded! Is God just to his creatures?"

With this sentence on his lips, he started abruptly from his seat, and left the house.

One day he found me painting some wild flowers, and was greatly interested in watching the progress I made in the group. Late in the afternoon of the following day he brought me a large bunch of splendid spring flowers.

"Draw these," said he; I have been all the way to the —— lake plains to find them for you."

Little Katie, grasping them one by one, with infantile joy, kissed every lovely blossom.

"These are God's pictures," said the hunter, "and the child, who is all nature, understands them in a minute. Is it not strange that these beautiful things are hid away in the wilderness, where no eyes but the birds of the air, and the wild beasts of the wood, and the insects that live upon them, ever see them? Does God provide, for the pleasure of such creatures, these flowers? Is His benevolence gratified by the admiration of animals whom we have been taught to consider as having neither thought nor reflection? When I am alone in the forest, these thoughts puzzle me." [. . .]

When our resolution was formed to sell our farm, and take up our grant of land in the backwoods, no one was so earnest in trying to persuade us to give up this ruinous scheme as our friend Brian B——, who became quite eloquent in his description of the trials and sorrows that awaited us. During the last week of our stay in the township of H——, he visited us every evening, and never bade us good-night without a tear moistening his cheek. We parted with the hunter as with an old friend; and we never met him again. His fate was a sad one. After we left that part of the country, he fell into a moping melancholy, which ended in self-destruction. But a kinder or warmer-hearted man, while he enjoyed the light of reason, has seldom crossed our path.

Adieu to the Woods

[T]hat was the last night I ever spent in the bush[9]—in the dear forest home which I had loved in spite of all the hardships which we had endured since we pitched our tent in the backwoods. It was the birthplace of my three boys, the school of high resolve and energetic action in which we had learned to meet calmly, and successfully to battle with the ills of life. Nor did I leave it without many regretful tears, to mingle once more with a world to whose usages, during my long solitude, I had become almost a stranger, and to whose praise or blame I felt alike indifferent. [. . .]

Many painful and conflicting emotions agitated my mind, but found no utterance in words, as we entered the forest path, and I looked my last upon that humble home consecrated by the memory of a thousand sorrows. Every object had become endeared to me during my long exile from civilised life. I loved the lonely lake, with its magnificent belt of dark pines sighing in the breeze; the cedar-swamp, the summer home of my dark Indian friends; my own dear little garden, with its rugged snake-fence which I had helped Jenny to place with my own hands, and which I had assisted the faithful woman in cultivating for the last three years, where I had so often braved the tormenting musquitoes, black-flies, and intense heat, to provide vegetables for the use of the family. Even the cows, that had given a breakfast for the last time to my children, were now regarded with mournful affection. [. . .]

Reader! It is not my intention to trouble you with the sequel of our history. I have given you a faithful picture of life in the backwoods of Canada, and I leave you to draw from it your own conclusions. To the poor, industrious working man it presents many advantages; to the poor gentleman, *none!* The former works hard, puts up with coarse, scanty fare, and submits, with a good grace, to hardships that would kill a domesticated animal at home. Thus he becomes independent, inasmuch as the land that he has cleared finds him in the common necessaries of life; but it seldom, if ever, in remote situations, accomplishes more than this. The gentleman can neither work so hard, live so coarsely, nor endure so many privations as his poorer but more fortunate neighbour. Unaccustomed to manual labour, his services in the field are not of a nature to secure for him a profitable return. The task is new to him, he knows not how to perform it well; and, conscious of his deficiency, he expends his little means in hiring labour, which his bush-farm can never repay. Difficulties increase, debts grow upon him, he struggles in vain to extricate himself, and finally sees his family sink into hopeless ruin.

If these sketches should prove the means of deterring one family from sinking their property, and shipwrecking all their hopes, by going to reside in the backwoods of Canada, I shall consider myself amply repaid for revealing the secrets of the prison-house, and feel that I have not toiled and suffered in the wilderness in vain.

[1852]

---

[9] In 1839, John Moodie was appointed sheriff of Hastings County. The Moodies settled in the town of Belleville, on Lake Ontario, in early 1840.

Forest Life in Canada West

[Anonymous review of Roughing It in the Bush *in Blackwood's Edinburgh Magazine, Vol. 72, January-June 1852.]*

Ladies of Britain, deftly embroidering in carpeted saloon, gracefully bending over easel or harp, pressing, with nimble finger, your piano's ivory, or joyously tripping in Cellarian circles, suspend, for a moment, your silken pursuits, and look forth into the desert at a sister's sufferings! May you never, from stern experience, learn fully to appreciate them. But, should fate have otherwise decreed, may you equal her in fortitude and courage. Meanwhile, transport yourselves, in imagination's car, to Canada's backwoods, and behold one, gently nurtured as yourselves, cheerfully condescending to rudest toils, unrepiningly enduring hardships you never dreamed of.

Not to such hardships was she born, nor educated for them. The comforts of an English home, the endearments of sisterly affection, the refinement of literary tastes, but ill prepared the emigrant's wife to work, in the rugged and inclement wilderness, harder than the meanest of the domestics, whom, in her own country, she was used to command. But where are the obstacles and difficulties that shall not be overcome by a strong will, a warm heart, a trusting and cheerful spirit?—precious qualities, strikingly combined by the lady of whose countless trials and troubles we have here an affecting and remarkable record.

The Far West of Canada is so remote a residence, and there is so much oblivion in a lapse of twenty years, that it may be necessary to mention who the authoress is who now appeals (successfully; or we are much mistaken) to the favour of her countrymen, and more especially of her countrywomen. Of a family well known in literature, Mrs Moodie is a sister of Miss Agnes Strickland, the popular and accomplished historical biographer.[10] In 1831, Miss Susanna Strickland published a volume of poems.[11] Had she remained in England, she in time, perhaps, might have rivalled her sister's fame as one of the most distinguished female writers of the day. But it was otherwise ordained. In 1832 she sailed, as Mrs Moodie, an emigrant to Canada. Under most unfavourable circumstances, she still from time to time took up the pen. The anxieties and accidents of her forest life, her regrets for the country she loved so well, and had left perhaps for ever, and, subsequently, the rebellion in Canada, suggested many charming songs and poems, some of which are still extremely popular in our North American colony. Years passed amidst hardships and sufferings. At last a brighter day dawned, and it is from a tranquil and happy home, as we gladly understand, that the

[10] Agnes Strickland (with her sister Eliza, who demanded anonymity) wrote the *Lives of the Queens of England, from the Norman Conquest.* The sisters further collaborated on four other works, including *Lives of the Queens of Scotland.*

[11] Susanna Moodie published *Enthusiasm and Other Poems* as well as *The History of Mary Prince* and *Negro Slavery Described by a Negro: Being the Narrative of Ashton Warner* in 1831.

settler's brave wife has transmitted this narrative of seven years' exertion and adventure. [. . .]

Most nobly, when the toil and anxiety came, did this high-hearted woman bear up against them. Severer hardships and trials were perhaps never endured, for so long a period, by one of her delicate sex. [. . .] Think of this, ye dainty dames, who, in like circumstances, heap your beds with feathers, and strew the street with straw. Think of the chilly forest, the windy log-house, the frosted potatoes, the five children, the weary, half-famished mother, the absence of all that gentle aid and comfort which wait upon your slightest ailment. Think of all these things, and, if the picture move you, remember that the like sufferings and necessities abound nearer home, within scope of your charity and relief.

[1852]

From Life in the Clearings versus the Bush

Introduction

In our work of "Roughing it in the Bush," I endeavoured to draw a picture of Canadian life, as I found it twenty years ago, in the Backwoods. My motive in giving such a melancholy narrative to the public, was prompted by the hope of deterring well-educated people, about to settle in this colony, from entering upon a life for which they were totally unfitted by their previous pursuits and habits.

To persons unaccustomed to hard labour, and used to the comforts and luxuries deemed indispensable to those moving in the middle classes at home, a settlement in the bush can offer few advantages.

It has proved the ruin of hundreds and thousands who have ventured their all in this hazardous experiment; nor can I recollect a single family of the higher class, that have come under my own personal knowledge, that ever realised an independence, or bettered their condition, by taking up wild lands in remote localities; while volumes might be filled with failures, even more disastrous than our own, to prove the truth of my former statements.

But while I have endeavoured to point out the error of gentlemen bringing delicate women and helpless children to toil in the woods, and by so doing excluding them from all social intercourse with persons in their own rank, and depriving the younger branches of the family of the advantages of education, which, in the vicinity of towns and villages, can be enjoyed by the children of the poorest emigrant, I have never said anything against the Real benefits to be derived from a judicious choice of settlement in this great and rising country. God forbid that any representations of mine should deter one of my countrymen from making this noble and prosperous colony his future home. But let him leave to the hardy labourer the place assigned to him by Providence, nor undertake, upon limited means, the task of pioneer in the great wilderness. Men of independent fortune can live anywhere. If such prefer a life in the woods, to the woods let them go; but they will soon find out that they could have employed the means in their power in a far more profitable manner than in chopping down trees in the bush.

There are a thousand more advantageous ways in which a man of property may invest his capital, than by burying himself and his family in the woods. There never was a period in the history of the colony that offered greater inducements to men of moderate means to emigrate to Canada than the present. The many plank-roads and railways in the course of construction in the province, while they afford high and remunerative wages to the working classes, will amply repay the speculator who embarks a portion of his means in purchasing shares in them. And if he is bent upon becoming a Canadian farmer, numbers of fine farms, in healthy and eligible situations, and in the vicinity of good markets, are to be had on moderate terms, that would amply repay the cultivator for the money and labor expended upon them. [. . .]

At the period when the greatest portion of "Roughing it in the Bush" was written, I was totally ignorant of life in Canada, as it existed in the towns and villages. Thirteen years' residence in one of the most thriving districts in the Upper Province[12] has given me many opportunities of becoming better acquainted with the manners and habits of her busy, bustling population, than it was possible for me ever to obtain in the green prison of the woods.

Since my residence in a settled part of the country, I have enjoyed as much domestic peace and happiness as ever falls to the lot of poor humanity. Canada has become almost as dear to me as my native land; and the home-sickness that constantly preyed upon me in the Backwoods, has long ago yielded to the deepest and most heartfelt interest in the rapidly increasing prosperity and greatness of the country of my adoption—the great foster mother of that portion of the human family whose fatherland, however dear to them, is unable to supply them with bread.

To the honest sons of labour Canada is, indeed, an El Dorado—a land flowing with milk and honey; for they soon obtain that independence which the poor gentleman struggles in vain to realise by his own labour in the woods.

The conventional prejudices that shackle the movements of members of the higher classes in Britain are scarcely recognised in Canada; and a man is at liberty to choose the most profitable manner of acquiring wealth, without the fear of ridicule and the loss of caste. [. . .]

[1853]

---

[12] In the 1840s, Belleville was a bustling town.

George Henry (Maungwudaus) was an Ojibway translator, Methodist preacher, impresario, and performer in the mid-nineteenth century. In the late 1820s, he attended the Methodist Mission School in Credit, Upper Canada, and later served as a preacher in various missions throughout the province. However, Henry was drawn to a more exciting career when, in 1844, he organized an Ojibway dance troupe and exhibition that toured Europe and the United States between 1845 and 1848. Henry's self-styled performance career bears comparison with Pauline Johnson's, including the adoption of Aboriginal "costume" to enhance his exotic mystique, and the performance of "war dances" to titillate European and American audiences. Tragically, his wife and three of his children died during the British portion of this tour. He wrote two accounts based on these experiences: *Remarks concerning the Ojibway Indians, by one of themselves, called Maungwudaus, who has been travelling in England, France, Belgium, Ireland, and Scotland* (1847) and *An Account of the Chippewa Indians, who have been travelling among the whites in the United States, England, Ireland, Scotland, France and Belgium* (1848); the excerpt included here is from the latter. These works are among the earliest recorded impressions of Europeans told from a Native perspective, and so are extremely important as a counterpoint to the innumerable representations of Native peoples in so much of Canadian literary history. They go some way to filling in the obvious silence in George Cartwright's text, where the Inuit people's skeptical impressions of England are related from Cartwright's viewpoint. Interestingly, according to the Library and Archives Canada description of a photograph of

Henry in its possession, taken in 1846 during his tour of England, he was one of the earliest Aboriginal people in Canada to be photographed. Henry's travel narrative is both humorous and incisive. His text is striking in the way it "defamiliarizes" readers' conventional views of Europeans, as, for example, when he describes the bearded Englishmen as looking "fierce and savage like our American dogs when carrying black squirrels in their mouths." His account of the Europeans as strange and in many cases vulgar, with "very big stomachs" and "the voice of a bull-frog," forms an insightful counterpoint to the many European accounts of North American Aboriginal peoples in similar terms. He also subtly highlights some of the hypocrisies of European attitudes about Native peoples' "immoral" lifestyles, particularly in his description of the London prostitutes, whom he designates "common wives" (the term used for Native women who became mistresses to the English and French traders in Canada): "They [the English] say that [the common wives] are allowed to walk in the streets every night for the safety of the married women." The condescension with which the Native delegates are treated by these prostitutes, and, in a subsequent scene, by some local townspeople when viewing a performing monkey, highlights Henry's keen sense of the ingrained biases in White attitudes toward Aboriginal people. His contrast of American liberality with English formality is also amusing, and forms an interesting complement to Susanna Moodie's depiction of Americans (and, for that matter, Native peoples) in *Roughing It in the Bush* (1852). Henry's is an important document in providing a picture of divergent peoples struggling to understand each other's customs and social mores.

From An Account of the Chippewa Indians

While on the sea our middle mast got blown away. The waves were like mountains; we did not get sea-sick, only got little hurt sometimes when thrown out of our berths. Sometime got a good ducking with salt water by the waves, pouring into our cabin. The flour and corn barrels got loose and knocked against one another and spilt all that was inside of them. The rats had great feasting. Every night after they had their bellies full they were very mischievous; they helped the waves in tormenting us, by biting us on our toes and noses. The sea in the night was like the blaze of fire.

We landed at Portsmouth on the 26th of the same month. Portsmouth is a great place for ships. We went to see Lord Nelson's war-ship and saw the place where he fell when he was killed.[1] The officers living in this sea-house were very kind to us. The great sea-war chief took us into the navy yard where they are making many war ships. Another war chief invited us and showed us all his warriors under him in the barracks.

From Portsmouth we went to London, and we remained a long time in this wonderful city; performed every day in the Egyptian Hall, in Piccadilly. This city is about ten miles broad, but some parts of it is about twenty miles long. Like musketoes in America in the summer season, so are the people in this city, in their numbers, and biting one another to get a living. Many very rich, and many very poor; about 900 births and about 1100 deaths every week in this city alone. There are many stone and iron bridges over the river Thames. The steamboats in this river are not so handsome as those in America. The St. Paul's church and the Council House are very large buildings indeed. Most of the houses rather dark in color on account of too much smoke.

Many ladies and gentlemen ride about in carriages. The carriages, servants and horses are covered with gold and silver. Hundreds of them walk about in the parks, the servants leading little dogs behind them to air them. The English women cannot walk alone; they must always be assisted by the men. They make their husbands carry their babies for them when walking.

Mr. Harris took us into the Queen's[2] house. She is a small woman but handsome. There are many handsomer women than she is. Prince Albert[3] is a handsome and well built man. Her house is large, quiet country inside of it. We got tired before we went through all the rooms in it. Great many warriors with their swords and guns stands outside watching for the enemy. We have been told that she has three or four other houses in other places as large. The one we

---

[1] Vice-Admiral Horatio Nelson, 1st Viscount Nelson (1758–1805), was a British admiral famous for his participation in the Napoleonic Wars, most notably in the Battle of Trafalgar.

[2] Queen Victoria (1819–1901) was the queen of the United Kingdom and Ireland from 1837 to 1901.

[3] Prince Albert, the prince consort (1819–61), was the husband of Queen Victoria.

saw they say is too small for her, and they are building a much larger one on one side of it.

When she goes out she has a great many warriors before and behind, guarding her; most of them seven feet tall. Their coats and caps are of steel; long white horse-hair waves on their heads. They wear long boots, long gloves, and white buckskin breeches. Their swords, guns, and everything about them are kept very clean and bright. Their horses are all black, and much silver and gold about them. They do not shave the upper part of their mouths, but let the beards grow long, and this makes them look fierce and savage like our American dogs when carrying black squirrels in their mouths.

The nobility and ministers and the Society of Friends[4] invited us most every day to take tea with them. Sometimes we were about two hours in eating; the plates, knives, forks, spoons and everything we used in eating were of gold and silver. The servants' heads were white powdered; they gave us many handsome presents, and caused us to see many things that others have never seen. [. . .] We went through the tunnel under the bed of the river Thames. The ships were sailing over us while walking below.

Our war-chief shot a buck in the Park, through the heart, and fell down dead three hundred yards, before four thousand ladies and gentlemen. This was done to amuse them. Travelling on the Great Western Railway, the Engine knocked down several rooks or crows while flying over the railway. We saw three men out of the Zoological Gardens going up to the country of stars. They had something very large in the shape of a bladder over their heads; they called it a balloon. One man said to us, 'You see now that we Englishmen can go and see the upper world with our bodies.' Lord Bloomfield invited us to see the big guns at Woolwich;[5] three of us got inside of one of them.

They say that there are eighty thousand common wives in the city of London. They say that they are allowed to walk in the streets every night for the safety of the married women. The English officers invited us to eat with them in the barracks in our native costume. When the tea got ready, the ladies were brought to the table like sick women; it took us about two hours in eating. The ladies were very talkative while eating; like ravens when feasting on venison. Indeed, they have a proverb which says, 'Thieves and robbers eat and drink a little, and make no noise when they eat.' They are very handsome; their waists, hands and feet are very small; their necks are rather longer than those of our women. They carry their heads on one side of the shoulder; they hold the knife and fork with the two forefingers and the thumb of each hand; the two last ones are of no use to them, only sticking out like our fish-spears, while eating.

The English officers are fine, noble, and dignified looking fellows. The voice of them when coming out of the mouth, sounds like the voice of a bull-frog. The only fault we saw of them, are their too many unneccessary [sic] ceremonies while

[4] The Religious Society of Friends, commonly known as the Quakers.

[5] Lieutenant-General Benjamin Bloomfield, 1st Baron Bloomfield, was the commanding officer of the garrison at Woolwich, the home of the Royal Artillery.

eating, such as allow me Sir, or Mrs. to put this into your plate. If you please Sir, thank you, you are very kind Sir, or Mrs. can I have the pleasure of helping you?

Many of the Englishmen have very big stomachs, caused by drinking too much ale and porter. Those who drink wine and brandy, their noses look like ripe strawberries.

When we got ready to leave, one of the officers said to us, our ladies would be glad to shake hands with you, and we shook hands with them. Then they were talking amongst themselves; then another officer said to us, 'Friends, our ladies think that you do not pay enough respects to them, they desire you to kiss them'; then we kissed them according to our custom on both cheeks. 'Why! they have kissed us on our cheeks; what a curious way of kissing this is.' Then another officer said to us, 'Gentlemen, our pretty squaws are not yet satisfied; they want to be kissed on their mouths.' Then we kissed them on their mouths; then there was a great shout amongst the English war-chiefs. Say-say-gon, our war-chief, then said in our language to the ladies: 'That is all you are good for; as for wives, you are good for nothing.' The ladies wanted me to tell them what the war-chief said to them. I then told them that he said he was wishing the officers would invite him very often, that he might again kiss the handsome ladies. Then they said, 'Did he? then we will tell our men to invite you again, for we like to be kissed very often; tell him so.' They put gold rings on our fingers and gold pins on our breasts, and when we had thanked them for their kindness, we got in our carriage and went to our apartments.

The great war-chief with the big nose, Duke of Wellington,[6] invited us, and he was very kind to us in his house. He and his son gave us handsome presents. [. . .]

The Archbishop of Canterbury Cathedral was very kind to us; he showed us everything in the Cathedral, curious and wonderful works of the ancient Britons. He said that this building is thirteen hundred years old. This is the most curious, the largest, and beautiful one we have seen. The top of its steeple our arrows could not reach. [. . .]

We crossed to Scotland and landed at the place called Ardrosson; we went to see R. Burns's[7] cottage, small, with straw-roof. We went to see Wallace's Oak Tree[8] near Paisley; went to Glasgow and Edinburgh. Edinburgh is large of the Scotch people; the new town is very handsome, but the old town is rather filthy. All the dirt is thrown in the streets before people get up, and carts take it away, but still the smell of it is most offensive all day. One of the chiefs told us that a Scotchman some years ago, who was born in the city, was away from it for some years, and returning to it he said, 'There is nothing like home'; and when he began to smell the streets, he said, 'Ah! sweet auld Edinburgh, I smell thee now.' The Scotch chiefs showed us the Crown of Scotland in the castle, also the Palace. We went to

---

[6] Duke of Wellington (1769–1852).

[7] Robert Burns (1759–96). Poet and lyricist who wrote in the Scottish vernacular and who is often considered to be the national poet of Scotland.

[8] Sir William Wallace, "Guardian of Scotland," was a hero of Scotland's Wars of Independence against England during the late thirteenth and early fourteenth centuries. Legend has it that William Wallace hid in the tree to avoid capture by his enemy. The ancient tree finally fell in a storm in 1856.

see about seventy young men, who are to be medicine men. They had thirty dead bodies, and they were skinning and cutting them same as we do with venison.

The Scotch people are very religious and industrious, very kind-hearted to strangers. They keep Sunday very strictly. A great many are teetotalers;[9] their country is mountainous. The old men and women are very fond of snuff;[10] they carry it in rams horns; they put one spoonful of it in each nostril at a time; this causes their words to sound nasal, something like pig grunting.

At Glasgow, two of my children died, another in Edinburgh; buried them in the burying ground of our friends the Quakers; and after we visited other towns at the North and South, we went to England again; my wife died at Newark. The vicar of that church was very kind to us, in allowing us to bury her remains near the church.

Riding through a town in our native costume, we saw a monkey performing in the street upon a music box, about fifty young men looking at him. He was dressed like a man. When the young men saw us, they began to make fun of us, and made use of very insulting language, making a very great noise;—at the same time when the monkey saw us he forgot his performances, and while we were looking at him, he took off his red cap and made a bow to us. A gentleman standing by, said to the audience, 'Look at the monkey take off his cap and make a bow in saluting those strangers; which of the two strangers will think are most civilized, you or the monkey? You ought to be ashamed of yourselves. You may consider yourselves better and wiser than those strangers, but you are very much mistaken. Your treatment to them tells them that you are not, and you are so foolish and ignorant, you know nothing about it. I have been travelling five years amongst these people in their own country, and I never, not once, was insulted, but I was always kindly treated and respected by every one of them. Their little children have far better manners than you. Young men, the monkey pays you well for all the pennies you have given him; he is worthy to become your teacher.' We then threw some money to the monkey, and he jumped down from his platform and picked up the money and jumped up again, and put the money into his master's mouth, and he made another bow to us as we were going away; at the same time heard one of the young men saying to his friends, 'See the teacher making another bow to the Indians.' 'Yes,' said another, 'this is to teach you, for you are the very one that was making fun and blackguarding the Indians.'

We visited New Castle upon Tyne, Hull, Leeds, York, Birmingham, and many other Towns; visited Shakespeare's house and his grave at Stratford on Avon. We visited Lord Byron's[11] house. Col. Wildman was very kind to us; went to Nottingham and to London again.

We left London the 23d of April, 1848, with the ship called Yorktown, of New York. Capt. Seba was very kind to us all the way. Sixteen children of the Germans

[9] One who abstains from any intoxicating liquor.

[10] Powdered tobacco inhaled through the nostrils.

[11] George Gordon, Lord Byron (1788–1824), was a leading British Romantic poet. Byron's house, Newstead Abbey, in Southwell, Nottinghamshire, was purchased by Colonel Thomas Wildman from Byron in 1817.

died on the way; also an English lady. Ourselves did not get sea sick. The waves were like mountains; saw seven whales and many porpoises; landed in New York city on the 4th of June, and we were very thankful to the Great Spirit for bringing us back again to America. [. . .]

In Ipswich [Massachusetts] we dined with our friends the Quakers, about sixty in number; their names are Alexanders and Ransoms. After we had eaten many good things and all the plates taken away, a small round but high cheese was put on the table, and one of the oldest Friends said to us, 'Now, friends, this is our English cheese; the poor of our people cannot afford to eat this. We never think that our dinner is finished until we have ate some of it; will thou have little of it.' I said yes. Will thou have little of it, &c., until every one of us had it before us, and we ate much of it, because it was from our friends. When our eating was over, a doctor, whose name is F.W. Johnson, placed on the table, what he calls microscope; it had three brass legs and a small glass to it, and when he had put a very small bit of the cheese we had to eat on a clean plate, he made us look at it through the little glass that was on the three legged brass, and we saw hundreds of worms moving in it. This made all our friends laugh, and we tried to laugh too, but we were very much frightened at the same time knowing that we must have swallowed thousands of them. When our friends saw that we were frightened, the medicine man dropped one drop of rain water in a clear glass, and he made us look at it again through the little glass, and we saw hundreds of living creatures swimming in it; some like beasts, some like snakes, some like fish, some had horns and some had no horns, some with legs and some had no legs; some had wheels on each side of their bodies, and with these they were moving about like steamboats, hooking, chasing, fighting, killing and eating one another. Then one of our oldest friends said to us, 'Now, friends, you must not think that this is the first time you have been eating worms. We swallow thousands of them every day either with food or water. They are floating in the air, and we inhale them, when we draw breath; thousands of them are also floating in our veins. The Great Spirit, who made us and all other beings is wonderful in power and wisdom. We sincerely hope that you will at all times love him, and obey what he tells you in your hearts.' We waited two or three days for the worms to bite. Sometimes we would be looking for them, thinking that they might have grown larger while they were in our bodies, but we did not feel their bites nor saw any of them. We have oftentimes been thinking since, that our friends must be something like bears, who love to eat living worms or maggots.

The Americans have been very kind to us in all places; they are not so fleshy as the English, but very persevering in all their ways. They pay more respect to their females than the English, and they like to see things belong to others without leave. The working classes of the English call their rich men 'Big Bugs,' but the Yankee call them, 'Top Notches.' They put their feet upon tables, chairs and chimney pieces when smoking their cigars or reading newspapers. They are not so much slaves to their civilization as the English; they like to be comfortable, something like ourselves, placing one leg upon the other knee, while basking ourselves in the sun. A real comfort is better than an artificial one to the human nature.

[1848]

CHARLES DAWSON SHANLY ■ (1811–1875)

Although Charles Dawson Shanly was born in Dublin, Ireland, and died in Florida, it is for his Gothic poem "The Walker of the Snow" (1859) that he is remembered in Canada. Shanly emigrated from Ireland to Upper Canada with his family in 1836. Joining the Board of Public Works of Lower Canada to work as a clerk in 1840, he remained with the board after the union of Upper and Lower Canada until 1857. At the same time, Shanly published creative work, often anonymously. For instance, he contributed unsigned poetry, satirical articles, and cartoons to the short-lived comic magazine out of Montreal *Punch in Canada* (1849–50). In 1857 Shanly moved to New York to work as a professional journalist, and wrote for the *Albion, New York Leader,* and *Atlantic Monthly*. He also assisted in founding *Vanity Fair* and later became its editor. His poem "The Walker of the Snow" was published anonymously in the *Atlantic Monthly* in 1859. Suffering from lung trouble, Shanly left New York for Arlington, Florida, only months before his death in 1875. He was buried in Arva, Ontario, near his family's homestead.

According to Sherrill Grace, "The Walker of the Snow" is a dramatic monologue "based on legends or folktales about the 'Shadow Hunter,' a figure who bears some resemblance to the Windigo of northern Ojibwa and Cree mythology." As the unnamed speaker of the poem addresses the "good Master," it is not entirely clear whether he has survived the experience he narrates. Readers, like the master, are held in the suspense of the tale and the obsession of the teller. Indeed, Shanly plays with the Gothic conventions of fireside ghost tales, where we never quite know if the speaker is a figure or a phantom himself. In this manner, "The Walker of the Snow" is reminiscent of S.T. Coleridge's "The Rime of the Ancient Mariner" (1798), and foreshadows the Gothic tradition in Canadian poems such as Robert Service's "The Cremation of Sam McGee" (1907). Grace argues of Shanly's poem that "he might be addressing us all from the depth of our inner fears about being alone . . . in the middle of the northern wilderness." John Burroughs included "The Walker of the Snow" in his collection *Locusts and Wild Honey* (1879) as an example of a poem that "fits well the distended pupil of the mind's eye about the camp-fire at night." The poem was also included in William Douw Lighthall's *Songs of the Great Dominion* (1889) and C.M. Whyte-Edgar's *A Wreath of Canadian Song* (1910) as an exemplary Canadian poem of a haunted nordicity and wilderness.

Literary critic Lisa Chalykoff argues that it was Burroughs's inclusion of the poem that made "The Walker of the Snow" known to painter William Blair Bruce (1859–1906), who acknowledges it as the source for his painting *The Phantom Hunter* (1888; Figure II-9, page 140). As Chalykoff notes, both this nocturnal, wintry poem and the painting it inspired depict a shadowy figure that, though human in form, seems distinctly otherworldly in origin.

The Walker of the Snow

SPEED on, speed on, good master!
  The camp lies far away;
We must cross the haunted valley
  Before the close of day.

How the snow-blight came upon me
  I will tell you as we go,—
The blight of the Shadow-hunter,
  Who walks the midnight snow.

To the cold December heaven
  Came the pale moon and the stars,   10
As the yellow sun was sinking
  Behind the purple bars.

The snow was deeply drifted
  Upon the ridges drear,
That lay for miles around me
  And the camp for which we steer.

'Twas silent on the hillside,
  And by the solemn wood
No sound of life or motion
  To break the solitude,   20

Save the wailing of the moose-bird
  With a plaintive note and low,
And the skating of the red leaf
  Upon the frozen snow.

And said I,—"Though dark is falling,
  And far the camp must be,
Yet my heart it would be lightsome,
  If I had but company."

And then I sang and shouted,
  Keeping measure, as I sped,   30
To the harp-twang of the snow-shoe
  As it sprang beneath my tread;

Nor far into the valley
  Had I dipped upon my way,
When a dusky figure joined me,
  In a capuchon[1] of gray,

---

[1] A hood or a head-dress.

Bending upon the snow-shoes,
　　With a long and limber stride;
And I hailed the dusky stranger,
　　As we travelled side by side. 40

But no token of communion
　　Gave he by word or look,
And the fear-chill fell upon me
　　At the crossing of the brook.

For I saw by the sickly moonlight,
　　As I followed, bending low,
That the walking of the stranger
　　Left no footmarks on the snow.

Then the fear-chill gathered o'er me,
　　Like a shroud around me cast, 50
As I sank upon the snow-drift
　　Where the Shadow-hunter passed.

And the otter-trappers found me,
　　Before the break of day,
With my dark hair blanched and whitened
　　As the snow in which I lay.

But they spoke not as they raised me;
　　For they knew that in the night
I had seen the Shadow-hunter,
　　And had withered in his blight. 60

Sancta Maria[2] speed us!
　　The sun is falling low,—
Before us lies the valley
　　Of the Walker of the Snow!

[1859]

---

2 "Holy Mary," another name for the Virgin Mary, the mother of Jesus Christ.

GEORGE COPWAY (KAH-GE-GA-GAH-BOWH) ■ (1818–1869)

George Copway was many things—a missionary, a cultural informant, a lecturer, and a writer. Copway presented himself as an example of the potent mix of Christianity and education. The son of the Ojibwa/Mississauga chief John Copway, who converted to Christianity in 1827, George Copway was taught at the Rice Lake Methodist mission, near Peterborough. He was also known as Kah-ge-ga-gah-bowh, "He who stands forever." In 1840 he married a White woman, Elizabeth Howell, the daughter of Toronto-area farmers. Copway himself was ordained as a Methodist missionary. In his autobiography, *Life, History and Travels of Kah-ge-ga-gah-bowh* (1847), Copway describes his childhood in the Rice Lake area. Here he details the changes to his family's life, including how his parents converted to Methodism. His text presents an interesting counterpoint to the works of Susanna Moodie and Catharine Parr Traill, who emigrated to that area of Upper Canada. While Moodie and Traill were sympathetic to the plight of Native peoples, they did not recognize their own complicity in displacing them from their land. Copway's text points to the challenges his people faced in the 1820s as a result of the influx of tens of thousands of British immigrants onto their hunting grounds. In the excerpt included here, he very clearly describes how Ojibwa families, following the conquest of the Hurons, claimed particular segments of Ontario as their territory, thus highlighting, in a very immediate way, the priority of Native communities before the arrival of the European settlers. Copway's autobiography blends communal history and personal experience as it incorporates traditions from oral storytelling and missionary taletelling. Copway's book was such a success that it went through seven printings in the year after publication. Following its appearance, Copway embarked on a series of speaking engagements as "the noble Christian convert," and often spoke in a full "Ojibwa costume," thereby anticipating the later performance career of Pauline Johnson. For a few years, he was a celebrated author in the United States, and briefly befriended by prominent American writers Henry Wadsworth Longfellow, James Fenimore Cooper, and Francis Parkman.

From Life, History and Travels of Kah-ge-ga-gah-bowh

The Christian will no doubt feel for my poor people, when he hears the story of one brought from that unfortunate race called the Indians. The lover of humanity will be glad to see that that once powerful race can be made to enjoy the blessings of life.

What was once impossible—or rather thought to be—is made possible through my experience. I have made many close observations of men, and things around me; but, I regret to say, that I do not think I have made as good use of my opportunities as I might have done. It will be seen that I know little— yet O how precious *that little!*—I would rather loose my right hand than be deprived of it.

I loved the woods, and the chase. I had the nature for it, and gloried in nothing else. The mind for letters was in me, *but was asleep*, till the dawn of Christianity arose, and awoke the slumbers of the soul into energy and action.

You will see that I served the imaginary gods of my poor blind father. I was out early and late in quest of the favors of the *Mon-e-doos* (spirits), who, it was said, were numerous—who filled the air! At early dawn I watched the rising of the *palace* of the Great Spirit—*the sun*—who, it was said, made the world!

Early as I can recollect, I was taught that it was the gift of the many spirits to be a good hunter and warrior; and much of my time I devoted in search of their favors. On the mountain top, or along the valley, or the water brook, I searched for some kind intimation from the spirits who made their residence in the noise of the waterfalls.

I dreaded to hear the voice of the angry spirit in the gathering clouds. I looked with anxiety to catch a glimpse of the wings of the Great Spirit, who shrouded himself in rolling white and dark clouds—who, with his wings, fanned the earth, and laid low the tall pines and hemlock in his course—who rode in whirlwinds and tornadoes, and plucked the trees from their woven roots—who drove the Bad Spirit from the surface of the earth, down to the dark caverns of the deep. Yet he was a kind spirit. My father taught me to call that spirit Ke-sha-mon-e-doo—*Benevolent spirit*—for his ancestors taught him no other name to give to that spirit who made the earth, with all its variety and smiling beauty. His benevolence I saw in the running of the streams, for the animals to quench their thirst and the fishes to live; the fruit of the earth teemed wherever I looked. Every thing I saw smilingly said Ke-sha-mon-ed-doo nin-ge-oo-she-ig—*the Benevolent spirit made me.*

Where is he? My father pointed to the sun. What is his will concerning me, and the rest of the Indian race? This was a question that I found no one could answer, until a beam from heaven shone on my pathway, which was very dark, when first I saw that there was a true heaven—not in the far-setting sun, where the Indian anticipated a rest, a home for his spirit—but in the bosom of the Highest.

I view my life like the mariner on the wide ocean, without a compass, in the dark night, as he watches the heavens for the north star, which his eye having discovered, he makes his way amidst surging seas, and tossed by angry billows into the very jaws of death, till he arrives safely anchored at port. I have been tossed with hope and fear in this life; no star-light shone on my way, until the men of God pointed me to a Star in the East, as it arose with all its splendor and glory. [. . .]

I have not the happiness of being able to refer to written records in narrating the history of my forefathers; but I can reveal to the world what has long been laid up in my memory; so that when "I go the way of all the earth," the crooked and singular paths which I have made in the world, may not only be a warning to others, but may inspire them with a trust in God. And not only a warning and a trust, but also that the world may learn that there once lived such a man as Kah-ge-ga-gah-bowh, when they read his griefs and his joys.

My parents were of the Ojebwa nation, who lived on the lake back of Cobourg, on the shores of Lake Ontario, Canada West. The lake called Rice Lake, where there was a great quantity of wild rice, and much game of different kinds, before the whites cleared away the woods, where the deer and the bear then resorted.

My father and mother were taught the religion of their nation. My father became a medicine man in the early part of his life, and always had by him the implements of war, which generally distinguish our head men. He was as good a hunter as any in the tribe. Very few brought more furs than he did in the spring. Every spring they returned from their hunting grounds. The Ojebwas each claimed, and claim to this day, hunting grounds, rivers, lakes, and whole districts of country. No one hunted on each other's ground. My father had the northern fork of the river Trent, above Bellmont lake.

My great-grandfather was the first who ventured to settle at Rice Lake, after the Ojebwa nation defeated the Hurons, who once inhabited all the lakes in Western Canada, and who had a large village just on the top of the hill of the Anderson farm, (which was afterwards occupied by the Ojebwas,) and which furnished a magnificent view of the lakes and surrounding country. He was of the *Crane tribe,* i.e. had a crane for his totem—*coat of arms*—which now forms the totem of the villagers, excepting those who have since come amongst us from other villages by intermarriage, for there was a law that no one was to marry one of the same totem, for all considered each other as being related. [. . .] The *Crane tribe* became the sole proprietors of this part of the Ojebwa land; the descendants of this tribe will continue to wear the distinguishing sign; except in a few instances, the chiefs are of this tribe.

My grandfather lived here about this time, and held some friendly intercourse with the whites. My father here learned the manners, customs, and worship of the nation. He, and others, became acquainted with the early settlers, and have ever been friendly with the whites. And I know the day when he used to shake the hand of the white man, and, *very friendly,* the white man would say, *"take some whiskey."* When he saw any hungering for venison, he gave them to eat; and some, in return for his kindness, have repaid him after they became good and great farmers.

My mother was of the *Eagle tribe;* she was a sensible woman; she was as good a hunter as any of the Indians; she could shoot the deer, and the ducks flying, as well as they. Nature had done a great deal for her, for she was active; and she was much more cleanly *[sic]* than the majority of our women in those days. She lived to see the day when most of her children were given up to the Lord in Christian baptism; while she experienced a change of heart, and the fullness of God in man, for she lived daily in the enjoyment of God's favors. I will speak more of her at a proper time, respecting her life and happy death.

My father still lives; he is from sixty-five to seventy years old, and is one of the chiefs of Rice Lake Indian Village. He used to love fire-water before he was converted to God, but now lives in the enjoyment of religion, and he is happy without the devil's spittle—*whiskey.* If Christianity had not come, and the grace of God had not taken possession of his heart, his head would soon have been laid low beneath the fallen leaves of the forest, and I, left, in my youthful days, an orphan. But to God be all the praise for his timely deliverance.

The reader will see that I cannot boast of an exalted parentage, nor trace the past history to some renowned warrior in days of yore, but let the above suffice. My fathers were those who endured much; who first took possession of the conquered lands of the Hurons.

I was born in *nature's wide domain!* The trees were all that sheltered my infant limbs—the blue heavens all that covered me. I am one of nature's children; I have always admired her; she shall be my glory; her features—her robes, and the wreath about her brow—the seasons—her stately oaks, and the evergreen—her hair—ringlets over the earth, all contribute to my enduring love of her; and wherever I see her, emotions of pleasure roll in my breast, and swell and burst like waves on the shores of the ocean, in prayer and praise to Him, who has placed me in her hand. It is thought great to be born in palaces, surrounded with wealth—but to be born in nature's wide domain is greater still!

I was born sometime in the fall of 1818, near the mouth of the river Trent, called in our language, Sah-ge-dah-we-ge-wah-noong, while my father and mother were attending the annual distribution of the presents from the government to the Indians.[1] I was the third of our family; a brother and sister being older, both of whom died. My brother died without knowledge of the Saviour, but my sister experienced the power of the loving grace of God. One brother, and two step-brothers, are still alive.

I remember the tall trees, and the dark woods—the swamp just by, where the little wren sang so melodiously after the going down of the sun in the west— the current of the broad river Trent—the skipping of the fish, and the noise of the rapids a little above. It was here I first saw the light; a little fallen-down shelter, made of evergreens, and a few dead embers, the remains of the last fire that shed its genial warmth around, were all that marked the spot. When I last visited it, nothing but fur [sic] poles stuck in the ground, and they were leaning on account of decay. Is this dear spot, made green by the tears of memory, any less enticing and hallowed than the palaces where princes are born? I would much more glory in this birth-place, with the broad canopy of heaven above me, and the giant arms of the forest trees for my shelter, than to be born in palaces of marble, studded with pillars of gold! Nature will be nature still, while palaces shall decay and fall in ruins. Yes, Niagara will be Niagara a thousand years hence! The rainbow, a wreath over her brow, shall continue as long as the sun, and the flowing of the river! While the work of art, however impregnable, shall in atoms fall.

[. . .] The hunting grounds of the Indians were secured by right, a law and custom among themselves. No one was allowed to hunt on another's land, without invitation or permission. If any person was found trespassing on the ground of another, all his things were taken from him, except a hand full of shot, powder sufficient to serve him in going *straight* home, a gun, a tomahawk, and a knife; all the fur, and other things, were taken from him. If he were found a second time trespassing, all his things were taken away from him, except food sufficient to subsist on while going home. And should he still come a third time to trespass on the same, or another man's hunting grounds, his nation, or tribe, are then informed of it, who take up his case. If still he disobey, he is banished from his tribe.

[1] *The Report on the Affairs of the Indians in Canada* (1847) of the Legislative Assembly of Canada notes that "from the earliest period of the connection between the Indians and the British Government it has been customary to distribute annually certain presents, consisting chiefly of clothing and ammunition." It continues to say that the objective in the first instance was "to conciliate the Indians, to ensure their services, and to supply their wants as warriors in the field; and afterwards, in times of peace, to secure their allegiance towards the British Crown, and their good will and peaceful behaviour towards the white settlers."

My father's hunting ground was at the head of Crow River, a branch of the River Trent, north of the Prince Edward District, Canada West. There are two branches to this river—one belongs to George Poudash, one of the principal chiefs of our nation; the other to my father; and the Crow River belongs to another chief by the name of John Crow. During the last war the Indians did not hunt or fish much for nearly six years, and at the end of that time there were large quantities of beaver, otter, minks, lynx, fishes, &c.

These hunting grounds abound with rivers and lakes; the face of the country is swampy and rocky; the deer and the bear abound in these woods; part of the surrendered territory is included in it. In the year 1818, 1,800,000 acres of it were surrendered to the British government. For how much, do you ask? For $2,960 per annum! What a *great sum* for British generosity!

Much of the back country remains unsold, and I hope the scales will be removed from the eyes of my poor countrymen, that they may see the robberies perpetrated upon them, before they surrender another foot of territory.

From these lakes and rivers come the best furs that are caught in Western Canada. Buyers of fur get large quantities from here. They are then shipped to New-York city, or to England. Whenever fruit is plenty, bears are also plenty, and there is much bear hunting. Before the whites came amongst us, the skins of these animals served for clothing; they are now sold from three to eight dollars a piece.

My father generally took one or two families with him when he went to hunt; all were to hunt, and place their gains into one common stock till spring (for they were often out all winter), when a division took place. [. . .]

I recollect the day when my people in Canada were both numerous and happy; and since then, to my sorrow, they have faded away like frost before the heat of the sun! Where are now that once numerous and happy people? The voice of but few is heard.

The Ojebwa nation, that unconquered nation, has fallen a prey to the withering influence of intemperance. Their buoyant spirits could once mount the air as on the wings of a bird. Now they have no spirits. They are hedged in, bound, and maltreated, by both the American and the British Governments. They have no other hope, than that at some day, they will be relieved from their privations and trials by death. The fire-water has rolled towards them like the waves of the sea. Alas! alas! my poor people! The tribe became dissipated, and consequently improvident, and often suffered intensely. [. . .]

[1847]

MARY ANN SHADD ■ (1823–1893)

Mary Ann Shadd is an important figure in nineteenth-century Canadian history. Known to her family and friends as "The Rebel," she was an abolitionist, an educational reformer, and a suffragette, as well as the first female newspaper editor in Canada West (now Ontario) and the first African-American female law student in North America. Unlike Thomas McCulloch and Joseph Howe in politics but like them in action, Shadd was pivotal in founding a newspaper that helped disseminate her political ideas. By 1854 she served as editor, publisher, and investigative reporter for the anti-slavery newspaper *The Provincial Freeman: Devoted to Anti-Slavery, Temperance, and General Literature*. The motto of the newspaper was "Self-reliance Is the True Road to Independence."

The woman who began the first racially integrated school in Canada was born into a family of free African-American abolitionists in Wilmington, Delaware, in 1823. While she was still young, her family moved to the more progressive state of Pennsylvania, where Shadd attended a Quaker boarding school. Her family's shoemaking shop in Pennsylvania was a stop on the Underground Railroad, serving as a shelter for fugitive slaves. From the age of sixteen, Shadd was dedicated to the education of her people. Following the Fugitive Slave Law of 1850 in America (which permitted slave owners to pursue their "property" to non-slave states and gave full legal support for the capture of slaves anywhere in the United States, as well as the sale of captured freed slaves), there was a mass exodus to Canada. Because of the anti-slavery legislation enacted in Canada in 1833, it was a refuge for both free men and women and runaway slaves from the United States. With her brother Isaac, Shadd emigrated in 1850 to Windsor, Canada West (formerly known as Upper Canada before the union of the Canadas in 1840), to escape the threat of unlawful enslavement. A vocal and eloquent opponent of slavery in America, she became a strong advocate for educational and social reform in Canada.

Whether fugitive or free, immigrant or colonial-born, Black people in Canada West were still subject to racial prejudice. This came socially in the proliferation of stereotypes of African-American people as licentious and violent, and publicly in the advocacy of separate educational facilities. In 1850, Canada West passed an act of government which gave "Coloured People" (as well as Protestants and Catholics) the option to open their own schools. This was a backhanded way of stating that educational facilities should be separate for those of different religious affiliations and races. While segregated schools were officially sanctioned, Shadd ardently advocated the integration of the student population. African-American immigrants themselves argued over the merits of educational segregation and integration. In the face of public opposition, aided by the American Missionary Association, Shadd opened the first integrated school in Windsor, Canada West.

Shadd subsequently published a page pamphlet entitled *A Plea for Emigration; or, Notes of Canada West, in Its Moral, Social, and Political Aspect: With Suggestions Respecting Mexico, West Indies, and Vancouver's Island for the Information of Colored Emigrants* (1852), excerpted here, in which she extolled the virtues of Canada. It was widely circulated in the United States. Unlike some (such as the segregationist Henry Bibb, publisher of *Voice of the Fugitive*) who believed that African-Americans in Canada were fugitives in exile, Shadd wrote about them as new Canadians with no place in America. Indeed she juxtaposes the tyranny of America with the utopian possibilities of Canada West. Making Canada an appealing alternative, she writes in grand terms of the farming and settlement possibilities and glosses over the problems of discrimination: "The soil [in Canada West] is unsurpassed and naturally superior to the adjoining Northern States." In addition, Shadd paints a positive portrait of relations among the races: "[C]oloured men prosecute all the different trades [. . .] and are not only unmolested, but sustained and encouraged in any business for which their qualifications and means fit them." Arguably, she writes in such hyperbolic terms in order to attract settlers.

Shadd's short marriage to Thomas Cary, a Toronto barber, lasted from 1856 to 1860. During most of the unconventional marriage, they lived 180 miles apart in Chatham and Toronto so they could each pursue their occupations. Sadly, her husband died at the age of thirty-five while Shadd was pregnant with their second child. As her major works were published before her marriage, Shadd is most commonly referred to by her maiden name. Following the death of her husband, disillusioned with the infighting among abolitionists, frustrated by the resistance to her role as editor of the newspaper (which forced her to relinquish her editorship when it was discovered that M.A. Shadd was a woman), and fed up with the reality of racism in Canada, Shadd left the 23 000-strong black

population of Canada West (1861) and moved to Detroit, where she worked as a teacher. Although she had already taught for many years, she received her teaching certificate in Detroit in 1862. Following the Emancipation Proclamation in the United States in 1863, she moved to Washington and became the first Black woman to enrol in law school. Teaching during the day and working on her law degree at night over many years, she received her LLB from Howard University at the age of sixty. Shadd's focus in her later years was on suffrage for women in such groups as the Coloured Women's Progressive Franchise Association.

Shadd's relevance to readers of Canadian literature lies in her role as the editor of The Provincial Freeman, and as an author of an emigration guide that stands provocatively beside that of Catharine Parr Traill, on one hand, and the government's promotional documents on the other. Several contemporary writers such as Dionne Brand and Rinaldo Walcott have paid homage to Shadd's influence.

From A Plea for Emigration

Introductory Remarks

The increasing desire on the part of the colored[1] people, to become thoroughly informed respecting the Canadas, and particularly that part of the province called Canada West—to learn of the climate, soil and productions, and of the inducements offered generally to emigrants, and to them particularly, since that the passage of the odious Fugitive Slave Law has made a residence in the United States to many of them dangerous in the extreme,—this consideration, and the absence of condensed information accessible to all, is my excuse for offering this tract to the notice of the public. The people are in a strait,—on the one hand, a pro-slavery administration, with its entire controllable force, is bearing upon them with fatal

[1] Shadd employs American spellings in her work so, for instance, she uses "color" rather than "colour."

effect: on the other, the Colonization Society,[2] in the garb of *Christianity* and *Philanthropy*, is seconding the efforts of the first named power, by bringing into the lists a vast social and immoral influence, this making more effective the agencies employed. Information is needed—Tropical Africa, the land of promise of the colonizationists, teeming as she is with the breath of pestilence, a burning sun and fearful maladies, bids them welcome; —she feelingly invites to moral and physical death, under a voluntary escort of their most bitter enemies at home. Again, many look with dreadful forebodings to the probability of worse than inquisitorial inhumanity in the Southern States, from the operation of the Fugitive Law. Certain that neither a home in Africa, nor the Southern States, is desirable under present circumstances, inquiry is made respecting Canada. I have endeavored to furnish information to a certain extent, to that end. And believing that more reliance would be placed upon a statement of facts obtained in the country, from reliable sources and from observation, than upon a repetition of statements made elsewhere, however honestly made, I determined to visit Canada, and to there collect such information as most persons desire. These pages contain the results of much inquiry—matter obtained both from individuals and from documents and papers of unquestionable character in the Province. Is saying its all true!

The Canadas—Climate, etc.

[. . .] In Canada West, the variation from a salubrious and eminently healthy climate, is nowhere sufficient to cause the least solicitude; on the contrary, exempt from the steady and enfeebling warmth of the southern latitudes, and the equally injurious characteristics of polar countries, it is highly conducive to mental and physical energy. Persons living in the vicinity of the Great lakes, and the neighboring districts, say that their winters are much less severe than when, in past years, vast forests covered that region—that very deep snows are less frequent than they were, and that owing to the great body of ice that accumulates in the Lakes, the people living in the States bordering, suffer more severely from the cold than Canadians,—the ice making more intense the north winds sweeping over it. [. . .] I have thought proper to allude to the cold, at first, from the reason that it is the feature in the climate most dwelt upon—the solicitude of friends, ignorant of this point, and of persons less disinterested, often appealing to fears having no foundation whatever, when the facts are fairly set forth. [. . .] In short, I believe that the climate opposes no obstacle to emigration, but that it is the most desirable known in

[2] The American Colonization Society (ACS) (Society for the Colonization of Free People of Color of America) was established in 1816 to assist freed slaves and "free people of color" to emigrate to Africa as an alternative to emancipation in the United States. Believing that free men and women would not be able to integrate into American society, ACS raised funds to help create a colony in West Africa (between 1822 and 1860 approximately twelve thousand people were transported to what became the independent nation of Liberia in 1847). ACS consisted of philanthropists, clergy, and abolitionists who wanted to free African slaves and their descendants and help them return to Africa. However, the society also consisted of slave owners who feared the possibility of insurrection led by freed slaves and so wanted them expelled from America. Some abolitionists opposed colonization because they saw it as a slaveholder's scheme.

so high a latitude, for emigrants generally, and colored people particularly. [. . .] In this province the regularity of the seasons promote health in a greater degree than in those countries subject to frequent changes, as in many of the United States, where cold and warm weather alternate in quick succession; and in the upper province especially, universal testimony to the healthiness of the climate obtains.

Labor—Trades

In Canada, as in other recently settled countries, there is much to do, and comparatively few for the work. The numerous towns and villages springing up, and the great demand for timber and agricultural products, make labor of every kind plenty: all trades that are practiced in the United States, are there patronized by whomsoever carried on—no man's complexion affecting his business, [. . .] he receives the public patronage the same as a white man. He is not obliged to work a little better, and at a lower rate—there is no degraded class to identify him with, therefore every man's work stands or falls according to merit, not as is his color. Builders, and other tradesmen, of different complexions, work together on the same building and in the same shop, with perfect harmony, and often the proprietor of an establishment is colored, and the majority or all the men employed are white. [. . .] It will suffice, that colored men prosecute all the different trades; are store keepers, farmers, clerks, and laborers; and are not only unmolested, but sustained and encouraged in any business for which their qualifications and means fit them; and as the resources of the country develop, new fields of enterprise will be opened to them, and consequently new motives to honorable effort.

Settlements—Dawn—Elgin

Much has been said of the Canadian colored settlements, and fears have been expressed by many that by encouraging exclusive settlements, the attempt to identify colored men with degraded men of like color in the States would result, and as a consequence, estrangement, suspicion, and distrust would be induced. Such would inevitably be the result, and will be, shall they determine to have entirely proscriptive settlements. Those in existence, so far as I have been able to get at facts, do not exclude whites from their vicinity; but that settlements may not be established of that character, is not so certain. Dawn, on the Suydenham [sic] River, Elgin, or King's Settlement, as it is called, situated about ten miles from Chatham, are settlements in which there are regulations in regard to morals and the purchase of lands bearing only on the colored people; but whites are not excluded because of dislike. When purchase was made of the lands, many white families were residents; at least, locations were not selected in which none resided. At first, a few sold out, fearing that such neighbours might not be agreeable; others, and they the majority, concluded to remain, and the result attests their superior judgement. Instead of an increase of vice, prejudice, improvidence, laziness, or a lack of energy, that many feared would characterize them, the infrequency of violations of law among so many, is unprecedented. Due attention to moral and intellectual culture has been given; the former prejudices on the part of the whites have given place to a perfect reciprocity of religious and social intercommunication. Schools are patronized equally; the gospel is common, and hospitality is shared alike by all. The school for the settlers at Elgin is so far superior to the one established for white children that the latter was discontinued, and, as before said, all send together, and visit in common the Presbyterian church there established. So of Dawn. That settlement is exceedingly flourishing, and the moral influence it exerts is good, though, owing to some recent arrangements, regulations designed to further promote its importance are being made. Land has increased in value in those settlements. Property that was worth but little, from the superior culture given by colored persons over the method before practised, and the increasing desires for country homes, is held much higher. Another fact that is worth a passing notice is that a spirit of competition is active in their vicinity. Efforts are now put forth to produce more to the acre, and to have the land and tenements present a tidy appearance.

That others than those designed to be benefitted by the organization, should be, is not reasonable, else might persons, not members of a society justly claim equal benefits with members. If Irishmen should subscribe to certain regulations on purchasing land, no neighbouring landholders could rightfully share with them in the result of that organization. But prejudice would not be the cause of exclusion. So it is of those two settlements; it cannot be said of them that they are caste institutions, so long as they do not express hostility to the whites; but the question of their necessity in the premises may be raised, and often is, by the settlers in Canada as well as in the States.

The "Institution" is a settlement under the direction of the A.M.E. [African Methodist Episcopal] Church; it contains, at present, two hundred acres, and is sold out in ten acre farms, at one dollar and fifty cents per acre, or one shilling less than cost. They have recently opened a school, in an unfinished state, also a burying ground. There are about fifteen families settled on the land, most of whom have cleared away a few trees, but it is not in a very prosperous condition, owing, it is said, to bad management of agents—a result to be looked for when a want of knowledge characterize them. This "Institution" bids fair to be one nucleus around which caste settlements will cluster in Canada. [. . .]

Political Rights—Election Law—The Oath

There is no legal discrimination whatever affecting colored emigrants in Canada, nor from any cause whatever are their privileges sought to be abridged. [. . .] The laws regulating elections, and relating to electors, are not similar in the two Canadas, but colored persons are not affected by them more than others. [The laws state that] "Only British subjects of the full age of twenty-one are allowed to vote. Electors may remove objection by producing certificate, or by taking the oath." These [laws] contain no proscriptive provisions, and there are none. Colored men comply with these provisions and vote in the administration of affairs. There is no difference made whatever; and even in the slight matter of taking the census it is impossible to get at the exact number of whites or colored, as they are not designated as such. There is, it is true, petty jealousy manifested at times by individuals, which is made use of by the designing; but impartiality and strict justice characterize proceedings at law, and the bearing of the laws. The oath, as prescribed by law, is as follows:

> "I, A.B., do sincerely promise and swear, that I will bear faithful and true allegiance to Her Majesty Queen Victoria, as lawful sovereign of the United Kingdom of Great Britain and Ireland, and of this Province of Canada, dependent on and belonging to the said United Kingdom, and that I will defend her to the uttermost of my power against all traitors, conspiracies and attempts whatever which shall be made against Her Person, Crown and Dignity, and that I will do my utmost endeavor to disclose and make known to Her Majesty, Her Heirs and Successors all treasons and traitorous conspiracies and attempts which I shall know to be against Her or any of them, and all this I do swear without any equivocation, mental evasion, or secret reservation, and, renouncing all pardons and dispensations from persons whatever, to the contrary. So help me God." [. . .]

The Thirty Thousand Colored Freemen of Canada

The colored subjects of her Majesty in the Canadas are, in general, in good circumstances; that is, there are few cases of positive destitution to be found among those permanently settled. [. . .] It is an easy manner to make out a case of prejudice in any country. We naturally look for it, and the conduct of many is calculated to cause unpleasant treatment, and to make it difficult for well mannered persons to get comfortable accommodations. There is a medium between servility and presumption, that recommends itself to all persons of common sense, of whatever rank and complexion; and if colored people would avoid the two extremes, there would be but few cases of prejudices to complain of in Canada. In cases in which tavern keepers and other public characters persist in refusing to entertain them, they can, in common with the traveling public generally, get redress from the law. [. . .]

Recapitulation

The conclusion arrived at in respect to Canada, by an impartial person, is, that no settled country in America offers stronger inducements to colored people. The climate is healthy, and they enjoy as good health as other settlers, or as the natives; the soil is of the first quality; the laws of the country give to them, at first, the same protection and privileges as to other persons not born subjects; and after compliance with Acts of Parliament affecting them, as taking oath, &c., they may enjoy "full privileges of British birth in the Province." The general tone of society is healthy; vice is discountenanced, and infractions of the law promptly punished; and, added to this, there is an increasing anti-slavery sentiment, and a progressive system of religion.

[1852]

Post-Confederation Period

Introduction: A New Nationality

> Come! let us construct a national literature for Canada, neither British, nor French, nor Yankeeish, but the offspring and heir of the soil, borrowing lessons from all lands, but asserting its own title throughout all!
> — Thomas D'Arcy McGee, "A National Literature for Canada" (1857)

"A Great New Northern Nation"

On 1 July 1867, the Toronto *Globe* ran a front-page story, "Confederation Day," heralding the inception of a new era. "With the first dawn of this gladsome midsummer morn, we hail the birthday of a new nationality," the paper proclaimed. "A united British America, with its four millions of people, takes its place this day among the nations of the world. . . . [O]ld things have passed away . . ." (1). The so-called "birth" of the new nation was celebrated across the four provinces that had been united to form the new Dominion of Canada: Nova Scotia, New Brunswick, Quebec, and Ontario. On the stroke of midnight, 1 July, the citizens of Ottawa were treated to a 101-gun salute (Donaldson 16). Cities and towns throughout the four provinces were scenes of celebration and fanfare. The celebrations concluded with elaborate fireworks displays held simultaneously in each province. "In the cities and large towns," writes Donald Creighton, "the spectacle always concluded with elaborate set pieces. The Montrealers arranged an intricate design with emblems representing the three uniting provinces—a beaver for Canada, a mayflower for Nova Scotia, and a pine for New Brunswick.

At Toronto the words 'God Save the Queen' were surrounded by a twined wreath of roses, thistles, shamrocks, and *fleur-de-lys*" ("First" 116).

Just one year earlier, on 20 October 1866, in one of his many inspirational speeches to "sell" the idea of Canada to the French-speaking Canadians in Canada East (Quebec), George-Étienne Cartier had announced: "My friends, a glorious era lies before us" (37). Cartier felt that in entering Confederation, Canadians were fulfilling an imperial mission by enabling "the realization of a plan designed by the first European to set foot in Canada: Jacques Cartier. . . . With Confederation, we will realize a vision of this great man: the coming together of all the provinces he discovered" (37). Similarly, Thomas D'Arcy McGee, in his speech before the Quebec Legislative Assembly of May 1860, prophesied: "I see in the not remote distance one great nationality bound, like the shield of Achilles, by the blue rim of ocean. . . . I see within the round of that shield the peaks of the Western Mountains and the crests of the Eastern waves. . . . I see a generation [of the future]" (ix-x). There was a sense that Canada was destined for greatness, that it was perhaps even destined to become the most powerful and esteemed nation of the British Empire.

But the pathway to the federation of the three colonies (split into four provinces) had not been a smooth one. Things had been looking precarious for the British North American colonies in the years before the proposed federation. Ever since the American Revolution in the late 1700s, the British North American colonies had defined themselves as being loyal to the British Crown and insisted on their distinctiveness from the Americans. Many Loyalists, including the numerous Iroquois men who had fought alongside the British under the leadership of Joseph Brant, had sought refuge in British North America in the aftermath of the revolution, settling what are today the provinces of New Brunswick, Nova Scotia, and Ontario. In 1812, American armies tried to invade British territory in North America; French Canadians and British settlers fought side by side with their Aboriginal allies, including the famous Shawnee war hero Tecumseh, to repulse the invasions. In 1840, in the wake of the rebellions led by William Lyon Mackenzie and Louis-Joseph Papineau three years earlier, Upper and Lower Canada had been joined to form the united province of "Canada"—even though people still continued to refer to the two areas as "Canada West" (or Upper Canada) and "Canada East" (or Lower Canada)—but the union was proving unsatisfactory to both. Canada, at this time, was governed by a single elected legislature with a moving capital, between Toronto and Quebec City, which was creating problems. From 1861 to 1865, a civil war was raging to the south in the United States, and the fear was that, once the battle for America had been resolved, the Republican armies would turn their attention to the territory to the north (especially since the British had lent their support to the South, which angered the American Republic). "[P]repare! Prepare! Prepare!" warned McGee in his speech to the Legislative Assembly of 9 February 1865. "[I]t is time for us to provide for our own security" (244, 245).

The thought, in the 1860s, of becoming annexed to the United States was an affront to the minds of most settlers in the provinces. One sees instances of this antipathy toward Americans in a good deal of the literature of the nineteenth century. In the 1830s, the Nova Scotian author Thomas Chandler Haliburton published his immensely popular satirical sketches of the "Yankee" entrepreneur with dubious ethics in his *Sam Slick* series. Susanna Moodie's portraits of the Americans she encounters in the Canadian backwoods in *Roughing It in the Bush* (1852), whom she represents as having no respect for British cultivation and manners, give a sense of the attitudes many British Canadians held toward Americans. In an 1862 speech in Quebec City, McGee, one of the most vocal defenders of the emerging sense of nationality in Canada, insisted on Canada's remaining distinct and independent of the United States: "I do not believe that it is our destiny to be engulphed [sic] into a Republican union, renovated and inflamed with the wine of victory. . . . [I]t seems to me we have theatre enough under our feet to act another and a worthier part. We can hardly join the Americans on our own terms, and we never ought to join them on theirs" ("Canadian" 33). Even after Confederation, when debates about the possibility of Canada's eventual amalgamation with the United States continued, Pauline Johnson wrote in her poem "Canadian Born": "The Yankee to the south of us must south of us remain."

Compounding the threat of American expansion was a series of attacks by the Fenians, a group of Irish rebels who were attempting a takeover of British territory in North America as part of their mission to coerce Britain into freeing Ireland of English rule. A faction of American Fenians sent invading forces across the border into Canada in 1866 and was stopped, but Canadians lived in fear of further incursions. The Fenian invasions of 1866 were one of the final events that clinched the idea of a union of the British provinces. In order to protect themselves, the colonies needed to be joined to better support each other in the event of further attack.

Thus it was that after much political wrangling, in 1864, the "Great Coalition" was established in the Canadian legislature between French and English, Liberals and Conservatives—represented by John A. Macdonald, George-Étienne Cartier, George Brown, and Alexander Galt—with "Confederation" as its mandate. When they learned that there was to be a September meeting in Charlottetown, P.E.I., of the four Atlantic colonies (Nova Scotia, New Brunswick, P.E.I., and Newfoundland) to discuss the possibility of an Atlantic alliance, the coalition members representing "Canada" invited themselves along, and proposed a union of all of the British North American provinces. The men engaged in this meeting, and in the following one held in Quebec City in October 1864, eventually became known as the "Fathers of Confederation" (see Figure III-3).

Nevertheless, support for the idea of Confederation was by no means unanimous among the participants. Newfoundland, the oldest colony in British North America, which had representatives present at the 1864 Charlottetown meeting, backed out of the deal when it became clear that the united nation would be centralized on the mainland and would be ruling Newfoundlanders from afar. Furthermore, from a purely economic standpoint a union with the

Canadian provinces did not seem feasible, given that London, England, was closer to St. John's than to the newly appointed capital of Ottawa (Morton 89). Prince Edward Island also decided to withdraw from the union, and Nova Scotia's entry into Confederation was precarious, with the province's former premier, Joseph Howe, opposing the deal at every turn. In a speech of 1866, Howe expressed his disdain for the proposed nation of Canada: "[A] more unpromising nucleus of a new nation can hardly be found on the face of the earth" ("Speeches" 445). Howe's opposition to Confederation lay in his fear that it would ultimately weaken Nova Scotia's ties with the British Empire. Christopher Dunkin, who represented the English of Canada East (i.e., Quebec), also insisted that the willed creation of "a new nationality" was impossible: "We have a large class whose national feelings turn towards London, whose very heart is there; another large class whose sympathies centre here at Quebec, or in a sentimental way may have some reference to Paris; another large class whose memories are of the Emerald Isle [Ireland]; and yet another whose comparisons are with Washington; but have we any class of people who are attached, or whose feelings are going to be directed with any earnestness to the city of Ottawa, the centre of the new nationality that is to be created?" (443). Furthermore, there was concern that it would be hard to sell the idea of a union with the British provinces to the Quebec Legislative Assembly. But actually, the idea of Confederation appealed to many French Canadians because the proposed federal system would initiate a return to the separation of Lower Canada from Upper Canada (the two had been joined under a single legislature in 1840), and thus would enable French Canadians to rule themselves at a provincial level and protect distinct legal, religious, cultural, and language rights.

Following a second meeting of the five colonies in Quebec City in October 1864, the representatives of New Brunswick, Nova Scotia, and Canada returned to their provincial legislatures to convince them to pass the new initiative. Feelings ran high, and the issue inspired some of the most impassioned and fiery public speeches in Canadian history, including those by McGee, as well as Howe's famous anti-Confederation "Men of Dartmouth" speech of 1867. The delegates had worked out the rules that would govern the new union, the British North America Act, which would become the basis of Canada's constitution. Once it had been passed by the provinces, the proposal had to be approved by Britain, though even then there were threats that New Brunswick, which was crucial in linking the mainland with Nova Scotia, might secede. In December 1866, Macdonald and other representatives travelled to London, England, to have the BNA Act approved by the Queen. Howe even went so far as to organize an anti-Confederation delegation to be in London at the same time that Macdonald and other politicians were there. However, Britain by this time was eager to withdraw its military forces from the colonies, and wholeheartedly supported the idea of a federation that would maintain imperial ties with the monarchy. But when the Canadians proposed to christen the nation "the Kingdom of Canada," the British warned that American anti-monarchist sensibilities might be provoked. New Brunswick leader Leonard Tilley offered a solution from the Bible, and provided Canada with its "national motto": "He shall have dominion also from sea to sea, and from the river unto the ends of the earth" (Psalms 72:8). Canada was proclaimed "the Dominion of Canada" and given a new motto, *A mari usque ad mare* (from sea to sea).

"From Sea to Sea": The Railway and the West

The post-Confederation period was one of the most eventful eras of Canadian history. It was a time of intense political wrangling, scandal, eager public debates, patriotic enthusiasm, colonial paternalism, and bitter self-criticism. Patriotic sentiment ran high in the years following the Dominion Day celebrations, even though the provinces continued to retain distinct regional identities. John A. Macdonald was elected as the nation's first prime minister, and negotiations were undertaken for the completion of the inter-colonial railway linking Montreal to Halifax. For much of his time in office, however, Macdonald's reign was plagued by difficulties. Howe continued to wage a campaign for Nova Scotia to secede from Confederation, while Prince Edward Island and Newfoundland still remained aloof. When, in 1870, the government of Canada acquired Rupert's Land, the vast territory in the northwest of the continent that had once been the Hudson's Bay Company holdings, Macdonald was in a quandary. On one hand, this was a prize acquisition, as it would enable him to realize the dream of linking "Canada" from sea to sea. On the other hand, with the exception of the colony of British Columbia on the Pacific Coast, the area was sparsely inhabited. Macdonald had suddenly become the absentee landlord of a territory much larger than Britain. In order to amalgamate the territory into the new dominion, and to ensure that the Northwest (today, Saskatchewan and Alberta) did not become annexed to the United States, the region had to be settled as quickly as possible. This imperative fuelled an enormous and expensive campaign of western settlement.

The first thing that was needed was a means of transporting settlers to the western prairies and linking them to the eastern "core" of the new nation. Thus began negotiations to build a vast railway—the longest in the world—that would link Canada "from sea to sea." The railway became a symbol of Macdonald's national dream, and a sign of the enormity of his vision for the new nation. As Macdonald himself put it during the election campaign of 1878: "Until this great work is completed, our Dominion is little more than a 'geographical expression'." Macdonald sought to create "a transcontinental British nation in North America—a workable alternative to the United States . . . [that] would be the spine of empire, an Imperial highway linking the British Isles with the Orient" (Berton, *National* 7). The epic nature of the enterprise, staged as a battle against the odds, forms the subject of E.J. Pratt's famous narrative poem "Towards the Last Spike" (1952), included in Volume II of this anthology. As the narrator of

Pratt's poem expresses it, "A nation, like the world, could not stand still" (line 44). However, even in Pratt's poem there is some discomfort about the destruction of the landscape that the railway brings with it. Far more critical, however, was the cartoon that appeared in the *Toronto Evening News* of 1885, "What It Must Come To" (Figure III-6). The relentless push of empire, and its concomitant destruction of Native peoples and cultures, took little notice of those whose interests it did not serve.

The enormous task of building the railway eventually went to a private syndicate: the Canadian Pacific Railway (CPR), which was incorporated on 16 February 1881. However, from the start the building of the transcontinental railway was plagued by setbacks. There was immense resistance to the plan from the leader of the Opposition, Alexander Mackenzie, soon to become Canada's second prime minister (1873–1878). Speaking in the House in 1871, Mackenzie called the venture "an act of insane recklessness" (qtd. in Berton, *National* 6). With the exception of the colony of British Columbia, the west was sparsely settled, which made a railway difficult to justify: who would use it? Geographically, there were seemingly insurmountable obstacles, including the vast stretch of Precambrian rock of the Canadian Shield, the enormous muskeg swamps, the sheer size of the prairie, and the Rocky Mountains. The most famous political stumbling block was the notorious "Pacific Scandal" of 1872, in which Macdonald was accused of having granted the contract to Montreal financier Hugh Allan (who was backed by American investors) in exchange for campaign funds. The scandal eventually, in 1873, forced the country's first prime minister to resign.

When the CPR was finally granted the contract in 1881, it was paid $25 million and given 25 million acres of land—land that was already inhabited by Métis and Aboriginal peoples—which it then sold to settlers and immigrants as a way of recouping some of the costs of building the railway. As a result, the railway company itself became involved in immigration and settlement initiatives, in part because a larger population in the Northwest would ensure increased revenue for the railway. As one of the developers of the railway put it in his autobiography, "If we build this road across the prairie, we will carry every pound of supplies that the settlers want and we will carry every pound of produce that the settlers wish to sell" (John Macoun, qtd. in Berton, *Last Spike* 18). Advertising posters for the CPR thus addressed themselves to prospective immigrants and settlers (Figures III-9 and III-11); the company even opened an Emigration Office in London, England, to promote Canada as a destination for British settlers (Figure IV-5), which later included a "Canada bus" that travelled to remote communities to encourage emigration (Distad 66–69). The CPR also advanced its interests (and, in many cases, overly idealistic images of Canadian settlement) throughout continental Europe, and printed brochures, pamphlets, posters, and newspaper advertisements in Danish, Dutch, Finnish, French, Gaelic, German, Norwegian, Swedish, and other languages (Choko 30). These settlement initiatives led to the arrival of 7,500 Mennonites in Manitoba between 1874 and 1880 (Distad 66), over 7,000 Doukhobors in 1899 in northern Saskatchewan (69), and thousands of Icelanders and Ukrainians on the western prairies between the 1870s and the First World War (Hjartarson 46, 48). In conjunction with these large-scale settlement initiatives, between 1880 and 1885 over 10,000 Chinese workers were brought to Canada to provide the labour for the construction of the railway and the clearing of terrain through the treacherous Rocky Mountains. They were joined by many Irish and European immigrant labourers. Hundreds of these workers lost their lives along the CPR lines, either in work-related accidents (including landslides that crushed their campsites) or from cholera and smallpox, but many others remained in Canada and went on to form part of the fabric of the growing nation.

Meanwhile, Macdonald had struck a deal with the colony of British Columbia to lure it into Confederation: he promised to link B.C. by rail to eastern Canada within ten years. British Columbia agreed, and entered Confederation in 1871. The Canadian government acceded to another, more controversial demand once the railway was completed: following pressure from British Columbians who were concerned about the number of Chinese people in their communities, it brought in the "Chinese head tax" as part of the Chinese Immigration Act of 1885 (Figure III-14). The institution of the head tax, and the even more extreme Chinese Exclusion Act of 1923, restricted further Chinese immigration and meant that many Chinese labourers who were already in Canada were prevented from having their families join them, which led to the tragic separation of families and the formation of a "bachelor society" in Canada, while many Chinese wives and children in China were left almost penniless. (See the header note to the Chinese Immigration Act and Edith Maude Eaton's "A Plea for the Chinaman" [1896] for a detailed discussion of racism toward Chinese immigrants in Canada.)

An unanticipated obstacle in the building of the CPR was the resistance the surveyors and politicians encountered from various local communities on the prairies. One of the strongest locations of resistance was in the area of the Red River Settlement. When the government sent in surveyors to divide the land into saleable lots in October 1869, and the newly appointed lieutenant-governor, William McDougall, appeared to establish his leadership over the territory, the Métis and White settlers who lived in the area were incensed. A Métis contingent, led by Louis Riel, confronted the surveying team. When Riel's requests for a hearing were refused, he seized the former Hudson's Bay Company post at Fort Garry and began to negotiate terms with the Dominion of Canada, including a land grant for the Métis and the protection of French-language rights. He hoped to establish terms upon which the Métis would enter Confederation as a distinct people and province; throughout his negotiations, he always insisted that they wanted to join Canada and remain loyal subjects of the British Queen. Just as the Canadian government was beginning to take the Métis claims for a separate province seriously, however, an unruly Protestant Orangeman named Thomas Scott, who had been taken prisoner, was executed by a Métis firing squad; Riel had not ordered the execution, but he condoned it. In response, Macdonald sent in troops and Riel was forced to flee to the United States. The Red River Rebellion, as it came to be known, had been quelled. Shortly after, in July 1870, Riel effectively got his wish: the area around the Red River Settlement entered Confederation as the (at that time) very small, bilingual province of Manitoba.

However, this was not the end of unrest in the west. In the 1880s, Métis settlers, who had been forced to move into the area of Saskatchewan, along with many of the Native communities of the area, were starving because the once-plentiful buffalo herds that had been a central source of food and clothing had been almost driven to extinction. Having lost their land and their livelihood, many of these people, including Plains Cree Chief Big Bear and his followers, became destitute. Another rebellion, led by Riel and Gabriel Dumont, erupted in Duck Lake, Saskatchewan, and other spots in March 1885, which ended in May with the arrest of Riel. Following the Red River uprising of 1869, the federal government, in sending troops out west, had seen first-hand the need for a transcontinental railway; when the second rebellion occurred in 1885, the still-incomplete rail lines were used to stifle it, giving Macdonald the support he needed for the completion of the line. Canada's military victory in crushing the Northwest Rebellion was a momentous event, heralded in local papers and celebrations. Isabella Valancy Crawford's poem "The Rose of a Nation's Thanks" is a celebration of the victorious Canadian troops returning home from the war. City streets were decorated with streamers to greet the returning troops. Other people were less sanguine. Pauline Johnson and Agnes Maule Machar, both from Ontario, published poems defending Riel and his supporters. French Canadians, who identified with the Métis community's concern for their cultural and religious differences, called for fair treatment of Riel. Macdonald was in an unenviable position, experiencing pressures on both sides from English Protestants and French Catholics. When the hammering of the CPR's "last spike" was finally completed on 5 November 1885, Riel was in jail, awaiting execution. Two weeks later, he was hanged outside the RCMP barracks in Regina, while many Canadians were still celebrating the completion of the railway that had been the instigator of his downfall.

The CPR and Canadian Iconography

It is not surprising that the building of the CPR has become etched in Canadian history as the event that made the nation. In effect, the railway created the Canada that we know today, since without its linking of the various provinces, a nation "from sea to sea" would not have been possible. Moreover, the CPR created towns along its prairie route, and often determined their shape since the hub of activity usually centred on the train station (see Figure IV-4). This was true of such major cities as Regina and Calgary. According to popular historian Pierre Berton, "some eight hundred villages, towns, and cities were eventually fostered in the three prairie provinces by the CPR" (Last Spike 19). However, the railway contributed to the "story" of Canada in another way as well: through its extensive advertising and publishing campaigns, which created and disseminated images of Canada across the country and around the globe.

Cultural theorist Benedict Anderson, in his influential book *Imagined Communities: Reflections on the Origins and Spread of Nationalism* (1983), argues that it was the advent of print that made possible the belief in an "imagined community" that was so central to national self-definition. The transmission of print enabled large numbers of readers who did not know one another, and who lived hundreds of miles apart, to read the same material and share the same cultural-historical information. Readers thus shared a common body of knowledge and a common sense of belonging, all contained within a clearly identifiable "national" boundary. Foremost in effecting this sense of community in Canada were newspapers and magazines, which appeared in great profusion in the period following Confederation, including such periodicals as *The Dominion Illustrated*, *Canadian Illustrated News*, the *Montreal Star*, and *La Presse* (all published out of Montreal), as well as a number of Toronto publications, including *Grip*, *Saturday Night*, *The Week*, the *Mail* (later merged with the *Globe* to form the *Globe and Mail*), and the *Canadian Monthly and National Review*.

There are at least three ways in which the CPR contributed to the "narrating" of Canada. First, with the completion of the railway, printed materials could be transported across great distances, and hence could link disparate segments of the continent. Before the railway, Canadians considered their world to be "regional rather than national" (Lamonde 4); now they could begin to think of themselves as part of a much larger national community. Second, the CPR was seminal in promoting immigration and luring settlers to the Canadian Northwest. Settlement was necessary in order for a cross-continental national community to exist. Third, the promotional and advertising materials propagated and printed by the CPR played a central role in the establishment of a recognizable Canadian iconography.

It is true that the CPR was more than just a railway. In launching its settlement campaign, the CPR initiated a phenomenal publicity (and propaganda) venture, publishing posters, brochures, pamphlets, and books, many of which were illustrated by professional artists and photographers, that promoted "Canada" transnationally and abroad. As with the emigration pamphlets of earlier generations, Canadians and potential Canadians alike were being sold the idea of Canada. The posters and other promotional material conveyed a picture of Canada as a land of freedom and plenty, not altogether different from the misleading promotional materials that were so prevalent in Britain in the 1820s and '30s, when Susanna Moodie and her family decided to emigrate. Posters represented beautiful farmlands with happy families (Figure III-11), which were nothing like the reality of the sod huts and severe droughts experienced by most new settlers. These materials were often imperialist in tenor, representing Canada as one of the "civilized" outposts in the British Empire (Figures III-9 and III-10). Similarly, CPR tourist propaganda played a key role in consolidating the enduring image of Canada (western Canada, in particular) as a land associated with such symbols as the Mounted Police (see Figure III-12), the beaver (which was for many years the logo of the CPR), the maple leaf, and the Rocky Mountains. Along the rail line the company established grand hotels, including the fabulous Château Frontenac in Quebec City, which was built on the cliff off the Plains of Abraham in order to be one of the first grand buildings that immigrants would see when they arrived in Canada by boat. The Banff Springs Hotel was another of these grand ventures, built near the now-famous hot springs in order to promote the area as a fashionable spa. The CPR also played a role in establishing national wilderness parks, which it then commercialized as holiday destinations, promoting the Rocky Mountains as a counterpart to the Swiss Alps complete with imported Swiss hiking guides.

CPR publicity materials also promoted the Canadian west as "Indian" territory. According to Francis, "In 1894, the CPR inaugurated Banff Indian Days [Figure III-13], an annual summer festival featuring displays of traditional Native cultural practices. The railway realized that wild Indians were a surefire tourist attraction, every bit as exciting as the tribes of darkest Africa, yet available from the safety and convenience of a railway car" (26). The irony, of course, is that the railway was built upon traditional Aboriginal lands, and was central in the destruction of Native peoples' lives. The Native people who dressed up and performed for the CPR's tourist travellers were forced to adopt this role as a form of employment because they were becoming increasingly impoverished by displacement from their lands and traditions.

It is also significant that the "Mounties" figure in so much of the CPR promotional material (see Figure III-12). The North West Mounted Police (the precursors of today's Royal Canadian Mounted Police) were initially formed in 1873 by John A. Macdonald in order to quell the unrest occurring between American whisky traders and the western Métis and Aboriginal peoples. These mounted riflemen had powers that extended beyond those of ordinary policemen; in order to maintain order on the frontier, they not only had the power to arrest suspects, but they also acted as judge and jury to try prisoners. The force, which established a number of forts throughout the Northwest, thereafter played a crucial role in clearing the way for the CPR, facilitating the settlement of the area, and enforcing the transfer of Aboriginal land title to the Canadian government (which was ironic, given that in the 1870s and '80s, men who enlisted in the force were rewarded with free land grants). Indeed, in most of the treaty negotiations, a Mounted Police official, dressed in ceremonial red serge, was present as a way of lending intimidating authority to the proceedings (see Duncan Campbell Scott's account in "The Last of the Indian Treaties"). In subsequent decades, the myth of the Mountie as a symbol of decency and hardy ruggedness, such as is evident in the role of Constable Benton Fraser in the popular television series *Due South* (1994–98), was used to establish Canada's distinctiveness from the United States. Central to this was the sense that the Mounted Police had "tamed" Canada's Aboriginal peoples through peaceful means, which in effect glosses over the fact that Native peoples were displaced and persecuted. The Mounties were also central, after 1885, in enforcing the dictates of the Indian Acts, and in the institution of the "pass system" (Aboriginal people were required to show identity passes each time they left their reserve land) that was put into effect following the 1885 rebellion.

In effect, the CPR was contributing to a narrative of Canada that would be told for years to come. Journalists and artists were allowed to travel the rails for free in the expectation that their works would provide good publicity for the railway. Some trains had specially equipped photography cars with mobile darkrooms where CPR photographers could develop and print their pictures while travelling (Hanna 4). Sara Jeannette Duncan's *A Social Departure: How Orthodocia and I Went Round the World by Ourselves* (1890), which began as a series of travel articles for the *Montreal Star*, celebrated the trip across Canada by rail. Duncan and her companion stopped in the major Canadian cities along the way, including Winnipeg and Vancouver, and even had the adventure of riding the "cowcatcher"[1] of the engine through the Rockies. Part of the context for this celebration of rail travel is the general enthrallment with technology and progress during the Victorian era. There was something of a railway mania throughout the British Empire during this time, although many romantically inspired writers were critical of this naive—and, in their view, soul-destroying—celebration of technology. This perspective is evident in such poems as Archibald Lampman's "The Railway Station" (1888) and Bliss Carman's allegorical "The Night Express" (1895). By contrast, E.J. Pratt's 1952 epic poem, "Towards the Last Spike," celebrates the building of the CPR as a heroic, if fraught, event in Canada's national history, even though Pratt was subsequently criticized by F.R. Scott in his short poem "All the Spikes but the Last" (1957) for failing to represent the Chinese workers in his epic. In 1967, Gordon Lightfoot was commissioned to produce a song for Canada's centenary celebrating the national spirit; the song, "The Canadian Railroad Trilogy," glorifies the epic vision of the CPR while also commemorating the unsung labourers who helped build it. More recently, Paulette Jiles's humorous novel *Sitting in the Club Car Drinking Rum and Karma-Kola* (1986) recounts a cross-Canada journey by train. Numerous Canadian novels also use the building of the railway and settlement of the west as their setting: texts such as Howard O'Hagan's *Tay John* (1939), Rudy Wiebe's *The Temptations of Big Bear* (1973) and *The Scorched-Wood People* (1977), and SKY Lee's *Disappearing Moon Cafe* (1990) fall into this category. More recent narratives that engage with the building of the CPR often retell the story from the perspective of the workers, rather than the decision makers. Lee's novel, for instance, opens with a character searching for the thousands of bones of the Chinese men who lost their lives while constructing the railway. "The CPR 'created' Canada," Daniel Francis writes, "not by binding it together with steel rails, but by inventing images of it that people then began to recognize as uniquely Canadian" (*National* 27).

---

[1] The piece projecting out from the front of the locomotive engine to clear the tracks of animals or debris.

"A State of Mind": The Creation of a Shared National Identity

"There is a wide difference, though comparatively few years span it, between a colonial and a Canadian," Sara Jeannette Duncan wrote in her essay "American Influence on Canadian Thought," published in the Toronto paper *The Week* in July 1887 (518). A lot had changed since Susanna Moodie and her sister Catharine Parr Traill had arrived in Canada in 1832 to establish themselves as backwoods pioneers. There was a new country to be drawn onto the global map. That country, now collectively known as the "Dominion of Canada," had elected its first prime minister. A route to the Far East (India, China, and Japan) across the North American continent had finally been achieved, thus fulfilling the goal of the European explorers two centuries before. And for the first time there were serious public debates about this new, albeit amorphous, thing called "Canadian literature." Moodie's 1871 introduction to the first Canadian edition of *Roughing It in the Bush* contrasts "Canada of the present" with "Canada of forty years ago" (525). Upon her arrival, Moodie's feeling for Canada was comparable to "that which the condemned criminal entertains for his cell" (135). Now, forty years later, she invoked a collective entity, "the Canadian people" (534), and celebrated a nation that was moving "towards the fulfilment of a great and glorious destiny" (528).

Not everyone agreed about this mission of destiny, and not everyone felt equally included in the self-image of this new nation, but nevertheless something had changed. According to literary critic Jonathan Kertzer, in modern and post-colonial nations such as Canada, "the state usually is created first, and a sustaining sense of nationhood must be forged afterward" (62–63). A nation exists when people believe it exists. People begin to learn certain national narratives and recognize particular symbols, which they then take to be inviolable; in the process, the narratives become self-constituting. Specifically, what had changed was that people *felt* that something had changed. In his 1892 review for *The Dial*, Charles G.D. Roberts could refer without qualification to "the ardent national sentiment so rapidly engaging the hearts of the great majority of our people" ("Future" 386). Included in this sentiment was a sense of Canada as a national community with distinguishing characteristics based on such things as distinct historical associations, cultural traditions, social etiquette, geographical climate, language, and political configurations. By 1940, writing in his essay "Canada as a State of Mind," Duncan Campbell Scott, one of the major poets of Canada's Confederation period, was able to state: "I . . . think of Canada, not as a geographical unit, or as a political entity, but as a State of Mind, a Dominion to which all the writers who have expressed the deeds and aspirations of times past have contributed" (469).

In popular historical accounts, the British North America Act is often described as the document that "created" Canada, which is an interesting choice of word: first, since "Canada" already existed (and had long existed in any number of manifestations, both for Aboriginal peoples and for the French, who had long referred to themselves as *les Canadiens*); and second, because it makes of Canada something of a wistful abstraction in the imaginations of those who envisioned it. It is often instructive to think of nations as imagined constructions, constructions that get "narrated" into being and subsequently take on a larger-than-life existence. Indeed, there are many who maintain that Canadian identity and longevity depended—and, perhaps, still depend—on such inventions. Canada was conjured into existence on 1 July, 1867. But it is to the creative writers, orators, and intellectuals of the period that we owe the solidification of what came to be defined as a Canadian tradition, contributing to what historian Eric Hobsbawm has called the foundation of an "invented tradition." More than a political document, the creation of Canada required a body of people who contributed to the consolidation of that abstraction in the minds of the citizenry. This is the period when the fantasy became an invokable reality, when Canada, so to speak, became a belief system. Many social and literary critics of the period were well aware of the elements that were necessary for the development of an "imagined community." "It is souls that make nations, not numbers," declares the speaker in Wilfred Campbell's 1899 poem "The Lazarus of Empire." Foremost was the fostering of a sense of identity that would span the territory of the huge nation. "What is essentially needed is a sentiment that will sweep like a baptismal wave from ocean to ocean and overpower all local, racial, and other influences" (226), wrote Campbell in his 31 December 1892 "At the Mermaid Inn" column for the *Globe*. The railway played a key role in this, particularly in its ability to transport printed materials (newspapers, magazines, books) across the country.

Of key importance to this vision of Canadian nationhood was a sense of continuing ties with the Mother Country, England,[2] balanced by an equally powerful sense of a unique North American identity that distinguished Canadians from the British as well as from the Americans. Macdonald, in his February 1865 speech to the Legislative Assembly, promoted the idea of the new nationality on this basis: "[B]y the proposed union, we [join people with] . . . experience in the ways of the New World—people who are as much Canadians, I may say, as we are—people who are imbued with the same feelings of loyalty to the Queen, and the same desire for the continuance of the connection with the Mother Country as we are, and at the same time, have a like feeling of ardent attachment for this, our common country . . ." (230). These sentiments are apparent in the creative writing of the period, if one contrasts the conclusion of Oliver Goldsmith's 1834 "The Rising Village" (with its invocation to "Happy Britannia!") with the poetry of this period that wrestles with the nature of Canada's independent status. This sense of national emergence is echoed in such poems as Roberts's "Canada" and "An Ode for the Canadian Confederacy" (1886), Johnson's "Canadian Born" (1903), Crawford's "Canada to England" (1874),

---

[2] This discussion focuses on the sentiments expressed by Anglo-Canadians during this period. French Canadians, at this time, had a much stronger and long-standing sense of themselves as a rooted "*Canadien*" people, distinct from European French traditions.

Machar's "The Canadian Fatherland" (1889), and Wilfred Campbell's "The Lazarus of Empire" (1899) and "Briton to Briton: An Appeal" (1905).

A combined sense of Canada's newness and indebtedness is evident in many nationalist pronouncements of this period. It informs the vision promoted by McGee in his impassioned defence of the "great new Northern nation" in 1862: "A Canadian nationality—not French-Canadian, nor British-Canadian, nor Irish-Canadian: patriotism rejects the prefix—is, in my opinion, what we should look forward to, that is what we ought to labour for, that is what we ought to be prepared to defend to the death" (33, 34). McGee's awareness of the exclusionary practices of sectarian allegiances, which he had experienced personally in his Fenian days, is clear in his exhortation that Canadians "must all liberalize— locally, sectionally, religiously, nationally" (33). "There is room enough in this country for one great free people," McGee stated, "but there is not room enough, under the same flag and the same laws, for two or three angry, suspicious, obstructive 'nationalities'" (33). McGee was also emphatic in his insistence that immigrant peoples should be included as equals within the new national vision, even though this vision was not, ultimately, put into practice in the treatment of Aboriginal Canadians and other groups such as Chinese immigrants, or always, for that matter, the Irish. Charles Mair, writing in the *Canadian Monthly* in August 1875, felt confident in contrasting the former absence of Canadian national sentiment with its flowering in the present: "There was a time when there was no fixed principle or national feeling in Canada; when men were Englishmen, Scotchmen, Irishmen, or Frenchmen, and when to be a Canadian was almost to hang the head. But that time has passed away. Young Canada has come to the front, and we are now a nation . . ." (163).

These were days when anything seemed possible . . . that is, if you were White, male, and born into the right family. An inclusive assimilationist rhetoric is evident in most of the statements promulgating the identity of the new nation, though it was generally assumed that the constituents included only the "White"—and, in some cases, White anglophone—citizenry. Many Quebeckers, for example, still chafed under the reins of British colonialism, and even though they were supposed to be equal partners in Confederation, they were still subject to the British sovereign and to solidly British attitudes about culture, language, religion, jurisprudence, and destiny. The French, however, were not the only people who were disgruntled. Women still had no access to the vote (women in Quebec were granted the franchise latest of all, in 1940), and were barred from certain educational establishments and professions. The era that saw the appearance of the "New Woman," embodied in different ways by such figures as Agnes Maule Machar and Sara Jeannette Duncan, was marked by fierce debates about the role of women in public life.

Meanwhile, the livelihood and culture of Aboriginal peoples were being curtailed by the increasingly restrictive legislation put into effect by the official Indian Act of 1876, which presumed to be acting in the name of "civilization" and humanitarianism while barring Native peoples from taking part as full citizens in the new national community (Native people, like women, were not allowed to vote). The marginalization of Aboriginal peoples was reinforced by the period's emphasis on the highly charged rhetoric of the "destiny" of the Canadian nation. In the language of the 1876 Indian Act, and in many of the literary writings of the period (such as those by Duncan Campbell Scott), Aboriginal people became identified as a "dying race" who were to be peacefully replaced by the colonial settlers. A perfect example of this is Scott's poem "Indian Place-Names," which invokes the Aboriginal names of Canadian places as the only remnant of a once-vibrant people, and suggests that these names have now been inherited by the White settlers.

The conversion of White colonials into "Canadians" also resulted in the exclusion of other groups who did not fit the predominant ideas of what a Canadian was, such as Chinese and other Asian immigrants, descendants of Black Loyalists, or settlers from eastern Europe. Indeed, the notion of the "ideal" Canadian settler extended to British, French, and many Nordic European nations (see, for example, the poster of the ideal Canadian settler in Figure III-11), while the prevailing, racist idea of "less ideal" immigrants applied to those of southern European, Middle Eastern, and Asian descent (see Clifford Sifton's "The Immigrants Canada Wants" in Section IV). The notion of a "shared nationality" or "shared destiny," which was invoked by many visionaries of the period, was therefore limited to a racially exclusive vision of the "new nationality" that was being forged. For those whose race and background enabled them to identify with this imagined community, however, it remained a compelling vision which joined together a sense of historical origins and destiny, imperial belonging and independence, national unity and regional diversity.

"The Poor Beggar Colonial": Canada's Political Future

One key issue that informed these debates about Canada's emerging identity was the sense that the new nation's political status was still not altogether clear. In her 30 September 1886 column in *The Week*, Duncan referred to "our present imperfect autonomy in 1867" (708). While discussions about Confederation were ongoing well into the twentieth century—Newfoundland held an election on the issue of joining Confederation in 1869, but did not join until 1949—even within the Dominion there were heated debates about Canada's political future. Many thought that Canada should strengthen its ties with Britain and include itself as part of a global imperial federation. Others, like Goldwin Smith, the editor of *The Week*, insisted that Canada's future lay in being annexed to the United States. The political choices were the same as those that had preceded Confederation: independence, stronger imperial ties to Britain, or annexation. There were heated intellectual battles between those, like Roberts, who supported independence, and those, like Smith, who advocated annexation with the United States. Roberts's political poem "Canada," Campbell's "The Lazarus of Empire," and Pauline

Johnson's "Canadian Born" are, among other things, a defence of Canadian independence. Eventually, many of those in favour of independence, such as Roberts, chose to support the cause of imperialism in order to avert the prospect of merging with the United States. In his grand election speech of 1891, just two months before he died, Macdonald uttered his famous proclamation: "A British subject I was born, a British subject I will die." Taken out of context, this statement appears to suggest Macdonald's lack of commitment to Canadian independence, though it was his way of insisting on Canadian sovereignty against the threat of American annexation.

Canadians' sense that their destiny was tied to the British Empire was propitious, since this era, from 1870 to 1914, is often described as the "heyday" of British imperialism, the period when the British Empire envisioned (and actualized) its increased expansion around the globe. Many of the CPR posters of the 1880s and '90s depict their "round-the-world" route as the embodiment of the British imperial global mission (Figure III-10), with Canada forming a central part of the imperial family. The CPR itself became a vast commercial empire, which included not only the railway tracks across the continent, but also a steamship line that would link Britain and Europe with Canada, and, at the other end of the country, would link Canada to China and Japan. In 1898 the Canadian government issued a Canadian stamp that depicted a map of the world on which the segments of the British Commonwealth are highlighted (Figure III-15). By this time, Britain had already established long-standing colonies in Canada, Australia, New Zealand, South Africa, India, and the Caribbean. In the 1880s, the competition among European powers for the accumulation of additional global territory led to what has been widely described as "the scramble for empire," particularly in Africa. The "scramble for Africa" culminated in the 1884 Berlin Conference, at which representatives of Great Britain, Portugal, Belgium, France, Holland, Italy, and Spain, among others, met at the invitation of Otto von Bismarck (the chancellor of Germany) to agree on the division of the continent between them and to establish rules for common trade between the countries. In 1899, the Anglo-Boer War erupted in South Africa, during which Canadian troops were called to South Africa to defend British territory against the Dutch.

Most Anglo-Canadians were explicit about their commitment to the British connection, particularly with the idea of the two countries sharing in a kind of hereditary cultural "greatness." Macdonald's 7 February 1891 speech in which he argued against reciprocity with the United States outlines what is gained by association with Britain and appeals to the foundations of Canada as a British (and hence, anti-American) state that was formed in contrast to the United States (74). The "imagined community" of Canada, the "Eldest Daughter of the Empire" (Lighthall xii), was thus imaginatively extended to become part of a proud hereditary tradition within a vast global imperial network. This is echoed, albeit somewhat satirically, in the political cartoon depicting the imperial lion cubs "answering the call" at the outbreak of World War I (Figure IV-6). There was even some suggestion that Canada could become the new centre of the empire. In keeping with the tenor of the times, William D. Lighthall, with a flourish, dedicated his major anthology of Canadian literature, *Songs of the Great Dominion* (1889), to "That Sublime Cause, the Union of Mankind, which the British peoples . . . will take to be the reason of existence of their empire."

At the same time, some contemporary writers were expressing disaffection with British imperial expansion and the management of the colonies. Joseph Howe, the pre-eminent anglophile, was disappointed when his dreams of Canada's equal participation in British government, such as he described in his 24 February 1854 speech on the preferred organization of the empire, proved a pipe dream. Colonials, it was clear, were on the fringes of the empire. This awareness of the colonies' inferior status in the eyes of the Old Country informs Campbell's description of "the poor beggar Colonial / Who feeds on the crumbs of [Britain's] fame" in his powerful poem "The Lazarus of Empire." Others were critical of the ways Britain was conducting its affairs in its imperial outposts. Duncan's numerous fictional writings about British India, for example, contain a piercing critique of the petty social politics and frivolities of the era of the British Raj. Even more bitter is Campbell's condemnation of Britain's lust for land in "Briton to Briton: An Appeal," written during the time of the Anglo-Boer War: "Is our world-wide task eternal? / Ever new lands to win?" asks the speaker of the poem. "Are we to scatter and scatter . . . / And all for a curse of commerce and trade?" The Anglo-Boer War was felt by many (particularly French Canadians) to be based not on the need to protect Britain, but on the lust for territorial accumulation, and some resented Canadians' participation in the war. Furthermore, the notion of a "shared destiny" across the British Empire was getting more and more difficult to sustain as Canadians gained an increased sense of themselves as a distinct people, even if this identity relegated them to the status of "colonials." "[W]ho are the rulers in truth, in right," continues Campbell's "Lazarus" poem. "And who are the conquered, pray?" The Lazarus metaphor would seem to suggest that "the poor beggar Colonial," notwithstanding his lowly stature, was to be resurrected for great things—though by whom is unclear. And whether this greatness was to be realized under the auspices of the British Empire remained to be seen.

"The Savour of the Soil": Defining a Canadian Literature

Simultaneous with the perceived need for an identifiable and bonding national identity was a sense of urgency to create and define a distinctly "Canadian" literature. The widespread assumption was that a national literature was a sign of national maturity. Hence, it was during this period that the terms "Canadian literature" and "Canadian author" as conceptual categories (albeit fraught ones) emerged into being. According to literary critic Desmond Pacey, "Never before had Canadians been as ready as in these first three decades after Confederation to welcome a native literary movement. . . . For thirty years, Canada's cultural development almost kept pace with her political and economic expansion" ("Confederation" 36). According to Walter Blackburn Harte's survey of Canadian literature in 1890, Canada was on the eve of "an intellectual revolution." As he put it, "the contemporary poets of Canada have placed a wide gulf between them and the preceding generation. . . . The poets are the precursors of a national upheaval" (qtd. in Bentley 248–49).

A number of factors contributed to this renaissance of Canadian literary production. In the first place, the generation that was born in the years immediately following Confederation (and who grew to maturity in the 1880s and '90s) was the first generation to be born "Canadian" nationals. "Canadian" authors, in other words, were an "emerging species," since prior to this period many authors who lived in what we now call Canada had been born abroad.[3] These writers were writing consciously about a landscape and country in which they had grown up as children, and which they felt had somehow contributed to their sense of who they were. The group of writers whom we now refer to as the "Confederation Poets," which included Charles G.D. Roberts, Bliss Carman, Archibald Lampman, Wilfred Campbell, and Duncan Campbell Scott, were seminal in the production of a Canadian literary identity during this period.

There was also a blossoming of literary periodicals and magazines at this time, which meant that Canadian authors could publish their work in Canada and have it read by their peers (although many writers continued to remain dependent on foreign presses for the publication of their books). The periodicals in which these authors published included *The Week*, the *Canadian Monthly and National Review*, *Grip*, and *Saturday Night*, not to mention the many newspapers that regularly published Canadian authors, including the *Globe*, the *Mail*, and the *Montreal Star*. It was during this period that Lampman, Scott, and Campbell wrote their influential "At the Mermaid Inn" column in the Toronto *Globe*. This period also saw the flourishing of many important women writers and feminist thinkers, who published alongside their male peers in these literary venues. These included the well-known poet Pauline Johnson, as well as Ethelwyn Wetherald, Susan Frances Harrison, Agnes Maule Machar, Sarah Anne Curzon, and Sara Jeannette Duncan, some of whom had professional careers as journalists. Many important cultural and intellectual institutions were established during these decades as well, including the Royal Society of Canada in 1882 and the Canadian Society of Authors in 1899 (Cambron and Gerson 130).

Many of the writers of this period saw themselves as contributing to a wider international discussion of literary form and cultural nationalism. The romantic nationalism informing these debates carried with it the assumption that nations could be recognized by their distinctive "national spirit" or "genius," which found expression in the nation's literature (see Kertzer 41–44). A national literature, most

---

[3] Of course, this definition of a "Canadian" author does not always apply, since many Canadian writers are first-generation immigrants.

authors and intellectuals agreed, was a sign of national "greatness." As McGee expounded in *The New Era* in 1857, "No literature, no national life,—this is an irreversible law." Similarly, Edward Hartley Dewart, in his introduction to his 1864 selection of Canadian poetry, insisted on the importance of literature to national unity: "It may be fairly questioned, whether . . . a people [may be] firmly united politically, without the subtle but powerful cement of a patriotic literature" (ix). It was more difficult, however, to agree upon what it was that constituted this notion of "Canadian literature." How was it to be defined? Did it have to have "Canadian" content? Should it be conversant with international literary and cultural movements, especially those in Britain and the United States? What made this even more difficult was the need to set Canadian literature apart from its antecedents: in the case of English Canada, from the long tradition of British literature that had exerted such a profound influence on Canadian writers and thinkers. R.G. Haliburton (son of Thomas Chandler Haliburton), commenting on poet and playwright Charles Mair's work in 1869, anticipated the views of the Modernists some decades later: "We must bid goodbye to the literary grave-cloths of former years, and strive to create a new school that will interpret the fresh new life of a young nation" (qtd. in Shrive xii). Haliburton echoed the thoughts of many cultural commentators of the period when he insisted on a literary language that would be appropriate to the new society and culture that was forming in Canada: "[F]or God's sake drop the old style. You're living in a new world and you must write in the language of the living to living men" (xiii).

Some of the most compelling and passionate debates of the period, particularly those between members of the Confederation Group of poets, concerned the so-called "Canadianness" of Canadian literature. The sense of urgency to create a distinctly "Canadian" literature meant that, for some people, the quality of a work of literature was secondary, as long as it was written by a Canadian or had Canadian subject matter. An additional question was that posed by Charles G.D. Roberts: could a work of Canadian literature "savour of the soil" if it was not concerned with "scenes and themes Canadian" ("Savour" 251)? In effect, these authors, particularly the poets, were in a quandary: they felt that they had to "de-colonialize" Canadian literature by purging it of its over-dependence on British influences while still maintaining universal literary and international standards. As a result, Canadian writers at this time, intent on creating a literature that would speak to their Canadian readership, emphasized distinctly Canadian themes and settings. These included a variety of things: scenes of the Canadian landscape (as in the nature poems of Roberts, Campbell, and Lampman); poems about Aboriginal peoples (as in Crawford's "Camp of Souls," or many of D.C. Scott's and Pauline Johnson's poems); and poems about Canadian historical figures and events (as, for example, in Johnson's and Machar's poems about the 1885 Northwest Rebellion or Campbell's and McGee's poems about the early explorers). Critics have suggested that Canadians, in the effort to forge a new national identity, found themselves in the predicament of consciously creating a cultural-historical tradition, and hence looked for elements that appeared "indigenous" to the Canadian locale: nature, history, Native peoples, and French-Canadian *habitants*, among others. These elements are evident in a good deal of Canadian writing.

However, the fact remained that these writers were still heavily influenced by traditional British verse forms, particularly the ideology and tropes of the British Romantic poets, such as John Keats and William Wordsworth. Roberts's "The Tantramar Revisited," for instance, echoes Wordsworth's famous 1798 poem "Lines Written a Few Miles above Tintern Abbey," where the speaker in the poem looks down upon a pastoral landscape from a height and recalls the time he spent there in his youth. Similarly, Johnson's powerful poem "A Cry from an Indian Wife," spoken by a Native woman whose husband has joined Riel's forces in the Northwest Rebellion, is written in the form of a dramatic mono-logue in the style of Robert Browning, with rhyming couplets and iambic pentameter. Roberts's essay, "The Poetry of Nature," published in *Forum* in 1897 and included in this anthology, provides a clear articulation of the Romantic tenets upheld by the Canadian poets of this period.

The challenge for these Canadian writers was to apply Romantic conventions and ideology to a uniquely "Canadian" landscape and context. English Romantic literature is generally dated from the 1790s to the 1850s, and is usually defined by its introspective quality, particularly its emphasis on nature as a spiritual (rather than a rational) force which inspires moments of reflection. It often invokes the power of memory, especially as it merges with the evocative power of the landscape, and hence tends to express nostalgia for the past. The well-known painting by Lucius O'Brien reproduced here, *Sunrise on the Saguenay* (1880), is a good example of pictorial Romantic landscape depiction (Figure III-16), whose qualities can be compared to the poetic output of the period. The movement also expresses itself in opposition to forces of modernity and industrialization, and usually includes a celebration of rustic or rural life as more authentic than urban living. Many of the poems of the period were social critiques of the ills of industrialization and the mass exodus to urban centres. Hence many writers of this period look back to an earlier, rural period in Canada's past. This is clearly evident in the short stories of Edward Thomson, in which one finds a celebration of French-Canadian rural life, as well as in the stories of Duncan Campbell Scott. More well-known examples of this genre are the beautiful, though sometimes vaguely unsettling, pastoral sonnets from Roberts's *Songs of the Common Day* (1893), as well as Lampman's famous poems "Heat," "Comfort of the Fields," and "Among the Timothy," which celebrate the landscape as an escape from the turmoil of urban civilization. In some instances, however, an edge of ambivalence in these poems hints at an underlying feeling that the retreat is impossible. Indeed, the most haunting and powerful condemnation of industrialized urban life occurs in Lampman's "The City of the End of Things," which describes the end of the world as the City's machines grind to a halt only to be watched over, for eternity, by the allegorical figure of the Idiot, a ghoulish, soulless creature slumped at the city gates.

In many cases, Canadian authors espoused a Romantic equation between national character and geography, as if the climate or landscape somehow created particular character types or literary approaches. This resonated in McGee's description of Canada as a "Northern nation" ("Canadian" 34) or in R.G. Haliburton's celebration of Canadians in 1869 as "the Northmen of the New World" (156). Mair, more explicitly, described how the northern Canadian climate would produce a "noble" race of people by "develop[ing] the broad shoulder, the tense muscle, and the clear brain, and which will build up the most herculean and robust nation upon earth" (164). The famous Canadian historian and political economist of the 1930s Harold Innis, in looking back at Canada's beginnings in the fur trade, argued that Canada had emerged not in spite of geography, but because of it (Winks xiv), thereby suggesting that Canada's distinctiveness from the United States had "natural" roots. By the post-Confederation period, writers were asserting the notion of an Anglo-Canadian "character type," which resulted from the confluence of particular geographical and social conditions. The "prototypical" Canadian was thus figured as an enterprising, hard-working, robust, and homespun individual— already emergent in Moodie's and Traill's descriptions of the ideal type of British settler—who rejected both English class snobbery and American materialism. Duncan, for example, spent a good portion of her writing career untangling the distinguishing qualities of the Canadian, American, and British characters, a topic that emerges in her novels in which Canadian or American girls visit England, as well as in her humorous novel *A Social Departure*, in which a Canadian and a British woman travel around the world together. Her 7 July 1887 piece for *The Week*, "American Influence on Canadian Thought," outlines some of these distinctions.

If Duncan's Canadian characters are more relaxed in manners than their British counterparts, "Canadian" literature was often anthropomorphized as the embodiment of the tamed yet unfettered wilderness. In order to be "autochthonous," Mair stated in 1875, Canadian literature had to "taste of the wood" (164). McGee, in his 1858 essay "Protection for Canadian Literature," invoked the importance of geography to the Canadian character and, by extension, to Canadian literary expression: "There is a glorious field upon which to work for the formation of our National Literature. It must assume the gorgeous coloring and the gloomy grandeur of the forest. It must partake of the grave mysticism of the Red man, and the wild vivacity of the hunter of western prairies. Its lyrics must possess the ringing cadence of the waterfall, and its epics be as solemn and beautiful as our great rivers" (23). By 1886, Duncan, writing in the *Washington Post*, confidently stated that a national literature "should have its roots in the national character and within national limits, and it should be, so to speak, racy of its native soil" (*Selected* 102). Similar sentiments were echoed by many of the Confederation poets, and reached their apotheosis in Lighthall's 1889 poetry anthology, *Songs of the Great Dominion*. In his introduction to the book, Lighthall makes a case for the new voice of Canada, as though the ancient land and its history have been resurrected in the poets of the day: "Through [these poems], taken all together, you may catch something of great Niagara falling, of brown rivers rushing with foam, of the crack of the rifle in the haunts of the moose and caribou, the lament of vanishing races singing their death-song as they are swept on to the cataract of oblivion . . . , shrill war-whoops of Iroquois battle, proud traditions of contests with the French and the Americans, stern and sorrowful cries of valour rising to curb rebellion" (xxi).

If it appears as though the writing of the Confederation poets emphasized Canada's natural geography at the expense of social and political events, it was this emphasis on the Canadian landscape that enabled them to articulate the distinctiveness of the new nationality, something that set Canada apart from England and the United States, which was in turn crucial in asserting Canada's independence as an autonomous nation. While landscape was not literally "in the blood," some, such as Roberts in his 1892 essay "The Savour of the Soil," made a case for the formative influence of place and geography in the constitution of Canadian literature. The expectation that Canadian literature would "savour of the soil from which it springs . . . means that we desire our literature to be genuine and original, not artificial and imitative" (251). As literary critic Roy Daniells puts it in his chapter for the *Literary History of Canada* (1965) on Confederation writers: "Those who turned to nature were not evading but seeking the true Canada. The only thing Canadians possessed that other people did not was the top half of the American continent. . . . Then, as now, the geological, geographical, topographic, and lyric features of the Canadian landscape were the fundamental facts of Canadian experience" (201). While there were other factors contributing to a distinct British North American identity, such as the unique social mores and a distinct form of Canadian English, Canadian geography remained that which most people, within Canada and beyond, could most easily identify as "Canadian" (something we see in the pervasive, clichéd images today of Canada as a land of wilderness, mountains, and snow).

However, despite the wealth of literary production in the period, there was still a good deal of uncertainty and discussion about the quality of the literature that was being produced, and the relation of that literature to other national literary traditions. A pervasive concern was that Canadians' focus on questions of national identity would result in an excessive and insular parochialism. While Roberts was one of the most active and ardent promoters of the new wave of Canadian literature, he nevertheless had some reservations about the excessive navel-gazing that such cultural nationalism brought with it. In his 1883 Alumni Address to the University of New Brunswick, "The Beginnings of a Canadian Literature," he stated his viewpoint succinctly: "[L]et me say a word concerning that perpetual injunction to our verse-writers to choose Canadian themes only. Now it must be remembered that the whole heritage of English Song is ours and that it is *not* ours to found a *new* literature. . . . All the greatest subject matter is free to the world's writers" (*Selected* 258). Later, in "The Savour of the Soil," he insisted, "It is not desirable . . . that Canadian literature should concern itself exclusively with scenes and themes Canadian. . . . It is an ignorant folly that would restrict a writer to his own surroundings in his choice of scene and theme" (251). However, Roberts also noted that Canadian writers' work must carry something distinctive to the Canadian locale which would set it apart from European models: "[T]he tone of the work, the quality of the handling, must be influenced by the surroundings and local sympathies of the workman" (258). These debates anticipate those of the Modernists some forty years later, when Canadian critic and poet A.J.M. Smith divided Canadian writers into two groups, the "native" and "cosmopolitan" (1943), and objected to the naive nationalism of the former. Roberts's short piece "A Note on Modernism" (1931) reveals his awareness of the links between these debates in his time and later, and thus provides an important counterpoint to the Modernists' often disparaging figuration of their literary predecessors as naive "maple-leaf" patriots (see, for example, F.R. Scott's 1927 poem "The Canadian Authors Meet" or Smith's "Rejected Preface" in Volume II of this anthology).

Indeed, many during this period were skeptical about the possibility of a Canadian literature existing a mere twenty or thirty years following Confederation. Although Walter Blackburn Harte predicted that Canada was on the eve of "an intellectual revolution" (qtd. in Bentley 248), many writers and critics were reluctant to become too complacent about the idea that they were in the midst of a literary renaissance. Goldwin Smith, in a comment that reflects his impatience with Canadian culture at the time, stated in *The Week* on 31 August 1894 that "no such thing as a literature Canadian *[sic]* in the local sense exists or is likely ever to exist. 'Canada' is a political expression. There is no literary unity, there is not even unity of language" (86). Smith held a rather atypical position among the writers of the time as a supporter of Canada's annexation to the United States, and his comments on Canada's tentative cultural status reflect this political position. However, even Lampman, in his oft-cited lecture "Two Canadian Poets," in which he notes the galvanizing effect of his first encounter with Roberts's *Orion and Other Poems* (1880), was hesitant to declare that Canadian literature was firmly established. Lampman critiques Roberts's patriotic poems on the basis that such nationalism is premature: "The time has not come for the production of any genuine national song. It is when the passion and enthusiasm of an entire people . . . enters into the soul of one man specially gifted, that a great national poem or hymn is produced" (107). As Duncan, in her 30 September 1886 piece in *The Week* pointedly expressed it, "We are still an eminently unliterary people" (707).

Part of this uncertainty about the status of Canadian literature was a result of the still limited prospects for writers within Canada at this time. Very few writers were able to earn a living from their writing, which forced many to accept government appointments, teaching positions, or other means of support. Secondly, many of these aspiring new authors were in search of places to publish their works. This was the heyday of the periodical press in Canada, which "provided the first national medium of mass communication" (Distad 293) and thereby played a significant role in the consolidation of a shared sense of a national community.

Nevertheless, authors interested in publishing book-length works were forced to seek publishers in the cosmopolitan centres abroad, namely London, Paris, New York, and Boston. Even though the 1880s and '90s are often celebrated as a "golden age" of Canadian writing, many writers chose to escape the limited opportunities and navel-gazing bent of the Canadian literary scene by moving abroad. This was the case for Charles G.D. Roberts, Bliss Carman, Ernest Thompson Seton, and Sara Jeannette Duncan, who spent most of their writing lives outside Canada. Roberts's "The Poet Is Bidden to Manhattan Island" exhorts Canadian poets to forsake their rural homeland and "pipe for them that pay the piper!" As Micheline Cambron and Carole Gerson put it, "[T]he price of success was often expatriation," a necessity that changed by the end of the First World War. In the last two decades of the nineteenth century, over 1.5 million Canadians left Canada for the United States (Bothwell and Granatstein 29). The exodus of Canadian authors and intellectuals during this period is comparable to what later became known as the "brain drain" in the 1960s and later, when Canadians expressed anxiety about the immigration to the United States of many of their most talented people.

A series of unfair copyright laws in effect in the colonies exacerbated the difficulties of publishing in Canada and may have furthered the impetus for the phenomenon of "self-exile" by Canadian writers. In 1842, the Literary Copyright Act was passed in Britain, which subjected Canadian materials to imperial copyright law until 1923. This meant that copyright laws focused on the rights of British authors and that "Britain and the United States competed as the main source of supply for the colonial market" (Parker 149). With the Foreign Reprints Act of 1847, American reprints of British books were legalized on the payment of a percentage to the British copyright holders. As a result, the Canadian market was flooded with cheap American reprints, which made it difficult for Canadian publishers (and authors) to compete. As McGee asked in his 1867 speech for the Montreal Literary Club, "The Mental Outfit of the New Dominion": "'Who reads a Canadian book?' I should answer frankly, very few, for Canadian books are exceedingly scarce" (15). As late as 1887, in her essay "American Influence on Canadian Thought," Duncan was still lamenting the excessive impact American interests were having on Canadian literary production. McGee stressed the importance of a Canadian literature for a Canadian citizenry: "The books that are made elsewhere, even in England, are not always the best fitted for us; they do not always run on the same mental gauge, nor connect with our trains of thought. . . . I do not object to such books . . . but it seems to me we do much need several other books calculated to our own meridian, and hitting home to our own society . . ." ("Mental" 16–17). McGee's use of the railway metaphor is significant given the galvanizing role the railway was to have in Canadians' emergent sense of national identity. In effect, it was the writers of the Confederation period who produced the first of the works that McGee was calling for: a literature that was both internationally situated and locally committed, emergent from and intended for the new Canadian populace.

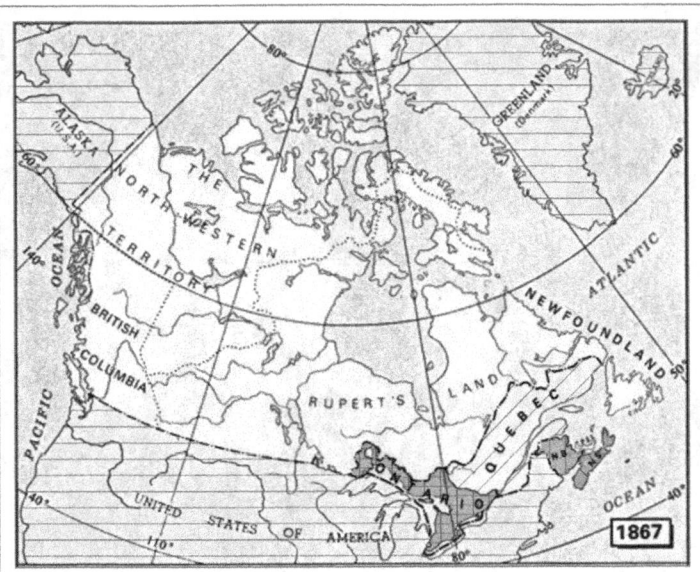

FIGURE III-1 Map of Canada in 1867, Following Confederation

Source: Original map data provided by The Atlas of Canada, http://atlas.gc.ca. ©2006. Produced under license from Her Majesty the Queen in Right of Canada, with permission of Natural Resources Canada.

FIGURE III-2 Map of Canada in 1870, Following the Acquisition of Rupert's Land (HBC Territory) and the Formation of Manitoba

Source: Original map data provided by The Atlas of Canada, http://atlas.gc.ca. ©2006. Produced under license from Her Majesty the Queen in Right of Canada, with permission of Natural Resources Canada.

FIGURE III-3 "The Fathers of Confederation" (oil painting, 1883–84), Robert Harris
This is one of the most famous images of Canadian political history, painted by Prince Edward
Island artist Robert Harris (1849–1919) to commemorate the founding of Canada. It was commissioned in 1883 as the official portrait of the Fathers of Confederation. The painting, entitled
*Conference at Québec in October 1864, to Settle the Basics of a Union of the British North
American Provinces*, in fact includes delegates from both the Quebec and Charlottetown
gatherings. John A. Macdonald is standing in the centre; Thomas D'Arcy McGee is seated at
the far right. The painting hung in the Parliament Buildings in Ottawa until it was destroyed
when the Centre Block caught fire in 1916. Many subsequent copies, including this one, were
made of the painting on the basis of Harris's early sketches for the work.

Source: Library and Archives Canada/C-002149.

CHILD CANADA TAKES HER FIRST STEP

MOTHER BRITANNIA: See! Why, the dear child can stand alone!
UNCLE SAM: Of course he can! Let go of him, Granny; if he falls I'll catch him!

FIGURE III-4 "Child Canada Takes Her First Step" (1870)

The depiction of Canada as a "child" of two adults, Britain and the United States, was a common one in the post-Confederation period, evident as well in such poems as Charles G.D. Roberts's "Canada" or Isabella Valancy Crawford's "Canada to England." This cartoon, originally published in the *Canadian Illustrated News* in June 1870, represents the debate that existed over Canada's political status, well after Confederation, as to whether Canada was to be independent, strengthen ties with the British Empire, or become annexed to the United States. The identification of both "adults" as anglophone underlines the way Canada was conceived as a British nation, even though the French were officially one of the founding groups at the time of Confederation. This bias is highlighted in such other imagery of the period as, for instance, Alexander Muir's famous anthem "The Maple Leaf for Ever" (1867). It is also noteworthy that "Child Canada" is clearly figured as Caucasian and appears to be wearing a Scottish tartan kilt.

Source: Charles and Cynthia Hou, *Great Canadian Political Cartoons, 1820 to 1914* (Vancouver: Moody's Lookout, 1997).

"ANTI-SECESH."

" Let me go, you old deceiver."
" By no means, my dear. What? leave, when our honeymoon is hardly over. Come, I'll let you
have a little more pin money "

FIGURE III-5 "Anti-Secesh" (1879)

This political cartoon, from the *Canadian Illustrated News* of 10 May 1879, shows the popular figuration of British Columbia as a young woman being wooed by John A. Macdonald. In some versions, the Lady of British Columbia is represented with two rivals: Canada and the United States. This metaphor occurs in the "Lady of British Columbia" section of E.J. Pratt's poem "Towards the Last Spike" (1952), included in Volume II.

Source: Library and Archives Canada/C-072110.

WHAT IT MUST COME TO
(With the Encroachment of Civilization)
OFFICER: [Sir John A. Macdonald]: Here, you copper colored gentlemen, no loafing allowed, you must either work or jump.

FIGURE III-6 "What It Must Come To" (1885)

This cartoon, published in the *Toronto Evening News* of 10 June 1885, took a remarkably courageous position in challenging the ways the advance of the CPR and settlement of the west, under the leadership of John A. Macdonald (here dressed as a British police officer), were pushing Aboriginal peoples to the brink of extinction. Just before this, in April 1885, the CPR had been used to transport troops to quell the Northwest Rebellion; by June, Louis Riel was being held in police custody awaiting trial. The train engine is emitting a trail of smoke labelled "Civilization." The words "Westward Ho!"—ironically inscribed on the sun—refer to British author Charles Kingsley's 1855 patriotic novel by the same title; the phrase also came to be used to describe migration to the United States.

Source: Charles and Cynthia Hou, *Great Canadian Political Cartoons, 1820–1914* (Vancouver: Moody's Lookout, 1997).

FIGURE III-7 "The Last Spike" (1885)

This is probably the most famous photograph in Canadian history. It was staged as the
official publicity shot to mark the completion of the Canadian Pacific Railway on 7 November
1885. The photo shows company director Donald Smith hammering in the ceremonial "last
spike" in Craigellachie, B.C. To his right stands company general manager William Cornelius
Van Horne; between them is chief engineer Sandford Fleming. In his first attempt to hammer
the spike, Smith bent it in half, so a second had to be substituted. Subsequently, the spike
had to be removed from the tracks for fear that it would be plundered by souvenir hunters.
No representative of the country was present at the ceremony. This is the photo that is commemorated in the conclusion to E.J. Pratt's 1952 epic poem "Towards the Last Spike,"
where the reverberations from the hammer's blow initiate "a massed continental chorus." The
first, bent spike was retained by Donald Smith's family and is currently held by the Canadian
National Museum of Science and Technology in Ottawa.

Source: Library and Archives Canada/C-003693.

FIGURE III-8 Workers' Photograph of the "Last Spike" Ceremony (1885)
As a counter to the official photograph of company director Donald Smith hammering the so-called "last spike," the railway workers staged their own photograph after the company officials had left. These are the "navvies" memorialized in Gordon Lightfoot's famous song about the railway, "The Canadian Railway Trilogy" (1967), the people who did the back-breaking labour and risked their lives in achieving what was to be memorialized as the "national dream." In his 1971 book *The Last Spike*, Pierre Berton calls them "the unknown soldiers in Van Horne's army." Like Lightfoot's song, however, the photograph does not show any of the thousands of Chinese men who were central in the construction of the CPR.

Source: Library and Archives Canada/C-014115.

FIGURE III-9 "The Golden Northwest" (poster, 1883)

The CPR played an enormous role in advertising the Canadian Northwest to prospective settlers and farmers. Here the western prairies are described as "a home for all people," and the image shows a Britannia figure shining the light of civilization onto the Canadian landscape. In many of these advertisements, the prairies were falsely promoted as a place where crops grew in plenty—hence the cornucopia of produce at the bottom of the picture.

Source: Canadian Pacific Railway Archives A.6418.

FIGURE III-10 "Around the World by the Canadian Pacific Route" (timetable, 1893)

The CPR developed a series of ocean liners that linked up with the cross-Canada train route. In this way, the railway saw itself as having opened up a trade and travel route to the East, such as had been dreamed of in the seventeenth and eighteenth centuries. The route connected the British Empire around the globe. The CPR, when connected with its subsidiary steamship line, advertised travel routes to Japan and China in the 1890s. It was a journey such as the one promoted here that Sara Jeannette Duncan embarked on in 1888, and that became the basis for her first novel, *A Social Departure* (1890). It is ironic that at the very time that the CPR was promoting tourist travel to China, the Canadian government was issuing restrictive legislation curtailing Chinese immigration to Canada, even though it was the Chinese workers who had been pivotal in constructing much of the western portion of the transcontinental railway line.

Source: Canadian Pacific Railway Archives A.18114.

FIGURE III-11 "Canada West: The New Homeland" (poster, 1923)

This poster encouraging settlement of the Canadian west presents an idealized and harmonious scene of order, ease, and plenty. The eroticized depiction of the ideal "White" Canadian settler is a central feature of much of the settlement propaganda of the late nineteenth and early twentieth centuries.

Source: Canadian Pacific Railway Archives BR.196.

FIGURE III-12 "Resorts in the Rockies" (menu cover, 1920s)
The Canadian Pacific Railway promoted tourism across Canada (and hence the increased
use of its rail lines) by building a series of grand hotels along the rail routes at various points
across the country. The Banff Springs Hotel, pictured here, was one of the earliest and most
magnificent of these resorts. These advertisements established the iconography of Canada
that is so widely in use today: images of mountains, moose, and Mounties. In this illustration,
a helpful Mountie shows a wealthy "lady" (dressed in upper-class riding gear) the location of
the Banff Springs Hotel.

Source: Canadian Pacific Railway Archives A.636.

FIGURE III-13 "Indian Days, Banff" (poster, 1925)

The CPR established "Indian Days" in some cities on its western route in order to entertain tourists travelling across the country. Native people were paid to dress up and "perform" for these tourists, an irony given the fact that the CPR had been instrumental in depriving Native peoples of their traditional lands—not to mention the fact that the Canadian government had issued an official ban on traditional Aboriginal celebrations during this time period (see the excerpts from the Indian Act in this section). This poster, designed by Wilfred Langdon Kihn, does not attempt to represent any particular Aboriginal community, but rather includes a conflation of various stereotypes of Aboriginal regalia (e.g., teepees, feathered headdresses, braids, papooses, and buffalo horns). While many of the figures wear traditional blankets, the central one is wrapped in the trademark striped Hudson's Bay Company blanket, thus hinting at the colonization of the people by the European traders and settlers.

Source: Canadian Pacific Railway Archives A.6145.

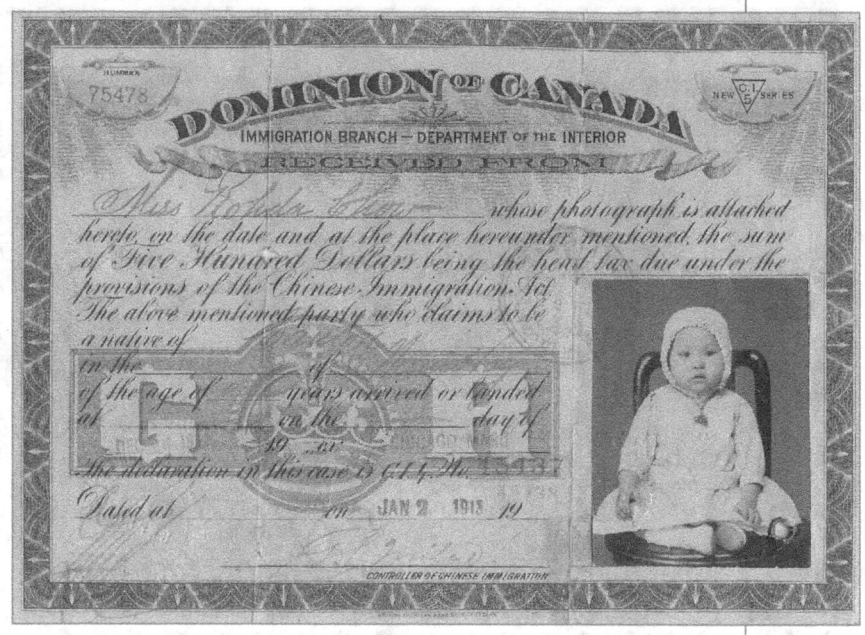

FIGURE III-14 Chinese Head Tax Certificate, 1913

Beginning in 1885, the Canadian government began imposing a head tax on every new Chinese immigrant arriving in Canada. The amount was raised from $50 in 1885, to $100 in 1900, to $500 in 1903 (the equivalent of two years' labour on the railway). The tax made it impossible for many Chinese people to become reunited with their families in Canada. Rhoda Chow, the subject of this certificate, later married and became Mrs. Rose Lee of Trail, BC.

Source: Head Tax Certificate courtesy of Mrs. Penny (Lee) Chong, daughter of Rose Lee.

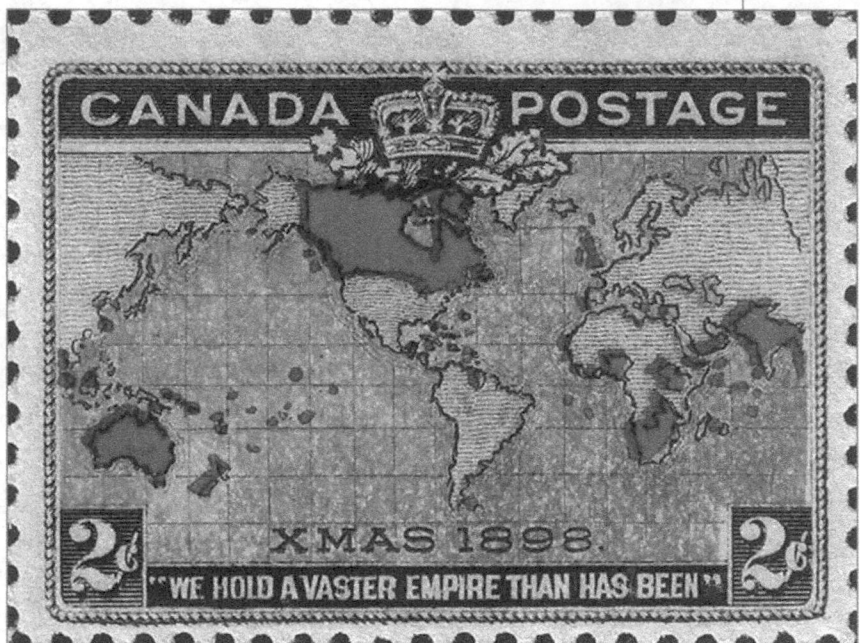

FIGURE III-15 "We Hold a Vaster Empire than Has Been" (1898)

This Canadian stamp, issued in 1898, shows the extent of the British Commonwealth in 1898. The map, which celebrates the British Empire, echoes many of the advertisements for the CPR "Round-the-World" tours, which depicted the railway and shipping lines as linking the various territories of the British Empire.

Source: ©Canada Post Corporation (1898). Reproduced with permission.

FIGURE III-16 *Sunrise on the Saguenay, Cape Trinity* **(oil on canvas, 1880), Lucius O'Brien (1832–1899)**

Lucius O'Brien's *Sunrise on the Saguenay* (1880) is a well-known example of nineteenth-century Romantic landscape depiction. The North American landscape is depicted as luminous and sublime, evoking the smallness of man before the grandeur of nature. It provides a useful complement to Susanna Moodie's description of her first view of the North American landscape from afar as her boat is approaching Grosse Isle and to Anna Jameson's descriptions of southern Ontario (both included in Section II). It is also an interesting companion piece to the landscape poems of the post-Confederation group of poets, such as Charles G.D. Roberts and Duncan Campbell Scott. The painting presents a view of Cape Trinity, overlooking a fjord on Quebec's Saguenay River. Born in Ontario, O'Brien was the first president of the Royal Canadian Academy of Arts in 1880. This painting was one of the National Gallery of Canada's first acquisitions.

Source: Lucius R. O'Brien, 1832–1899. *Sunrise on the Saguenay, Cape Trinity*, 1880. oil on canvas, 90 × 122 cm. National Gallery of Canada, Ottawa. Diploma work, deposited by the artist, Toronto, 1880.

FIGURES FOR SECTION III

289

MISS E. PAULINE JOHNSON.

Cochran

HAMILTON, ONT.   BRANTFORD, ONT.

FIGURE III-17 Publicity Photograph of Pauline Johnson in Her Performance Costume, Late 1892

This picture shows Johnson's buckskin stage dress with the bear-claw necklace and Iroquois wampum belt. Johnson would unpin her hair and wear this costume when presenting the "Indian" material from her poetic repertoire.

Source: Courtesy of Chiefswood National Historic Site, Six Nations of the Grand River.

FIGURE III-18 Pauline Johnson in English Dinner Dress, 1897

Johnson would change into a Victorian evening gown for the second half of her poetic performances, thus demonstrating her "Englishness."

Source: Courtesy of the Brant Museum and Archives.

En. Route — Abitibi River

FIGURE III-19 Duncan Campbell Scott in a Treaty Canoe, 1905
This photograph of Duncan Campbell Scott was taken during his trip to negotiate Treaty 9, which he describes in "The Last of the Indian Treaties." Scott would often compose poetry while being paddled by his Aboriginal guides.

Source: Archives of Ontario/10010557.

The British North America Act (BNA Act) is widely described as the document that "created" Canada. In effect, it was the brainchild of John A. Macdonald, George-Étienne Cartier, and George Brown, the party leaders of the united province of Canada who determined that joining the provinces of British North America was the best protection against annexation to the United States. In 1864, the Maritime provinces were already proposing a meeting to discuss an Atlantic union, and Macdonald invited himself and other representatives from Upper and Lower Canada to attend. It was at this meeting in Charlottetown, P.E.I., that he proposed a union of all of the eastern British North American colonies. This conference was followed by another one a month later in Quebec City (Figure III-3). It was in Quebec that the preliminary resolutions constituting the BNA Act were settled upon. Subsequently, Prince Edward Island and Newfoundland backed out of the deal. A delegation of sixteen men representing Canada, New Brunswick, and Nova Scotia travelled to London, England, in December 1866 to begin the process of ratification. The BNA Act was passed by the British Parliament in 1867, and on 1 July of that year (the day we now celebrate as Canada Day), the Dominion of Canada was officially proclaimed into existence.

The BNA Act described the separate provinces of Canada and set out the terms under which Canada would still maintain the British sovereign, at that time Queen Victoria, as its legal head of state, with the governor general as the Queen's representative in Canada. Most importantly, because Canada was constituted as a "federation" uniting a group of distinct provinces, the Act set out the distinctive jurisdictions and powers of the federal government and the individual provincial legislatures, and described the roles of the bodies of the federal government (the House of Commons and the Senate), which mimicked the format of the British parliamentary system. The federal system it outlined, however, was distinct from that of the United States (where federalism was proving a failure in view of the civil war that was tearing the country apart), since the central government would retain far greater powers than that of Washington. This was particularly important for the representatives from Quebec, who sought to preserve French Canadians' cultural and civic identity as it had been previously protected in the Quebec Act of 1774. In addition, according to the 1867 Act, Canada's foreign policy remained under British law, and any amendment to the Canadian constitution would need to be approved in Britain. Hence, Canada's colonial status remained intact; while as a nation it had substantial autonomy, it was not fully independent from the United Kingdom. This is a point that arises frequently in the writings of the Confederation period and early twentieth century. Sara Jeannette Duncan, for example, in the 30 September 1886 issue of *The Week*, wrote of "our present imperfect autonomy in 1867." In 1931, with the Statute of Westminster, these matters were altered, and Canada became an autonomous, equal member within the British Commonwealth. However, despite repeated attempts to unite the Canadian provinces on the issue, Canada was still not allowed to make amendments to its constitution. This was altered in 1982 when, under the leadership of Prime Minister Pierre Trudeau, the Canadian constitution was patriated (brought home) to Canada.

Ontario, Quebec, Nova Scotia, and New Brunswick came together with the passage of the BNA Act in 1867. Over the next 132 years, the other provinces and territories joined Confederation: Manitoba and the Northwest Territories in 1870; British Columbia in 1871; Prince Edward Island in 1873; the Yukon in 1898; and, in 1905, the provinces of Saskatchewan and Alberta. In 1949 Newfoundland entered Confederation, following a contentious referendum. Finally, in 1999, Nunavut was recognized as a separate territory.

From The British North America Act, 1867[1]

An Act for the Union of Canada, Nova Scotia, and New Brunswick, and the Government thereof, and for Purposes connected therewith. (29 March, 1867)

WHEREAS the Provinces of Canada, Nova Scotia and New Brunswick have expressed their Desire to be federally united into One Dominion under the Crown of the United Kingdom of Great Britain and Ireland, with a Constitution similar in Principle to the United Kingdom;

AND WHEREAS such a Union would conduce to the Welfare of the Provinces and promote the Interests of the British Empire;

AND WHEREAS on the Establishment of the Union by Authority of Parliament it is expedient, not only that the Constitution of the Legislative Authority in the Dominion be provided for, but also that the Nature of the Executive Government therein be declared;

AND WHEREAS it is expedient that Provision be made for the eventual Admission into the Union of other Parts of British North America [. . .]

II. Union

3. It shall be lawful for the Queen, by and with the Advice of Her Majesty's Most Honourable Privy Council, to declare by Proclamation that, on and after a Day therein appointed, not being more than Six Months after the passing of this Act, the Provinces of Canada, Nova Scotia and New Brunswick shall form and be One Dominion under the Name of Canada. [. . .]

5. Canada shall be divided into Four Provinces, named Ontario, Quebec, Nova Scotia and New Brunswick.

6. The parts of the Province of Canada (as it exists at the passing of this Act) which formerly constituted respectively the provinces of Upper and Lower Canada shall be deemed to be severed, and shall form Two separate Provinces. The Part which formerly constituted the Province of Upper Canada shall constitute the Province of Ontario, and the Part which formerly constituted the Province of Lower Canada shall Constitute the Province of Quebec.

7. The Provinces of Nova Scotia and New Brunswick shall have the same Limits as at the passing of this Act. [. . .]

[1] In 1982 the BNA Act was retitled the Constitution Act, 1982.

III. Executive Power

9. The Executive Government and Authority of and over Canada is hereby declared to continue and be vested in the Queen. [. . .]

11. There shall be a Council to aid and advise in the Government of Canada, to be styled the Queen's Privy Council for Canada;[2] and the Persons who are to be Members of that Council shall be from Time to Time chosen and summoned by the Governor General and sworn in as Privy Councillors, and Members thereof may be from Time to Time removed by the Governor General. [. . .]

13. The Provisions of this Act referring to the Governor General in Council shall be construed as referring to the Governor General acting by and with the Advice of the Queen's Privy Council for Canada. [. . .]

15. The Command-in-Chief of the Land and Naval Militia, and of all Naval and Military Forces, of and in Canada, is hereby declared to continue and be vested in the Queen.

16. Until the Queen otherwise directs, the Seat of Government of Canada shall be Ottawa.

IV. Legislative Power

17. There shall be One Parliament for Canada consisting of the Queen, and Upper House Styled [on] the Senate, and the House of Commons.

18. The privileges, immunities, and powers held, enjoyed, and exercised by the Senate and House of Commons, and by the Members thereof, shall be such as are from Time to Time defined by [an] Act of the Parliament of Canada, but so that any Act of the Parliament of Canada defining such privileges, immunities, or powers shall not confer any privileges, immunities, or powers exceeding those at the passing of the Act held, enjoyed and exercised by the Commons House of Parliament of the United Kingdom of Great Britain and Ireland, and by the members thereof.

[1867]

[2] The Queen's Privy Council for Canada, established by the BNA Act, is a council of advisers to the Queen of England who are appointed by the governor general.

JOHN A. MACDONALD ■ (1815–91)

There was a time when a transcontinental British North American nation was merely a figment of the imagination. John A. Macdonald, the man who conceived it and who would become the first elected prime minister of the new nation, knew what was needed to bring the idea to fruition: compromise and vision.

The challenges that lay before Macdonald in the years leading up to Confederation were immense. He had to unify the competing interests of English and French Canada, and allay French Canadians' legitimate fears that a union with the British provinces would pose a threat to their ancestral traditions and religious beliefs. He had to appease the fiercely loyal regional identities of the Atlantic provinces—particularly those of Nova Scotia and Newfoundland, two of the oldest colonies in British North America. In 1866, Nova Scotia politician Joseph Howe, a vocal opponent of Confederation from its beginnings, scoffed at the absurdity of this pipe dream to be called Canada: "[A] more unpromising nucleus of a new nation can hardly be found on the face of the earth." The provinces would be "insane" to join up, he declared, and he predicted that within less than a century, Canada would cease to exist. Meanwhile, the colony of British Columbia on the west coast was in danger of being annexed to the United States. The Red River colony (which before long would become the province of Manitoba) was a hotbed of unrest because the Métis population, who had lived on the land for generations, wanted to create a province of their own. To the south was the persistent military threat of the United States, which in the 1860s was engaged in a bloody civil war that was threatening to lead to a military invasion of Canada. Given these obstacles, Macdonald had to summon his rhetorical skill in order to sell the idea of national union.

Born in Scotland, Macdonald's family immigrated to Upper Canada when he was five years old. They settled in Kingston, Ontario, where Macdonald studied law and established his own law practice while in his early twenties. Eventually he was elected as a representative to the legislature of the united province of Canada, and by 1856 was the leader of Upper Canada. Although deeply committed to Canada's inherent connections with the British Empire, Macdonald realized not only that he had to respect the distinct nationality of Quebec, but also that he had to allow French Canadians to rule alongside the English

as equals. To this end, he established a Liberal-Conservative coalition government with the French conservatives, led by George-Étienne Cartier. When he learned that the Atlantic provinces were contemplating the possibility of a Maritime federation, Macdonald asked if representatives from Canada could attend, and a meeting was proposed in Prince Edward Island in September 1864. At the conference, Macdonald and Cartier launched their proposal for a union of the eastern British North American provinces. This was followed by a meeting in Quebec City where the rules that would govern the new federation, the BNA Act (the Constitution), were finalized. The various provincial leaders set to work convincing their separate legislatures of the advantages of Confederation. In his "Confederation" speech of February 1865, included here, Macdonald appealed to Canadians' pro-British feelings, to their allegiance to their ancestral heritages (French, English, and Irish), to their fears of the United States, and above all to their sense of destiny. The time was ripe for a federation, he proclaimed in his speech to the legislature, and people could not let the moment pass them by.

The Confederation speech, delivered in the Legislative Assembly, contains Macdonald's defence of the idea of a union of the eastern British North American provinces into an independent nation. Initially, he hoped to unite the province of Canada (the area that is today the provinces of Quebec and Ontario) with Nova Scotia, New Brunswick, Prince Edward Island, and Newfoundland (the latter two withdrew from the deal and entered Confederation some years later). He needed the approval of the Legislative assembly in order to be able to take the proposal to England for ratification. After four weeks of debate, the assembly approved the proposal, and a delegation of politicians representing the four provinces travelled to London in 1866. The Dominion of Canada was created by Queen's proclamation on 1 July 1867. On the same day, Macdonald was knighted by Queen Victoria for bringing about Confederation.

For Macdonald, this was only the beginning of the difficult task that lay ahead. Following on the heels of Confederation, Canada purchased the vast Hudson's Bay Company territory in the Northwest known as Rupert's Land. Macdonald, as historian Gordon Donaldson puts it, suddenly found himself "the absentee landlord of a third of the continent." He needed a way of bringing the huge western expanse of land under the national umbrella, while also, he hoped, luring British Columbia into union with the eastern provinces so that he could create a cross-continental British North American nation (as opposed to a "Yankee" one). Macdonald undertook what would be the crowning glory of his post-Confederation career: the building of the Canadian Pacific Railway and the western settlement initiatives that accompanied it. The Intercolonial Railway was already under way linking Ottawa with the Maritime provinces. The CPR would clinch British Columbia's entry into Confederation in 1871 with the promise of a railway, to be built within ten years, that would join the nation "from sea to sea."

As before, Macdonald was accused of fantasizing the impossible. While British Columbia agreed to the terms—it helped his cause that the British population of the province was adamantly opposed to joining the United States— the building of the railway was fraught with geographical difficulties (particularly in the Rocky Mountains) and, more contentiously, with political scandal. With

the Canadian government's acquisition of Rupert's Land, the Métis population on the prairies rebelled at the idea of becoming subjects to a group of eastern English Protestants. The Métis, under the provisional leadership of Louis Riel, saw no reason why they couldn't constitute a distinct province on par with Nova Scotia, which would negotiate its own terms for joining the federation. Macdonald's response to the Métis demands represents one of the failures in his career, and shows a lack of vision in a man who had previously been keenly aware of the necessity of mutual compromise and respect. When Canada ignored their demands, the Métis staged the Red River Rebellion of 1869–70, which was quelled by the influx of British and Canadian troops. Certain to be tried and hanged, Louis Riel fled to the United States.

Macdonald's government was plunged into another scandal when it was revealed that he had accepted financial donations to his 1872 election campaign in return for the CPR contract (and the bidders turned out to be American, no less). When Macdonald's government fell to Alexander Mackenzie's Liberals in 1873, things did not bode well for Macdonald's Canadian dream. However, a number of events played into Macdonald's hands. With the depression of the 1870s, Canadians became disillusioned about their prospects as an independent nation. Mackenzie's commitment to reciprocity with the United States angered many Canadian farmers and manufacturers, who felt that they would not be able to compete. Running for re-election in 1878, Macdonald rallied public confidence in Canadian sovereignty by developing what was known as the "National Policy," which instituted a series of tariffs to protect Canadian manufacturers against competition from the United States. Re-elected in 1878, Macdonald renewed his commitment to building the transcontinental railway and struck a new deal for the CPR with George Stephen, a Montreal financier, who offered to build the railway for $25 million and 25 million acres of land. When the enterprise ran out of money a few years later, Macdonald was at a loss to convince the Canadian government to lend the funds for its continuation. Paradoxically, Macdonald and the railway magnates were "saved" by Riel's reappearance in the west and the Northwest Rebellion of 1885. If the railway were extended across the prairies, Canadian troops could be rushed in to quell the rebels. And so it was. Riel and his supporters were arrested, and Riel was sentenced to hang. Macdonald's stance on Métis land claims is clearly spelled out in his 6 July 1885 speech to the House of Commons. In it, he disingenuously insists that the Métis have "the privileges of a white man," and says that they have no more claim to the land than any English settler. Acting as a kind of Pontius Pilate in the affair, Macdonald was pressured by English Canada to exact revenge, and he succumbed. Not only did he miss the opportunity of peacefully incorporating a Métis province into the Canadian federation, but his execution of Riel proved disastrous to his relations with French Canada, who defended the Métis leader as a courageous French Catholic visionary. This, combined with the many other controversies that Macdonald had to face over the course of his career and personal life, contributed to his lifelong drinking problem. Roy MacSkimming's 2007 novel *Macdonald* provides an evocative portrait of Macdonald's final months as he campaigns for re-election in 1891.

The main issues that Macdonald encountered during his two tenures as Canadian prime minister (1867–73 and 1878–91) would continue to arise in Canadian politics in the generations to follow: the tentative relations between Quebec and English Canada; the tortuous issue of free trade with the United States; the isolation of the west; and land claim settlements with Aboriginal peoples. Macdonald prided himself on his pragmatic tolerance of cultural and religious differences, and it was this stance that enabled him to reconcile the contending priorities of the various segments of Canada: "I never asked the question, and never will ask, what a man's religion, race or ancestry may be. If he is a capable man, 'the right man for the right place,' that is all I inquire into." Ironically, though he likely never acknowledged this to himself, Macdonald's generosity extended only to Europeans. The Métis settlers on the prairies were not accorded this measure of respect; neither were the Native peoples, whose rights were increasingly denied through various governmental Indian policies (culminating in the first Indian Act of 1876). Nor were the thousands of Chinese immigrants, who played such an important role in achieving national unity for the new nation via the building of the transcontinental railway, allowed full membership into the Canadian citizenry. In 1885, the Macdonald government issued the Chinese Immigration Act, one of the first of many statutes that would be used to curtail the immigration of Asians to Canada.

In his election speech of 1891, just two months before he died, Macdonald uttered his famous proclamation: "A British subject I was born, a British subject I will die." Taken out of context, this statement appears to suggest Macdonald's lack of commitment to Canadian independence, though in reality it was his way of insisting on Canadian sovereignty against the threat of annexation by the United States. His vision of a new nationality, albeit with some flaws, was seminal in the construction of a united Canada.

Confederation

Speech in the Legislative Assembly, 6 February 1865

The resolution is, "That the best interests and present and future prosperity of British North America will be promoted by a Federal Union under the Crown of Great Britain, provided such union can be effected on principles just to the several provinces." It seemed to all the statesmen assembled [. . .] that the best interests and present and future prosperity of British North America would be promoted by a Federal Union under the Crown of Great Britain. And it seems to me, as to them, and I think it will so appear to the people of this country, that, if we wish to be a great people; if we wish to form—using the expression which was sneered at the other evening—a great nationality, commanding the respect of the world, able to hold our own against all opponents, and to defend those institutions we prize: if we wish to have one system of government, and to establish a commercial union, with unrestricted free trade, between people of the five provinces, belonging, as they do, to the same nation, obeying the same Sovereign, owning the same allegiance, and being, for the most part, of the same blood and lineage: if we wish to be able to afford to each other the means of mutual defence and support against aggression and attack—this can only be obtained by a union of some kind between the scattered and weak boundaries composing the British North American Provinces. The very mention of the scheme is fitted to bring with it its own approbation. Supposing that in the spring of the year 1865, half a million people were coming from the United Kingdom to make Canada their home, although they brought only their strong arms and willing hearts; though they brought neither skill nor experience nor wealth, would we not receive them with open arms, and hail their presence in Canada as an important addition to our strength? But when, by the proposed union, we not only get nearly a million of people to join us—when they contribute not only their numbers, their physical strength, and their desire to benefit their position, but when we know that they consist of old-established communities, having a large amount of realized wealth,—composed of people possessed of skill, education and experience in the ways of the New World—people who are as much Canadians, I may say, as we are—people who are imbued with the same feelings of loyalty to the Queen, and the same desire for the continuance of the connection with the Mother Country as we are, and at the same time, have a like feeling of ardent attachment for this, our common country, for which they and we would alike fight and shed our blood, if necessary. When all this is considered, argument is needless to prove the advantage of such a union. [. . .]

The whole scheme of Confederation, as propounded by the Conference, as agreed to and sanctioned by the Canadian Government, and as now presented for the consideration of the people, and the Legislature, bears upon its face the marks of compromise. Of necessity there must have been a great deal of mutual concession. When we think of the representatives of five colonies,[1] all supposed to have different interests, meeting together, charged with the duty of protecting those interests and of pressing the views of their own localities and sections; it must be admitted that had we not met in a spirit of conciliation, and with an anxious desire to promote this union; if we had not been impressed with the idea contained in the words of the resolution—"That the best interests and present and future prosperity of British North America would be promoted by a Federal Union under the Crown of Great Britain,"—all our efforts might have proved to be of no avail. If we had not felt that, after coming to this conclusion, we were bound to set aside our private opinions on matters of detail, if we had not felt ourselves bound to look at what was practicable, not obstinately rejecting the opinions of others nor adhering to our own; if we had not met, I say, in a spirit of conciliation, and with an anxious, overruling desire to form one people under one government, we never would have succeeded. With these views, we press the question on this House and the country. I say to this House, if you do not believe that the union of the colonies is for the advantage of the country, that the joining of these five peoples into one nation, under one sovereign, is for the benefit of all, then reject the scheme. Reject it if you do not believe it to be for the present advantage and future prosperity of your-selves and your children. But if, after a calm and full consideration of this scheme, it is believed, as a whole, to be for the advantage of this province—if the House and country believe this union to be one which will ensure for us British Laws, British connection, and British freedom—and increase and develop the social, political and material prosperity of the country, then I implore this House and the country to lay aside all prejudices; and accept the scheme which we offer. [. . .]

The Conference having come to the conclusion that a legislative union, pure and simple, was impracticable, our next attempt was to form a government upon federal principles, which would give to the General Government the strength of a legislative and administrative union, while at the same time it preserved that liberty of action for the different sections which is allowed by a Federal Union. And I am strong in the belief—that we have hit upon the happy medium in those resolutions, and that we have formed a scheme of government which unites the advantages of both, giving us the strength of a legislative union and the sectional freedom of a federal union, with protection to local interests. In doing so we had the advantage of the experience of the United States.[2] It is the fashion now to enlarge on the defects of the Constitution of the United States, but I am not one of those who look upon it as a failure. [. . .] I am strongly of the belief that we have, in a great measure, avoided in this system which we propose

[1] i.e., Canada, New Brunswick, Nova Scotia, Prince Edward Island, and Newfoundland.
[2] The American Civil War (1861–65) had recently taken place in the United States. It was considered paramount, in formulating the British North America Act, to find some way of respecting local interests in order to prevent interprovincial strife; hence the proposal of a federal system of government.

for the adoption of the people of Canada, the defects which time and events have shown to exist in the American Constitution. [. . .] Changes come over nations and peoples in the course of ages. But, so far as we can legislate, we provide that, for all time to come, the Sovereign of Great Britain shall be the Sovereign of British North America. [. . .]

In the Constitution we propose to continue the system of Responsible Government, which has existed in this province since 1841, and which has long obtained in the Mother Country. This is a feature of our Constitution as we have it now, and as we shall have it in the Federation, in which, I think, we avoid one of the great defects in the Constitution of the United States. There the President, during his term of office, is in a great measure a despot, a one-man power, with the command of the naval and military forces—with an immense amount of patronage as head of the Executive, and with the veto power as a branch of the legislature, perfectly uncontrolled by responsible advisers, his cabinet being departmental officers merely, whom he is not obliged by the Constitution to consult with, unless he chooses to do so. With us the Sovereign, or in this country the Representative of the Sovereign, can act only on the advice of his ministers, those ministers being responsible to the people through Parliament. Prior to the formation of the American Union, as we all know, the different states which entered into it were separate colonies. They had no connection with each other further than that of having a common sovereign, just as with us at present. Their constitutions and their laws were different. They might and did legislate against each other, and when they revolted against the Mother Country they acted as separate sovereignties, and carried on the war by a kind of treaty of alliance against the common enemy. Ever since the union was formed the difficulty of what is called "State Rights" has existed, and this had much to do in bringing on the present unhappy war in the United States. [. . .]

One argument, but not a strong one, has been used against this Confederation, that it is an advance towards independence. Some are apprehensive that the very fact of our forming this union will hasten the time when we shall be severed from the mother country. I have no apprehension of that kind. I believe it will have the contrary effect. I believe that as we grow stronger, that, as it is felt in England we have become a people, able from our union, our strength, our population, and the development of our resources, to take our position among the nations of the world, she will be less willing to part with us than she would be now, when we are broken up into a number of insignificant colonies, subject to attack piece-meal without any concerted action or common organization of defence. I am strongly of opinion that year by year, as we grow in population and strength, England will more see the advantages of maintaining the alliance between British North America and herself. [. . .]

So long, too, as we form a portion of the British Empire, we shall have the example of her free institutions, of the high standard of the character of her statesmen and public men, of the purity of her legislation, and the upright administration of her laws. In this younger country one great advantage of our connection with Great Britain will be, that, under her auspices, inspired by her example, a portion of her empire, our public men will be actuated by principles similar to those which actuate the statesmen at home. [. . .]

It is our happiness to know the expression of the will of our Gracious Sovereign, through Her Ministers, that we have her full sanction for our deliberations, that Her only solicitude is that we shall adopt a system which shall be really for our advantage, and that She promises to sanction whatever conclusion after full deliberation we may arrive at as to the best mode of securing the well-being,—the present and future prosperity of British America. [. . .]

[1865]

THOMAS D'ARCY MCGEE ■ (1825–68)

It is difficult to fix a single label to Thomas D'Arcy McGee. He was a journalist, politician, orator, poet, literary critic, Canadian martyr, and, many have said, a visionary. He is celebrated as one of the Fathers of Confederation, yet he began his political career as an Irish nationalist, in opposition to the British Empire, and originally supported the annexation of Canada to the United States. In later years, he did an abrupt switch by enthusiastically promoting the British North American federation as the beginning of a "new northern nationality" that would be distinct from that of the United States. He was also an Anglo-Irishman living in French-speaking Montreal, who was elected to the Quebec legislature.

McGee was born in Ireland, but immigrated to the United States in 1842, where he worked on various newspapers. He returned to Ireland a few years later and edited the Irish nationalist newspaper the *Nation*, promoting Irish independence and supporting the Fenians, a group fighting for Irish liberation from Britain. When his involvement in an 1848 youth uprising resulted in a warrant for his arrest, he fled to the United States. In Boston and New York,

he founded various Irish-American newspapers and supported the cause of Irish immigrants. He moved to Montreal in 1857, where he published the journal *New Era*, and in 1858 was elected to the joint Legislative Assembly, eventually becoming a key figure in the negotiations for Confederation.

In the meantime, his political views became more moderate, and he eventually denounced the activities of the Fenians in the United States. The Fenians believed in armed resistance and a takeover of British property. They advocated the forced annexation of Canada (British territory) to the United States (independent territory). Their plan was to overthrow the government of Canada and to occupy the country until the British government granted independence to Ireland—a kind of international hostage-taking. A faction of American Fenians sent invading forces across the border into Canada in 1866; the invasion was stopped, but Canadians thereafter lived in fear of another Fenian raid. This fear, coupled with anxiety over the American Civil War raging south of the border, was one of the motivations for Confederation.

After this, McGee became an adamant opponent of the Fenians. Because he had been hoping for the integration of the Irish into Canadian society, he dreaded the effect the Fenians' behaviour would have on the treatment of Irish Catholics in English Canada. As is apparent in Susanna Moodie's account in *Roughing It in the Bush* (1852), the Irish were considered by many English settlers to be a subordinate class, and many employers refused to hire Irish labourers. However, the Irish had been steadily improving their social and economic condition, and McGee feared that the Fenian plots would blacklist all Irish people. His support of Confederation was motivated in part by his sense that it represented the only hope for the peaceful integration of a mixed grouping of peoples, not only between Protestants and Catholics (a divide which had already torn Ireland apart), or between French- and English-speakers, but also between different groups of British immigrants. As a result, McGee was denounced by the Fenians as a traitor to Ireland.

On 7 April 1868, after a late-night session in the House of Commons, McGee was assassinated in front of his rooming house on Sparks Street in Ottawa. James Patrick Whelan, a supposed Fenian sympathizer, was arrested and hanged for the crime in 1869 (this was the last public hanging to take place in Canada). Even today, Whelan's guilt remains in doubt, as the evidence against him was merely circumstantial. Many believe that he was a scapegoat and that the government wanted to pin the murder on an Irishman—a sad irony, given McGee's campaign to free Irish-Canadians from such prejudice. Whelan claimed to be innocent until the very end, and it is said that his ghost still haunts the Ottawa jail (today the Ottawa International Youth Hostel), where his body is buried beneath what is now a parking lot. The mystery surrounding McGee's assassination continues to form the subject of literary speculation. Pierre Brault's 1999 play *Blood on the Moon* is staged as a monologue delivered by Patrick Whelan on the eve of his execution. Jane Urquhart's 1993 novel *Away* includes the figure of McGee as a counterpart to the debilitating Old World commitments of the romanticized Irish settlers, and offers an imaginative "solution" to the mystery of his murder.

If John A. Macdonald was the brains behind Confederation, McGee became what historian Desmond Morton has called its "image-maker." Because he appealed to the imagination of the people, McGee was the prime force in mobilizing popular enthusiasm for Confederation. But what is most startling is the prophetic vision he had of a "great new Northern nation" before it had been clearly conceived of. Speaking before the Quebec Legislative Assembly in May 1860, McGee gazed into his crystal ball: "I see in the not remote distance one great nationality, bound, like the shield of Achilles, by the blue rim of ocean. I see it quartered into many communities, each disposing of its internal affairs, but all bound together by free institutions, free intercourse, and free commerce. I see within the round of that shield the peaks of the western mountains and the crests of the eastern waves, the winding Assiniboine, the five-fold lakes: the St. Lawrence, the Ottawa, the Saguenay, the St. John, and the basin of Minas. By all these flowing rivers, in all the valleys they fertilize, in all the cities they visit in their courses, I see a generation [of the future]." It is remarkable that McGee was able to foresee the consolidation of a "northern nation" that spanned from sea to sea, before the Hudson's Bay Company territory was even a part of the North

American colonies. Also remarkable is his anticipation of the political structure that would become entrenched in the BNA Act, outlining the relations of the provinces to the federal government.

McGee is also remembered for his inclusive vision of the newly forming Canadian society. At the time, one of the common arguments against Confederation was that it attempted to unite too disparate a group of people, who were separated by language, religion, ancestry, regional ties, and politics. McGee countered this by promoting the construction of a new nationality that would form a union of French, English, Scots, and Irish (while he expressed admiration for Native peoples, he does not include them in his formalized national vision). Historian Dennis Gruending refers to his vision as that of "an un-hyphenated Canadianism." As McGee put it in a speech in 1862, "A Canadian nationality—not French-Canadian, nor British-Canadian, nor Irish-Canadian; patriotism rejects the prefix—is, in my opinion, what we should look forward to. . . ."

McGee's vision of Canada was undoubtedly idealistic. He used his rhetorical powers to describe what he saw to be the founding of a great nation with unlimited possibilities. His 1865 speech to the Legislative Assembly, promoting the delegation that would be presenting the BNA Act for ratification in England, describes Canada thus: "There is not on the face of the earth a freer people than the inhabitants of these colonies. . . . This is a new land. . . . We have no aristocracy but of virtue and talent, which is the only true aristocracy." Here one finds clear echoes of the writings of Catharine Parr Traill and Susanna Moodie that described the new society that was forming in Canada.

Connected to this sense of a distinctive Canadian identity was McGee's feeling that a national identity required a national literature. He published numerous articles on the subject of the development of Canadian literature, and opposed the unfair copyright laws and tariffs that allowed British and American publishers to distribute cheap reprints throughout the colonies, while Canadian publishers were not given adequate copyright protection for their publications. McGee was writing from experience, since in 1858 he had published his collection, *Canadian Ballads and Occasional Verses,* in Montreal. While his poetry does not have the originality or New World confidence of such post-Confederation poets as Charles G.D. Roberts or Archibald Lampman, it is interesting for its treatment of immigrant experience and the notion of an identifiable Canadian culture informed by northern geography and Aboriginal spirituality. According to Canadian critic Carl Ballstadt, McGee's poems "endeavoured to show the potential for patriotic literature which resided in Canadian history by creating ballads on such famous persons as Jacques Cartier, Sebastian Cabot, Henry Hudson . . . as well as on legendary materials." McGee's article "Protection for Canadian Literature," published in the *New Era* in April 1858, recognizes the danger posed to the development of a Canadian literature from the inundation of British and American publications, and is an early expression of Canadian cultural protectionism such as would arise again in the 1960s and '70s.

In his 1867 speech to the Montreal Literary Club, "The Mental Outfit of the New Dominion," McGee asks: "'Who reads a Canadian book?' I should answer frankly, very few, for Canadian books are exceedingly scarce." He blames this on the flooding of Canadian markets by foreign publishers, as well as on Canadians' lack of confidence and commitment to their own culture: "The books that are made elsewhere, even in England, are not always the best fitted for us; they do not always run on the same mental gauge, nor connect with our trains of thought; they do not take us up at the by-stages of cultivation at which we have arrived, and where we are emptied forth as on a barren, pathless, habitationless heath. . . . I do not object to such books . . . but it seems to me we do much need several other books calculated to our own meridian, and hitting home to our own society. . . ." Here McGee describes the "colonial condition" of newly forming societies, much like Sara Jeannette Duncan in her 1887 essay,

"American Influence on Canadian Thought," included in this anthology. If his sense of the Canadian cultural milieu is bleak, it is notable for its contrast to the statements made by Canadian poets only twenty years later. While Charles G.D. Roberts and other members of the group of Confederation poets were, like McGee, also attempting to forge a distinct Canadian culture, they nevertheless felt themselves to be part of a lively cultural community dedicated to similar ends. A lot had changed since 1867.

Protection for Canadian Literature

[. . .] Every country, every nationality, every people, must create and foster a National Literature, if it is their wish to preserve a distinct individuality from other nations. If precautions are not taken to secure this end, the distinctive character and features of a people must disappear; they cannot survive the storms of time and the rude blasts of civil commotion. The popular mind must be trained and educated according to the physical appearances and social condition of the country; and the people who are so unfortunate as to possess no fountain from which they can procure the elixir of their existence, will soon disappear from the face of the earth, or become merged in some more numerous or more powerful neighbour.

The position of the people of Canada in this respect deserves more than passing attention. Every facility is afforded to the English or American publishers to inundate the country with their publications; whereas the Canadian publisher is obstructed by every possible means. So pernicious is the effect of this system that the North American Provinces with their present population have not a single publisher of even local fame, and have not as yet produced a name renowned in literature—if we except the Historian of Canada, Mr Garneau, Judge Haliburton,[1] and one or two others. Canada does not possess a periodical worthy of support—nor a literary newspaper—nor a review of any description. This is a gloomy prospect certainly, but the remedy lies in the hands of the public men of the country, and is much more important than some people would fain make us believe. We will be met with the assertion that Canada is not far enough advanced yet; that the material must triumph over the ideal in a young country where everything depends on energy, and where men have no time to spare from the toils of business for the pleasing pursuit of literature.

[1] François-Xavier Garneau (1809–66), the well-known French-Canadian historian, and Thomas Chandler Haliburton (1796–1865).

This is a false idea, imported from beyond the seas, and groundless in all its premises. It is to be found in the mouths of cockneys who speak disdainfully of the 'Colonies'; of persons who cannot see the importance of possessing a national literature; and of others who do not wish to see it.   *Only two*

Many—very many works of merit have appeared in Canada, in both languages; but few indeed have exceeded one edition. Some were with much difficulty got out by subscription, others were losing speculations to the parties concerned, while others, from the expenses attendant on their publication, and their necessary high prices, were unable to find purchasers. This has of course a most discouraging effect; the publisher will not risk in a matter which may affect his purse; the author becomes disgusted at the reward of his labors, and ceases his exertions, or else leaves their fruits unpublished. While the reading public can be supplied at a cheap rate from abroad, it is by no means probable that it will patronize a dearer home market.

Our readers will perceive, on reference to the Parliamentary notices of motions, that Mr McGee has taken the first step in this matter by giving notice of an enquiry whether the ministry have opened or intend to open any negotiations with the Imperial Government with a view to relieve Canadian Book Publishers from the restrictions of the Copyright Act.[2] This course of Administration in this respect will be watched with anxiety by every one who has a heart for the future nationality of Canada.

There is a glorious field upon which to work for the formation of our National Literature. It must assume the gorgeous coloring and the gloomy grandeur of the forest. It must partake of the grave mysticism of the Red man, and the wild vivacity of the hunter of western prairies. Its lyrics must possess the ringing cadence of the waterfall, and its epics be as solemn and beautiful as our great rivers. We have the materials—our position is favourable—northern latitudes like ours have ever been famed for the strength, variety and beauty of their literature, all we demand is, that free scope be allowed to the talent and enterprise of the country, instead of allowing an unhealthy foreign substitute to be presented to our people.

[*1858*]

[2]In his newspaper articles for the *New Era*, McGee frequently referred to himself in the third person.

AGNES MAULE MACHAR ■ (1837–1927)

Agnes Machar was one of the most important feminist and social reformist writers of nineteenth-century Canada. Her defence of the importance of education for women remains relevant to this day. "The question of higher female education," she proclaimed, "is simply that of the development of woman to the highest possible point of intellectual and moral excellence." Born in Kingston, Ontario, in 1837 into a Presbyterian family, Machar held firm Christian socialist views, which she applied to her ideas about civil society. Her causes included improved conditions for the working classes, equal access to education and employment for Canadian women, and animal rights and conservation. Machar was also a proud nationalist, who, like many intellectuals of this period, supported the maintenance of Canada's ties to imperial Britain, while also celebrating the burgeoning "local" Canadian culture. Her celebration of nature for its recuperative power and her condemnation of the social ills propagated by urban industrialization were in line with many of the Romantic poets of nineteenth-century Canada, such as Archibald Lampman and Wilfred Campbell. Her poems, collected in *Lays of the "True North" and Other Canadian Poems* (1899), take as their subject Canadian history and the landscape in order to celebrate an identifiably Canadian context.

Machar's family moved in influential social and intellectual circles. Her father, a Presbyterian minister, was the principal of Queen's University from 1846 to 1853. Visitors to the family home included John A. Macdonald, George Munro Grant, and, in later years, Pauline Johnson. Machar had immense intellectual and practical energy, and in her lifetime published more than five novels, six histories, and numerous essays and poems in such journals as *Rose-Belford's Canadian Monthly and National Review*, *The Week*, *The Canadian Magazine*, and others. Like many women of the period, she published under a pseudonym, "Fidelis" (and, in some cases, "Canadensis"), in order to mask her identity as a woman writer. One of Machar's best-known essays is "The New Ideal of Womanhood," a manifesto for women's rights in the spirit of Mary Wollstonecraft, which she published in June 1879 in *Rose-Belford's*. The essay takes a fierce stand against the deplorable prospects for unmarried women, who were condemned to be dependent on others for

their support and were often left financially destitute. She advocates access to education for women of all classes, and further access to such employment as would enable women to be financially self-sufficient. In short, she wanted women to have the opportunity to have nothing less than the full opportunity to realize their potential. She is also highly critical—and clever—in her "deconstruction" of the circular logic that many prominent writers and thinkers invoked in order to relegate women to a subordinate and dependent status. Machar did not advocate an overturning of gender roles, but rather supported a version of "maternal feminism" that saw women as a tempering influence "in an age of restless and clashing thought." In this, she is comparable to the feminist thinker Nellie McClung (see Section IV). She also analyzes the conventional representation of women in English literature, in which, she states, the "clinging-vine type" has been most predominant. The essays of Sara Jeannette Duncan and Pauline Johnson on women in literature, particularly Duncan's 28 October 1886 column in *The Week* and Johnson's 1892 essay "A Strong Race Opinion: On the Indian Girl in Modern Fiction" (the latter included in this anthology), are comparable to Machar's. In addition, Duncan's enigmatic essay on the modern woman published in her "Woman's World" column of the *Globe* in November 1886 provides an interesting counterpoint to Machar's, for Duncan's tongue-in-cheek account leaves open the question of the success of those reforms proposed by Machar.

Significantly, Machar's socially oriented Christianity was not limited to her writings. After her death, her estate was divided among many charitable causes, including the foundation of Machar House, which according to her will was to be "a home for old ladies past earning their own livelihood and without means or with insufficient means for their maintenance." The fate of these women calls to mind the final years of Machar's fellow writer, Pauline Johnson, who when suffering from breast cancer in her later years found herself destitute and unable to earn a living and was aided by the contributions of friends and readers. The Machar house, which opened in Kingston in 1930, still operates today.

Many of Machar's poems engage with national subjects. A year after "The New Ideal of Womanhood" appeared, Machar published her narrative poem about Laura Secord in the June 1880 issue of *Rose-Belford's*. The poem celebrates a female Canadian hero, without whose sagacity and courage the British would not have won against the American attack on Canada along the Niagara frontier in 1812. "Quebec to Ontario, A Plea for the Life of Riel, September, 1885," originally published in *The Week* in December 1887, is Machar's remarkable poem that advocates clemency for Louis Riel in his treason trial (which eventually resulted in his hanging on 16 November 1885). The poem is staged as an address from "Quebec" (which was sympathetic to the Catholic, French-speaking Riel) to "Ontario," and reveals Machar's empathy with French Canadians' continued sense of themselves as "a conquered people." The poem, published after Riel's trial in 1885, is a courageous piece that ran counter to much public opinion of the time, especially in Ontario. It can be read alongside Pauline Johnson's 1885 "A Cry from an Indian Wife" for its ability to see both sides of the conflict; Riel, too, considered himself fighting in "a patriot cause."

Machar is better known today as a Christian reformer and feminist than as a poet or novelist, though her writing engaged with the seminal issues of her time. Because she lived to be ninety, and her life spanned two centuries, Machar's life overlapped with many central literary and historical figures of the Confederation period and the turn of the century. In particular, she was an active supporter of fellow women writers Pauline Johnson, Isabella Valancy Crawford, and Marjorie Pickthall. Wilfred Campbell, reviewing her fiction in his 26 November 1892 "At the Mermaid Inn" column for the *Globe*, championed Machar not for her literary ability, but for her "strong and abiding interest in the social and religious problems of our present humanity." Machar had a vision of the future. As she puts it in "The New Ideal of Womanhood," "[T]here is little doubt that, in the long run, women will find themselves permitted to do whatever they shall prove themselves able to do well."

The New Ideal of Womanhood

Nothing in the progress of thought during the last generation has been more observable than the change in the ideal of womanhood. Of course there have always been exceptional women, in poetry as in real life—Portias and Cordelias, as well as Ophelias and Juliets.[1] Sir Walter Scott had his Rebecca and his Jeanie Deans, as well as his Rowena and his Lucy Ashton.[2] But on the whole, the ideal

[1] All four are female characters from the following plays by William Shakespeare (1564–1616): *The Merchant of Venice, King Lear, Hamlet,* and *Romeo and Juliet.*

[2] Female characters from novels by the Scottish author Sir Walter Scott (1771–1832); Rebecca and Rowena are characters in *Ivanhoe,* Jeanie Deans in *The Heart of Midlothian,* and Lucy Ashton in *The Bride of Lammermoor.*

woman of prose and poetry has usually been what has been called the 'clinging-vine type,' a creature of sentiment and emotion, absolutely dependent on man for any life worth living; the type evidently present to the mind of Milton (who perhaps had specially good reasons for preferring it) when he wrote,

'For contemplation he and valour formed,
For softness she, and sweet attractive grace.'[3]

It should not have been necessary indeed, one thinks—looking at such a heroine as Portia—to separate the 'sweet, attractive grace' from the tendency to 'contemplation'; but poetry is often one-sided for the sake of contrast—and Milton seems to have thought that the man could do all the necessary thinking for himself and the woman too. It is quite probable that this very couplet of Milton's—not seldom quoted—even yet has had a good deal to do with keeping up the limitations of the old ideal. [. . .]

It is curious, how pertinaciously the idea has been clung to by the opponents of reform, that it is the imagination and the affections which woman should chiefly cultivate; in the face of their own argument that her strong prejudices, which are of course the outcome of affection and imagination unregulated by sound judgment, must always disqualify her from forming an intelligent opinion on great social or political questions. Can the reason be, that they unconsciously desire to perpetuate the disqualification? Women, at all events, know, that the imagination and affections are, as a rule, the side of their nature which has least need to be cultivated in the sense of being stimulated, and unless they are to be balanced and regulated by sufficient development of the intellect or reason, as well as of the moral faculty, these good gifts may easily become perverted to their torture and destruction. Let the records of any lunatic asylum be examined, if evidence of this truth be required.

However, the fact is practically admitted now, that woman as well as man requires a harmonious and symmetrical development of all her faculties, and however beautiful the ideal of a 'common soul' may be, she must, for purposes of training and education, be regarded as a distinct and complete being. It is also being more and more admitted that she has a right to her share in the world's work, whether in what has been rightly considered her more especial sphere, or in any other for which she is fitted, and that, to fit her for the efficient discharge of her duties, she has a right to the highest and most invigorating mental discipline that can be made available. It is admitted, though not so generally as it might be, that the thorough and liberal education necessary to qualify her for taking part satisfactorily, in any kind of professional work to which her natural gifts may point, will be by no means thrown away on the wife and mother, any more than it is thrown away on the lad who may go into business instead of choosing a profession. We have too many testimonies, in the lives of eminent men, to the potent influence of a gifted and educated mother to doubt that the higher the intellectual plane of those who are the moulding power of the rising

[3] See John Milton (1608–74), *Paradise Lost* IV.296–97.

generation the higher will be the intellectual and moral average of that generation; for it is rarely indeed, that thorough education does not strengthen and develop the moral as well as the intellectual faculties of woman. [. . .]

However desirable a stimulus may be given to the cause of higher and more thorough education for girls, by the existence of the University examinations and certificates now within their reach, these will only defeat the object in view if they are regarded as an end instead of a means; if they merely turn out a number of female 'Admirable Crichtons,'[4] prodigies of scholarship or mathematical acquirement, without the desire or the power to pursue any branch of knowledge for its own sake, or turn their attainments to any useful end. [. . .]

Healthful study and healthful work, are a perpetual 'tonic which stimulates without exhausting.' And until this is understood, the drifting tendency which 'lets life run away in a dream,' must go on unchecked. The writer has heard girls of more than average ability, who had full opportunities of carrying on the work of self-culture, declare that 'the claims of society' upon them made it impossible to carry on any serious study. What were these claims of society, when analysed? Nothing but rounds of conventional 'calls' or little less conventional parties, nothing that contributed in the least to the true idea of society as the healthful interchange of thoughts and feelings, nothing certainly worth absorbing the whole of an intellectual being's life! We all know 'that where there's a will, there's a way.' It only needs a little enthusiasm for an interesting study, a study which appeals to the higher nature and higher tastes, to prove that the determination to secure it will provide unimagined treasures of time out of the fragments that have been lost for want of a saving motive. It is an American saying, that 'you have all the time there is,' but unfortunately, too many of us do not have all the time we might. And the reason is in a great measure an encouraged aimlessness in girls which would never be tolerated in boys. If a lad, however free from the necessity to labour, insists on spending his life in mere amusement, or even in light and trivial pursuits, public opinion is at once down on his guardians for permitting it, and the aimless man who lives only to kill time, receives, in general, no more respect than he deserves. But with regard to girls, there seems to exist an impression that nothing useful is to be expected of them so long as they are tolerably ornamental, that they are to be like the lilies of the field 'which toil not, neither do they spin.' There can be no question that the great majority of the very girls whose gifts of means, leisure and talent, place within their reach a high degree of self-culture, throw away all their golden opportunities, because their minds are imbued with the mistaken idea that they need have no object in life save to 'amuse themselves,' look as pretty as possible, and end by making a 'desirable' marriage. [. . .]

A good specimen of the tone in which a certain class of 'smart' writers are accustomed to refer to women and their attempts at self-improvement is

[4] Reference to James Crichton (1560–82), an infamous Scottish prodigy of the sixteenth century, who was known by the sobriquet "the Admirable Crichton."

the following, taken from a recent article in *Blackwood's Magazine*. He is describing the change which has passed over English provincial society, and the general enlargement of its ideas. He describes the dreary inanity of the convivial gatherings in the olden time, when, among details of their stupidity he tells us that 'a few fine ladies might get up on their hobbies, and chatter over the mania of the day, china, pug dogs, court trains, Shakespeare, Garrick[5] and the musical glasses—but their less fashionable sisters, when scandal ran short, could sit only in silence or compare notes over domestic grievances.' Now, he admits, there is an improvement, and this is his fashion of describing it. The younger son, he tells us, who formerly would have had little to speak of beyond farming and cows—'is now superficially, at least, a well informed gentleman.' 'His wife or sister, in the intervals of husband-hunting and lawn tennis, has found time to sit at the feet of philosophers and listen to the eloquence of popular lecturers. They manoeuvre for tickets for the Geographical Society and the Royal Institution, as their grandmothers used to do for vouchers to Almacks; and if they have but vague notions of the *sense* of modern speculation, at all events they have caught some echoes of its sound. They have their artistic and literary idols whom they worship; and in art and literature as well as religion, they profess some fashionable form of belief. Few of them can shine by good looks alone, and they are bound to cultivate a habit of babbling.'

That remarks so flippant and vulgar in tone should appear in a first-class magazine is only an illustration of the essentially low ideal of womanhood which still clings to many conservative minds. We need not spend time in inquiring why the proverbial husband-hunting proclivities of the young women are so unnecessarily dragged in, while the equally proverbial fortune-hunting propensities of younger sons are completely ignored. But whatever chaff may mingle with the grain of genuine self-culture in English women, there can hardly be two opinions as to the arrogance, the unchivalrous and unmanly spirit of the man who goes out of his way to bespatter with what mockery he may, any attempt—however rudimentary—of women to rise to some higher objects of interest than 'court trains' and 'pug dogs.' However, sneers, like hard words, break no bones, and women can afford to let their professed adorers in society laugh at them in print, while they are the gainers, and learn, even from hostile sneers, to avoid the little follies and pretensions which throw discredit on their genuine search after a truer culture. [. . .]

Into most girls' minds, however, this earnest purpose might be instilled by a more judicious training, and more especially by their being early made to realize the importance of so developing any natural gift or aptitude that it may become, not only a worthy interest throughout life, but also a source of honourable independence should it be their lot to require to maintain themselves. This is a

---

[5] David Garrick (1717–79), popular English actor, theatre manager, and playwright in the eighteenth century.

possibility that really lies before every girl almost as much as before every boy, since no individual woman can be certain of marriage, and even married life is subject to chances and changes, and to an abrupt termination. The cruelty of bringing up girls accustomed to every luxury in the assumption that they are always to enjoy the same without any care or thought of theirs, has been strikingly illustrated many times, but seldom more strikingly than in the result of the lamentable failure of the Glasgow Bank, when numbers of young ladies, unfitted by training for any lucrative method of earning a livelihood, were suddenly reduced to utter poverty. A writer in *Good Words*, in commenting upon this fact, observes most truly that 'the domestic tragedies which have come to pass within the last few weeks form a strong argument for women to lay aside the false and petty shame which forbids them to work in order to increase their means of livelihood. . . . Now is the time for women of all ages to get rid of the wretched, unworthy prejudice that work, not idleness, is a disgrace impeding their claims to gentle breeding—almost to womanliness.' Never, indeed, was there a more silly and unworthy prejudice than this, which, it may be hoped, will soon vanish before a truer ideal of what womanliness is! [. . .]

Nor is the *ennui* of ordinary female life less in need of a resource than the unresisted dominion of grief. The energetic business man, when buckling on his defences from the weather on a stormy morning, may be tempted to think his wife and daughters rather enviable in their sheltered lot; their immunity from the need of breasting wind and weather—their freedom to spend the day in lounging by the drawing-room fire, in novel reading or in some 'elegant' manufacture which nobody wants, and which is probably destined to encumber still further some unfortunate apartment already sufficiently distracted with a multiplicity of 'knick-knacks.' It never occurs to our good Paterfamilias that in a household of lively and energetic girls there may be activities or aspirations reaching beyond even crochet and crewel work, and by no means fully satisfied by the sensational light reading which they, unfortunately, too often affect. It never occurs to him that he himself would find intolerably dull the very existence which he expects them to enjoy; blank as it is in all interests other than the most transient and trifling ones. And many a girl, fitted for nobler interests, *does* chafe and fret under her silken bonds which yet she sees no way of breaking. [. . .]

Before, however, girls can be expected to prepare themselves, as a matter of course, for some remunerative employment, the facilities for such preparation must be made sufficient, the avenues to suitable employment must be set open, and the principle must be established that work should be paid for according to its intrinsic value, and not according to the sex of the worker. Facilities for preparing women for the higher departments of work are increasing rapidly. To what has been stated concerning these in a former article, it may be added that Harvard University has now opened to women an institution corresponding to the Cambridge Girton; in other words, it was placed within their reach the advantages of a first-class University. It was also a matter of interest in this connection, that six women have recently graduated in the honour-class at Cambridge. Of course, owing to many causes, the women who avail themselves of University advantages will be only the exceptional cases. [. . .]

But there is little doubt that, in the long run, women will find themselves permitted to do whatever they shall prove themselves able to do well—all *a priori* prejudices to the contrary notwithstanding. The world wants good work so much more than it wants old prejudices—that these must eventually yield to common sense, and the inevitable law of demand and supply. Even the much vexed question of the suffrage, so obstinate before mere agitation, will ultimately, doubtless, be settled by the women who quietly demonstrate their capability of discharging all other duties of life, and of organising and conducting even great undertakings with the calm and judicious judgment, the perseverance and the thorough conscientiousness of highly cultivated women, which, we believe, will not be found inferior to the same qualities in highly cultivated men. [. . .]

Women are often pathetically warned, that if they insist in competing with men they will lose the chivalrous consideration still extended to their physical weakness. Those who look beyond the small formal observances of 'society' may well wonder where this chivalrous consideration, as a rule, existed! It would appear that it is equal to handing a lady from one room to another, or to her carriage (especially if there be a footman in attendance), to picking up her scissors, or maintaining a certain show of deference in conversation, to be too often exchanged for a very different tone in the freedom of the smoking-room; but it cannot stand any tougher strain. To the woman who has her 'way to make in the world,' how rare a boon is the chivalrous, brotherly consideration of the stronger for the weaker, the kindly help and sympathy along the thorny path of life. [. . .] On the contrary, the moment that the principle of self interest comes into play, the average man is more ready to grind down, to over-reach, to underpay, to cheat outright a woman than a man, just because he thinks he can do it with more impunity. It is small wonder if women feel that the compensation of a thin veneer of social courtesy for the ability to earn an honest independence, is very like offering a stone for bread!

A feminine writer in the *Contemporary Review*, not long ago, expressed her fears lest the fast growing movement for training women to self-support and to cherish interests larger than personal ones, may in time so alter the nature and aspirations natural to woman, as to throw into confusion the whole existing scheme of human affairs and become the 'beginning of the end.' Of all the novel theories we have been recently favoured with, this seems one of the wildest, contradicted by all experience, ignoring the 'Divinity that shapes our ends,' and unsupported by any rational probability even then. So far as we have seen yet, the highest cultivation possible to man or woman has not gone in the direction of assimilating their characteristic differences in the least. Neither Mrs. Browning nor 'George Eliot,'[6] two of the most highly cultivated women that the world has seen—have been one iota the less womanly for all their cultivation. Working women of the lower classes are

[6] Elizabeth Barrett Browning (1806–61) and George Eliot (Mary Ann Evans, 1819–80), both well-known female English authors of the Victorian period.

not one whit the less devoted wives and mothers because before marriage they worked hard to earn their own living. Love, in some form or other, will almost always be lord of a woman's life, and a truly happy marriage its most perfect fruition. But a woman will be all the better fitted for marriage if her previous life has not been wasted on trivialities, if her mind and faculties have been trained and disciplined, and if her sacred treasure of affection has not been prematurely frittered away on 'make-believe' *affaires du coeur*. There will be fewer loveless and unhappy marriages, doubtless, when women feel themselves less dependent on marriage as a means of livelihood.

[1879]

Quebec to Ontario, A Plea for the Life of Riel, September, 1885

You have the land our fathers bought
    With blood, and toil, and pain,
De Monts' and Cartier's earnest thought—
    The life-blood of Champlain.[7]

From far Acadia's rock-bound strand
    To wide Ontario's shore,
Where Norman swords fought hand to hand
    The Iroquois of yore,

And those great western wilds afar,
    Where wandering Indians roam,   10
And where the hardy voyageur
    First reared his cabin home;—

All, all is yours; from east to west
    The British banner streams,
But in a conquered people's breast
    Will live its early dreams!

So, when your rich men grudge our poor
    Homes on their native plains,
The blood of the old voyageur
    Leaps boiling in our veins.   20

And one whose heart was fired at sight
    Of suffering and wrong

[7] The poem is spoken by a personified figure of "Quebec" (the "conquered people" mentioned in the fourth stanza) to the "British" people of Ontario. Pierre De Monts (1558–1628), along with Cartier and Champlain, was one of the early traders in New France; he was granted a trading monopoly in North America and, with Champlain, in 1605 established a settlement in Port Royal (in present-day Nova Scotia). Most people in Quebec wanted a reprieve for Louis Riel, which John A. Macdonald refused to grant. Here, "Quebec" aligns itself with Riel as a "patriot" fighting for his people.

Took arms, in evil hour, to fight,
   For weakness—with the strong.

His wild scheme failed; how could it stand
   Against such fatal odds?
And brave hearts sleep in yon far land
   Beneath the prairie sods!

He stands a traitor at the bar
   Of your cold modern laws,   30
And yet, to him who woke the war,
   It seemed a patriot cause!

Nay, more, perchance the sore distress
   That stirred the bitter fray,
Through *that*, has pierced to ears that else
   Had still been deaf to-day;—

While he who sought his people's weal,
   Who loved his nation well,
The prisoner of your fire and steel,
   Lies doomed in felon's cell!   40

Pity the captive in your hand,
   Pity the conquered race;
You—strong, victorious in the land—
   Grant us the victor's grace!

[1899]

ALEXANDER MUIR ■ (1830–1906)

The story of Alexander Muir and the maple leaf is not unlike that of Isaac Newton and the falling apple. Legend has it that Muir was out walking with a friend one autumn day in 1867, during the height of the excitement following Confederation, when a maple leaf landed on his sleeve and stuck there. When it resisted his efforts to brush it off, his friend told him that he had found the perfect emblem for his proposed Confederation poem: the maple leaf. Even though the maple leaf had already been used as a symbol of Canadian identity—when people in the procession welcoming the Prince of Wales in 1860 wore maple leaves on their clothing—Muir's poem was instrumental in fixing it in the Canadian imagination. Little did Muir know that his anthem, "The Maple Leaf Forever," which he submitted to a competition for patriotic poetry held by the Caledonian Society of Montreal (Muir's poem won second prize), would become one of the most popular anthems of late nineteenth- and early twentieth-century Canada, even rivalling the popularity of "O Canada!" As Sara Jeannette Duncan notes in her 30 September 1886 article for *The Week*, the song was regularly sung by school-children across the country. With the rise of Québécois nationalism in the 1960s, the song's pro-British bias became increasingly controversial: by celebrating General Wolfe as "the dauntless hero," it excluded French Canadians' loss of independence on the Plains of Abraham, against Wolfe, in 1759. A variant of the song, which some historians claim was Muir's original version, includes the French emblem of the *fleur-de-lis* and has as its chorus "The lily, thistle, shamrock, rose, / The maple leaf forever!" Nevertheless, the standard version's exclusion of Quebec is striking given that French Canada was a key partner in Confederation at the time the song was first printed, in late 1867 or early 1868. Moreover, the song's emblematic chorus, "The Thistle [Scotland], Shamrock [Ireland], Rose [England] entwine / The Maple Leaf [Canada] forever!" which envisions Canada as a union of British subjects, not only omits Aboriginal peoples, but also all of the other early groups of immigrants who settled Canada around the time of Confederation, such as Chinese and Doukhobor settlers. It is ironic indeed that Aboriginal peoples, who originated the tapping of maple trees to make maple syrup (today invoked as a typical "Canadian" product), are not included among the groups represented by the Maple Leaf.

The Maple Leaf Forever

In Days of yore, from Britain's shore,
Wolfe,[1] the dauntless hero came,
And planted firm Britannia's flag,
On Canada's fair domain.
Here may it wave, our boast, our pride,
And joined in love together,
The Thistle, Shamrock, Rose entwine,
The Maple Leaf forever!

The Maple Leaf, our emblem dear,
The Maple Leaf forever!   10
God save our Queen,[2] and Heaven bless,
The Maple Leaf forever!

At Queenston Heights and Lundy's Lane,[3]
Our brave fathers, side by side,
For freedom, homes, and loved ones dear,
Firmly stood and nobly died;
And those dear rights which they maintained,

---

[1] General James Wolfe (1727–59), the leader of the British forces who defeated the French on the Plains of Abraham in Quebec in 1759.

[2] Queen Victoria, who reigned from 1837 to 1901.

[3] The Battle of Queenston Heights (13 October 1812) and the Battle of Lundy's Lane (25 July 1814) took place during the War of 1812 when the United States invaded Canada. The combined British forces and local Canadian militias were victorious in both battles.

We swear to yield them never!
Our watchword evermore shall be
The Maple Leaf forever!   20

Chorus

May our Dominion still extend
From Cape Race to Nootka Sound;
May peace forever be our lot,
And plenteous store abound;
And may those ties of love be ours
Which discord cannot sever,
And flourish green o'er freedom's home,[4]
The Maple Leaf forever!

Chorus   30

On merry England's far-famed land
May kind Heaven sweetly smile;
God bless Old Scotland evermore,
And Ireland's Emerald Isle!
Then swell the song, both loud and long,
Till rocks and forest quiver,
God save our Queen, and Heaven bless
The Maple Leaf forever!

Chorus

[1867]

[4] The song here describes the colour of the maple leaf as "green"; in the nineteenth century, it was the green maple leaf that was most commonly celebrated, not the red colour of the dying leaf that Canada uses as its emblem today.

ANONYMOUS ■ (c.1869)

Newfoundland chose not to enter Confederation in 1867, but in 1869 the issue was revisited when the province held an election which focused on the question of whether to join with the new Dominion of Canada. Those in support of Confederation favoured the promise of reduced taxes on imported goods; those opposed defended the independence and pride of Newfoundland as Britain's oldest North American colony. The vote was strongly in favour of remaining independent. As late as 1931, following the Statute of Westminster, Newfoundland remained an independent dominion within the Commonwealth, of equal status to Canada. It was not until 1949, after a period of fractious debate that in some cases split apart families, that Newfoundland joined Confederation— an outcome that still remains a sore point for many contemporary Newfoundlanders (see Volume II). This song was composed and sung as part of the 1869 anti-Confederation campaign and remains a popular anthem in Newfoundland today.

The Anti-Confederation Song

Hurrah for our own native isle, Newfoundland!
Not a stranger shall hold one inch of its strand!
Her face turns to Britain, her back to the Gulf,
Come near at your peril, Canadian Wolf!

Ye brave Newfoundlanders who plough the salt sea,
With hearts like the eagle so bold and so free;
The time is at hand when you'll all have to say,
If Confederation will carry the day.

Cheap tea and molasses they say they will give,
All taxes take off that the poor man may live;   10
Cheap nails and cheap lumber our coffins to make,
And homespun to mend our old clothes when they break.

If they take off the taxes how then will they meet,
The heavy expense of the country's up-keep?
Just give them the chance to get us in the scrape,
And they'll chain us as slaves with pen, ink, and red tape.

Would you barter the right that your fathers have won,
Your freedom transmitted from father to son?
For a few thousand dollars of Canadian gold,
Don't let it be said that your birthright was sold.   20

[1869]

THE INDIAN ACT ■ (1876, 1927)

The Indian Act is one of the most controversial documents in Canadian legal history, as it singles out a particular group of people on the basis of their perceived race and gives the federal government management over their affairs. While ostensibly designed to protect Aboriginal land reserves and the interests of Aboriginal people, it in fact deprived Aboriginal peoples in Canada of their basic human rights and in many instances was used to implement racist policies. In short, the Indian Act was a government document that "legalized" the colonization and disenfranchisement of Native peoples. The primary assumption of the Indian Act is that indigenous people are not capable of making responsible decisions and managing their own affairs. The Act phrases its decrees in a paternalistic manner, presuming to be acting for the good of the "Indians" by treating them as children or wards of the state. In this, the Indian Act replicated Britain's treatment of many of its colonial subjects elsewhere (as, for example, in India and Africa), not to mention the treatment of women that had been common practice for centuries.

The main goal of the Indian Act was the assimilation of Aboriginal peoples into the mainstream of Canadian society. According to Duncan Campbell Scott, the deputy superintendent of Indian affairs in the early twentieth century, the goal was for "Indians [to] progress into civilization and finally disappear as a separate and distinct people, not by race extinction but by gradual assimilation with their fellow-citizens." The regulations instilled in the Indian Act, then, were seen as a transitional and protective measure which would be repealed once Native peoples had fully integrated into mainstream society. The Act thus forms part of the larger context of the "disappearing race" or "vanishing race" discourse of the nineteenth and early twentieth centuries, the self-serving notion (on the part of Europeans, Canadians, and the Canadian government) that the disappearance of distinct indigenous peoples was inevitable. As Scott put it in 1920: "Our object is to continue until there is not a single Indian in Canada that has not been absorbed into the body politic, and there is no Indian question, and no Indian department."

Although the 1867 BNA Act gave the federal government legal power over Native peoples, the first federal Indian Act was not passed until 1876, with subsequent amendments occurring over the years that followed. In fact, the Indian Act had had many earlier incarnations. The Royal Proclamation of 1763, following the British conquest of Canada, established the basis for Native land reserves in Canada. The proclamation stated that it was "essential to [British] Interest, and the Security of our Colonies, that the several Nations or Tribes of Indians with whom We are connected, and who live under Our Protection, should not be molested or disturbed in the Possession of such Parts of Our Dominions and Territories as, not having been ceded to or purchased by Us, are reserved to them, or any of them, as their Hunting Grounds." The Royal Proclamation, which was incorporated into the BNA Act, would become the basis of treaty negotiations between the British Crown and Aboriginal peoples thereafter. Up to 1830, because the British (and French) had been dependent on Native peoples as wartime allies, Indian administration was in the hands of the imperial military authorities, though after 1840 the individual colonies began to take over the management of Native communities. By 1860, Britain officially transferred the administration of "Indian Affairs" to the British North American colonies. In 1857, the Province of Canada passed the Gradual Civilization Act, introduced by John A. Macdonald, which initiated what would become the long-standing and controversial project of assimilation of Native peoples into White settler society. It was rejected by Native leaders who foresaw the erosion of Aboriginal cultural traditions and autonomy. The 1876 Indian Act consolidated these policies into one legal document, and gave ultimate authority for the management of Native peoples to the superintendent of Indian affairs. Attempts to assimilate Aboriginal people increased after this period, particularly following the Northwest Rebellion of 1885; as a result, subsequent amendments to the

In the process of "civilization," the Indigenous were forced onto lands. (handwritten margin note)

Act, as for example those of 1927, instituted further restrictions on Native peoples' social lives and cultural traditions.

One of the key segments of the Indian Act is the section devoted to the definition of "Indian status." Indian status was applied only under specific conditions, which meant that thousands of Aboriginal people were not officially considered "Indian" and therefore were denied the rights that were accorded to others. In effect, the term "Indian" included only pure-blood Indians living on reserve lands. It did not include the Inuit or Métis. The Indian Act was also an inherently patriarchal document that contradicted the matrilineal basis of many Native societies. For many Aboriginal groups, the bloodline or clan was passed down through the mother, and women were often the keepers of the group's history and traditions. The Indian Act, in contrast, applied European notions of patriarchal lineage and property claims. Hence, any Native woman who married a non-status Indian was automatically rendered "non-status," and therefore exempt from any of the privileges provided to status Indians. The children of such unions were similarly denied identification as "Indian," even though Canadian society continued to respond to "mixed-blood" individuals in predictably racist ways. By contrast, these restrictions did not apply to Native men who married non-status women.

The Indian Act was also used as a way of keeping Native peoples in check. Status Indians, as defined by the Indian Act, were denied the right to vote, were forbidden to use legal counsel, and were not allowed to sit on juries. Significantly, the definition of a "person," as summed up in

section 3.12 of the 1876 statute, is "an individual other than an Indian"; it was not until 1960 that all Aboriginal peoples in Canada were granted the right to vote in Canadian federal elections without losing status. Because one of the conditions of claiming "Indian status" and living on reserve land was a denial of the right to vote, journalist Heather Robertson has said that the "rent the Indians paid was the forfeiture of their right to Canadian citizenship." The long-term aim of the Act was the shedding of Indian identity. As historian Arthur J. Ray explains, "As a first step towards becoming a full-fledged Canadian citizen, an Indian had to prove that he was literate in English or French, of good moral character, and free of debt—terms most Canadians would have found it difficult to meet." Furthermore, the Indian Act could be changed at any time without consultation with Native peoples. As a result, subsequent amendments implemented increasingly restrictive measures related to Aboriginal cultural traditions. Cultural ceremonies such as the sun dance, potlatch, and pow-wows were either drastically curtailed or banned. Native people were not allowed to perform traditional dances or wear Native dress. They were subject to criminal charges if found in the possession of liquor, if they sought legal counsel, or if they took part in political demonstrations, and they were required to carry identity cards whenever they left their reserve lands. The most aggressive and tragic of the policies sanctioned by the Indian Act was the forced placement of Native children into church-run residential schools throughout Canada, which, according to the 1921 Indian Department report, "remove[d] from the Indian parent the responsibility for the care and education of his child."

Sounds like a passport! (handwritten margin note)

Undertaken in the interest of "civilizing" and Christianizing subsequent generations of Aboriginal people, the policy meant that children between the ages of seven and fifteen were forcibly removed from their families and were forbidden to communicate with their parents or speak their own languages.

In 1969, the infamous governmental "White Paper" on Indian policy was presented to abolish the notion of Indian status and the commitment to Indian reserves and treaties. This move was opposed by many Aboriginal groups who saw it as a governmental means of reneging on their treaty promises. The most notable revision was that of 1985, known as Bill C-31, which was initiated following the institution of the 1982 Canadian Charter of Rights and Freedoms. Bill C–31 removed the discriminatory definition of Indian status (especially as it applied to Native women) and reinstated those who had been denied privileges as a result of this policy. Today negotiations are under way to facilitate the transfer of the management of "Indian affairs" to Aboriginal peoples themselves through processes of Aboriginal self-government.

The paternalistic attitude toward Native peoples that is evident in the conceptualization of the Indian Act has long-standing roots in Canadian culture, and extends well before the institution of the Act in 1876. One sees similar attitudes, for example, in George Cartwright's relations with the Labrador Inuit, as well as in David Thompson's attempts to mystify Native people with his science, or even in Susanna Moodie's description of the noble "gentlemen" of the Canadian woods who remain impressed by her "civilized" European ways. A comparable stance is evident in the fiction and poetry of Duncan Campbell Scott, who, working in the Department of Indian Affairs for more than fifty years, was an integral figure in the implementation of the Indian Act's policies. Such early Native writers as Joseph Brant, George Copway, and Deskaheh perceived the hypocrisy in the government's paternalistic attitudes toward Aboriginal peoples, while in later years, many Aboriginal writers and public figures were fiercely critical of the Indian Act. In his 1969 critique, *The Unjust Society*, Native leader Harold Cardinal asserted that "instead of implementing the treaties and offering much-needed protection to Indian rights, [the Indian Act] subjugated to colonial rule the very people whose rights it was supposed to protect."

From The Indian Act (1876)

An Act to amend and consolidate the laws respecting Indians.

[*Assented to 12th April, 1876.*]

WHEREAS it is expedient to amend and consolidate the laws respecting Indians: Therefore Her Majesty, by and with the advice and consent of the Senate and House of Commons of Canada, enacts as follows:—

1. This Act shall be known and may be cited as "*The Indian Act, 1876;*" and shall apply to all the Provinces, and to the North West Territories, including the Territory of Keewatin.
2. The Minister of the Interior shall be Superintendent-General of Indian Affairs, and shall be governed in the supervision of the said affairs, and in the control

and management of the reserves, lands, moneys and property of Indians in Canada by the provisions of this Act.

Terms.

3. The following terms contained in this Act shall be held to have the meaning hereinafter assigned to them, unless such meaning be repugnant to the subject or inconsistent with the context:—

1. The term "band" means any tribe, band or body of Indians who own or are interested in a reserve or in Indian lands in common, of which the legal title is vested in the Crown, or who share alike in the distribution of any annuities or interest moneys for which the Government of Canada is responsible. [. . .]

2. The term "irregular band" means any tribe, band or body of persons of Indian blood who own no interest in any reserve or lands of which the legal title is vested in the Crown, who possess no common fund managed by the Government of Canada, or who have not had any treaty relations with the Crown.

3. The term "Indian" means

   First. Any male person of Indian blood reputed to belong to a particular band;

   Secondly. Any child of such person;

   Thirdly. Any woman who is or was lawfully married to such person:

   (a) Provided that any illegitimate child, unless having shared with the consent of the band in the distribution moneys of such band for a period exceeding two years, may, at any time, be excluded from the membership thereof by the band, if such proceeding be sanctioned by the Superintendent-General:

   (b) Provided that any Indian having for five years continuously resided in a foreign country shall with the sanction of the Superintendent-General, cease to be a member thereof and shall not be permitted to become again a member thereof, or of any other and, unless the consent of the band with the approval of the Superintendent-General or his agent, be first had and obtained; but this provision shall not apply to any professional man, mechanic, missionary, teacher or interpreter, while discharging his or her duty as such:

   (c) Provided that any Indian woman marrying any other than an Indian or a non-treaty Indian shall cease to be an Indian in any respect within the meaning of this Act, except that she shall be entitled to share equally with the members of the band to which she formerly belonged, in the annual or semi-annual distribution of their annuities, interest moneys and rents; but this income may be commuted to her at any time at ten years' purchase with the consent of the band:

[handwritten margin note: Woman are only "Indian" in their relation to men]

(d) Provided that any Indian woman marrying an Indian of any other band, or a non-treaty Indian shall cease to be a member of the band to which she formerly belonged and become a member of the band or irregular band of which her husband is a member:

(e) Provided also that no half-breed in Manitoba[1] who has shared in the distribution of half-breed lands shall be accounted an Indian; and that no half-breed of a family (except the widow of an Indian, or a half-breed who has already been admitted into a treaty), shall, unless under very special circumstances, to be determined by the Superintendent-General or his agent, be accounted an Indian, or entitled to be admitted into any Indian treaty.

4. The term "non-treaty Indian" means any person of Indian blood who is reputed to belong to an irregular band or who follows the Indian mode of life, even though such person be only a temporary resident in Canada.

5. The term "enfranchised Indian" means any Indian, his wife or minor unmarried child, who has received letters patent granting him in fee simple any portion of the reserve which may have been allotted to him, his wife and minor children, by the band to which he belongs, or any unmarried Indian who may have received letters patent for an allotment of the reserve.

6. The term "reserve" means any tract or tracts of land set apart by treaty or otherwise for the use or benefit of or granted to a particular band of Indians, of which the legal title is in the Crown, but which is unsurrendered, and includes all the trees, wood, timber, soil, stone, minerals, metals, or other valuables thereon or therein.

7. The term "special reserve" means any tract or tracts of land and everything belonging thereto set apart for the use or benefit of any band or irregular band of Indians, the title of which is vested in a society, corporation or community legally established, and capable of suing and being sued, or in a person or persons of European descent, but which land is held in trust for, or benevolently allowed to be used by, such band or irregular band of Indians.

8. The term "Indian lands" means any reserve or portion of a reserve which has been surrendered to the Crown. [. . .]

9. The term "Superintendent-General" means the Superintendent-General of Indian Affairs.

10. The term "agent" means a commissioner, superintendent, agent, or other officer acting under the instructions of the Superintendent-General.

---

[1] "Half-breed" was a derogatory term referring to people with one Aboriginal parent and one non-Aboriginal parent. Here it explicitly refers to the Métis of Manitoba, thereby excluding them from the definition of "Indian" according to the Indian Act.

11. The term "person" means an individual other than an Indian, unless the context clearly requires another construction.

Reserves.

4. All reserves for Indians or for any band of Indians, or held in trust for their benefit, shall be deemed to be reserved and held for the same purposes as before the passing of this Act, but subject to its provisions.

5. The Superintendent-General may authorize surveys, plans and reports to be made of any reserves for Indians, shewing and distinguishing the improved lands, the forests and land fit for settlement, and such other information as may be required; and may authorize that the whole or any portion of a reserve be subdivided into lots.

[1876]

From The Indian Act (revised statutes, 1927)

CHAPTER 98, sections 9, 10, 140, and 141.

9. The Governor in Council may establish
   1. (a) day schools in any Indian reserve for the children of such reserve;
      (b) industrial or boarding schools for the Indian children of any reserve or reserves or any district or territory designated by the Superintendent General. [. . .]

10. Every Indian child between the ages of seven and fifteen years who is physically able shall attend such day, industrial or boarding school as may be designated by the Superintendent General for the full periods during which such school is open each year.
   2. Such school shall be the nearest available school of the kind required, and no Protestant child shall be assigned to a Roman Catholic school or a school conducted under Roman Catholic auspices, and no Roman Catholic child shall be assigned to a Protestant school or a school conducted under Protestant auspices.
   3. The Superintendent General may appoint any officer or person to be a truant officer to enforce the attendance of Indian children at school, and for such purpose a truant officer shall be vested with powers of a peace officer, and shall have authority to enter any place where he has reason to believe there are Indian children between the ages of seven and fifteen years, and when requested by the Indian agent, a school teacher or the chief of a band shall examine into any case of truancy, shall warn the truants, their parents or guardians or the person with whom any Indian child resides, of the consequences of truancy, and notify the parent, guardian or such person in writing to cause the child to attend school.

4. Any parent, guardian or person with whom an Indian child is residing who fails to cause such child, being between the ages aforesaid, to attend school as required by this section after having received three days' notice so to do by a truant officer shall, on the complaint of the truant officer, be liable on summary conviction before a justice of the peace or Indian agent to a fine of not more than two dollars and costs, or imprisonment for a period not exceeding ten days or both, and such child may be arrested without a warrant and conveyed to school by the truant officer. [. . .]

140. Every Indian or other person who engages in, or assists in celebrating or encourages either directly or indirectly another to celebrate any Indian festival, dance or other ceremony of which the giving away or paying or giving back of money, goods or articles of any sort forms a part, or is a feature, whether such gift of money, goods or articles takes place before, at, or after the celebration of the same, or who engages or assists in any celebration or dance of which the wounding or mutilation of the dead or living body of any human being or animal forms a part or is a feature, is guilty of an offence and is liable on summary conviction to imprisonment for a term not exceeding six months and not less than two months.

2. Nothing in this section shall be construed to prevent the holding of any agricultural show or exhibition or the giving of prizes for exhibits thereat.

3. Any Indian in the province of Manitoba, Saskatchewan, Alberta or British Columbia, or in the Territories who participates in any Indian dance outside the bounds of his own reserve, or who participates in any show, exhibition, performance, stampede or pageant in aboriginal costume without the consent of the Superintendent General or his authorized agent, and any person who induces or employs any Indian to take part in such dance, show exhibition, performance, stampede or pageant, or induces any Indian to leave his reserve or employs any Indian for such a purpose, whether the dance, show, exhibition, stampede or pageant has taken place or not, shall on summary conviction be liable to a penalty not exceeding twenty-five dollars, or to imprisonment for one month, or to both penalty and imprisonment. [. . .]

141. Every person who, without the consent of the Superintendent General expressed in writing, receives, obtains, solicits or requests from any Indian any payment or contribution or promise of any payment or contribution for the purpose of raising a fund or providing money for the prosecution of any claim which the tribe or band of Indians to which such Indian belongs, or of which he is a member, has or is represented to have for the recovery of any claim or money for the benefit of the said tribe or band, shall be guilty of an offence and liable upon summary conviction for each such offence to a penalty not exceeding two hundred dollars and not less than fifty dollars or to imprisonment for any term not exceeding two months. [. . .]

[1927]

The Canadian national anthem has a curious and convoluted history. Not many Canadians realize that the French version of the song is the original one. In 1880, Quebec's National Congress of French Canadians commissioned Adolphe-Basile Routhier, a Quebec City judge and poet, to write a poem to celebrate the festivities of St. Jean-Baptiste Day, the French-Canadian national holiday, thirteen years after Confederation. Calixa Lavallée was asked to write the music, and he composed the tune that we sing to "O Canada!" today. The song was a hit when it made its debut in Quebec City on 24 June 1880, sparking a writer in the 17 April 1880 *Journal de Québec* to proclaim, "At last, we have a truly French-Canadian National Song!" Routhier published the poem in his 1882 collection of poems, *Les Échos,* but as a song it fell into relative obscurity in subsequent years. It was revived, by chance, in 1901 when a group of English schoolchildren sang the song in French to welcome the Duke and Duchess of Cornwall during their tour of Canada. This appears to have been the first time the song was heard in English Canada. Subsequently, numerous English versions were written, including one by Confederation poet Wilfred Campbell. The version that we use today was written by Montreal lawyer Robert Stanley Weir in 1908 to celebrate the 300th anniversary of Champlain's founding of Quebec City, and published in his 1917 collection of poems, *After Ypres and Other Verse* (the text reproduced here is from this collection). It is not a translation of the French version, which celebrates the historical exploits and glory of the French-Canadian people, but instead reflects English-Canadian patriotism.

Interestingly, as literary theorist Linda Hutcheon has pointed out, in the French version the nation is anthropomorphized as a presence that will protect the people, while in the English text, it is the people who defend the country. In essence, Canada has not one but two national anthems.

The anglophilic nature of Weir's multi-verse poem is evident in its epigraph, "That True North," taken from the English poet Alfred, Lord Tennyson's 1873 epilogue to *Idylls of the King* ("true," in this context, means "loyal"), where the speaker celebrates the British Empire and pays particular tribute to Canada, "that true North." Today, most Canadians are familiar with only the first verse of Weir's poem. Weir's and Routhier's versions of the song were popularly acknowledged as the national anthem of Canada by the beginning of the First World War, hence the ironic invocation of the anthem at the conclusion of Stephen Leacock's short story "The Marine Excursion of the Knights of Pythias" (1912). However, even though the song was composed in 1908, for copyright reasons it was not until 1 July 1980 that it was declared, in Parliament, the official National Anthem of Canada.

While the official anthem is a slightly altered version of Weir's original, the French text of "O Canada!" has remained unaltered. The English version of the song has been critiqued on a number of counts for excluding different groups of the Canadian population. Many contemporary parodies of the song have made much of the phrase "Our Home and Native Land," since the land was "native" to Aboriginal peoples and not to the English and French settlers commemorated in the poem (hence such parodic revisions as "Our home on Native land"). In addition, the patriarchal wording of "in all thy sons command" has been criticized by feminists and is sometimes replaced with "in all of our command"; what appears to be the Christianizing of the poem through the introduction of "God" in the revised version of the first verse has also been questioned.

Chant National

Adolphe-Basile Routhier (1839–1920)

O Canada! terre de nos aïeux,
Ton front est ceint de fleurons glorieux.
Car ton bras sait porter l'épée,
Il sait porter la croix;
Ton histoire est une épopée
Des plus brillants exploits;
Et ta valeur de foi trempée,
Protégera nos foyers et nos droits.

Sous l'oeil de Dieu, près du fleuve géant,
Le Canadien grandit en espérant.   10
Il est né d'une race fière;
Béni fut son berceau.
Le ciel a marqué sa carrière
Dans ce monde nouveau:
Toujours guidé par sa lumière,
Il gardera l'honneur de son drapeau.

De son patron, précurseur du vrai Dieu,
Il porte au front l'auréole de feu.
Ennemi de la tyrannie,
Mais plein de loyauté,   20
Il sait garder dans l'harmonie
Sa fière liberté,
Et par l'effort de son génie,
Sur notre sol asseoir la vérité.

Amour sacré du trône et de l'autel,
Remplis nos coeurs de ton souffle immortel.
Parmi les races étrangères
Notre guide est la loi;
Sachons être un peuple de frères
Sous le joug de la Foi;   30
Et répétons comme nos pères
Le cri vainqueur: Pour le Christ et le Roi!

[1880, 1882]

O Canada!

English translation of the first verse of the French version, Department of Canadian Heritage

O Canada! Land of our forefathers
Thy brow is wreathed with a glorious garland of flowers.
As is thy arm ready to wield the sword,
So also is it ready to carry the cross.
Thy history is an epic
Of the most brilliant exploits.
Thy valour steeped in faith
Will protect our homes and our rights.

O Canada!

Robert Stanley Weir (1856–1926)

"That True North."—*Tennyson*

O Canada! Our Home and Native Land!
True patriot-love in all thy sons command;
With glowing hearts we see thee rise,
The True North, strong and free,
And stand on guard, O Canada,
We stand on guard for thee.
O Canada, glorious and free!
We stand on guard for thee!

O Canada! Where pines and maples grow,   10
Great prairies spread and lordly rivers flow,
How dear to us thy broad domain,
From East to Western Sea;
Thou land of hope for all who toil!
Thou True North, strong and free!
O Canada, glorious and free!
We stand on guard for thee!

O Canada! Beneath thy shining skies
May stalwart sons and gentle maidens rise,
To keep thee steadfast through the years,   20
From East to Western Sea.
Our Fatherland, our Motherland!
Our True North, strong and free!
O Canada, glorious and free!
We stand on guard for thee!

Ruler supreme, Who hearest humble prayer,
Hold our dominion in Thy loving care.
Help us to find, O God, in Thee,
A lasting, rich reward,
As waiting for the Better Day   30
We ever stand on guard.
O Canada, glorious and free!
We stand on guard for thee!

[1908, 1917]

O Canada!

Official Lyrics, Department of Canadian Heritage (1968)

O Canada!
Our home and native land!
True patriot love in all thy sons command.
With glowing hearts we see thee rise,
The True North strong and free!
From far and wide,
O Canada, we stand on guard for thee.
God keep our land glorious and free!
O Canada, we stand on guard for thee.
O Canada, we stand on guard for thee.

[1968]

LOUIS RIEL ■ (1844–85)

Two momentous events occurred in the chilly November winter of 1885 in Canada's Northwest. The first was the long-awaited completion of the Canadian Pacific Railway. Gathered in the mist of Craigellachie in the Rocky Mountains of British Columbia, a group of railway officials stood for a photo shoot as the company president, Donald Smith, hammered the celebratory "last spike" into the tracks on 7 November 1885. The other event was the hanging of Louis Riel, the Métis leader who fought to preserve the land that he felt the CPR had stolen from his people.

Just one week after Canada had been joined "from sea to sea," and after numerous arguments, battles, deaths, and governmental appeals, on 16 November 1885, at 8:23 in the morning, Riel was hanged as a traitor to Canada in the RCMP barracks outside Regina, Saskatchewan. French Canadians had pleaded for a reprieve of Riel's sentence, but to no avail. John A. Macdonald, making one of the biggest blunders of his prime ministerial career, publicly stated that Riel would hang "though every dog in Quebec should bark in his favour." A November 1885 issue of the Montreal paper *Le Canard* ran a tribute on its editorial page: an epitaph for the fallen hero who was memorialized as a "Victim of Orange [Protestant] fanaticism and of devotion to the cause of his Métis brothers." That the CPR was blithely completed over the blood of Riel, and that it has become one of the crowning symbols of Canadian achievement, is a disturbing fact of Canadian history. The hanging of Riel had long-lasting effects, and intensified a rift in the relations between French and English, Catholics and Protestants, Natives and Whites, West and East that lingered for a long time after.

The Métis are people of mixed European (usually French) and Aboriginal ancestry, who were the descendants of the early fur traders and Native peoples in the West.[1] Many commentators have described the Métis as the prototypical Canadian people, since they represent a fusion of Aboriginal and European traditions.

Riel, born in the Red River Settlement of St. Boniface in October 1844, was of proud Métis lineage. A gifted student, at the age of fourteen he was sent to Montreal to study for the priesthood, but after his father died in 1864, he returned home and never completed his studies. Returning to the west in 1868, Riel became embroiled in the growing unrest along the Red River. The newly formed Dominion of Canada was about to purchase the former Hudson's Bay Company territory of Rupert's Land in the Northwest, and the large community of Métis and English "half-breeds," who had for generations made this land their home, were essentially being sold, as tenants, along with it. At just twenty-five years of age, Riel, well-educated and bilingual, was catapulted into the role of unofficial leader of the French-speaking Métis and English-speaking "half-breeds" and settlers of the Canadian west. When a Canadian survey team, along with the newly appointed lieutenant-governor of the region, William McDougall, was sent into the area in October 1869 and began segmenting the land that was already inhabited by Métis families, a group of Métis men, including Riel, confronted them. Soon after, he established a provisional government, and was chosen the leader of "the People of Rupert's Land and the Northwest." Having seized the Hudson's Bay Company post at Fort Garry in November 1869, Riel and his followers began to negotiate terms with the Dominion of Canada, including a land grant for the Métis and the protection of French-language rights. He hoped to establish terms upon which the Métis would enter Confederation as a distinct people and province; throughout his negotiations, he insisted that they wanted to join Canada and remain loyal subjects of the British Queen. However, just as the Canadian government was beginning to take the Métis claims for a separate province seriously, and it was arranged that a delegation would visit Ottawa that spring, Riel made a fatal miscalculation. When a Protestant Orangeman named Thomas Scott began to make trouble in March 1870, he was executed by a Métis firing squad. Although Riel didn't fire any bullets, he allowed the execution to take place. Macdonald sent in troops to regain control of the area, and Riel fled to the United States. The Red River Rebellion, as it came to be known, had been quelled.

Shortly after, in July 1870, Riel effectively got his wish: the area around the Red River Settlement entered Confederation as the (at that time) very small, bilingual province of Manitoba. Riel is widely hailed as the founder of the

[1] There has been enormous debate in recent years about the definition of "Métis" in Canada. Some commentators use the term to apply only to descendants of the Red River Métis peoples who were recipients of the Dominion Land Acts Scrip, and who were predominantly distributed in Manitoba, Saskatchewan, and Alberta. Others use the term to apply to additional regions, including Métis peoples in the Northwest Territories, Labrador, and Nova Scotia. Since our context here is the life and career of Louis Riel, we are discussing the Red River Métis in this section.

province. He reappeared in 1871 and offered the support of a Métis cavalry when the Fenians threatened to invade Manitoba. Although Macdonald preferred to avoid further trouble by having Riel remain in exile, a few years later Riel decided to run for federal election and, in 1873, was elected to the Canadian House of Commons; however, he was expelled from the house by Protestant protest. In 1875, the federal government issued an amnesty to Riel and his followers, including the man who actually murdered Thomas Scott, on the condition that they stay out of Canada for five years.

Over the succeeding decade, the government launched an immense campaign to populate the Canadian west with British, Canadian, and European settlers. It also undertook to negotiate treaties, with varying degrees of success, with the Cree and Assiniboine peoples. By this time, a combination of over-hunting and the destruction of their habitat had all but eradicated the once-abundant buffalo herds. As a result, the Native and Métis peoples were suffering from starvation. Many Métis families moved west into Saskatchewan (not yet part of Canada), but they had not been granted land rights. In the summer of 1884, a delegation from Saskatchewan visited Riel in Montana and begged him to again represent their cause to the government in Ottawa. When Riel entered the Northwest six days later, he was on a mission. Once again, he attempted to negotiate the terms for the North-West Territories (which included Saskatchewan and Alberta) to join Canada, along with accompanying land grants to the long-standing Métis and English settlers of the region, but repeatedly, his requests for a hearing with John A. Macdonald were denied. By spring 1885, he had gathered his small band, with the expert Métis marksman Gabriel

Dumont as their military leader, and a battle broke out with the North West Mounted Police in Duck Lake, Saskatchewan. Twelve Mounties were killed in the skirmish, along with five Métis men. Throughout, Riel was unarmed and managed to avert further slaughter by discouraging Dumont from pursuing the fleeing Canadian troops. Ironically, the CPR, which had become a liability for the Canadian government due to lack of funds, was now needed to transport armed troops to the west, and the rail line was finished in a hurry. In mid-April 1885, thousands of Canadian soldiers and police were transported along the just-completed CPR tracks and arrived in Qu'Appelle, near Batoche. After several battles and over 100 casualties, the military eventually triumphed over Riel's embattled forces in Batoche on the South Saskatchewan River. Riel was arrested, but because he had not actually fired any shots, he could not be charged with murder. Instead, he was charged with high treason for mounting an insurrection against the Canadian government. *Jn a place that wasn't part of Canada?*

It has been widely acknowledged that Riel's sanity was in question during the period of the Northwest Rebellion. Believing himself to be appointed by God as the saviour of his people, he christened himself the "Prophet of the New World," and instead of a gun carried a crucifix in battle. His proclamations, which included the establishment of a Canadian pope, led to his rejection by the Catholic Church. In his speech before the jury of July and August 1885, Riel insisted that he was fully sane, even though this ran counter to the case his defence attorneys were making. Had he done otherwise, his sentence would have been less severe. The trial itself, as Riel intimates in his jury address, was somewhat suspect. Because the trial took place in Regina (then capital of the

Northwest Territories) rather than in Winnipeg, Manitoba, different juridical regulations applied. Territorial law called for a jury of only six (as opposed to twelve) members, and the presiding magistrate was an adviser to the federal government, rather than an independent superior court judge. Furthermore, all of the jurors were English-speaking Protestants and there was no right to a French trial (as there would have been in Manitoba), which meant that Riel not only had to confront anti-Catholic prejudice, but he had to defend himself in English. The jury found him guilty, but recommended mercy. Despite numerous appeals, Riel was sentenced to hang.

The posthumous reputation of Louis Riel has undergone many changes since his sentencing in 1885. While for years he was considered both a madman and traitor, in more recent times Canadians have come to respect his fight for Métis land claims and political representation. In 2004, the CBC's "Greatest Canadian" competition, based on public polling, voted Louis Riel eleventh on the list. While he has long been celebrated as a martyr in French Canada, it should also be remembered that Quebeckers at the time supported the government's military initiative during the Northwest Rebellion; in fact, French-Canadian troops participated alongside English forces, while Quebec representatives in the House of Commons supported Riel's arrest. The difference was that the French asked for clemency. Macdonald, not wanting to yield to these pressures simply because Riel was French, nevertheless gave in to the pressures from English Canada. The decision had a lasting effect on the relations between French and English thereafter. Quebec voters withdrew their support from the Conservative Party and elected Wilfrid Laurier in 1896, the vivacious young Liberal leader who had

taken a stand against Macdonald on the Riel affair in 1885 and 1886. "Had I been born on the banks of the Saskatchewan I would myself have shouldered a musket to fight against the neglect of the government and the shameless greed of the speculators," Laurier proclaimed.

The issue of Métis rights and land claims still persists in Canada today. Maria Campbell's 1973 autobiographical novel, *Half-Breed*, describes the continued plight of the Saskatchewan Métis into the twentieth century. In *Lake of the Prairies: A Story of Belonging* (2002), Warren Cariou uncovers his family's Métis history that was hidden for generations. Fictional treatments of Louis Riel and the Métis rebellions include Margaret Laurence's *The Diviners* (1974), Rudy Wiebe's *The Scorched-Wood People* (1977), and Margaret Sweatman's *When Alice Lay Down with Peter* (2001). Riel has also inspired a number of poetic treatments, such as John Robert Colombo's "The Last Words of Louis Riel" (1967), Dorothy Livesay's "Prophet of the New World: A Poem for Two Voices" (1972), Don Gutteridge's *Riel: A Poem for Voices* (1972), Raymond Souster's "Louis Riel Addresses the Jury" (1977), Frank Davey's "Riel" (1985), and Kim Morrissey's collection *Batoche* (1989). Two poems written in the 1880s in support of Riel's cause were Pauline Johnson's "A Cry from an Indian Wife" and Agnes Machar's "Quebec to Ontario, A Plea for the Life of Riel," both of which are included in this section. By contrast, Isabella Valancy Crawford's "The Rose of a Nation's Thanks," published in the *Toronto Evening Telegram* in June 1885, is a tribute to the Canadian troops returning victorious following the Northwest Rebellion. In 1982, almost 100 years after the Northwest Rebellion, the Canadian Constitution officially recognized the Métis as one of the Aboriginal peoples of

Canada, and today statues of Riel stand on the grounds of the Parliament Buildings in Ottawa and in front of the Manitoba Legislature in Winnipeg. In 1998, a bill was passed by Parliament recognizing Riel as one of the Fathers of Confederation, almost 130 years after Manitoba became a province. With the acclaim for Aboriginal and Métis literatures that is evident in Canada today, Riel's words have proved prophetic: "My people will sleep for 100 years, and when they awake, it will be the artists who give them back their spirit."

Address to the Jury

Regina, Saskatchewan, 31 July/1 August 1885

Your Honors, gentlemen of the jury: It would be easy for me to-day to [plead] insanity, because the circumstances are such as to excite any man, and under the natural excitement of what is taking place to-day (I cannot speak English very well, but am trying to do so, because most of those here speak English), under the excitement which my trial causes me would justify me not to appear as usual, but with my mind out of its ordinary condition. I hope with the help of God I will maintain calmness and decorum as suits this honorable court, this honorable jury. [. . .]

To-day, although a man I am as helpless before this court, in the Dominion of Canada and in this world, as I was helpless on the knees of my mother the day of my birth.

The North-West is also my mother, it is my mother country and although my mother country is sick and confined in a certain way, there are some from Lower Canada who came to help her to take care of me during her sickness and I am sure that my mother country will not kill me more than my mother did forty years ago when I came into the world, because a mother is always a mother, and even if I have my faults if she can see I am true she will be full of love for me.

When I came into the North-West in July, the first of July 1884, I found the Indians suffering. I found the half-breeds eating the rotten pork of the Hudson Bay Company and getting sick and weak every day. Although a half-breed, and having no pretension to help the whites, I also paid attention to them. I saw they were deprived of responsible government, I saw that they were deprived of their public liberties. I remembered that half-breed meant white and Indian, and while I paid attention to the suffering Indians and the half-breeds I remembered that the greatest part of my heart and blood was white and I have directed my attention to help the Indians, to help the half-breeds and to help the whites to the best of my ability. We have made petitions, I have made petitions with others to the Canadian Government asking to relieve the condition of this country. We have taken time; we have tried to unite all classes, even if I may speak, all parties. Those who have been in close communication with me know I have suffered, that I have waited for months to bring some of the people of the Saskatchewan to an understanding of certain important points in our petition to the Canadian Government and I have done my duty. [. . .]

The agitation in the North-West Territories would have been constitutional, and would certainly be constitutional to-day if, in my opinion, we had not been attacked. Perhaps the Crown has not been able to find out the particulars, that we were attacked, but as we were on the scene it was easy to understand. When we sent petitions to the Government, they used to answer us by sending police, and when the rumors were increasing every day that Riel had been shot here or there, or that Riel was going to be shot by such and such a man, the police would not pay any attention to it. [. . .]

I know that through the grace of God I am the founder of Manitoba. I know that though I have no open road for my influence, I have big influence, concentrated as a big amount of vapour in an engine. I believe by what I suffered for fifteen years, by what I have done for Manitoba and the people of the North-West, that my words are worth something. If I give offence, I do not speak to insult. Yes, you are the pioneers of civilization, the whites are the pioneers of civilization, but they bring among the Indians demoralization. [. . .]

As to religion, what is my belief? [. . .] I did not wish to force my views, because in Batoche to the half-breeds that followed me I used the word, *carte blanche*. If I have any influence in the new world it is to help in that way and even if it takes 200 years to become practical, then after my death that will bring out practical results, and then my children's children will shake hands with the Protestants of the new world in a friendly manner. I do not wish these evils which exist in Europe to be continued, as much as I can influence it, among the half-breeds. I do not wish that to be repeated in America. That work is not the work of some days or some years, it is the work of hundreds of years.

My condition is helpless, so helpless that my good lawyers, and they have done it by conviction (Mr. Fitzpatrick[2] in his beautiful speech has proved he believed I was insane) my condition seems to be so helpless that they have recourse to try and prove insanity to try and save me in that way. If I am insane, of course I don't know it, it is a property of insanity to be unable to know it. [. . .]

I am glad that the Crown have proved that I am the leader of the half-breeds in the North-West. I will perhaps be one day acknowledged as more than a leader of the half-breeds, and if I am I will have an opportunity of being acknowledged as a leader of good in this great country. [. . .]

If it is any satisfaction to the doctors to know what kind of insanity I have, if they are going to call my pretensions insanity, I say humbly, through the grace of God, I believe I am the prophet of the new world. [. . .]

I have only a few more words to say, your Honors. Gentlemen of the jury, my reputation, my liberty, my life, are at your discretion. So confident am I, that I have not the slightest anxiety, not even the slightest doubt, as to your verdict. The calmness of my mind concerning the favorable decision which I expect, does not come from any unjustifiable presumption upon my part.

---

[2] Charles Fitzpatrick was one of Riel's defence lawyers. The defence hoped to get Riel acquitted through a plea of insanity, which Riel, as is clear in his speech to the jury, refused to accept.

I simply trust, that through God's help, you will balance everything in a conscientious manner, and that, having heard what I had to say, that you will acquit me. I do respect you, although you are only half a jury,[3] but your number of six does not prevent you from being just and conscientious; your number of six does not prevent me giving you my confidence, which I would grant to another six men. Your Honor, because you appointed these men, do not believe that I disrespect you. It is not by your own choice, you were authorised by those above you, by the authorities in the North-West; you have acted according to your duty, and while it is, in our view, against the guarantees of liberty, I trust the Providence of God will bring out good of what you have done conscientiously.

Although this court has been in existence for the last fifteen years, I thought I had a right to be tried in another court. I do not disrespect this court. I do respect it, and what is called by my learned and good lawyers, the incompetency of the court must not be called in disrespect, because I have all respect.

The only things I would like to call your attention to before you retire to deliberate are: 1st That the House of Commons, Senate and Ministers of the Dominion, and who make laws for this land and govern it, are no representation whatever of the people of the North-West.

2nd That the North-West Council generated by the Federal Government has the great defect of its parent.

3rd [That] [t]he number of members elected for the Council by the people make it only a sham representative legislature and no representative government at all.

British civilization which rules to-day the world, and the British constitution has defined such government as this is which rules the North-West Territories as irresponsible government, which plainly means that there is no responsibility, and by all the science which has been shown here yesterday you are compelled to admit if there is no responsibility, it is insane.

Good sense combined with scientific theories lead to the same conclusion. By the testimony laid before you during my trial, witnesses on both sides made it certain that petition after petition had been sent to the Federal Government, and so irresponsible is that Government to the North-West that in the course of several years besides doing nothing to satisfy the people of this great land, it has even hardly been able to answer once or to give a single response. That fact would indicate an absolute lack of responsibility, and therefore insanity complicated with paralysis.

The Ministers of an insane and irresponsible Government and its little one—the North-West Council—made up their minds to answer my petitions by surrounding me slyly and by attempting to jump upon me suddenly and upon

---

[3] There were only six jury members at Riel's trial according to North-West Territorial law. If the trial had been held in Manitoba, Riel would have had the right to a French trial, and would have been granted a superior court judge and twelve-person jury.

my people in the Saskatchewan. Happily when they appeared and showed their teeth to devour, I was ready: that is what is called my crime of high treason, and to which they hold me to-day.[4] Oh, my good jurors, in the name of Jesus Christ, the only one who can save and help me, they have tried to tear me to pieces.

If you take the plea of the defence that I am not responsible for my acts, acquit me completely since I have been quarrelling with an insane and irresponsible Government. If you pronounce in favor of the Crown, which contends that I am responsible, acquit me all the same. You are perfectly justified in declaring that having my reason and sound mind, I have acted reasonably and in self-defence, while the Government, my accuser, being irresponsible, and consequently insane, cannot but have acted wrong, and if high treason there is it must be on its side and not on my part. [. . .]

[1885]

[4] Riel was being charged with "high treason."

THE CHINESE IMMIGRATION ACT ■ (1885)

From the early days of national image-making in Canada, Chinese settlers were not included in the constructed image of the "White" nation. Yet it is possible that Chinese mariners explored and settled portions of the western and eastern coasts of North America well before Christopher Columbus's so-called "discovery" of the Americas in 1492. Remains of what may be ancient Chinese cities have been found on Cape Breton Island, and cairns that may have been built by Chinese monks have been discovered on the Queen Charlotte Islands, off the coast of British Columbia. Chinese emigration to Canada, as we think of it today, began in the 1850s during the British Columbia gold rushes (1857–58 along the Fraser River; and 1860–66 in the Cariboo). This means that people of Chinese origin have been part of the Canadian fabric since well before Confederation, which undermines the notion of Canada's so-called "founding nations" having been invaded by subsequent waves of immigrants.

The main influx of Chinese immigrants came during the building of the Canadian Pacific Railway in the 1880s. Between 1880 and 1885, over ten thousand Chinese workers arrived in Canada to provide the labour for the construction of the railway. Not only could Chinese labourers be paid low wages, but they were willing to undertake the treacherous work that railway building entailed, particularly in the dangerous Fraser Canyon. Hundreds of Chinese workers lost their lives in the process, either in work-related accidents (including landslides which crushed their campsites) or from cholera and smallpox. It has been said that for every mile of track, four Chinese labourers died. As soon as the railway was completed, however, the Canadian government, following pressure from British Columbians who were concerned about the number of

Chinese people in their communities because they were seen to be taking their jobs, issued the "Chinese head tax" as part of the Chinese Immigration Act of 1885 (see Figure III-14). All Chinese immigrants, including babies, were charged $50 before they were allowed to enter the country. In 1900, this amount was increased to $100, and in 1903 to $500, which was almost impossible for Chinese immigrants to pay (it was the equivalent of two years' labour on the railway). The imposition of the head tax, and the persistent racism toward Chinese people in Canada, is the subject of Edith Maude Eaton's (Sui Sin Far's) letter to the *Montreal Daily Star* of 1896, included later in this section. The head tax, and the even more extreme Chinese Exclusion Act of 1923, meant that many Chinese labourers who were already in Canada were not able to have their families join them, which led to the tragic separation of families and the formation of a "bachelor society" in Canada, while many Chinese wives and children in China were left almost penniless. In addition, the Chinese Immigration Act of 1885 stipulated that ships could land only one Chinese immigrant for every fifty tons of carrying capacity, and all Chinese immigrants were denied Canadian citizenship. Nor were the Chinese provided with the land grants on the prairies that were offered to British, American, and European settlers at this time. Indeed, even prior to the completion of the CPR, legislation in British Columbia during the 1870s and 1880s was overtly racist in prohibiting Chinese people from acquiring Crown lands or from holding public office. Contemporary novels such as SKY Lee's *Disappearing Moon Cafe* (1990),

Wayson Choy's *The Jade Peony* (1995) and *All That Matters* (2004), and Jack Hodgins's *Innocent Cities* (2000), as well as Fred Wah's "biotext" *Diamond Grill* (1996) and essays in *Faking It* (2000), contain fictionalized and non-fictionalized treatments of these periods in Chinese-Canadian history.

The institution of the Chinese Immigration Act in the same year as the completion of the long-awaited railway is a scandalous indication of the ways in which Canada was being imagined as a nation belonging to a very specific group of European settlers. The railway, in other words, came at great cost to the vision of the future Canadian citizenry, excluding, as it did, the Chinese and the Métis communities. The famous celebratory image of the hammering of the "Last Spike" (Figure III-7), which is described in E.J. Pratt's 1952 epic poem "Towards the Last Spike," did not include any Chinese labourers in the staged photo shoot. Outrage at this exclusion, both in the famous photo and in Pratt's poem (as well as, years later, in Gordon Lightfoot's well-known 1967 ballad, "The Canadian Railroad Trilogy"), is registered in F.R. Scott's 1957 poem, "All the Spikes but the Last," which asks, "Where are the thousands from China . . . / Did they fare so well in the land they helped to unite? . . . / Is all Canada has to say to them written in the Chinese/ Immigration Act?"

The Canadian legislation had antecedents in Australia (in 1857) and the United States (in 1882), where similar laws had been passed barring Chinese immigration. The Chinese Immigration Act was eventually repealed in 1947, when Chinese Canadians were finally given the right to vote. In total, the federal government amassed over $20 million (more than $1.2 billion today) from the Chinese head tax. In June 2006, Prime Minister Stephen Harper issued an apology for these anti-Chinese policies and offered compensation to living head-tax payers and spouses of deceased payers.

From An Act to Restrict and Regulate Chinese Immigration into Canada

Whereas it is expedient to make provision for restricting the number of Chinese immigrants coming into the Dominion and to regulate such immigration; and whereas it is further expedient to provide a system of registration and control over Chinese immigrants residing in Canada: Therefore Her Majesty, by and with the advice and consent of the Senate and House of Commons of Canada, enacts as follows: [. . .]

4. Subject to the provisions of section thirteen of this Act every person of Chinese origin shall pay into the Consolidated Revenue Fund of Canada, on entering Canada, at the port or other place of entry, the sum of fifty dollars, except the following persons who shall be exempt from such payment, that is to say, first: the members of the Diplomatic Corps, or other Government representatives and their suite and their servants, consuls and consular agents; and second: tourists, merchants, men of science and students, who are bearers of certificates of identity, specifying their occupation and their object in coming into Canada. [. . .]

5. No vessel carrying Chinese immigrants to any port in Canada shall carry more than one such immigrant for every fifty tons of its tonnage; and the owner of any such vessel, who carries any number in excess of the number allowed by this section, shall be liable to a penalty of fifty dollars for each person so carried in excess.

6. Every master of any vessel bringing Chinese immigrants to any port in Canada, shall be personally liable to Her Majesty for the payment of the fee imposed by section four of this Act in respect of any immigrant carried by such vessel, and shall deliver, together with the total amount of such fee, to the controller, immediately on his arrival in port and before any of his passengers or crew shall have disembarked, a complete and accurate list of his crew and passengers, showing their names in full, the country and place of their birth, and the occupation and last place of domicile of each passenger. [. . .]

10. The controller shall deliver to each Chinese immigrant who has been permitted to land, and in respect of whom the duty has been paid as hereinbefore provided, a certificate containing a description of such individual, the date of his arrival, the name of the port of his landing and an acknowledgment that the duty has been duly paid; and such certificate

shall be *prima facie* evidence of the right of the person presenting the same to enter the Dominion of Canada. [. . .]

13. The entrance fee or duty payable under this Act shall not apply to any Chinese person residing or being within Canada at the time of the coming into force of this Act, but every such Chinese person who desires to remain in Canada, may obtain, within twelve months after the passing of this Act, and upon the payment of a fee of fifty cents, a certificate of such residence, from the controller, or from a judge of a superior court, a justice of the peace, a police magistrate, a stipendiary magistrate, a recorder, or from the mayor or secretary-treasurer of the municipality in which he resides, or from any officer charged with the duty of carrying this Act into effect; and the person granting such certificate shall report the fact to the controller at the principal seaport of the Province in which such Chinese person resides. [. . .]

15. The controller shall, on the first day of January in each year, send to the Provincial Secretary of the Province wherein certificates of entry have been granted, a certified list of all Chinese immigrants to whom such certificates have been granted during the year next preceding.

16. Every Chinese person who wilfully evades or attempts to evade any of the provisions of this Act as respects the payment of duty, by personating any other individual, or who wilfully makes use of any forged or fraudulent certificate to evade the provisions of this Act, and every person who wilfully aids or abets any such Chinese person in any evasion or attempt at evasion of any of the provisions of this Act, is guilty of a misdemeanor, and liable to imprisonment for a term not exceeding twelve months, or to a penalty not exceeding five hundred dollars, or to both.

17. Every person who takes part in the organization of any sort of court or tribunal, composed of Chinese persons, for the hearing and determination of any offence committed by a Chinese person, or in carrying on any such organization, or who takes part in any of its proceedings, or who gives evidence before any such court or tribunal, or assists in carrying into effect any decision or decree, or order of any such court or tribunal, is guilty of a misdemeanor, and liable to imprisonment for any term not exceeding twelve months, or to a penalty not exceeding five hundred dollars, or to both: but nothing in this section shall be construed to prevent Chinese immigrants from submitting any differences or disputes to arbitration, provided such submission be not contrary to the laws in force in the Province in which such submission is made.

24. This Act may be cited as "*The Chinese Immigration Act, 1885.*"

[*1885*]

One of Canada's best-known early women poets, Isabella Valancy Crawford has been celebrated for what James Reaney and Northrop Frye called her "mythopoeic" portrayals of Canadian pioneering life, wilderness settings, and Ojibway legends. Her most famous work is her 1884 narrative poem, "Malcolm's Katie: A Love Story," which has long held a prominent place in nineteenth-century Canadian poetry. Accounts of Crawford's persona are somewhat contradictory: she could be both introverted and exuberant, self-effacing and ambitious. This may have been a response to the restrictive social expectations of women in Victorian times, when social propriety came into conflict with individual expression. She has been compared to such nineteenth-century women writers as Emily Brontë and Emily Dickinson because she lived a life of relative seclusion and eccentricity, yet composed highly passionate, indeed erotic, accounts of human psychological conflict.

Born in Dublin, Ireland, in December 1850, Crawford moved to Canada West in 1858 to the pioneer community of Paisley, Ontario, where her father embarked on an unsuccessful medical practice. James Reaney, in his introduction to Crawford's *Collected Poems* of 1972, suggests that this "collision" between a new landscape and the cultivation of her Dublin life had lasting effects and produced some of Crawford's most powerful imagery. Although he suffered from increasing financial constraints and a growing problem with alcoholism, her father was elected to the position of township treasurer in 1859. When it was discovered that he had misappropriated public funds, the family was disgraced. This was an experience that may have contributed to Crawford's noted social aloofness later in life. The family subsequently moved to Lakefield in Douro Township, near the homes of Samuel Strickland and Catharine Parr Traill, and then to Peterborough, where Crawford began her writing career in earnest.

Although she is the author of many short stories, which were her main source of income in later years, Crawford is best known for her poetry, which she published widely in the Toronto *Mail*, the *Globe*, the *Evening Telegram*, and other newspapers and periodicals of the day. After her father's death in 1875, Crawford and her mother moved to Toronto, where she hoped to earn a living from her writing. In Toronto, then the cultural centre of English Canada, Crawford was in good company, joining the ranks of such other well-known female authors as Sara Jeannette Duncan and Agnes Machar. In 1884, she published her first and only collection of poetry, *Old Spookses' Pass: Malcolm's Katie, and Other Poems*, but the book, while positively reviewed, was not a financial success. When Crawford died unexpectedly of heart failure in Toronto in 1887 at the young age of thirty-six, she was at the peak of her writing career, leaving her most ambitious work, *Hugh and Ion* (posthumously published in 1977), unfinished. "Canada to England," included here, was first published in the Toronto *Mail* in July 1874, and "The Camp of Souls" in the Toronto *Evening Telegram* in August 1880. Both were reprinted in Crawford's collected poems, edited by J.W. Garvin, in 1905.

Many of Crawford's works depict the tension of opposites: good versus evil; hope versus despair; Native versus European; wilderness versus settlement; pastoral versus urban. Such tensions are evident in "Malcolm's Katie," in which a period of redemptive suffering (wrought by the villain Alfred) is rewarded because of the selfless love of the two protagonists. The transposition of Eden to the New World location of the Canadian backwoods, such as one finds in "Malcolm's Katie," has echoes in Oliver Goldsmith's and Susanna Moodie's contradictory portraits of the rising social milieux in Canada. Crawford's work is thus of interest for its depiction of the transition from a pioneering society to that of more populous urban centres. Her poignant poem "The City Tree" presents an ambiguous picture of human encroachment into a once Edenic wilderness. Other poems engage with political issues of the day, such as "The Rose of a Nation's Thanks," originally published in 1885, which describes the return of Canadian troops after the Northwest Rebellion, or "Canada to England," which provides an idealized image of Canada coming into its own as a global nation with spiritual ties to England. This valorization of Canadian distinctiveness also occurs in Max's speech in "Malcolm's Katie," which sets up a clear opposition between the heroism of Old World warriors and that of the New World pioneers, who endure their own Herculean trials "[t]hro' tortuous lanes of blacken'd, smoking stumps; / And past great flaming brush heaps" (lines 78–79) to contribute to the building of a nation. That the act of settlement brings with it the inevitable destruction of the very Edenic landscape the poem celebrates is an irony the poem does not pursue.

Crawford's interest in conjuring the distinctiveness of the New World setting is also evident in her extensive use of Aboriginal legends and characters in her work. One of the most famous of these is the legend of Indian summer that is included in "Malcolm's Katie." Poems such as "The Camp of Souls" and "Said the Canoe" also use Aboriginal figures, while "Malcolm's Katie" echoes Henry Wadsworth Longfellow's famous poem, "The Song of Hiawatha," in describing the north and south winds as Aboriginal spirits. Crawford's use of such imagery thus appropriates Aboriginal subjects in the quest for an "indigenous" Canadian mythology, while still using traditional English verse forms. Native legends and traditions helped lend a metaphysical aura to the New World settings of her poems, yet she also sought to merge these traditions with the stories of European settlement that were her primary interest. Interestingly, in "The Camp of Souls," Crawford has the ghost of the Aboriginal warrior, Singing Leaves, returning to the "white man's hearth" to scatter the beneficence of Manitou.

These poems have made a lasting impression on Canadian readers for the vitality of their imagery. A.J.M. Smith, in his introduction to *The Book of Canadian Poetry* in 1943, singled out Crawford as one of the few predecessors of the Confederation Group who had a distinctively Canadian voice. "[H]er imagination catches fire . . . in her poems of the Canadian wilderness," he wrote. "If there is a Canadian poetry that exists as something distinct from English poetry, this—and this almost alone—is it."

The City Tree

I stand within the stony, arid town,
 I gaze forever on the narrow street,
I hear forever passing up and down
 The ceaseless tramp of feet.

I know no brotherhood with far-locked woods,
    Where branches bourgeon from a kindred sap,
Where o'er mossed roots, in cool, green solitudes,
    Small silver brooklets lap.

No emerald vines creep wistfully to me
    And lay their tender fingers on my bark;   10
High may I toss my boughs, yet never see
    Dawn's first most glorious spark.

When to and fro my branches wave and sway,
    Answ'ring the feeble wind that faintly calls,
They kiss no kindred boughs, but touch alway
    The stones of climbing walls.

My heart is never pierced with song of bird;
    My leaves know nothing of that glad unrest
Which makes a flutter in the still woods heard
    When wild birds build a nest.   20

There never glance the eyes of violets up,
    Blue, into the deep splendour of my green;
Nor falls the sunlight to the primrose cup
    My quivering leaves between.

Not mine, not mine to turn from soft delight
    Of woodbine breathings, honey sweet and warm;
With kin embattled rear my glorious height
    To greet the coming storm!

Not mine to watch across the free, broad plains
    The whirl of stormy cohorts sweeping fast,   30
The level silver lances of great rains
    Blown onward by the blast!

Not mine the clamouring tempest to defy,
    Tossing the proud crest of my dusky leaves—
Defender of small flowers that trembling lie
    Against my barky greaves!

Not mine to watch the wild swan drift above,
    Balanced on wings that could not choose between
The wooing sky, blue as the eye of love,
    And my own tender green!   40

And yet my branches spread, a kingly sight,
    In the close prison of the drooping air:
When sun-vexed noons are at their fiery height
    My shade is broad, and there

Come city toilers, who their hour of ease
    Weave out to precious seconds as they lie
Pillowed on horny hands, to hear the breeze
    Through my great branches die.

I see no flowers, but as the children race
    With noise and clamour through the dusty street,   50
I see the bud of many an angel face,
    I hear their merry feet.

No violets look up, but, shy and grave,
    The children pause and lift their crystal eyes
To where my emerald branches call and wave
    As to the mystic skies.

                                                          [1884]

The Camp of Souls

My white canoe, like the silvery air
    O'er the River of Death that darkly rolls
When the moons of the world are round and fair,
    I paddle back from the "Camp of Souls."
When the wishton-wish in the low swamp grieves
Come the dark plumes of red "Singing Leaves."[1]

Two hundred times have the moons of spring
    Rolled over the bright bay's azure breath
Since they decked me with plumes of an eagle's wing,
    And painted my face with the "paint of death,"   10
And from their pipes o'er my corpse there broke
The solemn rings of the blue "last smoke."

Two hundred times have the wintry moons
    Wrapped the dead earth in a blanket white;
Two hundred times have the wild sky loons
    Shrieked in the flush of the golden light
Of the first sweet dawn, when the summer weaves
Her dusky wigwam of perfect leaves.

Two hundred moons of the falling leaf
    Since they laid my bow in my dead right hand   20
And chanted above me the "song of grief"
    As I took my way to the spirit land;

[1] "Singing Leaves" is the name of the speaker in the poem.

Yet when the swallow the blue air cleaves
Come the dark plumes of red "Singing Leaves."

White are the wigwams in that far camp,
 And the star-eyed deer on the plains are found;
No bitter marshes or tangled swamp
 In the Manitou's happy hunting-ground!
And the moon of summer forever rolls
Above the red men in their "Camp of Souls." 30

Blue are its lakes as the wild dove's breast,
 And their murmurs soft as her gentle note;
As the calm, large stars in the deep sky rest,
 The yellow lilies upon them float;
And canoes, like flakes of the silvery snow,
Thro' the tall, rustling rice-beds come and go.

Green are its forests; no warrior wind
 Rushes on war trail the dusk grove through,
With leaf-scalps of tall trees mourning behind;
 But South Wind, heart friend of Great Manitou, 40
When ferns and leaves with cool dews are wet,
Blows flowery breaths from his red calumet.

Never upon them the white frosts lie,
 Nor glow their green boughs with the "paint of death";
Manitou smiles in the crystal sky,
 Close breathing above them His life-strong breath;
And He speaks no more in fierce thunder sound,
So near is His happy hunting-ground.

Yet often I love, in my white canoe,
 To come to the forests and camps of earth: 50
'Twas there death's black arrow pierced me through;
 'Twas there my red-browed mother gave me birth;
There I, in the light of a young man's dawn,
Won the lily heart of dusk "Springing Fawn."

And love is a cord woven out of life,
 And dyed in the red of the living heart;
And time is the hunter's rusty knife,
 That cannot cut the red strands apart:
And I sail from the spirit shore to scan
Where the weaving of that strong cord began. 60

But I may not come with a giftless hand,
 So richly I pile, in my white canoe,
Flowers that bloom in the spirit land,

Immortal smiles of Great Manitou.
When I paddle back to the shores of earth
I scatter them over the white man's hearth.

For love is the breath of the soul set free;
    So I cross the river that darkly rolls,
That my spirit may whisper soft to thee
    Of *thine* who wait in the "Camp of Souls."   70
When the bright day laughs, or the wan night grieves,
Come the dusky plumes of red "Singing Leaves."

[1905]

Canada to England

Gone are the days, old Warrior of the Seas,
When thine armed head, bent low to catch my voice,
Caught but the plaintive sighings of my woods,
And the wild roar of rock-dividing streams,
And the loud bellow of my cataracts,
Bridged with the seven splendours of the bow.
When Nature was a Samson yet unshorn,
Filling the land with solitary might,
Or as the Angel of the Apocalypse,
One foot upon the primeval bowered land,   10
One foot upon the white mane of the sea,
My voice but faintly swelled the ebb and flow
Of the wild tides and storms that beat upon
Thy rocky girdle,—loud shrieking from the Ind
Ambrosial-breathing furies; from the north
Thundering with Arctic bellows, groans of seas
Rising from tombs of ice disrupted by
The magic kisses of the wide-eyed sun.

The times have won a change. Nature no more
Lords it alone and binds the lonely land   20
A serf to tongueless solitudes; but Nature's self
Is led, glad captive, in light fetters rich
As music-sounding silver can adorn;
And man has forged them, and our silent God
Behind His flaming worlds smiles on the deed.
"Man hath dominion"—words of primal might;
"Man hath dominion"—thus the words of God.[2]

---

[2] An allusion to the "Dominion of Canada" and Canada's "national motto": "He shall have
dominion also from sea to sea, and from the river unto the ends of the earth" (Psalms 72:8).

If destiny is writ on night's dusk scroll,
Then youngest stars are dropping from the hand
Of the Creator, sowing on the sky   30
My name in seeds of light. Ages will watch
Those seeds expand to suns, such as the tree
Bears on its boughs, which grows in Paradise.

How sounds my voice, my warrior kinsman, now?
Sounds it not like to thine in lusty youth—
A world-possessing shout of busy men,
Veined with the clang of trumpets and the noise
Of those who make them ready for the strife,
And in the making ready bruise its head?
Sounds it not like to thine—the whispering vine,   40
The robe of summer rustling thro' the fields,
The lowing of the cattle in the meads,
The sound of Commerce, and the music-set,
Flame-brightened step of Art in stately halls,—
All the infinity of notes which chord
The diapason of a Nation's voice?

My infants' tongues lisp word for word with thine;
We worship, wed, and die, and God is named
That way ye name Him,—strong bond between
Two mighty lands when as one mingled cry,   50
As of one voice, Jehovah turns to hear.
The bonds between us are no subtle links
Of subtle minds binding in close embrace,
Half-struggling for release, two alien lands,
But God's own seal of kindred, which to burst
Were but to dash His benediction from
Our brows. "Who loveth not his kin,
Whose face and voice are his, how shall he love
God whom he hath not seen?"

[1905]

WILLIAM WILFRED CAMPBELL ■ (1860–1918)

In many respects, Wilfred Campbell was the most outspoken and opinionated of the Confederation Group of poets, which formed under the unofficial leadership of Charles G.D. Roberts in the 1880s and '90s. He is also one of the least remembered of the group. By most accounts, he was a jealous yet intellectually powerful man, fiercely protective of his reputation and difficult to get along with. Archibald Lampman, who on a number of occasions found himself on the receiving end of Campbell's wrath, described him as "raw, ragged and offensive" in a letter to E.W. Thomson. Because his immense success with his second collection of poetry, *Lake Lyrics and Other Poems* (1889), was not followed by a similar degree of acclaim, Campbell soon found himself losing ground to his increasingly successful poetic rivals Roberts, Lampman, and Bliss Carman. Never afraid to voice an opinion, Campbell became the most notorious member of the group when his ambition led him to turn on his peers in strident public attacks.

Born near Lake Ontario in Canada West (southern Ontario), Campbell was the son of an Anglican clergyman. He also trained in divinity in Toronto and Massachusetts, becoming an ordained minister in the mid-1880s. The Victorian age was marked by serious blows to religious faith, with the advent of scientific advances in geology, biology (particularly the evolutionary theories of Charles Darwin), and industrial technology. Campbell, like many others of this period, suffered a crisis of faith over the ensuing years, a theme that is evident in many of his poems. In effect, Campbell sought to harmonize contemporary scientific findings with his religious beliefs. In his 3 June 1893 "At the Mermaid Inn" column for the Toronto *Globe*, he defends the theory of evolution but attributes it to the "incomprehensible greatness" of the infinite. Like Thomas D'Arcy McGee, Campbell also recognized the dangers that religious sectarianism posed to any possibility of national unity in Canada. As a result, and like his fellow poets Carman and Roberts, Campbell turned to alternative spiritual philosophies as a way of seeking meaning in a seemingly amoral universe.

Already widely published in Canadian and American periodicals, Campbell resigned from the ministry in 1891 to take up a post in the federal civil service in Ottawa and devote himself to his literary career, even though the position paid less than his clerical duties. His early poems, lyrics about the area around Georgian Bay and Lake Huron, remain his most popular. They are notable for their startling imagery, and many of them, such as "The Winter Lakes," contain terrifying depictions of the natural landscape that evoke a sense of despair and bewilderment. The poems from his third collection, *The Dread Voyage* (1893), are darker in tone, and include such well-known works as "How One Winter Came in the Lake Region" and "The Dread Voyage." His remarkable dramatic monologue from this collection, "Unabsolved," is a confession of a member of one of the rescue parties of John Franklin, who saw the mast of Franklin's ship in the distance, but out of fear lied about his discovery. Although his poems "The Lazarus of Empire" and "Briton to Briton: An Appeal" are critical of ongoing British imperial expansion in the late nineteenth century, especially the latter's response to Canada's participation in the Anglo-Boer War (a war in part to increase British territory in South Africa), Campbell became an ardent imperialist toward the turn of the century, and advocated spiritual and economic ties between Britain and its colonies. This theme is increasingly evident in his later poems, especially in his collections *Beyond the Hills of Dream* (1899) and *Sagas of Vaster Britain* (1914), and his own *Collected Poems*, which he brought out in 1905.

Campbell was a close friend of two other Ottawa civil servants and members of the Confederation Group, Archibald Lampman and Duncan Campbell Scott. Because Campbell's income was inadequate to support his growing family, Lampman arranged for the three of them to collaborate on a weekly column in the Toronto *Globe* under the title "At the Mermaid Inn." Appearing between

February 1892 and July 1893, the column was a series of paragraphs and essays devoted to cultural and social issues of the day. In these columns, Campbell is highly critical of the naive patriotism that he saw to be rampant in contemporary cultural debates and literary publications, as, for example, in his contribution of 10 December 1892. While his commitment to Canada is unwavering, he called for the encouragement of a Canadian cultural identity that would transcend religious and regional differences and would be based on an intelligent fostering of a mature national identity: "What is essentially needed is a sentiment that will sweep like a baptismal wave from ocean to ocean and overpower all local, racial, and other influences," he wrote in the 31 December 1892 column. Unfortunately, the *Globe* series came to an abrupt end when Campbell published a mean-spirited parody of Lampman's poetry in the column.

The final blow to the Confederation Group followed a few years later, in 1895, in the wake of Campbell's publicly vented spleen at having had to bask in what he felt to be the undeserved glow of the others. This became known as the "War Among the Poets," the extended and notorious argument, printed in the pages of various Canadian newspapers and magazines, between the disaffected Campbell and other members of the group. Campbell's initial volley was an attack on his peers for an excessive devotion to form and technique over what he saw to be "genuine" poetic

expression. Attributing the success of Roberts and others to the fact that they were supported by academic audiences rather than by the Canadian populace at large, Campbell implicitly made a case for his own work, which he felt had been unjustly subordinated to the work of Lampman, Roberts, and Carman. What ensued was a very public, and at times vicious, "war" between the two camps, in which Campbell publicly accused Carman of plagiarism from the literary greats and condemned Roberts for "log-rolling," that is, for his conscious promotion of the work of his friends to the exclusion of any concern for real literary merit. That this argument had been brewing years earlier is evident in Sara Jeannette Duncan's ironic allusion to the "wicked company" known as the "Logrollas" in her 1887 essay included here. The argument also has interesting overlaps with the Canadian Modernist debates about poetic form and content a few decades later. There may have been a grain of truth in Campbell's accusations, yet he also ran the risk of allowing personal vitriol to undercut the very foundations of the national literary culture that he so urgently called for in his critical writings. As if to atone for his behaviour, in 1899 Campbell composed a moving elegy for Lampman entitled "Bereavement of the Fields," following the premature death of his friend that February. Curiously, in the poem he commemorates the "sweetness" of Lampman's nature poetry and not its haunting ambiguity, the very quality that so compellingly infuses Campbell's poems of the Great Lakes.

The Winter Lakes

Out in a world of death far to the northward lying,
   Under the sun and the moon, under the dusk and the day;
Under the glimmer of stars and the purple of sunsets dying,
   Wan and waste and white, stretch the great lakes away.

Never a bud of spring, never a laugh of summer,
 Never a dream of love, never a song of bird;
But only the silence and white, the shores that grow chiller and dumber,
 Wherever the ice winds sob, and the griefs of winter are heard.

Crags that are black and wet out of the grey lake looming,
 Under the sunset's flush and the pallid, faint glimmer of dawn;   10
Shadowy, ghost-like shores, where midnight surfs are booming
 Thunders of wintry woe over the spaces wan.

Lands that loom like spectres, whited regions of winter,
 Wastes of desolate woods, deserts of water and shore;
A world of winter and death, within these regions who enter,
 Lost to summer and life, go to return no more.

Moons that glimmer above, waters that lie white under,
 Miles and miles of lake far out under the night;
Foaming crests of waves, surfs that shoreward thunder,
 Shadowy shapes that flee, haunting the spaces white.   20

Lonely hidden bays, moon-lit, ice-rimmed, winding,
 Fringed by forests and crags, haunted by shadowy shores;
Hushed from the outward strife, where the mighty surf is grinding
 Death and hate on the rocks, as sandward and landward it roars.

                                             [1889]

How One Winter Came
in the Lake Region

For weeks and weeks the autumn world stood still,
 Clothed in the shadow of a smoky haze;
The fields were dead, the wind had lost its will,
And all the lands were hushed by wood and hill,
 In those grey, withered days.

Behind a mist the blear sun rose and set,
 At night the moon would nestle in a cloud;
The fisherman, a ghost, did cast his net;
The lake its shores forgot to chafe and fret,
 And hushed its caverns loud.   10

Far in the smoky woods the birds were mute,
 Save that from blackened tree a jay would scream,
Or far in swamps the lizard's lonesome lute
Would pipe in thirst, or by some gnarlèd root
 The tree-toad trilled his dream.

From day to day still hushed the season's mood,
   The streams stayed in their runnels shrunk and dry;
Suns rose aghast by wave and shore and wood,
And all the world, with ominous silence, stood
   In weird expectancy: 20

When one strange night the sun like blood went down,
   Flooding the heavens in a ruddy hue;
Red grew the lake, the sere fields parched and brown,
Red grew the marshes where the creeks stole down,
   But never a wind-breath blew.

That night I felt the winter in my veins,
   A joyous tremor of the icy glow;
And woke to hear the north's wild vibrant strains,
While far and wide, by withered woods and plains,
   Fast fell the driving snow.   30

[1893]

The Lazarus of Empire[1]

The Celt, he is proud in his protest,
   The Scot, he is calm in his place,
For each has a word in the ruling and doom
   Of the empire that honors his race:
And the Englishman, dogged and grim,
   Looks the world in the face as he goes,
And he holds a proud lip, for he sails his own ship,
   And he cares not for rivals nor foes;
But lowest and last, with his areas vast,
   And horizon so servile and tame,   10
Sits the poor beggar Colonial
   Who feeds on the crumbs of her fame.

He knows no place in her councils,
   He holds no part in the word
That girdles the world, with its thunders
   When the fiat of Britain is heard;
He beats no drums to her battles,
   He gives no triumphs her name,
But lowest and last, with his areas vast,
   He feeds on the crumbs of her fame.   20

---

[1] Campbell's note: "Written before the Boer War."

How long, O how long, the dishonor,
  The servile and suppliant place?
Are we Britons who batten upon her,
  Or degenerate sons of the race?
It is souls that make nations, not numbers,
  As our forefathers proved in the past,
Let us take up the burden of empire,
  Or nail our own flag to the mast.
Doth she care for us, value us, want us,
  Or are we but pawns in the game;   30
Where lowest and last, with our areas vast,
  We feed on the crumbs of her fame?

                                                    [1899]

CHARLES G.D. ROBERTS ■ (1860–1943)

Charles G.D. Roberts was the igniting force behind Canada's first consolidated literary movement, the group that we refer to today as the Confederation Poets. Confederation took place when Roberts was only seven years old, but the event was of formative importance to the boy in the 1870s, when nationalist sentiment was running high in Canada. In his adult years, Roberts became increasingly committed to the idea of a national literature for Canada. In truth, his approach in the 1880s was part of a wider movement of Romantic literary nationalism that was prevalent in the period, a movement that viewed literature to be an essential aspect of national identity and unity. This echoes Thomas D'Arcy McGee's 1858 essay "Protection for Canadian Literature," in which he argued that all countries "must create and foster a National Literature, if it is their wish to preserve a distinct individuality from other nations." In his Alumni Address delivered at the University of New Brunswick in 1883, entitled "The Beginnings of a Canadian Literature," Roberts likewise insisted that literature

"has in its hands the moulding of future character."

   We see this focus in many of his poems toward the end of the century, including "Canada" and "An Ode for the Canadian Confederacy," but it was really in his ardent support of his fellow writers that Roberts contributed to the growing development of a distinctive Canadian literature. Roberts was central in drawing together the poets of the Confederation Group, a group that included himself, his cousin Bliss Carman, Archibald Lampman, Duncan Campbell Scott, Frederick George Scott, and Wilfred Campbell. In the 1880s and '90s, he almost single-handedly forged the group's reputation, by eliciting reviews and promoting their work. "We are in the dawn, with night behind us," Roberts wrote triumphantly in a letter to fellow poet and literary critic William Douw Lighthall in June 1888.

   The poets of the post-Confederation period saw themselves as the avant-garde of a new Canadian literary and national movement. They, like the Modernists after them, were seeking to build a reputable and distinctive Canadian literary tradition: to make it innovative, fresh, distinctive, technically accomplished, and internationally celebrated. All were deeply indebted to the British Romantic poets, especially Shelley, Keats, and Wordsworth, as well as to the American Romantics Emerson and Thoreau. As is evident in Roberts's 1892 essay "The Savour of the Soil," these poets turned to the Canadian natural environment and local concerns in an effort to forge a national literature that would be unique to Canada, and therefore distinct from the British poetic tradition (which was not, Roberts emphasized, to insist that poets were to write *only* about Canada). This helps cast a more objective light on the unfavourable portrayal of the Confederation Poets provided in F.R. Scott's 1927 poem "The Canadian Authors Meet." As Roberts describes it in his 1931 "A Note on Modernism," these writers saw themselves to be as "modern" as many of the poets writing a generation later. Both groups were devoted to craftsmanship and the deprovincializing of Canadian literature; both believed in universal literary standards, while seeking to make their works less derivative. In his preface to his *Selected Poems* (1936), Roberts cited the English poet Humbert Wolfe: "There is no such thing [as modern verse] and never has been. . . . There are only oldish men in each generation misunderstanding what is being written now, side by side with youngish men misunderstanding what was written then."

Roberts was born in Douglas (near Fredericton), New Brunswick, though the family soon moved to the Tantramar region, near Sackville, where his father, an Anglican minister, was appointed rector. The Tantramar marshlands and tidal flats had a lifelong impact on Roberts, and they became the beloved landscape of his childhood and poetry, as is evident in such poems as "The Tantramar Revisited" and "The Salt-Flats." When Roberts entered the University of New Brunswick in 1876, he began to write poetry in earnest, publishing his first collection, *Orion and Other Poems* (1880), when he was only twenty. This book had an unprecedented impact on his generation. In his 1891 lecture "Two Canadian Poets," Archibald Lampman told of the remarkable effect *Orion* had on him when he first encountered it: "Like most of the young fellows about me I had been under the depressing conviction that we were situated hopelessly on the outskirts of civilization, where no art and no literature could be, and that it was useless to expect that anything great could be done by any of our companions, still more useless to expect that we could do it ourselves. . . . [*Orion*] was like a voice from some new paradise of art calling to us to be up and doing." According to J.D. Logan, *Orion* initiated "the First Renaissance in Canadian Literature"; it was heralded as the harbinger of a new era.

In November 1883, at the age of twenty-three, Roberts took on the position of editor of Goldwin Smith's new periodical *The Week*, published out of Toronto. *The Week* was one of the most important intellectual journals of the time in Canada, and was committed to the advancement of Canadian culture. While working on the journal, Roberts made the acquaintance of such contemporary writers as D.C. Scott, Lampman, and Campbell. However, his tenure there lasted only a few months (December 1883 to February 1884) because of his difference of opinion with Smith over one of the topical issues of the day: the prospect of Canada's independence. The political choices were the same as those that had preceded Confederation: independence, imperial ties to Britain, or annexation to the United States. There were heated intellectual battles between those, like Roberts, who supported independence, and those, like Smith, who advocated annexation to the United States. Roberts's political poem "Canada," for example, is a defence of Canadian independence, invoking the spirit of the infamous English and French generals Wolfe and Montcalm as unifying emblems from Canada's past. Roberts's review of Goldwin Smith's *Canada and the Canadian Question* (1891) in the *Dial* of 16 December 1892 fears the "extinction of a name we love" if Canada were to join the United States. Although by the late 1880s and early '90s, Roberts gradually came to align himself with imperial federation as a protection against American expansion, he favoured such federation only if it retained for Canada complete independence. In effect, this alliance combined his nationalism with his literary cosmopolitanism.

In 1885, Roberts was made a professor at King's College in Windsor, Nova Scotia, though he eventually tired of teaching and resigned from the position in 1895. He left his wife and family, and moved to New York in 1897, where he accepted the post of assistant editor of *The Illustrated American*. In 1907, he left for Europe, serving in the British and Canadian forces in the First World War, and did not return to Canada until 1925. He died in Toronto in 1943.

Roberts always stated that it was as a poet that he wanted to be remembered. He published *In Divers Tones* in 1886, a collection that revealed his interest in Canada, especially the Maritimes, as a resonant subject matter for poetry. He continued this approach in what many consider to be his best book of poems, *Songs of the Common Day* (1893), which contains a sonnet sequence depicting the yearly shift in seasons in the New Brunswick countryside. According to literary critic Desmond Pacey, it was with this collection that Roberts initiated "an

indigenous Canadian verse." In many of these poems, Roberts is concerned with the theme of transience, though, like William Wordsworth, he is especially attendant to the small beauties and glimpses of eternity that are to be found in the everyday. His "Prologue" to *Songs of the Common Day* contains a good description of his approach: he asks his muse who "[m]akes dull, familiar things divine" to show him "what beauty clings / In common forms, and find the soul / Of unregarded things!" His debt to the poetic theory of Wordsworth in the preface to *Lyrical Ballads*, and to William Blake's notion of seeing "a World in a Grain of Sand / And a Heaven in a Wild Flower" (from his poem "Auguries of Innocence"), is clearly evident in this passage. Moreover, Roberts's most oft-cited poem, "The Tantramar Revisited," is indebted in both style and theme to Wordsworth's "Lines Written a Few Miles Above Tintern Abbey" (1798), for both are narrated by a speaker looking down on a rustic scene and reminiscing about the time he spent there in his youth. Roberts's essay "The Poetry of Nature," published in *The Forum* in December 1897, describes the central tenets of his Romantic landscape aesthetic (see also the introduction to this section, which outlines some of the major concerns of the nature writing of this period).

In addition to his poetry, Roberts wrote numerous novels, many of them historical romances about Acadia that combined an interest in Canadian settings with a romantic re-imagining of Canada's French and English past. More importantly, with Ernest Thompson Seton, whose collection *Wild Animals I Have Known* appeared in 1898, Roberts is credited with originating the genre of the "realistic animal story," which has become a distinctive feature of Canadian literature. As Roberts explains in his introduction to *The Kindred of the Wild* (1902), included here, the realistic animal story was distinct from more conventional depictions of animals as anthropomorphized fairy-tale characters, or, alternatively, as mouthpieces for animal rights ideologies, as in Marshall Saunders's well-known novel from the period, *Beautiful Joe* (1894). Nor were the tales dry scientific accounts, but rather dramatic depictions of animals in their natural habitat. Roberts published over a dozen collections of such stories, which altogether included over two hundred tales, including *Earth's Enigmas* in 1896 and *The Kindred of the Wild* in 1902. The story included here, "When Twilight Falls on the Stump Lots," comes from the latter collection. While many of these tales explore the relation of man to the wilderness, they also contributed to the growing discussion of the aesthetic representation of animals that was raging at the turn of the century. Like Seton's stories, Roberts's were attacked for their inaccuracies and their attribution of human thinking to animals. In his 1903 article entitled "Real and Sham Natural History," American nature writer John Burroughs accused Seton and Roberts of creating overly sentimental portraits of animals. This became known as the "Nature Faker" controversy, the term applied by American president Theodore Roosevelt, who published his own criticisms of these writers in 1907. A prime question was whether such ostensibly "realistic" literary representations were objective depictions of animal behaviour, or humanized portraits of sympathetic human-like animals. These debates

included the question of whether animals could be said to "reason," and precisely how "instinct" was to be defined. Roberts's introduction to *The Kindred of the Wild*, "The Animal Story," contains his definition of the modern animal story. As one sees in his introduction, Roberts came down on the side of reason. In addition, Roberts's stories are tales of Darwinian struggle and death, a version of "nature red in tooth and claw," as Tennyson put it, which describe the inherent amorality of nature. In this way, the world view of his stories is often in distinct contrast to that of his poetry. However, his stories emphasize continuity; in each case, the natural world, if not the individual animals within it, endures.

Literary critic W.J. Keith states, "For many, Roberts and Canadian literature were practically synonymous." Even though Roberts spent a good portion of his life away from Canada, in part due to the better opportunities provided to writers in the United States and Britain (see his poem "The Poet Is Bidden to Manhattan Island"), Roberts remained attached to Canada. In a 20 October 1888 letter to Lighthall, Roberts waxed sentimental in his description of his dedication to Canadian literature: "Yea, indeed, let us who are true Canadians ever strengthen each others' *[sic]* hands. . . . The difficulty I feel is to keep sane & dignified in my tone when I speak of Canada. The name thrills me, and I have difficulty in keeping foolish tears out of my eyes when I am talking to my classes of Canadian possibilities and aspirations."

Canada

O Child of Nations, giant-limbed,
    Who stand'st among the nations now
Unheeded, unadored, unhymned,
    With unanointed brow,—

How long the ignoble sloth, how long
    The trust in greatness not thine own?
Surely the lion's brood is strong
    To front the world alone!

How long the indolence, ere thou dare
    Achieve thy destiny, seize thy fame—   10
Ere our proud eyes behold thee bear
    A nation's franchise, nation's name?

The Saxon force, the Celtic fire,
    These are thy manhood's heritage!
Why rest with babes and slaves? Seek higher
    The place of race and age.

I see to every wind unfurled
    The flag that bears the Maple-Wreath;[1]
Thy swift keels furrow round the world
    Its blood-red folds beneath;   20

Thy swift keels cleave the furthest seas;
    Thy white sails swell with alien gales;
To stream on each remotest breeze
    The black smoke of thy pipes exhales.

O Falterer, let thy past convince
    Thy future,—all the growth, the gain,
The fame since Cartier knew thee, since
    Thy shores beheld Champlain!

Montcalm and Wolfe! Wolfe and Montcalm!
    Quebec, thy storied citadel   30
Attest in burning song and psalm
    How here thy heroes fell!

O Thou that bor'st the battle's brunt
    At Queenston, and at Lundy's Lane,—[2]
On whose scant ranks but iron front
    The battle broke in vain!—

---

[1] A reference to Canada's unofficial flag at the time, the Canadian Red Ensign, which depicted a Canadian coat of arms above a maple wreath or garland. The flag had the Union Jack in the top left-hand corner with the Canadian coat of arms on the fly, thereby signifying Canada's dual status as both a British colony and an independent nation. It therefore provided an apt symbol for Canada's representation as a "Child of Nations" in this poem. The background of the flag was red, hence the poem's reference to "blood-red folds."

[2] Queenston Heights and Lundy's Lane, and in the next stanza, Chrysler's Farm and Chateauguay, are all locations of battles during the War of 1812 when the British/Canadian forces succeeded in repelling the Americans. The speaker is taking the reader through important moments in Canadian history.

Whose was the danger, whose the day,
   From whose triumphant throats the cheers,
At Chrysler's Farm, at Chateauguay,
   Storming like clarion-bursts our ears?   40

On soft Pacific slopes,—beside
   Strange floods that northward rave and fall,—
Where chafes Acadia's chainless tide—
   Thy sons await thy call.

They wait; but some in exile, some
   With strangers housed, in stranger lands;—
And some Canadian lips are dumb
   Beneath Egyptian sands.[3]

O mystic Nile! Thy secret yields
   Before us; thy most ancient dreams   50
Are mixed with far Canadian fields
   And murmur of Canadian streams.

But thou, my Country, dream not thou!
   Wake, and behold how night is done,—
How on thy breast, and o'er thy brow,
   Bursts the uprising sun!

[1886]

The Tantramar Revisited[4]

Summers and summers have come, and gone with the flight of the swallow;[5]
Sunshine and thunder have been, storm, and winter, and frost;
Many and many a sorrow has all but died from remembrance,
Many a dream of joy fall'n in the shadow of pain.
Hands of chance and change have marred, or moulded, or broken,
Busy with spirit or flesh, all I most have adored;
Even the bosom of Earth is strewn with heavier shadows,—
Only in these green hills, aslant to the sea, no change!
Here where the road that has climbed from the inland valleys and woodlands,

---

[3] Canadian forces aided Britain in Egypt during the 1880s.

[4] The Tantramar marshes are in the Bay of Fundy region of New Brunswick, on the border with Nova Scotia, where Roberts spent his childhood. The area is noted for its extensive and fertile tidal flats. Cumberland Point and Minudie, both mentioned in the poem, are towns in New Brunswick and Nova Scotia.

[5] Compare the beginning of this poem with the opening lines of Wordworth's "Lines Composed a Few Miles Above Tintern Abbey" (1798): "Five years have passed; five summers, with the length / Of five long winters! and again I hear / These waters, rolling from their mountain-springs." Both poems are spoken by a viewer looking down on the scene from afar and remembering his youth.

Dips from the hill-tops down, straight to the base of the hills,— 10
Here, from my vantage-ground, I can see the scattering houses,
Stained with time, set warm in orchards, and meadows, and wheat,
Dotting the broad bright slopes outspread to southward and eastward,
Wind-swept all day long, blown by the south-east wind.
Skirting the sunbright uplands stretches a riband of meadow,
Shorn of the laboring grass, bulwarked well from the sea,
Fenced on its seaward border with long clay dikes from the turbid
Surge and flow of the tides vexing the Westmoreland shores.
Yonder, toward the left, lie broad the Westmoreland marshes,—
Miles on miles they extend, level, and grassy, and dim, 20
Clear from the long red sweep of flats to the sky in the distance,
Save for the outlying heights, green-rampired Cumberland Point;
Miles on miles outrolled, and the river-channels divide them,—
Miles on miles of green, barred by the hurtling gusts.

Miles on miles beyond the tawny bay is Minudie.
There are the low blue hills; villages gleam at their feet.
Nearer a white sail shines across the water, and nearer
Still are the slim, grey masts of fishing-boats dry on the flats.
Ah, how well I remember those wide red flats, above tide-mark
Pale with scurf of the salt, seamed and baked in the sun! 30
Well I remember the piles of blocks and ropes, and the net-reels
Wound with the beaded nets, dripping and dark from the sea!
Now at this season the nets are unwound; they hang from the rafters
Over the fresh-stowed hay in upland barns, and the wind
Blows all day through the chinks, with the streaks of sunlight and sways them
Softly at will; or they lie heaped in the gloom of a loft.

Now at this season the reels are empty and idle; I see them
Over the lines of the dikes, over the gossiping grass.
Now at this season they swing in the long strong wind, thro' the lonesome
Golden afternoon, shunned by the foraging gulls. 40
Near about sunset the crane will journey homeward above them;
Round them, under the moon, all the calm night long,
Winnowing soft grey wings of marsh-owls wander and wander,
Now to the broad, lit marsh, now to the dusk of the dike.
Soon, thro' their dew-wet frames, in the live keen freshness of morning,
Out of the teeth of the dawn blows back the awakening wind.
Then, as the blue day mounts, and the low-shot shafts of the sunlight
Glance from the tide to the shore, gossamers jewelled with dew
Sparkle and wave, where late sea-spoiling fathoms of drift-net
Myriad-meshed, uploomed sombrely over the land. 50

Well I remember it all. The salt raw scent of the margin;
While, with men at the windlass, groaned each reel, and the net,

Surging in ponderous lengths, uprose and coiled in its station;
Then each man to his home,—well I remember it all!

Yet, as I sit and watch, this present peace of the landscape,—
Stranded boats, these reels empty and idle, the hush,
One grey hawk slow-wheeling above yon cluster of haystacks,—
More than the old-time stir this stillness welcomes me home.
Ah, the old-time stir, how once it stung me with rapture,—
Old-time sweetness, the winds freighted with honey and salt!   60
Yet will I stay my steps and not go down to the marsh-land,—
Muse and recall far off, rather remember than see,—
Lest on too close sight I miss the darling illusion,
Spy at their task even here the hands of chance and change.

[1886]

The Poet Is Bidden to Manhattan Island

Dear Poet, quit your shady lanes
   And come where more than lanes are shady.
Leave Phyllis to the rustic swains
   And sing some Knickerbocker lady.[6]
O hither haste, and here devise
   Divine *ballades* before unuttered.
Your poet's eyes *must* recognize
   The side on which your bread is buttered!

Dream not I tempt you to forswear
   One pastoral joy, or rural frolic.   10
I call you to a city where
   The most urbane are most bucolic.[7]
'Twill charm your poet's eyes to find
   Good husbandmen in brokers burly;—
Their stock is ever on their mind;
   To water it they rise up early.

Things you have sung, but ah, not seen—
   Things proper to the age of Saturn—
Shall greet you here; for we have been
   Wrought quaintly, on the Arcadian pattern.   20
Your poet's lips will break in song
   For joy, to see at last appearing

---

[6] i.e., New York woman. The reference is to the early Dutch settlers in New York.

[7] The extended, ironic conceit of the poem is the description of New York in pastoral, "bucolic" terms. "Husbandmen," two lines following, means "farmers" and plays on the double meaning of "stocks" (the stock market and livestock).

The bulls and bears,[8] a peaceful throng,
 While a lamb leads them—to the shearing!

And metamorphoses, of course,
 You'll mark in plenty, *à la* Proteus:[9]
A bear become a little horse—
 Presumably from too much throat-use!
A thousandfold must go untold;
 But, should you miss your farm-yard sunny,   30
And miss your ducks and drakes,[10] behold
 We'll make you ducks and drakes—of money!

Greengrocers here are fairly read.
 And should you set your heart upon them,
We lack not beets—but some are dead,
 While others have policemen on them.
And be the dewfall dear to you,
 Possess your poet's soul in patience!
Your *notes* shall soon be falling dew,—
 Most mystical of transformations!   40

Your heart, dear Poet, surely yields;
 And soon you'll leave your uplands flowery,
Forsaking fresh and bowery fields,
 For "pastures new"—upon the Bowery![11]
You've piped at home, where none could pay,
 Till now, I trust, your wits are riper.
Make no delay, but come this way,
 And pipe for them that pay the piper!

           [1886]

The Cow Pasture

I see the harsh, wind-ridden, eastward hill,
 By the red cattle pastured, blanched with dew;
 The small, mossed hillocks where the clay gets through;
The grey webs woven on milkweed tops at will.

---

[8] Reference to the rise and fall of the stock market.

[9] Proteus is a Greek god who could change shape.

[10] By "ducks and drakes," the speaker is referring both to water fowl and to a game played by skimming stones. The phrase "to play ducks and drakes" also means to behave irresponsibly or to squander one's wealth.

[11] An area in Manhattan.

The sparse, pale grasses flicker, and are still.
    The empty flats yearn seaward. All the view
    Is naked to the horizon's utmost blue;
And the bleak spaces stir me with strange thrill.

Not in perfection dwells the subtler power
    To pierce our mean content, but rather works   10
    Through incompletion, and the need that irks,—
Not in the flower, but effort toward the flower.
    When the want stirs, when the soul's cravings urge,
    The strong earth strengthens, and the clean heavens purge.

                                                          [1893]

The Mowing

This is the voice of high midsummer's heat.
    The rasping vibrant clamour soars and shrills
    O'er all the meadowy range of shadeless hills,
As if a host of giant cicadae beat
The cymbals of their wings with tireless feet,
    Or brazen grasshoppers with triumphing note
    From the long swath proclaimed the fate that smote
The clover and timothy-tops and meadowsweet.

The crying knives glide on; the green swath lies.
    And all noon long the sun, with chemic ray,   10
    Seals up each cordial essence in its cell,
That in the dusky stalls, some winter's day,
    The spirit of June, here prisoned by his spell,
    May cheer the herds with pasture memories.

                                                          [1893]

The Winter Fields

Winds here, and sleet, and frost that bites like steel,
    The low bleak hill rounds under the low sky.
    Naked of flock and fold the fallows lie,
Thin streaked with meagre drift. The gusts reveal
By fits the dim grey snakes of fence, that steal
    Through the white dusk. The hill-foot poplars sigh,
    While storm and death with winter trample by,
And the iron fields ring sharp, and blind lights reel.

Yet in the lonely ridges, wrenched with pain,
    Harsh solitary hillocks, bound and dumb,   10
Grave glebes close-lipped beneath the scourge and chain,

Lurks hid the germ of ecstasy—the sum
Of life that waits on summer, till the rain
Whisper in April and the crocus come.

[1893]

The Flight of the Geese

I hear the low wind wash the softening snow,
The low tide loiter down the shore. The night
Full filled with April forecast, hath no light.
The salt wave on the sedge-flat pulses slow.
Through the hid furrows lisp in murmurous flow
The thaw's shy ministers; and hark! The height
Of heaven grows weird and loud with unseen flight
Of strong hosts prophesying as they go!

High through the drenched and hollow night their wings
Beat northward hard on winter's trail. The sound   10
Of their confused and solemn voices, borne
Athwart the dark to their long Arctic morn,
Comes with a sanction and an awe profound,
A boding of unknown, foreshadowed things.

[1893]

The Poetry of Nature

'The poetry of earth is never dead,' wrote Keats;[12] and, though the statement sounds, at first thought, a dangerously sweeping one, there is no doubt that if he had been called upon to argue the point he would have successfully maintained his thesis. Regarded subjectively, the poetry of earth, or, in other words, the quality which makes for poetry in external nature, is that power in nature which moves us by suggestion, which excites in us emotion, imagination, or poignant association, which plays upon the tense-strings of our sympathies with the fingers of memory or desire. This power may reside not less in a bleak pasture-lot than in a paradisal close of bloom and verdure, not less in a roadside thistle-patch than in a peak that soars into the sunset. It works through sheer beauty or sheer sublimity; but it may work with equal effect through austerity or reticence or limitation or change. It may use the most common scenes, the most familiar facts and forms, as the vehicle of its most penetrating and most illuminating message. It is apt to make the drop of dew on a grass-blade as significant as the starred sphere of the sky.

The poetry of nature, by which I mean this 'poetry of earth' expressed in words, may be roughly divided into two main classes: that which deals with pure

---

[12] From John Keats, "On the Grasshopper and Cricket."

description, and that which treats of nature in some one of its many relations with humanity. The latter class is that which alone was contemplated in Keats's line. It has many subdivisions; it includes much of the greatest poetry that the world has known; and there is little verse of acknowledged mastery that does not depend upon it for some portion of its appeal.

The former class has but a slender claim to recognition as poetry, under any definition of poetry that does not make metrical form the prime essential. The failures of the wisest to enunciate a satisfactory definition of poetry make it almost presumptuous for a critic now to attempt the task; but from an analysis of these failures one may educe something roughly to serve the purpose. To say that *poetry is the metrical expression in words of thought fused in emotion*, is of course incomplete; but it has the advantage of defining. No one can think that anything other than poetry is intended by such a definition; and nothing is excluded that can show a clear claim to admittance. But the poetry of pure description might perhaps not pass without challenge, so faint is the flame of its emotion, so imperfect the fusion of its thought.

It is verse of this sort that is meant by undiscriminating critics when they inveigh against 'nature poetry,' and declare that the only poetry worth man's attention is that which has to do with the heart of man.

Merely descriptive poetry is not very far removed from the work of the reporter and the photographer. Lacking the selective quality of creative art, it is in reality little more than a presentation of some of the raw materials of poetry. It leaves the reader unmoved, because little emotion has gone to its making. Poetry of this sort, at its best, is to be found abundantly in Thomson's 'Seasons.'[13] At less than its best it concerns no one.

Nature becomes significant to man when she is passed through the alembic of his heart. Irrelevant and confusing details having been purged away, what remains is single and vital. It acts either by interpreting, recalling, suggesting, or symbolizing some phase of human feeling. Out of the fusing heat born of this contact comes the perfect line, luminous, unforgettable, with something of mystery in its beauty that eludes analysis. Whatever it be that is brought to the alembic—naked hill, or barren sand-reach, sea or meadow, weed or star,—it comes out charged with a new force, imperishable and active wherever it finds sympathies to vibrate under its currents. [. . .]

When man's heart and the heart of nature had become thus closely involved, the relationship between them and, consequently, the manner of its expression in song became complex almost beyond the possibilities of analysis. Wordsworth's best poetry is to be found in the utterances of the high-priest in nature's temple, interpreting the mysteries. The 'Lines Composed a Few Miles Above Tintern Abbey' are, at first glance, chiefly descriptive; but their actual function is to convey to a restless age, troubled with small cares seen in too close

[13] Reference to Scottish poet James Thomson's (1700–48) long nature poem, *The Seasons*.

perspective, the large, contemplative wisdom which seemed to Wordsworth the message of the scene which moved him.

Keats, his soul aflame with the worship of beauty, was impassioned toward the manifestations of beauty in the world about him; and, at the same time, he used these freely as symbols to express other aspects of the same compelling spirit. [. . .]

The main purpose of these brief suggestions is to call attention to the fact that nature-poetry is not mere description of landscape in metrical form, but the expression of one or another of many vital relationships between external nature and 'the deep heart of man.' It may touch the subtlest chords of human emotion and human imagination not less masterfully than the verse which sets out to be a direct transcript from life. The most inaccessible truths are apt to be reached by indirection. The divinest mysteries of beauty are not possessed exclusively by the eye that loves, or by the lips of a child, but are also manifested in some bird-song's unforgotten cadence, some flower whose perfection pierces the heart, some ineffable hue of sunset or sunrise that makes the spirit cry out for it knows not what. And whosoever follows the inexplicable lure of beauty, in colour, form, sound, perfume, or any other manifestation,—reaching out to it as perhaps a message from some unfathomable past, or a premonition of the future,—knows that the mystic signal beckons nowhere more imperiously than from the heights of nature-poetry.

[1897]

The Animal Story[14]

Alike in matter and in method, the animal story, as we have it to-day, may be regarded as a culmination. The animal story, of course, in one form or another, is as old as the beginnings of literature. Perhaps the most engrossing part in the life-drama of primitive man was that played by the beasts which he hunted, and by those which hunted him. They pressed incessantly upon his perceptions. They furnished both material and impulse for his first gropings toward pictorial art. When he acquired the kindred art of telling a story, they supplied his earliest themes; and they suggested the hieroglyphs by means of which, on carved bone or painted rock, he first gave his narrative a form to outlast the spoken breath. We may not unreasonably infer that the first animal story—the remote but authentic ancestor of "Mowgli" and "Lobo" and " Krag"[15] —was a story of some successful hunt, when success meant life to the starving family; or some desperate escape, when the truth of the narrative was attested, to the hearers squatted trembling about their fire, by the sniffings of the baffled bear or tiger at the rock-barred

[14] This essay formed the introduction to Roberts's 1902 story collection, *The Kindred of the Wild*. In it, he defines the characteristics of the modern animal story, but the introduction was also his defence against attacks on his stories for being too anthropomorphic.

[15] Reference to the orphaned boy, Mowgli, in Rudyard Kipling's *Jungle Book* stories and to two animal characters, "Lobo" (a wolf) and "Krag" (a ram), from stories by Ernest Thompson Seton (1860–1946).

mouth of the cave. Such first animal stories had at least one merit of prime literary importance. They were convincing. [. . .]

With the spread of freedom and the broadening out of all intellectual interests which characterise these modern days, the lower kindreds began to regain their old place in the concern of man. The revival of interest in the animals found literary expression (to classify roughly) in two forms, which necessarily overlap each other now and then, viz., the story of adventure and the anecdote of observation. Hunting as a recreation, pursued with zest from pole to tropics by restless seekers after the new, supplied a species of narrative singularly akin to what the first animal stories must have been,—narratives of desperate encounter, strange peril, and hairbreadth escape. Such hunters' stories and travellers' tales are rarely conspicuous for the exactitude of their observation; but that was not the quality at first demanded of them by fireside readers. The attention of the writer was focussed, not on the peculiarities or the emotions of the beast protagonist in each fierce, brief drama, but upon the thrill of the action, the final triumph of the human actor. The inevitable tendency of these stories of adventure with beasts was to awaken interest in animals, and to excite a desire for exact knowledge of their traits and habits. [. . .]

Altogether admirable and necessary as was this development at large, another, of richer or at least more spiritual significance, was going on at home. Folk who loved their animal comrades—their dogs, horses, cats, parrots, elephants—were observing, with the wonder and interest of discoverers, the astonishing fashion in which the mere instincts of these so-called irrational creatures were able to simulate the operations of reason. The results of this observation were written down, till "anecdotes of animals" came to form a not inconsiderable body of literature. The drift of all these data was overwhelmingly toward one conclusion. The mental processes of the animals observed were seen to be far more complex than the observers had supposed. Where instinct was called in to account for the elaborate ingenuity with which a dog would plan and accomplish the outwitting of a rival, or the nice judgment with which an elephant, with no nest-building ancestors behind him to instruct his brain, would choose and adjust the teak-logs which he was set to pile, it began to seem as if that faithful faculty was being overworked. To explain yet other cases, which no accepted theory seemed to fit, coincidence was invoked, till that rare and elusive phenomenon threatened to become as customary as buttercups. But when instinct and coincidence had done all that could be asked of them, there remained a great unaccounted-for body of facts; and men were forced at last to accept the proposition that, within their varying limitations, animals can and do reason. As far, at least, as the mental intelligence is concerned, the gulf dividing the lowest of the human species from the highest of the animals has in these latter days been reduced to a very narrow psychological fissure.

Whether avowedly or not, it is with the psychology of animal life that the representative animal stories of to-day are first of all concerned. Looking deep into the eyes of certain of the four-footed kindred, we have been startled to see therein a something, before unrecognised, that answered to our inner and intellectual, if not spiritual selves. We have suddenly attained a new and clearer vision. We have come face to face with personality, where we were blindly wont to predicate mere instinct and automatism. It is as if one should step carelessly out of one's back door, and marvel to see unrolling before his new-awakened eyes the peaks and seas and misty valleys of an unknown world. Our chief writers of animal stories at the present day may be regarded as explorers of this unknown world, absorbed in charting its topography. They work, indeed, upon a substantial foundation of known facts. They are minutely scrupulous as to their natural history, and assiduous contributors to that science. But above all are they diligent in their search for the motive beneath the action. Their care is to catch the varying, elusive personalities which dwell back of the luminous brain windows of the dog, the horse, the deer, or wrap themselves in reserve behind the inscrutable eyes of all the cats, or sit aloof in the gaze of the hawk and the eagle. The animal story at its highest point of development is a psychological romance constructed on a framework of natural science.

The real psychology of the animals, so far as we are able to grope our way toward it by deduction and induction combined, is a very different thing from the psychology of certain stories of animals which paved the way for the present vogue. Of these, such books as "Beautiful Joe" and "Black Beauty"[16] are deservedly conspicuous examples. It is no detraction from the merit of these books, which have done great service in awakening a sympathetic understanding of the animals and sharpening our sense of kinship with all that breathe, to say that their psychology is human. Their animal characters think and feel as human beings would think and feel under like conditions. This marks the stage which these works occupy in the development of the animal story.

The next stage must be regarded as, in literature, a climax indeed, but not the climax in this genre. I refer to the "Mowgli" stories of Mr. Kipling. In these tales the animals are frankly humanised. Their individualisation is distinctly human, as are also their mental and emotional processes, and their highly elaborate powers of expression. Their notions are complex; whereas the motives of real animals, so far as we have hitherto been able to judge them, seem to be essentially simple, in the sense that the motive dominant at a given moment quite obliterates, for the time, all secondary motives. Their reasoning powers and their constructive imagination are far beyond anything which present knowledge justifies us in ascribing to the inarticulate kindreds. To say this is in no way to depreciate such work, but merely to classify it. There are stories being written now which, for interest and artistic value, are not to be mentioned in the same breath with the "Mowgli" tales, but which nevertheless occupy a more advanced stage in the evolution of this genre.

[16] *Beautiful Joe* (1894) is a novel by the Nova Scotia author Marshall Saunders (1861–1947), a contemporary of Roberts. The story is narrated by a dog, Joe, and sought to enlist the same sympathies for animals that had earlier been aroused by Anna Sewell's novel *Black Beauty* (1877).

It seems to me fairly safe to say that this evolution is not likely to go beyond the point to which it has been carried to-day. In such a story, for instance, as that of "Krag, the Kootenay Ram," by Mr. Ernest Seton, the interest centres about the personality, individuality, mentality, of an animal, as well as its purely physical characteristics. The field of animal psychology so admirably opened is an inexhaustible world of wonder. Sympathetic exploration may advance its boundaries to a degree of which we hardly dare to dream; but such expansion cannot be called evolution. There would seem to be no further evolution possible, unless based upon a hypothesis that animals have souls. As souls are apt to elude exact observation, to forecast any such development would seem to be at best merely fanciful. [. . .]

[1902]

When Twilight Falls on the Stump Lots

The wet, chill first of the spring, its blackness made tender by the lilac wash of the afterglow, lay upon the high, open stretches of the stump lots. The winter-whitened stumps, the sparse patches of juniper and bay just budding, the rough-mossed hillocks, the harsh boulders here and there up-thrusting from the soil, the swampy hollows wherein a coarse grass began to show green, all seemed anointed, as it were, to an ecstasy of peace by the chrism[17] of that paradisal colour. Against the lucid immensity of the April sky the thin tops of five or six soaring ram-pikes aspired like violet flames. Along the skirts of the stump lots a fir wood reared a ragged-crested wall of black against the red amber of the horizon.

Late that afternoon, beside a juniper thicket not far from the centre of the stump lots, a young black and white cow had given birth to her first calf. The little animal had been licked assiduously by the mother's caressing tongue till its colour began to show of a rich dark red. Now it had struggled to its feet, and, with its disproportionately long, thick legs braced wide apart, was beginning to nurse. Its blunt wet muzzle and thick lips tugged eagerly, but somewhat blunderingly as yet, at the unaccustomed teats; and its tail lifted, twitching with delight, as the first warm streams of mother milk went down its throat. It was a pathetically awkward, unlovely little figure, not yet advanced to that youngling winsomeness which is the heritage, to some degree and at some period, of the infancy of all the kindreds that breathe upon the earth. But to the young mother's eyes it was the most beautiful of things. With her head twisted far around, she nosed and licked its heaving flanks as it nursed; and between deep, ecstatic breathings she uttered in her throat low murmurs, unspeakably tender, of encouragement and caress. The delicate but pervading flood of sunset colour had the effect of blending the ruddy-hued calf into the tones of the landscape; but the cow's insistent

[17] Sacramental oil.

blotches of black and white stood out sharply, refusing to harmonise. The drench of violet light was of no avail to soften their staring contrasts. They made her vividly conspicuous across the whole breadth of the stump lots, to eyes that watched her from the forest coverts.

The eyes that watched her—long, fixedly, hungrily—were small and red. They belonged to a lank she-bear, whose gaunt flanks and rusty coat proclaimed a season of famine in the wilderness. She could not see the calf, which was hidden by a hillock and some juniper scrub; but its presence was very legibly conveyed to her by the mother's solicitous watchfulness. After a motionless scrutiny from behind the screen of fir branches, the lean bear stole noiselessly forth from the shadows into the great wash of violet light. Step by step, and very slowly, with the patience that endures because confident of its object, she crept toward that oasis of mothering joy in the vast emptiness of the stump lots. Now crouching, now crawling, turning to this side and to that, taking advantage of every hollow, every thicket, every hillock, every aggressive stump, her craft succeeded in eluding even the wild and menacing watchfulness of the young mother's eyes.

The spring had been a trying one for the lank she-bear. Her den, in a dry tract of hemlock wood some furlongs back from the stump lots, was a snug little cave under the uprooted base of a lone pine, which had somehow grown up among the alien hemlocks only to draw down upon itself at last, by its superior height, the fury of a passing hurricane. The winter had contributed but scanty snowfall to cover the bear in her sleep; and the March thaws, unseasonably early and ardent, had called her forth to activity weeks too soon. Then frosts had come with belated severity, sealing away the budding tubers, which are the bear's chief dependence for spring diet; and worst of all, a long stretch of intervale meadow by the neighbouring river, which had once been rich in ground-nuts, had been ploughed up the previous spring and subjected to the producing of oats and corn. When she was feeling the pinch of meagre rations, and when the fat which a liberal autumn of blueberries had laid up about her ribs was getting as shrunken as the last snow in the thickets, she gave birth to two hairless and hungry little cubs. They were very blind, and ridiculously small to be born of so big a mother; and having so much growth to make during the next few months, their appetites were immeasurable. They tumbled, and squealed, and tugged at their mother's teats, and grew astonishingly, and made huge haste to cover their bodies with fur of a soft and silken black; and all this vitality of theirs made a strenuous demand upon their mother's milk. There were no more bee-trees left in the neighbourhood. The long wanderings which she was forced to take in her search for roots and tubers were in themselves a drain upon her nursing powers. At last, reluctant though she was to attract the hostile notice of the settlement, she found herself forced to hunt on the borders of the sheep pastures. Before all else in life was it important to her that these two tumbling little ones in the den should not go hungry. Their eyes were open now—small and dark and whimsical, their ears quaintly large and inquiring for their roguish little faces. Had she not been driven by the unkind season to so much hunting and foraging, she would have passed near all her time rapturously in the den under the pine root, fondling those two soft miracles of her world.

With the killing of three lambs—at widely scattered points, so as to mislead retaliation—things grew a little easier for the harassed bear; and presently she grew bolder in tampering with the creatures under man's protection. With one swift, secret blow of her mighty paw she struck down a young ewe which had strayed within reach of her hiding-place. Dragging her prey deep into the woods, she fared well upon it for some days, and was happy with her growing cubs. It was just when she had begun to feel the fasting which came upon the exhaustion of this store that, in a hungry hour, she sighted the conspicuous markings of the black and white cow.

It is altogether unusual for the black bear of the eastern woods to attack any quarry so large as a cow, unless under the spur of fierce hunger or fierce rage. The she-bear was powerful beyond her fellows. She had the strongest possible incentive to bold hunting, and she had lately grown confident beyond her wont. Nevertheless, when she began her careful stalking of this big game which she coveted, she had no definite intention of forcing a battle with the cow. She had observed that cows, accustomed to the protection of man, would at times leave their calves asleep and stray off some distance in their pasturing. She had even seen calves left all by themselves in a field, from morning till night, and had wondered at such negligence in their mothers. Now she had a confident idea that sooner or later the calf would lie down to sleep, and the young mother roam a little wide in search of the scant young grass. Very softly, very self-effacingly, she crept nearer step by step, following up the wind, till at last, undiscovered, she was crouching behind a thick patch of juniper, on the slope of a little hollow not ten paces distant from the cow and the calf.

By this time the tender violet light was fading to a grayness over hillock and hollow; and with the deepening of the twilight the faint breeze, which had been breathing from the northward, shifted suddenly and came in slow, warm pulsations out of the south. At the same time the calf, having nursed sufficiently, and feeling his baby legs tired of the weight they had not yet learned to carry, laid himself down. On this the cow shifted her position. She turned half round, and lifted her head high. As she did so a scent of peril was borne in upon her fine nostrils. She recognised it instantly. With a snort of anger she sniffed again; then stamped a challenge with her fore hoofs, and levelled the lance-points of her horns toward the menace. The next moment her eyes, made keen by the fear of love, detected the black outline of the bear's head through the coarse screen of the juniper. Without a second's hesitation, she flung up her tail, gave a short bellow, and charged.

The moment she saw herself detected, the bear rose upon her hindquarters; nevertheless she was in a measure surprised by the sudden blind fury of the attack. Nimbly she swerved to avoid it, aiming at the same time a stroke with her mighty forearm, which, if it had found its mark, would have smashed her adversary's neck. But as she struck out, in the act of shifting her position, a depression of the ground threw her off her balance. The next instant one sharp horn caught her slantingly in the flank, ripping its way upward and inward, while the mad impact threw her upon her back.

Grappling, she had her assailant's head and shoulders in a trap, and her gigantic claws cut through the flesh and sinew like knives; but at the desperate disadvantage of her position she could inflict no disabling blow. The cow, on the other hand, though mutilated and streaming with blood, kept pounding with her whole massive weight, and with short tremendous shocks crushing the breath from her foe's ribs.

Presently, wrenching herself free, the cow drew off for another battering charge; and as she did so the bear hurled herself violently down the slope, and gained her feet behind a dense thicket of bay shrub. The cow, with one eye blinded and the other obscured by blood, glared around for her in vain, then, in a panic of mother terror, plunged back to her calf.

Snatching at the respite, the bear crouched down, craving that invisibility which is the most faithful shield of the furtive kindred. Painfully, and leaving a drenched red trail behind her, she crept off from the disastrous neighbourhood. Soon the deepening twilight sheltered her. But she could not make haste; and she knew that death was close upon her.

Once within the woods, she struggled straight toward the den that held her young. She hungered to die licking them. But destiny is as implacable as iron to the wilderness people, and even this was denied her. Just a half score of paces from the lair in the pine root, her hour descended upon her. There was a sudden redder and fuller gush upon the trail; the last light of longing faded out of her eyes; and she lay down upon her side.

The merry little cubs within the den were beginning to expect her, and getting restless. As the night wore on, and no mother came, they ceased to be merry. By morning they were shivering with hunger and desolate fear. But the doom of the ancient wood was less harsh than its wont, and spared them some days of starving anguish; for about noon a pair of foxes discovered the dead mother, astutely estimated the situation, and then, with the boldness of good appetite, made their way into the unguarded den.

As for the red calf, its fortune was ordinary. Its mother, for all her wounds, was able to nurse and cherish it through the night; and with morning came a searcher from the farm and took it, with the bleeding mother, safely back to the settlement. There it was tended and fattened, and within a few weeks found its way to the cool marble slabs of a city market.

[1902]

In his day, Bliss Carman was the most popular of the Confederation Poets. Born in Fredericton, New Brunswick, he, like his cousin Charles G.D. Roberts, attended the University of New Brunswick, from which he graduated with a degree in classics in 1881. Carman's career was marked by indecisiveness and unrealized ambition. He attempted university study in England, but soon abandoned it. In 1886, he enrolled in Harvard University, but again didn't complete a degree. His various dreams of becoming a doctor, lawyer, or university lecturer gradually evaporated. However, the Harvard experience was a formative one, because it was there that Carman befriended Richard Hovey, a fellow poet and Bohemian. Together, the two poets wrote the "Vagabondia" series, a collection of four volumes of poetry (the fourth written by Carman alone), published between 1894 and 1912, which were to outsell any of Carman's other works.

The poems present a philosophy of life marked by an exuberant celebration of a carefree and unfettered existence in the outdoors. Carman is still known as the "Poet of Vagabondia," even though these works are not the most widely cited of his poems today. Ironically, Carman had the vagabond's life thrust upon him after his father's and mother's deaths in 1885 and 1886. Before this, Carman had been an intensely shy man who was unusually attached to his parents; with their death, he was forced into an unsettled life marked by restlessness, wandering, and financial duress. Throughout his life, he was given to bouts of melancholy and loneliness.

Carman's finest poems are those that voice this melancholic note, such as one finds in his early collections of poetry, *Low Tide on Grand Pré* (1893), *Behind the Arras* (1895), and *Ballads of Lost Haven* (1897). Carman was masterful at using hypnotic rhythms and cadences to conjure emotional effects, a technique that is evident in the haunting poems "Low Tide on Grand Pré" and "The Eavesdropper." From 1890 to 1892, he became the literary editor of the *Independent* in New York, the longest position of employment he ever held. Thereafter, Carman spent much of his time seeking ways to earn money. He did so through intermittent journalism, writing, and reading tours. However, he never settled into a permanent home. Following the death of his parents, when Carman left Canada for the United States, he would spend summers in Windsor, Nova Scotia, with his cousin Roberts, and the winters moving between the houses of various friends. In 1896, he met a Connecticut couple, Morris and Mary King, and settled in with them. It was Mary King who encouraged Carman's interest in the philosophy of unitrinianism—the doctrine that mind, body, and spirit are integrally linked and that great art must appeal to all three—which influenced Carman's poetry thereafter.

The First World War had an immense impact on Carman, as it had on many of his generation. He felt that he had witnessed the end of an era. Carman became disillusioned about the value of poetry in the face of the gravity of the time. His words in a letter to R.H. Hathaway in 1917 are prescient for his sense of the passing from one literary moment into another yet to come: "The greater and insistent problems of the tremendous times obliterate all other interests. Perhaps when the war is over, and we begin to arrange our ideals of life on a new basis, we shall have some fine poetry again. But I feel that when that time arrives, only new men . . . will be entitled to take part in the parliament of art. The Victorian days belong to history." In effect, Carman was anticipating the modernist movement of the post-war period.

The relationship between Carman's life and work is curiously antithetical. He was prone to melancholy, but his poetry is often marked by optimism. He praised the life of the perpetual vagabond, yet spent much of his life seeking a home. While Carman's poetry was immensely popular in his day, especially in the United States and England, it is less so today. Indeed, he was one of the most frequently anthologized of the Confederation Poets until the 1960s. The decline in his popularity may be due, in part, to the highly symbolist nature of his poetry, as is evident in the allegorical but esoteric nature of poems such as "The Eavesdropper" or "The Night Express." The latter poem uses the ambivalent symbol of a thundering passenger train, a frequent image in the literary works of the industrial era (see, by comparison, Lampman's "The Railway Station"), as a figure for the inexorable momentum of human destiny. His most celebrated poem, "Low Tide on Grand Pré," captures both sides of his character: it evokes the melancholy associated with the passage of youth, yet conjures a sense of mystical timelessness undergirding the transient. The imagery of the flood tide, particularly the expanse of the Bay of Fundy mudflats, expertly captures the shifts in the speaker's emotions as he mourns the passage of time and the woman he has lost. According to Canadian literary critic Desmond Pacey, "'Grand Pré' . . . is the most nearly perfect poem to come out of Canada in the nineteenth century."

Low Tide on Grand Pré[1]

The sun goes down, and over all
    These barren reaches by the tide
Such unelusive glories fall,
    I almost dream they yet will bide
    Until the coming of the tide.

And yet I know that not for us,
    By any ecstasy of dream,
He lingers to keep luminous
    A little while the grievous stream,
    Which frets, uncomforted of dream—   10

[1] An area in the Minas Basin in Nova Scotia where the Acadian people settled in the seventeenth century. In 1755, during the Seven Years War, the Acadians were expelled from the region by the British.

A grievous stream, that to and fro
    Athrough the fields of Acadie
Goes wandering, as if to know
    Why one beloved face should be
    So long from home and Acadie.

Was it a year or lives ago
    We took the grasses in our hands,
And caught the summer flying low
    Over the waving meadow lands,
    And held it there between our hands?   20

The while the river at our feet—
    A drowsy inland meadow stream—
At set of sun the after-heat
    Made running gold, and in the gleam
    We freed our birch upon the stream.

There down along the elms at dusk
    We lifted dripping blade to drift,
Through twilight scented fine like musk,
    Where night and gloom awhile uplift,
    Nor sunder soul and soul adrift.   30

And that we took into our hands
    Spirit of life or subtler thing—
Breathed on us there, and loosed the bands
    Of death, and taught us, whispering,
    The secret of some wonder-thing.

Then all your face grew light, and seemed
    To hold the shadow of the sun;
The evening faltered, and I deemed
    That time was ripe, and years had done
    Their wheeling underneath the sun.   40

So all desire and all regret,
    And fear and memory, were naught;
One to remember or forget
    The keen delight our hands had caught;
    Morrow and yesterday were naught.

The night has fallen, and the tide . . .
    Now and again comes drifting home,
Across these aching barrens wide,
    A sigh like driven wind or foam:
    In grief the flood is bursting home.   50

[1893]

The Eavesdropper

In a still room at hush of dawn,
    My Love and I lay side by side
And heard the roaming forest wind
    Stir in the paling autumn-tide.

I watched her earth-brown eyes grow glad
    Because the round day was so fair;
While memories of reluctant night
    Lurked in the blue dusk of her hair.

Outside, a yellow maple tree,
    Shifting upon the silvery blue 10
With tiny multitudinous sound,
    Rustled to let the sunlight through.

The livelong day the elvish leaves
    Danced with their shadows on the floor;
And the lost children of the wind
    Went straying homeward by our door.

And all the swarthy afternoon
    We watched the great deliberate sun
Walk through the crimsoned hazy world,
    Counting his hilltops one by one. 20

Then as the purple twilight came
    And touched the vines along our eaves,
Another Shadow stood without
    And gloomed the dancing of the leaves.

The silence fell on my Love's lips;
    Her great brown eyes were veiled and sad
With pondering some maze of dream,
    Though all the splendid year was glad.

Restless and vague as a gray wind
    Her heart had grown, she knew not why. 30
But hurrying to the open door,
    Against the verge of western sky

I saw retreating on the hills,
    Looming and sinister and black,
The stealthy figure swift and huge
    Of One who strode and looked not back.

[1893]

Winter

When winter comes along the river line
And Earth has put away her green attire,
With all the pomp of her autumnal pride,
The world is made a sanctuary old,
Where Gothic trees uphold the arch of gray,
And gaunt stone fences on the ridge's crest
Stand like carved screens before a crimson shrine,
Showing the sunset glory through the chinks.
There, like a nun with frosty breath, the soul,
Uplift in adoration, sees the world   10
Transfigured to a temple of her Lord;
While down the soft blue-shadowed aisles of snow
Night, like a sacristan[2] with silent step,
Passes to light the tapers of the stars.

[1916]

Wild Geese

To-night with snow in the November air,
Over the roof I heard that startling cry
Passing along the highway of the dark—
The Wild Geese going South. Confused commands
As of a column on the march rang out
Clamorous and sharp against the frosty air.
And with an answering tumult in my heart
I too went hurrying out into the night
Was it from some deep immemorial past
I learned those summoning signals and alarms,   10
And still must answer to my brothers' call?
I knew the darkling hope that bade them rise
From Northern lakes, and with courageous hearts
Adventure forth on their uncharted quest.

[1929]

[2] A person in charge of a church's sacred objects.

SARA JEANNETTE DUNCAN ■ (1861–1922)

Sara Jeannette Duncan was born into the era of the "New Woman" in the late nineteenth century, when women across England and North America were radically rethinking their roles in society and arguing that they should be granted the same privileges as men, including access to education, the pursuit of a career, engagement in athletic activities, and the right to vote. There were heated debates about these issues in the nineteenth century, and Duncan, who held firmly feminist views and was determined to earn her living as a journalist, was, with fellow Canadian Agnes Maule Machar, fully immersed in these debates. In her 12 November 1886 article for the Toronto *Globe*, she was outspoken about her vision of women's prospects: "Careers, if possible, and independence anyway, we must all have, as musicians, artists, writers, teachers, lawyers, doctors, ministers, or something."

Duncan was born in Brantford, Ontario (then Canada West), to a prosperous dry-goods and furniture dealer. She and Pauline Johnson moved in many of the same circles in Brantford. Following the unveiling of the Joseph Brant memorial in 1886, Duncan interviewed Johnson for the *Globe*. Like Johnson, Duncan also modified her name to make it more "exotic": she was christened Sarah Janet but adopted "Sara Jeannette" in 1886 as the byline for her early published work. In 1882, she completed teacher training but, like Charles G.D. Roberts and Archibald Lampman, had little enthusiasm for the profession and instead pursued a career in journalism. It was a difficult undertaking for a woman in her day, when many women held menial jobs in the printing industry but were rarely given positions as major reporters or editors. In 1884 she convinced a series of newspapers to publish her reports of the New Orleans World's Fair; her success at this venture led to her becoming a regular contributor to the *Washington Post* in 1885 and 1886. In July 1886, Duncan left Washington to become the first woman to be employed full-time by the Toronto *Globe*, where she published the "Woman's World" column under the name "Garth Grafton." By September, she was also writing a regular column, "Saunterings," for

Goldwin Smith's influential Toronto paper, *The Week*.

In her newspaper article "How an American Girl Became a Journalist," Duncan invented a fictionalized autobiographical character, Margery Blunt, whose "Secret Purpose was to distinguish herself in literature." These words are easily applicable to Duncan, who was single-minded in her pursuit of a writing career at a time when the prospects for serious women journalists were scarce. Not content to be relegated to the subject matter of conventional "women's pages," Duncan wrote outspoken and courageous commentaries on such issues as women's rights, the suffrage movement, unfair copyright legislation, universities, national identity, American imperialism, and the status of Canadian literature. Many of Duncan's newspaper articles were audacious, as she was not afraid to put her feminist and literary opinions in print. Her cutting statements about the dearth of Canadian literary culture, or her comments about Canadian nationality, are impressive for their perspicacity. This is true of her many pieces written for the *Globe* and *The Week*. "We are still an eminently unliterary people," she wrote in frustration in the 30 September 1886 issue of *The Week*. "The Province of Ontario is one great camp of the Philistines." Her critique of the Canadian colonial mentality, which she identified by its attitude of complacency, inertia, and parochialism, echoes the satirical depictions of the Nova Scotia "Bluenoses" published by Thomas Chandler Haliburton fifty years earlier. Much work needed to be done, she maintained, to shake Canadians out of their excessive humility and intellectual torpor.

Duncan's political acumen and social incisiveness set her apart from many of her peers. At times, her writings are so ironic that it is difficult to know how to read them. Her 17 November 1886 article for the *Globe* on the "advantages" of being a modern woman, included here, is a parodic piece which appears to celebrate the small gains achieved by the New Woman of the period while underscoring the futility of women's access to higher education when their prospects remain so curtailed by marriage, domesticity, and the inability to vote. The piece applauds the educational reforms that have been extended to women, thus echoing Machar's account in "The New Ideal of Womanhood" (1879), and anticipates Lucy Maud Montgomery's description, in *Anne of Green Gables* (1908), of Anne's education under the reformist school teacher Miss Stacy, whose program includes nature studies and physical fitness. Duncan's message is so subtly couched in this piece that it is easy to miss the irony that underlies the article, an approach that is comparable to the arch satire of a piece like Jonathan Swift's "A Modest Proposal." The conclusion of the article hints at the fierce opposition to the "New Women" that had been expressed by so many prominent Canadian male figures, including Goldwin Smith and, later, Stephen Leacock, who decried what they saw to be the increasing "feminization" of the age. Duncan's acerbic and ironizing wit characterizes much of her newspaper reporting and fiction.

By 1887, Duncan had moved to Montreal to become a columnist for the *Star*. The following year she became the newspaper's parliamentary correspondent in Ottawa, and was one of only two women in the male-dominated press gallery. In the fall of 1888, she undertook a trip around the world with fellow journalist Lily Lewis, which formed the basis of a series of travel articles for the Montreal *Star*. This journey, which began as a westward trek across Canada aboard the recently completed CPR, followed the "round the world" route promoted by

much of the Canadian Pacific advertising and propaganda (see Figure III-10), including a voyage across the Pacific to Japan, India, and Egypt. These pieces were later revised into fictionalized form and published as her first, and enormously successful, book, *A Social Departure: How Orthodocia and I Went Round the World by Ourselves* (1890). The title of the book is ironic, since it was hardly "orthodox" for a woman of the period to be undertaking such a journey, and the two protagonists of the book (one Canadian, one British) are representative of the daring "New Woman" of the age, riding on the cowcatchers of trains and landing themselves in various unlikely adventures. For all her social and political shrewdness, however, Duncan was not above the racism of her day, and her portrayals of Aboriginal and Asian peoples are often stereotyped and pejorative in this work.

It was during the Indian portion of the trip that Duncan met her future husband, Everard Cotes, whom she married in 1890. After this, Duncan lived in India from 1890 to 1915. Many of her works have India as their setting, including *The Simple Adventures of a Memsahib* (1893), *Set in Authority* (1906), and the short story collection *The Pool in the Desert* (1903). During this time, Duncan made periodic trips to Canada, and became increasingly interested in the distinctions between national types, especially between Americans, Canadians, and the British. She explored this theme in a number of humorous novels from this period, including *An American Girl in London* (1891), *A Voyage of Consolation* (1898), and *Those Delightful Americans* (1902). In a 1905 letter to literary critic Archibald MacMechan, Duncan expressed her "conviction of the individuality of the Canadian type" and yearned to return to Canada in order to "work at it from closer range." This she was able to do in two subsequent novels. One of these, *Cousin Cinderella* (1908), follows the amusing experiences of an unmarried Canadian girl who is learning the ways of London society. *The Imperialist* (1904), which today many critics consider Duncan's best novel, is set in the fictional town of Elgin, Ontario, based on Duncan's hometown of Brantford. The novel's detailed exploration of the Canadian political situation at the end of the nineteenth century, as well as its depiction of its heroine, Advena Murchison, as an intellectual "New Woman" of the era, led to the novel's lukewarm reception by many reviewers who were scornful of its Canadian setting and the female author's interest in politics. "[A] woman attempting politics must be judged leniently," stated a patronizing review in the *Canadian Magazine* in April 1904.

In her writings on Canadian culture, Duncan was well aware of the threat of American capitalism, particularly when it affected the distribution of books and periodicals in Canada, for cheap American editions were inundating the market and contributing to a form of "cultural imperialism" (precisely the same complaint Canadians would raise in the 1960s and '70s—see, for example, the excerpts from Margaret Atwood's *Survival* [1972], included in Volume II of this anthology). It was difficult for Canadian publishers and authors to compete, given the higher production costs and smaller audience. Duncan addresses this concern in her 7 July 1887 piece from *The Week*, "American Influence on Canadian Thought" (which can be paired with Thomas D'Arcy McGee's "Protection for Canadian Literature"), but it also arises in her fictional works, as when Lorne Murchison, in *The Imperialist*, proclaims that "the armies of the south have already crossed the border" in the form of "American enterprise [and] American capital." Nevertheless, Duncan also realized that Canadians needed to be part of a global culture, which means that, like Charles G.D. Roberts and other prominent literary thinkers of her day, she was not advocating a form of Canadian isolationism. As she put it in January 1886, "A literature should have its roots in the national character and within national limits. . . . But to give it growth, variety and comprehensive character, it has to be fed from without." Even while living in India, Duncan remained actively conversant in world politics and wrote frequent pieces for the *Indian Daily News*. She eventually moved to England in 1915, where she died following a bout of pneumonia on 22 July 1922. Over the course of her career, she wrote more than twenty novels, and it is primarily as a novelist that she is celebrated today; yet Duncan's newspaper writings reveal her to be one of the most astute political and social commentators of her era.

Woman's World

As you are probably well aware, my sisters, to-morrow is Thanksgiving Day.[1] It is not so very long since we imported the laudable custom of our American cousins, but quite long enough for one of its chief features to have taken such strong hold upon our affections as to make the approach of the occasion very evident to every housekeeper. Thanksgiving turkey, with all that doth accompany or flow therefrom, may be said to have become an incorporated fact in

[1] Beginning in the late 1870s, Thanksgiving Day was celebrated in November in Canada, comparable to that in the United States. It was not moved to its present date in October until 1908.

Canadian domesticity. We have not gone the length of compounding mince meat out of its due season, as the New Englanders do, nor have we taken the typical Thanksgiving pumpkin pie into our affections to any great extent as yet, but we have shown remarkable unanimity in adopting the dinner extraordinary as an indispensable feature of all true gratitude. It is both stimulative and illustrative and we have not been slow to appreciate these advantages.

So by your plenished larder, and your hot cheeks, and your floury apron, and the arrival of half a score of friends and relations, you know very well that to-morrow you will be called upon to give thanks with the rest of the people of this Dominion of Canada for all your manifold and multiplied mercies, national, social, family, civil, and religious. I have no doubt you will lump them. People always do, although the particularity with which they enumerate their tribulations is most painstaking. This department has frequently been given over to such enumeration, but will seize the present propitious occasion to make a few specifications of the other sort.

To begin at the very beginning your start in the world was made under auspices for which you would have been grateful doubtless, at the time, if you had been able to form any idea of the woes you escaped. You were not constantly jig-trotted on your nurse's knee to induce repose of mind and body. You were not swathed in uncounted yards of baby linen, which would have utterly repressed your reasonable and infantile desire to kick, and left your natural spirits no outlet but your lungs. You were not made acquainted with distilled liquor and the necessity of prohibition as a preventive of cruelty to infants, at the early age of three days. You were not fed until your small organs of deglutition and digestion utterly rebelled and your whole wretched little internal structure arose in a colicky protest. You were not put to sleep by the assistance of laudanum and Mrs. Winslow,[2] and occasionally, when you wept for it, you were given a mouthful of water! All of which was reversed in the experience of the babies of the last generation.

Froebel hadn't influenced modern educational ideas as he did later when you were a very small girl, and there were no kindergartens.[3] But your father and mother knew that romping and fresh air were important factors in your development, and while you may have learned your alphabet under the old system, you were not compelled to sit in the house and sew samplers and keep your petticoats clean, your slippers in shape, and your hair in curl, because you were a little girl. You climbed apple trees and fences and tore your clothes and raced and rioted and had as generally good and uproarious a time as your brothers had. Perhaps you even played hockey with them—I did, with crooked sticks and wrinkled horse-chestnuts, in intervals of taffy-making, over a big kitchen floor. And all this helped to lay the foundation for your excellent constitution which meets the wear and tear of the world's demand upon it so well to-day.

---

[2] A reference to "Mrs. Winslow's Soothing Syrup," a common opiate sold for teething babies.

[3] Friedrich Wilhem August Froebel (1782–1852) founded the modern education system for children, including the institution of early "play" education known as kindergarten.

But the small creatures in pinafores of your mother's day were served not so.

When you went to school you were permitted to learn Latin if you wanted to, and to revel in the higher mathematics if you were so inclined. You had the fun of beating your cousin Tom at trigonometry, and topping the class in an examination in Greek prose. Science invited you, and you ruined three aprons, nearly deprived yourself of your right thumb, and burst twenty-seven glass tubes in learning how to make a certain acid with a most inexpressible smell. True, you couldn't make it now, even if you wanted to, and you don't remember much of your chemical research, and you couldn't analyze your own baking powder,[4] nevertheless one Julia Jones who researched at the same time you did now occupies an excellent position in a ladies' college by virtue of the opportunity. Then you could have matriculated if you had so decided, and if it had not been for Jack no doubt you would have been to-day a graduate of a university of which he is now the president, and faculty, and Senate combined.

Which educational advantages were not known to the maidens of the last generation.

Jack was not the first who attempted to interfere with your university career by several people. But the possibility of other than domestic channels for your womanly activity made you critical and careful. So you said "No" till you couldn't help "Yes," which is a course so admirable that it is here held up for emulation by every young woman whose eyes rest upon your causes for thanksgiving. You could afford to wait till Jack came or to dispense with a matrimonial prospect altogether, although Jack was an incident you rather hoped for and have never regretted.

But in the olden time the girl who refused a man who was willing and able to support her in comfort assumed a responsibility for her future that is rather alarming to think of.

And now that you and Jack are housekeeping, haven't you got a patent cradle, and an improved kitchen range, and hot and cold water, and stationary wash tubs, and a magic sewing machine silent and dexterous, and a carpet-sweeper, and a book which tells you how to furnish a house artistically with red flannel and empty flour barrels for three hundred and fifty dollars, and photogravures and Public Library books, and ten cent editions of the philosophers, and the prospect of casting an early and unbiassed vote, and the sweetest baby girl in the world who will have a great many more advantages than her mother ever had!

Yes, if you follow Old Aunt Chloe's advice and "Tink ob y'er mercies,"[5] it is very evident that your meditations will be long and not unprofitable to-morrow; and it is tolerably certain, too, that however Jack may rail at the deplorable feminine tendencies of the age, upon hearing your enumeration of them, his thankfulness will not be less than yours.

[1886]

---

[4] The original text in the *Globe* has "baking power" at this point, which appears to be a typographical error for "powder."

[5] Aunt Chloe is the wife of Uncle Tom in Harriet Beecher Stowe's (1811–96) anti-slavery novel *Uncle Tom's Cabin* (1852).

American Influence on Canadian Thought

Of Canada's literary past it seems invidious to say very much more. The few eminent names which make it possible for us to point to any achievement at all in the department of letters have been so often shown to be chiefly imported, and the remainder have been so many times lumped in a sentence tagged with some expression of indifference or contempt, that to add to the mass of deprecation that already attaches to this feature of our history is to do a useless, gratuitous thing, not void of offence, as useless, gratuitous things are apt not to be—a thing, moreover, very like scolding a child for lacking the characteristics of a man. It would be more agreeable, and doubtless more acceptable, to take a look about our literary garden in its present season, uprooting in our righteous imagination all the rank growths that take the sap out of the soil, and pushing aside the great quantity of dead leaves that encumber it, to rejoice together over the new and tender beginnings that we should not fail to find. To do this however—you may not be aware of it, so I impart the fact to you in confidence—would be to class ourselves at once in the public estimation among that great, flourishing, and wicked company of people the just call "Logrollas."[6] The Logrollas were not known to antiquity, or even to early modern times, but sprang quite recently upon the public ready-made from the spleen of one of those reformers of criticism whom criticism has treated badly. The Logrollas consist of everybody who has ever had a favourable opinion of anybody else, and been rash enough to put it in print. As almost every writer has committed this indiscretion at some time of his life, it will be easily seen that the Logrollas are a large and influential class; and as nobody is too great or too small to escape the imputation of belonging to it, the danger inseparable from the discussion of contemporary Canadian literature must be apparent. In order to check, to the humble extent within our power, the growth of this already very widespread evil, we must avoid its very appearance. If therefore, you have a literary predilection that might fairly be called personal, go bury it.

But we may take it for granted that a general strain of hopefulness for our future in authorship, and of speculation as to its character, may be indulged in without suspicion of any sordid motive; and since it is about the only direction of literary comment that will bear this saying we hasten to take it.

The future existence of Canada as a nation seems imperilled just now by the forces that lie behind a grave doubt. The future existence of a Canadian national literature is not openly threatened, but it is none the less in danger. In fact the influences assailing literary effort here have nothing to do with the blandishments of the Annexationists.[7] If Canada becomes part of the Union in the very infancy of her literature, of course it will grow to the full stature of an American; but even if she does

[6] Duncan is playing on the expression "log-rollers," a termed applied by Wilfred Campbell in his condemnation of Charles G.D. Roberts and others for nepotism and mutual promotion.

[7] i.e., those Canadians who supported annexation to the United States.

SARA JEANNETTE DUNCAN

380

not, it is greatly to be feared that the offspring of her brain may show more than cousinship for its relations over the border. More than one generation of people who talked of England or Scotland or Ireland as "home," people of refinement, scholarly tastes, and a certain amount of leisure, have taken in hand the construction of a Canadian literature. Their ideals were British, their methods were British, their market was chiefly British, and they are mostly gathered to their British fathers, leaving the work to descendants, whose present, and not whose past, country is the actual, potential fact in their national life. There is a wide difference, though comparatively few years span it, between a colonial and a Canadian, and we may not unnaturally look for a corresponding difference in their literary productions. That the difference will be, for a long time at least, not perceptible as between British and Canadian, but rather as between British and American, may be expected for several reasons.

The most obvious of these is perhaps the great number of American books and magazines that find ready readers here. The literary faculty is more imitative than any other, especially in the earlier stages of its endeavour, and it is prone to imitate first in the direction of its own liking. This direction may be readily guessed at by a comparison of the number of English and American contemporary writers familiar to the present generation of Canadian readers, by which the latter will be found to preponderate in almost anybody's experience. [. . .] It is not, however, the taste or the literary culture implied in the fact, but the fact itself that is pertinent to our argument. Once Canadian minds are thoroughly impregnated with American matter, American methods, in their own work, will not be hard to trace.

It is pertinent here to consider the difference in the price of English and American publications, which is great, and doubtless often induces the bookbuyer to choose the lesser good at the cheaper rate. The English publisher finds it to his interest to bring out a first edition of an average successful novel at 31s. 6d. His American brother knows it to be very remunerative to publish a book of the same class at $1.50. The same duty on both books makes the price to the Canadian thirty per cent higher. He buys the American book in part because it is the cheapest, but in greater part because he is in every respect the sort of person whose existence in great numbers in the United States makes its publication profitable. The lack of moneyed leisure is not the only condition of life common to Americans and Canadians. If it were, American literature would be as impotent, at any price, to change the character of Canadian literature as it is to effect a literary revolution in England. But, like the Americans, we have a certain untrammelled consciousness of new conditions and their opportunities, in art as well as in society, in commerce, in government. Like them, having a brief past as a people, we concentrate the larger share of thought, energy, and purpose upon our future. We have their volatile character, as we would have had without contact with them; volatility springs in a new country as naturally as weeds. We have greatly their likings and their dislikings, their ideas and their opinions. In short, we have not escaped, as it was impossible we should escape, the superior influence of a people overwhelming in numbers, prosperous in business, and aggressive in political and social faith, the natural conditions of whose life we share, and with whom we are brought every day into closer contact.

Imitation and sympathy having diverted the Canadian *littérateur* somewhat from the ways of his forefathers, it remains for him to consider his market. The magazines being the great vehicles, he will look with awed despair upon the brilliant list from which the *Contemporary* or the *Nineteenth Century* draws its monthly quota, and with which his obscure patronymic must compete, handicapped with that damning adjective, "colonial." And he turns with comfort to the half score of New York publications, each of which contains names unknown yesterday, and to be forgotten tomorrow, where his chance is indeed better, as the number of Canadians at present contributing to these periodicals proves. Having selected his market, he forthwith proceeds to write up to it, or down to it, as the case may be. As the great northern magazine phalanx is dictating now to the literary movement in the South its limits and its character, so will it some day dictate to a similar movement in Canada. The market for Canadian literary wares of all sorts is self-evidently New York, where the intellectual life of the continent is rapidly centralising. It is true that it will never be a great or a profitable market until some original process of development is applied to the transplanted romance of our North-west, to the somewhat squat and uninteresting life of Ontario, to our treasure trove, Quebec; but when this is done, we may be sure that it will be with an eye upon immediate American appreciation, and in the spirit and methods of American literary production.

[1887]

From A Social Departure: How Orthodocia and I Went Round the World by Ourselves

[...] I met Orthodocia originally on a sandy point of the peninsula of Yucatan. She looked very pretty, I remember, picking up muddy conch shells all shiny and pink inside, and running to her aunty chaperon with them for admiration. I remember, too, that she did not get the admiration, but a scolding. "Look," said the chaperon, "look at your front breadth!" Orthodocia was eighteen then, but she looked at her front breadth, and went away very low in her mind, and sat down remotely on the Peninsula of Yucatan and made a dreadful mess of her back one. It was this little incident, I think, that drew me to Orthodocia.

It does not in the least matter what had happened in the four years between Yucatan and the port of Montreal last September, where I met Orthodocia again. You will believe that a good deal had happened when you understand that she was quite by herself, and prepared for a trip round the world with a person her relatives had been in the habit of mentioning as "that American young lady," which was me. Naturally you will think of matrimony first, which casualty would have enabled Orthodocia to go to the planet Mars alone, I believe, with the full approval of all her friends and acquaintances. But matrimony had not befallen her. [...]

I have said that Orthodocia arrived in Montreal prepared for a trip round the world. This, considering her baggage, is an inadequate statement. It would have taken her comfortably through the universe with much apparel to spare, I should say, in a rough estimate. All the quartermasters who were not watching over her person were engaged in superintending the removal of her effects, relieved at intervals by the ship's officers. There were two long attenuated boxes, and two short apoplectic ones. There was a small brown hair trunk, and a large black tin case. There was a collection of portmanteaux, and a thing she called a despatch-box, that properly belonged to her papa. There were two tin cylinders containing millinery, I believe. And there was a sitz bath[8] tub—a beautiful round, shining, symmetrical sitz bath tub. I cannot conscientiously say that Orthodocia's full name was painted on that object. In the brief instant I gave to its contemplation, I certainly saw a legend of some sort in white letters, but it may have been only the Devonshire address from which it had innocently wandered, in which case it may have been restored by this time to its native Wigginton. For there is no use in concealing the fact that in the course of my long, serious, private conversation with the drayman offering the lowest contract for removing Orthodocia's luggage, I enjoined him carefully to lose that sitz bath, and he did. [. . .]

Orthodocia was a disappointment to my family circle. It was probably because I had always spoken of her as "Miss Love," maintained a guarded silence as to her age and personal appearance, and discreetly allowed the fact to escape me that she had an ambition to become a Poor Law Guardian, that she was expected to arrive a mature person somewhat over thirty, with political opinions and views upon dress reform, and the habit of wearing black alpaca and unknown horrors which she would call "goloshes." Instead of which, as you know, she was only twenty-two, with a pinkness and healthiness which subtracted a year or two from that; she hadn't a theory about her except that one should say one's prayers and look as well as possible under all circumstances, and her inexperience in the practical concerns of life seemed appalling. True, she could walk ten miles in her broad-toed boots, and slay any member of the family with a tennis-ball at a hundred yards, but these qualifications, original and valuable as they seemed, hardly gave my friends the sense of security they expected to derive from Orthodocia's chaperonage. It is very "American" for young ladies to travel alone, but not such a common thing in my part of the continent that it could be acceded to without a certain amount of objection on the part of their friends and relatives. [. . .] We argued that propriety was entirely relative, and that naturally impropriety in North America would be quite the correct thing in the antipodes. Who would look after our luggage? We suggested, with the gently disciplinary air of two who have their quarrel just, that there was only one

---

[8] A sitz bath is a type of bath in which only the hips and buttocks are soaked in water or saline solution. It is used to treat hemorrhoids and to ease discomfort from infections.

change of cars, so to speak, between Montreal and Yokohama, and that the C.P.R. porters were reliable. [. . .]

"What," said Orthodocia, in the days of discussion that followed, "is the 'Seepiar'?"

"The C.P.R.," I answered her, "is the most masterly stroke of internal economy a Government ever had the courage to carry out, and the most lunatic enterprise a Government was ever foolhardy enough to hazard. It was made for the good of Canada, it was made for the greed of contractors. It has insured our financial future, it has bankrupted us for ever. It is our boon and our bane. It is an iron bond of union between our East and our West—if you will look on the map you will discover that we are chiefly east and west—and it is an impotent strand connecting a lot of disaffected provinces. This is a coalition Liberal-Conservative definition of the C.P.R., which is the slang or household expression for Canadian Pacific Railway. In the language of the vulgar—'you pays your money and you takes your choice.'"

"I'm sure it doesn't matter," said Orthodocia, in a manner that caused me to give up her education in Canadian economics on the spot.

We were both quite aware, however, when we made our last farewells out of the car window in the noisy lamp-lit darkness of Montreal station, the September night that saw us off, that the C.P.R. would take us over the prairies and across the Rockies, and finally to a point along the shore of the Pacific Ocean, somewhere in British Columbia, we believed, where in the course of time we should find a ship. It was our intention to commit ourselves to the ship, but there speculation ceased and purpose vanished away, for who hath foreknowledge of the Pacific, or can prophesy beyond the rim of it? We had been so grievously embarrassed by kind-hearted people who wanted to know our plans in detail, with dates attached, that we refused at last to entertain a single plan or date or detail—we would send them, we said, when they had been carried out, which would be much more satisfactory. In the six days' journey across the continent we would get out occasionally and wait for the next train where the landscape looked inviting; but whenever we paused this way we would let them know. And thus we sped away.

It was Orthodocia's first experience of a Pullman[9] sleeper, and I dare say she found it exciting. I know I did. For economy's sake we had taken a lower berth together instead of luxuriating in a whole section; and as we sat in a vacant place across the car she watched the transformation of our own seat into a bed with disfavour from the beginning. "Extremely stuffy!" she said, "extremely stuffy!" When the upper berth was shut down and the curtains drawn she thought it

[9] By the end of the nineteenth century, the Pullman Palace Car Company produced the most ornate sleeping cars in existence. They boasted high-backed seats, French upholstery, plush carpeting, and carved mahogany panelling. By day, each lower berth was converted into two facing seats. At night, the seats turned into beds and the upper berths that had been closed during the day were unfolded and made up into beds as well.

time to interfere. "Please put the top bed up," she said to the negro porter;[10] "we can't possibly sleep that way!"

"Sawry not tuh be able tuh 'commodate yuh, Miss; but dat berth's took by a gen'leman in de smokin' car at present, Miss."

"I suppose there is some mistake," said Orthodocia to me, whereupon I was obliged to tell her that the proceeding was perfectly regular, and that the gentleman in the smoking car would probably be a large oleomarginous[11] person who would snore hideously, diffuse an odour of stale tobacco, and drop his boots at intervals during the night into our berth. Orthodocia then stated her intention of sitting up all night, a course from which she was dissuaded by the appearance of claimants for the only two seats that were left. Then the gentleman came in from the smoking car, and turned out to be a perfectly inoffensive little English curate, as new to the customs of the aborigines as Orthodocia, and quite as deeply distressed. "Perhaps—perhaps you would prefer my sitting up?" he said unhappily. "Oh no," said Orthodocia, "*I'll* sit up." "But really"—protested the curate. "It's not of the slightest consequence," Orthodocia interrupted frigidly, and sat down on the edge of our berth, while the frightened little man scrambled up to his with the aid of a step-ladder. Orthodocia told me next morning that she sat there a long time waiting for the boots, but as nothing appeared she concluded that he must have slept in them. The curtains that screen the berths are buttoned loosely together, and the usual method of reconnoitring before making a sortie in the direction of the toilet-room is to thrust one's head out between the buttons. It was very early in the morning when Orthodocia did this: no sound was to be heard but the rattling of the train; and she did it very deliberately and very stealthily. She looked carefully in all directions, and was just about to depart, when an upward glance made her withdraw precipitately. For there above her was the anxious countenance and dishevelled locks of the curate, also scanning the situation and looking for the step-ladder. I suppose, if I had not been willing, after performing my own toilet, to hold the top curtains together while Orthodocia made her exit, both she and the curate might have been there still.

We entered after that, the little curate and Orthodocia and I, into the most amicable relations, for it took us two days to get to Winnipeg, which was our first

---

[10]The majority of the porters who worked in the Pullman sleeping cars on CPR trains were African-American or African-Canadian men (hence the reference to the "negro porter" here). The early days of the transcontinental railways coincided with the emancipation of slaves in America. George Pullman took advantage of those he saw as cheap labour, and hired many former slaves to work in his sleeper cars. Due to enduring racial discrimination in Canada and the United States, the railway was one of the few places where Black men could find steady employment. For many decades, thousands of men worked as porters on the trains in the United States and Canada. Because of long working hours, low rates of pay (with a reliance on tips), and exclusion from White-only unions of railway workers, the porters joined together to form the Order of Sleeping Car Porters (OSCP) in 1918. The CPR porters were fully unionized in 1945. Here, Duncan is trying to replicate an African-American accent.

[11] i.e., oily or fatty; derived from the word *oleomargarine*.

stopping-place, and nobody can sit within three feet of a small thin pale Ritualist, an alien in the Canadian North-West, for two days, without feeling sorry for him and wishing to mitigate his lot in every possible way. So we fed him with chicken sandwiches from our hamper and made him cups of tea with our spirit lamp, and he in return gave us each three throat lozenges and some excellent spiritual nourishment in the form of tracts. He was going, he said, to labour in Assiniboia among the Indians, and hoped it would not be long before he could expostulate with them in their own tongue. In fact, he had quite expected to have picked up something of the language by this time. Possibly I could speak a little Cree? He was disappointed, I think, to find that the aboriginal dialects did not survive more widely.

The country for the first day was very grim and barren and dreary. We rushed along through a wilderness of rocks and stunted shrubs, juniper chiefly. The great boulders thrust themselves through the scanty grasses like gaunt shoulders through a ragged gown. Now and then a spray of yellowing maple or of reddening oak broke the grey monotony, or the rocks blossomed into lichens, but this only gave an accent to the general desolation. And steadily travelling with us all along the sky-line went a fringe of blackened firs, martyred memorials of forest fires. That alliterative expression belongs properly to the curate, whose depression was frightful about this time, and whom I saw write it down in his note-book. I hope that any of the curate's English relations who may read this chapter and be able to identify the phrase by one of his letters, will charitably refrain from communicating the plagiarism to the public. It is a very little one.

But next day we hurried along the north shore of Lake Superior, and the country grew in colour and boldness and significance. We could almost touch the great wet masses of stone the railway pierced, and there were tangled forest depths to look into, and always some glimpse of the majesty of the lake. It had many moods, sometimes blue and still and tender over headlands far away, sometimes deep and darkling in great inlets that gave back the tamarack and the pine clinging to their sheer rocky sides, sometimes sending long white waves dashing among broken boulders within a few feet of the road. I think when the world grew orthodox, they exiled Pan to the north shore of Lake Superior, its beauty is so conscious, so strong, so eternal.

On the morning of the third day we began to see fences and an occasional cow, and then we rejoiced, for we knew we were nearing Winnipeg and the Manitoban approach to civilisation. At about ten o'clock we arrived. I don't think the emigration agents have left much to say seriously about Winnipeg, which they probably call the "Prairie City," and chromo-lithograph in other ways with their usual skill, so I will treat it from Orthodocia's point of view, which cannot be called serious. Her first surprise was a cab—a four-wheeler, with two horses. The next was the popular style of architecture. "Queen Anne!" she said under her breath. "I distinctly understood that the settlers lived in loghuts!" She asked to be driven at once to the Hudson Bay trading post, to see the

Indians bringing in their peltries and exchanging them for guns and knives—a scene which she said she had always imagined with pleasure. I took her to the Hudson Bay trading post because I wanted to gratify her and to buy a pair of six-button Jouvin's[12] at the same time; and, of course, there wasn't an Indian anywhere in the vicinity of that extremely fashionable establishment, or a peltry either. Our Winnipeg hostess lived in one of the Queen Anne houses, and I could perceive Orthodocia's astonishment rising within her as she observed the ordinary interior garnishings of Turkish rugs and Japanese vases and Spode teacups. "I rather expected," she said to me privately, "deers' horns and things." And when I sarcastically suggested wampum and war hatchets, she answered with humble sincerity, "Yes." Orthodocia's wonder culminated at an afternoon "At home" at Government House, where, as the local paper put it next day, "the wealth and fashion" of Winnipeg gathered together to drink claret-cup and amuse itself. There were the Governor and his A.D.C.'s, there was a Bishop, there were the matrimonial adjuncts of the Governor and the Bishop, equally impressive; there was a Canadian Knight and his dame, there were judges and barristers, and officers and visiting celebrities, and a rumour of a real lord in one end of what the local paper called the "spacious apartments." I was rather glad Orthodocia didn't find any Indian chiefs there, as she expected, though perhaps she would have preferred that sensation; and I was distinctly gratified when I passed her in conversation with a younger son in corduroys at the reception, looking glum, who had just come out to waste his substance in Manitoba, and heard him inform her that "Weally, you know, for natives—it's weally wathah wum."

The reason he found it "wathah wum," was because he had a shooting jacket on and people were looking at him. They all wear corduroys at first—to dances and the opera indiscriminately, by way of helping the "natives" to feel on an equality with them. But in the course of time they commonly go back to the usages of civilisation.

[. . .] Orthodocia and I had our first glimpse of the Rockies from the window of the "ladies' toilet-room" between the splashes of the very imperfect ablutions one makes in such a place. It was just before sunrise, and all we could see was a dull red burning in the sky behind the wandering jagged edge of what might have been the outer wall of some Titanic prison. Orthodocia raised her hands in admiration, and began to quote something. I didn't, one of mine being full of soap, and ransacked my mind in vain for any beautiful sentiment to correspond with Orthodocia's. I found the towel though, which was of more consequence at the time; and then we both hurried forth upon the swaying rear platform of the car to join our exclamations with those of a fellow-passenger, whom we easily recognised to be the man from Little Rock, "Arkansaw."[13]

[12] A type of glove developed by the French inventor Xavier Jouvin in 1834. Jouvin invented a press that could cut gloves of a precise size.

[13] This character was introduced shortly before this as a man snoring in the upper berth across the aisle from the two women. Here Duncan is setting up a contrast between the attitudes and manners of American, British, and Canadian characters.

As we stood there on the end of the car and looked out at the great amphitheatre, with the mountains sitting solemnly around it, regarding our impudent noisy toy of steam and wheels, we remembered that we should see mountains with towers and minarets—mountains like churches, like fortifications, like cities, like clouds. And we saw them all, picking out one and then another in the calm grandeur of their lines far up along the sky. Orthodocia cavilled a little at the impertinence of any comparison at all. She thought that a mountain—at all events, one of these great western mountains, down the side of which her dear little England might rattle in a landslip—could never really look like anything but a mountain. It might have a superficial suggestion of something else about its contour, but this, Orthodocia thought, ought to be wholly lost in the massive, towering, eternal presence of the mountain itself.

"Let us go into abstractions for our similes," said Orthodocia; "let us compare it to a thought, to a deed, that men have thrust high above the generations that follow and sharp against the ages that pass over, and made to stay for ever there, and not to some poor fabrication of stone and mortar that dures but for a century or so, and whose builder's proudest boast might well be that he had made something like a mountain!"

"That's so!" said the man from Little Rock, "Arkansaw."

Orthodocia shuddered, and consulted her muse further in silence, while the dull red along the frontier east burned higher, flinging a tinge of itself on the foam of the narrow pale-green river that went tearing past, and outlining purple hulks among the mountains that lay between. There was something theatrical about the masses of unharmonised colour, the broad effects of light and shadow, the silent pose of everything. It seemed a great drop-curtain that Nature would presently roll up to show us something else. And in a moment it did roll up or roll away, and was forgotten in one tall peak that lifted its snow-girt head in supremest joy for the first baptism of the sun. It was impossible to see anything but the flush of light creeping down and over that far solemn height, tracing its abutments and revealing its deep places. It seemed so very near to God that a wordless song came from it, set in chords we did not know. But all the air was sentient with the song. . . .

"How many feet, naow, do you suppose they give that mountain?" said the man from Little Rock, "Arkansaw."

Orthodocia and I stood not upon the order of our going, but went at once, vowing that it would be necessary to live to be very old in order to forgive that man.

Field is a little, new place on the line, chiefly hotel, where I remember a small boy who seemed to run from the foot of one mountain to the foot of another to unlock a shanty and sell us some apples at twenty-five cents a pound. But Field is chiefly memorable to us as being the place where the engine-driver accepted our invitation to ride with him. He was an amiable engine-driver, but he required a great deal of persuasion into the belief that the inlaid box upholstered in silk plush and provided with plate-glass windows that rolled along behind, was not indisputably the best place from which to observe the scenery. "You see, if you was on the ingin' an anythin' 'appened you'd come to smash certain," he observed cheerfully but implacably. "Besides, it's ag'inst the rules."

Whereupon we invoked the aid of a certain Superintendent of Mechanics, who was an obliging person and interceded for us. "Lady Macdonald did it," he said, instancing the wife of our Premier,[14] "and if these young ladies can hold on"—he looked at us doubtfully, and Orthodocia immediately gave him several examples of her extraordinary nerve. We coveted a trip on the pilot—in vulgar idiom the cow-catcher—a heavy iron projection in front of the engines in America, used to persuade wandering cattle of the company's right of way. My argument was that in case of danger ahead we could obviously jump. The engineer appreciated it very reluctantly, and begged us on no account to jump, obviously or any way. And we said we wouldn't, with such private reservations as we thought the situation warranted. Finally we were provided with a cushion apiece and lifted on. To be a faithful historian I must say that it was an uncomfortable moment. We fancied we felt the angry palpitations of the monster we sat on, and we couldn't help wondering whether he might not resent the liberty. It was very like a personal experiment with the horns of a dragon, and Orthodocia and I found distinct qualms in each other's faces. But there was no time for repentance; our monster gave a terrible indignant snort, and slowly, then quickly, then with furious speed, sent us forth into space.

Now, I have no doubt you expect me to tell you what it feels like to sit on a piece of black iron, holding on by the flagstaff, with your feet hanging down in front of a train descending the Rockies on a grade that drops four and a half feet in every hundred. I haven't the vocabulary—I don't believe the English language has it. There is no terror, as you might imagine, the hideous thing that inspires it is behind you. There is no heat, no dust, no cinder. The cool, delicious mountain air flows over you in torrents. You are projected swiftly into the illimitable, stupendous space ahead, but on a steady solid basis that makes you feel with some wonder that you are not doing anything very extraordinary after all, though the Chinese navvies along the road looked at Orthodocia and me as if we were. That, however, was because Orthodocia's hair had come down and I had lost my hat, which naturally would not tend to impress the Celestial mind with the propriety of our mode of progression. We were intensely exhilarated, very comfortable and happy, and felt like singing something to the rhythmic roar of the train's accompaniment. We did sing and we couldn't hear ourselves. The great armies of the pines began their march upwards at our feet. On the other side the range of the stately Selkirks rose, each sheer and snowy against the sky. A river foamed along beside us, beneath us, beyond us. We were ahead of everything, speeding on into the heart of the mountains, on into a wide sea of shining mist with white peaks rising out of it on all sides, and black firs pointing

[14] Lady Agnes Macdonald, second wife of Prime Minister John A. Macdonald, rode the cow-catcher of the CPR through the Rockies in July 1886, shortly after the opening of the transcontinental passenger service. Her daring adventure started a trend.

raggedly up along the nearer slopes. A small cave in a projecting spur, dark as Erebus;[15] the track went through it, and in an instant so did we, riding furiously into the echoing blackness with a wild thought of the possible mass of fallen in *débris* which was not there.

Orthodocia and I wondered simultaneously, as we found out afterwards, what we should do if the rightful occupant of the cow-catcher—namely, the cow—should appear to claim it. It was impossible to guess. I concluded that it would depend upon how much room the cow insisted upon taking up. If we could come to terms with her, and she didn't mind going "heads and tails," she would find a few inches available between us; otherwise—but it would be unpleasant in any event to be mixed up in an affair of the sort. Cows suggested bears, not from any analogy known to natural history, but because a bear on that road was a good deal more probable an episode than a cow. Supposing a bear suddenly hurled into our society, would he feel fear, or amazement, or wrath? Would he connect us in displeased astonishment with the immediate cause of his disaster, or would he sympathise with us as fellow-victims trapped further back? In either case, would he make any demonstration? These considerations so worked upon my mind that I actually expected the bear. In imagination I saw him tramping through the undergrowth to meet the great surprise of his life and of mine, and my sympathy was divided between us. I dwelt with fascination upon certain words of an American author—"And the bear was coming on,"[16] and I thought of the foolhardiness of travelling on a cow-catcher without a gun. With an imaginary rifle I despatched the gross receipts of the cow-catcher for a week with great glory. I wondered what would be said in our respective home circles if the bear really came on. And as we alighted at The Glacier I confided to Orthodocia my bitter regret that he did not come.

[1890]

[15] In Greek mythology, Erebus, meaning primordial darkness, was the son of Chaos. In some accounts, Erebus is associated with the underworld, and sometimes used as a synonym for Hades.

[16] See Charles Dudley Warner's *In the Wilderness* (Boston, 1878), which contains the line "The bear was coming on" as a kind of refrain as the author humorously describes being pursued by a bear in the Adirondacks.

E. PAULINE JOHNSON (TEKAHIONWAKE) ■ (1861–1913)

"Never let anyone call me a white woman," Pauline Johnson told fellow writer Ernest Thompson Seton in 1894. "There are those who think they pay me a compliment in saying that I am just like a white woman. My aim, my joy, my pride is to sing the glories of my own people." The youngest daughter of a Mohawk chief and a British mother, throughout her life Johnson found herself caught between two cultures and two loyalties. She came from illustrious lineage on both sides. Her mother, Emily Howells, had immigrated to the United States with her father, who was a vocal abolitionist and worked in the Underground Railroad. Emily's cousin William Dean Howells became the renowned editor of the American magazine *Harper's*. Johnson's father, Chief George Johnson, was one of a line of hereditary chiefs, whose grandfather Jacob Tekahionwake (rechristened Johnson) had been among the thousands of Iroquois who fled to Canada with Joseph Brant following the American Revolution. The British government granted the Six Nations Loyalists a reserve along the Grand River in southwestern Ontario. Further, Jacob's son, John "Smoke" Johnson (Pauline's grandfather), fought with the British troops in the War of 1812 in defence of Canada, stealing out under cover of night to set fire to the American city of Buffalo. His son, George, who would become Pauline's father, was both a Mohawk chief and an official translator for the colonial government.

When George Johnson and Emily Howells announced their engagement, people were shocked. Emily's family was worried about the scandal of her marrying an "Indian"; George's family was upset because his marriage to a White woman would mean the hereditary chieftainship would be lost (since it was passed down through the matrilineal line and chiefs were appointed by women). Nevertheless, the couple were living proof that a merging of cultures was possible; they married in 1853 and had four children, the youngest of whom was Pauline. The family lived in a mansion, "Chiefswood," on the Six Nations Reserve (near Brantford, Ontario), built when the couple were married. They enjoyed a high standard of living for the period, employed household servants, and held a prominent social status in both the Native and non-Native communities.

Due to George Johnson's status as a representative of the Six Nations, Chiefswood became the stopping point for governors general and other celebrities. Raising her children to become refined Victorian gentlemen and ladies, Emily Johnson educated them in social etiquette and the great tradition of English literature. From her father and grandfather, Johnson learned the stories of her Mohawk ancestors, and grew up with immense pride in her Mohawk ancestry.

Johnson likely inherited her love of oratory and performance from her father, who was known for his self-possession and style, particularly his love of ceremonial dress. Nevertheless, because of her official "Indian" status, as set out in the various Indian Acts from 1860 onwards, Johnson and her Iroquois relatives were considered "non-citizens" according to Canadian law. This is a bitter irony given Johnson's anglicized upbringing and her subsequent prominence in Canadian literary history.

From early on, Johnson dreamed of being a writer. Following her father's death in 1884, the family experienced financial constraints and moved to a smaller house in Brantford. It was during these years that Johnson began publishing poems in the *Brantford Expositor*, *The Week*, the *Globe*, and *Saturday Night*. When invited to compose a poem in memory of Brantford's founder, the Iroquois hero Joseph Brant, in October 1886, Johnson entered the limelight in a public ceremony with her "Ode to Brant," which was read aloud by a local man. The next day, Johnson was interviewed and lauded by fellow writer

Sara Jeannette Duncan in the Toronto *Globe*. The pivotal moment in Johnson's career, however, came on 16 January 1892, when she was invited to take part in a public "Evening with Canadian Authors" that was being organized by Frank Yeigh for the Young Men's Liberal Club in Toronto. The event was to be a celebration of Canada's literary identity, and included such well-known authors as Duncan Campbell Scott, William Wilfred Campbell, and Agnes Maule Machar. Johnson, the least-known writer of the group, wowed the audience with her dramatic performance of "A Cry from an Indian Wife," a poem she had composed seven years earlier during the height of the Northwest Rebellion and published in the 18 June 1885 issue of *The Week*. The poem stood out from the conventional fare of the period. It is a dramatic monologue spoken by the wife of a Native man taking part in the Northwest Rebellion. Johnson was an immediate success and was called back on stage to perform an encore. A review in the *Globe* two days later stated that her poetry "was like the voice of the nations who once possessed this country . . . speaking through this cultured, gifted, soft-voiced descendant."

This event marked the launch of Johnson's career as a performance poet. Frank Yeigh became Johnson's manager, and a few weeks later, on 19 February 1892, he advertised a solo reading in Toronto by Johnson, billing her as "the Indian poetess." Johnson quickly realized that she had captured a niche, and that she could put her Native heritage to good effect. In a letter to her friend Archie Kains, she stated that her goal was to "upset the Indian Extermination and Non-education theory, in fact to stand by my blood and my race." Growing increasingly tired of the stereotyped notions about Aboriginal peoples, Johnson published

an article in the 22 May 1892 edition of the *Sunday Globe*, entitled "A Strong Race Opinion: On the Indian Girl in Modern Fiction." In it, she critiqued the conventional depictions of helpless Indian maidens and the frequent conflation of all Native peoples into one common "tribe." Shortly afterwards, she submitted her short story, "A Red Girl's Reasoning," about a marriage between a White man and a mixed-race woman, to *The Dominion Illustrated*'s story competition and won; published in February 1893, it was her first piece of fiction to appear in print. In it, and in "As It Was in the Beginning" (first published in *Saturday Night* in 1899), she provided an alternative to the Indian maiden stories that had so exasperated her. It was also in the early 1890s that Johnson composed what became her most famous poem, "The Song My Paddle Sings," a sensuous account of a woman at home in nature canoeing through the rapids. The poem struck a chord with Canadian audiences and became a popular campfire song.

As Johnson's performance career picked up steam, she felt that she needed something to increase the dramatic impact of her act, and hit upon the perfect solution: she decided to dress in "Indian" costume when reciting her poems about Native characters. The costume that Johnson devised was of her own design (Figure III-17). She attached her grandmother's silver trade brooches to the neckline, and hung rabbit skins from the front and sleeves. As extra adornments, she included around her waist her father's hunting knife, an Iroquois wampum belt, and a Huron scalp that had belonged to her grandfather. Later she added a feather to her hair and a necklace of bear claws given to her by Seton. Johnson's new public persona was an instant success.

Between October 1892 and May 1893 she gave over 100 recitals across Ontario, and in the summer of 1893, toured eastern Canada and the United States. Her performances were unprecedented. The first half of her show included her passionate "Indian" poems, which she would perform in Native costume with her hair loose about her shoulders. Then, following a brief intermission, she would return on stage dressed as a proper English lady, in an elegant evening gown and pinned-up hair, for the recital of her nature poems (Figure III-18). Audiences were enthralled by the two apparently contrasting sides of her persona.

Johnson's Ontario tour was followed, in 1894, by a two-month stint in London, England, where she performed her poetry for British aristocrats. This led to the publication of her first collection of poems, *The White Wampum* (1895). The interview included here was conducted during this trip. It was in England that Johnson decided to rename herself after her great-grandfather; hereafter, she performed under her English name and her Mohawk one, "Tekahionwake." After a brief return to Brantford that same year, she embarked on a major cross-Canada tour with co-performer Owen Smily. The pair travelled by the recently completed CPR, and for two months performed in a series of venues across the country, from Orillia, Ontario, to Victoria, British Columbia. It was on this journey, when Johnson was for the first time exposed to the breadth and variety of the Canadian landscape, that she composed her self-critical poem "His Majesty, the West Wind," in which she looks back upon "The Song My Paddle Sings" and critiques her naive view of the prairie climate. The publication of "West Wind" caused some furor among critics, who felt that Johnson was being too flippant about her poetic status.

Johnson's career from 1895 to 1909 became a never-ending series of performance tours across Canada, the United States, and again England in 1906, as Johnson struggled to support herself financially. While in London, Johnson met Chief Joe Capilano, from the Squamish nation, who was present with a delegation to oppose restrictions that had been imposed upon British Columbia Native peoples by the Canadian government. She developed a friendship with Capilano, and his tales became the basis of her 1911 story collection, *Legends of Vancouver*. In 1903, she published her second collection of poetry, *Canadian Born*, and she produced a volume of her collected poems, *Flint and Feather*, in 1912. She eventually moved to Vancouver, and retired from touring in 1909. Johnson died of breast cancer on 7 March 1913 and is buried in Vancouver's Stanley Park where there is now a monument to her. Her funeral attracted hundreds of mourners, both Native and non-Native, who lined the city's streets to say their farewells. She willed her buckskin costume to the Vancouver Museum, where it is on display to the public. Her childhood home, Chiefswood, is now a museum containing many of her manuscripts and other possessions. Her story collections, *The Moccasin Maker* and *The Shagganappi*, were both published posthumously in 1913.

While Johnson's stated aim was to promote the cause of Canada's Aboriginal peoples, as well as to counter received stereotypes about them, many critics have accused her of promoting such stereotypes in her own performances in order to cater to popular demand. Her stage costume was a mélange of various "Indian" symbols, and her performances included war whoops and threatening postures (many of which shocked her bourgeois audiences) and thus evoked an image of Native savagery. Moreover, her switch into refined evening dress in the course of her performance enacted the very assimilation (and presumed disappearance) of Native peoples that she so much opposed. Likewise, her "Indian" poems are written in the tradition of British poetry, including dramatic monologues written in heroic couplets ("A Cry from an Indian Wife" and "Ojistoh"). One might argue that Johnson was getting her message across in the only way possible: by catering to audience demand, she was also able to slip in her political message about Native disenfranchisement. Her own frustration at the audience's expectation of exoticism comes out in a letter to a friend when she writes, "[T]he public will not listen to lyrics, will in fact not have me as an entertainer if I give them nothing but rhythm, cadence, beauty, thought. I could do so much better if they'd only let me." Johnson's British refinement made her "safe" to her bourgeois Canadian audiences, who were fascinated by Aboriginal peoples but did not necessarily want to credit their grievances. Ultimately, Johnson sought some way for Native peoples and Europeans to live harmoniously together and exchange cultural traditions. Her so-called "conflicted" identity, which she had also witnessed in her father's life, existed mainly because of the presumptions that were imposed on Native peoples by other Canadians. While she was proud of her Mohawk heritage, Johnson, like her father, was also a committed Canadian nationalist and British Loyalist. Moreover, her family's social status set her apart from many of the Aboriginal members of the Six Nations Reserve. Her poem "Canadian Born" reveals that she saw membership in the British Empire as the glue that could unify all Canadians, Native and non-Native alike. As her biographer Charlotte Gray puts it, Johnson "blurred boundaries that her contemporaries saw as impermeable." The political courage of Johnson's message is evident not only in her early poem "A Cry from an Indian Wife," in which she unequivocally condemns the European theft of Native lands, but also in "The Cattle Thief" and many of her public statements, as for example in her interview with the London *Gazette* in 1894. In his memoir of Johnson, Seton recalls her impassioned belief that Native peoples were swindled out of their rightful claims to the land: "But for our few numbers, our simple faith that others were as true as we to keep their honor bright and hold as bond inviolable their plighted word, we should have owned America to-day."

While some of her contemporaries felt that Johnson had cheapened herself by playing up her Native ancestry and making a performance out of her indigeneity, she was one of the most famous Canadian writers of the day, and was a unique voice in the post-Confederation period when few writers were taking Canadians to task for their biased treatment of Aboriginal peoples. Charles G.D. Roberts, much to Johnson's delight, declared her "the aboriginal voice of Canada." As literary critic D.M.R. Bentley states in his study of the Confederation Poets, while Johnson was not officially recognized as a member of the group (in part because she was a woman), she received "international recognition of the sort to which no member of the Confederation group ever aspired or could possibly emulate."

A Cry from an Indian Wife[1]

My Forest Brave, my Red-skin love, farewell;
We may not meet to-morrow; who can tell
What mighty ills befall our little band,
Or what you'll suffer from the white man's hand?
Here is your knife! I thought 'twas sheathed for aye.
No roaming bison calls for it to-day;
No hide of prairie cattle will it maim;
The plains are bare, it seeks a nobler game:
'Twill drink the life-blood of a soldier host.
Go; rise and strike, no matter what the cost.   10
Yet stay. Revolt not at the Union Jack,
Nor raise thy hand against this stripling pack
Of white-faced warriors, marching West to quell
Our fallen tribe that rises to rebel.
They all are young and beautiful and good;
Curse to the war that drinks their harmless blood.
Curse to the fate that brought them from the East
To be our chiefs—to make our nation least
That breathes the air of this vast continent.
Still their new rule and council is well meant.   20
They but forget we Indians owned the land
From ocean unto ocean; that they stand
Upon a soil that centuries agone
Was our sole kingdom and our right alone.
They never think how they would feel to-day,
If some great nation came from far away,
Wrestling their country from their hapless braves,
Giving what they gave us—but wars and graves.
Then go and strike for liberty and life,
And bring back honour to your Indian wife.   30
Your wife? Ah, what of that, who cares for me?
Who pities my poor love and agony?
What white-robed priest prays for your safety here,
As prayer is said for every volunteer
That swells the ranks that Canada sends out?
Who prays for vict'ry for the Indian scout?
Who prays for our poor nation lying low?
None—therefore take your tomahawk and go.

[1] The poem is spoken by the wife of a warrior who is embarking to fight on the side of Louis Riel in the Northwest Rebellion of 1885. It was published in the 18 June 1885 issue of *The Week* during the height of the rebellion, before the surrender of Big Bear.

My heart may break and burn into its core,
But I am strong to bid you go to war.   40
Yet stay, my heart is not the only one
That grieves the loss of husband and of son;
Think of the mothers o'er the inland seas;
Think of the pale-faced maiden on her knees;
One pleads her God to guard some sweet-faced child
That marches on toward the North-West wild.
The other prays to shield her love from harm,
To strengthen his young, proud uplifted arm.
Ah, how her white face quivers thus to think,
Your tomahawk his life's best blood will drink.   50
She never thinks of my wild aching breast,
Nor prays for your dark face and eagle crest
Endangered by a thousand rifle balls,
My heart the target if my warrior falls.
O! coward self I hesitate no more;
Go forth, and win the glories of the war.
Go forth, nor bend to greed of white men's hands,
By right, by birth we Indians own these lands,
Though starved, crushed, plundered, lies our nation low.
Perhaps the white man's God has willed it so.[2]   60

[1885, 1895]

The Song My Paddle Sings

West wind, blow from your prairie nest,
Blow from the mountains, blow from the west.
The sail is idle, the sailor too;
O! wind of the west, we wait for you.
— Blow, blow!
I have wooed you so,
But never a favour you bestow.
You rock your cradle the hills between,
But scorn to notice my white lateen.

I stow the sail, unship the mast: 10
I wooed you long but my wooing's past;
My paddle will lull you into rest.
O! drowsy wind of the drowsy west,

---

[2] This poem was first published in *The Week* of 18 June 1885. Originally, the last four lines read as follows: "O! coward self—I hesitate no more. / Go forth—and win the glories of the war. / O! heart o'erfraught—O! nation lying low— / God, and fair Canada have willed it so."

—Sleep, sleep,
By your mountain steep,
Or down where the prairie grasses sweep!
Now fold in slumber your laggard wings,
For soft is the song my paddle sings. *

August is laughing across the sky,
Laughing while paddle, canoe and I,   20
Drift, drift,
Where the hills uplift
On either side of the current swift.

The river rolls in its rocky bed;
My paddle is plying its way ahead;
Dip, dip,
While the waters flip
In foam as over their breast we slip.

And oh, the river runs swifter now;
The eddies circle about my bow.   30
Swirl, swirl!
How the ripples curl
In many a dangerous pool awhirl!

And forward far the rapids roar,
Fretting their margin for evermore.
Dash, dash,
With a mighty crash,
They seethe, and boil, and bound, and splash.

Be strong, O paddle! be brave, canoe!
The reckless waves you must plunge into.   40
Reel, reel,
On your trembling keel,
But never a fear my craft will feel.

We've raced the rapid, we're far ahead!
The river slips through its silent bed.
Sway, sway,
As the bubbles spray
And fall in tinkling tunes away.

And up on the hills against the sky,
A fir tree rocking its lullaby,   50
Swings, swings,
Its emerald wings,
Swelling the song that my paddle sings.

[1892, 1895]

His Majesty, the West Wind

Once in a fit of mental aberration
I wrote some stanzas to the western wind,[3]
A very stupid, maudlin invocation,
That into ears of audiences I've dinned.

A song about a sail, canoe and paddle,
Recited I, in sailor flannels dressed,
And when they heard it people would skiddadle,
Particularly those who had been west.

For they, alas, had knowledge, I was striving
To write of something I had never known,   10
That I had ne'er experienced the driving
Of western winds across a prairie blown.

I never thought when grinding out those stanzas,
I'd live to swallow pecks of prairie dust,
That I'd deny my old extravaganzas,
And wish his Majesty distinctly—cussed.

[1894]

The Cattle Thief

They were coming across the prairie, they were galloping hard and fast;
For the eyes of those desperate riders had sighted their man at last—
Sighted him off to Eastward, where the Cree encampment lay,
Where the cotton woods fringed the river, miles and miles away.
Mistake him? Never! Mistake him? the famous Eagle Chief!
That terror to all the settlers, that desperate Cattle Thief—
That monstrous, fearless Indian, who lorded it over the plain,
Who thieved and raided, and scouted, who rode like a hurricane!
But they've tracked him across the prairie; they've followed him hard
    and fast;
For those desperate English settlers have sighted their man at last.   10

Up they wheeled to the tepees, all their British blood aflame,
Bent on bullets and bloodshed, bent on bringing down their game;
But they searched in vain for the Cattle Thief: that lion had left his lair,
And they cursed like a troop of demons—for the women alone were there.
'The sneaking Indian coward,' they hissed; 'he hides while yet he can;

---

[3] This poem is Johnson's critical response to "The Song My Paddle Sings," which had first been published two years before this, in the 27 February 1892 issue of *Saturday Night*. Johnson wrote this poem after travelling across Canada in 1894 and experiencing the "west wind" first-hand.

He'll come in the night for cattle, but he's scared to face a *man*.'
'Never!' and up from the cotton woods rang the voice of Eagle Chief;
And right out into the open stepped, unarmed, the Cattle Thief.
Was that the game they had coveted? Scarce fifty years had rolled
Over that fleshless, hungry frame, starved to the bone and old; 20
Over that wrinkled, tawny skin, unfed by the warmth of blood.
Over those hungry, hollow eyes that glared for the sight of food.

He turned, like a hunted lion: 'I know not fear,' said he;
And the words outleapt from his shrunken lips in the language of the Cree.
'I'll fight you, white-skins, one by one, till I kill you *all*,' he said;
But the threat was scarcely uttered, ere a dozen balls of lead
Whizzed through the air about him like a shower of metal rain,
And the gaunt old Indian Cattle Thief dropped dead on the open plain.
And that band of cursing settlers gave one triumphant yell,
And rushed like a pack of demons on the body that writhed and fell. 30
'Cut the fiend up into inches, throw his carcass on the plain;
Let the wolves eat the cursed Indian, he'd have treated us the same.'
A dozen hands responded, a dozen knives gleamed high,
But the first stroke was arrested by a woman's strange, wild cry.
And out into the open, with a courage past belief,
She dashed, and spread her blanket o'er the corpse of the Cattle Thief;
And the words outleapt from her shrunken lips in the language of the Cree,
'If you mean to touch that body, you must cut your way through *me*.'
And that band of cursing settlers dropped backward one by one,
For they knew that an Indian woman roused, was a woman to let alone. 40
And then she raved in a frenzy that they scarcely understood,
Raved of the wrongs she had suffered since her earliest babyhood:
'Stand back, stand back, you white-skins, touch that dead man to your
    shame;
You have stolen my father's spirit, but his body I only claim.
You have killed him, but you shall not dare to touch him now he's dead.
You have cursed, and called him a Cattle Thief, though you robbed him
    first of bread—
Robbed him and robbed my people—look there, at that shrunken face,
Starved with a hollow hunger, we owe to you and your race.
What have you left to us of land, what have you left of game,
What have you brought but evil, and curses since you came? 50
How have you paid us for our game? how paid us for our land?
By a *book*, to save our souls from the sins *you* brought in your other hand.
Go back with your new religion, we never have understood
Your robbing an Indian's *body*, and mocking his *soul* with food.
Go back with your new religion, and find—if find you can—
The *honest* man you have ever made from out a *starving* man.

You say your cattle are not ours, your meat is not our meat,
When *you* pay for the land you live in, *we'll* pay for the meat we eat.
Give back our land and our country, give back our herds of game;
Give back the furs and the forests that were ours before you came; 60
Give back the peace and the plenty. Then come with your new belief,
And blame, if you dare, the hunger that *drove* him to be a thief.'

[1895]

E. PAULINE JOHNSON (TEKAHIONWAKE)

400

The Corn Husker

Hard by the Indian lodges, where the bush
  Breaks in a clearing, through ill-fashioned fields,
She comes to labour, when the first still hush
  Of autumn follows large and recent yields.

Age in her fingers, hunger in her face,
  Her shoulders stooped with weight of work and years,
But rich in tawny colouring of her race,
  She comes a-field to strip the purple ears.

And all her thoughts are with the days gone by,
  Ere might's injustice banished from their lands 10
Her people, that to-day unheeded lie,
  Like the dead husks that rustle through her hands.

[1903]

Canadian Born

We first saw light in Canada, the land beloved of God;
We are the pulse of Canada, its marrow and its blood:
And we, the men of Canada, can face the world and brag
That we were born in Canada beneath the British flag.

Few of us have the blood of kings, few are of courtly birth,
But few are vagabonds or rogues of doubtful name and worth;
And all have one credential that entitles us to brag—
That we were born in Canada beneath the British flag.

We've yet to make our money, we've yet to make our fame,
But we have gold and glory in our clean colonial name; 10
And every man's a millionaire if only he can brag
That he was born in Canada beneath the British flag.

No title and no coronet is half so proudly worn
As that which we inherited as men Canadian born.
We count no man so noble as the one who makes the brag
That he was born in Canada beneath the British flag.

The Dutch may have their Holland, the Spaniard have his Spain,
The Yankee to the south of us must south of us remain;
For not a man dare lift a hand against the men who brag
That they were born in Canada beneath the British flag.   20

[1903]

A Strong Race Opinion: On the Indian Girl in Modern Fiction

Every race in the world enjoys its own peculiar characteristics, but it scarcely follows that every individual of a nation must possess these prescribed singularities, or otherwise forfeit in the eyes of the world their nationality. Individual personality is one of the most charming things to be met with, either in a flesh and blood existence, or upon the pages of fiction, and it matters little to what race an author's heroine belongs, if he makes her character distinct, unique and natural.

The American book heroine of today is vari-coloured as to personality and action. The author does not consider it necessary to the development of her character, and the plot of the story to insist upon her having American-coloured eyes, an American carriage, an American voice, American motives, and an American mode of dying; he allows her to evolve an individuality ungoverned by nationalisms—but the outcome of impulse and nature and a general womanishness.

Not so the Indian girl in modern fiction, the author permits her character no such spontaneity, she must not be one of womankind at large, neither must she have an originality, a singularity that is not definitely 'Indian.' I quote 'Indian' as there seems to be an impression amongst authors that such a thing as tribal distinction does not exist among the North American aborigines.

The term 'Indian' signifies about as much as the term 'European,' but I cannot recall ever having read a story where the heroine was described as 'a European.' The Indian girl we meet in cold type, however, is rarely distressed by having to belong to any tribe, or to reflect any tribal characteristics. She is merely a wholesome sort of mixture of any band existing between the Mic Macs of Gaspé and the Kwaw-Kewlths of British Columbia, yet strange to say, that notwithstanding the numerous tribes, with their aggregate numbers reaching more than 122,000 souls in Canada alone, our Canadian authors can cull from this huge revenue of character, but one Indian girl, and stranger still that this lonely little heroine never had a prototype in breathing flesh-and-blood existence!

It is a deplorable fact, but there is only one of her. The story-writer who can create a new kind of Indian girl, or better still portray a 'real live' Indian girl who will do something in Canadian literature that has never been done, but once. The general author gives the reader the impression that he has concocted the plot, created his characters, arranged his action, and at the last moment has been seized with the idea that the regulation Indian maiden will make a very harmonious background whereon to paint his pen picture, that, he, never having met this interesting individual, stretches forth his hand to his library shelves, grasps the first Canadian novelist he sees, reads up his subject, and duplicates it in his own work.

After a half dozen writers have done this, the reader might as well leave the tale unread as far as the interest touches upon the Indian character, for an unvarying experience tells him that this convenient personage will repeat herself with monotonous accuracy. He knows what she did and how she died in other romances by other romancers, and she will do and die likewise in his (she always does die, and one feels relieved that it is so, for she is too unhealthy and too unnatural to live).

The rendition of herself and her doings gains no variety in the pens of manifold authors, and the last thing that they will ever think of will be to study 'The Indian Girl' from life, for the being we read of is the offspring of the writer's imagination and never existed outside the book covers that her name decorates. [. . .]

She is never dignified by being permitted to own a surname, although, extraordinary to note, her father is always a chief. [. . .] [T]his surnameless creature is possessed with a suicidal mania. Her unhappy, self-sacrificing life becomes such a burden to both herself and the author that this is the only means by which they can extricate themselves from a lamentable tangle, though, as a matter of fact suicide is an evil positively unknown among Indians. [. . .]

The hardest fortune that the Indian girl of fiction meets with is the inevitable doom that shadows her love affairs. She is always desperately in love with the young white hero, who in turn is grateful to her for services rendered the garrison in general and himself in particular during red days of war. In short, she is so much wrapped up in him that she is treacherous to her own people, tells falsehoods to her father and the other chiefs of her tribe, and otherwise makes herself detestable and dishonourable. Of course, this white hero never marries her! Will some critic who understands human nature, and particularly the nature of authors, please tell the reading public why marriage with the Indian girl is so despised in books and so general in real life? Will this good far-seeing critic also tell us why the book-made Indian makes all the love advances to the white gentleman, though the real wild Indian girl (by the way, we are never given any stories of educated girls, though there are many such throughout Canada) is the most retiring, reticent, noncommittal being in existence! [. . .]

Perhaps, sometimes an Indian romance may be written by someone who will be clever enough to portray national character without ever having come in contact with it. [. . .] But such things are rare, half of our authors who write up Indian stuff have never been on an Indian reserve in their lives, have never met a 'real live' Redman, [. . .] what wonder that their conception of a people that they are ignorant of, save by heresay, is dwarfed, erroneous and delusive.

And here follows the thought—do authors who write Indian romances lo‘. the nation they endeavour successfully or unsuccessfully to describe? Do they, like Tecumseh, say, 'And I, who love your nation, which is just, when deeds deserve it,'[4] or is the Indian introduced into literature but to lend a dash of vivid colouring to an otherwise tame and sombre picture of colonial life: it looks suspiciously like the latter reason, or why should the Indian always get beaten in the battles of romances, or the Indian girl get inevitably the cold shoulder in the wars of love?

Surely the Redman has lost enough, has suffered enough without additional losses and sorrows being heaped upon him in romance. [. . .] Let us not only hear, but read something of the North American Indian 'besting' some one at least once in a decade, and above all things let the Indian girl of fiction develop from the 'doglike,' 'fawnlike,' 'deer-footed,' 'fire-eyed,' 'crouching,' 'submissive' book heroine into something of the quiet, sweet womanly woman she is, if wild, or the everyday, natural, laughing girl she is, if cultivated and educated; let her be natural, even if the author is not competent to give her tribal characteristics.

[1892]

Fate of the Red Man: An English Journalist's Chat with Pauline Johnson[5]

"You ask me why I have come to England," said Miss E. Pauline Johnson, the young Iroquois poetess and reciter, Tekahionwake, to the writer last week. "I have come here because my Indian people are very much misunderstood among you English. You do not believe them to be poetic, artistic, and as beautifully moral in their religion as they are. You have a poor idea of the grandeur of the Red Man's nature, and you do him an injustice."

"An injustice? I thought the Indians were so well treated in Canada!" I exclaimed.

"Yes, the Canadian government treats us with the greatest consideration, while the United States government does not study the Indians at all. We of the Six Nations tribe—that is, the Iroquois tribe made up of the Mohawk, Cayuga, Oneida, Onondaga, Seneca, and Tuscarora—have our own government. We are, of course, under white law, but the Canadian government never does a thing without asking the chiefs of the Iroquois in council, and when the chiefs pass a bill in our council it is submitted to the Canadian parliament. But there is never any dissension. They do not impose on us, and we do not impose on them. But then, we are one reserve out of hundreds."

---

4 Tecumseh (1768–1813) was a Shawnee chief who fought alongside the British in the War of 1812. Johnson is quoting from Charles Mair's (1838–1927) play *Tecumseh: A Drama* (1886): "And I, who love your nation, which is just, / When deeds deserve it, will adopt you here" (II.i).

5 This interview in the London *Gazette* was conducted during Johnson's 1894 stay in London, England.

⊃ the Indian an injustice by the way you think, and speak and write of n Iroquois and, of course, I think the Iroquois are the best Indians in and birth, just as you English think you are better than the Turks. Do ....ow that the Iroquois have done more in the last hundred years than it took the native Britons all their time to do? Indian families who fifty years ago were worshipping the Great Spirit, in the old Indian way, have turned out professional men and finely-educated women who hold responsible positions. One of the best government land surveyors Canada has is a full-blooded young Indian, and one of the best assistants in the Indian department at Ottawa is a little Mohawk lady. You cannot, perhaps, count such cases by scores, but they show of what the Red Man is capable. He is no savage if only given a chance."

"How is he handicapped now?"

"For one thing, by the awful class of white people near our reserves. When an Indian mixes in cultured white society, he becomes, in five years, a cultured man. When I was a child I was never allowed to have any white friends except those of the missionary's family. They drag the Indian down. Yet I would not say that the Indians have now any real grievance, so far as the government is concerned, though they had at the time of the Northwest rebellion. The only thing is this. Suppose we came over to England as a powerful people. Suppose you gave us welcome to English soil, worshipped us as gods, as we worshipped you white people when you first came to Canada; and suppose we encroached upon your homeland and drove you back and back, and then said, 'Oh, well, we will present you with a few acres'—a few acres of your own dear land. What would you think of it all? So we think. We are without a country. I cannot say America is my country. The whole continent belongs to us by right of lineage. We welcomed you as friends, we worshipped you, and you drove us up into a little corner.

"But you white men may well think better of the Indian than you do. Why, do you know that the Iroquois have one of the most marvelous constitutions that the world has seen? Hiawatha—not the god that dear dead Longfellow painted him, but the greatest statesman Indian civilization ever produced—he found the Indians in eternal feud with one another, killing each other out. [. . .] He got them to agree, and they amalgamated and fought en masse. Instead of fighting among themselves, they fought for the British. To get quarrelling Indian tribes together to do that, and give them a constitution which has lasted for four hundred years, was no small achievement.

"I will read you what Horatio Hale, the American historian, says: 'The laws and policy framed by Hiawatha and his associates more than four centuries ago are still in force among their descendants on the Grand River Reserve, near Brantford, Ontario. The territory has shrunk by many sales made at the well-meant instance of the protecting government to an extent of little more than 20,000 acres, with a population of some 3,000 souls. But in this small domain the chiefs are still elected, the councils are still conducted, and the civil policy is decided as nearly as possible by the rules of their ancient league. Not many persons are aware that there exists in the heart of Canada this relic of the oldest constitutional government of America—a free commonwealth, older even than any in Europe, except those of England and Switzerland, and perhaps two small semi-independent republics which lurk in the fastnesses of the Pyrenees and the Apennines.' [. . .]

"And it makes one feel sad to think that, despite all these historic associations and national character, the Indian is going to die out like the Pole and the Jew. Yes, I know the Iroquois are increasing in numbers a little now; but while we are today, say, 5,000, there must have been 80,000 of us a hundred years ago. The same sad tale must be told of the Crees, the Blackfeet, and the Sioux—all of splendid lineage. The Onondaga are blue-blooded—not a drop of any other blood in them, and they generally remain conservative in their habits. They will not embrace Christianity. I know an Onondaga family which can count back nine hundred years in direct line, and a great many Crees and Sioux Indians are the same. The Tuscaroras have a little Osage blood in them, I think—some Florida Indian blood."

"But come, Miss Johnson," I said rallying her; "you yourself would hardly be leading your present life of culture had it not been for the white man's invasion."

"Perhaps not the same kind of life; but there are two of me. Sometimes I feel I must get away to the Highlands among a people who seem somehow akin to mine." [. . .]

[1894]

As It Was in the Beginning

They account for it by the fact that I am a Redskin, but I am something else, too—I am a woman.

I remember the first time I saw him. He came up the trail with some Hudson's Bay trappers, and they stopped at the door of my father's tepee. He seemed even then, fourteen years ago, an old man; his hair seemed just as thin and white, his hands just as trembling and fleshless as they were a month since, when I saw him for what I pray his God is the last time.

My father sat in the tepee, polishing buffalo horns and smoking; my mother, wrapped in her blanket, crouched over her quill-work, on the buffalo-skin at his side; I was lounging at the doorway, idling, watching, as I always watched, the thin, distant line of sky and prairie; wondering, as I always wondered, what lay beyond it. Then he came, this gentle old man with his white hair and thin, pale face. He wore a long black coat, which I now know was the sign of his office, and he carried a black leather-covered book, which, in all the years I have known him, I have never seen him without.

The trappers explained to my father who he was, the Great Teacher, the heart's Medicine Man, the 'Blackcoat' we had heard of, who brought peace where there was war, and the magic of whose black book brought greater things than all the Happy Hunting Grounds of our ancestors.

He told us many things that day, for he could speak the Cree tongue, and my father listened, and listened, and when at last they left us, my father said for him to come and sit within the tepee again.

He came, all the time he came, and my father welcomed him, but my mother always sat in silence at work with the quills; my mother never liked the Great 'Blackcoat.'

His stories fascinated me. I used to listen intently to the tale of the strange new place he called 'heaven,' of the gold crown, of the white dress, of the great music; and then he would tell of that other strange place—hell. My father and I hated it; we feared it, we dreamt of it, we trembled at it. Oh, if the 'Blackcoat' would only cease to talk of it! Now I know he saw its effect upon us, and he used it as a whip to lash us into his new religion, but even then my mother must have known, for each time he left the tepee she would watch him going slowly away across the prairie; then when he was disappearing into the far horizon she would laugh scornfully, and say:

'If the white man made this Blackcoat's hell, let him go to it. It is for the man who found it first. No hell for Indians, just Happy Hunting Grounds. Blackcoat can't scare me.'

And then, after weeks had passed, one day as he stood at the tepee door he laid his white, old hand on my head and said to my father: 'Give me this little girl, chief. Let me take her to the mission school; let me keep her, and teach her of the great God and His eternal heaven. She will grow to be a noble woman, and return perhaps to bring her people to the Christ.'

My mother's eyes snapped. 'No,' she said. It was the first word she ever spoke to the 'Blackcoat.' My father sat and smoked. At the end of a half-hour he said: 'I am an old man, Blackcoat. I shall not leave the God of my fathers. I like not your strange God's ways—all of them. I like not His two new places for me when I am dead. Take the child, Blackcoat, and save her from hell.'

The first grief of my life was when we reached the mission. They took my buckskin dress off, saying I was now a little Christian girl and must dress like all the white people at the mission. Oh, how I hated that stiff new calico dress and those leather shoes! But, little as I was, I said nothing, only thought of the time when I should be grown, and do as my mother did, and wear the buckskins and the blanket.

My next serious grief was when I began to speak the English, that they forbade me to use any Cree words whatever. The rule of the school was that any child heard using its native tongue must get a slight punishment. I never understood it, I cannot understand it now, why the use of my dear Cree tongue could be a matter for correction or an action deserving punishment.

She was strict, the matron of the school, but only justly so, for she had a heart and a face like her brother's, the 'Blackcoat.' I had long since ceased to call him that. The trappers at the post called him 'St. Paul,' because, they told me, of his self-sacrificing life, his kindly deeds, his rarely beautiful old face; so I, too, called him 'St. Paul,' though oftener 'Father Paul,' though he never liked the latter title, for he was a Protestant. But as I was his pet, his darling of the whole school, he let me speak of him as I would, knowing it was but my heart speaking in love. His sister was a widow, and mother to a laughing yellow-haired little boy of about my own age, who was my constant playmate and who taught me much of English in his own childish way. I used to be fond of this child, just as I was fond of his mother and of his uncle, my 'Father Paul,' but as my girlhood passed away, as womanhood came upon me, I got strangely wearied of them all; I longed, oh, God, how I longed for the old wild life! It came with my womanhood, with my years.

What mattered it to me now that they had taught me all their ways?—their tricks of dress, their reading, their writing, their books. What mattered it that 'Father Paul' loved me, that the traders at the post called me pretty, that I was a pet of all, from the factor to the poorest trapper in the service? I wanted my own people, my own old life, my blood called out for it, but they always said I must not return to my father's tepee. I heard them talk amongst themselves of keeping me away from pagan influences; they told each other that if I returned to the prairies, the tepees, I would degenerate, slip back to paganism, as other girls had done; marry, perhaps, with a pagan—and all their years of labour and teaching would be lost.

I said nothing, but I waited. And then one night the feeling overcame me. I was in the Hudson's Bay store when an Indian came in from the north with a large pack of buckskin. As they unrolled it a dash of its insinuating odour filled the store. I went over and leaned above the skins a second, then buried my face in them, swallowing, drinking the fragrance of them, that went to my head like wine. Oh, the wild wonder of that wood-smoked tan, the subtlety of it, the untamed smell of it! I drank it into my lungs, my innermost being was saturated with it, till my mind reeled and my heart seemed twisted with a physical agony. My childhood recollections rushed upon me, devoured me. I left the store in a strange, calm frenzy, and going rapidly to the mission house I confronted my Father Paul and demanded to be allowed to go 'home,' if only for a day. He received the request with the same refusal and the same gentle sigh that I had so often been greeted with, but this time the desire, the smoke-tan, the heart-ache, never lessened.

Night after night I would steal away by myself and go to the border of the village to watch the sun set in the foothills, to gaze at the far line of sky and prairie, to long and long for my father's lodge. And Laurence—always Laurence—my fair-haired, laughing, child playmate, would come calling and calling for me: 'Esther, where are you? We miss you; come in, Esther, come in with me.' And if I did not turn at once to him and follow, he would come and place his strong hands on my shoulders and laugh into my eyes and say, 'Truant, truant, Esther; can't *we* make you happy?'

My old child playmate had vanished years ago. He was a tall, slender young man now, handsome as a young chief, but with laughing blue eyes, and always those yellow curls about his temples. He was my solace in my half-exile, my comrade, my brother, until one night it was, 'Esther, Esther, can't *I* make you happy?'

I did not answer him; only looked out across the plains and thought of the tepees. He came close, close. He locked his arms about me, and with my face pressed up to his throat he stood silent. I felt the blood from my heart sweep to my very finger-tips. I loved him. O God, how I loved him! In a wild, blind instant it all came, just because he held me so and was whispering brokenly, 'Don't leave me, don't leave me, Esther; *my* Esther, my child-love, my playmate, my girl-comrade, my little Cree sweetheart, will you go away to your people, or stay, stay for me, for my arms, as I have you now?'

No more, no more the tepees; no more the wild stretch of prairie, the intoxicating fragrance of the smoke-tanned buckskin; no more the bed of buffalo hide, the soft, silent moccasin; no more the dark faces of my people, the dulcet cadence of the sweet Cree tongue—only this man, this fair, proud, tender man who held me in his arms, in his heart. My soul prayed his great white God, in that moment, that He would let me have only this. It was twilight when we re-entered the mission gate. We were both excited, feverish. Father Paul was reading evening prayers in the large room beyond the hallway; his soft, saint-like voice stole beyond the doors, like a benediction upon us. I went noiselessly upstairs to my own room and sat there undisturbed for hours.

The clock downstairs struck one, startling me from my dreams of happiness, and at the same moment a flash of light attracted me. My room was in an angle of the building, and my window looked almost directly down into those of Father Paul's study, into which at that instant he was entering, carrying a lamp. 'Why, Laurence,' I heard him exclaim, 'what are you doing here? I thought, my boy, you were in bed hours ago.'

'No, uncle, not in bed, but in dreamland,' replied Laurence, arising from the window, where evidently he, too, had spent the night hours as I had done.

Father Paul fumbled about a moment, found his large black book, which for once he seemed to have got separated from, and was turning to leave, when the curious circumstance of Laurence being there at so unusual an hour seemed to strike him anew. 'Better go to sleep, my son,' he said simply, then added curiously, 'Has anything occurred to keep you up?'

Then Laurence spoke: 'No, uncle, only—only, I'm happy, that's all.'

Father Paul stood irresolute. Then: 'It is—?'

'Esther,' said Laurence quietly, but he was at the old man's side, his hand was on the bent old shoulder, his eyes proud and appealing.

Father Paul set the lamp on the table, but, as usual, one hand held that black book, the great text of his life. His face was paler than I had ever seen it—graver.

'Tell me of it,' he requested.

I leaned far out of my window and watched them both. I listened with my very heart, for Laurence was telling him of me, of his love, of the new-found joy of that night.

'You have said nothing of marriage to her?' asked Father Paul.

'Well—no; but she surely understands that—'

'Did you speak of *marriage*?' repeated Father Paul, with a harsh ring in his voice that was new to me.

'No, uncle, but—'

'Very well, then, very well.'

There was a brief silence. Laurence stood staring at the old man as though he were a stranger; he watched him push a large chair up to the table, slowly seat himself; then mechanically following his movements, he dropped on to a lounge. The old man's head bent low, but his eyes were bright and strangely fascinating. He began:

'Laurence, my boy, your future is the dearest thing to me of all earthly interests. Why you *can't* marry this girl—no, no, sit, sit until I have finished,' he added, with raised voice, as Laurence sprang up, remonstrating. 'I have long since decided that you marry well; for instance, the Hudson's Bay factor's daughter.'

Laurence broke into a fresh, rollicking laugh. 'What, uncle,' he said, 'little Ida McIntosh? Marry that little yellow-haired fluff ball, that kitten, that pretty little dolly?'

'Stop,' said Father Paul. Then with a low, soft persuasiveness, 'She is *white*, Laurence.'

My lover started. 'Why, uncle, what do you mean?' he faltered.

'Only this, my son: poor Esther comes of uncertain blood; would it do for you— the missionary's nephew, and adopted son, you might say—to marry the daughter of a pagan Indian? Her mother is hopelessly uncivilized; her father has a dash of French somewhere—half-breed, you know, my boy, half-breed.' Then, with still lower tone and half-shut, crafty eyes, he added: 'The blood is a bad, bad mixture, *you know that*; you know, too, that I am very fond of the girl, poor dear Esther. I have tried to separate her from evil pagan influences; she is the daughter of the Church; I want her to have no other parent; but you never can tell what lurks in *a caged animal that has once been wild*. My whole heart is with the Indian people, my son; my whole heart, my whole life, has been devoted to bringing them to Christ, *but it is a different thing to marry with one of them*.'

His small old eyes were riveted on Laurence like a hawk's on a rat. My heart lay like ice in my bosom.

Laurence, speechless and white, stared at him breathlessly.

'Go away somewhere,' the old man was urging; 'to Winnipeg, Toronto, Montreal; forget her, then come back to Ida McIntosh. A union of the Church and the Hudson's Bay will mean great things, and may ultimately result in my life's ambition, the civilization of this entire tribe, that we have worked so long to bring to God.'

I listened, sitting like one frozen. Could those words have been uttered by my venerable teacher, by him whom I revered as I would one of the saints in his own black book? Ah, there was no mistaking it. My white father, my life-long friend who pretended to love me, to care for my happiness, was urging the man I worshipped to forget me, to marry with the factor's daughter—because of what? Of my red skin; my good, old, honest pagan mother; my confiding French-Indian father. In a sec- ond all the care, the hollow love he had given me since my childhood, were as things that never existed. I hated that old mission priest as I hated his white man's hell. I hated his long, white hair; I hated his thin, white hands; I hated his body, his soul, his voice, his black book—oh, how I hated the very atmosphere of him!

Laurence sat motionless, his face buried in his hands, but the old man continued, 'No, no; not the child of that pagan mother; you can't trust her, my son. What would you do with a wife who might any day break from you to return to her prairies and her buckskins? *You can't trust her.*' His eyes grew smaller, more glittering, more fascinating then, and leaning with an odd, secret sort of movement towards Laurence, he almost whispered, 'Think of her silent ways, her noiseless step; the girl glides about like an apparition; her quick fingers, her wild longings—I don't know why, but with all my fondness for her, she reminds me sometimes of a strange—*snake.*'

Laurence shuddered, lifted his face, and said hoarsely: 'You're right, uncle; perhaps I'd better not; I'll go away, I'll forget her, and then—well, then—yes, you are right, it *is* a different thing to marry one of them.' The old man arose. His feeble fingers still clasped his black book; his soft white hair clung about his forehead like that of an Apostle; his eyes lost their peering, crafty expression; his bent shoulders resumed the dignity of a minister of the living God; he was the picture of what the traders called him—'St. Paul.'

'Good-night, son,' he said.

'Good-night, uncle, and thank you for bringing me to myself.'

They were the last words I ever heard uttered by either that old arch-fiend or his weak, miserable kinsman. Father Paul turned and left the room. I watched his withered hand—the hand I had so often felt resting on my head in holy benedictions—clasp the door-knob, turn it slowly, then, with bowed head and his pale face wrapped in thought, he left the room—left it with the mad venom of my hate pursuing him like the very Evil One he taught me of.

What were his years of kindness and care now? What did I care for his God, his heaven, his hell? He had robbed me of my native faith, of my parents, of my people, of this last, this life of love that would have made a great, good woman of me. God! how I hated him!

I crept to the closet in my dark little room. I felt for a bundle I had not looked at for years—yes, it was there, the buckskin dress I had worn as a little child when they brought me to the mission. I tucked it under my arm and descended the stairs noiselessly. I would look into the study and speak good-bye to Laurence; then I would—

I pushed open the door. He was lying on the couch where a short time previously he had sat, white and speechless, listening to Father Paul. I moved towards him softly. God in heaven, he was already asleep. As I bent over him the fullness of his perfect beauty impressed me for the first time; his slender form, his curving mouth that almost laughed even in sleep, his fair, tossed hair, his smooth, strong-pulsing throat. God! how I loved him!

Then there arose the picture of the factor's daughter. I hated her. I hated her baby face, her yellow hair, her whitish skin. 'She shall not marry him,' my soul said. 'I will kill him first—kill his beautiful body, his lying, false heart.' Something in my heart seemed to speak; it said over and over again, 'Kill him, kill him; she will never have him then. Kill him. It will break Father Paul's heart and blight his life. He has killed the best of you, of your womanhood; kill *his* best, his pride, his hope—his sister's son, his nephew Laurence.' But how? how?

What had that terrible old man said I was like? A *strange snake.* A snake? The idea wound itself about me like the very coils of a serpent. What was this in the beaded bag of my buckskin dress? This little thing rolled in tan that my mother had given me at parting with the words, 'Don't touch much, but some time maybe you want it!' Oh! I knew well enough what it was—a small flint arrowhead dipped in the venom of some *strange snake*.

I knelt beside him and laid my hot lips on his hand. I worshipped him, oh, how, how I worshipped him! Then again the vision of *her* baby face, *her* yellow hair—I scratched his wrist twice with the arrow-tip. A single drop of red blood oozed up; he stirred. I turned the lamp down and slipped out of the room—out of the house.

I dream nightly of the horrors of the white man's hell. Why did they teach me of it, only to fling me into it?

Last night as I crouched beside my mother on the buffalo-hide, Dan Henderson, the trapper, came in to smoke with my father. He said old Father Paul was bowed with grief, that with my disappearance I was suspected, but that there was no proof. Was it not merely a snake bite?

They account for it by the fact that I am a Redskin.

They seem to have forgotten I am a woman.

[1913]

ARCHIBALD LAMPMAN ■ (1861–1899)

Archibald Lampman is considered by many critics to be the finest of the Confederation Poets, which may at first seem surprising given the brevity of his life (he died from pneumonia and heart complications at the age of thirty-seven) and his relatively sparse poetic output. Born in Morpeth, Ontario, to an Anglican minister father and a highly cultured mother, Lampman moved to Gore's Landing on Rice Lake in 1867, where he made the acquaintance of Catharine Parr Traill and Susanna Moodie. At the age of seven, Lampman suffered a bout of rheumatic fever that damaged his heart irreparably. Thereafter, like his beloved English poet John Keats, Lampman was plagued by weak health. From early on, Lampman showed a precocious intelligence, which enabled him to win a scholarship to Trinity College in Toronto in 1879. It was during this period, in 1881, that he was inspired to begin writing poetry, after reading Charles G.D. Roberts's *Orion and Other Poems* (1880). After graduating from Trinity in 1882, and following a brief and unsatisfying stint of high school teaching, Lampman accepted a post in the civil service in Ottawa in January 1883. Appointed a clerk in the Post Office Department, Lampman continued in this job for more than fifteen years. Though the position was marked by tedium and low pay, it afforded him ample time to write poetry. He soon became acquainted with Duncan Campbell Scott, another Ottawa civil servant, and they struck up a close and rewarding friendship that had an immense impact on both their poetic careers. Together they undertook numerous canoeing expeditions in the Ontario and Quebec wilderness. Lampman's early poem "Morning on the Lièvre" was inspired by one of these adventures. Indeed, it was Scott who was responsible for gathering and publishing Lampman's poems following Lampman's early death at the close of the century.

Lampman's lecture "Two Canadian Poets" was delivered to the Ottawa Literary and Scientific Society in February 1891. In it, he describes the galvanizing effect of Roberts's 1880 *Orion and Other Poems* when he was an undergraduate at Trinity in 1881. For Lampman, Roberts was proof that a Canadian could write great literature. However, writing a decade later in 1891, Lampman averred that there was not yet a sufficient body of good writing that could be deemed a "Canadian literature," though he singles out Roberts and the poet George Frederick Cameron as paving the way for such a development. This may seem a startling statement for the man who was dubbed "the foremost of the young poets of America" in the 1889 Toronto *Globe* and hailed as "the greatest poet that Canada has produced" by D.G. Logan in 1924. Lampman's characteristic modesty in "Two Canadian Poets" is also evident in his famous assessment of himself, written in a letter to fellow writer E.W. Thomson on 29 August 1895, as "a minor poet of a superior order." In fact, in making such claims Lampman was engaging in the strenuous debates of the time on the topic of Canada's literary maturity. Sara Jeannette Duncan had proclaimed in the pages of *The Week* in 1886 that Canadians were an "unliterary people," while Goldwin Smith, in *Canada and the Canadian Question* (1891), had insisted that Canada was a mere "political expression" that was not held together by national sentiment or common outlook. Lampman, aware of these debates and of those concerning Canada's political independence, celebrates Canadian national identity, but is keen to distance himself from what he terms "blatant patriotism." Like Roberts and William Wilfred Campbell, he did not countenance the automatic celebration of things just because they were

Canadian, but sought an intelligent response to Canadian writing. In this vein, he critiques Roberts's patriotic poems for their prematurity: "The time has not come for the production of any genuine national song. It is when the passion and enthusiasm of an entire people . . . enters into the soul of one man specially gifted, that a great national poem or hymn is produced."

Lampman published only two collections of poetry in his lifetime: *Among the Millet* in 1888, which he published at his own expense, and *Lyrics of Earth* in 1896. A third collection, *Alcyone*, which he was working on before he died, was published posthumously by D.C. Scott in 1899. Based on the excellence of *Among the Millet*, E.W. Thomson, writing in the Toronto *Globe* in March 1890, addressed an editorial to the prime minister, John A. Macdonald, suggesting that Lampman's literary importance merited a more illustrious and better-paying position in the civil service. Nothing came of this request, but a few years later Lampman decided to supplement his income by writing a column for the Toronto *Globe*, entitled "At the Mermaid Inn." The column, which was shared by Lampman, Scott, and Campbell, included the writers' thoughts on various cultural and social issues of the day. "At the Mermaid Inn," which commenced in February 1892, concluded abruptly on 1 July 1893 when Campbell published a vicious satire of Lampman's poetry.

One sees in Lampman's poems the Romantic concern with the therapeutic potential of nature as a restorative retreat from the bustle of city life and petty, quotidian concerns. Such poems as "The Frogs" and "Among the Timothy" deal with this theme. It is not so much the landscape description that is of interest in these works (though they were certainly lauded for their depiction of a distinctly Canadian geography), but rather the effect of the surroundings on the mental state of the observer. In this, Lampman shares similarities with the British Romantics such as Wordsworth and Keats. Keats, in particular, was a central influence on Lampman's writings. In an 1894 letter to Thomson, Lampman wrote: "Keats has always had such a fascination for me and has so permeated *my* whole mental outfit that I have an idea that he has found a sort of faint reincarnation in me." This was partly due to the fact that both poets were plagued by poor health, and some critics have suggested that Lampman may have anticipated his own early death in his celebration of Keats as a spiritual precursor. However, Lampman also admired the visionary nature of Keats's poetry, in which moments of solitary contemplation in nature are accompanied by a kind of reverie that yields a transcendent vision, an experience that is rendered the more powerful by a haunting sense of transience or loss. Canadian critic Barrie Davies, in his 1970 dissertation on Lampman, astutely described Lampman's frustration with his reputation this way: "Lampman felt he was praised for all the wrong reasons; that the reviews tell us more about the taste of his society; that they smoothed over in blank appraisals all evidences of struggle and commitment. In other words, society took from Lampman's poems whatever comforted and flattered their preservative instincts and simply refused to see in them anything more abrasive." This may account for the often oversimplified celebration of Lampman as a nature poet, such as one finds in Campbell's moving elegy for his friend, "Bereavement of the Fields," at the expense of his profound exploration of uncertainty in the midst of nature's beauty.

While Lampman is widely celebrated as one of Canada's foremost nature poets, his writings, like Roberts's, also demonstrate an increasing social vision, particularly in his critique of capitalism and political corruption, evident in such poems as "To a Millionaire" and "The Modern Politician." In these poems, Lampman reveals both his socialist inclinations and his disillusioned Romanticism. Indeed, his work is poised between Romantic and Modernist visions of the world. D.M.R. Bentley describes this position as "the cusp between the Romantic withdrawal into Nature that enables communion with self and cosmos and a Modern sense of human aloneness in a universe whose meaning can never be known." In this vein, Lampman's nightmarish poem "The City of the End of Things" provides an apocalyptic depiction of the end of the industrialized world that prefigures the modernist visions of T.S. Eliot and W.B. Yeats.

The complex nature of Lampman's outlook, which oscillates between affirmation and melancholy, has led to contradictory assessments of his poetry. There has been extended discussion of the extent of Lampman's melancholic vision, but his close friend D.C. Scott repeatedly maintained that Lampman was not a melancholic man. In "The Modern School of Poetry in England," Lampman insists, "Life is not a dreary thing." Similarly, in his 1896 essay "Happiness" he writes: "We spend long lives in the pursuit of objects which we seldom attain, but always before us are the glories of anticipation, and behind us the magical playhouse of memory." Lampman, as he puts it in his own poem "Winter-Store," was drawn by "a nameless hunger of the soul," a keen sense of the paradoxical nature of human existence. In nature, he sought what he called "the eternal movement of life," and in this he shares a philosophical perspective with the best of Roberts's writings, as well as with Carman's "Low Tide on Grand Pré." He could be given to statements of great optimism, as one sees in the poem "Outlook" or in his fine essay "Happiness," yet also to moments of intense depression, as one finds in the powerful sonnet "Despondency." This split vision is often emblematized in his poetry in the divide between Nature and the City. If Lampman was able to celebrate the wonder of being alive, his experience was often marred by an awareness of life's inevitable passage. It is this paradoxical vision, what poet Ralph Gustafson refers to as Lampman's "sensitive unrest," that lends his poetry such power.

Among the Timothy

Long hours ago, while yet the morn was blithe,
    Nor sharp athirst had drunk the beaded dew,
A mower came, and swung his gleaming scythe
      Around this stump, and, shearing slowly, drew
      Far round among the clover, ripe for hay,
        A circle clean and gray;
And here among the scented swathes that gleam,
      Mixed with dead daisies, it is sweet to lie
      And watch the grass and the few-clouded sky,
        Nor think but only dream.   10

For when the noon was turning, and the heat
    Fell down most heavily on field and wood,
I too came hither, borne on restless feet,
      Seeking some comfort for an aching mood.
      Ah! I was weary of the drifting hours,
        The echoing city towers,
The blind gray streets, the jingle of the throng,
      Weary of hope that like a shape of stone
      Sat near at hand without a smile or moan,
        And weary most of song.   20

And those high moods of mine that sometime made
    My heart a heaven, opening like a flower
A sweeter world where I in wonder strayed,
      Begirt with shapes of beauty and the power
      Of dreams that moved through that enchanted clime
        With changing breaths of rhyme,
Were all gone lifeless now, like those white leaves
      That hang all winter, shivering dead and blind
      Among the sinewy beeches in the wind,
        That vainly calls and grieves.   30

Ah! I will set no more mine overtaskèd brain
    To barren search and toil that beareth nought,

For ever following with sore-footed pain
   The crossing pathways of unbournèd thought;
      But let it go, as one that hath no skill,
         To take what shape it will,
An ant slow-burrowing in the earthy gloom,
   A spider bathing in the dew at morn,
   Or a brown bee in wayward fancy borne
      From hidden bloom to bloom.   40

Hither and thither o'er the rocking grass
   The little breezes, blithe as they are blind,
Teasing the slender blossoms pass and pass,
   Soft-footed children of the gipsy wind,
      To taste of every purple-fringèd head
         Before the bloom is dead;
And scarcely heed the daisies that, endowed
   With stems so short they cannot see, up-bear
   Their innocent sweet eyes distressed, and stare
      Like children in a crowd.   50

Not far to fieldward in the central heat,
   Shadowing the clover, a pale poplar stands
With glimmering leaves that, when the wind comes, beat
   Together like innumerable small hands,
      And with the calm, as in vague dreams astray,
         Hang wan and silver-gray;
Like sleepy maenads,[1] who in pale surprise,
   Half-wakened by a prowling beast, have crept
   Out of the hidden covert, where they slept,
      At noon with languid eyes.   60

The crickets creak, and through the noonday glow,
   That crazy fiddler of the hot mid-year,
The dry cicada plies his wiry bow
   In long-spun cadence, thin and dusty sere;
      From the green grass the small grasshoppers' din
         Spreads soft and silvery thin;
And ever and anon a murmur steals
   Into mine ears of toil that moves alway,
   The crackling rustle of the pitch-forked hay
      And lazy jerk of wheels.   70

And so I lie and feel the soft hours wane,
   To wind and sun and peaceful sound laid bare,

---

[1] In Greek mythology, the frenzied female worshippers of Dionysus, the god of wine.

That aching dim discomfort of the brain
        Fades off unseen, and shadowy-footed care
        Into some hidden corner creeps at last
                To slumber deep and fast;
And gliding on, quite fashioned to forget,
        From dream to dream I bid my spirit pass
        Out into the pale green ever-swaying grass
                To brood, but no more fret.   80

And hour by hour among all shapes that grow
        Of purple mints and daisies gemmed with gold
In sweet unrest my visions come and go;
        I feel and hear and with quiet eyes behold;
        And hour by hour, the ever-journeying sun,
                In gold and shadow spun,
Into mine eyes and blood, and through the dim
        Green glimmering forest of the grass shines down,
        Till flower and blade, and every cranny brown,
                And I are soaked with him.   90

[1888]

Outlook

Not to be conquered by these headlong days,
        But to stand free: to keep the mind at brood
        On life's deep meaning, nature's altitude
Of loveliness, and time's mysterious ways;
At every thought and deed to clear the haze
        Out of our eyes, considering only this,
        What man, what life, what love, what beauty is,
This is to live, and win the final praise.

Though strife, ill fortune and harsh human need
        Beat down the soul, at moments blind and dumb   10
        With agony; yet, patience—there shall come
                Many great voices from life's outer sea,
Hours of strange triumph, and, when few men heed,
        Murmurs and glimpses of eternity.

[1888]

The Railway Station

The darkness brings no quiet here, the light
        No waking: ever on my blinded brain

The flare of lights, the rush, and cry, and strain,
The engines' scream, the hiss and thunder smite:
I see the hurrying crowds, the clasp, the flight,
    Faces that touch, eyes that are dim with pain:
    I see the hoarse wheels turn, and the great train
Move labouring out into the bourneless night.

So many souls within its dim recesses,
    So many bright, so many mournful eyes: 10
Mine eyes that watch grow fixed with dreams and guesses;
    What threads of life, what hidden histories,
What sweet or passionate dreams and dark distresses,
    What unknown thoughts, what various agonies!

[1888]

The City of the End of Things

Beside the pounding cataracts
Of midnight streams unknown to us
'Tis builded in the leafless tracts
And valleys huge of Tartarus.[2]
Lurid and lofty and vast it seems;
It hath no rounded name that rings,
But I have heard it called in dreams
The City of the End of Things.

Its roofs and iron towers have grown
None knoweth how high within the night,   10
But in its murky streets far down
A flaming terrible and bright
Shakes all the stalking shadows there,
Across the walls, across the floors,
And shifts upon the upper air
From out a thousand furnace doors;
And all the while an awful sound
Keeps roaring on continually,
And crashes in the ceaseless round
Of a gigantic harmony.   20
Through its grim depths re-echoing
And all its weary height of walls,
With measured roar and iron ring,
The inhuman music lifts and falls.

---

[2] The ancient Greek hell or underworld.

Where no thing rests and no man is,
And only fire and night hold sway;
The beat, the thunder and the hiss
Cease not, and change not, night nor day.

And moving at unheard commands,
The abysses and vast fires between,   30
Flit figures that with clanking hands
Obey a hideous routine;
They are not flesh, they are not bone,
They see not with the human eye,
And from their iron lips is blown
A dreadful and monotonous cry;
And whoso of our mortal race
Should find that city unaware,
Lean Death would smite him face to face,
And blanch him with its venomed air: 40
Or caught by the terrific spell,
Each thread of memory snapt and cut,
His soul would shrivel and its shell
Go rattling like an empty nut.

It was not always so, but once,
In days that no man thinks upon,
Fair voices echoed from its stones,
The light above it leaped and shone:
Once there were multitudes of men,
That built that city in their pride,   50
Until its might was made, and then
They withered age by age and died.
But now of that prodigious race,
Three only in an iron tower,
Set like carved idols face to face,
Remain the masters of its power;
And at the city gate a fourth,
Gigantic and with dreadful eyes,
Sits looking toward the lightless north,
Beyond the reach of memories;   60
Fast rooted to the lurid floor,
A bulk that never moves a jot,
In his pale body dwells no more,
Or mind or soul,—an idiot!
But sometime in the end those three
Shall perish and their hands be still,

And with the master's touch shall flee
Their incommunicable skill.
A stillness absolute as death
Along the slacking wheels shall lie,   70
And, flagging at a single breath,
The fires shall moulder out and die.
The roar shall vanish at its height,
And over that tremendous town
The silence of eternal night
Shall gather close and settle down.
All its grim grandeur, tower and hall,
Shall be abandoned utterly,
And into rust and dust shall fall
From century to century;   80
Nor ever living thing shall grow,
Nor trunk of tree, nor blade of grass;
No drop shall fall, no wind shall blow,
Nor sound of any foot shall pass:
Alone of its accursèd state,
One thing the hand of Time shall spare,
For the grim Idiot at the gate
Is deathless and eternal there.

[1899]

Winter Evening

To-night the very horses springing by
Toss gold from whitened nostrils. In a dream
The streets that narrow to the westward gleam
Like rows of golden palaces; and high
From all the crowded chimneys tower and die
A thousand aureoles. Down in the west
The brimming plains beneath the sunset rest,
One burning sea of gold. Soon, soon shall fly
The glorious vision, and the hours shall feel
A mightier master; soon from height to height,   10
With silence and the sharp unpitying stars,
Stern creeping frosts, and winds that touch like steel,
Out of the depth beyond the eastern bars,
Glittering and still shall come the awful night.

[1899]

To a Millionaire

The world in gloom and splendour passes by,
And thou in the midst of it with brows that gleam,
A creature of that old distorted dream
That makes the sound of life an evil cry.
Good men perform just deeds, and brave men die,
And win not honour such as gold can give,
While the vain multitudes plod on, and live,
And serve the curse that pins them down: But I
Think only of the unnumbered broken hearts,
The hunger and the mortal strife for bread,   10
Old age and youth alike mistaught, misfed,
By want and rags and homelessness made vile,
The griefs and hates, and all the meaner parts
That balance thy one grim misgotten pile.

[1900]

The Modern Politician

What manner of soul is his to whom high truth
Is but the plaything of a feverish hour,
A dangling ladder to the ghost of power!
Gone are the grandeurs of the world's iron youth,
When kings were mighty, being made by swords.
Now comes the transit age, the age of brass,
When clowns into the vacant empires pass,
Blinding the multitude with specious words.
To them faith, kinship, truth and verity,
Man's sacred rights and very holiest thing,   10
Are but the counters at a desperate play,
Flippant and reckless what the end may be,
So that they glitter, each his little day,
The little mimic of a vanished king.

[1900]

Two Canadian Poets: A Lecture[3]

In the last twenty years great advances have been made in this country, and many
things have been accomplished which are a sourse [sic] of hope and comfort to
those who are beginning to feel for Canada the enthusiasm of Fatherland[.] Already
there are many among us whose fathers and grandfathers have lived and died upon

[3] This lecture was delivered by Lampman in February 1891 for the Literary and Scientific Society
in Ottawa.

this soil, who are neither British, French nor German, but simply Canadians. For them everything connected with the honour and well-being of their country has come to be a matter of daily interest. The enthusiasm of Fatherland, the attachment to native soil, the love of the name of our country[,] is one of those generous impulses which have always been a moral necessity and an encouraging help to people who do not live by bread alone. It is getting rather customary in our time to underrate patriotism as one of the virtues, and to substitute in its place cosmopolitanism or the enthusiasm for the advancement of all mankind, making no distinction in favour of any country. Nothing could be finer than that; but unfortunately our energies, if made to cover too wide a ground, are apt to lose themselves in mere speculation, and to fall short of practical effect. Perhaps it is safer therefore to be interested chiefly in the well fare of our own country, provided that we do nothing to hinder the just advancement of that of others. At any rate the true spirit of patriotism has always been a considerable factor in the best upward movements of the human race. Let us however discountenance blatant patriotism as we would discountenance everything that is suspicious and ridiculous. Dr. Johnson's old saying about patriotism holds true in a new country like ours more markedly than in any other, and there are a greater number of those who find that it pays to be extremely zealous about their Fatherland.[4] Already there is a good deal of talk in the public press which reminds one a little of Elijah Pogram and Jefferson Brick.[5] At this time when our country's destiny, its very independent existence perhaps, is a matter of doubt and anxiety, it behooves us to be silent and do no boasting, but look seriously about us for the wisest thing to be said and done at each crisis.

A good deal is being said about Canadian Literature, and most of it takes the form of question and answer as to whether a Canadian Literature exists. Of course it does not. It will probably be a full generation or two before we can present a body of work of sufficient excellence as measured by the severest standards, and sufficiently marked with local colour, to enable us to call it a Canadian Literature. It is only within the last quarter of a century that the United States have produced anything like a distinctive American Literature. There was scarcely any peculiar literary quality in the work of the age of Longfellow, and Hawthorne to mark it decidedly as American[.][6] But within the last twenty five or thirty years, along with the evolution of a marked American race, certain noticeable American peculiarities of mind and character have been developed, which have strongly affected literary expression. Our country is still in the house-building land-breaking stage, and all its energies must go to the laying of a foundation of material prosperity upon which a future culture may be built. Those capable minds, which in old and long-civilized countries might be drawn into literature, in Canada are forced into the more practical paths[.] They are engaged in making fortunes and founding

---

[4] Probably a reference to Samuel Johnson's (1709–84) famous saying, "Patriotism is the last refuge of a scoundrel" (cited in James Boswell's biography of Johnson).

[5] Both characters from Charles Dickens's *Martin Chuzzlewit*.

[6] Henry Wadsworth Longfellow (1807–82) and Nathaniel Hawthorne (1804–64), both important writers in the canon of American national literature.

families. Their descendents [*sic*], the people who shall inherit the fortune, leizure [*sic*], station secured by them will be the writers or the readers of the age when a Canadian Literature comes to be. At present our people are too busy to read, too busy at least to read with discernment, and where there are no discerning readers there will be no writers. Also our educational institutions—even our best universities—are yet too raw to develop a literary spirit. All they can now be expected to do is to furnish the country with smart lawyers, competent physicians, able business men. As we advance in age and the settled conditions of life, these things will be gradually changed[.] There will arise a leizured class, a large body of educated people, who will create a market for literature and a literary atmosphere. And when that happens a literature will be produced for them. If our country becomes an independent compacted, self-supporting nation, which is, or ought to be, the dream of all of us, its social and climatic conditions will in the course of time evolve a race of people, having a peculiar national temperament and bent of mind, and when that is done we shall have a *Canadian* literature[.]

It is no doubt futile to speculate on the character of a thing as yet so remote as a Canadian Literature; yet one might hazard a thought or two on that subject. We know that climatic and scenic conditions have much to do with the moulding of national character. In the climate of this country we have the pitiless severity of the climate of Sweden with the sunshine and the sky of the north of Italy, a combination not found in the same degree anywhere else in the world. The northern winters of Europe are seasons of terror and gloom; our winters are seasons of glittering splendour and incomparable richness of colour. At the same time we have the utmost diversity of scenery, a country exhibiting every variety of beauty and grandeur. A Canadian race, we imagine, might combine the energy, the seriousness, the perseverance of the Scandinavians with something of the gayety, the elasticity, the quickness of spirit of the south. If these qualities could be united in a literature, the result would indeed be something novel and wonderful.

[. . .] In the last decade or two a small quantity of work of very decided excellence has been produced by Canadians. If we confine our view to pure literature a great part of this small quantity of excellent work has been done in verse. It is natural that the poet should be the most conspicuous product of the awakening literary impulse in a new country like ours. The philosopher, the historian, the critic, the novelist are more likely to represent a long established civilization. In a new and sparcely [*sic*] settled land the urgent problems of life do not force themselves on the attention of men as they do in the midst of dense populations. Consequently though they may interest themselves in the study of philosophy as a matter of culture, they are not likely to produce much original work of that sort. The field for the historian is also not very extensive. The critic has no place because he has nothing to examine. Even the novelist is likely to be a later product; for it is in the press of the older civilizations, where life in all its variety throngs about him, that he finds birth, food and stimulus. But for the poet the beauty of external nature and the aspects of the most primitive life are always a sufficient inspiration. On the border of civilization the poet is pretty sure to be the literary pioneer[.] For the poet of external nature no country is richer in inspiration than ours. For the balladist or the narrative writer we have at least as good a field as our neighbours of the United States. For the dramatic poet, if a dramatic poet could be produced in our age, there are I should think several excellent subjects in [the] history of old French Canada. [. . .]

As regards Mr. Roberts['] work I have always had a personal feeling which perhaps induces me to place a higher estimate upon it in some respects than my hearers will care to accept. To most younger Canadians, who are interested in literature, especially those who have written themselves, Mr. Roberts occupies a peculiar position. They are accustomed to look up to him as in some sort the founder of a school, the originator of a new era in our poetic activity. I hope my hearers will pardon me, if I go out of my way to illustrate this fact by describing the effect Mr. Roberts' poems produced upon me when I first met with them.

It was almost ten years ago, and I was very young, an undergraduate at College. One May evening somebody lent me *Orion and Other Poems* then recently published. Like most of the young fellows about me I had been under the depressing conviction that we were situated hopelessly on the outskirts of civilization, where no art and no literature could be, and that it was useless to expect that anything great could be done by any of our companions, still more useless to expect that we could do it ourselves. I sat up all night reading and re-reading "Orion" in a state of the wildest excitement and when I went to bed I could not sleep. It seemed to me a wonderful thing that such work could be done by a Canadian, by a young man, one of ourselves. It was like a voice from some new paradise of art calling to us to be up and doing. A little after sunrise I got up and went out into the College grounds. The air, I remember, was full of the odour and cool sunshine of the spring morning. The dew was thick upon the grass. All the birds of our Maytime seemed to be singing in the oaks, and there were even a few adder-tongues and trilliums still blossoming on the slope of the little ravine. But everything was transfigured for me beyond description, bathed in an old world radiance of beauty, the magic of the lines that were sounding in my ears, those divine verses, as they seemed to me, with their Tennyson-like richness and strange, earth-loving Greekish flavour. I have never forgotten that morning, and its influence has always remained with me. [. . .]

[1891]

DUNCAN CAMPBELL SCOTT ■ (1862–1947)

Duncan Campbell Scott is today considered the most controversial of the Confederation Poets. This is ironic given that, of all the members of what Charles G.D. Roberts christened his little "band" of Canadian writers, he led the most settled life. Scott's infamous and hotly debated reputation arises from the profoundly divided nature of his writings about Canada's Aboriginal peoples. His life itself was split between his fascination with Native cultures and an official mandate, as part of his work for the Department of Indian Affairs, to "continue until there is not a single Indian in Canada that has not been absorbed into the body politic" and "Indians . . . finally disappear as a separate and distinct people." In both his poetry and nonfiction writing, Scott gave voice to a profound ambivalence about what he termed "the Indian problem." His writings are marked by a simultaneous mix of enthrallment and fear, both of which were fed by his awareness of the hypocrisy of many governmental policies toward Native peoples, policies that he was instrumental in generating and implementing.

Born in Ottawa in 1862, Scott was the son of a Methodist minister who worked as a missionary among Native communities in the small villages of Ontario and Quebec. The family's itinerant lifestyle exposed Scott to a variety of societies and cultures, from French-Canadian *habitants* and lumbermen to various Native peoples. He quickly developed the art of camouflage, an ability to fit in and adapt to the unexpected, which may have contributed to his shy and modest persona in later life. These early childhood experiences also contributed to his love of wilderness adventure. Because the family was large and a minister's salary was meagre, Scott's hopes of entering university to study medicine were dashed when, in 1879, he had to earn a living. His father arranged for him to be interviewed by Prime Minister John A. Macdonald, following which Scott was given a position as a clerk in the Department of Indian Affairs. Although Scott entertained vague hopes of saving enough money to pay for his medical training, his success in the civil service led to a series of promotions and a career that ultimately lasted fifty-two years, until his retirement in 1932. It was during his time in the civil service, in the 1880s and '90s, that Scott met fellow poet Archibald Lampman, who worked in the Post Office

Department. Scott told literary critic E.K. Brown that it was his friendship with Lampman that inspired him to begin writing poetry. The two became close friends, meeting regularly to discuss literature and music (Scott was an accomplished pianist), writing a column together in the Toronto *Globe* ("At the Mermaid Inn"), and undertaking numerous canoeing and camping expeditions throughout Quebec and Ontario. Following Lampman's death in 1899, Scott tirelessly devoted himself to promoting Lampman's reputation, publishing *The Memorial Edition* of Lampman's poems in 1900, which included a personal memoir of his friend.

While Scott, like Lampman, may have felt constrained by life in the civil service, the position offered certain advantages. As he advanced to a position of seniority in the Department of Indian Affairs, eventually reaching the post of deputy superintendent in 1913, he made extended trips to Native settlements for treaty negotiations and other policy matters. Scott loved being out in nature, and these trips provided him with inspiration for his poetry. As he outlines in "The Last of the Indian Treaties," his essay describing his 1905 trip to James Bay to negotiate Treaty 9, on many of these excursions he enjoyed the status of a kind of visiting dignitary. As he was paddled across lakes in enormous canoes (see Figure III-19), he would often compose elaborate poems about the landscape and people he was encountering. Such was the case with "The Half-Breed Girl" and "The Height of Land," which were based on his northern excursions of 1905 and 1906 respectively (as was "Powassan's Drum," written many years later in 1925). However, in "The Last of the Indian Treaties," published in *Scribner's Magazine* in 1906, Scott also expresses a sense of the complexity of his position.

He realizes that the Native peoples have been subdued by the Europeans and he understands the skepticism of the chiefs when they appear bemused by the latest promises of the government officials. What is rarely acknowledged in the critiques of Scott's Indian Affairs work is that he was quite aware of the contradictions inherent in government policy. As he wrote in 1923, the policy's goal "is to protect the Indian, to guard his identity as a race and at the same time to apply methods which will destroy that identity and lead eventually to his disappearance as a separate division of the population." Yet "The Last of the Indian Treaties" is also an excellent example of self-justification. By the end, he maintains the rightness of his mission, though it may be a case of protesting too much. To be sure, Scott's official position on Native peoples was the assimilationist one of his time, based on an implicit notion of White superiority. In his view, Native peoples were destined to become subsumed within the White population, and it was the mission of British civil law to facilitate this outcome through peaceful means. His projection of the hopeless future for Aboriginal peoples and cultures is thus not altogether different from Lord Durham's insistence, in 1839, on the need for assimilating French Canadians until they had "disappeared."

In his official statements for the Department of Indian Affairs, Scott supported the banning of Native gatherings and dances (including the sun dance and potlatch), the establishment of residential schools (despite his awareness of the miserable conditions at many of the schools), and the complete assimilation of Aboriginal people. He was also involved in 1924 in raiding the home of Six Nations leader Deskaheh and dissolving the traditional government of the Six Nations Confederacy (see Section IV for an excerpt from Deskaheh's last speech).

However, in private he expressed some reservations about the policies that he was enforcing. In a 1941 letter to E.K. Brown, Scott admitted that he was sympathetic to "aboriginal ideals" but was bound by "[the Indian Act] which I did not originate." It is difficult to establish how much responsibility is to be laid on Scott for the Indian policies he supported. In his creative writing, including "The Last of the Indian Treaties," he laments the lost nobility of Native cultures. His portrait of the Iroquois woman in his poem "Watkwenies," for example, contrasts her proud past with the abject circumstances of the present. Similarly, his famous sonnet "The Onondaga Madonna" presents a striking portrait of a Native woman, yet concludes with a sense of impending doom, not just for Aboriginal peoples, but also for the White men who have had a hand in their destruction. The poem has been described as an example of the "vanishing race" theory, in that it laments the demise of Aboriginal peoples while ostensibly "preserving" them in a work of art. Such notions of the imminent demise of the race were built on a sometimes unstated desire for the complete effacement of Aboriginal peoples. Also, at its paternalistic base is an essential fear of the Native "Other," and the settler's unacknowledged guilt at having displaced indigenous North Americans. The baby signals his "nation's doom" because he is of mixed heritage, while at the same time "the primal warrior gleam[s] from his eyes," as he poses a lingering threat to the Europeans since he may enact his revenge on his conquerors. This kind of ambivalence pervades much of Scott's writing about Native peoples. In "Powassan's Drum," it reaches its culmination in Scott's depiction of the nightmare vision that is conjured by the Aboriginal shaman of the poem. Armand Garnet Ruffo's "Poem for Duncan Campbell Scott" (see Volume II) presents a view of Scott from the perspective of the Aboriginal people he sought to "talk treaty" with.

Most of Scott's "Indian poems" are contained in his 1898 and 1905 collections, *Labor and the Angel* and *New World Lyrics and Ballads*. In 1893 he published his first collection, *The Magic House and Other Poems*, though it is the later collections that are more widely cited. Of all the Confederation Poets, Scott was the most stylistically experimental and varied in his choice of subject matter: from descriptive landscape poems, to tales of Native life, to mystical dream visions, to lyrical elegies, to longer narrative poems. His 1898 poem, "The Piper of Arll," stands out as a strange allegory about the fate of the poet, while "Night Hymns" is a haunting yet lulling poem of canoeing against the backdrop of an oncoming storm. In poems such as "Night Hymns" and "The Height of Land," the latter of which Scott considered one of his best works, Scott sought to reconcile himself with the deep pathos of human life by meditating on the contingencies of historical time and the poet's role in capturing the "golden and inappellable" moments that point beyond individual consciousness. In "Poetry and Progress," his 1922 presidential address to the Royal Society, Scott states that poetry's role is to express "the complex emotions of life in terms of purest beauty." In his view, much of the modernist school of poetry was too concerned with the "false freedom" of revolt to capture the true spirit of poetic expression. And yet, Scott also saw in this movement a shift in powers: "Revolt is essential to progress. . . . The latest mission of revolt has . . . served to show us that our poetic utterance was becoming formalized."

Like Roberts, Scott also made a reputation for himself as an accomplished writer of short stories. In 1896 he published *In the Village of Viger*, a collection of linked stories that centres on the inhabitants of a French-Canadian village. The stories provide affectionately ironic, and sometimes vaguely eerie, renderings of a regional setting and its many inhabitants: a milliner, a widow, a pedlar, an innkeeper, and others. Scott's work is a clear precursor of Stephen Leacock's *Sunshine Sketches of a Little Town* (1912), although the content of Scott's stories is far darker than Leacock's, as many of his characters are plagued by madness or depression. In this, the stories in *Viger* anticipate the much weirder tales in his 1923 collection, *The Witching of Elspie*, in which Scott explores his interest in the supernatural. While Scott's fascination with nightmarish tales of terror and the uncanny is evident in such poems as "The Piper of Arll" and "Powassan's Drum," it achieved fuller treatment in these tales. The stories do not concern Native people as much as instances of suspicion and violence that arise when White men find themselves in isolated wilderness settings. They are reminiscent of the stories of the American author Edgar Allan Poe, but with a Canadian twist. As Scott puts it in one of his stories, his interest is "the petty passions of man displayed before the grand calm of nature." A tale such as "In the Year 1806" thus forms part of a tradition of Canadian psychological "wilderness Gothic," such as one finds in Susanna Moodie's fears in the backwoods (1852), in Charles Dawson Shanly's "The Walker of the Snow" (1859), in Roberts's curious tales in *Earth's Enigmas* (1896), and further forward, in such poems as Earle Birney's "Bushed" (1952) or Margaret Atwood's *The Journals of Susanna Moodie* (1970).

Although in "Poetry and Progress" Scott lamented the absence of any overt feelings of national identity in the post-Confederation period, he identified himself, with Lampman and Marjorie Pickthall, as stalwartly contributing to the "struggle for self-expression in a new country." Looking back on his writing career in 1929, Scott asked that "if any of my work may be remembered for a while[,] I wish that Canadians might remember the things I have written about the aspect and charm of this land of ours, for I am a Canadian to the marrow of my bones. . . ."

The Onondaga[1] Madonna

She stands full-throated and with careless pose,
This woman of a weird and waning race,
The tragic savage lurking in her face,
Where all her pagan passion burns and glows;
Her blood is mingled with her ancient foes,
And thrills with war and wildness in her veins;
Her rebel lips are dabbled with the stains
Of feuds and forays and her father's woes.

And closer in the shawl about her breast,
The latest promise of her nation's doom,   10
Paler than she her baby clings and lies,
The primal warrior gleaming from his eyes;
He sulks, and burdened with his infant gloom,
He draws his heavy brows and will not rest.

[1898]

The Piper of Arll

There was in Arll a little cove
Where the salt wind came cool and free:
A foamy beach that one would love,
If he were longing for the sea.

A brook hung sparkling on the hill,
The hill swept far to ring the bay;
The bay was faithful, wild or still,
To the heart of the ocean far away.

There were three pines above the comb
That, when the sun flared and went down,   10
Grew like three warriors reaving home
The plunder of a burning town.

A piper lived within the grove,
Tending the pasture of his sheep;

[1] One of the Iroquois nations.

His heart was swayed with faithful love,
From the springs of God's ocean clear and deep.

And there a ship one evening stood,
Where ship had never stood before;
A pennon bickered red as blood,
An angel glimmered at the prore.[2]   20

About the coming on of dew,
The sails burned rosy, and the spars
Were gold, and all the tackle grew
Alive with ruby-hearted stars.

The piper heard an outland tongue,
With music in the cadenced fall;
And when the fairy lights were hung,
The sailors gathered one and all,

And leaning on the gunwales dark,
Crusted with shells and dashed with foam,   30
With all the dreaming hills to hark,
They sang their longing songs of home.

When the sweet airs had fled away,
The piper, with a gentle breath,
Moulded a tranquil melody
Of lonely love and longed-for death.

When the fair sound began to lull,
From out the fireflies and the dew,
A silence held the shadowy hull,
Until the eerie tune was through.   40

Then from the dark and dreamy deck
An alien song began to thrill;
It mingled with the drumming beck,
And stirred the braird[3] upon the hill.

Beneath the stars each sent to each
A message tender, till at last
The piper slept upon the beach,
The sailors slumbered round the mast.

Still as a dream till nearly dawn,
The ship was bosomed on the tide;   50

[2] *prore* is an archaic term for a ship's prow; the reference is to an angel figurehead on the prow of the ship.

[3] *beck*, a stream; *braird*, the young shoots of grass or crops.

The streamlet, murmuring on and on,
Bore the sweet water to her side.

Then shaking out her lawny sails,
Forth on the misty sea she crept;
She left the dawning of the dales,
Yet in his cloak the piper slept.

And when he woke he saw the ship,
Limned black against the crimson sun;
Then from the disc he saw her slip,
A wraith of shadow—she was gone.   60

He threw his mantle on the beach,
He went apart like one distraught,
His lips were moved—his desperate speech
Stormed his inviolable thought.

He broke his human-throated reed,
And threw it in the idle rill;
But when his passion had its mead,
He found it in the eddy still.

He mended well the patient flue,
Again he tried its varied stops;   70
The closures answered right and true,
And starting out in piercing drops,

A melody began to drip
That mingled with a ghostly thrill
The vision-spirit of the ship,
The secret of his broken will.

Beneath the pines he piped and swayed,
Master of passion and of power;
He was his soul and what he played,
Immortal for a happy hour.   80

He, singing into nature's heart,
Guiding his will by the world's will,
With deep, unconscious, childlike art
Had sung his soul out and was still.

And then at evening came the bark
That stirred his dreaming heart's desire;
It burned slow lights along the dark
That died in glooms of crimson fire.

The sailors launched a sombre boat,
And bent with music at the oars;   90

The rhythm throbbing every throat,
And lapsing round the liquid shores,

Was that true tune the piper sent,
Unto the wave-worn mariners,
When with the beck and ripple blent
He heard that outland song of theirs.

Silent they rowed him, dip and drip,
The oars beat out an exequy,[4]
They laid him down within the ship,
They loosed a rocket to the sky.   100

It broke in many a crimson sphere
That grew to gold and floated far,
And left the sudden shore-line clear,
With one slow-changing, drifting star.

Then out they shook the magic sails,
That charmed the wind in other seas,
From where the west line pearls and pales,
They waited for a ruffling breeze.

But in the world there was no stir,
The cordage slacked with never a creak,   110
They heard the flame begin to purr
Within the lantern at the peak.

They could not cry, they could not move,
They felt the lure from the charmed sea;
They could not think of home or love
Or any pleasant land to be.

They felt the vessel dip and trim,
And settle down from list to list;
They saw the sea-plain heave and swim
As gently as a rising mist.   120

And down so slowly, down and down,
Rivet by rivet, plank by plank;
A little flood of ocean flown
Across the deck, she sank and sank.

From knee to breast the water wore,
It crept and crept; ere they were ware
Gone was the angel at the prore,
They felt the water float their hair.

---

[4] A funeral ceremony.

They saw the salt plain spark and shine,
They threw their faces to the sky;   130
Beneath a deepening film of brine
They saw the star-flash blur and die.

She sank and sank by yard and mast,
Sank down the shimmering gradual dark;
A little drooping pennon last
Showed like the black fin of a shark.

And down she sank till, keeled in sand,
She rested safely balanced true,
With all her upward gazing band,
The piper and the dreaming crew.   140

And there, unmarked of any chart,
In unrecorded deeps they lie,
Empearled within the purple heart
Of the great sea for aye and aye.

Their eyes are ruby in the green
Long shaft of sun that spreads and rays,
And upward with a wizard sheen
A fan of sea-light leaps and plays.

Tendrils of or and azure creep,
And globes of amber light are rolled,   150
And in the gloaming of the deep
Their eyes are starry pits of gold.

And sometimes in the liquid night
The hull is changed, a solid gem,
That glows with a soft stony light,
The lost prince of a diadem.

And at the keel a vine is quick,
That spreads its bines and works and weaves
O'er all the timbers veining thick
A plenitude of silver leaves.   160

[1898]

Night Hymns on Lake Nipigon[5]

Here in the midnight, where the dark mainland and island
Shadows mingle in shadow deeper, profounder,

---

[5] A large lake to the northeast of Thunder Bay, Ontario.

Sing we the hymns of the churches, while the dead water
   Whispers before us.

Thunder is travelling slow on the path of the lightning;
One after one the stars and the beaming planets
Look serene in the lake from the edge of the storm-cloud;
   Then have they vanished.

While our canoe, that floats dumb in the bursting thunder,
Gathers her voice in the quiet and thrills and whispers,   10
Presses her prow in the star-gleam, and all her ripple
   Lapses in blackness.

Sing we the sacred ancient hymns of the churches,
Chanted first in old-world nooks of the desert,
While in the wild, pellucid Nipigon reaches
   Hunted the savage.

Now have the ages met in the Northern midnight,
And on the lonely, loon-haunted Nipigon reaches
Rises the hymn of triumph and courage and comfort,
   Adeste Fideles.   20

Tones that were fashioned when the faith brooded in darkness,
Joined with sonorous vowels in the noble Latin,
Now are married with the long-drawn Ojibwa,
   Uncouth and mournful.

Soft with the silver drip of the regular paddles
Falling in rhythm, timed with the liquid, plangent
Sounds from the blades where the whirlpools break and are carried
   Down into darkness;

Each long cadence, flying like a dove from her shelter
Deep in the shadow, wheels for a throbbing moment,   30
Poises in utterance, returning in circles of silver
   To nest in the silence.

All wild nature stirs with the infinite, tender
Plaint of a bygone age whose soul is eternal,
Bound in the lonely phrases that thrill and falter
   Back into quiet.

Back they falter as the deep storm overtakes them,
Whelms them in splendid hollows of booming thunder,
Wraps them in rain, that, sweeping, breaks and onrushes
   Ringing like cymbals.   40

[1905]

Indian Place-Names

The race has waned and left but tales of ghosts,
That hover in the world like fading smoke
About the lodges: gone are the dusky folk
That once were cunning with the thong and snare
And mighty with the paddle and the bow;
They lured the silver salmon from his lair,
They drove the buffalo in trampling hosts,
And gambled in the tepees until dawn,
But now their vaunted prowess all is gone,
Gone like a moose-track in the April snow.   10
But all the land is murmurous with the call
Of their wild names that haunt the lovely glens
Where lonely water falls, or where the street
Sounds all day with the tramp of myriad feet;
Toronto triumphs; Winnipeg flows free,
And clangs the iron height where gaunt Quebec
Lies like a lion in a lily bed,
And Restigouche takes the whelmed sound of sea,
Meductic falls, and flutes the Mirimichi;
Kiskisink where the shy mallard breeds   20
Breaks into pearls beneath his whirling wings,
And Manitowapah sings;
They flow like water, or like wind they flow,
Waymoucheeching, loon-haunted Manowan,
Far Mistassini by her frozen wells,
Gold-hued Wayagamac brimming her wooded dells:
Lone Kamouraska, Metapedia,
And Metlakahtla ring a round of bells.

[1905]

Powassan's Drum[6]

Throb—throb—throb—throb;—
Is this throbbing a sound
Or an ache in the air?
Pervasive as light,
Measured and inevitable,

---

[6] According to Stan Dragland, this poem, composed in 1925, was inspired by the 1905 treaty trip that Scott describes in "The Last of the Indian Treaties." In that essay, Scott notes how "occasionally the sound of a conjuror's drum far away pervaded the day like an aerial pulse."

It seems to float from no distance,
But to live in the listening world—
Throb—throb—throb—throb—throbbing
The sound of Powassan's Drum.

He crouches in his dwarf wigwam   10
Wizened with fasting,
Fierce with thirst,
Making great medicine
In memory of hated things dead
Or in menace of hated things to come,
And the universe listens
To the throb—throb—throb—throb—
Throbbing of Powassan's Drum.

The world seems lost and shallow,
Seems sunken and filled with water,   20
With shores lightly moving
Of marish grass and slender reeds.
Through it all goes
The throbbing of Powassan's Drum.

Has it gone on forever,
As the pulse of Being?
Will it last till the world's end
As the pulse of Being?
He crouches under the poles
Covered with strips of birchbark   30
And branches of poplar and pine,
Piled for shade and dying
In dense perfume,
With closed eyelids
With eyes so fierce,
Burning under and through
The ancient worn eyelids,
He crouches and beats his drum.

The morning star formed
Like a pearl in the shell of darkness;   40
Light welled like water from the springs of morning;
The stars in the earth shadow
Caught like whitefish in a net;
The sun, the fisherman,
Pulling the net to the shore of night,
Flashing with the fins of the caught stars;—
All to the throbbing of Powassan's Drum.

The live things in the world
Hear it and are silent.
They hide silent and charmed   50
As if guarding a secret;
Charmed and silent hiding a rich secret,
Throbbing all to the
Throb—throb—throbbing of Powassan's Drum.

Stealthy as death the water
Wanders in the long grass,
And spangs of sunlight
Slide on the slender reeds
Like beads of bright oil.
The sky is a bubble blown so tense   60
The blue has gone grey
Stretched to the throb—throb—throb—throb—
Throbbing of Powassan's Drum.

Is it a memory of hated things dead
That he beats—famished—
Or a menace of hated things to come
That he beats—parched with anger
And famished with hatred—?

The sun waited all day.
There was no answer.   70
He hauled his net
And the glint of the star-fins
Flashed in the water of twilight;
There was no answer.
But in the northeast
A storm cloud reaches like a hand
Out of the half darkness.
The spectral fingers of cloud
Grope in the heavens,
And at moments, sharp as pain,   80
A bracelet of bright fire
Plays on the wrist of the cloud.
Thunder from the hollow of the hand
Comes almost soundless, like an air pressure,
And the cloud rears up
To the throbbing of Powassan's Drum.
An infusion of bitter darkness
Stains the sweet water of twilight.

Then from the reeds stealing,
A shadow noiseless,   90
A canoe moves noiseless as sleep,
Noiseless as the trance of deep sleep
And an Indian still as a statue,
Moulded out of deep sleep,
Headless, still as a headless statue
Moulded out of deep sleep,
Sits modelled in full power,
Haughty in manful power,
Headless and impotent in power.
The canoe stealthy as death   100
Drifts to the throbbing of Powassan's Drum.
The Indian fixed like bronze
Trails his severed head
Through the dead water
Holding it by the hair,
By the plaits of hair,
Wound with sweet grass and tags of silver.
The face looks through the water
Up to its throne on the shoulders of power,
Unquenched eyes burning in the water,   110
Piercing beyond the shoulders of power
Up to the fingers of the storm cloud.

Is this the meaning of the magic—
The translation into sight
Of the viewless hate?
Is this what the world waited for
As it listened to the throb—throb—throb—throb—
Throbbing of Powassan's Drum?

The sun could not answer.
The tense sky burst and went dark   120
And could not answer.
But the storm answers.
The murdered shadow sinks in the water.
Uprises the storm
And crushes the dark world;
At the core of the rushing fury
Bursting hail, tangled lightning
Wind in a wild vortex
Lives the triumphant throb—throb—throb—throb—
Throbbing of Powassan's Drum.   130

[1926]

The Last of the Indian Treaties

[. . .] In the early days the Indians were a real menace to the colonization of Canada. [. . .] So all the Indian diplomacy of that day was exercised to keep the tomahawk on the wall and the scalping knife in the belt. It was a rude diplomacy at best, the gross diplomacy of the rum bottle and the material appeal of gaudy presents, webs of scarlet cloth, silver medals, and armlets.

Yet there was at the heart of these puerile negotiations, this control that seemed to be founded on debauchery and license, this alliance that was based on a childish system of presents, a principle that has been carried on without cessation and with increased vigilance to the present day—the principle of the sacredness of treaty promises. Whatever has been written down and signed by king and chief both will be bound by so long as "the sun shines and the water runs." The policy, where we can see its outcome, has not been ineffectual, and where in 1790 stood clustered the wigwams and rude shelters of Brant's people[7] now stretch the opulent fields of the township of Tuscarora; and all down the valley of the Grand River there is no visible line of demarcation between the farms tilled by the ancient allies in foray and ambush who have become confederates throughout a peaceful year in seed-time and harvest.

The treaty policy so well established when the confederation of the provinces of British North America took place has since been continued and nearly all civilized Canada is covered with these Indian treaties and surrenders. A map colored to define their boundaries would show the province of Ontario clouted with them like a patch-work blanket; as far north as the confines of the new provinces of Saskatatchewan [sic] and Alberta the patches lie edge to edge. Until lately, however, the map would have shown a large portion of the province of Ontario uncovered by the treaty blanket. Extending north of the watershed that divides the streams flowing into Lakes Huron and Superior from those flowing into Hudson Bay, it reached James Bay on the north and the long curled ribbon of the Albany River, and comprised an area of 90,000 square miles, nearly twice as large as the State of New York.[8] [. . .]

In June, 1905, the writer was appointed one of three commissioners to visit the Indian tribes and negotiate a treaty. Our route lay inland from Dinorwic, a small station on the Canadian Pacific Railway two hundred miles east of Winnipeg, to reach the Lac Seul water system, to cross the height of land, to reach Lake St. Joseph, the first great reservoir of the Albany River. Our flotilla consisted of three canoes, two large Peterboroughs and one birch-bark thirty-two feet long which could easily hold eleven or twelve men and 2,500 pounds of baggage and supplies, as well as the treasure-chest which was heavy with thirty

---

[7] Joseph Brant (1742–1807), Mohawk leader and warrior who fought on the side of the British in the American War of Independence and negotiated for the Six Nations Grand River Reserve in Ontario. See his letter in Section II.

[8] Scott is here writing about the negotiations for finalizing Treaty 9 in northwestern Ontario.

thousand dollars in small notes. Our party included three commissioners, a physician, an officer of the Hudson's Bay Company who managed all the details of transport and commissariat, and two constables of the Dominion police force. I am bound to say the latter outshone the members of the commission itself in the observance of the Indians. The glory of their uniforms and the wholesome fear of the white man's law which they inspired spread down the river in advance and reached James Bay before the commission. I presume they were used as a bogey by the Indian mothers, for no children appeared anywhere until the novelty had somewhat decreased and opinion weakened that the magnificent proportions and manly vigor of our protectors were nourished upon a diet of babies.

Our crew of half-breeds and Indians numbered not less than twelve and sometimes seventeen, so that the strength of the party never fell below nineteen and was often twenty-four. [. . .]

It was about two o'clock one afternoon that we sighted Osnaburgh, a group of Hudson Bay buildings clustered on the lakeshore, and upon higher ground the little wooden church of the Anglican mission. Everyone expected the usual welcome, for the advent of a paymaster is always announced by a fusillade, yells, and the barking of dogs. But even the dogs of Osnaburgh gave no sound. The Indians stood in line outside the palisades, the old blind chief, Missabay, with his son and a few of the chief men in the centre, the young fellows on the outskirts, and the women by themselves, separated as they are always. A solemn hand-shaking ensued; never once did the stoicism of the race betray any interest in the preparations as we pitched our tents and displayed a camp equipage, simple enough, but to them the matter of the highest novelty; and all our negotiations were conducted under like conditions—intense alertness and curiosity with no outward manifestation of the slightest interest. Everything that was said and done, our personal appearance, our dress and manners, were being written down as if in a book; matter which would be rehearsed at many a campfire for generations until the making of the treaty had gathered a lore of its own; but no one could have divined it from visible signs. [. . .]

To individuals whose transactions had been heretofore limited to computation with sticks and skins our errand must indeed have been dark.

They were to make certain promises and we were to make certain promises, but our purpose and our reasons were alike unknowable. What could they grasp of the pronouncement on the Indian tenure which had been delivered by the law lords of the Crown, what of the elaborate negotiations between a dominion and a province which had made the treaty possible, what of the sense of traditional policy which brooded over the whole? Nothing. So there was no basis for argument. The simpler facts had to be stated, and the parental idea developed that the King is the great father of the Indians, watchful over their interests, and ever compassionate. After gifts of tobacco, as we were seated in a circle in a big room of the Hudson's Bay Company's House, the interpreter delivered this message to Missabay and the other chiefs, who listened unmoved to the recital of what the Government would give them for their lands.

Eight dollars to be paid at once to every man, woman and child; and forever afterward, each year, "so long as the grass grows and the water runs" four dollars each: and reserves of one square mile to every family of five or in like proportion; and schools for their children; and a flag for the chief.

"Well for all this," replied Missabay, "we will have to give up our hunting and live on the land you give us, and how can we live without hunting?" So they were assured that they were not expected to give up their hunting-grounds, that they might hunt and fish throughout all the country just as they had done in the past, but they were to be good subjects of the King, their great father, whose messengers we were. That was satisfying, and we always found that the idea of a reserve became pleasant to them when they learned that so far as that piece of land was concerned they were the masters of the white man, could say to him, "You have no right here; take your traps, pull down your shanty and begone."

At Fort Hope, Chief Moonias was perplexed by the fact that he seemed to be getting something for nothing; he had his suspicions maybe that there was something concealed in a bargain where all the benefit seemed to be on one side. "Ever since I was a little boy," he said, "I have had to pay well for everything, even if it was only a few pins or a bit of braid, and now you come with money and I have to give nothing in exchange." He was mightily pleased when he understood that he was giving something that his great father the King would value highly.

Missabay asked for time to consider, and in their tents there was great deliberation all night. But in the morning the chiefs appeared, headed by Missabay, led by Thomas, his son, who attended the blind old man with the greatest care and solicitude. [. . .] Their decision was favorable. "Yes," said Missabay, "we know now that you are good men sent by our great father the King to bring us help and strength in our weakness. All that we have comes from the white man and we are willing to join with you and make promises which will last as long as the air is above the water, as long as our children remain who come after us." [. . .]

As soon as the treaty had been signed a feast had been promised by the commissioners and the comestibles had been issued by the Hudson's Bay Company. [. . .] There is a rigid etiquette at these feasts; the food is piled in the centre of the surrounding Indians, the men in the inner circle, the women and children in the outer. When everyone is assembled the food is divided as fairly as possible and until each person is served no one takes a mouthful, the tea grows cold, the hot pork rigid, and half the merit of the warm food vanishes, but no one breaks the rule. They still wait patiently until the chiefs address them. At Osnaburgh while Missabay walked to and fro striking his long staff on the ground and haranguing them in short reiterant sentences—the same idea expressed over and over, the power and goodness of the white man, the weakness of the Indian, the kindness of the King, their great father—there they sat and stoically watched the food turn clammy! With us the cloth is cleared and the speeches follow; with the Albany River Indians every formality precedes the true purpose of the feast, the eating of it. [. . .]

The effect of education and of contact with a few of the better elements of our civilization were noticeable at Albany and Moose Factory. There was a certain degree of cleanliness in the preparation of food, the Indians were better dressed, and although the fur trade is a sort of slavery, a greater self-reliance was apparent. The crew that took the commission from Moose Factory to Abitibi were constant in their vespers and every evening recited a litany, sang a hymn and made a prayer. There was something primitive and touching in their devotion, and it marks an advance, but these Indians are capable of leaving a party of travellers suddenly, returning to Moose Factory in dudgeon if anything displeases them, and the leader of the prayers got very much the better of one of the party in an affair of peltries. But any forecast of Indian civilization which looks for final results in one generation or two is doomed to disappointment. Final results may be attained, say, in four centuries by the merging of the Indian race with the whites, and all these four things—treaties, teachers, missionaries, and traders—with whatever benefits or injuries they bring in their train, aid in making an end.

The James Bay treaty will always be associated in my mind with the figure of an Indian who came in from Attawapiskat to Albany just as we were ready to leave. The pay-lists and the cash had been securely packed for an early start next morning, when this wild fellow drifted into the camp. Père Fafard, he said, thought we might have some money for him. He did not ask for anything, he stood, smiling slightly. He seemed about twenty years of age, with a face of great beauty and intelligence, and eyes that were wild with a sort of surprise—shy at his novel position and proud that he was of some importance. His name was Charles Wabinoo. We found it on the list and gave him his eight dollars. When he felt the new crisp notes he took a crucifix from his breast, kissed it swiftly, and made a fugitive sign of the cross. "From my heart I thank you," he said. There was the Indian at the best point of a transitional state, still wild as a lynx, with all the lore and instinct of his race undimmed, and possessed wholly by the simplest rule of the Christian life, as yet unspoiled by the arts of sly lying, paltry cunning, and the lower vices which come from contact with such of our debased manners and customs as come to him in the wilderness.

[1906]

In the Year 1806

In the year 1806 there was a small and unimportant outpost of the North West Company at Lac Achigan. It had been located there by the policy of the fur trade in an attempt to gain ground from the Hudson's Bay Company in a territory famous for the quality of its mink-skins, but without much success. The situation of the Post seemed unfortunate. The rival company had located upon a spot loved of old by the Indians, and Lac Achigan was to them no more than scores of lakes. An Indian at Lac Achigan was merely in transit to Fort la Touche, which flew the Hudson's Bay Company's flag.

The Lac Achigan post had been held during the winter by a trader called Nairn, Andrew Nairn, and his helper, Alec Pendarvies.

When the spring came and the time had elapsed when the Indians should have brought in their furs, the last and absolute failure of the adventure became apparent. But the springtime revealed more than that. Fate had thrown together for a year two men who were as ill assorted a couple as might be. Pendarvies came from the high parts of Wales; a quick-thinking, thin-skinned fellow, chary of speech, but full of broodings and weak proud imaginings. Nairn was a lowland Scot; a teasing man, without a trace of fine feeling, and, withal, a tremendous talker. His ceaseless babble was filled with sharp personalities.

The denouement in the clash of these two personalities was foregone. Pendarvies had passed through a winter of agonies and had emerged into the spring changed as only such agonies can change. His lean, drawn face was cadaverous; his soul stood just behind his eyes trying to escape. He looked as if he had passed through a maddening illness. Nairn was fatter, his long red beard was silky and sleek, and he was blind to the change in his companion. He was so fond of the sound of his own hard voice that he had not perceived that since the seventeenth of February Alec Pendarvies had never spoken to him. It was then the tenth of May.

In the morning of that day Nairn said to Pendarvies: "I am awa' to the Fort, do ye ken, don't stand there like a loon. I'm going to sell the Hudson's Bay Company our furs as are not worth taking out and then we'll pack up and be off. Ye doited idiot! did ye no have your breakfast that ye're sucking in yer cheeks and chewing them like that?" Pendarvies paid no heed. Nairn began one peculiar form of torture; he would sing all his Scotch songs to Pendarvies' name. This time it was "Annie Laurie"—[9]

"Pendarvies' braes are bonny
When early fas the dew
And 'twas there P. E. N. Darvies
Gied her his promise true.
'Twas P. E. N. Darvies,
'Twas P. E. N. Darvies,
'Twas there P. E. N. Darvies
Gied her his promise true."

A familiar, tingling shudder ran through Alec's frame. Hate, hate, hate, inarticulate, blasting, consuming. He felt the familiar shudder quiver in his neck and jaws! All other consciousness fell into a mist; he paid no heed to the preparations for departure. "I'll be back in three days, do ye ken? Have an eye to things when I'm gone." He did not expect an answer and Alec heard him go off singing down the trail between the wands of the poplars just sprayed with green,— "Pendarvies' braes are bonny"—the high, ringing, mocking tones!

[9] "Annie Laurie" is a traditional Scottish song, the first verse of which runs as follows: "Maxwellton's braes are bonnie, / Where early fa's the dew, / And 'twas there that Annie Laurie / Gi'ed me her promise true."

Long after the silence closed around him Alec still sat on the bench in the sun; gradually he began to realise that he was alone, alone for the first time in thirteen months, free of the presence that he loathed. He dropped his head in his hands. The release of the torture was too swift. He could have borne more of the torture, but not this sudden end of it. He was free for three days. How could he measure that idea? Alone, alone, for three days. It was a bit of time; he tried to measure it. It had no end.

Then something snapped within his mind. He sprang to his feet; he did not know what he was doing. He waved his arms and tried to shout; he shook his fists high in the air. Then he ran furiously down to the lake near the boat landing and rushed into the water up to his knees. He clung to the boat landing and walked out farther; then he found that he was in the water and began to laugh and pulled himself out on the boat landing and laughed idiotically till his ribs ached.

Then he came to himself and found that he was stretched on the boat landing and the moon was up—a large moon on the lake. He tried to pull his rabbit-skin robe over him and felt his chill damp trousers instead of the soft fur. Still he did not move. His eyes stared at the moon and he tried to remember what it was. That groping effort ceased and long afterwards he felt as if something was striking him in the face. It was the sun, high over the water. Stupefied, he sat up and made a great effort to draw his legs under him. There was a mist. Yes, but he was free; that came to him in a flash. He would go to the house; he saw it towering like a castle above him. What he wanted was something to eat. He found some cold fried fish and bannock. He ate with gusto. He was free, free.

How long after that, as he sat at the table staring at the wall, did he notice something reflected in the looking glass? He moved his head about, but could only see it at a certain angle; then he recognised it and screamed violently—once, twice. It was Nairn's wallet; he had left it on the table. The mist came again, drifting—but after long intervals small clear spaces appeared. He could think. Free, free—but Nairn's wallet—he had forgotten his wallet. He saw the wallet in the looking glass—free, yes, for three days; but he would come back for his wallet; he could do no business without his wallet. Had he just gone or was it years and years ago?—Then nothing but mist. He heard a sound in the mist. Nairn's voice! It was only a few minutes ago he had left;—he was coming back for his wallet, singing—listen, listen—a smothered sound— "Pendarvies' braes are bonny." Lost now, lost. No, clearer, nearer— "Pendarvies' braes are bonny."

He laughed a cunning, small laugh—No, no, Nairn, wouldn't you leave me for three days even? He had taken a rifle off the rack. The door was there where the sunlight was pouring through. He knew he was a deadly shot. He stood at the door. The voice came strong and clear—"And for sweet P. E. N. Darvies I'd lay me down and die." Nairn's figure came out clearly on the trail through the poplars and Alec fired. The body threw up one hand and fell back heavily. The mist came again.

He found himself on the bench in the sun. He remembered—free, free, yes, he was free now for three days; no, no, Mr. Nairn, for longer than three days. He chuckled with low laughter, low and cunning. Stop! What would he do with the body? He was in the poplars now, and there it was on the trail. The eyes were open. He was not afraid of it, but he was in a hurry. He bent over and placed his arm under the small of the back and lifted a little; the body was yet warm and lissome; it fell back. He was terribly hurried. There was a little natural meadow in a circle of poplars. He was digging there with a spade. The sweat poured from him. Hours he worked—sunset came and went; he worked in the dark, then the moon gave him light. Then he came to hard clay. He could go down no deeper; he could walk about in the grave. How much longer? He was cold, cold to the bone, but the sun was bright enough. If he could get through that mist. He remembered now he had something to perform: a great important act that was decided upon so long ago that he had almost forgotten. He was to bury a dead man, and he must find something to wrap him in. One of the old canvas boat covers would do. He rolled the stiff body in it and dragged it to the grave. There was plenty of room, but ages were in the mist before he found the spade and covered all in, close and well.

How much time was measured? He found his elbows on the table and he was chewing and he had an unfamiliar feeling. He put his hand to his head. His cap! Yes, he always wore his cap, he even slept in his cap, and he had lost his cap; he began to grope for it. Well, it was lost, that was all. Then he remembered everything. No, no, Mr. Nairn, you couldn't leave me alone for three days. Well, you'll be longer than three days where you are now. He laughed with dry satisfaction.

Suddenly he saw the looking glass and something else—no, not the wallet reflected there. He tip-toed over, then he sprang back defending himself with his arms and elbows. It was Nairn's face in the glass. He pressed his back against the opposite wall and tried to push through the wall. Then he caught up things that were near him and tried to hit the glass and break it. He threw hundreds of things and at last one was well aimed. The glass shivered to the floor, only a small V-shaped splinter remained in the frame. He went towards it stealthily. He threw himself back—even in the splinter he could see Nairn's face, like a miniature.

There was a great gulf of mist. Then a dull knocking began—he was very near the lake, but it was stiff and glittering. He picked up a paddle and struck it, once and twice with all his force. It cracked like a mirror from side to side with a piercing sound.

All was in perfect calm, a long, slow, soothing calm, and he sat on the bench by the wall. Time had lost its significance for him, but he was living in light and calm. He had been released into deep wondrous calm. In the quiet he heard a sound, a sound of singing. He could distinguish the words, "Pendarvies' braes are bonny." He heard it just once, or did he hear? Then an appearance seemed to glide along amid the poplars. The figure of Nairn, the figure of Nairn! He rose on his tip-toes and backed off, brushing the air away as if to brush away the figure. He knew that he had killed Nairn and buried him; so this was Nairn's ghost. He could see the lips moving, but could not hear a word that was said. Time was lost. Suddenly he felt himself held by a horrible thing, the phantom had him. He struggled and broke away from it.

Measure a deep darkness. He was over the grave in the meadow. He had done a cunning thing; he had possession of the rifle and the ghost had vanished. No, there it was, floating about the house, peering from the door. He could shoot it easily at any time. A long pause, a little whispering stir in the poplars. He turned quickly; there was the ghost in the trees, but before he could gain the rifle it had disappeared. Then he saw the spade. He would get the grave ready, when he killed the ghost he could bury them together. Now that he had the idea everything seemed easy. He worked like mad, throwing out the earth tirelessly. He looked up once in a while and laughed, low and inwardly, when he saw the phantom seated not very far away watching intently. "This goes well," he chuckled. "As soon as I come to the canvas boat cover I'll shoot you and you come down here too."

By and by he struck that hard clay again. Then he unearthed a bit of cloth; it was the boat cover. No, it was not the boat cover; it was something soft and small; he picked it up; his cap. There was a pause. His cap? What then? He had lost his cap; his cap was next the hard clay; all earthy he put it on his head. Then his cap must have been under the body; he must have thrown the body out. He clambered over the earth; nothing was there. He took up the gun. Well, he would shoot the ghost; he could bury the ghost. It had vanished. Measure the immeasurable, the deeps of the darkness. He was on the boat landing and the lake was below him. He was tired beyond any mortal conception of weariness. He was parched with thirst and reached his hand to the water. It was stiff as glass and as he leaned over and looked down, up peered the face of Nairn. That was all.

The trader ventured at last to the boat landing and felt safe when he gained possession of the rifle, but it was not capped and the old charge was still in it. He was not troubled with tenderness, but he carried Alec's body carefully to the house and laid it on the bench and placed it decently and reposefully. Nothing had been disturbed in the house, nothing had been touched but the rifle, the looking glass hung unbroken on the wall and there were fragments of food on the table and his wallet, which he had not intended to take with him. In the little meadow, where he had watched Alec so long clutching the spade and the gun, the earth was not disturbed and the spade was lying where Alec had dropped it. In the morning he went there and dug a grave deep as the hard clay. Then he bethought him of some old, but stout canvas boat-covers and wrapping the body in one he buried it. The moon had risen before he found that he had covered the grave close and smoothed it well.

[1923]

EDITH MAUDE EATON (SUI SIN FAR) ■ (1865–1914)

Edith Maude Eaton, who published under several pseudonyms including the Chinese name "Sui Sin Far" (which translates as "Water Lily"), is widely heralded as one of the first writers of Asian descent in North America to write about the experiences of Chinese North Americans during the nineteenth and early twentieth centuries. She was born in England to Chinese and English parents at a time when such intercultural marriages were uncommon. When she was a child, her family immigrated to North America, eventually settling in Montreal in 1872. At the age of eighteen, Eaton was working in the composing room of the *Montreal Daily Star*. Eaton was devoted to her mother and was determined to counter the extensive prejudice toward her mother's people. Publishing as E.E. or Edith Eaton, she was a regular contributor to such periodicals and newspapers as *The Dominion Illustrated*, the *Montreal Daily Witness*, and the *Montreal Daily Star*. Her 15 March 1890 article "The Land of the Free," published in the *Montreal Daily Witness*, is the first recognized piece of journalism she composed in defence of the Chinese people in Canada. By the late 1890s, she was publishing articles and works of fiction as Sui Sin Far. Many of her stories contain central characters of "Eurasian," or mixed Chinese and European, ancestry. In her stories, Eaton took on issues of racism, bicultural and biracial marriage, and women's independence.

Since there were more publication opportunities for Canadian writers in the United States than in Canada, Eaton sent many of her pieces to American periodicals, often deleting the references that would identify her settings as Canadian Chinatowns. As an adult, Eaton lived most of her life in the United States, settling in Seattle, San Francisco, and eventually Boston. It was while living in Boston, in 1912, that Eaton published a book-length collection of her stories, entitled *Mrs. Spring Fragrance*. Many of these stories were republished in 1995 in a volume that also includes some of Eaton's journalistic writings. In the course of her career, Eaton published over seventy short stories and newspaper articles that challenged the

pervasive discrimination against Chinese North Americans. In 1913, she returned to Montreal (where a memorial commemorates her work for Chinese Canadians), and she died there in April 1914.

Eaton's work is particularly impressive when set within the context of the extreme anti-Asian sentiment in late nineteenth-century North America. Thousands of Chinese labourers had been brought to Canada and the United States to work on the railways and in mining operations, but because the predominant idea of Canada was as a "White" nation, Asian immigrants were deemed undesirable and were not granted the same rights as other settlers. As a result, the federal government instituted a "head tax" in 1885 whose purpose was to curtail further immigration from China. Eaton's 21 September 1896 article in the *Montreal Daily Star*, "A Plea for the Chinaman," is an impassioned appeal to English and French Canadians to regard Chinese Canadians as equal citizens and to repeal the head tax. It is notable for highlighting the hypocrisy of many governmental policies, especially since Chinese labourers were initially recruited as a source of cheap labour and then were subsequently considered a threat precisely because they were willing to work harder and for lower wages than other settlers. In addition, Eaton emphasizes the humanity and morality of Chinese people in contrast to the illogical racism of the government policy-makers. She states the source of the prejudice very bluntly: "The chief reason for the prejudice against the Chinese," Eaton asserts, is that they look different.

Eaton hoped that her writing would help to foster mutual understanding between peoples of European and Asian ancestry. In her autobiographical sketch "Leaves from the Mental Portfolio of an Eurasian," she expressed her belief that "prejudice can be eradicated by association." Like her contemporary Pauline Johnson, her mixed ethnicity put her in a position of having experienced both prejudice and privilege first-hand. As she wrote in "Leaves from the Mental Portfolio of an Eurasian," "I give my right hand to the Occidentals and my left to the Orientals, hoping that between them they will not utterly destroy the insignificant 'connecting link.'" Her work bears interesting comparison with that of Fred Wah, especially his 1996 collection, *Diamond Grill* (see Volume II), which is also concerned with the experience of being of mixed Chinese/European heritage in Canada. Eaton's ultimate argument in "A Plea for the Chinaman" is for people to look beyond their differences to the common humanity that they share. "Individuality is more than nationality," she insists.

A Plea for the Chinaman: A Correspondent's Argument in His Favor

The Mongolian Defended from the Charges Made against Him by Members of Parliament from British Columbia

To the Editor of the Star:

Sir,—Every just person must feel his or her sense of justice outraged by the attacks which are being made by public men upon the Chinese who come to this country. It is a shame because the persecutors have every weapon in their hands and the persecuted are defenceless. They do not understand in a full sense all that their revilers charge them with and they have no representative men to answer the charges. [. . .]

It makes one's cheeks burn to read about men of high office standing up and abusing a lot of poor foreigners behind their backs and calling them all the bad names their tongues can utter. They know that the Chinese cannot answer them and they go on fully armed, using all their weapons. It's very brave, I must say, to fight with the air. A fine spectacle for the world to look at. But I suppose they don't care. They've got a party at home to cheer them.

I will now go over the ground a little. I speak from experience, because I know the Chinamen in all characters, merchants, laundrymen, laborers, servants, smugglers and smuggled, also as Sunday School scholars and gamblers. They have faults, but they also have virtues. Nations are made up of all sorts.

It is proposed to impose a tax of five hundred dollars upon every Chinaman coming into the Dominion of Canada.[1] The reasons urged for imposing such a tax are that the presence of the Chinese affects the material and moral interests

---

[1] The Chinese head tax was raised to $500 in 1903.

of the Canadian people, that the Chinese work cheap and therefore white men cannot compete with them, that they are gamblers and grossly immoral, that they introduce disease, cost the public much money and delay the development of the country.

The presence of the Chinaman does affect the material interests of this country, for he is a good and steady workman and has helped and is still helping to build our railways, mine our ores and in various branches of agriculture and manufacturing is proving a source of wealth to those who employ him. He does good to our laboring class for he acts as an incentive to them to be industrious and honest. I say honest, because he seeks to gain no advantage over other laborers, simply comes to compete with them—and competition is always good. The Chinaman stands on his merits; if he were of no benefit to this country he would soon have no reason to wish to remain here, for you may be sure, if incapable of performing the tasks required of him, he would not be given employment, for Canadians do not employ Chinamen for love; they take them for the use they can make of them.

As to working cheap, I believe if the matter was investigated, you would find out that the white men are willing to accept the same wages per week as the Chinamen, but they refuse to put in as much work for the wages. If the white man has to live, so also has the Chinaman, and I know that in Montreal the Chinese live well, and a great many of those I am acquainted with are former residents of British Columbia and have not changed their manner of living since coming East. I have seen on their breakfast tables great bowls of rice and dishes of beautiful light omelet, besides many European comestibles and I have noticed and have been told by themselves that they frequently order fowl and fish from the markets and the best of meats and vegetables. I am speaking of laundrymen, not merchants. Of course, the very poor ones are more frugal, but I can assure you a Chinaman lives merrily when he has the means.

Now, as to the charges of immorality brought against the Chinese. There are over five hundred Chinamen in Montreal, besides a transient population, and I have never heard during a residence here of many years of any one of these Chinese being accused of saying or doing that which was immoral, in the sense in which I understand the word "immoral." It is true some of the Chinamen who have been contaminated by white men and American lawyers, become swindlers and perjurers, and help their contaminators, who are just like leeches, to bleed the poor Chinese laborers who are desirous of passing into the States, and from which by a disgraceful law they are barred out, but the main body of the Chinamen are straightforward, hard-working fellows. Their worst fault is that they are somewhat cynical with regard to the honesty of white men, but that is not surprising when we consider that nearly all the white men with whom they come in contact think of nothing but squeezing money out of them by some means or other. Even the law restricting them from entering America looks as if it was got up for the sole purpose of giving unprincipled lawyers and corrupt Government officers a chance to do some boodling. [. . .]

When Mr. Maxwell[2] speaks of the vices of the Chinese corrupting the whole body politic of British Columbia one has to smile. It is so absurd. Surely those who are "controlled by the higher influences of civilization" cannot succumb to those who obey "the lower forces of barbarism." The Chinaman may be willing to attend Sunday school and learn all that you can teach him, but I am quite certain that it never enters his head to convert you to his way of thinking.

I am afraid Mr. Maxwell knew very little about what he was speaking when he took up the Chinese question. He knew that he wanted to get certain advantages for a party of British Columbians, and he put all his heart and soul into gaining his object, forgetting that there are two sides to every story, or if he did remember, assuring himself that no one else would.

"I have but to say the word, and it will be believed," said he to his constituents on the eve of his departure for Ottawa.

The influence of the Chinese people in a moral sense is null, and I have yet to meet the man or woman who will tell me that a Chinaman influenced him or her to do that against which moral sense rebelled.

The Chinese receive instruction gladly when it comes their way, but they do not ask for it, and as to imparting to others their opinions and beliefs, the pride or humility of the race forbids anything approaching that. The quiet dignity of the Chinese is worthy of admiration, and Mr. Maxwell ought to be ashamed of himself for sneering at them for being docile and easily managed. Perhaps he does not know that the Chinese are taught to treat the rude with silent contempt. A Chinaman does not knock a man down or stab him for the sake of an insult. He will stand and reason, but unless forced, though not by any means a coward, he will not fight. In China a man who unreasonably insults another has public opinion against him, whilst he who bears and despises the insult is respected. There are signs that in the future we in this country may attain to the high degree of civilization which the Chinese have reached, but for the present we are far away behind them in that respect.

"No self-respecting people," said Mr. Maxwell, "wish to have dumped into their midst the scum of eastern barbarism."

I am sorry to have to again show up Mr. Maxwell's ignorance of his subject. The Chinese who come to our shores are not "scum." They are mostly steady, healthy country boys from the Canton district. There are none of them paupers. They come here furnished with a modest sum of money and with the hope of adding thereto by honest labor. [. . .]

The Chinese have many worthy characteristics; they are good natured—all the world knows that. They have a keen sense of humor—I could tell many good stories showing that up. They easily forgive those who insult or wrong them—that is proved every day. They are hospitable and are at heart gentlemen. In the spring of this year I visited New York's Chinatown. I went alone,

---

[2] George Ritchie Maxwell was a Liberal MP for Vancouver who was lobbying to raise the Chinese head tax.

and though a woman and a perfect stranger was received by the Chinese there with the greatest kindness and courtesy. For two weeks I dwelt amongst them, trotted up and down Mott, Pell and Doyer streets, saw the Chinese theatres and Joss Houses, visited all the little Chinese women, talked pigeon English to them, examined their babies, dined with a Chinese actress, darted hither and thither through the tenements of Chinatown, and during that time not the slightest disrespect or unkindness was shown to me. I was surprised, for I was in the slum portion of the city of New York, and dreadful tales had been told me of what I should meet and see there. I had been told that Chinatown was a dangerously wicked place; I had been warned that if I went in there alone I would never come out alive or sound in mind or body. My warders were like Mr. Maxwell and his colleagues—they did not know the Chinese people. I went there and returned the better for my visit. I had proved to my satisfaction what I had always believed, that the Chinese people are a more moral and a much happier lot than those who are strangers to them make them out to be.

Human nature is the same all the world over, and the Chinaman is as much a human being as those who now presume to judge him; and if he is a human being, he must be treated like one, and that we should not be doing were we to fine him five hundred dollars simply for being himself—a Chinaman. If a Chinaman breaks a law—a just law—a law which is a law to all Canadians, and which all Canadians are liable to be punished for, I would say at once that he should pay the penalty, but there is no justice in fining him just for what he is—a Chinaman. We should be broader-minded. What does it matter whether a man be a Chinaman, an Irishman, an Englishman or an American. Individuality is more than nationality. "A man's a man for all that."[3] Let us admire a clever Chinaman more than a stupid Englishman, and a bright Englishman more than a dull Chinaman.

Why should Canadians in their own land fear to compete with foreigners, when they know that the foreigners are not liked, and if they, the Canadians, worked as well, there would be no chance for the Chinese whatever. If they really want to keep the Chinese out, let them do so by fair means, not by foul. Let the Canadians make an agreement with Canadians that Chinese labor will not be utilized in Canada. Then the Chinese would soon make themselves scarce; but so long as Canadian employers employ Chinese laborers, so long is a sign up telling all the world that Chinese labor is needed and wanted in Canada, and it is only a desire on the part of Mr. Maxwell to please the rowdy element of the Dominion which leads him to pretend that the Chinese are not of benefit to the country in which they are sojourning.

Some complain that they object to the Chinese because they will not settle here, nor associate with other races. That objection is also a pretence, for we well know that if such a notion as settling here ever entered the Chinaman's head, our treatment of him would soon knock it out. "He does

---

[3] See Robert Burns (1759–96), "Song: For a' that and a' that."

not associate with our race at all," they cry. Well, we don't and we won't associate with him. "He comes here to make money, and with the intention of returning sooner or later," says another. In that he follows the example set him by the westerners; there are many foreigners in China, and, with the exception of the missionaries, they are all there with the avowed purpose of making money. The ports of China are full of foreign private adventurers. After they have made their "pile" they will return to their homes—which are not in China.

I believe the chief reason for the prejudice against the Chinese, I may call it the real and only solid reason for all the dislike shown to the Chinese people[,] is that they are not considered good looking by white men; that is, they are not good looking according to a Canadian or American standard for looks. This reason may be laughed at and considered womanish, but it is not a woman's reason, it is a man's. Women do not care half as much for personal appearance as do men. I am speaking very seriously, and if you will send a commission to investigate the Chinese trouble in British Columbia—if the Government will—they will find the matter to be as I say. That the Chinese do not please our artistic taste is really at the root of all the evil there, and from it springs the other objections to the Chinese. It is a big shame, I feel, and I think it is the duty of all enlightened men to combat with and overcome this very real and serious prejudice. Do not the sages say that beauty is a matter of opinion, and so if Wong Chang does not appear to our eyes as lovely to behold as Mr. Maxwell, there are those in his own land who would probably think the reverse. Besides, Wong Chang is here for utility and not for ornament.

I am convinced that an honest commission will find no real cause to further tax the Chinese. Indeed, if as conscientious as a commission can be, it will advise the fifty dollar tax already imposed be lifted.[4]

Of course, there will be found many to stand up as witnesses against the Chinamen, but if watched closely it will be discovered that such witnesses belong to a class which is determined to find fault with the Chinaman no matter what he does or does not do.

Will the Government of Canada pander to that certain class? Will it forget the debt of gratitude America and British America owes to China—China, who sent her men to work for us when other labor was not obtainable.

If it is loyal to that England, whose shores, as Mr. Fraser says, "are free to all comers, irrespective of race, creed or color," it will answer decidedly, No.

Montreal, September 19   E.E.

[1896]

---

4 In 1885, the Chinese Immigration Act had instituted a $50 head tax.

Turn of the Century

Introduction: Canada on the World Stage

> We are under the suzerainty of the King of England. We are his loyal subjects. We bow the knee to him. But the King of England has no more rights over us than are allowed by our own Canadian parliament. If this is not a nation, what then, is a nation?
> —Wilfrid Laurier to the Toronto Conservative Club (1910)

The Changing Shape of Canadian Society

In a speech to the Ottawa Canadian Club in 1904, Prime Minister Wilfrid Laurier uttered his famous pronouncement on Canada's future: "As the nineteenth century was that of the United States, so I think the twentieth century shall be filled by Canada." In recent years, this proclamation has been phrased in simpler terms. "The twentieth century will belong to Canada," Laurier is often thought to have said. True enough, the early years of the new century brought with them a sense of promise. In his spirited 1907 essay, "Greater Canada: An Appeal," Stephen Leacock invoked "the inevitable greatness of Canada. . . . Here stand we, six million people, heirs to the greatest legacy in the history of mankind, owners of half a continent" (135). Similarly, in her 1904 novel *The Imperialist*, Sara Jeannette Duncan had one of her protagonists, the great advocate of imperialism Lorne Murchison, utter an impassioned prophecy of Canada's global centrality in the years to come: "In the scrolls of the future it is already written that the centre of the Empire must shift—and where, if not to Canada?" (262). The prevailing mood of optimism that characterized the first decade of the new century, however, was replaced by one of horror and disillusionment with the advent of the First World War in 1914. In the early part of this period, popular writers such as Leacock, L.M. Montgomery, and Robert Service rode the wave of prosperity and hope for the nation. Following the war, the tone shifted dramatically and the seeds of a modernist discontent and incredulity were sown.

Historians such as Robert Craig Brown and Ramsay Cook have written of the early years of the twentieth century as a period of transformation, optimism, and relative prosperity. As the noted literary historian Archibald MacMechan put it in his 1924 study *Headwaters of Canadian Literature*, between the end of the nineteenth century and the outbreak of the First World War, "Canadians who had been accustomed, all their lives, to think of Canada as a poor country had to readjust their thinking to fit the concept of Canada as a rich country" (189). But the changes were more than conceptual ones. Canada, as a nation, was coming into its own. Following the election of Wilfrid Laurier, Canada's first French-Canadian prime minister, in 1896, Canada's international reputation as an independent nation emerged. Events in the First World War solidified this sense of national sovereignty. In England in 1897 during the Queen's Jubilee, Laurier was celebrated in the *Daily Mail* thus: "For the first time on record a politician of the New World has been recognized as the equal of the great men of the Old Country." Laurier's desire to move Canada beyond the confines of a colony was echoed at home. Leacock, for instance, characterized Canada in similar terms in his article "Greater Canada: An Appeal": "Canada, as a *colony*, was right enough in the days of good old Governor Simcoe, when your emigrant officer sat among the pine stumps of his Canadian clearing and reared his children in the fear of God and in the love of England— right enough then, wrong enough and destructive enough now. We cannot continue as we are." While Leacock, Laurier, and the political elite were contesting the role of colonialism in Canada, the British Empire was still going strong. By 1914, the empire encompassed nearly a quarter of the world's land surface.

According to historian Robert Bothwell, from the turn of the century until the outbreak of the First World War, Canada experienced the greatest economic boom in its short history (*Canada* 55). Perhaps the most spectacular change was Canada's transformation from a rural agricultural nation to an industrialized one, characterized by an emphasis on mining operations, pulp and paper mills, forestry, and manufacturing. This brought with it the migration of people from rural locations to large urban centres, contributing not only to the establishment of a substantial proletariat and incipient labour movement, but also to such alarming conditions as urban slums, child labour, health hazards, and urban crime. The shift in Canadians' social world can be charted in Leacock's two well-known story collections from this period. *Sunshine Sketches of a Little Town*, written in 1912, conveys a sense of nostalgia for small-town Ontario, which in the book is described as a thing of the past. *Arcadian Adventures with the Idle Rich*, published in 1914, depicts the materialism and corruption of urban industrial life, particularly the growing divide between the rich and the poor. This mass movement of people to the cities was of particular concern to Quebeckers, who worried about their ability to maintain their cultural and religious distinctiveness.

Coincident with increased industrialization were new technological advances that were heralded as the wave of the future. The telegraph, the telephone, radio, cinema, electric light, pharmaceuticals, central heating, indoor plumbing, the vacuum cleaner, vitamins, the mass-produced automobile (the Model T Ford), stainless steel, and the airplane, among other inventions, altered the face of the everyday world Canadians inhabited. Around the world, it was becoming easier to move across large spaces in less time than in previous eras. International advances in technology were accompanied by significant intellectual developments: James Frazer's highly influential work of comparative mythology, *The Golden Bough: A Study in Magic and Religion*, came out in 1890 and was greatly expanded in 1915; Sigmund Freud's *The Interpretation of Dreams* was published in 1900; Max Planck originated quantum theory in 1900; 1901 saw the first wireless communication across the Atlantic, conducted by the Italian scientist Guglielmo Marconi from the top of Signal Hill in St. John's, Newfoundland; Albert Einstein published three papers outlining his theory of relativity in 1905; and the list goes on. Such advances were seen as signs of progress that were meant to make life easier, safer, and more comprehensible. This perception was shattered with the advent of the war.

One of the major changes that Canada experienced in the opening decades of the twentieth century was a large increase in population. Now that the transcontinental railway was fully operating, it was seen to be time to fill up the sparsely populated country in order to consolidate a working national citizenry from coast to coast. At Confederation, the population was under 4 million; by 1911, it had jumped to more than 7 million. This was largely the result of a massive influx of immigrants to the new country, many from northern Europe. The expansion of Canadian territory during this period aided the immigration wave. In 1905, the provinces of Alberta and Saskatchewan were formed, and the northern areas of the western provinces were opened up to settlement. Laurier's appointed minister of the interior, Clifford Sifton, undertook a monumental immigration campaign, promoting western Canada throughout Europe and the United States as "the Last Best West" and providing immigrants with free land grants of 160 acres. While anxiety prevailed about the ethnic tensions that such heterogeneous immigration would bring, there was a general sense that populating the prairie provinces was crucial to Canada's national growth and prosperity, especially given the need for farmers and general labourers on the prairie wheat fields and farmlands. A sense of superiority toward these "simple" people was widespread on the part of English Canadians. In a 1922 article in *Maclean's* magazine, Sifton retrospectively describes his vision of the ideal immigrant as "a stalwart peasant in a sheep-skin coat, born on the soil, whose forefathers have been farmers for ten generations, with a stout wife and a half-dozen children" (see Sifton's article in this section). Canada was attractive, in part, because by now the free land in the American west, particularly in Oklahoma and North Dakota, had already been portioned out.

The first decade of the century produced the first net gain of immigration over emigration since Confederation (Bothwell and Granatstein 38–39). In 1913 alone, over 400,000 immigrants arrived in Canada. In 1911, almost half of the prairie population originated from outside of Canada (Nelles 155). Many of these new immigrants were Ukrainians, Icelanders, Poles, Scandinavians, and Germans; in combination with earlier arrivals of Mennonites and Doukhobors in Canada's west, they contributed to the increasingly multicultural constitution of Canada.

As in the previous century, emigration pamphlets were written to attract settlers to the prairies. For instance, in the Ukraine, Osyp Oleskiv's *About Free Lands* and *On Emigration* provided information about western Canada as a place of viable settlement for Ukrainian farmers. These pamphlets were highly successful. Between 1891, when the first wave of Ukrainian immigrants came to Canada, and the outbreak of the First World War, approximately 170,000 Ukrainians settled in the west. During the same period, 35,000 Germans came to Manitoba and an estimated 95,000 Germans immigrated to Saskatchewan. Among the first Russians to settle in the country were the Doukhobors, members of a sect whose pacifism and communal lifestyle were under threat of harassment and persecution in Czarist Russia. Sifton did not seek immigrants from southern Europe at this time because he considered them to be ill-suited to the hardships of prairie settlement and pioneering. Nevertheless, thousands of Italians came to Canada as migrant workers during these years.

Few, if any, of these early European immigrants published long accounts of their settlement or artistic works in English. Such writing did not come about until the late 1920s and into the 1930s and 1940s, with works by authors such as Frederick Philip Grove (*Over Prairie Trails*, 1922), Laura Goodman Salverson (*Confessions of an Immigrant's Daughter*, 1939), and Vera Lysenko (*Men in Sheepskin Coats*, 1947). In her observations of life in western Canada, *Janey Canuck in the West* (1910), Emily Murphy comments that "on the streets of Winnipeg, there are people who smile at you in English, but speak in Russian. There are rushful, pushful people from 'the States,' stiff-tongued Germans, ginger-headed Icelanders, Galicians, Norwegians, Poles, and Frenchmen, all of whom are rapidly becoming irreproachably Canadian. In all there are sixty tongues in the pot." Here Murphy refers obliquely to the melting pot of cultural assimilation. John Murray Gibbon's famous theory of Canada as a "cultural mosaic" was not introduced until 1938. In the early part of the century, the popular view was to regard assimilation as a form of "civility" extended to new immigrants, thus building toward a recognizably Canadian polity based on a British model. However, in *White Civility: The Literary Project of English Canada* (2006), literary critic Daniel Coleman argues that the Canadian literary community was (generally) committed to reinforcing notions of White citizenship during the optimistic nation-building years of the late nineteenth and early twentieth centuries.

In *Colour Coded: A Legal History of Racism in Canada* (1999), legal historian Constance Backhouse points out how central a concept race was in this period as she describes the instructions for the 1901 census, when all Canadians were to be identified by a colour—White, Black, Yellow, or Red. Backhouse explodes the myth of a "raceless" society in Canada and shows how for the first half of the twentieth century, the Canadian justice system was built on White privilege. The lack of suffrage for Chinese Canadians, Japanese Canadians, and "Hindus" is an example of a more widespread sense of racial superiority that governed the country. The assimilationist policies of previous generations endured during this period. Immigrants from many parts of the world were increasingly unwelcome in Canada during this time. The Immigration Act of 1910, for instance, conferred on the government the authority to exclude "immigrants belonging to any race deemed unsuited to the climate or requirements of Canada." The Act also increased the federal government's power to deport individuals on the grounds of political instability. Potential Chinese immigrants continued to be targeted when the Chinese head tax was increased in 1900 to $100 and again in 1903 to $500. Anti-Asian riots rocked the city of Vancouver in 1907. Anti-Semitism was rife, especially in the major centres of Toronto and Montreal where large Jewish populations had become established. One notorious incident in British Columbia in 1914 was the arrival of 376 British subjects (12 Hindus, 24 Muslims, and 340 Sikhs) of Indian origin on board the *Komagata Maru* (see Figure IV-6). Sharon Pollock's 1976 play, *The Komagata Maru Incident*, is a fictional rendering of this event, and the film *Continuous Journey* (2004) by Ali Kazimi traces the history and impact of the event through documents and personal stories.

In addition to immigration policies, the government continued to implement new and more restrictive measures into the Indian Act during the early decades of the twentieth century to curtail the rights of Native peoples. The government's paternalism and its support of assimilation were also evident in its educational policies. According to the 1996 *Report of the Royal Commission on Aboriginal Peoples*, "[T]he tragic legacy of residential education began in the late nineteenth century with a three-part vision of education in the service of assimilation. It included, first, a justification for removing children from their communities and disrupting Aboriginal families; second, a precise pedagogy for re-socializing children in the schools; and third, schemes for integrating graduates into the non-Aboriginal world." The report notes how for Duncan Campbell Scott, the most influential senior bureaucrat in the Department of Indian Affairs in the first three decades of the twentieth century, education was "by far the most important of the many subdivisions of the most complicated Indian problem" (qtd. in *Report* 10). Education was seen to hold significant promise as a potential solution to the "problem." In 1908, the minister of the interior and superintendent general of Indian affairs, Frank Oliver, identified education as the method that would "elevate the Indian from his condition of savagery" and "make him a member of the state, and eventually a citizen in good standing" (qtd. in *Report* 10). Other policies such as the continued banning of cultural ceremonies were also meant to aid in the assimilation of First Nations people, the

Métis, and the Inuit. Leaders such as Deskaheh, whose speech is included in this section, fought for land rights and for equal rights but met with either inaction or non-recognition on the part of the government (and even with the stiffening of laws, as was the case in Deskaheh's situation).

Compounding the sense that traditional French- and British-Canadian cultural values might be eroded by a strong indigenous population and by the huge influx of European and Asian immigrants was a general feeling that social and religious structures were at risk from other sources. Increased industrialization and urbanization, combined with the decline in religious belief that followed in the wake of the theories of evolution promoted by Charles Darwin in the nineteenth century and Sigmund Freud's scandalous pronouncements on human psychology in the early twentieth century, brought with them a move away from traditional family and religious values. The rapidly changing nature of Canadian social values and the fear of the degeneracy of urban life initiated a widespread social reform movement, often conducted under the auspices of religious organizations. Known as the "Social Gospel," the Protestant reform movement had as its mission the improvement of social injustices that had accompanied urban industrialization. This movement focused on two issues: economic hardship and social vices, particularly alcohol. During this period, the prohibition or temperance movement, aimed at outlawing the selling and consumption of liquor, made great strides under the leadership of such figures as Nellie McClung and Emily Murphy. These early feminists were ardent proponents of temperance because they saw a direct link between alcohol consumption and violence against women and children. Prohibition was put into effect in the provinces of Nova Scotia and Prince Edward Island before the First World War, and instituted in the remaining provinces during the war. Leacock mocks the temperance campaign in his 1915 article "The Woman Question," and pokes fun at people's hypocrisies in response to the movement in his short story "The Marine Excursion of the Knights of Pythias" (1912), when characters smuggle liquor onto the boat.

Many women who campaigned for prohibition also became active in the suffragist movement for the franchise (the vote). The Woman's Christian Temperance Union, for example, steadfastly embraced the cause of women's suffrage. This is the era that is now spoken of as the period of first-wave feminism (in comparison to second-wave feminism, which refers to the "women's liberation" movement of the 1960s and '70s). Coincidentally, the suffragist cause was aided by the onset of the First World War, partly because women argued that their inherent pacifism and maternalism would enable them to contribute to national politics in the interests of peace, but also because women experienced increased independence during the war, after entering the labour force in huge numbers to replace the thousands of men who had gone overseas. As Cecily Devereux notes in her introduction to *Anne of Green Gables*, the feminist politics of the early twentieth century differed from the "New Woman" rhetoric of an earlier era in its concern with "'advancing' women towards political and social agency" (29). This is evident in Jessie Georgina

Sime's short story "Munitions!" which describes the sense of freedom that came with women's participation in the public workforce during this period. Of particular interest is the way women's political objectives were promoted "on the basis of a nationally and, usually, racially identified maternity" (Devereux 29). The rhetoric of "maternalism" was linked to a conception of the improvement of the Anglo-Saxon "race," and was thus mobilized to support the advancement of the British Empire. One sees this ideology at work in L.M. Montgomery's novel *Anne of Green Gables* (1908), over the course of which Anne is gradually being tailored to become a good—that is, educated, cultivated, and physically strong—mother. This agenda is also apparent in Montgomery's short story, "The Education of Betty" (1920), included here. As Devereux states, "[W]omen had to be empowered politically and socially in order to protect their own work of child-bearing" and to protect the Anglo-Saxon race at large "from moral and physical degeneration" (29–30). Intelligent, healthy mothers produced intelligent, healthy children. This rhetoric was also tied up with the discourse of eugenics, such as was advocated by Emily Murphy as a court magistrate and Nellie McClung as a member of the Alberta Legislature. Devereux has recently linked these ideas in a provocative book entitled *Growing a Race: Nellie McClung and the Fiction of Eugenic Feminism* (2005).

McClung's 1916 essay "Speaking of Women" provides a good outline of these maternal feminist principles. Even more powerful, however, was her satirical enactment of the "Women's Parliament," staged in Winnipeg in 1914 with other members of the Manitoba Political Equality League. The play inverts the political situation when Manitoba premier Rodmond Roblin refused the petition of women suffragists; in the script, men approach an all-female parliament requesting the vote. McClung fictionalized this event as "The Play" in her 1921 novel *Purple Springs*. Sime's story collection, *Sister Woman* (1919), from which "Munitions!" is taken, also illuminates the realities of women's poverty and marginalization within Canadian society during this period. As a result of McClung's intervention, among others, Manitoba was the first province, in 1916, to grant women the right to vote in provincial elections. Slowly, the demands of women were heeded. In 1917, all female relatives of Canadian servicemen were granted a limited franchise, as part of Prime Minister Robert Borden's attempt to garner the "patriotic vote" (Bothwell et al. 158). This half-hearted and self-serving measure outraged Canadian feminists, until, in 1918, women were finally granted the legal right to vote in federal elections; the first Canadian woman to be elected to the federal parliament was Agnes Macphail in 1921. Nevertheless, many provinces, between 1916 and 1940, lagged behind in granting women the franchise. Women in Quebec did not have the right to vote until 1940. It is useful to note in comparison that in 1893 New Zealand was the first nation to allow all women to vote, including Maori women, at a federal level. South Australia had the franchise for land-owning women in local elections as early as 1861, and for all women in the state without restrictions in 1894. It was extended to all women in the Commonwealth of Australia in 1902.

One after another, states and territories of the United States, starting with the Wyoming territory in 1869, allowed women to vote at the local and state level. The United States as a whole granted women's suffrage in 1920.

Related to the fight for voting rights was the "Persons Case" in Canada, which insisted on the right of women to be recognized as "persons" in the eyes of the law and hence given access to the same rights and privileges as men, including the right to be appointed to the Senate. The Supreme Court Act included a segment that allowed any five interested persons to request a ruling on a constitutional point, leading Alberta activist Emily Murphy to gather a group of women known as the "Famous Five" (also including Irene Parlby, Nellie McClung, Henrietta Muir Edwards, and Louise McKinney) to bring a petition to the Canadian Supreme Court in 1928 asking that women be recognized as "persons" in the Canadian constitution. When their petition was overturned, the group took their case to England where it was decided that women were to be recognized as "persons" according to the British North America Act—an interpretation that was not, however, granted to Aboriginal people (men or women) at that time (and ultimately not until 1960, in fact, when voting rights were granted without restriction).

The sense of Canada's having entered a "new era" was augmented by the political reign of its new prime minister, Wilfrid Laurier, from 1896 to 1911. Laurier was a new kind of leader—francophone, Catholic, charismatic, and modern. His political career is noted for two things: his ability to straddle the interests of both French and English Canada, and his insistence on Canada's autonomy within the British Empire. As both a passionate anglophile and a proud French Canadian, Laurier was committed to the bicultural conception of Canada. In his famous speech on the principles of Liberalism delivered in Quebec City to Le Club Canadien on 26 June 1877, Laurier proclaimed that even though French Canadians were a "conquered race" (4), the French were themselves the originators of the true concept of liberty, and in Canada, he maintained, these principles applied equally to French and English. Concluding on a sentimental note, he mentioned the statue of Wolfe and Montcalm in Quebec City: "In what country under the sun could you find the names of the victor and vanquished honored in the same degree" (28). His speech offers a grand vision of the union of French and English (29).

One of Laurier's most strenuous causes was that of national independence. His notion of the twentieth century "belonging" to Canada assumed a Canada that had international sovereignty apart from England. Central to this was his insistence on Canada being able to control its foreign policy, including its participation in international disputes. This issue came to a head with the outbreak of the Anglo-Boer War in October 1899. When the long-standing Dutch settlers (Boers) resisted the imperial presence of the British outlanders in South Africa, Britain declared war to protect this outpost of its substantial empire. What resulted was essentially a civil war between two White Christian nations. British colonial secretary Joseph Chamberlain called for Canada to come to Britain's aid as an affirmation of the solidarity of the empire. Canadians, many of whom were first-generation British immigrants, insisted that Canada must send a contingent to defend British territory. French Canadians did not consider this a valid cause, particularly since Britain itself was not being threatened. They were especially opposed to entering wars to maintain British imperialism, the very power that had once conquered their ancestors on the Plains of Abraham in the expansion of the British Empire. One might say that the modern French-Canadian nationalist movement emerged partially in response to the Anglo-Boer War, particularly following the protest and resignation of one of Laurier's French cabinet ministers, Henri Bourassa, who was intensely opposed to Canada's participation in the war. Laurier was caught in a bind: "If he knuckled under to the British, his own people would call him a traitor; at the same time, his instincts to maintain an arm's length relationship within the Empire would lose him the support of the rest of Canada" (Berton 23). In response, he compromised, arranging for a volunteer contingent of Canadian soldiers that would fight in South Africa under British orders. Canada's vexed response to this war was a prelude to what was to come.

The Road to Sovereignty: First World War, 1914–18

In his 10 December 1892 "At the Mermaid Inn" column in the Toronto *Globe*, Wilfred Campbell insists on the need for a "grave national crisis" to bring about meaningful national unity in Canada (208). Ironically, this came in the wake of what was undoubtedly the single most catastrophic event of the period from 1900 to 1920: the First World War. To many, the war is regarded as having helped in the consolidation of Canada's national self-confidence and international reputation; it produced a sense of national pride and contributed to the developing myth of Canadian integrity, lawfulness, and distinctiveness from the Americans (since the Americans entered the war toward the end of the conflict). More concretely, it set in motion the first steps toward the official establishment of Canadian national sovereignty. However, it was also internally divisive and psychologically cataclysmic. The huge losses of men—over 60,000 Canadians were killed in the war—and the sheer horror and pointlessness of these deaths left a generation of Canadians jaded and disillusioned. As Bliss Carman wrote in a letter to his friend R.H. Hathaway in 1917, "The greater and insistent problems of [these] tremendous times obliterate all other interests. . . . The Victorian days belong to history."

Canada automatically entered the war in August 1914 as part of the British Empire. An August 1914 cartoon in *The Vancouver Daily Province* depicts the whelps of the British lion responding to the call (see Figure IV-7). In the autumn of that year, Canada sent over 30,000 troops as a contribution to Britain's war effort, the largest army that had ever crossed the Atlantic from west to east. By the end of the war, the total of the Canadian expeditionary recruits amounted to 600,000. The late entry of the United States into the war in 1917 helped consolidate Canada's reputation as an independent and proud nation. At the outset, English-Canadian support for the "war to end all wars" was enormous, especially because many of the initial volunteers were British-born or had close allegiances to Britain (Bothwell and Granatstein 53). According to the Canadian historian Gordon Donaldson, in the first wave of recruitment, "two of every three recruits were not native Canadians but immigrants from the British Isles" (93).

From the beginning, the organization of Canadian troops was somewhat haphazard, as the Canadians formed part of the British Army in Europe. As the war continued and casualties mounted, people became increasingly uncertain of Canada's role overseas. As C.M. Wallace puts it in his description of Canadians' initial response to the war, "Myopic popular fervour masked the fact that at the outset Canadians had no common understanding of the role their country was to play. Was Canada simply a colony giving loyal support to the Mother Country, or was she a nation in her own right fighting in the defence of the same noble principles as the other Allies? This question was vitally important because upon its answer depended the character and extent of Canadian involvement" (236). This question was not resolved until 1931, when the Statute of Westminster was passed in Britain granting Canada independent control over its foreign policy. Many people in Quebec, while initially supportive of the war, became skeptical and wondered about their role, as French Canadians, in the British war effort. As French-Canadian nationalist and politician Henri Bourassa put it at that time, "Those who disembowelled your fathers on the Plains of Abraham are asking you today to go and get killed for them" (qtd. in Donaldson 76). Two of the most catastrophic battles for Canadians were the Battle of the Somme in 1916, in which the Newfoundland Regiment (serving not with the Canadian forces, since Newfoundland was not yet a part of Canada, but under British command) was decimated, and the Battle of Vimy Ridge in 1917, in which well over 10,000 Canadian soldiers were killed (followed by further losses of over 15,000 in the offensive at Passchendaele). The capture of Vimy, which was made possible by the planning and coordination of the Canadian troops, contributed to the growing sense of Canadian courage and sagacity. The monolithic Vimy Memorial, designed by Walter Allward in 1926, stands to commemorate the Canadian effort in defence of France; the construction of the memorial, which took over 10 years to build, forms the subject of Jane Urquhart's 2001 novel *The Stone Carvers*. Following the victory at Vimy, the Canadian Corps was put under the command of Canadian brigadier-general Arthur Currie, the first time a Canadian (rather than British) commander was given this post.

Within Canada, the war had significant ramifications. The most divisive issue it provoked was the question of conscription. In a speech to the Halifax Canadian Club on 18 December 1914, Prime Minister Robert Borden, who had defeated Laurier in 1911, confidently declared that "there has not been, there will not be, compulsion or conscription." However, the war lasted much longer than anyone expected, and as it progressed, fewer recruits could be convinced to sign on. Early in 1916, Borden committed to sending 500,000 more recruits to England. In 1917, he announced his decision to institute conscription, thereby unleashing a national crisis. Initially he promised not to extend conscription to Canadian farmers, but eventually this promise was retracted too. The response in Quebec was that of outrage. Riots took place in the streets. When troops from Toronto were sent in to quell the resistance, four civilians were killed. The Montreal paper *Le Devoir*, edited by Bourassa, was threatened with government censorship because of its anti-conscription position (Keshen 354). It was also in this year that a federal income tax, the precursor of today's income tax, was put into effect as a "temporary war tax" or "conscription of wealth" to boost the war effort (Cook 411). In response to the conscription crisis of 1917, Borden recruited other pro-conscription members of Parliament, both Liberal and Conservative, and formed the Union Government coalition. While the "Unionist Coalition" won the election in 1917 under Borden's leadership, it lost strength following the end of the war in 1918. In the 1921 election, most of the Liberals who had joined Borden's unionist forces returned to the Liberal Party under the leadership of the new prime minister, William Lyon Mackenzie King.

The First World War is widely celebrated for having provided Canadians with a proud international reputation as independent, principled, and courageous people, and, paradoxically, as international peacekeepers. Many of Canada's political gains during this period can be attributed to the interventions of Borden himself. During the war, the leaders of the colonies were given no information concerning the war's progress except what they could glean from censored British newspapers. When Borden insisted that he needed to be kept abreast of developments in Europe, he was dismissed. With outrage, he protested against the fact that the hundreds of thousands of Canadian soldiers were being treated like "toy automata." "Is this war being waged by the United Kingdom alone, or is it being waged by the whole Empire?" he pointedly asked the High Commission in London (qtd. in Donaldson 96). During the Imperial War Conference of 1917, Borden teamed up with other British colonies, including South Africa, Australia, New Zealand, and Newfoundland, to insist on the full recognition of the dominions as autonomous nations rather than as extensions of Britain. This initiative effectively led to the Statute of Westminster in 1931, which guaranteed these nations' independence within the newly constituted "Commonwealth." At the international peace conference that followed the war, Borden was insistent that Canada would sign the peace treaty as an independent member and attain its own seat within the League of Nations. When British prime minister David Lloyd George and American president Woodrow Wilson questioned the proposal, Borden was furious: "The Dominions have maintained their place before the world during the past five years through sacrifices which no nation outside of Europe has known. I am confident that the people of Canada will not tamely submit to a dictation which declares that Liberia or Cuba, Panama or Hedjaz, Haiti or Equador must have a higher place . . . than can be accorded to their own country" (qtd. in Donaldson 97–98). At the very least, Canada merited equal representation, he argued. "So far as Borden was concerned," writes historian Desmond Morton, "his country had just won her War for Independence" (181).

In effect, then, it was not so much a pro-war positioning that unified Canadians during the war, but the sense of rallying as one body. This sentiment is encapsulated in John McCrae's famous war poem "In Flanders Fields," written in 1915. As Nancy Holmes argues, the poem does not celebrate the "glory of war" (28); rather, it "expresse[s] regret and confusion but also use[s] the torch of hopeful connection" as the voices of the dead insist on their continuity with the living (29). The poem thus invokes an imagined and unified national populace, much as the Confederation writers had been calling for in the 1880s and '90s; Canadians, it suggests, have a responsibility to their compatriots. The Union Government coalition used the first two stanzas of the poem on its election pamphlets in order to appeal to the sense of duty to the nation that the poem evokes.

Many poets and writers responded to the war in the years that followed. L.M. Montgomery's *Rilla of Ingleside* (1921) explores the effects of the Great War on the Canadian population. Literary critic Amy Tector notes that although Montgomery is reluctant to directly challenge militarist propaganda, she deliberately juxtaposes the pastoral ideal of Ingleside with the war-torn landscape of Flanders. Frederick George Scott's 1922 memoir, *The Great War as I Saw It*, and his 1917 volume of poetry, *In the Battle Silences*, are among the most interesting early Canadian accounts of the First World War. Other important war literature includes Francis Marion Beynon's autobiographical anti-war novel *Aleta Day* (1919), Peregrine Acland's *All Else Is Folly* (1929), Charles Yale Harrison's *Generals Die in Bed* (1930), and Philip Child's *God's Sparrows* (1937). In more recent years, John Gray and Eric Peterson's 1981 play, *Billy Bishop Goes to War*, tackles Canadians' ambivalent response to warfare and heroism through its treatment of the real-life First World War flying ace Billy Bishop. Timothy Findley's 1977 novel, *The Wars*, also takes as its subject questions of authority and history-making in its treatment of Robert Ross's experiences on the First World War battlefield, as does his disturbing short story "Stones" (1988), about a psychologically scarred First World War veteran. David MacFarlane's *The Danger Tree* (1991), Frances Itani's *Deafening* (2003), and Joseph Boyden's *Three Day Road* (2005) are three recent works that continue to explore the legacy of the horrors wrought by the Great War on family, love, and friendship.

Beyond the controversy in Quebec, Canadians generally were supportive of the war effort, not only of the expeditionary forces, but also through their war measures on the home front: factory work, munitions production, food rationing, prohibition, and Red Cross packages. Nevertheless, the war also proved internally divisive. French and English Canadians had initially been divided over the extent of their allegiance to Britain, but the launching of conscription in 1917–18 introduced an irreconcilable rift. December 1917 also brought tragedy on the home front when a munitions ship exploded in the Halifax harbour, devastating the city and leaving 1600 dead and 6000 homeless (Hugh MacLennan's 1941 novel, *Barometer Rising*, is set during the Halifax explosion). There was also an extended program of government-instituted censorship, one of the most blatant travesties of democracy in the country's history, under the orders of the chief censor, Ernest J. Chambers. Truths about the war—in newspapers, films, photography, music, even letters—were covered up in order to ensure continued support of the war effort. The misrepresentation of the realities of war, including the enormous number of losses and fatalities, was particularly unscrupulous in a Canadian context where, in contrast to Britain, Canadians did not see the steady procession of wounded men returning from the front. Some newspapers and magazines were shut down altogether, and the penalty was fine or imprisonment (Keshen 354). Robert Service's dispatches for the Ottawa *Journal*, written while he worked as an ambulance driver during the war, were suppressed for fear that they would discourage new recruits (Berton 162–63). In addition, during the war there were repeated instances of racism against targeted immigrant groups, particularly those of German or Austrian extraction. It was during the First World War, for example, that the name of Berlin, Ontario, was changed to Kitchener because of its German associations. This prejudice was extended to other groups after the war when European "Bolsheviks" were wrongly accused of sowing the seeds of labour unrest throughout the country.

The labour movement gained momentum following the war during a period of extensive unemployment. Across Canada, there was widespread labour unrest in the absence of any access to collective bargaining or union recognition (fourteen large strikes occurred across Canada between 1901 and 1913), culminating in the Winnipeg General Strike of 1919 when nearly 30,000 workers walked off the job, paralyzing the city. Winnipeg was left with no postal service, no streetcars, no newspapers, no gasoline, and no milk delivery for almost six weeks (15 May to 26 June). Further, most restaurants and shops in the city closed their doors for the duration of the strike. Even those in the public service (firefighters, police officers, and employees of the water works) left their posts. Workers' demands included higher wages, union recognition, and workers' rights. After negotiations failed, the strike was quelled by the national army and the North West Mounted Police in a day that turned bloody. A striker was killed, at least thirty sus-tained injuries, and thousands of Canadian workers were left demoralized. The sentiments harnessed in the strike were at least partially responsible in the 1930s and '40s for the foundation of a political labour party—the Co-operative Commonwealth Federation (CCF), a precursor to today's New Democratic Party—that called for the socialization of banks and the public ownership of communication, transportation, and natural resources.

In addition to labour unrest across the country, one of the most devastating events in the post-war period was the 1918–19 global pandemic of Spanish flu that spread in the aftermath of the war. The irony is that soldiers returning home to celebrate the miracle of having survived the horrors of Europe may in fact have been spreading the virus. Most of the victims, like those who died in the war itself, were in the prime of life. According to Kevin Kerr, whose 2002 play *Unity (1918)* is about the effects of the post-war flu epidemic on a community in Saskatchewan, "more people died in four weeks of the flu than did in four years of fighting" (8). Ultimately, the Spanish flu claimed more lives than the Great War itself—well over 20 million people worldwide.

The fire that levelled the Parliament Buildings in Ottawa in February 1916 only added to the sense of a world that was crumbling (some newspapers at the time described the tragedy as an act of German sabotage). Nevertheless, despite the devastations wrought by the war, the strikes, the influenza pandemic, and even the fire, Canada emerged with a stronger and more vibrant sense of itself as a unique and independent national community, capable of holding its own in an international forum. A 1918 political cartoon in the *Halifax Herald* depicts Canada's slow growth toward national recognition during the course of the war (Figure IV-8). Symbolic acclamation of Canada's national sovereignty came in 1921 when Canada was granted an official coat of arms by the British Crown (Figures IV-1 and IV-2). Canada was no longer a British imperial outpost.

At Home and Abroad: The Rise of Canadian Literature

The evolution of national consciousness that had been growing in the latter decades of the nineteenth century and which culminated in the twentieth century following the First World War was accompanied by a burgeoning of Canadian literary production. Books by Canadians addressing Canadian themes and topics were in increasing demand by the turn of the century. Indeed, an international market was developing for stories with Canadian characters and settings. For the first time, a few Canadian authors were selling their books by the hundred thousand copies. Robert Service, for instance, rode the wave of pre-war hope and prosperity in the Yukon as he followed the trails of the gold rush and published the rustic adventure poems in *Songs of a Sourdough* (1907) to worldwide success. The book made him one of the wealthiest authors in the world.

The first decades of the twentieth century saw works by a number of Canadian authors become national and international bestsellers. Such Canadian authors as Montgomery, Service, McClung, McCrae, and Ralph Connor enjoyed international fame during this period. McClung's early novel, *Sowing Seeds in Danny* (1908), for example, sold over 100,000 copies. The review of Leacock's *Sunshine Sketches of a Little Town* in *The Vancouver Daily Province* of 5 October 1912 maintained that the book would "be read with as much pleasure in England and the United States" as it would in Canada. Likewise, the Montreal *Daily Herald* of 21 July 1908 insisted that the Canadian setting of Montgomery's *Anne of Green Gables* would "appeal to the whole English-speaking world." Although sales figures do not measure aesthetic or literary merit, they do show the extensive international recognition and popularity of Canadian writers at this time.

During this period, there was an enlarged readership for books due to the better education and financial status of the Canadian populace, as well as to the advent of public lending libraries. An enlarged readership in Canadian terms, however, was not large enough to make a financial success out of any but the most popular writers. By the end of the First World War, most Canadians were literate and the reading public spanned most socio-economic groups (Parker 17; Bothwell et al. 188). However, the reading public was reading, and buying, mostly American and British authors as well as Canadian books published abroad. Although there were over four hundred publishers operating in Canada in 1900, they mainly focused on textbooks, trade books, and the distribution of works of fiction by American and British writers (Mount 22). It was difficult for Canadian publishers to assume the risk of publishing an unknown Canadian writer.

Before the turn of the century, most writers had to find publishers abroad in England or the United States, contributing to what was perceived as a "brain drain" of Canada's foremost thinkers. Archibald Lampman, in his 4 March 1893 "At the Mermaid Inn" column, admitted that "Canadians . . . are obliged, or at least irresistibly tempted, to carry their force and enterprise of character elsewhere. They also had to hew out their fortunes in foreign lands. . . . No doubt a time will come when the more populous life and increasing interests of our own country will keep a larger proportion of its enterprising spirits within its own borders" (269–70). After the turn of the century, there was still a strong sense that Canadian writers (as well as actors, artists, and musicians) had to leave Canada to seek recognition and reward in cultural centres such as London, New York, Berlin, and Paris. Emerging and established writers alike still sent their manuscripts to New York or London for consideration. Many of these writers became what literary historian Nick Mount calls "literary emigrants," choosing to move to where the literary scene was more dynamic and the publishers of new fiction and poetry were more plentiful than in Canada. Contrary to the prevalent lament that the development of Canadian literature was stalled when its writers left the country, in *When Canadian Literature Moved to New York* (2005) Mount argues that Canadian literature benefited from the American publishing industry, which enabled Canadian writers to appear in print when adequate outlets were unavailable in Canada. In fact, he goes so far as to argue that while in America (and Europe, one could add), these writers laid a viable foundation for further Canadian literary development.

At the beginning of the new century there were also increasing numbers of writers who had turned to America or England to be published, but who were able to return to Canada after they became successful. Montgomery is a foremost example. She originally tried five Canadian publishers for *Anne of Green Gables* (1908) before her manuscript was finally accepted by an American one. By 1917 she was successful enough that she could move to a Canadian publisher, shifting her work from her Boston publisher, L.C. Page, to the Toronto firm of McClelland, Goodchild, and Stewart, the Canadian publishing company founded in 1906. In addition to the success of works of literature for adults, Canadian children's books, which started to achieve recognition at this time, were read by people who wanted stories about the land they had grown up in as children, so that they might pass on their traditions and memories to subsequent generations.

It is also in this period that one sees "the beginning of serious study of English-Canadian writers" (Cambron 130), both in the publication of critical works on the topic of Canadian literature and in the introduction of university courses in the subject. The first university course in English-Canadian literature appears to have been taught by J.B. Reynolds to an affiliate of the University of Guelph in 1906–07, followed the next year by Susan E. Vaughan at McGill (Pacey 68; see also Fee and Monkman 1086). By the early 1920s, courses in Canadian literature were being taught by Alexander MacMechan at Dalhousie University and J.D. Logan at Acadia, with universities across the country following suit shortly after. Nevertheless, the presence of Canadian literature as an established and respected field within university English departments did not take serious hold until the 1960s and '70s.

It is difficult to affix an encompassing label to the literature of this period, which saw such diverse writings as the political essays and feminist fiction of McClung, the social realist stories of Sime, the regional idylls of Montgomery, the social satire of Leacock, and the romanticized ballads of Service. Nevertheless, the Romantic meditation on the elevation of the human spirit in response to nature had largely been left behind in favour of a more whimsical outlook, yet one that was often grounded in Canadian social contexts. Indeed, much of this literature celebrates Canadian locations and people, prompting reviewers to praise the "Canadianness" of the work, as did, for example, the reviewer of *Anne of Green Gables* for the November 1908 *Canadian Magazine*, who applauded the book for being "thoroughly Canadian." Many writers of this period wrote what has been called "local-colour" fiction and poetry (Smiley 816), delineated with affectionate humour and, in some cases, social satire and critique. Satirical self-deprecation became a recognizably Canadian trait at this time (with, admittedly, a backwards nod to Thomas Chandler Haliburton and Thomas McCulloch), most evident in the work of Leacock. Although this was the period that marked the beginning of literary and poetic modernism worldwide (including such writers as W.B. Yeats, Thomas Hardy, Henry James, Joseph Conrad, James Joyce, and Virginia Woolf), with its emphasis on existential concerns, nihilism, and formal innovation, literary modernism did not fully take hold in Canada until after the First World War. Canadian writing of the early decades of the twentieth century tended to be more in the form of idealist realism, as one finds in the writings of Leacock, Connor, or Montgomery, and less of the more gritty realism of later years (such as one sees, for instance, in the work of Frederick Philip Grove, Sinclair Ross, Morley Callaghan, or even the later work of Robert Service). Montgomery herself characterized the *Anne* novels as a series that "belong[ed] to the green, untroubled pastures and still waters of the world before the war" (qtd. in Edwards and Litster 32); her 1921 novel, *Rilla of Ingleside*, by contrast, depicts an Anne who has been severely dispirited by the outbreak of hostilities in Europe. After the First World War, and in the wake of European and American modernism, the period of relative innocence and optimism that we associate with the early decades of twentieth-century Canada was quickly left behind.

FIGURE IV-1 Unofficial Coat of Arms (1904)

When the Dominion of Canada was formed in 1867, each of the original four provinces (Ontario, Quebec, Nova Scotia, and New Brunswick) was granted arms, but the Dominion itself was not. Instead, the provincial arms were quartered for federal use, appearing first on the Great Seal of Canada. This shield implicitly became the arms identifying the Dominion of Canada. As other provinces joined Confederation, the arms of the new provinces were added to this federal composite design. Before long, the design became far too complex and unwieldy for its intended purpose of simple identification, as this 1904 version, when there were seven provinces, shows. Eventually, the Canadian government submitted a request to the British sovereign for a grant of arms. The request was approved and the arms assigned to Canada were declared in the proclamation of King George V in 1921.

Source: Royal Heraldry Society.

FIGURE IV-2 Official Canadian Coat of Arms (1921-1994)

The Royal Coat of Arms of Canada (formally known as the Arms of Her Majesty in Right of Canada) was proclaimed by King George V on 21 November 1921. Approved in 1994, the present design also includes a red ribbon behind the shield with the motto of the Order of Canada written in gold lettering, "*Desiderantes Meliorem Patriam*" ("they desire a better country"). The coat of arms consists of nine symbolic parts: the Shield, Ribbon, Helm, Crest and Crown, Supporters, Motto, Mount, and Blazon. The design of the arms of Canada reflects the royal symbols of Great Britain and France: the three royal lions of England, the royal lion of Scotland, the royal Irish harp of Tara, and the royal fleur-de-lis of France. On the bottom portion of the shield is a sprig of three Canadian maple leaves representative of Canadians of all other origins. The original maple leaves were green, signifying youth, rather than the red of the autumn leaves that we use today. The colour was changed in 1957. There are no symbolic representations of the Aboriginal peoples of Canada on the Royal Coat of Arms. The country's motto, "*A Mari Usque Ad Mare*" ("from sea to sea"), is written on the ribbon at the bottom. At the base of the arms are the floral emblems associated with the Canadian monarchy: the English rose, the Scottish thistle, the Irish shamrock, and the French fleur-de-lis. It is these emblems, minus the fleur-de-lis, that are invoked in Alexander Muir's famous Canadian anthem from 1867, "The Maple Leaf for Ever." The coat of arms is used by Canada on federal government possessions such as buildings, official seals, money, passports, proclamations, and publications, as well as on the badges of some members of the Canadian Forces.

Source: Reproduced with the permission of the Government of Canada, 2008.

FIGURE IV-3 Map of Canada in 1905

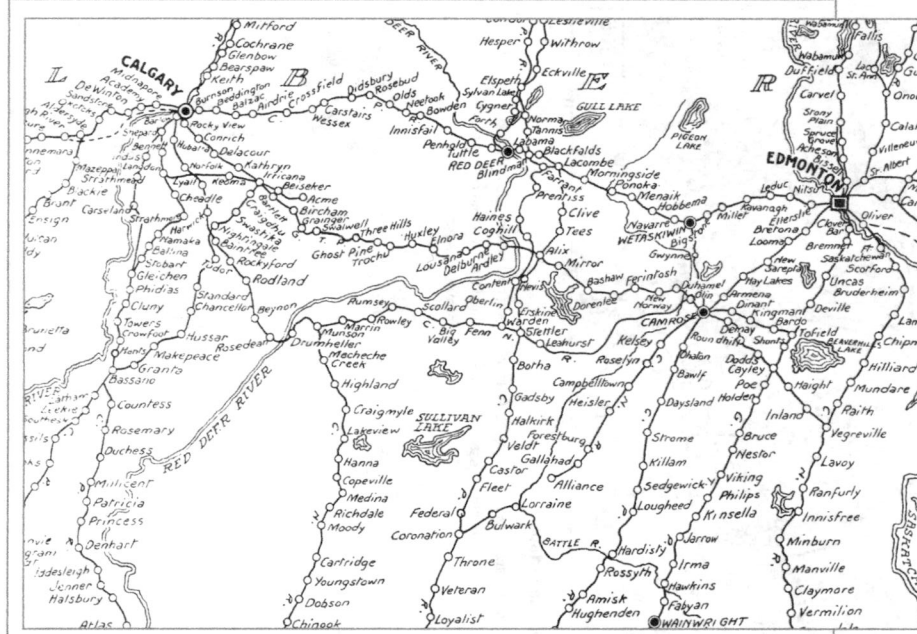

FIGURE IV-4 Railway Map of Alberta (1916)

This detail from the 1916 map illustrates the province's development along the lines of the railway. The towns are spaced quite evenly along the railway line to provide easy access points for the transportation of grain and people. This map shows the extent to which Western development and the railway are interwined. Just as towns grew up around the train station as the central point of meeting and commerce, the province grew along the railway lines.

Source: Association of Canadian Map Libraries and Archives.

FIGURE IV-5 The Canadian Emigration Office in London, England, July 1911
The Canadian Department of the Interior's immigration campaign included the establishment of this office in London, England. The office promoted Canada as a land of opportunity for farmers and families, with carefully photographed displays of fruits and vegetables offered as proof of the fertility and richness of prairie land. Note that this office is advertising 160-acre farms for free in Western Canada as an inducement to emigrate from England.

Source: Library and Archives Canada/C-063257.

FIGURE IV-6 The *Komagata Maru* Incident (1914)

In 1914 the *Komagata Maru* was chartered by Gurdit Singh, a Singapore-based Sikh business-man. The ship's passage was intended as a direct challenge to the "continuous journey" provi-sion of the Immigration Act of 1910, which required immigrants to travel to Canada directly from their country of origin, rather than by way of another foreign port, and required them to enter with at least $200. Article 38 of the Act prohibits the entry of "any immigrant who has come to Canada otherwise than by continuous journey from the country of which he is a native" and bars "immigrants belonging to any race deemed unsuited to the climate or requirements of Canada." It was widely understood that the regulation was created to curtail emigration from India. As there were no direct connections to Canada from India, immigration to Canada was effectively blocked. The *Komagata Maru*, however, had not left from India but rather had departed from Hong Kong. On 23 May 1914, the ship arrived in Burrard Inlet, Vancouver, with 376 passengers aboard, mainly from the Punjab region of India: 340 Sikhs, 24 Muslims, and 12 Hindus, seeking to enter Canada. Canadian authorities stopped the passengers from landing. Under guard by troops and a gunboat, they were kept in the harbour for nearly two months while they tried to negotiate entry into the country as fellow members of the British Empire. In the end, only 24 of the passengers were allowed to enter and stay in Canada. Ordered out of the harbour through an act of intervention by Prime Minister Robert Borden, and escorted by the navy ship *The Rainbow*, the *Komagata Maru* was forced to sail to India. When the ship arrived in Calcutta, it was sent to dock many miles out of the city with the idea that the passengers would be put on a train to Punjab. Seen as agitators by the rulers of British India for their effort to enter Canada, the passengers were placed under guard. There was also an attempt to arrest the leaders. In the end, the passengers protested and the police opened fire, killing nineteen and wounding nine others.

The events surrounding the *Komagata Maru* remain an example of the racism, injustice, and inequality that continued in Canada into the turn of the century. A plaque commemorating the seventy-fifth anniversary of the departure of the *Komagata Maru* was erected in the Sikh Gurdwara (temple) in Vancouver on 23 July 1989. Responding to increasing calls for redress, in August 2006, Prime Minister Stephen Harper stated that "the government of Canada acknowledges the *Komagata Maru* incident and we will soon undertake consultations with the Indo-Canadian community on how best to recognize this sad moment in our history."

ANSWERING THE CALL
" The whelps of the lion are joining their sire."

SIGNS OF THE TIMES
John Bull alters the sign again.

FIGURE IV-8 "Signs of the Times" (1918)

Canada's international status changed over the course of the First World War. Having auto-matically joined the war effort in August 1914 as part of the British Empire, by 1918 Canada achieved symbolic independence. During the Imperial War Conference of 1917, Canadian Prime Minister Robert Borden insisted on recognition of the colonial Dominions as autonomous nations, rather than as extensions of Britain. By 1918, at the international peace conference that followed the war, Borden was insistent that Canada should sign the peace treaty as an independent member and attain its own seat within the League of Nations. This cartoon, published in the *Halifax Herald* on 3 August 1918, shows the changing relationship of Canada to Britain. Here John Bull (the national personification of England), dressed in First World War military attire, keeps repainting the sign to indicate Canada's altered status.

Source: Charles and Cynthia Hou, *Great Canadian Political Cartoons, 1820 to 1914* (Vancouver:
Moody's Lookout, 1997).

Although the promotion of immigration to Canada began in the early nineteenth century, the government of Prime Minister Wilfrid Laurier in the early twentieth century was particularly innovative and aggressive in its campaign to bring people to the expanding nation. At fairs and expositions, in travelling tents, and on speaking tours, immigration agents in Britain and Europe advertised Canada as the "Last Best West" and "the Land of Milk and Honey." The agents working on behalf of the Canadian government (or transportation companies offering services to Canada) made presentations to packed halls of potential immigrants, presenting beautiful images of the Rocky Mountains and thriving settled farmland. They even sometimes carried bushels of Canadian wheat and barley to show the prosperity and economic potential of the country.

Clifford Sifton (MP for Brandon North), who headed the Department of the Interior and was superintendent general of Indian affairs in Laurier's government (from 1896 to 1905), was central to this promotion of immigration. It was Sifton who initiated the vigorous and successful policy that is outlined in his 1 April 1922 retrospective article in *Maclean's* excerpted here. Sifton notes that his goal was to search for a "quality" immigrant who could endure hardship on the land. Although Sifton was particular as to where such an immigrant could best come from (northern Britain, America, and northern Europe), his favoured choice of immigrant was based primarily on occupation (farmer). His description of the "class of settlers that are not wanted in Canada," namely city-dwellers and artisans, echoes Susanna Moodie's and Catharine Parr Traill's similar distinctions almost a century earlier. His successor, Frank Oliver (MP for Edmonton and Edmonton West), minister of the interior from 1905 to 1911, heavily criticized Sifton's policies for disregarding what he believed were the necessities of an Anglo-Canadian society based on British ideals. Oliver thus changed the focus of Canadian immigration policy (with the Immigration Acts of 1906 and 1910) by implementing a plan that sought immigrants on the basis of ethnicity or "race." Oliver's department wanted to encourage British immigrants above all other prospective groups, in order to maintain what it viewed as the racial integrity of the country. The Immigration Act of 1906 bars anyone who, for medical or moral reasons, might constitute a drain on the state. In addition, the Immigration Act of 1910 is clear in its desire to exclude potential immigrants based on race or class. Indeed, section 38 is where the "continuous journey" clause challenged by the men on the *Komagata Maru* (see Figure IV-6) was introduced.

The Immigrants Canada Wants

It is a consoling thought, sanctified by long usage, that if everything is not satisfactory with regard to Immigration it can always be blamed on the government or the tariff. The fact remains, however, that a country can only get the kind of immigrants which are suitable to it and can only hold and assimilate them if they have been wisely chosen. [. . .]

People who do not know anything at all about the policy which was followed by the department of the Interior under my direction quite commonly make the statement that my policy for Immigration was quantity and not quality. As a matter of fact that statement is the direct opposite of the fact. In those days settlers were sought from three sources; one was the United States. The American settlers did not need sifting; they were of the finest quality and the most desirable settlers. In Great Britain we confined our efforts very largely to the North of England and Scotland, and for the purpose of sifting the settlers we doubled the bonuses to the agents in the North of England, and cut them down as much as possible in the South. The result was that we got a fairly steady stream of people from the North of England and from Scotland and they were the very best settlers in the world. I do not wish to suggest that we did not get many very excellent people from the more southerly portions of England, but they were people who came on their own initiative largely, which was the best possible guarantee of success.

Our work was largely done in the North. Then, came the continent—where the great emigrating center was Hamburg. Steamships go there to load up with people who are desirous of leaving Europe. The situation is a peculiar one. If one should examine twenty people who turn up at Hamburg to emigrate he might find one escaped murderer, three or four wasters and ne'er-do-wells, some very poor shop-keepers, artisans or laborers and there might be one or two stout, hardy peasants in sheep-skin coats. Obviously the peasants are the men that are wanted here. Now, with regard to these twenty men, no one knows anything about them except the shipping agents. These men are sent in from outlying local agencies all over Europe. They arrive at Hamburg and the booking agents have their names and full descriptions of who they are and where they came from. No one else has this information.

We made an arrangement with the booking agencies in Hamburg, under which they winnowed out this flood of people, picked out the agriculturists and peasants and sent them to Canada, sending nobody else. We paid, I think, $5 per head for the farmer, and $2 per head for the other members of the family.

[. . .] The policy was completely and perfectly successful while it lasted. There was not one-half of one per cent of the people we got from Hamburg who were not actual agriculturists. Almost without exception they went on farms and practically without exception they are on their farms yet, if they are alive. If not, their children are there. [. . .]

When I speak of quality I have in mind, I think, something that is quite different from what is in the mind of the average writer or speaker upon the question of Immigration. I think a stalwart peasant in a sheep-skin coat, born on the soil, whose forefathers have been farmers for ten generations, with a stout wife and a half-dozen children, is good quality. A Trades Union artisan who will not work more than eight hours a day and will not work that long if he can help it, will not work on a farm at all and has to be fed by the public when work is slack is, in my judgment, quantity and very bad quantity. I am indifferent as to whether or not he is British born. It matters not what his nationality is; such men are not wanted in Canada, and the more of them we get the more trouble we shall have.

For some years after the changes in policy which followed my retirement from office, Canada received wholesale arrivals of all kinds of immigrants. As above stated, there was no selection. Particularly from the continent it is quite clear that we received a considerable portion of the off-scourings and dregs of society. They formed colonies in Ottawa, Montreal, Toronto, Winnipeg and other places and some of them and their children have been furnishing work for the police ever since.

The situation at Hamburg is practically the same now as it was then, except that there is a larger proportion of ne'er-do-wells and scalawags who desire to get away from Europe. The peasants can be brought there and they wish to emigrate, but it is imperative that an effective method be adopted for making a selection. We want the peasants and agriculturists; we do not want the wasters and criminals. [. . .]

I have a very emphatic opinion, based on the observation of something like thirty years, about the class of settlers that are not wanted in Canada. It is said there are millions of town dwellers, artisans, small shopkeepers, laborers and so forth on the continent of Europe who are anxious to come to Canada. Everyone will sympathize with their condition and desire that they should find a place where they will lead a happier life; but we do not want them in Canada under any conditions whatever. These people are essentially town dwellers. They have no idea in the world of going out in a country like Canada and fighting the battle of the pioneer. If they come here they will swell the ranks of the unemployed; they will create slums; they will never go upon the land; they will not add anything to the production of the country and we shall have an insoluble problem and festering sore upon our hands, which, if the experience of the past is any guide, will remain as long as Canada endures.

There is talk, also, about getting a large number of people from the manufacturing towns of England and Scotland. We do not want mechanics from the Clyde—riotous, turbulent, and with an insatiable appetite for whiskey. We do not want artisans from the southern towns of England who know absolutely nothing about farming. There is nothing in these schemes suggested for educating them and making farmers of them, and then sending them out to fight the battle of the pioneer's life. It is the next thing to a crime to put these men under such conditions. The pioneers have to be of the toughest fibre that can be found. Let no one imagine that you can get people in huge numbers from the towns and make farmers of them. If an attempt is made to do so there will be a worse problem created than that which exists now. I may be told that there are some cases in which mechanics and townspeople have been successful. The Barr colony, for instance. That is quite true. But they were not gathered up by immigration propaganda, spoonfed and coddled into coming to Canada. They were people who came themselves, paid their own way, stood on their own feet, and, imbued with the determination to make a home and the true spirit of the pioneer, in many cases they succeeded admirably. Let it not be imagined from this fact that you can gather up tens of thousands of people who have neither any desire for, nor adaptability to, the life which is ahead of them and turn them into farmers. It takes two generations to convert a town-bred population into an agricultural one, and it is not likely to be done on any considerable scale except under the pressure of starvation. In any event it takes two generations to do it. Canada has no time for that operation. We have not two generations to spare. [. . .]

I am of the deliberate opinion that about 500,000 farmers could be actually put on land in the next ten years by a thorough, systematic and energetic organization, backed with all needful legal authority and money. If four are allowed to a family, that would represent two million people actually added to the agricultural population in ten years. Twenty years from now it would represent, with natural increase, a population of six or seven millions. If that is done, then the railway problem is solved and the problem of the payment of the national debt is solved, provided the government ceases to make fresh additions to the debt by extravagant expenditures. [. . .]

In Norway, Sweden, Denmark, Belgium, Bohemia, Hungary and Galicia there are hundreds of thousands of hardy peasants, men of the type above described, farmers for ten or fifteen generations, who are anxious to leave Europe and start life under better conditions in a new country. These men are workers. They have been bred for generations to work from daylight to dark. They have never done anything else and they never expect to do anything else. We have some hundreds of thousands of them in Canada now and they are among our most useful and productive people.

[1922]

EMILY MURPHY ■ (1868–1933)

Emily Murphy has been called the quintessential example of a "Canadian New Woman" by critics and supporters alike. She was a writer and a journalist, as well as a legal reformer who became the first female police magistrate in the British Empire. She engaged with the most important issues of the period, including the role of women in society, temperance, eugenics, narcotics, and the growth of western Canada. Murphy was a prolific writer who published in Canadian, American, and English periodicals under a variety of pseudonyms including Janey Canuck; Earl or Earlie York; Emily Chetwood; Emily Ferguson; and Mrs. Arthur Murphy; as well as Judge, Magistrate, or Mrs. Emily

Murphy. As the leader of the "Famous Five" group of women (Murphy, Henrietta Muir Edwards, Louise McKinney, Irene Parlby, and Nellie McClung), she is best known for her twelve-year battle for the recognition of women as "persons" under the British North America Act. This vocal advocate for equality between the sexes has also recently been brought to task for her role supporting forced sterilization of mentally challenged people, her racist attitudes to non-European immigrants, and her virulent stand on drugs and addiction. While Murphy was fighting the "persons" case for women's equality, she published a collection of essays entitled *The Black Candle* (1922), under the name of Janey Canuck. This book has recently met with sharp criticism on two fronts: it displays racial prejudice and it advocates strict anti-drug laws that led directly to the criminalization of drugs in Canada.

Born into a prominent legal family in Cookstown, Ontario, in 1868, Emily Ferguson was educated at Bishop Strachan School in Toronto. She first met her future husband, Arthur Murphy, when she was just fifteen years old. They married when she was nineteen. As a young Anglican minister's wife, she penned stories under the name "Janey Canuck." Travelling first to England, where she wrote *The Impressions of Janey Canuck Abroad* (1901), published under the name Emily Ferguson, Murphy became vitally interested in matters of social justice. Moving in 1907 to Edmonton, Alberta, Murphy continued her political activism while combining family life, writing, and a multitude of reform activities in the interests of women and children. A prolific contributor of book reviews and articles to Canadian magazines and newspapers, she published several more popular books of personal sketches to add to the original *Janey Canuck Abroad*, including *Janey Canuck in the West* (1910), *Open Trails* (1912), and *Seeds of Pine* (1914). Murphy was also prominent in the suffrage movement, and a long-time executive member of the Canadian Women's Press Club (serving as its president from 1913 to 1920), the National Council of Women of Canada, the Federated Women's Institutes of Canada (becoming its first national president), and over twenty other professional and volunteer organizations.

Janey Canuck in the West consists of sketches of her travels across the prairies. Included here is her description of the Doukhobor settlement in Saskatchewan. It is particularly valuable in the amount of detail Murphy gives about the community, as it is a good description of a group of immigrants who are not regularly acknowledged in literary circles because of a dearth of accounts of settlement by the Doukhobors themselves. Murphy's celebration of the Doukhobors as ideal Canadian prairie settlers is comparable to Clifford Sifton's praise of the "hardy peasants in sheep-skin coats." Still, it is important to note the degree to which Murphy is editorializing about "them" in ethnographic terms from her position as the wife of an Anglican minister. The sketch tells as much about Murphy and her values (particularly around domestic themes such as clothing, divisions of labour, and cooking) as it does about the Doukhobors. To the modern eye, "Janey Canuck" seems far more encumbered in her corsets and undergarments than the Doukhobor women in their headkerchiefs.

From Janey Canuck in the West

With the Dukhobors

It was seven o'clock when we sighted the Dukhobor village of Vosnesenia. It is built on rising ground, and the site has been well chosen. The drainage is perfect. Ditches on either side of the village carry the water to a small creek that winds through the lowland.

Arriving at Vosnesenia, we went to Eli's house. He has frequently worked for us, and the Padre[1] says his house is one of the cleanest and most comfortable in the village.

The houses are arranged on both sides of a wide street, and are foreign in every line. They are one-storied, and of unsawn lumber plastered with clay. They are whitewashed, and frescoed with vivid dadoes. Sometimes the roofs project into verandas, which are ornamented with carving. The blinds are on the outside, and consist of several thicknesses of hemp. These have a superlative advantage. Early callers know whether the inmates are ready or not to receive them.

The Padre went into the house to know if we might spend the night with them. I was presently surrounded by men, women and children, and borne triumphantly indoors, all the while feeling that I was being examined with a directness that was disconcerting. They took off my headgear, fur coat, and golf-jacket, and finally tackled my footgear. Then they all laughed at the great heap of dry-goods I had shed. My hatpins afforded them especial amusement. They pushed them in and out of my cap many times.

When our "grub" box was brought in, I sallied to the kitchen to get tea ready. The stove was made of baked clay. It was what Mr. Arnold Haultain[2] has described as "an ungainly but highly satisfactory stove." I put a handful of tea in the pot, and gave it to one of the women to steep. She poured half a cupful of water on, and then proceeded to pour it off. I was afraid of losing my brew, but unnecessarily, for this was only to free the leaves of dust and other impurities—surely a laudable and sanitary precaution.

I cooked bacon in my own pan, and fried some potatoes. One of the little girls held her nose during the cooking process. Eli told me she did not like "the stank."

The Dukhobors are vegetarians, and urge with their kind that we "make graveyards of our stomachs." I explained to Eli that the Israelites ate angels' food in the wilderness, and remained stiff-necked and uncircumcised in heart.

"Me no understand," said Eli. He is a sly fellow, this Eli, and does not like to be drawn out.

[1] Janey Canuck's name for her minister husband.

[2] T. Arnold Haultain (1857–1941), minor Canadian writer. Author of *Two Country Walks in Canada* (1910).

The table off which the Dukhobors eat is small. With them, dining is clearly not a function. They spread a white cloth over the table in our honour. They also set down a plate of their bread. In colour it resembled New Orleans treacle, and had we no fine stomachic sensibilities I am sure we should have found it highly nutritive. I do not know what they put in it, but should say its component parts are similar to those of bread I once ate in Germany, consisting of three parts specially prepared sawdust and one part rye-flour.

The women of the household washed my dishes. How many women were there? I do not know. There were four generations of them. Some of the houses have five.

The news had spread that we were in the village, and soon all the young men and maidens gathered to see us. They were taking us in, and it would doubtless have been a thorn in our pride if we knew what they thought of us.

The girls entered, and made a stately bow, which I must practise. It is beautiful. The women wear short postillion-like jackets of black sateen. Their skirts are short, and made without gores, being gathered in, even succeeded in blending purple, red and green in a happy triple alliance.

The unmarried women—even the baby girls—wear white kerchiefs on their heads, and the married women coloured ones. These kerchiefs are never doffed. I do not know why, but in likelihood to show they are unquestionably worshipful of their lords.

On the whole, their dress spells comfort. Their arm-holes are easy; their skirts do not drag; their bodies are not jails of bones and steels, and they wear no cotton-batting contrivances. [. . .]

Most of the Dukhobors can speak a few words of English, and all are anxious to become proficient so that they may go to our villages to work. On this occasion, John, a young Dukhobor who had worked in a Canadian store, and who speaks English fluently, acted as interpreter.

I asked them to sing for us. Their music is not of the "popular" variety, and in volume would suffice for a marching regiment. All the sounds seem to come from their head and throat. They do not move their lips, or very slightly, so that I found it difficult to know who was singing. The airs are weird and vagrant. It is astonishing how long they can hold one note. The Dukhobors never use musical instruments. They sang the 77th Psalm, lullabies, and songs of freedom. [. . .]

When I expressed a wish to retire, the guests bowed themselves out, and one of the women made our bed. It consisted of a feather mattress as soft as marshmallows, and a heap of pillows and blankets. The mattress was very short, being calculated to accommodate only the body and not the legs. It was laid on a wooden bench which was about five feet wide, and ran nearly all the way round the room.

The men retired to one apartment, the women to another, and Eli and his wife to a third. A woman and baby lay at our feet, and a boy opposite. The baby was placed in a square bed or box which was suspended from the ceiling, something like a bird-cage.

While I was undressing, the women returned and examined my clothing with apparent interest. My golf-skirt, with brilliant plaid lining, and my underskirts were handed round, rubbed between the fingers and commented upon. They seemed much pleased with the ribbons running through my underwear, but were shocked and, at the same instant, amused by my corsets. They nudged each other, grinned, and shrugged their shoulders. These corsets were of the long-hipped style, had two pairs of yellow suspenders, and carried a patent busk-protector.[3]

Then they showed me what they wore. Taking all things into consideration, I wouldn't exchange.

After we lay down, the women returned once more with articles for sale. We bought some socks and woollen mittens. The mittens were white, and had white fleece knitted inside, making them as warm as fur.

Heavens! but the heat was awful. No Pullman car was ever comparable, nor baker's oven for that matter. The women kept piling on dry tamarack wood at intervals all night. I gasped and suffocated, and thought longingly of the dress mentioned by Rabelais[4] as "nothing before, nothing behind, with sleeves of the same."

And the cat walked over me most of the night, for in an ill-guided moment I had fed it with meat, and so it was showing me some cupboard love. [. . .]

These thrifty women sew without machines, spin, knit, and make their own baskets and linen. They reap in the harvest fields too, and, if need be, can take a hand at the plough.

By unfriendly critics, much has been made of the fact that the Dukhobor women perform the arduous work of harnessing themselves to the plough, but this is entirely at their own suggestion.

At first the women were greatly in the majority, as their fathers, sons, and husbands were in Siberian exile, and much of the work had, therefore, to be done by the womenfolk. It was when only a few draught horses were available, and these were needed to haul logs from a distance so that homes might be built before the rigours of winter set in, that the women volunteered, with true Spartan fortitude, to break up the land. [. . .]

As I watch the easy, muscular movement of the women kneading the meal, it is borne in on me that they have no need for dumb-bells nor any reason for physical culture.

Dr. Johnson[5] is credited with saying that much can be done with a Scotsman if you catch him young. The same would apply to the Dukhobors. The children are bright, receptive, and keen for work, and will be singing "The Maple Leaf" before another decade.

[3] A "busk protector" is a layer of material that covers the "busk" (a piece of wood, whalebone, ivory, horn, or steel slotted into the front of stays to hold the torso erect in a corset) and prevents it from snapping with wear. It was the latest innovation in corsets at this time.

[4] French Renaissance writer François Rabelais (1483–1553) describes the garments of King Shrovetide in these terms in *Gargantua and Pantagruel IV*.

[5] Dr. Samuel Johnson (1709–84), poet, essayist, biographer, and lexicographer, is credited with this saying in James Boswell's *Life of Johnson* (1791).

The boys are the same as other boys, in that they stare, wriggle, snuffle, grin behind your back, and are as hard to hold as quicksilver.

The girls are round, brown, and dimpled, and as well developed physically as their brothers. They are not warm-happed, cuddled, and health-fooded like our children, and so infant mortality is not high among them. Overlooked, almost forgotten, these little wildings gather to themselves sap and sinew like children of the cave-dwellers. It is the shrewd way of God.

I am convinced that these people from the shores of the Black Sea will make excellent citizens. They do not steal—or very seldom—fight, drink intoxicants, smoke, or swear. Their lives are saturated with ideas of thrift and small economies. They hold themselves slaves of neither priest nor landlord, and their history is a story of sturdy struggling for independence. [. . .]

Their system is communistic. The crops and money are all stored in one fund. This practice cannot be set aside as entirely visionary and unworkable when the whole Christian Church kept it without violation for more than two hundred years. Besides, it is something very akin to this system that is advocated to-day by leading Socialists in all parts of the world.

There are some very apparent benefits in this Dukhobor method, too. The people are not isolated on lonely steadings miles and miles from any one. This loneliness is undoubtedly the greatest trial our settlers have to endure. He was a wise statesman who said it was not a parish council the country needed so much as a parish circus.

In these Dukhobor villages, the people practically constitute one large family, and know each other's outgoings and incomings, fortunes and misfortunes. It is their habit to visit each other in the evenings, to sew, gossip, sing, or while away the time as wisdom may dictate or fancy lead.

Their system has another superlative advantage. The wolf is never at the door. Their storehouses have superfluities for none, but an abundance for all.

It looks, though, as if the iron of worldly ambition has at last got a wedge in their souls. The land which the Government allotted to them is about to be thrown open to settlers. The Government is wholly justified in this action. It is neither wise nor fair to leave a large area of country fallow and unproductive while other people need it.

But the forfeiture will probably prove too severe a strain on the principles of the community, and the likelihood is that the people will make entries for homesteads.

Their beautiful ideals will be whittled down by the jack-knife of all-pervading expediency. Their little Arcadias will be broken up, and presently their women, too, will be affecting hatpins, corsets, and yellow garters. The pity of it!

Hitherto the sciences and arts have been a quality unfelt, because unknown. They lost some few things; but in losing they gained more. They were wise with the supreme wisdom of simplicity.

[1910]

In the final sentence of Jessie Georgina Sime's story collection *Sister Woman* (1919), the narrator runs her fingers over the keys of her typewriter and feels them "lovingly." In this act of giving herself over to writing instead of human love, the narrator highlights her need for artistic expression over all else. She thus shows herself to be a precursor of modernist values and contemporary mores. For forty years after Sime came to Canada she was by her own definition a "near-Canadian," who wrote about the experiences of urban women and men on the margins of Canadian society. Born in Scotland into a literary family (her parents, James Sime and Jessie Aitken Wilson, were both writers), Sime grew up in literary circles that included family friends George Meredith, Thomas Hardy, and W.B. Yeats. Influenced by the socially minded ideas of George Bernard Shaw and William Morris, in her early years Sime wrote a column for the Pall Mall *Gazette* and book reviews for the *Atheneum*. However, near the end of the nineteenth century, financial misfortune caused her to take up a position as a secretary in a doctor's office in Edinburgh. Immigrating to Montreal in 1907, she again worked in a doctor's office. A firm advocate of women's independence through work, Sime focused on writing about the benefits and pitfalls of the changing roles available to women in the new century.

Always concerned with the position of working women, in 1916 Sime published *The Mistress of All Work*, a household handbook for single working women. She subsequently published the novels *Our Little Life: A Novel of To-Day* (1921) and *Orpheus in Quebec* (1942). It is in her collection of stories, *Sister Woman* (1919), however, that Sime is seen to have made her most profound statement on women's lives and modern urban society. In "Munitions!," one of the most successful stories in *Sister Woman*, Sime writes about those whom critic Sandra Campbell calls "the hardy, shrewd, nurturing, lower-class women of Montreal, native and immigrant alike." Campbell notes how the stories deal with psychic and social pressures faced by working class women as a result of the rapid industrialization and urbanization which Sime witnessed in Montreal. Emerging out of her experience as a secretary in a gynecologist's office (in Edinburgh and in Montreal) before she became a professional writer, the stories in *Sister Woman* deal with pregnancy, illegitimacy, venereal disease, sexuality, maternity, and "female fatigue," as well as adultery, prostitution, and working poverty. Sime strongly criticizes the exploitation of women workers in a post-war society in stories about women's labour: dressmaking, domestic service, factory work, office work, and work in retail. Yet she also shows the freedom and possibility attached to such positions (as in the hopeful scene on the bus to the factory in "Munitions!"). Literary critic Ann Martin maintains that "by exploring the new possibilities that the twentieth-century metropolis and its technologies offered to women," Sime provides "another perspective on the sense of social and personal estrangement that we have come to regard as a prominent feature of the literature of the day." So, for Martin, Sime shows the alienating aspects of the metropolis, but also assertions of independent identity in the modern city.

The title of the collection is taken from Sime's epigraph to the book from the Scottish poet Robert Burns's "Address to the Unco Guid": "Then gently scan your brother man, / Still gentler, sister woman." Setting up gender as a primary concern within the text, Sime creates a dialogue with an ironic twist between the narrator and her interlocutor in the prologue:

> "Well," I said, after a long pause for consideration, "I'll—I'll skirt the question if you like."
> "The Woman's Question?" he inquired.
> "The woman's and the man's," I said. "It's the same thing. There's no difference."

> "That," he said, "sounds
> That's the most articulate
> ever heard a woman say
> At that we laughed aga...
> people like each other and are happy
> they laugh easily. [. . .] I took the
> cover off my typewriter and sat down
> before it. . . .

While the 1919 publication date of *Sister Woman* places the book at the end of what this anthology designates the "turn-of-the-century" period, Sime's explorations of urban modernity and modern subjectivity, as well as the text's major aesthetic concerns and the forthright treatment of sexuality and society, situate the stories within the framework of an incipient modernism in Canada.

Munitions!

Bertha Martin sat in the street car in the early morning going to her work. Her work was munitions. She had been at it exactly five weeks.

She sat squeezed up into a corner, just holding on to her seat and no more, and all round her were women and girls also working at munitions—loud, noisy, for ever talking—extraordinarily happy. They sat there filling the car with their two compact rows, pressed together, almost in one another's laps, joking, chewing tobacco—flinging the chewed stuff about.

It wasn't in the least that they were what is technically known as "bad women." Oh no—no! If you thought that, you would mistake them utterly. They were decent women, good, self-respecting girls, for the most part "straight girls"—with a black sheep here and there, to be sure, but where aren't there black sheep here and there? And the reason they made a row and shrieked with laughter and cracked an unseemly jest or two was simply that they were turned loose. They had spent their lives caged, most of them, in shop or house, and now they were drunk with the open air and the greater freedom and the sudden liberty to do as they liked and damn whoever stopped them.

Bertha Martin looked round at her companions. She saw the all sorts that make the world. Here and there was a pretty, young, flushed face, talking—talking—trying to express something it felt inside and couldn't get out. And here and there Bertha Martin saw an older face, a face with a knowledge of the world in it and that something that comes into a woman's eyes if certain things happen to her, and never goes out of them again. And then Bertha Martin saw quite elderly women, or so they seemed to her—women of forty or so, decent bodies, working for someone besides themselves—they had it written on their faces; and she saw old women—old as working women go—fifty and more, sitting there with their long working lives behind them and their short ones in front. And now and then some woman would draw her snuff-box from her shirt-waist and it would pass up and down the line and they would all take great pinches of the brown, pungent powder and stuff it up their noses—and laugh and laugh. . . . Bertha Martin looked round the car and she couldn't believe it was she who was sitting in it.

It was the very early spring. The white March sunshine came streaming into the car, and when Bertha, squeezed sideways in her corner, looked through the window, she saw the melting snow everywhere—piles and piles of it uncleared because the men whose job it was to clear it were at the war. She saw walls of snow by the sides of the streets—they went stretching out into infinity. And the car went swinging and lurching between them, out through the city and into the country where the factory was. There were puddles and little lakes of water everywhere; winter was melting away before the birth of another spring.

Bertha looked. She looked up into the clear—into the crystal clearness of the morning sky. It was the time of the spring skies of Canada—wonderful, delicate, diaphanous skies that come every spring to the Northern Land—skies the colour of bluebells and primroses—transparent, translucent, marvellously beautiful. Bertha looked up into the haze of colour—and she smiled. And then she wondered why she smiled.

It was the very early springtime.

Just five weeks before and Bertha had been a well-trained servant in a well-kept, intensely self-respecting house—a house where no footfall was heard on the soft, long-piled rugs; where the lights were shaded and the curtains were all drawn at night; where the mistress lay late in bed and "ordered" things; where life was put to bed every night with hot bottles to its feet; where no one ever spoke of anything that mattered; where meals were paramount. There had Bertha Martin lived five long, comfortable years.

She had gone about her business capably. She had worn her uniform like any soldier—a white frock in the mornings and a cap upon her head, and her hair had been orderly, her apron accurately tied. She had been clean. There were no spring skies in sight—or else she had not looked to see them. She had got up—not too unreasonably early—had had her early morning cup of tea with the other servants, had set the dining-room breakfast, waited on it—quiet—respectful—as self-respecting as the house. And in the afternoons there she had been in her neat black gown with her cap and apron immaculate—her hair still orderly and unobtrusive—everything about her, inside and out, still self-respecting and respectful. She had "waited on table," cleaned silver, served tea, carried things everlastingly in and out, set them on tables, taken them off again, washed them, put them away, taken them out again, reset tables with them—it was a circular game with never any end to it. And she had done it well. "Martin is an excellent servant," she had heard the lady of the house say once. "I can trust her thoroughly."

One afternoon in the week she went out. At a certain hour she left the house; at another certain hour she came back again. If she was half-an-hour late she was liable to be questioned: "Why?" And when she had given her explanation then she would hear the inevitable "Don't let it occur again." And Sunday—every other Sunday—there was the half day, also at certain hours. Of course—how otherwise could a well-run house *be* well run? And down in the kitchen the maids would dispute as to whether you got out half-an-hour sooner last time and so must go half-an-hour later this—they would quarrel and squabble over the silliest little things. Their horizon was so infinitesimally small, and they were so much too comfortable—they ate so much too much and they did so far too little—what could they do but squabble? They were never all on speaking-terms at one time together. Either the old cook was taking the housemaid's part or she and the housemaid were at daggers drawn; and they all said the same things over and over and over again—to desperation.

Bertha Martin looked up at the exquisite sky—and she smiled. The sun came streaming in, and the girls and women talked and jabbered and snuffed and chewed their tobacco and spat it out. And sometimes when the car conductor put his head in at the door they greeted him with a storm of chaff—a hail of witticisms—a tornado of personalities. And the little French-Canadian, overpowered by numbers, would never even try to break a lance with them. He would smile and shrug and put his hand up to his ears and run the door back between himself and them. And the women would laugh and clap their hands and stamp with their feet and call things to him—shout. . . .

Bertha turned to the girl next her—nearly atop of her—and looked her over. She was a fragile-looking, indoors creature—saleslady was written all over her—with soft rings of fair curled hair on her temples, and a weak, smiling mouth, and little useless feet in her cheap, high-heeled pumps. She was looking intently at a great strap of a girl opposite, with a great mouth on her, out of which was reeling a broad story.

"My, ain't she the girl!" said Bertha's little neighbour; and with the woman's inevitable gesture, she put her two hands up to her hair behind, and felt, and took a hairpin out here and there and put it in again.

She turned to Bertha.

"Say, ain't she the girl alright? Did you hear?"

Bertha nodded.

The little indoors thing turned and glanced at Bertha—took her in from head to foot with one feminine look.

"You gittin' on?" she said.

"Fine!" said Bertha.

The eyes of the women met. They smiled at one another. Fellow-workers—out in the world together. That's what their eyes said: Free! And then the little creature turned away from Bertha—bent forward eagerly. Another of the stories was coming streaming out.

"Ssh! . . . ssh!" cried some of the older women. But their voices were drowned in the sea of laughter as the climax took possession of the car. The women rocked and swayed——they clutched each other—they shrieked.

"Where's the harm?" the big strap cried.

Five weeks ago and Bertha had never heard a joke like that. Five weeks ago she would hardly have taken in the utter meaning of that climax. Now! Something in her ticked—something went beating. She smiled not at the indecency, not at the humour. What Bertha smiled at was the sense of liberty it gave her. She could hear stories if she liked. She could *act* stories if she liked. She was earning money—good money—she was capable and strong. Yes, she was strong, not fragile like the little thing beside her, but a big, strong girl—twenty-four—a woman grown—alive.

It seemed a long, dim time ago when all of them sat round that kitchen table to their stated meals at stated hours. Good, ample, comfortable meals. Plenty of time to eat them. No trouble getting them—that was the cook's affair—just far too much to eat and too much time to eat it in. Nothing to think about. Inertia. A comfortable place. What an age ago it seemed! And yet she had expected to spend her life like that—till she married someone! She never would have thought of "giving in her notice" if it hadn't been for Nellie Ford. How well Bertha remembered it—that Sunday she met Nellie—a Nellie flushed, with shining eyes.

"I'm leaving," Nellie had said to her. "I'm leaving—for the factory!"

And Bertha had stopped, bereft of words.

"*The factory* . . . !" she had said. That day the factory had sounded like the bottomless pit. "The factory . . . !"

"Come on," Nellie had said, "come on—it's fine out there. You make good money. Give in your notice—it's the life."

And Bertha had listened helplessly, feeling the ground slipping.

"But, Nellie—" she kept saying.

"It's the life," Nellie had kept reiterating; "it's the life, I tell you. Come on, Bert, *sure* it's the life. Come on—it's great out there. We'll room together if you'll come."

Then Nellie had told her hurriedly, brokenly, as they walked along that Sunday afternoon, all that she knew about the factory. What Agnes Dewie, that was maid to Lady Something once—what *she* said. "It was great!" That's what she said. "Liberty," said Agnes Dewie, "a room you paid for, good money, disrespect to everything, nothing above you—freedom. . . ."

Nellie had panted this out to Bertha. "Come on, come *on*, Bert," she had said; "it's time we lived."

And slowly the infection had seized on Bertha. The fever touched her blood—ran through it. Her mental temperature flew up. She was a big girl, a slow-grower, young for her years, with a girl's feelings in her woman's body. But Nellie Ford had touched the spring of life in her. After that Sunday when Bertha looked round the quiet, self-respecting house—she hated it. She hated the softness of it—the quietness—hated the very comfort. What did all these things matter? Nellie Ford had said: "It's time we *lived*. . . ."

Bertha gazed upward through the window of the car—twisted and turned so that she could look right into the morning blue. The car was clear of city life. It sped along a country road. Fields were on either side, and only now and then a solitary house. Great trees stretched out bare branches.

Then in that far-off life came the giving in of the notice. Bertha remembered the old cook's sour face—that old sour face past every hope of life and living. Could one grow to look like that? Can such things be? "You'll live to rue the day, my lady!" said the cook. And Bertha remembered how the lady at the head of things had said: "Do you realise that you'll *regret* leaving a good place like this?" And then, more acidly: "I wouldn't have believed it of you, Martin." And as she turned to go: "If you choose to reconsider —"

Regret! Reconsider! Never again would she hear bells and have to answer them. Never again would someone say to her: "Take tea into the library, Martin." Never again need she say: "Yes, ma'am." Think of it! Bertha smiled. The sun came streaming in on her—she smiled.

Liberty! Liberty to work the whole day long—ten hours at five and twenty cents an hour—in noise and grime and wet. Damp floors to walk on. Noise— distracting noise all round one. No room to turn or breathe. No time to stop. And then at lunchtime no ample comfortable meal—some little hurried hunch of something you brought with you. Hard work. Long hours. Discomfort. Strain. That was about the sum of it, of all that she had gained . . . but then, the sense of freedom! The joy of being done with cap and apron. The feeling that you could draw your breath—speak as you liked—wear overalls like men—curse if you wanted to.

Oh, the relief of it! The going home at night, dead-tired, to where you had your room. Your own! The poor, ill-cooked suppers—what a taste to them! The deep, dreamless sleep. And Sunday—if you ever got a Sunday off—when you could lie abed, no one to hunt you up, no one to call you names and quarrel with you. Just Nellie there.

What did it matter if you had no time to stop or think or be? What did anything matter if life went pulsing through you amidst dirt and noise and grime? The old life—that treading round with brush and dust-pan—that making yourself noiseless with a duster: "Martin, see you dust well *beneath* the bed." "Yes, ma'am." And now the factory! A new life with other women working round you—bare-armed—grimy—roughened—unrestrained. What a change! What a sense of broadening out! What . . . !

Bertha Martin smiled. She smiled so that a woman opposite smiled back at her; and then she realised that she was smiling. She felt life streaming to her very finger-tips. She felt the spring pass through her being—insistent and creative. She felt her blood speak to her—say things it never said when she was walking softly in the well-ordered house she helped to keep for five long, comfortable years. "Selfish to leave me." That was what the lady of the house had said to her. "Selfish—you're all selfish. You think of nothing but yourselves."

Well—why not? What if that were true? Let it go anyway. That half-dead life was there behind . . . and Bertha Martin looked out at the present. The car went scudding in the country road. There was the Factory—the Factory, with its coarse, strong, beckoning life—its noise—its dirt—its men.

Its men! And suddenly into Bertha Martin's cheek a wave of colour surged. Yesterday—was it yesterday?—that man had caught her strong, round arm as she was passing him—and held it.

Her breath came short. She felt a throbbing. She stopped smiling—and her eyes grew large.

It was the very early spring.

Then suddenly the flock of women rose—felt in the bosoms of their shirtwaists for their cigarettes and matches—surged to the door—talking—laughing—pushing one another—the older ones expostulating.

And, massed together in the slushy road, they stood, lighting up, passing their matches round—happy—noisy—fluttered—not knowing what to do with all the life that kept on surging up and breaking in them—waves of it—wave on wave. Willingly would they have fought their way to the Munitions Factory. If they had known the *Carmagnole*[1] they would have danced it in the melting snow. . . .

It was the spring.

[1919]

[1] "La Carmagnole" is the name of a song and dance that was popular among the French revolutionists during the French Revolution (1789–99).

STEPHEN LEACOCK ■ (1869–1944)

Stephen Leacock was, and still is, one of Canada's most celebrated comic writers. According to David Staines, the editor of Leacock's letters, "he was the best-known and bestselling humorist in English from 1910 to almost 1930." Literary critic Desmond Pacey called Leacock "an ironist and satirist, who alone in his generation, saw through the hypocrisy and pretension of his society." His writing about economic issues and small-town Ontario still resonates today. Established in Leacock's honour two years after his death, the Stephen Leacock Memorial Medal is still awarded annually for the best book of humour written by a Canadian.

Leacock was born in Swanmore, England, in 1869, and immigrated to Canada with his family in 1876. He was educated at Upper Canada College, Strathroy Collegiate Institute, and the University of Toronto, from which he received a B.A. in 1891. Given that his father abandoned the family in 1887, leaving Leacock's mother with the care of eleven children, it is remarkable that Leacock was able to accomplish what he did. To help his mother support the family, he accepted a teaching position at Upper Canada College, Toronto, where he taught modern languages from 1889 to 1899. In 1899 he "gave up school teaching in disgust" to pursue graduate studies at the University of Chicago. When he obtained his doctor of philosophy degree in political science and political economy in 1903, Leacock joined McGill University's Department of Economics and Political Science as a professor. Five years later he was appointed the William Dow Professor of Political Economy and chair of the department. He held this position until his retirement in 1936. Leacock's reputation as a political scientist was secured with the 1906 publication of *Elements of Political Science*, which became a standard university textbook for decades. Following the publication of this book and his later fictional works, Leacock was a much sought-after public speaker who conducted frequent lecture tours in Canada and England.

Leacock was a traditionalist and an imperialist, whose belief in civilization and progress was tempered by his unease about the growth of materialism. His commitment to the British Empire, like that of many writers in the post-Confederation period, was based on his sense that Britain stood for a strong tradition of humanist and communal values. In 1907, he took a year's leave of absence from McGill to conduct a speaking tour of the British Empire to promote imperial unity under the auspices of the Cecil Rhodes Trust. "Greater Canada: An Appeal," published in the same volume of *The University Magazine* (1907) as work by John McCrae, Duncan Campbell Scott, Pelham Edgar, and Andrew Macphail, comes out of this time and expresses his discomfort with Canada's persistent colonial insecurity. His attempt to shake Canadians out of their intellectual and ethical torpor echoes the writings of Thomas Chandler Haliburton and Thomas McCulloch in the nineteenth century, and continues many of the arguments raised during the

post-Confederation period about Canada's imperial connections. Ironically, the grandiose terms in which he describes Canada in this essay parallel the rhetoric of the local Mariposans in their delusions about their town.

Leacock's traditionalism is evident in his ardent position against suffrage for women. He wrote a strongly anti-suffrage article in the October issue of *Maclean's Magazine* of 1915—"The Woman Question"—in response to Nellie McClung's *In Times Like These* (1915), a bestselling collection of suffrage essays and speeches that discuss women's struggles for political recognition. In effect, women were protesting "against the world's estimate of woman's position," as McClung puts it in her 1916 essay, "What Do Women Think of War?". Leacock makes clear that he is content with such a position, and that he thinks women should be as well; nevertheless, his comments about the meagre gains that women have achieved with the advent of the industrial and technological age bear comparison with Sara Jeannette Duncan's ironic account of women's progress in her 17 November 1886 "Woman's World" essay, and, interestingly, with Jessie Sime's short story based on a similar period of transition, "Munitions!" McClung wrote a response to Leacock entitled "Speaking of Women" in the May 1916 issue of *Maclean's*. The two essays are highly entertaining, but the humour is clearly barbed; selections from both essays are included in this section.

The enduring popularity of Leacock's fiction comes from his use of gentle irony and social satire, which is evident throughout his work. He is most remembered for his tales of small-town life and literary sketches. *Literary Lapses: A Book of Sketches* (1910), *Sunshine Sketches of a Little Town*

(1912), and *Arcadian Adventures with the Idle Rich* (1914) were among the first of his many popular books. *Sunshine Sketches of a Little Town* is a short story cycle that conveys a sense of nostalgia for small-town Canadian life. Its fictional setting, the Canadian town of Mariposa, is based on Orillia, Ontario, where Leacock had a summer home on Lake Couchiching. Nevertheless, Leacock claimed to be writing about a universal Canadian locale, and the success of *Sunshine Sketches* testifies to the resonance Mariposa has had not only in Canada, but throughout the United States and England. In his preface to the book, Leacock writes: "In regard to the present work I must disclaim at once all intention of trying to do anything so ridiculously easy as writing about a real place and real people. Mariposa is not a real town. On the contrary, it is about seventy or eighty of them. You may find them all the way from Lake Superior to the sea, with the same square streets and the same maple trees and the same churches and hotels, and everywhere the sunshine of the land of hope." Pacey argues that it is in this book that Leacock's "best qualities—his benevolence, his common sense, his humanity, his whimsical yet ironic observation— come to focus." At the time of the book's publication, the townspeople of Orillia were upset by Leacock's portrayal, for they felt themselves to be the object of his critique. True enough, it is sometimes difficult to tell where the narrator of the sketches places himself. Is he an equally ridiculous member of the community, or is he being scornful of the "locals"? In "The Marine Excursion of the Knights of Pythias," Leacock makes particular fun of people's petty vanities and delusions of grandeur. Orillia has long since forgiven Leacock, and is now home to the

Leacock Association and the National Leacock Historic Museum.

Arcadian Adventures with the Idle Rich, published two years after *Sunshine Sketches*, depicts the materialism and corruption of urban industrial life, particularly the growing divide between rich and poor. Critic Gerald Lynch explains that the city of Plutoria in *Arcadian Adventures* and Mariposa in *Sunshine Sketches* represent the two opposite poles of Leacock's artistic vision. Mariposa is a small Canadian town that allows for human folly, whereas Plutoria is an unnamed American metropolis that supports "absurd individualism." The two short story cycles illustrate the scope of Leacock's humour, from the mild and gentle satire of provincialism (in *Sunshine Sketches*) to the stronger and sharper ridicule of a plutocratic society (in *Arcadian Adventures*). The final story in *Sunshine Sketches*, "L'Envoi: A Train to Mariposa," exhibits what Robertson Davies saw as a deep vein of melancholia that works as a precursor to *Arcadian Adventures*.

In Canadian letters, Leacock follows most closely in the footsteps of his literary predecessor Haliburton and his creation Sam Slick. In the 1916 publication of *Essays and Literary Studies*, Leacock summarizes his own views on humour:

[T]he final stage of the development of humour is reached when amusement no longer arises from a single "funny" idea, meaningless contrast, or odd play upon words, but rests upon a prolonged and sustained conception of the incongruities of human life itself. On this higher plane humour and pathos mingle and become one. To the Creator perhaps in retrospect the little story of man's creation and his fall seems sadly droll.

Leacock might also be placed in the Canadian tradition of the short story cycle, from Duncan Campbell Scott's *In the Village of Viger* (1896), to which *Sunshine Sketches* bears a clear resemblance, to the contemporary linked short story collections of such writers as Alice Munro, Margaret Laurence, Rohinton Mistry, and David Adams Richards.

Leacock received honorary degrees from Queen's University, Dartmouth, Brown, the University of Toronto, Bishop's University, and, after his retirement, from McGill itself. In spite of his public role as a humorist, Leacock himself was a serious man, particularly following the death of his wife in 1925 from breast cancer. Following his wife's death, he raised their disabled son on his own. It is said that the reason he was such a prolific writer was in part that he wanted to set enough money aside for his son's care following his own death. Leacock continued writing until his death from throat cancer in 1944.

Still celebrated as Canada's premier satirist, Leacock has clearly had a lasting impact on Canadian literature. Indeed, along with Haliburton (and, one might argue, Sara Jeannette Duncan), he is often heralded as the progenitor of a national tradition of Canadian irony, as has been explored by the Canadian literary theorist Linda Hutcheon in the 1980s and '90s. The tone of Leacock's work is self-mocking; it is the expression of a people who have become confident enough in their uniqueness to make fun of themselves.

The Marine Excursion of the Knights of Pythias

Half-past six on a July morning! The Mariposa Belle is at the wharf, decked in flags, with steam up ready to start.

Excursion day!

Half-past six on a July morning, and Lake Wissanotti lying in the sun as calm as glass. The opal colours of the morning light are shot from the surface of the water.

Out on the lake the last thin threads of the mist are clearing away like flecks of cotton wool.

The long call of the loon echoes over the lake. The air is cool and fresh. There is in it all the new life of the land of the silent pine and the moving waters. Lake Wissanotti in the morning sunlight! Don't talk to me of the Italian lakes, or the Tyrol or the Swiss Alps. Take them away. Move them somewhere else. I don't want them.

Excursion Day, at half-past six of a summer morning! With the boat all decked in flags and all the people in Mariposa on the wharf, and the band in peaked caps with big cornets tied to their bodies ready to play at any minute! I say! Don't tell me about the Carnival of Venice[1] and the Delhi Durbar.[2] Don't!

---

[1] First recorded in 1268, the Venice Carnival is an annual festival in the city of Venice, Italy. People wear ornate costumes to the many masked balls of the festival.

[2] "Delhi Durbar" refers to the "Court of Delhi" or the extravagant festivities set up to commemorate the coronation of Queen Victoria as empress of India (1877); the coronation of King Edward VII and Queen Alexandra as emperor and empress of India in 1903; and in 1911 to commemorate the coronation of King George V and Queen Mary as emperor and empress of India.

I wouldn't look at them. I'd shut my eyes! For light and colour give me every time an excursion out of Mariposa down the lake to the Indian's Island out of sight in the morning mist. Talk of your Papal Zouaves[3] and your Buckingham Palace Guard![4] I want to see the Mariposa band in uniform and the Mariposa Knights of Pythias[5] with their aprons and their insignia and their picnic baskets and their five-cent cigars!

Half-past six in the morning, and all the crowd on the wharf and the boat due to leave in half an hour. Notice it!—in half an hour. Already she's whistled twice (at six, and at six fifteen), and at any minute now, Christie Johnson will step into the pilot house and pull the string for the warning whistle that the boat will leave in half an hour. So keep ready. Don't think of running back to Smith's Hotel for the sandwiches. Don't be fool enough to try to go up to the Greek Store, next to Netley's, and buy fruit. You'll be left behind for sure if you do. Never mind the sandwiches and the fruit! Anyway, here comes Mr. Smith himself with a huge basket of provender that would feed a factory. There must be sandwiches in that. I think I can hear them clinking. And behind Mr. Smith is the German waiter from the caff with another basket—indubitably lager beer; and behind him, the bar-tender of the hotel, carrying nothing, as far as one can see. But of course if you know Mariposa you will understand that why he looks so nonchalant and empty-handed is because he has two bottles of rye whiskey under his linen duster. You know, I think, the peculiar walk of a man with two bottles of whiskey in the inside pockets of a linen coat. In Mariposa, you see, to bring beer to an excursion is quite in keeping with public opinion. But, whiskey,—well, one has to be a little careful.

Do I say that Mr. Smith is here? Why, everybody's here. There's Hussell the editor of the *Newspacket*, wearing a blue ribbon on his coat, for the Mariposa Knights of Pythias are, by their constitution, dedicated to temperance; and there's Henry Mullins, the manager of the Exchange Bank, also a Knight of Pythias, with a small flask of Pogram's Special in his hip pocket as a sort of amendment to the constitution. And there's Dean Drone, the Chaplain of the Order, with a fishing-rod (you never saw such green bass as lie among the rocks at Indian's Island), and with a trolling line in case of maskinonge, and a landing net in case of pickerel, and with his eldest daughter, Lilian Drone, in case of young men. There never was such a fisherman as the Rev. Rupert Drone.

Perhaps I ought to explain that when I speak of the excursion as being of the Knights of Pythias, the thing must not be understood in any narrow sense. In Mariposa practically everybody belongs to the Knights of Pythias just as they do to everything else. That's the great thing about the town and that's what makes it so different from the city. Everybody is in everything.

---

[3] Formed in defence of the Papal States in 1860, they served in part as guards to Pope Pius IX and are noted for their grey and red uniforms.

[4] The guards of Buckingham Palace, the official royal residence in London, England.

[5] The Order of Knights of Pythias is an international non-sectarian fraternal order, established in Washington in 1864. The principles of the Order of Knights of Pythias are "friendship, charity, and benevolence."

You should see them on the seventeenth of March,[6] for example, when everybody wears a green ribbon and they're all laughing and glad,—you know what the Celtic nature is,—and talking about Home Rule.

On St. Andrew's Day[7] every man in town wears a thistle and shakes hands with everybody else, and you see the fine old Scotch honesty beaming out of their eyes.

And on St. George's Day![8] —well, there's no heartiness like the good old English spirit, after all; why shouldn't a man feel glad that he's an Englishman?

Then on the Fourth of July[9] there are stars and stripes flying over half the stores in town, and suddenly all the men are seen to smoke cigars, and to know all about Roosevelt and Bryan and the Philippine Islands.[10] Then you learn for the first time that Jeff Thorpe's people came from Massachusetts and that his uncle fought at Bunker Hill[11] (it must have been Bunker Hill,—anyway Jefferson will swear it was in Dakota all right enough); and you find that George Duff has a married sister in Rochester and that her husband is all right; in fact, George was down there as recently as eight years ago. Oh, it's the most American town imaginable is Mariposa,—on the fourth of July.

But wait, just wait, if you feel anxious about the solidity of the British connection, till the twelfth of the month, when everybody is wearing an orange streamer in his coat and the Orange-men[12] (every man in town) walk in the big procession. Allegiance! Well, perhaps you remember the address they gave to the Prince of Wales on the platform of the Mariposa station as he went through on his tour to the west. I think that pretty well settled that question.

So you will easily understand that of course everybody belongs to the Knights of Pythias and the Masons and Odd-fellows,[13] just as they all belong to the Snow Shoe Club and the Girls' Friendly Society.

And meanwhile the whistle of the steamer has blown again for a quarter to seven:—loud and long this time, for any one not here now is late for certain, unless he should happen to come down in the last fifteen minutes.

[6] March 17 is St. Patrick's Day, celebrating the patron saint of Ireland.

[7] St. Andrew is the patron saint of Scotland. St. Andrew's Day is celebrated on 30 November of each year.

[8] St. George is the patron saint of England, celebrated on 23 April.

[9] July 4 is Independence Day in the United States of America, celebrating the adoption of the Declaration of Independence, 4 July 1776.

[10] During the American presidential campaign of 1900, the Republican vice-presidential candidate Theodore Roosevelt and the Democratic presidential candidate William Jennings Bryan differed on their views of American actions in the Philippine Islands. Roosevelt spoke of the need for "expansionism" and Bryan campaigned against American "imperialism" in the Philippines.

[11] The Battle of Bunker Hill (1775) took place in Boston during the American Revolutionary War.

[12] On 12 July the Orange Order (Protestant fraternal organization) marches to celebrate the victory of the Protestant William of Orange over Catholic King James at the Battle of the Boyne (1690).

[13] The Masons and the Oddfellows are international fraternal organizations with millions of members worldwide.

What a crowd upon the wharf and how they pile on to the steamer! It's a wonder that the boat can hold them all. But that's just the marvellous thing about the Mariposa Belle.

I don't know,—I have never known,—where the steamers like the Mariposa Belle come from. Whether they are built by Harland and Wolff of Belfast, or whether, on the other hand, they are not built by Harland and Wolff of Belfast, is more than one would like to say offhand.

The Mariposa Belle always seems to me to have some of those strange properties that distinguish Mariposa itself. I mean, her size seems to vary so. If you see her there in the winter, frozen in the ice beside the wharf with a snowdrift against the windows of the pilot house, she looks a pathetic little thing the size of a butternut. But in the summer time, especially after you've been in Mariposa for a month or two, and have paddled alongside of her in a canoe, she gets larger and taller, and with a great sweep of black sides, till you see no difference between the Mariposa Belle and the Lusitania.[14] Each one is a big steamer and that's all you can say.

Nor do her measurements help you much. She draws about eighteen inches forward, and more than that,—at least half an inch more, astern, and when she's loaded down with an excursion crowd she draws a good two inches more. And above the water,—why, look at all the decks on her! There's the deck you walk on to, from the wharf, all shut in, with windows along it, and the after cabin with the long table, and above that the deck with all the chairs piled upon it, and the deck in front where the band stand round in a circle, and the pilot house is higher than that, and above the pilot house is the board with the gold name and the flag pole and the steel ropes and the flags; and fixed in somewhere on the different levels is the lunch counter where they sell the sandwiches, and the engine room, and down below the deck level, beneath the water line, is the place where the crew sleep. What with steps and stairs and passages and piles of cordwood for the engine,—oh no, I guess Harland and Wolff didn't build her. They couldn't have.

Yet even with a huge boat like the Mariposa Belle, it would be impossible for her to carry all of the crowd that you see in the boat and on the wharf. In reality, the crowd is made up of two classes,—all of the people in Mariposa who are going on the excursion and all those who are not. Some come for the one reason and some for the other.

The two tellers of the Exchange Bank are both there standing side by side. But one of them,—the one with the cameo pin and the long face like a horse,— is going, and the other,—with the other cameo pin and the face like another horse,—is not. In the same way, Hussell of the *Newspacket* is going, but his brother, beside him, isn't. Lilian Drone is going, but her sister can't; and so on all through the crowd.

---

[14] Launched in 1906, RMS *Lusitania*, at 32,000 tons, was the largest passenger vessel on transatlantic service. Three years after this story was first published, in the middle of the First World War, the ship was sunk by a German U-boat, killing over a thousand people on board (1915).

And to think that things should look like that on the morning of a steamboat accident.

How strange life is!

To think of all these people so eager and anxious to catch the steamer, and some of them running to catch it, and so fearful that they might miss it,—the morning of a steamboat accident. And the captain blowing his whistle, and warning them so severely that he would leave them behind,—leave them out of the accident! And everybody crowding so eagerly to be in the accident.

Perhaps life is like that all through.

Strangest of all to think, in a case like this, of the people who were left behind, or in some way or other prevented from going, and always afterwards told of how they had escaped being on board the Mariposa Belle that day!

Some of the instances were certainly extraordinary.

Nivens, the lawyer, escaped from being there merely by the fact that he was away in the city.

Towers, the tailor, only escaped owing to the fact that, not intending to go on the excursion he had stayed in bed till eight o'clock and so had not gone. He narrated afterwards that waking up that morning at half-past five, he had thought of the excursion and for some unaccountable reason had felt glad that he was not going.

The case of Yodel, the auctioneer, was even more inscrutable. He had been to the Oddfellows' excursion on the train the week before and to the Conservative picnic the week before that, and had decided not to go on this trip. In fact, he had not the least intention of going. He narrated afterwards how the night before someone had stopped him on the corner of Nippewa and Tecumseh Streets (he indicated the very spot) and asked: "Are you going to take in the excursion to-morrow?" and he had said, just as simply as he was talking when narrating it: "No." And ten minutes after that, at the corner of Dalhousie and Brock Streets (he offered to lead a party of verification to the precise place) somebody else had stopped him and asked: "Well, are you going on the steamer trip to-morrow?" Again he had answered: "No," apparently almost in the same tone as before.

He said afterwards that when he heard the rumour of the accident it seemed like the finger of Providence, and he fell on his knees in thankfulness.

There was the similar case of Morison (I mean the one in Glover's hardware store that married one of the Thompsons). He said afterwards that he had read so much in the papers about accidents lately,—mining accidents, and aeroplanes and gasoline,—that he had grown nervous. The night before his wife had asked him at supper: "Are you going on the excursion?" He had answered: "No, I don't think I feel like it," and had added: "Perhaps your mother might like to go." And the next evening just at dusk, when the news ran through the town, he said the first thought that flashed through his head was: "Mrs. Thompson's on that boat."

He told this right as I say it—without the least doubt or confusion. He never for a moment imagined she was on the Lusitania or the Olympic or any other boat. He knew she was on this one. He said you could have knocked him down where he stood. But no one had. Not even when he got half-way down,—on his knees, and it would have been easier still to knock him down or kick him. People do miss a lot of chances.

Still, as I say, neither Yodel nor Morison nor anyone thought about there being an accident until just after sundown when they—

Well, have you ever heard the long booming whistle of a steamboat two miles out on the lake in the dusk, and while you listen and count and wonder, seen the crimson rockets going up against the sky and then heard the fire bell ringing right there beside you in the town, and seen the people running to the town wharf?

That's what the people of Mariposa saw and felt that summer evening as they watched the Mackinaw life-boat go plunging out into the lake with seven sweeps to a side and the foam clear to the gunwale with the lifting stroke of fourteen men!

But, dear me, I am afraid that this is no way to tell a story. I suppose the true art would have been to have said nothing about the accident till it happened. But when you write about Mariposa, or hear of it, if you know the place, it's all so vivid and real that a thing like the contrast between the excursion crowd in the morning and the scene at night leaps into your mind and you must think of it.

But never mind about the accident,—let us turn back again to the morning.

The boat was due to leave at seven. There was no doubt about the hour,—not only seven, but seven sharp. The notice in the *Newspacket* said: "The boat will leave sharp at seven;" and the advertising posters on the telegraph poles on Missinaba Street that began "Ho, for Indian's Island!" ended up with the words: "Boat leaves at seven sharp." There was a big notice on the wharf that said: "Boat leaves sharp on time."

So at seven, right on the hour, the whistle blew loud and long, and then at seven fifteen three short peremptory blasts, and at seven thirty one quick angry call,—just one,—and very soon after that they cast off the last of the ropes and the Mariposa Belle sailed off in her cloud of flags, and the band of the Knights of Pythias, timing it to a nicety, broke into the "Maple Leaf for Ever!"

I suppose that all excursions when they start are much the same. Anyway, on the Mariposa Belle everybody went running up and down all over the boat with deck chairs and camp stools and baskets, and found places, splendid places to sit, and then got scared that there might be better ones and chased off again. People hunted for places out of the sun and when they got them swore that they weren't going to freeze to please anybody; and the people in the sun said that they hadn't paid fifty cents to be roasted. Others said that they hadn't paid fifty cents to get covered with cinders, and there were still others who hadn't paid fifty cents to get shaken to death with the propeller.

Still, it was all right presently. The people seemed to get sorted out into the places on the boat where they belonged. The women, the older ones, all gravitated into the cabin on the lower deck and by getting round the table with needlework, and with all the windows shut, they soon had it, as they said themselves, just like being at home.

All the young boys and the toughs and the men in the band got down on the lower deck forward, where the boat was dirtiest and where the anchor was and the coils of rope.

And upstairs on the after deck there were Lilian Drone and Miss Lawson, the high school teacher, with a book of German poetry,—Gothey[15] I think it was,— and the bank teller and the younger men.

In the centre, standing beside the rail, were Dean Drone and Dr. Gallagher, looking through binocular glasses at the shore.

Up in front on the little deck forward of the pilot house was a group of the older men, Mullins and Duff and Mr. Smith in a deck chair, and beside him Mr. Golgotha Gingham, the undertaker of Mariposa, on a stool. It was part of Mr. Gingham's principles to take in an outing of this sort, a business matter, more or less,—for you never know what may happen at these water parties. At any rate, he was there in a neat suit of black, not, of course, his heavier or professional suit, but a soft clinging effect as of burnt paper that combined gaiety and decorum to a nicety.

"Yes," said Mr. Gingham, waving his black glove in a general way towards the shore, "I know the lake well, very well. I've been pretty much all over it in my time."

"Canoeing?" asked somebody.

"No," said Mr. Gingham, "not in a canoe." There seemed a peculiar and quiet meaning in his tone.

"Sailing, I suppose," said somebody else.

"No," said Mr. Gingham. "I don't understand it."

"I never knowed that you went on to the water at all, Gol," said Mr. Smith, breaking in.

"Ah, not now," explained Mr. Gingham; "it was years ago, the first summer I came to Mariposa. I was on the water practically all day. Nothing like it to give a man an appetite and keep him in shape."

"Was you camping?" asked Mr. Smith.

"We camped at night," assented the undertaker, "but we put in practically the whole day on the water. You see we were after a party that had come up here from the city on his vacation and gone out in a sailing canoe. We were dragging. We were up every morning at sunrise, lit a fire on the beach and cooked breakfast, and then we'd light our pipes and be off with the net for a whole day. It's a great life," concluded Mr. Gingham wistfully.

---

15 The narrator is referring to the German author Johann Wolfgang von Goethe (1749–1832), best known for his plays *Faust I* (1808) and *Faust II* (1832). The narrator's mispronunciation of the name is meant to indicate an uneducated person with pretensions to high culture.

"Did you get him?" asked two or three together.

There was a pause before Mr. Gingham answered.

"We did," he said,— "down in the reeds past Horseshoe Point. But it was no use. He turned blue on me right away."

After which Mr. Gingham fell into such a deep reverie that the boat had steamed another half-mile down the lake before anybody broke the silence again.

Talk of this sort,—and after all what more suitable for a day on the water?— beguiled the way.

Down the lake, mile by mile over the calm water, steamed the Mariposa Belle. They passed Poplar Point where the high sand-banks are with all the swallows' nests in them, and Dean Drone and Dr. Gallagher looked at them alternately through the binocular glasses, and it was wonderful how plainly one could see the swallows and the banks and the shrubs,—just as plainly as with the naked eye.

And a little further down they passed the Shingle Beach, and Dr. Gallagher, who knew Canadian history, said to Dean Drone that it was strange to think that Champlain had landed there with his French explorers three hundred years ago;[16] and Dean Drone, who didn't know Canadian history, said it was stranger still to think that the hand of the Almighty had piled up the hills and rocks long before that; and Dr. Gallagher said it was wonderful how the French had found their way through such a pathless wilderness; and Dean Drone said that it was wonderful also to think that the Almighty had placed even the smallest shrub in its appointed place. Dr. Gallagher said it filled him with admiration. Dean Drone said it filled him with awe. Dr. Gallagher said he'd been full of it ever since he was a boy; and Dean Drone said so had he.

Then a little further, as the Mariposa Belle steamed on down the lake, they passed the Old Indian Portage where the great grey rocks are; and Dr. Gallagher drew Dean Drone's attention to the place where the narrow canoe track wound up from the shore to the woods, and Dean Drone said he could see it perfectly well without the glasses.

Dr. Gallagher said that it was just here that a party of five hundred French had made their way with all their baggage and accoutrements across the rocks of the divide and down to the Great Bay. And Dean Drone said that it reminded him of Xenophon[17] leading his ten thousand Greeks over the hill passes of Armenia down to the sea. Dr. Gallagher said that he had often wished he could have seen and spoken to Champlain, and Dean Drone said how much he regretted to have never known Xenophon.

And then after that they fell to talking of relics and traces of the past, and Dr. Gallagher said that if Dean Drone would come round to his house some night he would show him some Indian arrow heads that he had dug up in his garden.

[16] In 1615, Samuel de Champlain passed through the area of present-day Orillia on his way to fight in the Iroquois wars further south.

[17] *Anabasis*, by Greek writer Xenophon (431–355 BC), tells the story of the Ten Thousand—a large army who were commissioned by Cyrus the Younger in his bid to seize the throne of Persia.

And Dean Drone said that if Dr. Gallagher would come round to the rectory any afternoon he would show him a map of Xerxes' invasion of Greece. Only he must come some time between the Infant Class and the Mothers' Auxiliary.

So presently they both knew that they were blocked out of one another's houses for some time to come, and Dr. Gallagher walked forward and told Mr. Smith, who had never studied Greek, about Champlain crossing the rock divide.

Mr. Smith turned his head and looked at the divide for half a second and then said he had crossed a worse one up north back of the Wahnipitae and that the flies were Hades,—and then went on playing freezeout poker with the two juniors in Duff's bank.

So Dr. Gallagher realized that that's always the way when you try to tell people things, and that as far as gratitude and appreciation goes one might as well never read books or travel anywhere or do anything.

In fact, it was at this very moment that he made up his mind to give the arrows to the Mariposa Mechanics' Institute,—they afterwards became, as you know, the Gallagher Collection. But, for the time being, the doctor was sick of them and wandered off round the boat and watched Henry Mullins showing George Duff how to make a John Collins without lemons, and finally went and sat down among the Mariposa band and wished that he hadn't come.

So the boat steamed on and the sun rose higher and higher, and the freshness of the morning changed into the full glare of noon, and they went on to where the lake began to narrow in at its foot, just where the Indian's Island is,—all grass and trees and with a log wharf running into the water. Below it the Lower Ossawippi runs out of the lake, and quite near are the rapids, and you can see down among the trees the red brick of the power house and hear the roar of the leaping water.

The Indian's Island itself is all covered with trees and tangled vines, and the water about it is so still that it's all reflected double and looks the same either way up. Then when the steamer's whistle blows as it comes into the wharf, you hear it echo among the trees of the island, and reverberate back from the shores of the lake.

The scene is all so quiet and still and unbroken, that Miss Cleghorn,—the sallow girl in the telephone exchange, that I spoke of—said she'd like to be buried there. But all the people were so busy getting their baskets and gathering up their things that no one had time to attend to it.

I mustn't even try to describe the landing and the boat crunching against the wooden wharf and all the people running to the same side of the deck and Christie Johnson calling out to the crowd to keep to the starboard and nobody being able to find it. Everyone who has been on a Mariposa excursion knows all about that.

Nor can I describe the day itself and the picnic under the trees. There were speeches afterwards, and Judge Pepperleigh gave such offence by bringing in Conservative politics that a man called Patriotus Canadiensis wrote and asked for some of the invaluable space of the Mariposa *Times-Herald* and exposed it.

I should say that there were races too, on the grass on the open side of the island, graded mostly according to ages,—races for boys under thirteen and girls over nineteen and all that sort of thing. Sports are generally conducted on that plan in Mariposa. It is realized that a woman of sixty has an unfair advantage over a mere child.

Dean Drone managed the races and decided the ages and gave out the prizes; the Wesleyan minister helped, and he and the young student, who was relieving in the Presbyterian Church, held the string at the winning point.

They had to get mostly clergymen for the races because all the men had wandered off, somehow, to where they were drinking lager beer out of two kegs stuck on pine logs among the trees.

But if you've ever been on a Mariposa excursion you know all about these details anyway.

So the day wore on and presently the sun came through the trees on a slant and the steamer whistle blew with a great puff of white steam and all the people came straggling down to the wharf and pretty soon the Mariposa Belle had floated out on to the lake again and headed for the town, twenty miles away.

I suppose you have often noticed the contrast there is between an excursion on its way out in the morning and what it looks like on the way home.

In the morning everybody is so restless and animated and moves to and fro all over the boat and asks questions. But coming home, as the afternoon gets later and later and the sun sinks beyond the hills, all the people seem to get so still and quiet and drowsy.

So it was with the people on the Mariposa Belle. They sat there on the benches and the deck chairs in little clusters, and listened to the regular beat of the propeller and almost dozed off asleep as they sat. Then when the sun set and the dusk drew on, it grew almost dark on the deck and so still that you could hardly tell there was anyone on board.

And if you had looked at the steamer from the shore or from one of the islands, you'd have seen the row of lights from the cabin windows shining on the water and the red glare of the burning hemlock from the funnel, and you'd have heard the soft thud of the propeller miles away over the lake.

Now and then, too, you could have heard them singing on the steamer,—the voices of the girls and the men blended into unison by the distance, rising and falling in long-drawn melody: "O— Can-a-da—O—Can-a-da."

You may talk as you will about the intoning choirs of your European cathedrals, but the sound of "O Ca-na-da," borne across the waters of a silent lake at evening is good enough for those of us who know Mariposa.

I think that it was just as they were singing like this: "O—Can-a-da," that word went round that the boat was sinking.

If you have ever been in any sudden emergency on the water, you will understand the strange psychology of it,—the way in which what is happening seems to become known all in a moment without a word being said. The news is transmitted from one to the other by some mysterious process.

At any rate, on the Mariposa Belle first one and then the other heard that the steamer was sinking. As far as I could ever learn the first of it was that George Duff, the bank manager, came very quietly to Dr. Gallagher and asked him if he thought that the boat was sinking. The doctor said no, that he had thought so earlier in the day but that he didn't now think that she was.

After that Duff, according to his own account, had said to Macartney, the lawyer, that the boat was sinking, and Macartney said that he doubted it very much.

Then somebody came to Judge Pepperleigh and woke him up and said that there was six inches of water in the steamer and that she was sinking. And Pepperleigh said it was perfect scandal and passed the news on to his wife and she said that they had no business to allow it and that if the steamer sank that was the last excursion she'd go on.

So the news went all round the boat and everywhere the people gathered in groups and talked about it in the angry and excited way that people have when a steamer is sinking on one of the lakes like Lake Wissanotti.

Dean Drone, of course, and some others were quieter about it, and said that one must make allowances and that naturally there were two sides to everything. But most of them wouldn't listen to reason at all. I think, perhaps, that some of them were frightened. You see the last time but one that the steamer had sunk, there had been a man drowned and it made them nervous.

What? Hadn't I explained about the depth of Lake Wissanotti? I had taken it for granted that you knew; and in any case parts of it are deep enough, though I don't suppose in this stretch of it from the big reed beds up to within a mile of the town wharf, you could find six feet of water in it if you tried. Oh, pshaw! I was not talking about a steamer sinking in the ocean and carrying down its screaming crowds of people into the hideous depths of green water. Oh, dear me, no! That kind of thing never happens on Lake Wissanotti.

But what does happen is that the Mariposa Belle sinks every now and then, and sticks there on the bottom till they get things straightened up.

On the lakes round Mariposa, if a person arrives late anywhere and explains that the steamer sank, everybody understands the situation.

You see when Harland and Wolff built the Mariposa Belle, they left some cracks in between the timbers that you fill up with cotton waste every Sunday. If this is not attended to, the boat sinks. In fact, it is part of the law of the province that all the steamers like the Mariposa Belle must be properly corked,—I think that is the word,—every season. There are inspectors who visit all the hotels in the province to see that it is done.

So you can imagine now that I've explained it a little straighter, the indignation of the people when they knew that the boat had come uncorked and that they might be stuck out there on a shoal or a mud-bank half the night.

I don't say either that there wasn't any danger; anyway, it doesn't feel very safe when you realise that the boat is settling down with every hundred yards that she goes, and you look over the side and see only the black water in the gathering night.

Safe! I'm not sure now that I come to think of it that it isn't worse than sinking in the Atlantic. After all, in the Atlantic there is wireless telegraphy, and a lot of trained sailors and stewards. But out on Lake Wissanotti,—far out, so that you can only just see the lights of the town away off to the south,—when the propeller comes to a stop,—and you can hear the hiss of steam as they start to rake out the engine fires to prevent an explosion,—and when you turn from the red glare that comes from the furnace doors as they open them, to the black dark that is gathering over the lake,—and there's a night wind beginning to run among the rushes,—and you see the men going forward to the roof of the pilot house to send up the rockets to rouse the town,— safe? Safe yourself, if you like; as for me, let me once get back into Mariposa again, under the night shadow of the maple trees, and this shall be the last, last time I'll go on Lake Wissanotti.

Safe! Oh yes! Isn't it strange how safe other people's adventures seem after they happen. But you'd have been scared, too, if you'd been there just before the steamer sank, and seen them bringing up all the women on to the top deck.

I don't see how some of the people took it so calmly; how Mr. Smith, for instance, could have gone on smoking and telling how he'd had a steamer "sink on him" on Lake Nipissing and a still bigger one, a side-wheeler, sink on him in Lake Abbitibbi.

Then, quite suddenly, with a quiver, down she went. You could feel the boat sink, sink,—down, down,—would it never get to the bottom? The water came flush up to the lower deck, and then—thank heaven,—the sinking stopped and there was the Mariposa Belle safe and tight on a reed bank.

Really, it made one positively laugh! It seemed so queer and, anyway, if a man has a sort of natural courage, danger makes him laugh. Danger? pshaw! fiddlesticks! everybody scouted the idea. Why, it is just the little things like this that give zest to a day on the water.

Within half a minute they were all running round looking for sandwiches and cracking jokes and talking of making coffee over the remains of the engine fires.

I don't need to tell at length how it all happened after that.

I suppose the people on the Mariposa Belle would have had to settle down there all night or till help came from the town, but some of the men who had gone forward and were peering out into the dark said that it couldn't be more than a mile across the water to Miller's Point. You could almost see it over there to the left,—some of them, I think, said "off on the port bow," because you know when you get mixed up in these marine disasters, you soon catch the atmosphere of the thing.

So pretty soon they had the davits swung out over the side and were lowering the old lifeboat from the top deck into the water.

There were men leaning out over the rail of the Mariposa Belle with lanterns that threw the light as they let her down, and the glare fell on the water and the reeds. But when they got the boat lowered, it looked such a frail, clumsy thing as one saw it from the rail above, that the cry was raised: "Women and children first!" For what was the sense, if it should turn out that the boat wouldn't even hold women and children, of trying to jam a lot of heavy men into it?

So they put in mostly women and children and the boat pushed out into the darkness so freighted down it would hardly float.

In the bow of it was the Presbyterian student who was relieving the minister, and he called out that they were in the hands of Providence. But he was crouched and ready to spring out of them at the first moment.

So the boat went and was lost in the darkness except for the lantern in the bow that you could see bobbing on the water. Then presently it came back and they sent another load, till pretty soon the decks began to thin out and everybody got impatient to be gone.

It was about the time that the third boat-load put off that Mr. Smith took a bet with Mullins for twenty-five dollars, that he'd be home in Mariposa before the people in the boats had walked round the shore.

No one knew just what he meant, but pretty soon they saw Mr. Smith disappear down below into the lowest part of the steamer with a mallet in one hand and a big bundle of marline in the other.

They might have wondered more about it, but it was just at this time that they heard the shouts from the rescue boat—the big Mackinaw lifeboat—that had put out from the town with fourteen men at the sweeps, when they saw the first rockets go up.

I suppose there is always something inspiring about a rescue at sea, or on the water.

After all, the bravery of the lifeboat man is the true bravery,—expended to save life, not to destroy it.

Certainly they told for months after of how the rescue boat came out to the Mariposa Belle.

I suppose that when they put her in the water the lifeboat touched it for the first time since the old Macdonald Government placed her on Lake Wissanotti.

Anyway, the water poured in at every seam. But not for a moment,—even with two miles of water between them and the steamer,—did the rowers pause for that.

By the time they were half-way there the water was almost up to the thwarts, but they drove her on. Panting and exhausted (for mind you, if you haven't been in a fool boat like that for years, rowing takes it out of you), the rowers stuck to their task. They threw the ballast over and chucked into the water the heavy cork jackets and lifebelts that encumbered their movements. There was no thought of turning back. They were nearer to the steamer than the shore.

"Hang to it, boys," called the crowd from the steamer's deck, and hang they did.

They were almost exhausted when they got them; men leaning from the steamer threw them ropes and one by one every man was hauled aboard just as the lifeboat sank under their feet.

Saved! by Heaven, saved, by one of the smartest pieces of rescue work ever seen on the lake.

There's no use describing it; you need to see rescue work of this kind by lifeboats to understand it.

Nor were the lifeboat crew the only ones that distinguished themselves.

Boat after boat and canoe after canoe had put out from Mariposa to the help of the steamer. They got them all.

Pupkin, the other bank teller, with a face like a horse, who hadn't gone on the excursion,—as soon as he knew that the boat was signalling for help and that Miss Lawson was sending up rockets,—rushed for a row boat, grabbed an oar (two would have hampered him), and paddled madly out into the lake. He struck right out into the dark with the crazy skiff almost sinking beneath his feet. But they got him. They rescued him. They watched him, almost dead with exhaustion, make his way to the steamer, where he was hauled up with ropes. Saved! Saved!!

They might have gone on that way half the night, picking up the rescuers, only, at the very moment when the tenth load of people left for the shore,—just as suddenly and saucily as you please, up came the Mariposa Belle from the mud bottom and floated.

FLOATED?

Why, of course she did. If you take a hundred and fifty people off a steamer that has sunk, and if you get a man as shrewd as Mr. Smith to plug the timber seams with mallet and marline, and if you turn ten bandsmen of the Mariposa band on to your hand pump on the bow of the lower decks—float? why, what else can she do?

Then, if you stuff in hemlock into the embers of the fire that you were raking out, till it hums and crackles under the boiler, it won't be long before you hear the propeller thud—thudding at the stern again, and before the long roar of the steam whistle echoes over to the town.

And so the Mariposa Belle, with all steam up again and with the long train of sparks careering from the funnel, is heading for the town.

But no Christie Johnson at the wheel in the pilot house this time.

"Smith! Get Smith!" is the cry.

Can he take her in? Well, now! Ask a man who has had steamers sink on him in half the lakes from Temiscaming to the Bay, if he can take her in? Ask a man who has run a York boat down the rapids of the Moose when the ice is moving, if he can grip the steering wheel of the Mariposa Belle? So there she steams safe and sound to the town wharf!

Look at the lights and the crowd! If only the federal census taker could count us now! Hear them calling and shouting back and forward from the deck to the shore! Listen! There is the rattle of the shore ropes as they get them ready, and there's the Mariposa band,—actually forming in a circle on the upper deck just as she docks, and the leader with his baton,—one—two—ready now,—

"O CAN-A-DA!"

[1912]

Greater Canada: An Appeal

Now, in this month of April, when the ice is leaving our rivers, the ministers of Canada take ship for this the fourth Colonial Conference at London.[18] What do they go to do? Nay, rather what shall we bid them do? We—the six million people of Canada, unvoiced, untaxed, in the Empire, unheeded in the councils of the world,—we, the six million colonials sprawling our over-suckled infancy across a continent,—what shall be our message to the motherland? Shall we still whine of our poverty, still draw imaginary pictures of our thin herds shivering in the cold blasts of the North, their shepherds huddled for shelter in the log cabins of Montreal and Toronto? Shall we still beg the good people of England to bear yet a little longer, for the poor peasants of their colony, the burden and heat of the day? Shall our ministers rehearse this worn-out fiction of our 'acres of snow,'[19] and so sail home again, still untaxed, to the smug approval of the oblique politicians of Ottawa? Or, shall we say to the people of England, "The time has come; we know and realize our country. We will be your colony no longer. Make us one with you in an Empire, Permanent and Indivisible."

This last alternative means what is commonly called Imperialism. It means a united system of defence, an imperial navy for whose support somehow or other the whole Empire shall properly contribute, and with it an imperial authority in whose power we all may share. To many people in Canada this imperialism is a tainted word. It is too much associated with a truckling subservience to English people and English ideas and the silly swagger of the hop-o'-my-thumb junior officer. But there is and must be for the true future of our country, a higher and more real imperialism than this—the imperialism of the plain man at the plough and the clerk in the counting house, the imperialism of any decent citizen that demands for this country its proper place in the councils of the Empire and in the destiny of the world. In this sense, imperialism means but the realization of a Greater Canada, the recognition of a wider citizenship.

I, that write these lines, am an Imperialist because I will not be a Colonial. This Colonial status is a worn-out, by-gone thing. The sense and feeling of it has

[18] Colonial Conferences were assemblies of representatives of the self-governing members of the British Empire (Dominion governments) concerned with defence and economic policy that occurred in 1887, 1897, 1902, 1907, and subsequently (called Imperial Conferences after 1907) until the Second World War. After the war, Imperial Conferences were replaced by biennial Commonwealth Conferences.

[19] Reference to the French author Voltaire's description of Canada as "quelques arpents de neige" in his satirical novel *Candide* (1759).

become harmful to us. It limits the ideas, and circumscribes the patriotism of our people. It impairs the mental vigor and narrows the outlook of those that are reared and educated in our midst. [. . .]

Some time ago Theodore Roosevelt, writing with the pardonable irresponsibility of a Police Commissioner of New York and not as President of the United States, said of us here in Canada, that the American feels towards the Canadian the good natured condescension that is felt by the free-born man for the man that is not free. Only recently one of the most widely circulated of American Magazines, talking in the same vein, spoke of us Canadians as a "subject people." These are, of course, the statements of extravagance and ignorance; but it is true, none the less, that the time has come to be done with this *colonial* business, done with it once and forever. We cannot in Canada continue as we are. We must become something greater or something infinitely less. We can no longer be an appanage[20] and outlying portion of something else. Canada, as a *colony*, was right enough in the days of good old Governor Simcoe,[21] when your emigrant officer sat among the pine stumps of his Canadian clearing and reared his children in the fear of God and in the love of England—right enough then, wrong enough and destructive enough now. We cannot continue as we are. In the history of every nation as of every man there is no such thing as standing still. There is no pause upon the path of progress. There is no stagnation but the hush of death.

And for this progress, this forward movement, what is there first to do? How first unravel this vexed skein of our colonial and imperial relations? This, first of all. We must realize, and the people of England must realize, the inevitable greatness of Canada. This is not a vain-glorious boast. This is no rhodomontade.[22] It is simple fact. Here stand we, six million people, heirs to the greatest legacy in the history of mankind, owners of half a continent, trustees, under God Almighty, for the fertile solitudes of the west. A little people, few in numbers, say you? Ah, truly such a little people! Few as the people of the Greeks that blocked the mountain gates of Europe to the march of Asia, few as the men of Rome that built a power to dominate the world, nay, scarce more numerous than they in England whose beacons flamed along the cliffs a warning to the heavy galleons of Spain.[23] Aye, such a little people, but growing, growing, growing, with a march that shall make us ten millions to-morrow, twenty millions in our children's time and a hundred millions ere yet the century runs out. [. . .]

This then for the size and richness of our country. Would that the soul and spirit of its people were commensurate with its greatness. For here as yet we fail. Our politics, our public life and thought, rise not to the level of our opportunity. The mud-bespattered politicians of the trade, the party men and party managers, give us in place of patriotic statescraft the sordid traffic of a tolerated jobbery. For

[20] A piece of land given by the sovereign to lesser family members.

[21] John Graves Simcoe was the first lieutenant-governor of Upper Canada, 1791–96.

[22] Vain and empty boasting.

[23] When the Spanish Armada was sighted in the English Channel in July 1588, warning beacons were lit all along the south coast of England.

bread, a stone. Harsh is the cackle of the little turkey-cocks of Ottawa, fighting the while as they feather their mean nests of sticks and mud, high on their river bluff. Loud sings the little Man of the Province, crying his petty Gospel of Provincial Rights, grudging the gift of power, till the cry spreads and town hates town and every hamlet of the country side shouts for its share of plunder and of pelf. This is the tenor of our politics, carrying as its undertone the voice of the black-robed sectary, with narrow face and shifting eyes, snarling still with the bigotry of a by-gone day. This is the spirit that we must purge. This is the demon we must exorcise; this the disease, the cankerworm of corruption, bred in the indolent securities of peace, that must be burned from us in the pure fire of an Imperial patriotism, that is no theory but a passion. This is our need, our supreme need of the Empire—not for its ships and guns, but for the greatness of it, the soul of it, aye for the very danger of it.

Of our spirit, then, it is not well. [. . .] We cannot sit passive to watch our growth. Good or bad, straight or crooked, we must make our fate.

Nor is it ever possible or desirable that we in Canada can form an independent country. The little cry that here and there goes up among us is but the symptom of an aspiring discontent, that will not let our people longer be colonials. 'Tis but a cry forced out by what a wise man has called the growing pains of a nation's progress. Independent, we could not survive a decade. Those of us who know our country realize that beneath its surface smoulder still the embers of racial feud and of religious bitterness. Twice in our generation has the sudden alarm of conflict broken upon the quiet of our prosperity with the sound of a fire bell in the night. Not thus our path. Let us compose the feud and still the strife of races, not in the artificial partnership of an Independent Canada, but in the joint greatness of a common destiny.

Nor does our future lie in Union with those that dwell to the Southward. The day of annexation to the United States is passed. Our future lies elsewhere. Be it said without concealment and without bitterness. They have chosen their lot; we have chosen ours. Let us go our separate ways in peace. Let them still keep their perennial Independence Day, with its fulminating fireworks and its Yankee Doodle. We keep our Magna Charta and our rough and ready Rule Britannia, shouting as lustily as they! The propaganda of Annexation is dead. Citizens we want, indeed, but not the prophets of an alien gospel. To you who come across our western border we can offer a land fatter than your Kansas, a government better than Montana, a climate kinder than your Dakota. Take it, Good Sir, if you will: but if, in taking it, you still raise your little croak of annexation, then up with you by the belt and out with you, breeches first, through the air, to the land of your origin! This in all friendliness.

Not Independence then, not annexation, not stagnation: nor yet that doctrine of a little Canada that some conceive,— half in, half out of the Empire, with a mimic navy of its own; a pretty navy this,—poor two-penny collection, frolicking on its little way strictly within the Gulf of St. Lawrence, a sort of silly adjunct to the navy of the Empire, semi-detached, the better to be smashed at will. As well a Navy of the Province, or the Parish, home-made for use at home, docked every Saturday in Lake Nipigon! [. . .]

Thus stands the case. Thus stands the question of the future of Canada. Find for us something other than mere colonial stagnation, something sounder than independence, nobler than annexation, greater in purpose than a Little Canada. Find us a way. Build us a plan, that shall make us, in hope at least, an Empire Permanent and Indivisible.

[1907]

The Woman Question

I was sitting the other day in what is called the Peacock Alley of one of our leading hotels, drinking tea with another thing like myself, a man. At the next table were a group of Superior Beings in silk, talking. I couldn't help overhearing what they said,—at least not when I held my head a little sideways.

They were speaking of the war.

"There wouldn't have been any war," said one, "if women were allowed to vote."

"No, indeed," chorused all the others.

The woman who had spoken looked about her defiantly. She wore spectacles and was of the type that we men used to call, in days when we still retained a little courage, an Awful Woman.

"When women have the vote," she went on, "there will be no more war. The women will forbid it."

She gazed about her angrily. She evidently wanted to be heard. My friend and I hid ourselves behind a little fern and trembled.

But we listened. We were hoping that the Awful Woman would explain how war would be ended. She didn't. She went on to explain instead that when women have the vote there will be no more poverty, no disease, no germs, no cigarette smoking and nothing to drink but water.

It seemed a gloomy world.

"Come," whispered my friend, "this is no place for us. Let us go to the bar."

"No," I said, "leave me. I am going to write an article on the Woman Question. The time has come when it has got to be taken up and solved."

So I set myself to write it.

The woman problem may be stated somewhat after this fashion. The great majority of the women of to-day find themselves without any means of support of their own. [. . .] This is true also of men. But the men can acquire means of support. They can hire themselves out and work. Better still, by the industrious process of intrigue rightly called busyness, or business, they may presently get hold of enough of other people's things to live without working. Or again, men can, with a fair prospect of success, enter the criminal class, either in its lower ranks as a house breaker, or in its upper ranks, through politics. Take it all in all a man has a certain chance to get along in life.

A woman, on the other hand, has little or none. The world's work is open to her, but she cannot do it. She lacks the physical strength for laying bricks or digging coal. If put to work on a steel beam a hundred feet above the ground, she would fall off. For the pursuit of business her head is all wrong. Figures confuse her. She lacks sustained attention and in point of morals the average woman is, even for business, too crooked.

This last point is one that will merit a little emphasis. Men are queer creatures. They are able to set up a code of rules or a standard, often quite an artificial one, and stick to it. They have acquired the art of playing the game. Eleven men can put on white flannel trousers and call themselves a cricket team, on which an entirely new set of obligations, almost a new set of personalities, are wrapped about them. Women could never be a team of anything.

So it is in business. Men are able to maintain a sort of rough and ready code which prescribes the particular amount of cheating that a man may do under the rules. This is called business honesty, and many men adhere to it with a dog-like tenacity, growing old in it, till it is stamped on their grizzled faces, visibly. They can feel it inside them like a virtue. So much will they cheat and no more. Hence men are able to trust one another knowing the exact degree of dishonesty they are entitled to expect.

With women it is entirely different. They bring to business an unimpaired vision. They see it as it is. It would be impossible to trust them. They refuse to play fair.

Thus it comes about that woman is excluded, to a great extent, from the world's work and the world's pay.

There is nothing really open to her except one thing,—marriage. She must find a man who will be willing, in return for her society, to give her half of everything he has, allow her the sole use of his house during the daytime, pay her taxes, and provide her clothes.

This was, formerly and for many centuries, not such a bad solution of the question. The women did fairly well out of it. It was the habit to marry early and often. The "house and home" was an important place. The great majority of people, high and low, lived on the land. The work of the wife and the work of the husband ran closely together. [. . .]

Then came the modern age, beginning let us say about a hundred and fifty years ago. The distinguishing marks of it have been machinery and the modern city. The age of invention swept the people off the land. It herded them into factories, creating out of each man a poor miserable atom divorced from hereditary ties, with no rights, no duties, and no place in the world except what his wages contract may confer on him. Every man for himself, and sink or swim, became the order of the day. It was nicknamed 'industrial freedom.' The world's production increased enormously. It is doubtful if the poor profited much. They obtained the modern city,—full of light and noise and excitement, lively with crime and gay with politics,—and the free school where they learned to read and write, by which means they might hold a mirror to their poverty and take a good look at it. They lost the quiet of the country side, the murmur of the brook and the inspiration of the open sky. These are unconscious things, but the peasant who has been reared among them, for all his unconsciousness, pines and dies without them. It is doubtful if the poor have gained. The chaw-bacon rustic who trimmed a hedge in the reign of George the First, compares well with the pale slum-rat of the reign of George V.

But if the machine age has profoundly altered the position of the working man, it has done still more with woman. It has dispossessed her. Her work has been taken away. The machine does it. It makes the clothes and brews the beer. The roar of the vacuum cleaner has hushed the sound of the broom. The proud proportions of the old-time cook, are dwindled to the slim outline of the gas-stove expert operating on a beefsteak with the aid of a thermometer. And at the close of day the machine, wound with a little key, sings the modern infant to its sleep, with the faultless lullaby of the Victrola.[24] The home has passed, or at least is passing out of existence. In place of it is the 'apartment'—an incomplete thing, a mere part of something; where children are an intrusion, where hospitality is done through a caterer, and where Christmas is only the twenty-fifth of December.

All this the machine age did for woman. For a time she suffered—the one thing she had learned, in the course of centuries, to do with admirable fitness. With each succeeding decade of the modern age things grew worse instead of better. The age for marriage shifted. A wife instead of being a help-mate had become a burden that must be carried. It was no longer true that two could live on less than one. The prudent youth waited till he could 'afford' a wife. Love itself grew timid. Little Cupid exchanged his bow and arrow for a book on arithmetic and studied money sums. [. . .] Thus the unmarried woman, a [quite] distinct thing from the 'old maid' of ancient times, came into existence, and multiplied and increased till there were millions of her.

Then there rose up in our own time, or within call of it, a deliverer. It was the Awful Woman with the Spectacles, and the doctrine that she preached was Woman's Rights. She came as a new thing, a hatchet in her hand, breaking glass. But in reality she was no new thing at all, and has her lineal descent in history from age to age. The Romans knew her as a sybil and shuddered at her. The Middle Ages called her a witch and burnt her. The ancient law of England named her a scold and ducked her in a pond. But the men of the modern age, living indoors and losing something of their ruder fibre, grew afraid of her. The Awful Woman,—meddlesome, vociferous, intrusive,—came into her own.

Her softer sisters followed her. She became the leader of her sex. "Things are all wrong," she screamed, "with the *status* of women." Therein she was quite right. "The remedy for it all," she howled, "is to make women 'free,' to give

---

[24] Internal horn phonographs introduced by the Victor Talking Machine Company in 1906 were the latest in musical technology at the time of this essay.

women the vote. When once women are 'free' everything will be all right." Therein the woman with the spectacles was, and is, utterly wrong.

The women's vote, when they get it, will leave women much as they were before.

Let it be admitted quite frankly that women are going to get the vote. Within a very short time all over the British Isles and North America,—in the States and the nine provinces of Canada,—woman [sic] suffrage will soon be an accomplished fact. It is a coming event which casts its shadow, or its illumination, in front of it. The woman's vote and total prohibition are two things that are moving across the map with gigantic strides. Whether they are good or bad things is another question. They are coming. [. . .]

In and of itself, a vote is nothing. It neither warms the skin nor fills the stomach. Very often the privilege of a vote confers nothing but the right to express one's opinion as to which of two crooks is the crookeder.

But after the women have obtained the vote the question is, what are they going to do with it? The answer is, nothing, or at any rate nothing that men would not do without them. Their only visible use of it will be to elect men into office. Fortunately for us all they will not elect women. Here and there perhaps at the outset, it will be done as the result of a sort of spite, a kind of sex antagonism bred by the controversy itself. But speaking broadly the women's vote will not be used to elect women to office. Women do not think enough of one another to do that. If they want a lawyer they consult a man, and those who can afford it have their clothes made by men, and their cooking done by a chef. As for their money, no woman would entrust that to another woman's keeping. They are far too wise for that.

So that the woman's vote will not result in the setting up of female prime ministers and of parliaments in which the occupants of the treasury bench cast languishing eyes across at the flushed faces of the opposition. From the utter ruin involved in such an attempt at mixed government, the women themselves will save us. They will elect men. They may even pick some good ones. It is a nice question and will stand thinking about.

But what else, or what further can they do, by means of their vote and their representatives to "emancipate" and "liberate" their sex?

Many feminists would tell us at once that if women had the vote they would first and foremost throw everything open to women on the same terms as men. Whole speeches are made on this point, and a fine fury thrown into it, often very beautiful to behold.

The entire idea is a delusion. Practically all of the world's work is open to women now, wide open. *The only trouble is that they can't do it.* There is nothing to prevent a woman from managing a bank, or organizing a company, or running a department store, or floating a merger, or building a railway,—except the simple fact that she can't. Here and there an odd woman does such things, but she is only the exception that proves the rule. Such women are merely—and here I am speaking in the most decorous biological sense,—"sports." The ordinary woman cannot do the ordinary man's work. She never has and never will. The reasons why she can't are so many, that is, she *'can't'* in so many different ways, that it is not worth while to try to name them.

Here and there it is true there are things closed to women, not by their own ability but by the law. This is a gross injustice. There is no defence for it. The province in which I live, for example, refuses to allow women to practise as lawyers. This is wrong. Women have just as good a right to try at being lawyers as they have at anything else. But even if all these legal disabilities, where they exist, were removed (as they will be under a woman's vote) the difference to women at large will be infinitesimal. A few gifted "sports" will earn a handsome livelihood, but the woman question in the larger sense will not move one inch nearer to solution.

The feminists, in fact, are haunted by the idea that it is possible for the average woman to have a life patterned after that of the ordinary man. They imagine her as having a career, a profession, a vocation,—something which will be her "life work" just as selling coal is the life work of the coal merchant.

If this were so, the whole question would be solved. Women and men would become equal and independent. It is thus indeed that the feminist sees them, through the roseate mist created by imagination. Husband and wife appear as a couple of honorable partners who share a house together. Each is off to business in the morning. The husband is, let us say, a stock broker: the wife manufactures iron and steel. The wife is a Liberal, the husband a Conservative. At their dinner they have animated discussions over the tariff till it is time for them to go to their clubs. [. . .]

The whole thing is mere fiction. It is quite impossible for women,—the average and ordinary women,—to go in for having a career. Nature has forbidden it. The average woman must necessarily have,—I can only give the figures roughly,—about three and a quarter children. She must replace in the population herself and her husband with something over to allow for the people who never marry and for the children that do not reach maturity. If she fails to do this the population comes to an end. Any scheme of social life must allow for these three and a quarter children and for the years of care that must be devoted to them. The vacuum cleaner can take the place of the housewife. It cannot replace the mother. No man ever said his prayers at the knees of a vacuum cleaner, or drew his first lessons in manliness and worth from the sweet old-fashioned stories that a vacuum cleaner told. Feminists of the enraged kind may talk as they will of the paid attendant and the expert baby-minder. Fiddlesticks! These things are a mere supplement, useful enough but as far away from the realities of motherhood as the vacuum cleaner itself. But the point is one that need not be labored. Sensible people understand it as soon as said. With fools it is not worth while to argue. [. . .]

[1915]

Every 11 November, "In Flanders Fields" by Lieutenant-Colonel John McCrae, M.D., is recited thousands of times across Canada. Composed in a few peaceful moments on the front lines of the second Battle of Ypres in 1915, "In Flanders Fields" was written shortly after the burial of McCrae's former student and friend Lieutenant Alexis Helmer of Ottawa, and first published in the 8 December 1915 issue of *Punch*. Born in Guelph, Ontario, in 1872, McCrae was educated at the University of Toronto, from which he graduated with a medical degree in 1898. Following service in South Africa (during the Anglo-Boer War, 1899–1900), McCrae moved to Montreal where he taught pathology at McGill University. At this time his poetry was frequently published in *The University Magazine* alongside the work of Stephen Leacock and Duncan Campbell Scott.

Following the outbreak of the First World War in 1914, McCrae enlisted with the Canadian Forces as a medical officer. He served until his death from pneumonia while in France on active duty in 1918. The former editor of *The University Magazine*, Sir Andrew Macphail, published twenty-nine of McCrae's poems posthumously in a slim collection entitled *In Flanders Fields and Other Poems* (1919). This volume also contains letters from McCrae to his mother, Janet McCrae, in Guelph, Ontario, from the frontlines of the Battle of Ypres when "In Flanders Fields" was written. In his letters home, McCrae describes the horrors of the battle when "for seventeen days and seventeen nights none of us have had our clothes off, nor our boots even, except occasionally."

In his portrait of McCrae entitled "An Essay in Character," Macphail describes how he himself was serving at the 6th Canadian Field Ambulance Headquarters in Flanders when he first read the poem. Although the poem was anonymous, Macphail, as his former editor, recognized it as belonging to McCrae. The poem's early haunting pastoral imagery gives way to a final patriotic plea for the passing of the torch. Macphail notes that "it is little wonder that 'In Flanders Fields' has become the poem of the army. The soldiers have learned it with their hearts, which is quite different from committing [it] to memory. It circulates, as a song should circulate, by the living word of mouth, not by printed characters. . . . Nor has any piece of verse in recent years been more widely used in the civilian world." The poem met with an appreciative audience at home in Canada as well. In the 1917 election, the first two stanzas of "In Flanders Fields" were used on election pamphlets promoting the "Union Government" coalition of Liberal and Conservative members of Parliament, led by Prime Minister Robert Borden, who campaigned in support of continuing the war effort.

Although "In Flanders Fields" has been criticized for being too romantic and jingoistic by recent critics and poets, it is important not to underestimate the resonance of the poem at the time of publication. Indeed, in the contemporary popular imagination, it is likely still the single best-known work of Canadian poetry. It is due to McCrae's poem that the poppy was adopted as the symbol of war remembrance, not only in Canada, but in the United States and throughout the British Commonwealth.

In Flanders Fields

In Flanders fields the poppies blow
Between the crosses, row on row,
    That mark our place; and in the sky
    The larks, still bravely singing, fly
Scarce heard amid the guns below.

We are the Dead. Short days ago
We lived, felt dawn, saw sunset glow,
    Loved and were loved, and now we lie,
    In Flanders fields.

Take up our quarrel with the foe: 10
To you from failing hands we throw
    The torch; be yours to hold it high.
    If ye break faith with us who die
We shall not sleep, though poppies grow
    In Flanders fields.

[1919]

Letters

Friday, April 23rd, 1915.

As we moved up last evening, there was heavy firing about 4.30 on our left, the hour at which the general attack with gas was made when the French line broke. We could see the shells bursting over Ypres. [. . .]

As we sat on the road we began to see the French stragglers—men without arms, wounded men, teams, wagons, civilians, refugees—some by the roads, some across country, all talking, shouting—the very picture of debacle. I must say they were the "tag enders" of a fighting line rather than the line itself. They streamed on, and shouted to us scraps of not too inspiriting information while we stood and took our medicine, and picked out gun positions in the fields in case we had to go in there and then. The men were splendid; not a word; not a shake, and it was a terrific test. Traffic whizzed by—ambulances, transport, ammunition, supplies, dispatch riders—and the shells thundered into the town, or burst high in the air nearer us, and the refugees streamed. Women, old men, little children, hopeless, tearful, quiet or excited, tired, dodging the traffic,—and the wounded in singles or in groups. Here and there I could give a momentary help, and the ambulances picked up as they could. So the cold moonlight night wore on—no change save that the towers of Ypres showed up against the glare of the city burning; and the shells still sailed in. [. . .]

Of one's feelings all this night—of the asphyxiated French soldiers—of the women and children—of the cheery, steady British reinforcements that moved up quietly past us, going up, not back—I could write, but you can imagine.

[. . .] Along the roads we went, and made our place on time, pulled up for ten minutes just short of the position, where I put Bonfire[1] with my groom in a farmyard, and went forward on foot—only a quarter of a mile or so—then we advanced. Bonfire had soon to move; a shell killed a horse about four yards away from him, and he wisely took other ground. Meantime we went on into the position we were to occupy for seventeen days, though we could not guess that. I can hardly say more than that it was near the Yser Canal. We got into action at once under heavy gunfire. [. . .]

Sunday, May 2nd, 1915.

Heavy gunfire again this morning. Lieut. H—— was killed at the guns. His diary's last words were, "It has quieted a little and I shall try to get a good sleep." I said the Committal Service over him, as well as I could from memory. A soldier's death! Batteries again registering barrages or barriers of fire at set ranges. At 3 the Germans attacked, preceded by gas clouds. Fighting went on for an hour and a half, during which their guns hammered heavily with some loss to us. The French lines are very uneasy, and we are correspondingly anxious. The infantry fire was very heavy, and we fired incessantly, keeping on into the night. Despite the heavy fire I got asleep at 12, and slept until daylight which comes at 3.

Sunday, May 9th, 1915.

At 4 we were ordered to get ready to move, and the Adjutant picked out new retirement positions; but a little later better news came, and the daylight and sun revived us a bit. As I sat in my dugout a little white and black dog with tan spots bolted in over the parapet, during heavy firing, and going to the farthest corner began to dig furiously. Having scraped out a pathetic little hole two inches deep, she sat down and shook, looking most plaintively at me. A few minutes later, her owner came along, a French soldier. Bissac was her name, but she would not leave me at the time. When I sat down a little later, she stole out and shyly crawled in between me and the wall; she stayed by me all day, and I hope got later on to safe quarters.

Firing kept up all day. In thirty hours we had fired 3600 rounds, and at times with seven, eight, or nine guns; our wire cut and repaired eighteen times. Orders came to move, and we got ready. At dusk we got the guns out by hand, and all batteries assembled at a given spot in comparative safety. We were much afraid they would open on us, for at 10 o'clock they gave us 100 or 150 rounds, hitting the trench parapet again and again. However, we were up the road, the last wagon half a mile away before they opened. One burst near me, and

---

[1] McCrae's horse.

splattered some pieces around, but we got clear, and by 12 were out of the usual fire zone. Marched all night, tired as could be, but happy to be clear.

I was glad to get on dear old Bonfire again. We made about sixteen miles, and got to our billets at dawn. I had three or four hours' sleep, and arose to a peaceful breakfast. We shall go back to the line elsewhere very soon, but it is a present relief, and the next place is sure to be better, for it cannot be worse. Much of this narrative is bald and plain, but it tells our part in a really great battle. [. . .]

[1919]

DESKAHEH (LEVI GENERAL OR HI-WYI-ISS) ■ (1873–1925)

Levi General was a Haudenosaunee/ Iroquois farmer and statesman particularly remembered for his persistent efforts to protect the treaty rights of the Six Nations at the Grand River settlement. He was one of the first indigenous leaders to approach the international community on behalf of an indigenous nation, when he appealed to the League of Nations in Geneva (a precursor to the United Nations) to recognize the rights of the Six Nations Iroquois Confederacy. Shortly after the First World War, the Canadian government had decided to replace the Council of Six Nations with the Indian Act system of governance. Deskaheh (General assumed the title when he became a chief) was adamantly opposed to the assimilationist goals of the government. His determination to preserve treaty rights compelled him to travel to England in 1921 to appeal to King George V for an intervention but he was denied an audience with the monarch.

In 1923, using a passport from the Six Nations Iroquois Confederacy, he journeyed to Switzerland on behalf of the confederacy to apply for membership in the League of Nations and to make an appeal on behalf of a "small nation of the world." In "The Redman's Appeal for Justice," he made the case of the

binding nature of the treaty agreements over land, jurisdiction, and the right of a small nation to govern itself according to its custom and tradition. He spent over a year in Geneva, preparing petitions, seeking meetings with foreign delegates, and speaking out about the injustices Canada had committed against its former Iroquois allies. Despite receiving the support of some members (including Persia, Estonia, Ireland, and Panama), Deskaheh was denied an official hearing at the League of Nations. Instead, he is said to have rented a hall to give himself a venue to state his case. He spoke to a crowd of thousands and garnered popular, if not political, support for his cause. According to legal historian Grace Woo, Duncan Campbell Scott, the deputy superintendent of Indian affairs, prepared a response to "The Redman's Appeal for Justice," even though it had never been formally accepted at the League. In February 1924, Scott's defence of Canada's policies was distributed to the members of the League, despite the fact that the petition to which it was responding had been blocked.

In October 1924, at the behest of Indian Affairs, the RCMP dissolved the traditional government of the Six Nations, seized important documents, and confiscated wampums. As the two-row wampum belt represents the treaty between the Iroquois and the government, its confiscation indicates the symbolic act of breaking the treaty. Failing to bring about change as a diplomat at the League of Nations, and feeling threatened by Canadian government legislation, Deskaheh went into voluntary exile on the Tuscarora Reservation near Buffalo, New York. The speech here was presented over radio in Rochester, N.Y., on 10 March 1925, and many say that Deskaheh died of "heartbreak" a few months afterwards. It was his final public speech, an incisive condemnation of the ways the Iroquois Confederacy had been betrayed by the British, Canadian, and American governments. Responding to the accusation that Native peoples are "victims of superstition," Deskaheh cleverly turned the tables on his accusers: "Any superstition of which the Grand River People have been victims [has been] . . . in their trust in the honor of governments who boast of a higher civilization."

Deskaheh's Last Speech

Nearly everyone who is listening to me is a pale face, I suppose. I am not. My skin is not red but that is what my people are called by others. My skin is brown, light brown, but our cheeks have a little flush and that is why we are called red skins. We don't mind that. There is no difference between us, under the skins, that any expert with a carving knife has ever discovered.

My home is on the Grand River. Until we sold off a large part, our country extended down to Lake Erie, where, 140 winters ago, we had a little sea-shore of our own and a birch-bark navy. You would call it Canada. We do not. We call the little ten-miles square we have left the "Grand River Country." We have the right to do that. It is ours. We have the written pledge of George III that we should have it forever as against him or his successors and he promised to protect us in it. We didn't think we would ever live long enough to find that a British promise was not good. An enemy's foot is on our country, and George V knows it for I told him so, but he will not lift his finger to protect us nor will any of his ministers. [. . .]

In some respects, we are just like you. We like to tell our troubles. You do that. You told us you were in great trouble a few winters ago because a great big giant with a big stick was after you.[1] We helped you whip him. Many of our young men volunteered and many gave their lives for you.[2] You were very willing to let them fight in the front ranks in France. Now we want to tell our troubles to you.

I do not mean that we are calling on your governments—we are tired of calling on the governments of pale-faced peoples in America and in Europe. We have tried that and found it was no use. They deal only in fine words. [. . .] We have a little territory left—just enough to live and die on.

[1] The First World War.

[2] See also Joseph Boyden's novel *Three Day Road* (2005) in which he tells the story of two Cree men serving in the First World War.

Don't you think your governments ought to be ashamed to take that away from us by pretending it is part of theirs? You ought to be ashamed if you let them. Before it is all gone, we mean to let you know what your governments are doing. If you are a free people you can have your own way. The governments at Washington and Ottawa have a silent partnership of policy. It is aimed to break up every tribe of Red-men so as to dominate every acre of their territory. Your high officials are the nomads today—not the Red People. Your officials won't stay home. Over in Ottawa, they call that policy "Indian Advancement." Over in Washington, they call it "Assimilation." We who would be the helpless victims say it is tyranny. [. . .]

We want none of your laws and customs that we have not willingly adopted for ourselves. We have adopted many. You have adopted some of ours—votes for women, for instance. We are as well behaved as you and you would think so if you knew us better. We would be happier today, if left alone, than you who call yourselves Canadians and Americans. We have no jails and do not need them. You have many jails, but do they hold all the criminals you convict? And do you convict or prosecute all your violators of the thousands of laws you have?

Your governments have lately resorted to new practices in their Indian policies. In the old days, they often bribed our chiefs to sign treaties to get our lands. Now they know that our remaining territory can easily be gotten away from us by first taking our political rights away in forcing us into your citizenship, so they give jobs in their Indian offices to the bright young people among us who will take them and who, to earn their pay, say that our people wish to become citizens with you and that we are ready to have our tribal life destroyed and want your governments to do it. But that is not true. Your governments of today learned that method from the British. The British have long practiced it on weaker peoples in carrying out their policy of subjugating the world, if they can, to British Imperialism. Under cover of it, your lawmakers now assume to govern other peoples too weak to resist your courts. There is no three-mile limits or twelve-mile limits to strong governments who wish to do that. About three winters ago, the Canadian government set out to take mortgages on farms of our returned soldiers to secure loans made to them intending to use Canadian courts to enforce these mortgages in the name of Canadian authority within our country. When Ottawa tried that, our people resented it. We knew that would mean the end of our government. Because we did so, the Canadian government began to enforce all sorts of Dominion and Provincial laws over us and quartered armed men among us to enforce Canadian laws and customs upon us. We appealed to Ottawa in the name of our right as a separate people and by right of our treaties, and the door was closed in our faces. We then went to London with our treaty and asked for the protection it promised and got no attention. Then we went to the League of Nations at Geneva with its covenant to protect little peoples and to enforce respect for treaties by its members and we spent a whole year patiently waiting but got no hearing.

To punish us for trying to preserve our rights, the Canadian government has now pretended to abolish our government by Royal Proclamation, and has pretended to set up a Canadian-made government over us, composed of the few traitors among us who are willing to accept pay from Ottawa and do its bidding. Finally, Ottawa officials, under pretense of a friendly visit, asked to inspect our precious wampum belts, made by our Fathers centuries ago as records of our history, and when shown to them, these false-faced officials seized and carried away those belts as bandits take away your precious belongings. [. . .] The Ottawa government thought that with no wampum belts to read in the opening of our Six Nations Councils, we would give up our home rule and self-government, the victims of superstition. Any superstition of which the Grand River People have been victims are not in reverence for wampum belts, but in their trust in the honor of governments who boast of a higher civilization. [. . .]

We are not as dependent in some ways as we were in the early days. We do not need interpreters now. We know your language and can understand your words for ourselves and we have learned to decide for ourselves what is good for us. It is bad for any people to take the advice of an alien people as to that.

Your Mothers, I hear, have a good deal to say about your government. Our Mothers have always had a hand in ours. Maybe you can do something to help us now. If you white mothers are hard-hearted and will not, perhaps you boys and girls who are listening and who have loved to read stories about our people—the true ones, I mean—will help us when you grow up if there are any of us left then to be helped. If you are bound to treat us as though we were citizens under your government, then those of your people who are land-hungry will get our farms away from us by hooks and crooks under your property laws and in your courts that we do not understand and do not wish to learn. We would then be homeless and have to drift into your big cities to work for wages, to buy bread, and have to pay rent, as you call it, to live on this earth and to live in little rooms in which we would suffocate. We would then be scattered and lost to each other and lost among so many of you. Our boys and girls would then have to intermarry with you, or not at all. If consumption[3] took us off or if we brought no children into the world, or our children mixed with the ocean of your blood, then there would be no Iroquois left. [. . .]

This is the story of the Mohawks, the story of the Oneidas, of the Cayugas—I am a Cayuga—of the Onondagas, the Senecas, and the Tuscaroras. They are the Iroquois. Tell it to those who have not been listening. Maybe I will be stopped from telling it. But if I am prevented from telling it over, as I hope to do, the story will not be lost. I have already told it to thousands of listeners in Europe—it has gone into the records where your children can find it when I may be dead

[3] Tuberculosis.

or be in jail for daring to tell the truth. I have told this story in Switzerland—they have free speech in little Switzerland. One can tell the truth over there in public, even if it is uncomfortable for some great people.

This story comes straight from Deskaheh, one of the chiefs of the Cayugas. I am the speaker of the Council of the Six Nations, the oldest League of Nations now existing. It was founded by Hiawatha. It is a League which is still alive and intends, as best it can, to defend the rights of the Iroquois to live under their own laws in their own little countries now left to them, to worship their Great Spirit in their own way, and to enjoy the rights which are as surely theirs as the white man's rights are his own. [. . .]

[1925]

NELLIE MCCLUNG ■ (1873–1951)

Nellie McClung was a part of the social and moral reform movements prevalent in western Canada in the early 1900s that sought improvement to the rights of Canadian women and families. Her concerns ranged from problems of rural life and conditions in cities and factories to temperance, eugenics, and women's suffrage. Living through the First World War, the Depression, and the Second World War, McClung responded to what she viewed as social injustice at every stage of her life.

The sixth child of an Irish father and a Scottish mother, Helen Letitia Mooney (called Nellie) was born in Grey County, Ontario, and raised on a homestead farm in rural Manitoba. Young Nellie, an opinionated girl, rebelled against the prevailing attitude that women should not be educated or hold opinions on subjects outside the domestic sphere. In rebellion, she decided to become a teacher. She accomplished this by going to school in rural Manitoba, and then gaining entrance to the Winnipeg Normal School where she trained to be a teacher. According to biographer Mary Lile Benham, for her first Christmas as a teacher, McClung was given a gift of the works of Charles Dickens. As she read Dickens's treatment

of poverty, humanity, and exploitation, she later recalled that "a light shone around me" and she realized that a writer could be "an interpreter, a revealer of secrets, a heavenly surgeon, a sculptor who can bring an angel out of a stone. . . . I wanted to do for the people around me what Dickens had done for his people."

She married Robert Wesley McClung in 1896 and moved to Winnipeg in 1911. Together they had five children. While living in rural Manitoba, McClung began to write seriously. When her first novel, *Sowing Seeds in Danny*, was published in 1908, it became a bestseller and sold over 100,000 copies, earning almost $25,000. She continued to publish both fiction and non-fiction regularly throughout her life. In addition to her writing, during her Winnipeg years McClung garnered a reputation as a public speaker, primarily on the subjects of temperance and women's issues. Introduced to it by her mother-in-law, McClung was active in the Woman's Christian Temperance Union (WCTU) throughout her career. She argued that there was an irrefutable link between violence against women and children and alcohol consumption. For McClung, women's rights and temperance went hand-in-hand, which was one of the things that Stephen Leacock objected to in his published response to her. According to literary critic Cecily Devereux, McClung "emerged as a popular spokesperson for the kind of feminism that has often been character-ized as 'maternal.' Maternal feminism undertook a radical undermining of the patriarchal structures of most ideological apparatuses—education, law, organized religion, labour—although it did so through what many critics have seen as a deeply conservative affirmation and social reification of an idea of women as inherently motherly, wanting not only to bear children for the good of the state but to turn the idealized domestic practices of the patriarchal mother upon the nation."

In 1912, McClung and several other educated middle-class women formed the Women's Political Equality League. Two years later, the league asked the Manitoba legislature, specifically Premier Rodmond Roblin, for voting rights for women and was turned down. Roblin was openly hostile to the suffra-gist movement, disallowing more than seventy suffrage petitions and appar-ently sending party stooges to disrupt public meetings at which women pre-sented their views on suffrage. In response, the league staged a mock parliament—the "Women's Parliament"—at Winnipeg's Walker Theatre with McClung acting the role of the premier (Roblin) and other women playing parts as members of Parliament. The curtain opened to reveal the Parliament receiving petitions—includ-ing the request for a law to ban men's six-inch collars and scarlet ties. Next, a group of men arrived with a wheelbar-row full of petitions, asking for votes for men. After the delegation presented their case, the premier spoke. Inverting Roblin's own words by replacing "women" with "men," McClung showed

the absurdity of some of his arguments. "The Play," reprinted here from McClung's 1921 novel *Purple Springs*, is a fictionalized version of the events of that evening. The "thick-set" man who calls himself Robertson Jones in the story, with dark glasses, a battered hat, and a "much bedraggled waterproof," is meant to be Rodmond Roblin.

The success of the "Women's Parliament" lent energy and popular support to the league's campaign. In the election race of the following year, McClung and other prominent social reformers campaigned on behalf of the Liberal leader, T.C. Norris, who had agreed to extend the franchise to women if he won the election. He made good on his promise when he defeated Roblin's Conservatives. After receiving a petition with almost 40,000 signatures, collected for presentation to the legislature in December 1915, the Manitoba Legislature extended the vote to women on 29 January 1916. Manitoba thus became the first Canadian province to allow women the right to vote and to run for public office. Lillian Benyon Thomas (under the name "Lillian Laurie") wrote in her "Women's Page" column in the *Weekly Free Press*, "It is all over now, even the shouting. The women of Manitoba are now citizens, persons, human beings, who have groped politi-cally out of the class of criminals, children, idiots and lunatics."

Published in the heat of the battle for suffrage, McClung's bestselling *In Times Like These* (1915) is a collection of suffrage essays and speeches that rep-resents women's struggle for political recognition during these years. It endures as an important document of "first-wave feminism" in Canada. That the book provoked a virulent response from Stephen Leacock in the October issue of *Maclean's* of that year (see "The Woman Question") only testifies to the social obstacles and ingrained attitudes women were fighting against. In effect, women were protesting "against the world's estimate of woman's position," as McClung puts it in "What Do Women Think of War?" In the May 1916 issue of *Maclean's*, McClung published an article about the Alberta suffrage victory that was also a response to Leacock ("Speaking of Women," included here). In it, she engages directly with Leacock's critiques yet very diplomatically does not mention his name.

After moving to Edmonton, Alberta, with her family in 1915, McClung continued to campaign for suffrage. This was achieved in Alberta in 1916 and in much of the rest of Canada in the following few years. Elected as a Liberal (opposition) member of the Alberta Legislature from 1921 to 1926, she promoted a number of social reforms, including medical and dental care for children and married women's property rights. Like Canada's first female magistrate, Emily Murphy, McClung also advocated the legislation of forced sterilization for "young simple-minded girls" and those who were designated "feeble minded." McClung's arguments helped lead to the passage of the Sexual Sterilization Act in 1928. Until the law was repealed in 1972, over 2,800 people were sterilized, most without consent. In 1928, advocates of sterilization believed that mental illness, epilepsy, alcoholism, some criminal behaviour, and social defects were genetically determined and inherited. It was believed by the prominent

eugenicists that sterilization of those who were "mentally deficient" would be of benefit to those who were "incapable of intelligent parenthood" and would help keep the gene pool strong. This in turn would lead to a stronger society. Five years after Alberta, British Columbia passed its own sexual sterilization act, which remained in place until 1973.

In 1927 McClung joined Emily Murphy in her fight to have women recognized as "persons." The "Famous Five" Albertan women, including Irene Parlby, Henrietta Muir Edwards, and Louise McKinney as well as McClung and Murphy, petitioned the Supreme Court of Canada to examine the meaning of the word "persons" in section 24 of the 1867 British North America Act to see if it included women in its definition. When the Supreme Court ruled that women were not persons, the five women appealed to the Judicial Committee of England's Privy Council, the highest court of appeal for Canada at that time. In October 1929, the Judicial Committee came to the unanimous conclusion that "the word 'persons' in Section 24 includes both the male and female sex." According to them, the exclusion of women from public office was "a relic of days more barbarous than ours."

McClung's ideas were widely circulated in the Canadian press both through reports of her work and in her own political writing. McClung continued to fight for social justice until she died in Victoria, B.C., in 1951.

From Purple Springs

The Play

"Sorry, sir," said the man in the box-office of the Grand, "but the house has been sold out for two days now. The standing room has gone too."

"Can you tell me what this is all about, that every one is so crazy to see it?" the man at the wicket asked, with studied carelessness. He was a thick-set man, with dark glasses, and wore a battered hat, and a much bedraggled waterproof.

"The women here have got up a Parliament, and are showing tonight," said the ticket-seller. "They pretend that only women vote, and women only sit in Parliament. The men will come, asking for the vote, and they'll get turned down good and plenty, just like the old man turned them down."

"Did the Premier turn them down?" asked the stranger. "I didn't hear about it."

"Did he? I guess, yes—he ripped into them in his own sweet way. Did you ever hear the old man rage? Boy! Well, the women have a girl here who is going to do his speech. She's the woman Premier, you understand, and she can talk just like him. She does everything except chew the dead cigar. The fellows in behind say it's the richest thing they ever heard. The old boy will have her shot at sunrise, for sure."

"He won't hear her," said the man in the waterproof, with sudden energy. "He won't know anything about it."

"Sure he will. The old man is an old blunderbuss, but he's too good a sport to stay away. They're decorating a box for him, and have his name on it. He can't stay away."

"He can if he wants to," snapped the other man. "What does he care about this tommyrot—he'll take no notice of it."

"Well," said the man behind the wicket, "I believe he'll come. But say, he sure started something when he got these women after him. They're the sharpest-tongued things you ever listened to, and they have their speeches all ready. The big show opens tonight, and every seat is sold. You may get a ticket though at the last minute, from some one who cannot come. There are always some who fail to show up at the last. I can save you a ticket if this happens. What name?"

"Jones," said the gentleman in the waterproof. No doubt the irritation in his voice was caused by having to confess to such a common name. "Robertson Jones. Be sure you have it right," and he passed along the rail to make room for two women who also asked for tickets.

The directors of the Women's Parliament knew the advertising value of a mystery, being students of humanity, and its odd little ways. They knew that people are attracted by the unknown; so in their advance notices they gave the names of all the women taking part in the play, but one. The part of the Premier—the star part—would be taken by a woman whose identity they were "not at liberty to reveal." Well-known press women were taking the other parts, and their pictures appeared on the posters, but no clue was given out as to the identity of the woman Premier.

Long before sundown, the people gathered at the theatre door, for the top gallery would open for rush seats at seven. Even the ticket holders had been warned that no seat would be held after eight o'clock.

Through the crowd came the burly and aggressive form of Robertson Jones, still wearing his dark glasses, and with a disfiguring strip of court plaster across his cheek. At the wicket he made inquiry for his ticket, and was told to stand back and wait. Tickets were held until eight o'clock.

In the lobby, flattening himself against the marble wall, he waited, with his hat well down over his face. Crowds of people, mostly women, surged past him, laughing, chattering, feeling in their ridiculous bags for their tickets, or the price of a box of chocolates at the counter, where two red-gold blondes presided.

Inside, as the doors swung open, he saw a young fellow in evening dress, giving out handbills, and an exclamation almost escaped him. He had forgotten all about Peter Neelands!

Robertson Jones, caught in the eddies of women, buffeted by them, his toes stepped upon, elbowed, crowded, grew more and more scornful of their intelligence, and would probably have worked his way out—if he could, but the impact of the crowd worked him forward.

"A silly, cackling hen-party," he muttered to himself. "I'll get out of this—it's no place for a man—Lord deliver me from a mob like this, with their crazy tittering. There ought to be a way to stop these things. It's demoralizing—it's unseemly."

It was impossible to turn back, however, and he found himself swept inside. He thought of the side door as a way of escape, but to his surprise, he saw the whole Cabinet arriving there and filing into the boxes over which the colors of the Province were draped; every last one of them, in evening dress.

That was the first blow of the evening! Every one of them had said they would not go—quite scornfully—and spoke of it as "The Old Maids' Convention"—Yet they came!

He wedged his way back to the box office, only to find that there was no ticket for him. Every one had been lifted. But he determined to stay.

Getting in again, he approached a man in a shabby suit, sitting in the last row.

"I'll give you five dollars for your seat," he whispered.

"Holy smoke!" broke from the astonished seat-holder, and then, recovering from his surprise, he said, "Make it ten."

"Shut up then, and get out—here's your money," said Mr. Jones harshly, and in the hurriedly vacated seat, he sat down heavily.

Behind the scenes, the leader of the Women's Party gave Pearl[1] her parting words:

"Don't spare him, Pearl," she said, with her hand around the girl's shoulder, "it is the only way. We have coaxed, argued, reasoned, we have shown him actual cases where the laws have worked great injustice to women. He is blind in his own conceit, and cannot be moved. This is the only way—we can break his power by ridicule—you can do it, Pearl. You can break down a wall of prejudice to-night that would take long years to wear away. Think of cases you know, Pearl, and strike hard. Better to hurt one, and save many! This is a play—but a deadly serious one! I must go now and make the curtain speech."

---

[1] Pearl is the protagonist of *Purple Springs* and the name of the character who most closely resembles McClung. Here Pearl plays the role of the premier, just as McClung had done when the Women's Political Equality League staged the "Women's Parliament" in Winnipeg in 1914.

"This is not the sort of Parliament we think should exist," she said, before the curtain, "this is the sort of Parliament we have at the present time—one sex making all the laws. We have a Parliament of women tonight, instead of men, just to show you how it looks from the other side. People seem to see a joke better sometimes when it is turned around."

Robertson Jones shrugged his shoulders in disgust. What did they hope to gain, these freaks of women, with their little plays and set little speeches. Who listened or noticed? No one, positively no one.

Then the lights went out in the house, and the asbestos curtain came slowly down and slowly crept into the ceiling again, to re-assure the timorous, and the beautiful French garden, with its white statuary, and fountain, against the green trees, followed its plain asbestos sister, and the Women's Parliament was revealed in session.

The Speaker, in purple velvet, with a sweeping plume in her three-cornered hat, sat on the throne; pages in uniform answered the many calls of the members, who, on the Government side were showing every sign of being bored, for the Opposition had the floor, and the honorable member from Mountain was again introducing her bill to give the father equal guardianship rights with the mother. She pleaded eloquently that two parents were not any too many for children to have. She readily granted that if there were to be but one parent, it would of course be the mother, but why skimp the child on parents? Let him have both. It was nature's way. She cited instances of grave injustice done to fathers from having no claim on their offspring.

The Government members gave her little attention. They read their papers, one of the Cabinet Ministers tatted,[2] some of the younger members powdered their noses, many ate chocolates. Those who listened, did so to sneer at the honorable member from Mountain, insinuating she took this stand so she might stand well with the men. This brought a hearty laugh, and a great pounding of the desks.

When the vote was taken, the House divided along party lines. Yawningly the Government members cried "No!"

Robertson Jones sniffed contemptuously; evidently this was a sort of Friday afternoon dialogue, popular at Snookum's Corners, but not likely to cause much of a flutter in the city.

There was a bill read to give dower rights to men, and the leader of the Opposition made a heated defence of the working man who devotes his life to his wife and family, and yet has no voice in the disposition of his property. His wife can sell it over his head, or will it away, as had sometimes been done.

The Attorney General, in a deeply sarcastic vein, asked the honorable lady if she thought the wife and mother would not deal fairly—even generously with her husband. Would she have the iron hand of the law intrude itself into the sacred precincts of the home, where little cherub faces gather round the hearth,

---

[2] A form of crocheting with lace.

under the glow of the glass-fringed hanging lamp. Would she dare to insinuate that love had to be buttressed by the law? Did not a man at the altar, in the sight of God and witnesses, endow his wife with all his goods? Well then—were those sacred words to be blasphemed by an unholy law which compelled her to give back what he had so lovingly given? When a man marries, cried the honorable Attorney General, he gives his wife his name—and his heart—and he gives them unconditionally. Are not these infinitely more than his property? The greater includes the less—the tail goes with the hide! The honorable leader of the Opposition was guilty of a gross offense against good taste, in opening this question again. Last session, the session before, and now this session, she has harped on this disagreeable theme. It has become positively indecent.

The honorable leader of the Opposition begged leave to withdraw her motion, which was reluctantly granted, and the business of the House went on.

A page brought in the word that a delegation of men were waiting to be heard.

Even the Opposition laughed. A delegation of men, seemed to be an old and never-failing joke.

Some one moved that the delegation be heard, and the House was resolved into a committee of the whole, with the First Minister in the chair.

The First Minister rose to take the chair, and was greeted with a round of applause. Opera glasses came suddenly to many eyes, but the face they saw was not familiar. It was a young face, under iron gray hair, large dark eyes, and a genial and pleasant countenance.

For the first time in the evening, Mr. Robertson Jones experienced a thrill of pleasure. At least the woman Premier was reasonably good looking. He looked harder at her. He decided she was certainly handsome, and evidently the youngest of the company.

The delegation of men was introduced and received—the House settled down to be courteous, and listen. Listening to delegations was part of the day's work, and had to be patiently borne.

The delegation presented its case through the leader, who urged that men be given the right to vote and sit in Parliament. The members of the Government smiled tolerantly. The First Minister shook her head slowly and absent-mindedly forgot to stop. But the leader of the delegation went on.

The man who sat in the third seat from the back found the phrasing strangely familiar. He seemed to know what was coming. Sure enough, it was almost word for word the arguments the women had used when they came before the House. The audience was in a pleasant mood, and laughed at every point. It really did not seem to take much to amuse them.

When the delegation leader had finished, and the applause was over, there was a moment of intense silence. Every one leaned forward, edging over in their seats to get the best possible look.

The Woman Premier had risen. So intent was the audience in their study of her face, they forgot to applaud. What they saw was a tall, slight girl whose naturally brilliant coloring needed no make-up; brilliant dark eyes, set in a face whose coloring was vivid as a rose, a straight mouth with a whimsical smile. She gave the audience one friendly smile, and then turned to address the delegation.

She put her hands in front of her, locking her fingers with the thumbs straight up, gently moving them up and down, before she spoke.

The gesture was familiar. It was the Premier's own, and a howl of recognition came from the audience, beginning in the Cabinet Ministers' box.

She tenderly teetered on her heels, waiting for them to quiet down, but that was the occasion for another outburst.

"Gentlemen of the Delegation," she said, when she could be heard, "I am glad to see you!"

The voice, a throaty contralto, had in it a cordial paternalism that was as familiar as the Premier's face.

"Glad to see you—come any time, and ask for anything you like. You are just as welcome this time as you were the last time! We like delegations—and I congratulate this delegation on their splendid, gentlemanly manners. If the men in England had come before their Parliament with the frank courtesy you have shown, they might still have been enjoying the privilege of meeting their representatives in this friendly way.

"But, gentlemen, you are your own answer to the question; you are the product of an age which has not seen fit to bestow the gift you ask, and who can say that you are not splendid specimens of mankind? No! No! Any system which can produce the virile, splendid type of men we have before us today, is good enough for me, and," she added, drawing up her shoulders in perfect imitation of the Premier when he was about to be facetious, "if it is good enough for me— it is good enough for anybody."

The people gasped with the audacity of it! The impersonation was so good— it was weird—it was uncanny. Yet there was no word of disrespect. The Premier's nearest friends could not resent it.

Word for word, she proceeded with his speech, while the theatre rocked with laughter. She was in the Premier's most playful, God-bless-you mood, and simply radiated favors and goodwill. The delegation was flattered, complimented, patted on the head, as she dilated on their manly beauty and charm.

In the third seat from the back, Mr. Robertson Jones had removed his dark glasses, and was breathing like a man with double pneumonia. A dull, red rage burned in his heart, not so much at anything the girl was saying, as the perfectly idiotic way the people laughed.

"I shouldn't laugh," a woman ahead of him said, as she wiped her eyes, "for my husband has a Government job and he may lose it if the Government members see me, but if I don't laugh, I'll choke. Better lose a job than choke."

"But my dear young friends," the Premier was saying, "I am convinced you do not know what you are asking me to do;" her tone was didactic now; she was a patient Sunday School teacher, laboring with a class of erring boys, charitable to their many failings and frailties, hopeful of their ultimate destiny, "you do not know what you ask. You have not thought of it, of course, with the natural thoughtlessness of your sex. You ask for something which may disrupt the whole course of civilization. Man's place is to provide for his family, a hard enough task in these strenuous days. We hear of women leaving home, and we hear it with deepest sorrow. Do you know why women leave home? There is a reason. Home is not made sufficiently attractive. Would letting politics enter the home help matters. Ah no! Politics would unsettle our men. Unsettled men mean unsettled bills—unsettled bills mean broken homes—broken vows—and then divorce."

Her voice was heavy with sorrow, and full of apology for having mentioned anything so unpleasant.

Many of the audience had heard the Premier's speech, and almost all had read it, so not a point was lost.

An exalted mood was on her now—a mood that they all knew well. It had carried elections. It was the Premier's highest card. His friends called it his magnetic appeal.

"Man has a higher destiny than politics," she cried, with the ring in her voice that they had heard so often, "what is home without a bank account? The man who pays the grocer rules the world. Shall I call men away from the useful plow and harrow, to talk loud on street corners about things which do not concern them. Ah, no, I love the farm and the hallowed associations—the dear old farm, with the drowsy tinkle of cow-bells at eventide. There I see my father's kindly smile so full of blessing, hardworking, rough-handed man he was, maybe, but able to look the whole world in the face. . . . You ask me to change all this."

Her voice shook with emotion, and drawing a huge white linen handkerchief from the folds of her gown, she cracked it by the corner like a whip, and blew her nose like a trumpet.

The last and most dignified member of the Cabinet, caved in at this, and the house shook with screams of laughter. They were in the mood now to laugh at anything she said.

"I wonder will she give us one of his rages," whispered the Provincial Secretary to the Treasurer.

"I'm glad he's not here," said the Minister of Municipalities, "I'm afraid he would burst a blood vessel; I'm not sure but I will myself."

"I am the chosen representative of the people, elected to the highest office this fair land has to offer. I must guard well its interests. No upsetting influence must mar our peaceful firesides. Do you never read, gentlemen?" she asked the delegation, with biting sarcasm, "do you not know of the disgraceful happenings in countries cursed by manhood suffrage? Do you not know the fearful odium into which the polls have fallen—is it possible you do not know the origin of that offensive word 'Poll-cat'; do you not know that men are creatures of habit—give them an inch—and they will steal the whole sub-division, and although it is quite true, as you say, the polls are only open once in four years— when men once get the habit—who knows where it will end—it is hard enough to keep them at home now! No, history is full of unhappy examples of men in public life; Nero, Herod, King John—you ask me to set these names before your young people. Politics has a blighting, demoralizing influence on men. It dominates them, hypnotizes them, pursues them even after their earthly career is over. Time and again it has been proven that men came back and voted—even after they were dead."

The audience gasped at that—for in the Premier's own riding, there were names on the voters' lists, taken, it was alleged, from the tomb-stones.

"Do you ask me to disturb the sacred calm of our cemeteries?" she asked, in an awe-stricken tone—her big eyes filled with the horror of it. "We are doing very well just as we are, very well indeed. Women are the best students of economy. Every woman is a student of political economy. We look very closely at every dollar of public money, to see if we couldn't make a better use of it ourselves, before we spend it. We run our elections as cheaply as they are run anywhere. We always endeavor to get the greatest number of votes for the least possible amount of money. That is political economy."

There was an interruption then from the Opposition benches, a feeble protest from one of the private members.

The Premier's face darkened; her eyebrows came down suddenly; the veins in her neck swelled, and a perfect fury of words broke from her lips. She advanced threateningly on the unhappy member.

"You think you can instruct a person older than yourself, do you—you, with the brains of a butterfly, the acumen of a bat; the backbone of a jelly-fish. You can tell me something, can you? I was managing governments when you were sitting in your high chair, drumming on a tin plate with a spoon." Her voice boomed like a gun. "You dare to tell me how a government should be conducted."

The man in the third seat from the back held to the arm of the seat, with hands that were clammy with sweat. He wanted to get up and scream. The words, the voice, the gestures were as familiar as his own face in the glass.

Walking up and down, with her hands at right angles to her body, she stormed and blustered, turning eyes of rage on the audience, who rolled in their seats with delight.

"Who is she, Oh Lord. Who is she?" the Cabinet ministers asked each other for the hundredth time.

"But I must not lose my temper," she said, calming herself and letting her voice drop, "and I never do—never—except when I feel like it—and am pretty sure I can get away with it. I have studied self-control, as you all know—I have had to, in order that I may be a leader. If it were not for this fatal modesty, which on more than one occasion has almost blighted my political career, I would say I believe I have been a leader, a factor in building up this fair province; I would say that I believe I have written my name large across the face of this Province."

The government supporters applauded loudly.

"But gentlemen," turning again to the delegation, "I am still of the opinion even after listening to your cleverly worded speeches, that I will go on just as I have been doing, without the help you so generously offer. My wish for this fair, flower-decked land is that I may long be spared to guide its destiny in world affairs. I know there is no one but me—I tremble when I think of what might happen [to] these leaderless lambs—but I will go forward confidently, hoping that the good ship may come safely into port, with the same old skipper on the bridge. We are not worrying about the coming election, as you may think. We rest in confidence of the result, and will proudly unfurl, as we have these many years, the same old banner of the grand old party that had gone down many times to disgrace, but thank God, never to defeat."

The curtain fell, as the last word was spoken, but rose again to show the "House" standing, in their evening gowns. A bouquet of American beauty roses was handed up over the foot-lights to the Premier, who buried her face in them, with a sudden flood of loneliness. But the crowd was applauding, and again and again she was called forward.

The people came flocking in through the wings, pleading to be introduced to the "Premier," but she was gone.

In the crowd that ebbed slowly from the exits, no one noticed the stout gentleman with the dark glasses, who put his hat on before he reached the street, and seemed to be in great haste.

The comments of the people around him, jabbed him like poisoned arrows, and seared his heart like flame.

"I wonder was the Premier there," one man asked, wiping the traces of merriment from his glasses, "I've laughed till I'm sore—but I'm afraid he wouldn't see the same fun in it as I do."

"Well, if he's sport enough to laugh at this, I'll say he's some man," said another.

"That girl sure has her nerve—there isn't a man in this city would dare do it."

"She'll get his goat—if he ever hears her—I'd advise the old man to stay away."

"That's holding a mirror up to public life all right."

"But who is she?"

"The government will be well advised to pension that girl and get her out of the country—a few more sessions of the Women's Parliament, and the government can quit."

He hurried out into the brilliantly lighted street, stung by the laughter and idle words. His heart was bursting with rage, blind, bitter choking. He had been laughed at, ridiculed, insulted—and the men, whom he had made—had sat by applauding.

John Graham[3] had, all his life, dominated his family circle, his friends, his party, and for the last five years had ruled the Province. Success, applause, wealth, had come easily to him, and he had taken them as naturally as he accepted the breath of his nostrils. They were his. But on this bright night in

---

[3] In the story John Graham is meant to be the "real" name of Robertson Jones, the character based on Premier Rodmond Roblin.

NELLIE MCCLUNG

532

May, as he went angrily down the back street, unconsciously striking the pavement with his cane, with angry blows, the echo of the people's laughter in his ears was bitter as the pains of death.

[1921]

Speaking of Women

[. . .] Men are still haunted by the ghost of that old fear that there may not be enough of some things to go around if too many people have the same chance of obtaining a share. They join in the thanksgiving of the old blessing: "Six potatoes among the four of us; Thank the Lord there ain't any more of us."

This deep-rooted fear, that any change may bring personal inconvenience, lies at the root of much of the opposition to all reform.

Men held to slavery for long years, condoning and justifying it, because they were afraid that without slave labor life would not be comfortable. Certain men have opposed the advancement of women for the same reason; their hearts have been beset with the old black fear that, if women were allowed equal rights with men, some day some man would go home and find the dinner not ready, and the potatoes not even peeled! But not many give expression to this fear, as a reason for their opposition. They say they oppose the enfranchisement of women because they are too frail, weak and sweet to mingle in the hurly-burly of life; that women have far more influence now than if they could vote, and besides, God never intended them to vote, and it would break up the home, and make life a howling wilderness; the world would be full of neglected children (or none at all) and the homely joys of the fireside would vanish from the earth.

I remember once hearing an eloquent speaker cry out in alarm, "If women ever get the vote, who will teach us to say our prayers?"

Surely his experience of the franchised class had been an unfortunate one when he could not believe that anyone could both vote and pray!

That women are physically inferior to men is a strange reason for placing them under a further handicap, and we are surprised to find it advanced in all seriousness as an argument against woman suffrage. The exercising of the ballot does not require physical strength or endurance. Surely the opponents of woman suffrage do not mean to advocate that a strong fist should rule; just now we are a bit sensitive about this, and such doctrine is not popular. Might is not right; with our heart's blood we declare it is not!

No man has the right to citizenship on his weight, height, or lifting power; he exercises this right because he is a human being, with hands to work, brain to think, and a life to live.

It is to save women from toil and fatigue and all unpleasantness that the chivalrous ones would deny her the right of exercising the privileges of citizenship; though just how this could be brought about is not stated. Women are already in the battle of life; thirty per cent of the adult women of Canada and the United States are wage earners, and the percentage grows every day. How does the lack of the ballot help them? Is it any comfort to the woman who feels the sting of social injustice to reflect that she, at least, had no part in making such a law? Or do the poor women who go through the deserted streets in the grey dawn to their homes, alone and unprotected after their hard night's work at office-cleaning, ever proudly reflect that at least they have never had to drag their skirts in the mire of the polls, or be stared at by rude men as they approach the ballot box?

The physical disability of women is an additional reason for their having the franchise. The ballot is such a simple, easy way of expressing a preference or wish so "genteel," ladylike and dignified. [. . .]

Whether able or not able, women are out in the world, meeting its conditions, bearing its conditions, fighting their own battles, and always under a handicap.

Now the question is, what are we going to do about it?

One way, pursued by many, is to turn blind eyes to conditions as they are, and "haver" away about how frail and sweet women are; and that what they need is greater dependence. This babble of marriage and home for every woman sounds soothing, but does not seem to lead anywhere. Before the war, there were a million and a half more women than men in the Old Country alone—what will the proportion be when the war, with its fearful destruction of men, is over? One would think, to read the vaporings which pass as articles on the suffrage question, that good reliable husbands will be supplied upon request, if you would only write your name and address plainly and enclose a stamped envelope.

It is certainly true that the old avenues of labor have been closed to women. The introduction of machinery has done this, for now the work is done in factories, which formerly was done by hand labor. Women have not deserted their work, but the work has been taken from them. Sometimes it is said that women are trying to usurp men's place in the world; and if they were, it would be merely an act of retaliation, for men have already usurped women's sphere. We have men cooks, milliners, hairdressers, dressmakers, laundrymen—yes, men have invaded women's sphere. It is inevitable and cannot be changed by words of protest. People do well to accept the inevitable.

Men and women have two distinct spheres, when considered as men and women, but as human beings there is a great field of activity which they may—and do occupy in common. Now it is in this common field of activity that women are asking for equal privileges. There is not really much argument in pointing out that women cannot lay bricks, nor string electric wire, and therefore can never be regarded as man's equal in the matter of citizenship. Man cannot live by bricks alone! And we might with equal foolishness declare that because a man (as a rule) cannot thread a needle, or "turn a heel," therefore he should not ever be allowed to vote. Life is more than laying bricks or threading needles, for we have diverse gifts given to us by an all-wise Creator!

The exceptional woman can do many things, and these exceptions simply prove that there is no rule. There is a woman in the Qu'Appelle Valley who runs a big wheat farm and makes money. The Agricultural Editor of the *Manitoba Free Press*[4] is a woman who is acknowledged to be one of the best crop experts in Canada. Figures do not confuse her! Even if the average woman is not always sure of the binomial theorem, that does not prove that she is incapable of saying who shall make the laws under which she shall live.

But when all other arguments fail, the anti-suffragist can always go back to the "saintly motherhood" one, and "the hand that rocks." There is the perennial bloom that flourishes in all climates. Women are the mothers of the race—therefore they can be nothing else. When once a woman has a child, they argue, she must stay right on the job of raising it. Children have been blamed for many things very unjustly, and one of the most outstanding of these is that they take up all their mother's time, and are never able to care for themselves: that no one can do anything for the child but the mother; not even caring for it once every four years. From observation and experience, I wish to state positively that children do grow up—indeed they do—far too soon. The delightful days of babyhood and childhood are all too short, and they grow independent of us: and in a little while the day comes, no matter how hard we try to delay it, when they go out from us, to make their own way in the world, and we realize, with a queer stabbing at our hearts, that in the going of our first-born, our own youthfulness has gone too! And it seems such a cruel short time since he was born!

Yes, it is true. Children do grow up. And when they have gone from their mother, she still has her life to live.

The strong, active, virile woman of fifty, with twenty good years ahead of her, with a wealth of experience and wisdom, with a heart mellowed by time and filled with that large charity which only comes by knowledge—is a force to be reckoned with in the uplift of the world.

But if a woman has had the narrow outlook on life all the way along—if her efforts have been all made on behalf of her own family, she cannot quickly adjust herself to anything else, even when her family no longer need her. There is no sadder sight than the middle-aged woman left alone and purposeless when her family have gone. "I am a woman of fifty, strong, healthy—a college graduate," I once heard a woman say. "My children no longer need me—my attentions embarrass them—I gave them all my thought, all my time—I stifled every ambition to serve them. Now I am too old to gain new interests. I am a woman without a job."

Yet this type of woman, who had no thought beyond her own family circle, has been exalted greatly as the perfect mother, the "living sacrifice," the "perfect slave" of her children.

---

[4] In 1901 E. Cora Hind (1861–1942) was hired as an agriculture reporter for the *Manitoba Free Press*. She soon became the commercial and agricultural editor. From 1904 she published twenty-nine annual predictions on the prairie wheat crop that were used around the world to help determine the price of Canadian wheat. With McClung and Lillian Beynon Thomas, she also helped to form the Political Equality League in 1912.

It was a daring woman who claimed that she had a life of her own; and a perfect right to her own ambitions, hopes, interests, and desires.

But time goes on, and the world moves; and the ways of the world are growing kinder to women. Here and there in a sheltered eddy in the stream of life, where the big currents never are felt, you will find the old mossy arguments that women are intended to be wageless servants dependent upon man's bounty, with no life or hopes of their own. But the currents of life grow stronger and stronger in these terrible days, and the moss is being broken up, and driven out into the turbulent water.

On March 1st, at 3 o'clock in the afternoon, the Woman Suffrage Bill was given its second reading in the legislature of Alberta, and the women of the province gathered in large numbers to hear the debate. For over an hour before the galleries were opened, women waited at the foot of the stairs; white-haired women, women with little children by the hand, women with babies in their arms, smartly-dressed women, alert, tailor-made business women; quiet, dignified and earnest; they were all there; they filled the galleries; they packed every available space. Many were unable to find a place in the gallery, and stood outside in the corridors. "I consider it an honor to stand anywhere in the building," one bright-eyed old lady said when someone expressed their regret at not having a seat for her, "and I can read the speeches to-morrow, and imagine that I heard them."

When the Premier rose to move the second reading of the Bill the silence of the legislative chamber was tense, and the great mass of humanity in the galleries did not appear to breathe. The Premier, in a straightforward way, outlined the reasons for the granting of the franchise; he did not speak of it as a favor, a boon, a gift, or a privilege, but a right, and declared that the extension of the franchise was an act of justice; he did not once refer to us as the "fair sex," or assure us of his deep respect for us. The Leader of the Opposition, whose advocacy of woman franchise dates back many years, seconded the reading of the Bill; and short speeches were made by other members. There was only one who opposed it; one timorous brother declared it would break up the home.

On the same day that the Bill got its second reading, and at the same hour, the women of Calgary met together to discuss what women should do with the vote; and they drafted a platform, which must commend itself to all thinking people. Each subject discussed was for human betterment, and social welfare.

Women will make mistakes, of course,—and pay for them. That will be nothing new—they have always paid for men's mistakes. It will be a change to pay for their own. Democracy has its failures—it falls down utterly sometimes, we know, but not so often, or so hopelessly, as any other form of government. There have been beneficent despotisms, when a good king ruled absolutely. But unfortunately the next king was not good, and he drove the country to ruin. [. . .]

Democracy has its faults; the people may run the country to the dogs, but they will run it back again. People, including women, will make mistakes, but in paying for them they will learn wisdom.

[1916]

Lucy Maud Montgomery, born in Prince Edward Island in 1874, is renowned worldwide as the creator of Anne of Green Gables—perhaps the single most recognizable character in Canadian fiction. Before Montgomery was two years old, her mother died of tuberculosis, and shortly afterwards, her father moved to Saskatchewan for work. Raised by her strict maternal grandparents in Cavendish, P.E.I., until she was fifteen, Montgomery grew up with an overflowing imagination and a love of storytelling, even joining with friends in a "Story Club" such as the one featured in her novel *Anne of Green Gables* (1908). Named Lucy after her grandmother and Maud after Princess Alice Maud Mary (Queen Victoria's daughter), Montgomery preferred family and friends to call her Maud (or "Maud with no 'e'," as she joked). At fifteen she moved to Saskatchewan to live with her father and step-family. When that was unsuccessful, Montgomery returned to P.E.I. to live with her grandparents and teach piano. Apparently, however, in the style of her best characters, the noise was so great that her grandparents agreed to help pay her college tuition. She attended Prince of Wales College in Charlottetown, and obtained her teaching certificate by completing a two-year program in one year. In 1895 and 1896 she studied literature at Dalhousie University in Halifax, Nova Scotia. After a few years of teaching in rural P.E.I., she decided to try her hand at earning a living from her pen. This was clearly a good decision. Montgomery wrote twenty-four books, over five hundred short stories, and more than five hundred poems. Her most famous book, *Anne of Green Gables*, has been published in over twenty languages and has sold more than a million copies. The red-headed girl with the fiery temperament has become a fixture of Canadian iconography.

By 1901 Montgomery was employed at a Halifax newspaper, *The Daily Echo*, but was not content to write "potboilers." In 1905, she began writing *Anne of Green Gables*. It took rejections from five publishers to find one who was willing to publish it. After the fifth rejection, Montgomery was reportedly so disappointed that she put the manuscript in an old hatbox and set it in the cupboard. Finally, the American publisher L.C. Page & Company accepted the manuscript, and the novel was published in 1908. Upon publication, *Anne of Green Gables* met with immediate and resounding success. As literary biographer Elizabeth MacLeod notes, "[S]oon Maud became famous worldwide and, to her amazement, not only with children. Canada's Governor General and Great Britain's Prime Minister were fans. Mark Twain, who wrote about Tom Sawyer and Huckleberry Finn, even sent her a fan letter." Twain called Anne the "most lovable childhood heroine since the immortal Alice." By 1910, Montgomery received $7,000 a year in royalty payments for *Anne*. This rose to $13,000 a year in 1914. This was a fortune, as MacLeod points out, when the average worker in P.E.I. earned less than $300 a year.

Even though she had not originally planned a series, the success of *Anne of Green Gables* and its sequel, *Anne of Avonlea* (1909), brought demands from her publishers for further sequels. After *Rilla of Ingleside* (the story of Anne's daughter) appeared in 1921, Montgomery wrote, "I am sick of [Anne] and wonder that the public isn't too." But, as biographer Mollie Gillen explains, the public was not sick of Anne, and as late as 1936 and

1939 two more *Anne* books appeared: *Anne of Windy Poplars* and *Anne of Ingleside*. It may be indicative of Montgomery's growing impatience with her character that Anne becomes more conformist as one moves through the novels. Subsequently, Montgomery began a new series based on a character who was closer to her own heart: *Emily of New Moon* (1923), *Emily Climbs* (1925), and *Emily's Quest* (1927). "People were never right in saying I was Anne," Montgomery wrote, "but in some respects they will be right if they write me down as Emily."

Also of interest is Montgomery's concern with the education of women at the turn of the century—a topic that had been widely debated in the previous decades, notably by the well-known Christian feminist thinker Agnes Maule Machar. Montgomery, unlike her feminist contemporaries Emily Murphy and Nellie McClung, was not an advocate for women's suffrage, though like both women, she did believe in the inherent maternalism of women and in the importance of education in making women better mothers. In effect, while her story "The Education of Betty," published in *Further Chronicles of Avonlea* (1920), expresses resistance to the limited roles imposed on women at the time, it retreats from a too radical feminist agenda through its conclusion of true love in marriage. It is, therefore, difficult to decide whether Montgomery advocates an escape from predetermined gender roles for women or whether she reinforces women's limited position within society. Betty, like Anne, is characterized by spunk, spontaneity, self-sufficiency, and forthrightness (much like the Canadian women in Sara Jeannette Duncan's fiction). The editor of a scholarly edition of *Anne of Green Gables*, Cecily Devereux, argues that Montgomery "negotiates in problematic ways early twentieth-century tensions between restrictive ideas of femininity and first-wave feminist politics." So too does "The Education of Betty," for it signals Montgomery's enduring commitment to the intertwining of education and romance. The story also plays on the myth of Pygmalion and Galatea, in which a teacher/creator falls in love with his student/creation.

After a secret engagement that lasted five years, and shortly after her grandmother's death in 1911, Montgomery married Ewan Macdonald. They moved to Ontario where he had accepted a position as the minister of St. Paul's Presbyterian Church, Leaskdale (in Uxbridge Township). There the couple had three sons, one of whom died at birth. Although Montgomery remained in Ontario until her death in 1942, most of her books are set in P.E.I. She was buried at the Cavendish Community Cemetery in P.E.I.

The enduring international success of *Anne of Green Gables* and its many sequels is staggering. Today, with thousands of active *Anne of Green Gables* fan clubs and websites, there is virtually a cult of Anne. Attention comes from all parts of the globe, from Charlottetown to Stockholm to Osaka. An interesting cultural phenomenon is the particular fascination Anne holds for Japanese women. The first translation of the novel into Japanese, by Hanako Muraoka, was published in 1952. It has remained in print ever since. Within P.E.I., the tourist industry has capitalized on the popularity of Montgomery's writing, and consistently markets the province as the home of Anne and Green Gables. According to Parks Canada promotional material, each year hundreds of thousands of visitors from around the world visit the "Lucy Maud Montgomery Cavendish National Historic Site" and the house which inspired the setting for the novels.

The house of the fictional characters is open to tours online and in person.

Critical interest in Montgomery seems to be on the rise and does not appear to be abating soon. Nevertheless, as Devereux observes, Montgomery herself felt excluded from the male, modernist literary estab... English Canada, even thoug... much better-known and her... more widely read than that... other author in Canada."

The Education of Betty

When Sara Currie married Jack Churchill I was broken-hearted . . . or believed myself to be so, which, in a boy of twenty-two, amounts to pretty much the same thing. Not that I took the world into my confidence; that was never the Douglas way, and I held myself in honor bound to live up to the family traditions. I thought, then, that nobody but Sara knew; but I dare say, now, that Jack knew it also, for I don't think Sara could have helped telling him. If he did know, however, he did not let me see that he did, and never insulted me by any implied sympathy; on the contrary, he asked me to be his best man. Jack was always a thoroughbred.

I was best man. Jack and I had always been bosom friends, and, although I had lost my sweetheart, I did not intend to lose my friend into the bargain. Sara had made a wise choice, for Jack was twice the man I was; he had had to work for his living, which perhaps accounts for it.

So I danced at Sara's wedding as if my heart were as light as my heels; but, after she and Jack had settled down at Glenby I closed The Maples and went abroad . . . being, as I have hinted, one of those unfortunate mortals who need consult nothing but their own whims in the matter of time and money. I stayed away for ten years, during which The Maples was given over to moths and rust, while I enjoyed life elsewhere. I did enjoy it hugely, but always under protest, for I felt that a broken-hearted man ought not to enjoy himself as I did. It jarred on my sense of fitness, and I tried to moderate my zest, and think more of the past than I did. It was no use; the present insisted on being intrusive and pleasant; as for the future . . . well, there was no future.

Then Jack Churchill, poor fellow, died. A year after his death, I went home and again asked Sara to marry me, as in duty bound. Sara again declined, alleging that her heart was buried in Jack's grave, or words to that effect. I found that it did not much matter . . . of course, at thirty-two, one does not take these things to heart as at twenty-two. I had enough to occupy me in getting The Maples into working order, and beginning to educate Betty.

Betty was Sara's ten-year-old daughter, and she had been thoroughly spoiled. That is to say, she had been allowed her own way in everything and, having inherited her father's outdoor tastes, had simply run wild. She was a thorough tomboy, a thin, scrawny little thing without a trace of Sara's beauty. Betty took after her father's dark, tall race and, on the occasion of my first introduction to her, seemed to be all legs and neck. There were points about her, though, which I considered promising. She had fine, almond-shaped, hazel eyes, the smallest

L.M. MONTGOMERY

.d most shapely hands and feet I ever saw, and two enormous braids of thick, nut-brown hair.

For Jack's sake I decided to bring his daughter up properly. Sara couldn't do it, and didn't try. I saw that, if somebody didn't take Betty in hand, wisely and firmly, she would certainly be ruined. There seemed to be nobody except myself at all interested in the matter, so I determined to see what an old bachelor could do as regards bringing up a girl in the way she should go. I might have been her father; as it was, her father had been my best friend. Who had a better right to watch over his daughter? I determined to be a father to Betty, and do all for her that the most devoted parent could do. It was, self-evidently, my duty.

I told Sara I was going to take Betty in hand. Sara sighed one of the plaintive little sighs which I had once thought so charming, but now, to my surprise, found faintly irritating, and said that she would be very much obliged if I would.

"I feel that I am not able to cope with the problem of Betty's education, Stephen," she admitted. "Betty is a strange child . . . all Churchill. Her poor father indulged her in everything, and she has a will of her own, I assure you. I have really no control over her, whatever. She does as she pleases, and is ruining her complexion by running and galloping out of doors the whole time. Not that she had much complexion to start with. The Churchills never had, you know." . . . Sara cast a complacent glance at her delicately tinted reflection in the mirror. . . . "I tried to make Betty wear a sunbonnet this summer, but I might as well have talked to the wind."

A vision of Betty in a sunbonnet presented itself to my mind, and afforded me so much amusement that I was grateful to Sara for having furnished it. I rewarded her with a compliment.

"It is to be regretted that Betty has not inherited her mother's charming color," I said, "but we must do the best we can for her under her limitations. She may have improved vastly by the time she has grown up. And, at least, we must make a lady of her; she is a most alarming tomboy at present, but there is good material to work upon . . . there must be, in the Churchill and Currie blend. But even the best material may be spoiled by unwise handling. I think I can promise you that I will not spoil it. I feel that Betty is my vocation; and I shall set myself up as a rival of Wordsworth's 'nature,'[1] of whose methods I have always had a decided distrust, in spite of his insidious verses."

Sara did not understand me in the least; but, then, she did not pretend to.

"I confide Betty's education entirely to you, Stephen," she said, with another plaintive sigh. "I feel sure I could not put it into better hands. You have always been a person who could be thoroughly depended on."

---

[1] Wordsworth's poetry was famous for its celebration of the nurturing influence of nature in ways that resisted the institutional constraints of structured education. In his poem "Ode: Intimations on Immortality from Recollections of Early Childhood," Wordsworth expounded his theory about children being born into the world in an ideal state, "trailing clouds of glory," and in the process of growing up and becoming "educated" gradually losing their innocence.

Well, that was something by way of reward for a life-long devotion. I felt that I was satisfied with my position as unofficial adviser-in-chief to Sara and self-appointed guardian of Betty. I also felt that, for the furtherance of the cause I had taken to heart, it was a good thing that Sara had again refused to marry me. I had a sixth sense which informed me that a staid old family friend might succeed with Betty where a stepfather would have signally failed. Betty's loyalty to her father's memory was passionate and vehement; she would view his supplanter with resentment and distrust; but his old familiar comrade was a person to be taken to her heart.

Fortunately for the success of my enterprise, Betty liked me. She told me this with the same engaging candor she would have used in informing me that she hated me, if she had happened to take a bias in that direction, saying frankly:

"You are one of the very nicest old folks I know, Stephen. Yes, you are a ripping good fellow!"

This made my task a comparatively easy one; I sometimes shudder to think what it might have been if Betty had not thought I was a "ripping good fellow." I should have stuck to it, because that is my way; but Betty would have made my life a misery to me. She had startling capacities for tormenting people when she chose to exert them; I certainly should not have liked to be numbered among Betty's foes.

I rode over to Glenby the next morning after my paternal interview with Sara, intending to have a frank talk with Betty and lay the foundations of a good understanding on both sides. Betty was a sharp child, with a disconcerting knack of seeing straight through grindstones; she would certainly perceive and probably resent any underhand management. I thought it best to tell her plainly that I was going to look after her.

When, however, I had encountered Betty, tearing madly down the beech avenue with a couple of dogs, her loosened hair streaming behind her like a banner of independence, and had lifted her, hatless and breathless, up before me on my mare, I found that Sara had saved me the trouble of an explanation.

"Mother says you are going to take charge of my education, Stephen," said Betty, as soon as she could speak. "I'm glad, because I think that, for an old person, you have a good deal of sense. I suppose my education has to be seen to, some time or other, and I'd rather you'd do it than anybody else I know."

"Thank you, Betty," I said gravely. "I hope I shall deserve your good opinion of my sense. I shall expect you to do as I tell you, and be guided by my advice in everything."

"Yes, I will," said Betty, "because I'm sure you won't tell me to do anything I'd really hate to do. You won't shut me up in a room and make me sew, will you? Because I won't do it."

I assured her I would not.

"Nor send me to a boarding-school," pursued Betty. "Mother's always threatening to send me to one. I suppose she would have done it before this, only she knew I'd run away. You won't send me to a boarding-school, will you, Stephen? Because I won't go."

"No," I said obligingly. "I won't. I should never dream of cooping a wild little thing, like you, up in a boarding-school. You'd fret your heart out like a caged skylark."

"I know you and I are going to get along together splendidly, Stephen," said Betty, rubbing her brown cheek chummily against my shoulder. "You are so good at understanding. Very few people are. Even dad darling didn't understand. He let me do just as I wanted to, just because I wanted to, not because he really understood that I couldn't be tame and play with dolls. I hate dolls! Real live babies are jolly; but dogs and horses are ever so much nicer than dolls."

"But you must have lessons, Betty. I shall select your teachers and superintend your studies, and I shall expect you to do me credit along that line, as well as along all others."

"I'll try, honest and true, Stephen," declared Betty. And she kept her word.

At first I looked upon Betty's education as a duty; in a very short time it had become a pleasure . . . the deepest and most abiding interest of my life. As I had premised, Betty was good material, and responded to my training with gratifying plasticity. Day by day, week by week, month by month, her character and temperament unfolded naturally under my watchful eye. It was like beholding the gradual development of some rare flower in one's garden. A little checking and pruning here, a careful training of shoot and tendril there, and, lo, the reward of grace and symmetry!

Betty grew up as I would have wished Jack Churchill's girl to grow—spirited and proud, with the fine spirit and gracious pride of pure womanhood, loyal and loving, with the loyalty and love of a frank and unspoiled nature; true to her heart's core, hating falsehood and sham—as crystal-clear a mirror of maidenhood as ever man looked into and saw himself reflected back in such a halo as made him ashamed of not being more worthy of it. Betty was kind enough to say that I had taught her everything she knew. But what had she not taught me? If there were a debt between us, it was on my side.

Sara was fairly well satisfied. It was not my fault that Betty was not better looking, she said. I had certainly done everything for her mind and character that could be done. Sara's manner implied that these unimportant details did not count for much, balanced against the lack of a pink-and-white skin and dimpled elbows; but she was generous enough not to blame me.

"When Betty is twenty-five," I said patiently—I had grown used to speaking patiently to Sara—"she will be a magnificent woman—far handsomer than you ever were, Sara, in your pinkest and whitest prime. Where are your eyes, my dear lady, that you can't see the promise of loveliness in Betty?"

"Betty is seventeen, and she is as lanky and brown as ever she was," sighed Sara. "When I was seventeen I was the belle of the county and had had five proposals. I don't believe the thought of a lover has ever entered Betty's head."

"I hope not," I said shortly. Somehow, I did not like the suggestion. "Betty is a child yet. For pity's sake, Sara, don't go putting nonsensical ideas into her head."

"I'm afraid I can't," mourned Sara, as if it were something to be regretted. "You have filled it too full of books and things like that. I've every confidence in your judgment, Stephen—and really you've done wonders with Betty. But don't you think you've made her rather too clever? Men don't like women who are too clever. Her poor father, now—he always said that a woman who liked books better than beaux was an unnatural creature."

I didn't believe Jack had ever said anything so foolish. Sara imagined things. But I resented the aspersion of blue-stockingness[2] cast on Betty.

"When the time comes for Betty to be interested in beaux," I said severely, "she will probably give them all due attention. Just at present, her head is a great deal better filled with books than with silly premature fancies and sentimentalities. I'm a critical old fellow—but I'm satisfied with Betty, Sara—perfectly satisfied."

Sara sighed. "Oh, I dare say she is all right, Stephen. And I'm really grateful to you. I'm sure I could have done nothing at all with her. It's not your fault, of course—but I can't help wishing she were a little more like other girls."

I galloped away from Glenby in a rage. What a blessing Sara had not married me in my absurd youth! She would have driven me wild with her sighs and her obtuseness and her everlasting pink-and-whiteness. But there—there—there— gently! She was a sweet, good-hearted little woman; she had made Jack happy; and she had contrived, heaven only knew how, to bring a rare creature like Betty into the world. For that, much might be forgiven her. By the time I reached The Maples and had flung myself down in an old, kinky, comfortable chair in my library I had forgiven her, and was even paying her the compliment of thinking seriously over what she had said.

Was Betty really unlike other girls? That is to say, unlike them in any respect wherein she should resemble them? I did not wish this; although I was a crusty old bachelor, I approved of girls, holding them the sweetest things the good God has made. I wanted Betty to have her full complement of girlhood in all its best and highest manifestation. Was there anything lacking?

I observed Betty very closely during the next week or so, riding over to Glenby every day and riding back at night, meditating upon my observations. Eventually, I concluded to do what I had never thought myself in the least likely to do. I would send Betty to a boarding-school for a year. It was necessary that she should learn how to live with other girls.

I went over to Glenby the next day and found Betty under the beeches on the lawn, just back from a canter. She was sitting on the dappled mare I had given her on her last birthday, and was laughing at the antics of her rejoicing dogs around her. I looked at her with pleasure; it gladdened me to see how much, nay, how totally a child she still was, despite her Churchill height. Her hair, under her velvet cap, still hung over her shoulders in the same thick plaits; her face had the firm

---

[2] The term "blue stocking" refers to women with intellectual interests. The term originated in reference to the Blue Stocking Society, a nickname for a women's literary club in London in the late eighteenth century.

leanness of early youth, but its curves were very fine and delicate. The brown skin, that worried Sara so, was flushed through with dusky color from her gallop; her long, dark eyes were filled with the beautiful unconsciousness of childhood. More than all, the soul in her was still the soul of a child. I found myself wishing that it could always remain so. But I knew it could not; the woman must blossom out some day; it was my duty to see that the flower fulfilled the promise of the bud.

When I told Betty that she must go away to a school for a year, she shrugged, frowned and consented. Betty had learned that she must consent to what I decreed, even when my decrees were opposed to her likings, as she had once fondly believed they never would be. But Betty had acquired confidence in me to the beautiful extent of acquiescing in everything I commanded.

"I'll go, of course, since you wish it, Stephen," she said. "But why do you want me to go? You must have a reason—you always have a reason for anything you do. What is it?"

"That is for you to find out, Betty," I said. "By the time you come back, you will have discovered it, I think. If not, it will not have proved itself a good reason and shall be forgotten."

When Betty went away I bade her good-by without burdening her with any useless words of advice.

"Write to me every week, and remember that you are Betty Churchill," I said.

Betty was standing on the steps above, among her dogs. She came down a step and put her arms about my neck.

"I'll remember that you are my friend, and that I must live up to you," she said. "Good-by, Stephen."

She kissed me two or three times—good, hearty smacks! did I not say she was still a child?—and stood waving her hand to me as I rode away. I looked back at the end of the avenue and saw her standing there, short-skirted and hat-less, fronting the lowering sun with those fearless eyes of hers. So I looked my last on the child Betty.

That was a lonely year. My occupation was gone and I began to fear that I had outlived my usefulness. Life seemed flat, stale, and unprofitable. Betty's weekly letters were all that lent it any savor. They were spicy and piquant enough. Betty was discovered to have unsuspected talents in the epistolary line. At first she was dolefully homesick, and begged me to let her come home. When I refused—it was amazingly hard to refuse—she sulked through three letters, then cheered up and began to enjoy herself. But it was nearly the end of the year when she wrote:

"I've found out why you sent me here, Stephen—and I'm glad you did."

I had to be away from home on unavoidable business the day Betty returned to Glenby. But the next afternoon I went over. I found Betty out and Sara in. The latter was beaming. Betty was so much improved, she declared delightedly. I would hardly know "the dear child."

This alarmed me terribly. What on earth had they done to Betty? I found that she had gone up to the pineland for a walk, and thither I betook myself speedily. When I saw her coming down a long, golden-brown alley, I stepped behind a tree to watch her—I wished to see her, myself unseen. As she drew near I gazed at her with pride, and admiration and amazement—and, under it all, a strange, dreadful, heart-sinking, which I could not understand and which I had never in all my life experienced before—no, not even when Sara had refused me.

Betty was a woman! Not by virtue of the simple white dress that clung to her tall, slender figure, revealing lines of exquisite grace and litheness; not by virtue of the glossy masses of dark brown hair heaped high on her head and held there in wonderful shining coils; not by virtue of added softness of curve and daintiness of outline; not because of all these, but because of the dream and wonder and seeking in her eyes. She was a woman, looking, all unconscious of her quest, for love.

The understanding of the change in her came home to me with a shock that must have left me, I think, something white about the lips. I was glad. She was what I had wished her to become. But I wanted the child Betty back; this womanly Betty seemed far away from me.

I stepped out into the path and she saw me, with a brightening of her whole face. She did not rush forward and fling herself into my arms as she would have done a year ago; but she came towards me swiftly, holding out her hand. I had thought her slightly pale when I had first seen her; but now I concluded I had been mistaken, for there was a wonderful sunrise of color in her face. I took her hand—there were no kisses this time.

"Welcome home, Betty," I said.

"Oh, Stephen, it is so good to be back," she breathed, her eyes shining.

She did not say it was good to see me again, as I had hoped she would do. Indeed, after the first minute of greeting, she seemed a trifle cool and distant. We walked for an hour in the pine wood and talked. Betty was brilliant, witty, self-possessed, altogether charming. I thought her perfect and yet my heart ached. What a glorious young thing she was, in that splendid youth of hers! What a prize for some lucky man—confound the obtrusive thought! No doubt we should soon be overrun at Glenby with lovers. I should stumble over some forlorn youth at every step! Well, what of it? Betty would marry, of course. It would be my duty to see that she got a good husband, worthy of her, as men go. I thought I preferred the old duty of superintending her studies. But there, it was all the same thing—merely a post-graduate course in applied knowledge. When she began to learn life's greatest lesson of love, I, the tried and true old family friend and mentor, must be on hand to see that the teacher was what I would have him be, even as I had formerly selected her instructor in French and botany. Then, and not until then, would Betty's education be complete.

I rode home very soberly. When I reached The Maples, I did what I had not done for years . . . looked critically at myself in the mirror. The realization that I had grown older came home to me with a new and unpleasant force. There were marked lines on my lean face, and silver glints in the dark hair over my temples. When Betty was ten she had thought me "an old person." Now, at eighteen, she probably thought me a veritable ancient of days. Pshaw, what did it matter? And yet . . . I thought of her as I had seen her, standing under the pines, and something cold and painful laid its hand on my heart.

My premonitions as to lovers proved correct. Glenby was soon infested with them. Heaven knows where they all came from. I had not supposed there was a quarter as many young men in the whole county; but there they were. Sara was in the seventh heaven of delight. Was not Betty at last a belle? As for the proposals . . . well, Betty never counted her scalps in public; but every once in a while a visiting youth dropped out and was seen no more at Glenby. One could guess what that meant.

Betty apparently enjoyed all this. I grieve to say that she was a bit of a coquette. I tried to cure her of this serious defect, but for once I found that I had undertaken something I could not accomplish. In vain I lectured. Betty only laughed; in vain I gravely rebuked, Betty only flirted more vivaciously than before. Men might come and men might go, but Betty went on forever. I endured this sort of thing for a year, and then I decided that it was time to interfere seriously. I must find a husband for Betty . . . my fatherly duty would not be fulfilled until I had . . . nor, indeed, my duty to society. She was not a safe person to have running at large.

None of the men who haunted Glenby was good enough for her. I decided that my nephew, Frank, would do very well. He was a capital young fellow, handsome, clean-souled, and whole-hearted. From a worldly point of view, he was what Sara would have termed an excellent match; he had money, social standing, and a rising reputation as a clever young lawyer. Yes, he should have Betty, confound him!

They had never met. I set the wheels going at once. The sooner all the fuss was over the better. I hated fuss, and there was bound to be a good deal of it. But I went about the business like an accomplished matchmaker. I invited Frank to visit The Maples and, before he came, I talked much . . . but not too much . . . of him to Betty, mingling judicious praise and still more judicious blame together. Women never like a paragon. Betty heard me with more gravity than she usually accorded to my dissertations on young men. She even condescended to ask several questions about him. This I thought a good sign.

To Frank I had said not a word about Betty; when he came to The Maples I took him over to Glenby and, coming upon Betty wandering about among the beeches in the sunset, I introduced him without any warning.

He would have been more than mortal if he had not fallen in love with her upon the spot. It was not in the heart of man to resist her . . . that dainty, alluring bit of womanhood. She was all in white, with flowers in her hair, and, for a moment, I could have murdered Frank or any other man who dared to commit the sacrilege of loving her.

Then I pulled myself together and left them alone. I might have gone in and talked to Sara . . . two old folks gently reviewing their youth while the young folks courted outside . . . but I did not. I prowled about the pine wood, and tried to forget how blithe and handsome that curly-headed boy, Frank, was, and what a flash had sprung into his eyes when he had seen Betty. Well, what of it? Was not that what I had brought him there for? And was I not pleased at the success of my scheme? Certainly I was! Delighted!

Next day Frank went to Glenby without even making the poor pretense of asking me to accompany him. I spent the time of his absence overseeing the construction of a new greenhouse I was having built. I was conscientious in my supervision; but I felt no interest in it. The place was intended for roses, and roses made me think of the pale yellow ones Betty had worn at her breast one evening the week before, when, all lovers being unaccountably absent, we had wandered together under the pines and talked as in the old days before her young womanhood and my gray hairs had risen up to divide us. She had dropped a rose on the brown floor, and I had sneaked back, after I had left her in the house, to get it, before I went home. I had it now in my pocket-book. Confound it, mightn't a future uncle cherish a family affection for his prospective niece?

Frank's wooing seemed to prosper. The other young sparks, who had haunted Glenby, faded away after his advent. Betty treated him with most encouraging sweetness; Sara smiled on him; I stood in the background, like a benevolent god of the machine, and flattered myself that I pulled the strings.

At the end of a month something went wrong. Frank came home from Glenby one day in the dumps, and moped for two whole days. I rode down myself on the third. I had not gone much to Glenby that month; but, if there were trouble Betty-ward, it was my duty to make smooth the rough places.

As usual, I found Betty in the pineland. I thought she looked rather pale and dull . . . fretting about Frank, no doubt. She brightened up when she saw me, evidently expecting that I had come to straighten matters out; but she pretended to be haughty and indifferent.

"I am glad you haven't forgotten us altogether, Stephen," she said coolly. "You haven't been down for a week."

"I'm flattered that you noticed it," I said, sitting down on a fallen tree and looking up at her as she stood, tall and lithe, against an old pine, with her eyes averted. "I shouldn't have supposed you'd want an old fogy like myself poking about and spoiling the idyllic moments of love's young dream."

"Why do you always speak of yourself as old?" said Betty, crossly, ignoring my reference to Frank.

"Because I am old, my dear. Witness these gray hairs."

I pushed up my hat to show them the more recklessly.

Betty barely glanced at them.

"You have just enough to give you a distinguished look," she said, "and you are only forty. A man is in his prime at forty. He never has any sense until he is forty—and sometimes he doesn't seem to have any even then," she concluded impertinently.

My heart beat. Did Betty suspect? Was that last sentence meant to inform me that she was aware of my secret folly, and laughed at it?

"I came over to see what has gone wrong between you and Frank," I said gravely.

Betty bit her lips.

"Nothing," she said.

"Betty," I said reproachfully, "I brought you up . . . or endeavored to bring you up . . . to speak the truth, the whole truth, and nothing but the truth. Don't tell me I have failed. I'll give you another chance. Have you quarreled with Frank?"

"No," said that maddening Betty, "*he* quarreled with me. He went away in a temper and I do not care if he never comes back!"

I shook my head.

"This won't do, Betty. As your old family friend, I still claim the right to scold you until you have a husband to do the scolding. You mustn't torment Frank. He is too fine a fellow. You must marry him, Betty."

"Must I?" said Betty, a dusky red flaming out on her cheek. She turned her eyes on me in a most disconcerting fashion. "Do *you* wish me to marry Frank, Stephen?"

Betty had a wretched habit of emphasizing pronouns in a fashion calculated to rattle anybody.

"Yes, I do wish it, because I think it will be best for you," I replied, without looking at her. "You must marry sometime, Betty, and Frank is the only man I know to whom I could trust you. As your guardian, I have an interest in seeing you well and wisely settled for life. You have always taken my advice and obeyed my wishes; and you've always found my way the best, in the long run, haven't you, Betty? You won't prove rebellious now, I'm sure. You know quite well that I am advising you for your own good. Frank is a splendid young fellow, who loves you with all his heart. Marry him, Betty. Mind, I don't *command*. I have no right to do that, and you are too old to be ordered about, if I had. But I wish and advise it. Isn't that enough, Betty?"

I had been looking away from her all the time I was talking, gazing determinedly down a sunlit vista of pines. Every word I said seemed to tear my heart, and come from my lips stained with lifeblood. Yes, Betty should marry Frank! But, good God, what would become of me!

Betty left her station under the pine tree, and walked around me until she got right in front of my face. I couldn't help looking at her, for if I moved my eyes she moved, too. There was nothing meek or submissive about her; her head was held high, her eyes were blazing, and her cheeks were crimson. But her words were meek enough.

"I will marry Frank if you wish it, Stephen," she said. "You are my friend. I have never crossed your wishes, and, as you say, I have never regretted being always guided by them. I will do exactly as you wish in this case also, I promise you that. But, in so solemn a question, I must be very certain what you *do* wish. There must be no doubt in my mind or heart. Look me squarely in the eyes, Stephen—as you haven't done once to-day, no, nor once since I came home from school—and, so looking, tell me that you wish me to marry Frank Douglas and I will do it! *Do* you, Stephen?"

I had to look her in the eyes, since nothing else would do her; and, as I did so, all the might of manhood in me rose up in hot revolt against the lie I would have told her. That unfaltering, impelling gaze of hers drew the truth from my lips in spite of myself.

"No, I don't wish you to marry Frank Douglas, a thousand times no!" I said passionately. "I don't wish you to marry any man on earth but myself. I love you—I love you, Betty. You are dearer to me than life—dearer to me than my own happiness. It was your happiness I thought of—and so I asked you to marry Frank because I believed he would make you a happy woman. That is all!"

Betty's defiance went from her like a flame blown out. She turned away and drooped her proud head.

"It could not have made me a happy woman to marry one man, loving another," she said, in a whisper.

I got up and went over to her.

"Betty, whom do you love?" I asked, also in a whisper.

"You," she murmured meekly—oh, so meekly, my proud little girl!

"Betty," I said brokenly, "I'm old—too old for you—I'm more than twenty years your senior—I'm—"

"Oh!" Betty wheeled around on me and stamped her foot. "Don't mention your age to me again. I don't care if you're as old as Methuselah.[3] But I'm not going to coax you to marry me, sir! If you won't, I'll never marry anybody—I'll live and die an old maid. You can please yourself, of course!"

She turned away, half-laughing, half-crying; but I caught her in my arms and crushed her sweet lips against mine.

"Betty, I'm the happiest man in the world—and I was the most miserable when I came here."

"You deserved to be," said Betty cruelly. "I'm glad you were. Any man as stupid as you deserves to be unhappy. What do you think I felt like, loving you with all my heart, and seeing you simply throwing me at another man's head. Why, I've always loved you, Stephen; but I didn't know it until I went to that detestable school. Then I found out—and I thought that was why you had sent me. But, when I came home, you almost broke my heart. That was why I flirted so with all those poor, nice boys—I wanted to hurt you, but I never thought I succeeded. You just went on being *fatherly*. Then, when you brought Frank here, I almost gave up hope; and I tried to make up my mind to marry him; I should have done it if you had insisted. But I had to have one more try for happiness first. I had just one little hope to inspire me with sufficient boldness. I saw you, that night, when you came back here and picked up my rose! I had come back, myself, to be alone and unhappy."

"It is the most wonderful thing that ever happened—that you should love me," I said.

[3] The oldest man mentioned in the Bible: "And all the days of Methuselah were nine hundred sixty and nine years: and he died" (Genesis 5:27).

"It's not—I couldn't help it," said Betty, nestling her brown head on my shoulder. "You taught me everything else, Stephen, so nobody but you could teach me how to love. You've made a thorough thing of educating me."

"When will you marry me, Betty?" I asked.

"As soon as I can fully forgive you for trying to make me marry somebody else," said Betty.

It was rather hard lines on Frank, when you come to think of it. But, such is the selfishness of human nature that we didn't think much about Frank. The young fellow behaved like the Douglas he was. Went a little white about the lips when I told him, wished me all happiness, and went quietly away, "gentleman unafraid."

He has since married and is, I understand, very happy. Not as happy as I am, of course; that is impossible, because there is only one Betty in the world, and she is my wife.

[1920]

ROBERT SERVICE ■ (1874–1958)

Robert Service's obituary in the Pittsburgh *Sun-Telegraph* of 16 September 1958 read: "A great poet died last week in Lancieux, France, at the age of 84." While the word "great" is disputable, the international love of Service's poetry in evidence here is not. He was a "people's poet," also known as the "Canadian Kipling," who tapped into the popular desire for a good story, a love of easy rhyme, a need for melodramatic and often humorous tales about the common man and woman, and a fascination with the wild North. His best-known poetry immortalized the eccentricity and adventure of the Klondike Gold Rush of 1896–99. Not only was Service a popular sensation, he was also a commercial success. In *Prisoners of the North*, the popular historian Pierre Berton (who had been a neighbour of Service during his own Yukon childhood) writes that "the literary gold he panned was better than any prospector's."

Service was born in Preston, Lancashire, England, to Scottish parents. After growing up in Glasgow and working in a bank for several years, he moved to Canada at the age of twenty-one in search of adventure. He is said to have had $15 in his pocket and a dream of becoming a cowboy. Working at odd jobs around British Columbia (such as being a "cow-juice-jerker" [a dairy farm hand], a storekeeper, and a tutor in the Cowichan valley) from 1896 to 1904, Service met a variety of working people. However, it wasn't until he moved to the Yukon that Service began to write the poetry that made him famous. After failing the University of Victoria entrance exam, Service was hired by the Canadian Imperial Bank of Commerce and posted to its branch in Whitehorse. He was later posted to Dawson City. Banker by day, poet by night, story has it that Service penned his famous poem "The Shooting of Dan McGrew" during a slow period at the bank, then tossed it into a drawer with a number of other poems. Not convinced that his poems were worthy of wide publication, he decided to produce a slim collection at his own expense to give as Christmas presents to his friends. When the Toronto publisher William Briggs received the poems, he realized the potential of the work and returned Service's money, publishing *Songs of a Sourdough* soon after (1907). The collection was reissued as *The Spell of the Yukon and Other Verses* later in the year, when it was published in the United States by a New York publisher. These poems took the form of fictionalized narratives about local Yukoners. For instance, the namesake of his most famous character, Sam McGee, was a Dawson prospector whose name Service had lifted from the bank's ledger and who actually came from Lindsay, Ontario. The real McGee left the Yukon in 1909 and is said to have spent much of his life responding to queries about whether he was "warm enough yet." With poems like "The Cremation of Sam McGee," Service gained an international following. Calling himself "a rhyme-rustler, rugged and shameless," he was as surprised as anyone about the success of his poems.

With the success of his first two collections of poems about the Yukon, *Songs of a Sourdough* (1907) and *Ballads of a Cheechako* (1909), he earned more than enough money to quit his job at the bank and become a full-time writer and traveller. In 1912 he published another celebrated collection, *Rhymes of a Rolling Stone*. His published work is eclectic. It includes thirteen books of poetry, six novels, two memoirs, and even a book on physical fitness (*Why Not Grow Young? Keeping Fit at Fifty* [1928]). Living in Paris before the First World War, Service met the literary and intellectual elite of the day, and wrote *The Pretender: The Story of the Latin Quarter* (1914). In a manner similar to Stephen Leacock's *Arcadian Adventures with the Idle Rich*, published in the same year, Service exposed the pretensions of the elite. Left-leaning all his life (he was a socialist in his youth), Service was committed to

voicing the stories of the people. Over the years he spent time as a war correspondent for the *Toronto Star*, an ambulance driver during the First World War (when he wrote another bestseller, *Rhymes of a Red Cross Man* [1916]), and a scriptwriter and novelist in Hollywood. During the Second World War, Service and his family lived in Vancouver (1940–45), but they returned to France after the war. He died in Lancieux, Brittany, and is buried there in the local cemetery.

Service's cabin in Dawson City was preserved as a tourist site by the Imperial Order of the Daughters of the Empire in 1917 in an effort to raise money for the war. It remains a tourist destination and is now operated by the National Historic Sites Branch of Parks Canada to commemorate where the "bard of the Klondike" lived from November 1909 to June 1912.

Service's poems played a central role in consolidating the popular mystique of the Canadian North as an alluring land of high drama, extreme conditions, raw emotions, and desperate men. In this, his imaginary northern landscape echoes those that were concocted in the wake of the disastrous Franklin expedition in the late 1800s (see Figure I-10), while "The Cremation of Sam McGee" recalls Charles Dawson Shanly's famous poem of Gothic doubling from 1859, "The Walker of the Snow" (see Section II and Figure II-9). According to critic Sherrill Grace, Service's Yukon is misrepresentative, depicting "an almost exclusively male world" populated by reckless men, deceitful women, and an absence of Aboriginal peoples. Nevertheless, Service succeeded in casting the "spell of the Yukon" on generations of readers. As he writes in his poem of the same title, "[T]here's some as would trade it / For no land on earth—and I'm one."

The Cremation of Sam McGee

ROBERT SERVICE

There are strange things done in the midnight sun
  By the men who moil for gold;
The Arctic trails have their secret tales
  That would make your blood run cold;
The Northern Lights have seen queer sights,
  But the queerest they ever did see
Was that night on the marge of Lake Lebarge
  I cremated Sam McGee.

Now Sam McGee was from Tennessee, where the cotton blooms and blows.
Why he left his home in the South to roam round the Pole, God only knows.   10
He was always cold, but the land of gold seemed to hold him like a spell;
Though he'd often say in his homely way that he'd "sooner live in hell."

On a Christmas Day we were mushing our way over the Dawson trail.
Talk of your cold! through the parka's fold it stabbed like a driven nail.
If our eyes we'd close, then the lashes froze till sometimes we couldn't see;
It wasn't much fun, but the only one to whimper was Sam McGee.

And that very night, as we lay packed tight in our robes beneath the snow,
And the dogs were fed, and the stars o'erhead were dancing heel and toe,
He turned to me, and "Cap," says he, "I'll cash in this trip, I guess;
And if I do, I'm asking that you won't refuse my last request."   20

Well, he seemed so low that I couldn't say no; then he says with a sort of moan:
"It's the cursèd cold, and it's got right hold till I'm chilled clean through to the
  bone.
Yet 'tain't being dead, it's my awful dread of the icy grave that pains;
So I want you to swear that, foul or fair, you'll cremate my last remains."

A pal's last need is a thing to heed, so I swore I would not fail;
And we started on at the streak of dawn; but God! he looked ghastly pale.
He crouched on the sleigh, and he raved all day of his home in Tennessee;
And before nightfall a corpse was all that was left of Sam McGee.

There wasn't a breath in that land of death, and I hurried, horror-driven,
With a corpse half-hid that I couldn't get rid, because of a promise given;   30
It was lashed to the sleigh, and it seemed to say: "You may tax your brawn and
  brains,
But you promised true, and it's up to you to cremate those last remains."

Now a promise made is a debt unpaid, and the trail has its own stern code.
In the days to come, though my lips were dumb, in my heart how I cursed that
  load.
In the long, long night, by the lone firelight, while the huskies, round in a ring,
Howled out their woes to the homeless snows—O God! how I loathed the thing.

And every day that quiet clay seemed to heavy and heavier grow;
And on I went, though the dogs were spent and the grub was getting low;
The trail was bad, and I felt half mad, but I swore I would not give in;
And I'd often sing to the hateful thing, and it hearkened with a grin. 40

Till I came to the marge of Lake Lebarge, and a derelict there lay;
It was jammed in the ice, but I saw in a trice it was called the "Alice May."
And I looked at it, and I thought a bit, and I looked at my frozen chum;
Then "Here," said I, with a sudden cry, "is my cre-ma-tor-eum."

Some planks I tore from the cabin floor, and I lit the boiler fire;
Some coal I found that was lying around, and I heaped the fuel higher;
The flames just soared, and the furnace roared—such a blaze you seldom see;
And I burrowed a hole in the glowing coal, and I stuffed in Sam McGee.

Then I made a hike, for I didn't like to hear him sizzle so;
And the heavens scowled, and the huskies howled, and the wind began to
  blow. 50
It was icy cold, but the hot sweat rolled down my cheeks, and I don't know why;
And the greasy smoke in an inky cloak went streaking down the sky.

I do not know how long in the snow I wrestled with grisly fear;
But the stars came out and they danced about ere again I ventured near;
I was sick with dread, but I bravely said: "I'll just take a peep inside.
I guess he's cooked, and it's time I looked"; . . . then the door I opened wide.

And there sat Sam, looking cool and calm, in the heart of the furnace roar;
And he wore a smile you could see a mile, and he said: "Please close that door.
It's fine in here, but I greatly fear you'll let in the cold and storm—
Since I left Plumtree, down in Tennessee, it's the first time I've been warm." 60

> There are strange things done in the midnight sun
>   By the men who moil for gold;
> The Arctic trails have their secret tales
>   That would make your blood run cold;
> The Northern Lights have seen queer sights,
>   But the queerest they ever did see
> Was that night on the marge of Lake Lebarge
>   I cremated Sam McGee.

[1907]

Maracle, Brian. "The First Words." *Our Story: Aboriginal Voices on Canada's Past*. Pref. Rudyard Griffiths. Toronto: Doubleday, 2004. 13–31.

I. Narratives of Encounter

Primary Texts

Brébeuf, Jean de. "The Huron Carol" ["Jesous Ahatonhia"]. 1926. Trans. Jesse Edgar Middleton. *The Book of Common Praise*. Rev. ed. London: Oxford UP, 1938. 742–43.

—. "The Huron Carol." Trans. John Steckley. 1984. "Original Huron Carol." In "The Huron Carol." unpublished essay, n.d. 8–11.

Cartier, Jacques. *The Voyages of Jacques Cartier, 1534, 1535–36, 1541*. Ed. and introd. Ramsay Cook. Toronto: U of Toronto P, 1993.

Cartwright, George. *Captain Cartwright and His Labrador Journal*. Ed. Charles Wendell Townsend. London: Williams & Norgate, 1911.

Champlain, Samuel de. *The Voyages and Explorations of Samuel de Champlain (1604–1616), Narrated by Himself.* Trans. Annie Nettleton Bourne. Ed. Edward Gaylord Bourne. 2 vols. Toronto: Courier, 1911.

—. *Voyages to New France*. Trans. Michael Macklem. Introd. Edward Miles. Ottawa: Oberon, 1971.

—. The Voyages to the Great River St. Lawrence by the Sieur de Champlain, Captain in the Royal Navy, from the year 1608 to 1612. Book II of The Voyages: 1608–1612. 1613. In *The Works of Samuel de Champlain*. Ed. H.P. Biggar. 6 vols. Vol. 2: 1608–1613. Toronto: Champlain Society, 1925.

Franklin, Sir John. *Narrative of a Journey to the Shores of the Polar Sea in the Years 1819, 20, 21, and 22*. Edmonton: Hurtig, 1969.

Hearne, Samuel. *A Journey from Prince of Wales's Fort in Hudson's Bay to the Northern Ocean, 1769, 1770, 1771, 1772*. Ed. Richard Glover. Toronto: Macmillan, 1958.

The Jesuit Relations and Allied Documents: A Selection. Ed. S.R. Mealing. Carleton Library Series. Ottawa: Carleton UP, 1985.

The Jesuit Relations: Natives and Missionaries in Seventeenth-Century North America. Ed. Allan Greer. Bedford Series in History and Culture. Boston: Bedford/St. Martin's, 2000.

"Lady Franklin's Lament." Accessed 14 April 2005 <www.folkinfo.org.> [From Kennedy, D. *Martin Carthy: A Guitar in Folk Music*. Petersham, New Punchbowl Music, 1987.]

Qaqortingneq. Testimony given to Knud Rasmussen. *Across Arctic America: Narrative of the Fifth Thule Expedition*, by Knud Rasmussen. 1927. New York: Greenwood, 1969. 239–41.

Thompson, David. *David Thompson's Narrative, 1784–1812*. Ed. Richard Glover. Toronto: Champlain Society, 1962.

—. *Narrative of His Explorations in Western America, 1784 to 1812*. Ed. Joseph Burr Tyrell. Toronto: Champlain Society, 1916.

—. *Travels in Western North America, 1784–1812*. Ed. Victor G. Hopwood. Toronto: Macmillan, 1971.

Tooktoocheer. Testimony given to Lieutenant Frederick Schwatka. *Schwatka's Search: Sledging in the Arctic in Quest of Franklin Records*, by William Gilder. New York: Scribner's, 1881. 106–08.

Tuk-ke-ta and Ow-wer. Testimony given to Charles Francis Hall. *Unravelling the Franklin Mystery: Inuit Testimony*, by David C. Woodman. Montreal: McGill-Queen's UP, 1991. 124–26.

Secondary Texts

Atwood, Margaret. *Strange Things: The Malevolent North in Canadian Literature*. Oxford: Clarendon, 1995.

—. *Survival: A Thematic Guide to Canadian Literature*. Toronto: Anansi, 1972.

Blais, Christian. "Marc Lescarbot's *Les muses de la Nouvelle France* (1609)." Fleming et al. 31–33.

Chiasson, Paul. *The Island of Seven Cities: Where the Chinese Settled When They Discovered North America*. Toronto: Random House , 2006.

A Dictionary of Canadians on Historical Principles. Toronto: Gage, 1967.

Fleming, Patricia Lockhart, Gilles Gallichan, and Yvan Lamonde, eds. *History of the Book in Canada: Volume I: Beginnings to 1840*. Toronto: U of Toronto P, 2004.

Frye, Northrop. "Conclusion to a *Literary History of Canada*." 1965. *The Bush Garden: Essays on the Canadian Imagination*. Toronto: Anansi, 1971. 213–51.

—. "Haunted by Lack of Ghosts: Some Patterns in the Imagery of Canadian Poetry." *The Canadian Imagination: Dimensions of a Literary Culture.* Ed. David Staines. Cambridge: Harvard UP, 1977. 22–45.

Goldie, Terry. *Fear and Temptation: The Image of the Indigene in Canadian, Australian, and New Zealand Literatures.* Montreal: McGill-Queen's UP, 1989.

Grace, Sherrill E. *Canada and the Idea of North.* Montreal: McGill-Queen's UP, 2001.

Gray, Charlotte. *The Museum Called Canada: 25 Rooms of Wonder.* Toronto: Random House, 2004.

Greenblatt, Stephen. *Marvelous Possessions: The Wonder of the New World.* Chicago: U of Chicago P, 1991.

Hannon, Leslie F. *The Discoverers: The Seafaring Men Who First Touched the Coasts of Canada.* Toronto: McClelland, 1971.

Harris, R. Cole. *Historical Atlas of Canada: Volume I: From the Beginning to 1800.* Toronto: U of Toronto P, 1987.

Holland, Clive. "Franklin, Sir John." *Dictionary of Canadian Biography Online.* Accessed 6 June 2006 <http://www.biographi.ca>.

Honour, Hugh. *The European Vision of America.* Cleveland: Cleveland Museum of Art, 1975.

—. *The New Golden Land: European Images of America from the Discoveries to the Present Time.* New York: Pantheon, 1975.

Hopwood, Victor G. "Explorers by Land to 1867." *Literary History of Canada: Canadian Literature in English.* 2nd ed. Vol. I. Toronto: U of Toronto P, 1976. 19–53.

—. "Explorers by Sea: The West Coast." *Literary History of Canada: Canadian Literature in English.* 2nd ed. Vol. I. Toronto: U of Toronto P, 1976. 54–65.

Innis, Harold A. *The Fur Trade in Canada: An Introduction to Canadian Economic History.* Rev. ed. Toronto: U of Toronto P, 1962.

Kerr, D.G.G. *A Historical Atlas of Canada.* Toronto: Thomas Nelson, 1960.

King, Thomas. "Godzilla vs. Post-Colonial." *Unhomely States: Theorizing English-Canadian Postcolonialism.* Ed. Cynthia Sugars. Peterborough: Broadview, 2004. 183–90.

Klinck, Carl F., ed. *Literary History of Canada: Canadian Literature in English.* 2nd ed. Vol. I. Toronto: U of Toronto P, 1976.

Kröller, Eva-Marie. "Exploration and Travel." *The Cambridge Companion to Canadian Literature.* Ed. Eva-Marie Kröller. Cambridge: Cambridge UP, 2004. 70–93.

Laberge, Aimée. *Where the River Narrows.* Toronto: HarperPerennial, 2003.

Lowes, John Livingston. *The Road to Xanadu: A Study in the Ways of the Imagination.* 1927. Princeton: Princeton UP, 1986.

MacEwen, Gwendolyn. *Afterworlds.* Toronto: McClelland, 1987.

MacLaren, I.S. "English Writings About the New World." Fleming et al. 33–44.

—. "Samuel Hearne's Accounts of the Massacre at Bloody Fall, 17 July 1771." *ARIEL* 22.1 (1991): 25–51.

McClintock, Anne. *Imperial Leather: Race, Gender, and Sexuality in the Colonial Contest.* New York: Routledge, 1995.

McGoogan, Ken. *Ancient Mariner: The Amazing Adventures of Samuel Hearne, the Sailor Who Walked to the Arctic Ocean.* Toronto: HarperFlamingo, 2003.

McGrath, Robin. "Samuel Hearne and the Inuit Oral Tradition." *Studies in Canadian Literature* 18.2 (1993): 94–109.

Menzies, Gavin. *1421: The Year China Discovered the World.* New York: Bantam, 2002.

Monkman, Leslie. *A Native Heritage: Images of the Indian in English-Canadian Literature.* Toronto: U of Toronto P, 1981.

—. "Visions and Revisions: Contemporary Writers and Exploration Accounts of Indigenous Peoples." *The Native in Literature: Canadian and Comparative Perspectives.* Ed. Thomas King, Cheryl Calver, and Helen Hoy. Toronto: ECW, 1987. 80–98.

Morantz, Alan. *Where Is Here? Canada's Maps and the Stories They Tell.* Toronto: Penguin/Pearson, 2002.

Moreau, Bill. "Exploration Literature." *Encyclopedia of Literature in Canada.* Ed. William H. New. Toronto: U of Toronto P, 2002. 346–50.

New, W.H. *A History of Canadian Literature.* Houndmills: Macmillan, 1989.

Ray, Arthur J. *I Have Lived Here Since the World Began: An Illustrated History of Canada's Native People.* Toronto: Lester, 1996.

Rayburn, Alan. *Naming Canada: Stories About Place Names from Canadian Geographic.* Toronto: U of Toronto P, 1994.

Steckley, John. "Huron Carol." Unpublished manuscript, n.d.

Thorner, Thomas, ed. *"A Few Acres of Snow": Documents in Canadian History, 1577–1867.* Peterborough: Broadview, 1997.

Trigger, Bruce G. *Natives and Newcomers: Canada's "Heroic Age" Reconsidered.* Kingston: McGill-Queen's UP, 1985.

Turner, Margaret. *Imagining Culture: New World Narrative and the Writing of Canada.* Montreal: McGill-Queen's UP, 1995.

Warkentin, Germaine, ed. *Canadian Exploration Literature: An Anthology.* Toronto: Oxford UP, 1993.

—. "Exploration Literature in English." *The Oxford Companion to Canadian Literature.* 2nd ed. Ed. Eugene Benson and William Toye. Don Mills: Oxford UP, 1997. 372–80.

Warwick, Jack. "New France, Writing in." *The Oxford Companion to Canadian Literature.* 2nd ed. Ed. Eugene Benson and William Toye. Don Mills: Oxford UP, 1997. 799–805.

Wiebe, Rudy. *Playing Dead: A Contemplation Concerning the Arctic.* Edmonton: NeWest, 1989.

Woodman, David C. "Inuit Accounts and the Franklin Mystery." *Echoing Silence: Essays on Arctic Narrative.* Ed. John Moss. Ottawa: U of Ottawa P, 1997. 53–60.

—. *Unravelling the Franklin Mystery: Inuit Testimony.* Montreal: McGill-Queen's UP, 1991.

II. Narratives of Emigration, Settlement, and Invasion

Primary Texts

Brant, Joseph. "Letter of 10 Dec. 1798." *An Anthology of Canadian Native Literature in English*. Ed. Daniel David Moses and Terry Goldie. 2nd ed. Don Mills: Oxford UP, 2002. 14–15.

Copway, George. *The Life, History, and Travels of Kah-Ge-Ga-Gah-Bowh*. Albany: Weed and Parsons, 1847.

Goldsmith, Oliver. *The Rising Village*. St. John, NB: John McMillan, 1834.

—. *The Rising Village*. Ed. Gerald Lynch. London, ON: Canadian Poetry Press, 1989.

Haliburton, Thomas Chandler. *The Clockmaker; or, the Sayings and Doings of Samuel Slick of Slickville*. London: Richard Bentley, 1839.

Hecht, Anne. [Anonymous original]. "Advice to Mrs. Mowat." *Canadian Poetry: From the Beginnings Through the First World War*. Ed. Carol Gerson and Gwendolyn Davies. Toronto: McClelland, 1994. 41–43.

Henry, George. *An Account of the Chippewa Indians, who have been travelling among the whites, in the United States, England, Ireland, Scotland, France and Belgium*. 1848. *First People, First Voices*. Ed. Penny Petrone. Toronto: U of Toronto P, 1983. 87–94.

Jameson, Anna Brownell. *Winter Studies and Summer Rambles*. New York: Wiley and Putnam, 1839.

King, Boston. *The Life of Boston King: Black Loyalist, Minister, and Master Carpenter*. Ed. Ruth Holmes Whitehead and Carmelita A.M. Robertson. Halifax: Nimbus Publishing and the Nova Scotia Museum, 2002.

McCulloch, Thomas. *Letters of Mephibosheth Stepsure, Reprinted from the Acadian Recorder of the years 1821 and 1822*. Halifax: H.W. Blackadar, 1862.

Moodie, Susanna. *Life in the Clearings Versus the Bush*. New York: Dewitt and Davenport, 1854.

—. *Roughing It in the Bush, or, Life in Canada*. London: Richard Bentley, 1852.

—. *Roughing It in the Bush*. Ed. Elizabeth Thompson. Ottawa: Tecumseh, 1997.

Review of *Roughing It in the Bush*. *Blackwood's Edinburgh Magazine* LXXI (Jan.-June 1852): 355.

Shadd (Cary), Mary Ann. *A Plea for Emigration, or, Notes of Canada West*. Detroit: George Pattison, 1852.

Shanly, Charles Dawson. "The Walker of the Snow." *Atlantic Monthly* May 1859: 631.

Traill, Catharine Parr. *The Backwoods of Canada*. 1836. Intro. Michael Peterman. Ottawa: Carleton UP, 1997.

Secondary Texts

Arthur, George. *The Arthur Papers*. Toronto: Toronto Public Libraries, 1957.

Atwood, Margaret. *The Journals of Susanna Moodie*. Toronto: Oxford UP, 1970.

Ballstadt, Carl, Elizabeth Hopkins, and Michael Peterman, eds. *Susanna Moodie: Letters of a Lifetime*. Toronto: U of Toronto P, 1985.

Bentley, D.M.R., ed. *Early Long Poems on Canada*. London: Canadian Poetry Press, 1993.

Blodgett, E. D. "Francophone Writing." Kröller 49–69.

Brown, Wallace. "Victorious in Defeat: The American Loyalists in Canada." Wallace et al. 231–40.

Brydon, Diana. "Canada and Postcolonialism: Questions, Inventories, and Futures." Moss 49–77.

Canadian Broadcasting Corporation. "Rebellion and Reform." *Canada: A People's History*. Accessed March 2007 <http://history.cbc.ca/history/? MIval=EpContent.html&episode_id=7&series_id= 1&lang=E&chapter_id=2>.

Chalykoff, Lisa. "Tracing C.D. Shanly's 'The Walker of the Snow.'" *Canadian Literature* 160 (Spring 1999): 187–89.

Chiasson, Anselme, and Nicolas Landry. "French Colonization (1534–1713)." *The Canadian Encyclopedia* <http://thecanadianencyclopedia. com>.

Clarke, George Elliott, ed. *Eyeing the North Star: Directions in African-Canadian Literature*. Toronto: McClelland, 1997.

Conrad, Margaret, Alvin Finkel, with Cornelius Jaenen. *History of the Canadian Peoples: Beginnings to 1867*. Toronto: Copp Clark, 1998.

Copway, George (Kah-Ge-Ga-Gah-Bowh). *Traditional History and Characteristic Sketches of the Ojibwa Nation*. London: Charles Gilpin, 1850.

Coupland, Reginald, ed. *The Durham Report*. Oxford: Clarendon, 1945.

Craig, Gerald. "Conservatives and Rebels: 1836–37." Wallace et al. 365–89.

Davies, Richard A. "Haliburton, Thomas Chandler." *Encyclopedia of Literature in Canada*. Ed. W.H. New. Toronto: U of Toronto P, 2002. 469–72.

Durham, John George Lambton, Earl of. *Report on the Affairs of British North America from the Earl of Durham*. Toronto: Robert Stanton, 1839.

Dvorak, Marta. "Fiction." Kröller 155–76.

Egan, Susanna, and Gabriele Helms. "Life Writing." Kröller 216–40.

Errington, Jane. "'Woman … Is a Very Interesting Creature': Some Women's Experiences in Early Upper Canada." Francis and Smith 240–53.

Fiamengo, Janice. "Regionalism and Urbanism." Kröller 241–62.

Fleming, Patricia Lockhart, Gilles Gallichan, and Yvan Lamonde, eds. *History of the Book in Canada: Volume 1: Beginnings to 1840*. Toronto: U of Toronto P, 2004.

Francis, R. Douglas, and Donald B. Smith, eds. *Reading Canadian History: Pre-Confederation*. Toronto: Nelson Thomson, 2002.

Friskney, Janet B. "Christian Faith in Print." Fleming et al. 138–44.

Gerson, Carole, and Gwendolyn Davies, eds. *Canadian Poetry: From the Beginnings Through the First World War*. Toronto: McClelland, 1994.

Glickman, Susan. "Afterword." *Roughing It in the Bush*. Toronto: McClelland, 1993. 535–43.

Goldie, Terry. *Fear and Temptation: The Image of the Indigene in Canadian, Australian, and New Zealand Literatures*. Montreal: McGill-Queen's UP, 1989.

Goldsmith, Oliver. *The Deserted Village*. London: W. Griffin, 1970.

—. *Traveller and Deserted Village*. London: Macmillan, 1951.

Grace, Sherrill. *Canada and the Idea of North*. Montreal: McGill-Queen's UP, 2002.

Grant, John Miller. *To Emigrants: Canada: Its Advantages to Settlers*. London: Algar and Street, W. Wesley, 1856.

Gray, Charlotte. *Sisters in the Wilderness: The Lives of Susanna Moodie and Catharine Parr Traill*. Toronto: Viking, 1999.

Graymount, Barbara. "Thayendanegea," *Dictionary of Canadian Biography*. Toronto: U of Toronto P, 1983. 804.

Greer, Allan. "1837–38: Rebellion Reconsidered." Wallace et al. 390–404.

Hill, Lawrence. *The Book of Negroes*. Toronto: HarperCollins, 2007.

—. "Freedom Bound." *The Beaver* Feb./March 2007. Accessed 2 March 2007 <http://www.history society.ca/bea.asp?subsection=fea>.

Information Published by His Majesty's Commissioners for Emigration Respecting the British Colonies in North America. London: Charles Knight, 1832.

Klinck, Carl F, ed. *Literary History of Canada*. Toronto: U of Toronto P, 1965.

Kröller, Eva-Marie, ed. *The Cambridge Companion to Canadian Literature*. Cambridge: Cambridge UP, 2004.

Lawson, Alan. "From Asymptote to Zeugma." *Postcolonizing the Commonwealth: Studies in Literature and Culture*. Ed. Rowland Smith. Waterloo: Wilfrid Laurier UP, 2000. 19–38.

Library and Archives of Canada. "Moving Here, Staying Here. The Canadian Immigrant Experience." Accessed March 2007 <http://www.collectionscanada.ca/immigrants/021017–110.05-e. php>.

Manitoba: The Home for Agriculturists, Stock Raisers, Dairymen, and all who Desire Comfort and Prosperity. Winnipeg: Manitoba Provincial Government, 1889.

McLachlan, Alexander. *The Emigrant*. Ed. D.M.R. Bentley. London, ON: Canadian Poetry Press, 1991.

—. "Young Canada Or Jack's as Good as His Master." *Canadian Poetry: From the Beginnings Through the First World War*. Ed. Carole Gerson and Gwendolyn Davies. Toronto: McClelland, 1994. 95–96.

Mennonite Historical Society of Canada. "Who Are the Mennonites?" Accessed May 2006 <http://www.mhsc.ca/index.asp?content=http://www.mhsc.ca/mennos/hcanada.html>.

Mills, David. "Durham, John George Lambton, 1st Earl of." *The Canadian Encyclopedia*. Toronto: McClelland, 1999. 707.

Morton, Desmond. *A Short History of Canada*. Toronto: McClelland, 1997.

Moss, Laura, ed. *Is Canada Postcolonial? Unsettling Canadian Literature*. Waterloo: Wilfrid Laurier UP, 2003.

Murray, Heather. *Come, Bright Improvement!: The Literary Societies of Nineteenth-Century Ontario*. Toronto: U of Toronto P, 2002.

—. "Great Works and Good Works: The Toronto Women's Literary Club, 1877–83." *Historical Studies in Education* 11:2 (Fall 1999). Accessed 27 Feb. 2007 <http://www.edu.uwo.ca/hse/99murray.html>.

New, W.H. *A History of Canadian Literature*. Montreal: McGill-Queen's UP, 2003.

—. ed. *Encyclopedia of Literature in Canada*, Toronto: U of Toronto P, 2002.

Nish, Cameron. "The 1760s." *Colonists and Canadiens, 1760–1867*. Ed. J.M.S. Careless. Toronto: Gage, 1971. 1–19.

Nova Scotia Archives and Record Management. "African Nova Scotians." Accessed March 2007 <http://www.gov.ns.ca/nsarm/virtual/africanns/ch4.asp>.

Nova Scotia Museum. "Birchtown, 1784." Accessed May 2006 <http://museum.gov.ns.ca/arch/sites/birch/btown.htm>.

O'Callaghan, E.B., ed. *Documents Relative to the Colonial History of the State of New York*. 15 vols. Albany, 1853–87. 670–71. Accessed March 2007 <http://historymatters.gmu.edu/d/8071/>.

Ontario Archives. "John Graves Simcoe." Accessed May 2006 <http://www.archives.gov.on.ca/english/exhibits/simcoe/john.htm>.

—. "Travels with Elizabeth Simcoe." Accessed Aug. 2007 <http://www.archives.gov.on.ca/english/exhibits/simcoe/index.html>.

Ouellett, Fernand. "The Failure of the Insurrectionary Movement, 1837–1839." Wallace et al. 341–63.

Panofsky, Ruth. "Case Study: Thomas Chandler Haliburton's *The Clockmaker*." Fleming et al. 352–54.

Paxton, James. "The Myth of the Loyalist Iroquois: Joseph Brant and the Invention of a Canadian Tradition." Unpublished paper presented at the Iroquois Research Conference on October 6, 2002. Accessed March 2007 <http://www.wampumchronicles.com/josephbrant.html>.

Perkins, Pam. "Frances Brooke, Emily Montague, and Other Travellers: Representing Eighteenth-Century North America." *The History of Emily Montague*. Ed. Laura Moss. Ottawa: Tecumseh Press, 2001. 421–36.

—. "Imagining Eighteenth-Century Quebec: British Literature and Colonial Rhetoric." Moss 151–62.

Potter, Janice. "Patriarchy and Paternalism: The Case of the Eastern Ontario Loyalist Women." Wallace et al. 240–59.

Report of the Select Committee on Emigration in 1826. London: John Murray, 1827.

Robeson, Virginia, ed. *Upper Canada in the 1830s*. Toronto: Ontario Institute for Studies in Education, 1977.

Said, Edward. *Culture and Imperialism*. Toronto: Random House, 1993.

Smith, Donald. "Copway, George." *Canadian Encyclopedia*. Toronto: McClelland, 1999. 566.

Staines, David. "Poetry." Kröller 134–54.

Storey, Norah, ed. *The Oxford Companion to Canadian History and Literature*. Toronto: Oxford UP, 1967.

Taras, David, and Beverly Rasporich, eds. *A Passion for Identity: An Introduction to Canadian Studies*. Scarborough, ON: Nelson, 1997.

Thompson, Elizabeth, ed. *Roughing It in the Bush*. Ottawa: Tecumseh, 1997.

Thorner, Thomas, ed. *"A Few Acres of Snow": Documents in Canadian History, 1577–1867*. Peterborough: Broadview, 1997.

Walker, Frank Norman. "Charles Dawson Shanly." *Dictionary of Canadian Biography Online*. Accessed 20 March 2007 <http://www.biographi.ca/EN/ShowBio.asp?BioId=39380&query=Shanly>.

Wallace, C.M., R.M. Bray, and A.D. Gilbert, eds. *Reappraisals in Canadian History: Pre-Confederation*. Toronto: Prentice Hall, 1996.

Whitehead, Ruth Holmes. *The Old Man Told Us: Excerpts from Micmac History: 1500–1950*. Halifax: Nimbus Publishing, 1991.

Wilton, Carol. *Popular Politics and Political Culture in Upper Canada 1800–1850*. Montreal: McGill-Queen's UP, 2000.

Wise, S.F. "God's Peculiar Peoples." *The Shield of Achilles: Aspects of Canada in the Victorian Age*. Ed. W.L. Morton. Toronto: McClelland, 1968. 36–61.

Wordsworth, William, and Samuel Taylor Coleridge. "Preface." *Lyrical Ballads, with Pastoral and Other Poems*. 1802. *Lyrical Ballads and Other Selected Poems* Introd. Martin Scofield. Ware: Wordsworth Editions, 2003. 5–8.

Wulf, Karin A. *Not All Wives: Women of Colonial Philadelphia*. Philadelphia: U of Pennsylvania P, 2005.

III. Post-Confederation Period

Primary Texts

"The Anti-Confederation Song." *The Old-Time Songs and Poetry of Newfoundland*. Ed. Gerald S. Doyle. St John's: Gerald S. Doyle Ltd., 1940.

Campbell, William Wilfred. *Beyond the Hills of Dream*. Boston: Houghton Mifflin, 1899.

—. *The Dread Voyage: Poems*. Toronto: William Briggs, 1893.

—. *Lake Lyrics and Other Poems*. St. John, NB: J. & A. McMillan, 1889.

—. *The Poems of Wilfred Campbell*. Toronto: William Briggs, 1905.

—. *Selected Poetry and Essays*. Ed. Laurel Boone. Waterloo: Wilfrid Laurier UP, 1987.

—. "10 December 1892." *At the Mermaid Inn: Wilfred Campbell, Archibald Lampman, Duncan Campbell Scott in The Globe 1892–93*. Ed. Barrie Davies. Toronto: U of Toronto P, 1979. 207–09.

Carman, Bliss. *Four Sonnets*. Boston: Small, Maynard, 1916.

—. *Low Tide on Grand Pré: A Book of Lyrics*. New York: Charles L. Webster, 1893.

—. *The Poems of Bliss Carman*. Ed. John Robert Sorfleet. Toronto: NCL, 1976.

—. *Sanctuary: Sunshine House Sonnets*. Toronto: McClelland, 1929.

The Chinese Immigration Act, 1885. *Documenting Canada: A History of Modern Canada in Documents*. Ed. Dave De Brou and Bill Waiser. Saskatoon: Fifth House, 1992. 151–53.

Crawford, Isabella Valancy. *The Collected Poems of Isabella Valancy Crawford*. Ed. John W. Garvin. Toronto: William Briggs, 1905. Rpt. with Introd. by James Reaney. Toronto: U of Toronto P, 1972.

—. *Malcolm's Katie: A Love Story*. 1884. Ed. D.M.R. Bentley. London: Canadian Poetry Press, 1987.

—. *Old Spookses' Pass: Malcolm's Katie, and Other Poems*. Toronto: James Bain, 1884.

—. *Selected Stories of Isabella Valancy Crawford*. Ed. Penny Petrone. Ottawa: U of Ottawa P, 1975.

Davies, Barrie, ed. *At the Mermaid Inn: Wilfred Campbell, Archibald Lampman, Duncan Campbell Scott in The Globe 1892–93*. Toronto: U of Toronto P, 1979.

Duncan, Sara Jeannette. "American Influence on Canadian Thought." *The Week* 7 July 1887: 518.

—. "How an American Girl Became a Journalist." *Selected Journalism* 6–13.

—. *The Imperialist*. London: Constable, 1904.

—. "Saunterings." *The Week* 30 Sept. 1886: 707–08.

—. "Saunterings." *The Week* 28 Oct. 1886: 771–72.

—. *Selected Journalism*. Ed. Thomas E. Tausky. Ottawa: Tecumseh, 1978.

—. *A Social Departure: How Orthodocia and I Went Round the World by Ourselves*. New York: Appleton, 1890.

—. "Woman's World." [Interview with Pauline Johnson.] *Globe* 14 Oct. 1886: 6.

—. "Woman's World." *Globe* 17 Nov. 1886: 6.

Eaton, Edith Maude [Sui Sin Far]. *Mrs. Spring Fragrance and Other Writings*. Ed. Amy Ling and Annette White-Parks. Urbana: U of Illinois P, 1995.

The Indian Act, 1876 and 1927. Accessed 13 June 2006 <www.collectionscanada.ca/aboriginal> and <www.collections.ic.gc.ca/aboriginaldocs/stat/>.

Johnson, E. Pauline (Tekahionwake). *Collected Poems and Selected Prose*. Ed. Carole Gerson and Veronica Strong-Boag. Toronto: U of Toronto P, 2002.

—. "A Cry from an Indian Wife." *The Week* 18 June 1885: 457.

—. "The Fate of the Red Man: An English Journalist's Chat with Pauline Johnson." *The Gazette* [London] Summer 1894. Rpt. in the *Ottawa Daily Free Press* 21 June 1894: 3.

—. *Flint and Feather*. Toronto: Musson, 1912.

—. "His Majesty, the West Wind." *The Globe* 15 Dec. 1894: 18.

—. *The Moccasin Maker*. Toronto: Briggs, 1913.

—. "A Strong Race Opinion: On the Indian Girl in Modern Fiction." *The Globe* 22 May 1892: 1.

Lampman, Archibald. *Alcyone*. Ottawa: James Ogilvy, 1899.

—. *Among the Millet and Other Poems*. Ottawa: J. Durie, 1888.

—. *The Essays and Reviews of Archibald Lampman.* Ed. D.M.R. Bentley. London: Canadian Poetry Press, 1996.

—. *The Poems of Archibald Lampman.* Ed. Duncan Campbell Scott. Toronto: Musson, 1900.

—. "Two Canadian Poets: A Lecture." *The Essays and Reviews of Archibald Lampman.* 91–114.

Macdonald, John A. "On Reciprocity." *Great Canadian Speeches.* Ed. Dennis Gruending. Markham, ON: Fitzhenry & Whiteside, 2004. 72–75.

—. "Speech before the House of Commons, July 6, 1885." Library and Archives Canada. 26 pages. Accessed 15 June 2006 <www.collectionscanada.ca/primeministers/h4–4090-e.html>.

—. "Speech in the Legislative Assembly, February 6, 1865." *The Colonial Century: English-Canadian Writing Before Confederation.* 1973. Ed. A.J.M. Smith. Ottawa: Tecumseh, 1986. 226–40.

Machar, Agnes Maule. *Lays of the "True North" and Other Canadian Poems.* London: Elliot Stock, 1899.

—. "The New Ideal of Womanhood." *Rose-Belford's Canadian Monthly and National Review* June 1879: 659–676.

McGee, Thomas D'Arcy. "A Canadian Nationality." 1862. *Who Speaks for Canada? Words That Shape a Country.* Ed. Desmond Morton and Morton Weinfeld. Toronto: McClelland, 1998. 32–34.

—. "The Mental Outfit of the New Dominion." 1867. *1825–D'Arcy McGee–1925: A Collection of Speeches and Addresses.* Ed. Charles Murphy. Toronto: Macmillan, 1937. 1–21.

—. "A National Literature for Canada." *The New Era* 17 June 1857: 2.

—. *Poems.* London: Sadlier, 1870.

—. "A Prophetic Vision." Speech in the Legislative Assembly, May 2nd, 1860. *1825–D'Arcy McGee–1925: A Collection of Speeches and Addresses.* Ed. Charles Murphy. Toronto: Macmillan, 1937. ix-x.

—. "Protection for Canadian Literature." *The New Era* 24 April 1858: 2. Rpt. in *The Search for English-Canadian Literature: An Anthology of Critical Articles from the Nineteenth and Early Twentieth Centuries.* Ed. Carl Ballstadt. Toronto: U of Toronto P, 1975. 21–24.

—. "Speech in the Legislative Assembly, February 9, 1865." *The Colonial Century: English-Canadian Writing Before Confederation.* Ed. A.J.M. Smith. 1973. Ottawa: Tecumseh, 1986. 242–49.

Muir, Alexander. "The Maple Leaf Forever." Library and Archives of Canada. Accessed 12 July 2007 <http://www.collectionscanada.ca/obj/m5/f2/csm05606.pdf >.

"O Canada!" Department of Canadian Heritage. Accessed 8 Nov. 2007 <www.pch.gc.ca>.

Riel, Louis. *The Diaries of Louis Riel.* Ed. Thomas Flanagan. Edmonton: Hurtig, 1976.

—. *The Queen v. Louis Riel: Canada's Greatest State Trial.* Introd. Desmond Morton. Toronto: U of Toronto P, 1974.

Roberts, Charles G.D. "The Beginnings of a Canadian Literature." *Selected Poetry and Critical Prose: Charles G.D. Roberts.* Ed. W.J. Keith. Toronto: U of Toronto P, 1974. 243–59.

—. *The Collected Letters of Charles G.D. Roberts.* Ed. Laurel Boone. Fredericton: Goose Lane, 1989.

—. *The Collected Poems of Sir Charles G.D. Roberts: A Critical Edition.* Ed. Desmond Pacey. Wolfville, NS: Wombat, 1985.

—. *Earth's Enigmas.* 1895. New York: Books for Libraries, 1969.

—. "The Future of Canada." Review of *Canada and the Canadian Question,* by Goldwin Smith. *The Dial* 16 Dec. 1892: 385–87.

—. *In Divers Tones.* Boston: Lothrop, 1886.

—. *The Kindred of the Wild: A Book of Animal Life.* Boston: L.C. Page, 1902.

—. "A Note on Modernism." 1931. *Selected Poetry and Critical Prose: Charles G.D. Roberts.* Ed. W.J. Keith. Toronto: U of Toronto P, 1974. 296–301.

—. *Orion, and Other Poems.* Philadelphia: Lippincott, 1880.

—. "The Poetry of Nature." *The Forum* [New York] Dec. 1897. 442–45.

—. "The Savour of the Soil." *The Dominion Illustrated Monthly* May 1892: 251–53.

—. *Selected Poetry and Critical Prose.* Ed. W.J. Keith. Toronto: U of Toronto P, 1974.

—. *Songs of the Common Day and Ave! an Ode for the Shelley Centenary.* Toronto: William Briggs, 1893.

Routhier, A.B. *Les Échos.* Quebec City: Typographie de P.-G. Delisle, 1882.

Scott, Duncan Campbell. *Addresses, Essays, and Reviews.* 2 vols. Ed. Leslie Ritchie. Introd. Stan Dragland. London: Canadian Poetry Press, 2000.

—. *The Circle of Affection and Other Pieces in Prose and Verse.* Toronto: McClelland, 1947.

—. *In the Village of Viger.* Boston: Copeland and Day, 1896.

—. *In the Village of Viger and Other Stories.* Introd. Stan Dragland. Toronto: NCL, 1973.

—. *Labor and the Angel.* Boston: Copeland and Day, 1898.

—. "The Last of the Indian Treaties." *Scribner's* 40 (1906): 573–83. Rpt. in *The Circle of Affection* 109–22.

—. "Memoir." *The Poems of Archibald Lampman.* Ed. Duncan Campbell Scott. Toronto: Musson, 1900. xi-xxv.

—. *New World Lyrics and Ballads.* Toronto: Morang, 1905.

—. *The Poems of Duncan Campbell Scott.* Toronto: McClelland, 1926.

—. "Poetry and Progress." *The Circle of Affection* 123–47.

—. *The Witching of Elspie: A Book of Stories.* Toronto: McClelland, 1923.

Weir, Robert Stanley. *After Ypres and Other Verse.* Toronto: Musson Book Co, 1917.

Secondary Texts

Adams, John Coldwell. *Sir Charles God Damn: The Life of Sir Charles G.D. Roberts.* Toronto: U of Toronto P, 1986.

Anderson, Benedict. *Imagined Communities: Reflections on the Origin and Spread of Nationalism.* Rev. ed. London: Verso, 1991.

Ballstadt, Carl, ed. *The Search for English-Canadian Literature: An Anthology of Critical Articles from the Nineteenth and Early Twentieth Centuries.* Toronto: U of Toronto P, 1975.

—. "Thomas D'Arcy McGee as a Father of Canadian Literature." *Studies in Canadian Literature* 1.1 (1976). Accessed 26 June 2006 <http://www.lib.unb.ca/Texts/SCL>.

Beck, J. Murray "Howe, Joseph." *Dictionary of Canadian Biography Online.* Accessed 23 June 2006 <www.biographi.ca>.

—. *Joseph Howe: Voice of Nova Scotia.* Toronto: McClelland, 1964.

Benson, Eugene, and William Toye, eds. *The Oxford Companion to Canadian Literature.* 2nd ed. Toronto: Oxford UP, 1997.

Bentley, D.M.R. *The Confederation Group of Canadian Poets, 1880–1897.* Toronto: U of Toronto P, 2004.

—. Introduction. *Malcolm's Katie: A Love Story*, by Isabella Valancy Crawford. London: Canadian Poetry Press, 1987. xi-lxi.

Berton, Pierre. *The Last Spike: The Great Railway: 1881–1885.* Toronto: McClelland, 1971.

—. *The National Dream: The Great Railway: 1871–1881.* Toronto: McClelland, 1970.

Boone, Laurel. "Campbell, William Wilfred." *Dictionary of Canadian Biography Online.* Accessed 27 July 2006 < http://www.biographi.ca>.

Bothwell, Robert, and J.L. Granatstein. *Our Century: The Canadian Journey in the Twentieth Century.* Toronto: McArthur, 2000.

Braz, Albert. *The False Traitor: Louis Riel in Canadian Culture.* Toronto: U of Toronto P, 2003.

Brown, Craig, ed. *The Illustrated History of Canada.* Toronto: Key Porter, 1997.

Brown, E.K. "Archibald Lampman." *On Canadian Poetry.* Toronto: Ryerson, 1943. 80–108.

—. "Duncan Campbell Scott: A Memoir." *Responses and Evaluations: Essays on Canada.* Ed. David Staines. Toronto: NCL, 1977. 112–44.

Burns, Robin B. "McGee, Thomas D'Arcy." *Dictionary of Canadian Biography Online.* Accessed 26 June 2006 <www.biographi.ca>.

Burroughs, John. "Real and Sham Natural History." *Atlantic Monthly* March 1903: 298–309.

Cambron, Micheline, and Carole Gerson. "Literary Authorship." Lamonde et al. 119–34.

Campbell, Wanda. "Agnes Maule Machar." Canadian Poetry Press. 24 pages. Accessed 3 October 2006 <www.uwo.ca/english/canadianpoetry/hidden_rooms/agnes_maule_machar.htm>.

"Canadian Literature: An Evening with Canadian Authors." *Globe* 18 Jan. 1892: 5. [Review of Pauline Johnson's performance in Toronto.]

Cardinal, Harold. *The Unjust Society.* Edmonton: Hurtig, 1969.

Cartier, George-Étienne. "I Am Also a French Canadian." *Who Speaks for Canada? Words That Shape a Country.* Ed. Desmond Morton and Morton Weinfeld. Toronto: McClelland, 1998. 36–38.

Choko, Marc H., and David L. Jones. *Posters of the Canadian Pacific.* Richmond Hill, ON: Firefly, 1994.

Colombo, John Robert. *The Penguin Treasury of Popular Canadian Poems and Songs.* Toronto: Penguin, 2002.

Compton Brouwer, Ruth. "Machar, Agnes Maule." *Dictionary of Canadian Biography Online.* Accessed 3 October 2006 <www.biographi.ca>.

"Confederation Day." *Globe* [Toronto] 1 July 1867: 1–9.

Connor, Carl Y. *Archibald Lampman: Canadian Poet of Nature.* Ottawa: Borealis, 1977.

Creighton, Donald. "Confederation and Expansion." *Reappraisals in Canadian History: Post Confederation.* 3rd ed. Ed. C.M. Wallace and R.M. Bray. Scarborough, ON: Prentice Hall, 1999. 3–12.

—. "The First of July, 1867." *The Spirit of Canada.* Ed. Barbara Hehner. Toronto: Stoddart, 1999. 115–16. [From his book, *John A. Macdonald: The Young Politician* (1952).]

Dagg, Melvin H. "Scott and the Indians." Dragland, *Duncan Campbell Scott* 181–92.

Daniells, Roy. "Confederation to the First World War." *Literary History of Canada: Canadian Literature in English.* Ed. Carl F. Klinck. Toronto: U of Toronto P, 1965. 191–207.

Davies, Barrie. "The Alien Mind: A Study of the Poetry of Archibald Lampman." Diss. Univ. of New Brunswick, 1970.

Dawson, Michael. *The Mountie: From Dime Novel to Disney.* Toronto: Between the Lines, 1998.

Dean, Misao, ed. *Early Canadian Short Stories: Short Stories in English Before World War I.* Ottawa: Tecumseh, 2000.

De Brou, Dave, and Bill Waiser, eds. *Documenting Canada: A History of Modern Canada in Documents.* Saskatoon: Fifth House, 1992.

Dewart, Edward Hartley. "Introductory Essay." *Selections from Canadian Poets.* 1864. Literature of Canada Poetry and Prose in Reprint series. Toronto: U of Toronto P, 1973. ix-xix.

Distad, Merrill. "Print and the Settlement of the West." Lamonde et al. 62–71.

Donaldson, Gordon. *The Prime Ministers of Canada.* Toronto: Doubleday, 1994.

Dragland, Stan, ed. *Duncan Campbell Scott: A Book of Criticism.* Ottawa: Tecumseh, 1974.

—. *Floating Voice: Duncan Campbell Scott and the Literature of Treaty 9.* Concord, ON: Anansi, 1994.

Drew, Lois. "Redeeming Riel." 10 pages. Accessed 27 June 2006 <http://www.uwo.ca/english/canadianpoetry/cpjrn/vol31/drew.htm>.

Dudek, Louis. "Crawford's Achievement." *The Crawford Symposium.* Ed. Frank Tierney. Ottawa: U of Ottawa P, 1979. 123–25.

Dunkin, Christopher. "Monday, February 27." *"A Few Acres of Snow": Documents in Canadian History, 1577–1867.* Ed. Thomas Thorner. Peterborough: Broadview, 1997. 438–44.

Farmiloe, Dorothy. *Isabella Valancy Crawford: The Life and the Legends.* Ottawa: Tecumseh, 1983.

Ferens, Dominika. *Edith and Winnifred Eaton: Chinatown Missions and Japanese Romances.* Urbana: U of Illinois P, 2002.

Flanagan, Thomas. *Louis "David" Riel: "Prophet of the New World."* Toronto: U of Toronto P, 1979.

Fowler, Marian. *Redney: A Life of Sara Jeannette Duncan.* Toronto: Anansi, 1983.

Francis, Daniel. *The Imaginary Indian: The Image of the Indian in Canadian Culture.* Vancouver: Arsenal Pulp, 1992.

—. *National Dreams: Myth, Memory, and Canadian History.* Vancouver: Arsenal Pulp, 1997.

Frye, Northrop. "The Narrative Tradition in English-Canadian Poetry." *Canadian Anthology.* 3rd ed. Ed. Carl F. Klinck and Reginald E. Watters. Toronto: Gage, 1974. 603–08.

Galvin, Elizabeth McNeill. *Isabella Valancy Crawford: We Scarcely Knew Her.* Toronto: Natural Heritage, 1994.

Geddes, Gary. "Piper of Many Tunes: Duncan Campbell Scott." *Duncan Campbell Scott: A Book of Criticism.* Ed. Stan Dragland. Ottawa: Tecumseh, 1974. 165–77.

Gerson, Carole, and Kathy Mezei, eds. *The Prose of Life: Sketches from Victorian Canada.* Downsview: ECW Press, 1981.

Goldie, Terry. *Fear and Temptation: The Image of the Indigene in Canadian, Australian, and New Zealand Literatures.* Montreal: McGill-Queen's UP, 1989.

Gray, Charlotte. *Flint & Feather: The Life and Times of E. Pauline Johnson, Tekahionwake.* Toronto: HarperFlamingo, 2002.

Greunding, Dennis, ed. *Great Canadian Speeches.* Markham, ON: Fitzhenry & Whiteside, 2004.

Gustafson, Ralph. "Among the Millet." *Archibald Lampman.* Ed. Michael Gnarowski. Critical Views on Canadian Writers Series. Toronto: Ryerson, 1970. 142–53.

Gwyn, Sandra. *The Private Capital: Ambition and Love in the Age of Macdonald and Laurier.* Toronto: McClelland, 1984.

Haliburton, R.G. "On Northern Culture." *The Search for English-Canadian Literature: An Anthology of Critical Articles from the Nineteenth and Early Twentieth Centuries.* Ed. Carl Ballstadt. Toronto: U of Toronto P, 1975. 154–56.

Hanna, Jonathan, Robert C. Kennell, and Carol Lacourte. *Portraits of Canada: Photographic Treasures of the CPR.* Calgary: Fifth House, 2006.

Hjartarson, Paul. "Print Culture, Ethnicity, and Identity." Lamonde et al. 43–54.

Hobsbawm, Eric, and Terence Ranger, eds. *The Invention of Tradition.* Cambridge: Cambridge UP, 1992.

Horrall, S.W. *The Pictorial History of the Royal Canadian Mounted Police.* Toronto: McGraw-Hill, 1973.

Hou, Charles, and Cynthia Hou. *Great Canadian Political Cartoons, 1820–1914.* Vancouver: Moody's Lookout Press, 1997.

Howe, Joseph. *The Speeches and Public Letters of Joseph Howe.* 2 vols. Ed. Joseph Andrew Chisholm. Halifax: Chronicle, 1909.

—. "Speeches and Letters, 1866." *"A Few Acres of Snow": Documents in Canadian History, 1577–1867.*

Ed. Thomas Thorner. Peterborough: Broadview, 1997. 445–47.

Hurst, Alexandra J. *The War Among the Poets: Issues of Plagiarism and Patronage Among the Confederation Poets.* London: Canadian Poetry Press, 1994.

Hutcheon, Linda. "Self-Inscriptions: Reading the Texts of the Nation." *Témoignages: Reflections on the Humanities.* Ottawa: CFH, 1993. 141–49.

Innis, Harold. *The Fur Trade in Canada: An Introduction to Canadian Economic History.* Fwd. Robin W. Winks. Rev. ed. Toronto: U of Toronto P, 1962.

Johnston, Sheila M.F. *Buckskin & Broadcloth: A Celebration of E. Pauline Johnson— Tekahionwake, 1861–1913.* Toronto: Natural Heritage, 1997.

Jones, David Laurence. *Tales of the CPR.* Calgary: Fifth House, 2002.

Keith, W.J. *Canadian Literature in English.* Rev. ed. 2 vols. Erin, ON: Porcupine's Quill, 2006.

—. *Charles G.D. Roberts.* Toronto: Copp Clark, 1969.

Keller, Betty. *Pauline: A Biography of Pauline Johnson.* Toronto: Douglas and McIntyre, 1981.

Kertzer, Jonathan. *Worrying the Nation: Imagining a National Literature in English Canada.* Toronto: U of Toronto P, 1998.

Klinck, Carl F. *Wilfred Campbell: A Study in Late Provincial Victorianism.* 1942. Ottawa: Tecumseh, 1977.

Lamonde, Yvan, Patricia Lockhart Fleming, and Fiona A. Black, eds. *History of the Book in Canada: Volume II: 1840–1918.* Toronto: U of Toronto P, 2005.

Laurier, Wilfrid. *Wilfrid Laurier on the Platform 1871–1890.* Ed. Ulric Barthe. Quebec: Turcotte & Menard, 1890.

Lighthall, William Douw. Introduction. *Songs of the Great Dominion: Voices from the Forests and Waters, the Settlements and Cities of Canada.* London: Walter Scott, 1889. xxi–xxxvii.

Logan, J.D., and Donald G. French. *Highways of Canadian Literature: A Synoptic Introduction to the Literary History of Canada (English) from 1760 to 1924.* Toronto: McClelland, 1924.

Lutts, Ralph. H., ed. *The Wild Animal Story.* Philadelphia: Temple UP, 1998.

Lynn, Helen, ed. *An Annotated Edition of the Correspondence Between Archibald Lampman and Edward William Thomson (1890–1898).* Ottawa: Tecumseh, 1980.

Mair, Charles. "The New Canada." *Canadian Monthly and National Review* 8 (Aug. 1875): 156–64.

McMullen, Lorraine, and Sandra Campbell, eds. *Aspiring Women: Short Stories by Canadian Women, 1880–1900.* Ottawa: U of Ottawa P, 1993.

McNaught, Kenneth. *The Penguin History of Canada.* Harmondsworth: Penguin, 1988.

Moodie, Susanna. *Roughing It in the Bush; or, Life in Canada.* 1852. Toronto: McClelland, 1989.

—. "Introductory Chapter to the 1871 Edition." *Roughing It in the Bush.* Toronto: McClelland, 1989. 525–34.

Morton, Desmond. *A Short History of Canada.* 3rd rev. ed. Toronto: McClelland, 1997.

—, and Morton Weinfeld, eds. *Who Speaks for Canada? Words That Shape a Country.* Toronto: McClelland, 1998.

New, W.H. *A History of Canadian Literature.* Houndsmills: Macmillan, 1989.

Osborne, Brian S. "The World of Agnes Maule Machar (1837–1927): Social Reform, Nation, Empire, Nature." Kingston Historical Society. 5 pages. Accessed 3 October 2006 <www.heritagekingston.org/wok/machar.html>.

Pacey, Desmond. "The Confederation Era (1867–1897)." *Creative Writing in Canada: A Short History of English-Canadian Literature.* 2nd ed. Toronto: McGraw-Hill Ryerson, 1961. 35–88.

—. *Ten Canadian Poets: A Group of Biographical and Critical Essays.* Toronto: Ryerson, 1958.

Parker, George L. "English-Canadian Publishers and the Struggle for Copyright." Lamonde et al. 148–59.

Ray, Arthur J. *I Have Lived Here Since the World Began: An Illustrated History of Canada's Native People.* Toronto: Key Porter, 1996.

Reaney, James. "Isabella Valancy Crawford." *Our Living Tradition, Second and Third Series.* Ed. Robert L. McDougall. Toronto: U of Toronto P, 1959. 268–88.

—. "Isabella Valancy Crawford, 1850–87." Introduction. *The Collected Poems of Isabella Valancy Crawford.* Toronto: U of Toronto P, 1972. vii–xxxiv.

Robertson, Heather. *Reservations Are for Indians.* Toronto: James Lewis & Samuel, 1970.

Roosevelt, Theodore. "Nature Fakers." *Everybody's Magazine* 17 (Sept. 1907): 427–30.

Ross, Malcolm, ed. *Poets of the Confederation.* Toronto: McClelland, 1960.

The Royal Proclamation, October 7, 1763. Accessed 23 June 2006 <www.colon.org/Constitutions/Canada/English/PreConfederation/rp_1763.html>.

Seton, Ernest Thompson. "Tekahionwake." Introduction. *The Shagganappi.* Toronto: Ryerson, 1913. 7–9.

—. *Wild Animals I Have Known.* 1898. Toronto: NCL, 1977.

Shrive, Norman. Introduction. *Dreamland and Other Poems; Tecumseh: A Drama.* Literature of Canada: Poetry and Prose in Reprint series. Toronto: U of Toronto P, 1974. vii–xxxii.

Smith, A.J.M. Introduction. *The Book of Canadian Poetry: A Critical and Historical Anthology.* Chicago: U of Chicago P, 1943. 3–31.

—, ed. *The Colonial Century: English-Canadian Writing Before Confederation.* Introd. George L. Parker. Ottawa: Tecumseh, 1986.

Smith, Goldwin. *Canada and the Canadian Question.* London: Macmillan, 1891.

—. "What Is the Matter with Canadian Literature?" 1894. *The Search for English-Canadian Literature: An Anthology of Critical Articles from the Nineteenth and Early Twentieth Centuries.* Ed. Carl Ballstadt. Toronto: U of Toronto P, 1975. 85–88.

Stanley, George F.G. "Riel, Louis." *The Canadian Encyclopedia Online.* Accessed 27 June 2006 <www.thecanadianencyclopedia.com>.

Strong-Boag, Veronica, and Carole Gerson. *Paddling Her Own Canoe: The Times and Texts of E. Pauline Johnson (Tekhionwake).* Toronto: U of Toronto P, 2000.

Tausky, Thomas E. *Sara Jeannette Duncan: Novelist of Empire.* Port Credit: P.D. Meany, 1980.

Thomas, Lewis H. "Riel, Louis." *Dictionary of Canadian Biography Online.* Accessed 30 June 2006 <www.biographi.ca>.

Thorner, Thomas, ed. *"A Few Acres of Snow": Documents in Canadian History, 1577–1867.* Peterborough: Broadview, 1997.

"Trial of Louis Riel." *Wikipedia.* 3 pages. Accessed 30 June 2006 <http://en.wikipedia.org/wiki/Trial_of_Louis_Riel>.

"The Trial of Louis Riel: A Chronology." 4 pages. Accessed 27 June 2006 <http://www.law.umkc.edu/faculty/project/ftrials/riel/rielchronology.html.>

Wadland, John Henry. *Ernest Thompson Seton: Man in Nature and the Progressive Era 1880–1915.* New York: Arno, 1978.

Wallace, C.M. and R.M. Bray, eds. *Reappraisals in Canadian History: Post Confederation.* 3rd ed. Scarborough, ON: Prentice Hall, 1999.

Ware, Tracy, ed. *A Northern Romanticism: Poets of the Confederation.* Ottawa: Tecumseh, 2000.

White-Parks, Annette. *Sui Sin Far/Edith Maude Eaton: A Literary Biography.* Urbana: U of Illinois P, 1995.

Winks, Robin W. Foreword. *The Fur Trade in Canada: An Introduction to Canadian Economic History,* by Harold A. Innis. Rev. ed. Toronto: U of Toronto P, 1962. vii–xv.

IV. Turn of the Century

Primary Texts

Deskaheh (Levi General or Hi-wyi-iss). "Last Speech: 10 March 1925." *First People, First Voices.* Ed. Penny Petrone. Toronto: U of Toronto P, 1983. 151–54.

Leacock, Stephen. *Arcadian Adventures with the Idle Rich.* London: John Lane, 1914.

—. *Essays and Literary Studies.* New York: John Lane, 1916.

—. "Greater Canada: An Appeal." *University Magazine* 6 (1907): 132–41.

—. *Sunshine Sketches of a Little Town.* London: John Lane, The Bodley Head, 1912.

—. *Sunshine Sketches of a Little Town.* Ed. Gerald Lynch. Ottawa: Tecumseh, 1996.

—. *Sunshine Sketches of a Little Town.* Ed. Carl Spadoni. Peterborough: Broadview, 2002.

—. "The Woman Question." *Maclean's* Oct. 1915: 7–9.

McClung, Nellie. "The Play." *Purple Springs*. Toronto: Thomas Allen, 1921. 273–80.

—. "Speaking of Women." *Maclean's* May 1916: 25–26, 96–97.

McCrae, John. *In Flanders Fields and Other Poems*. Ed. Sir Andrew MacPhail. Toronto: William Briggs, 1919.

Montgomery, L.M. "The Education of Betty." *Further Chronicles of Avonlea*. Boston: L.C. Page, 1920. 188–215.

Murphy, Emily F. "With the Dukhobors." *Janey Canuck in the West*. 3rd ed. Toronto: Cassell and Company, 1910. Accessed Jan. 2007 <http://digital.library. upenn.edu/women/murphy/west/west. html#XXIV>.

Service, Robert. *Songs of a Sourdough*. Toronto: William Briggs, 1907.

—. *The Spell of the Yukon and Other Verses*. New York: Barse and Hopkins, 1907.

Sifton, Clifford. "The Immigrants Canada Wants." *Maclean's* April 1, 1922: 16, 32–34.

Sime, J.G. "Munitions!" *Sister Woman*. 1919. Ed. Sandra Campbell. Ottawa: Tecumseh, 1992. 35–45.

Secondary Texts

Alberta Online Encyclopedia. "Eugenics in Alberta." Accessed February 2007 <http://www.abheritage. ca/abpolitics/people/influ_eugenics.html>.

Backhouse, Constance. *Colour-Coded: A Legal History of Racism in Canada*. Toronto: U of Toronto P, 1999.

Benham, Mary Lile. *Nellie McClung*. Markham: Fitzhenry & Whiteside, 2000.

Berton, Pierre. *Marching as to War: Canada's Turbulent Years, 1899–1953*. Toronto: Anchor, 2002.

—. *Prisoners of the North*. Toronto: Anchor, 2005.

Bothwell, Robert, Ian Drummond, and John English. *Canada, 1900–1945*. Toronto: U of Toronto P, 1987.

Bothwell, Robert, and J.L. Granatstein. *Our Century: The Canadian Journey in the Twentieth Century*. Toronto: McArthur, 2000.

Brown, Robert Craig, and Ramsay Cook. *Canada 1896–1921: A Nation Transformed*. Canadian Centenary Series 14. Toronto: McClelland, 1974.

Cambron, Micheline, and Carole Gerson. "Literary Authorship." Lamonde et al. 119–34.

Campbell, Wilfred. "10 December 1892." *At the Mermaid Inn: Wilfred Campbell, Archibald Lampman, Duncan Campbell Scott in* The Globe *1892–93*. Ed. Barrie Davies. Toronto: U of Toronto P, 1979. 207–09.

Canadian Heritage. "Ceremonial and Canadian Symbols Promotion." Accessed Feb. 2007 <http://www.pch.gc.ca/progs/cpsc-ccsp/ sc-cs/arm2_e.cfm>.

Carman, Bliss. *Letters*. Ed. H. Pearson Gundy. Montreal: McGill-Queen's UP, 1981.

Coleman, Daniel: *White Civility: The Literary Project of English Canada*. Toronto: U of Toronto P, 2006.

Cook, Ramsay. "The Triumph and Trials of Materialism 1900–1945." *The Illustrated History of Canada*. Ed. Craig Brown. Toronto: Key Porter, 1997. 375–466.

Dart, Ron. "Robert Service: People's Poet." Accessed Feb. 2007 <http://www.vivelecanada.ca/article.php/ 20060403130053273/print>.

Davies, Robertson, ed. *Stephen Leacock*. Canadian Writers 7. Toronto: McClelland, 1970.

Devereux, Cecily. *Growing a Race: Nellie McClung and the Fiction of Eugenic Feminism*. Montreal: McGill-Queen's UP, 2005.

—. "Introduction." *Anne of Green Gables*. Peterborough: Broadview, 2004.

—. "Nellie McClung." *The Literary Encyclopedia*. 25 Nov. 2004. The Literary Dictionary Company. Accessed Feb. 2007 <http://www.litencyc.com/php/ speople.php?rec=tru&UID=3030>.

Diogenes. Review of *Sunshine Sketches of a Little Town*, by Stephen Leacock. *Vancouver Daily Province* 5 Oct. 1912: 6.

Donaldson, Gordon. *The Prime Ministers of Canada*. Toronto: Doubleday, 1994.

Duncan, Sara Jeannette. *The Imperialist*. 1904. Toronto: McClelland, 1990.

Edwards, Owen Dudley, and Jennifer H. Litster. "The End of Canadian Innocence: L.M. Montgomery and the First World War." *L.M. Montgomery and Canadian Culture*. Ed. Irene Gammel and Elizabeth Epperly. Toronto: U of Toronto P, 1999. 31–46.

Explore North. "Robert Service and His Cabin." Accessed Feb. 2007 <http://explorenorth.com/ library/service/bl-servicecabin.htm>.

Fee, Margery, and Leslie Monkman. "Teaching Canadian Literature." *Encyclopedia of Literature in Canada*. Ed. William H. New. Toronto: U of Toronto P, 2002. 1084–89.

Gillen, Mollie. *Lucy Maud Montgomery*. Don Mills: Fitzhenry & Whiteside, 1978.

Grace, Sherrill. *Canada and the Idea of North*. Montreal: McGill-Queen's UP, 2002.

Grekul, Jana, Harvey Krahn, and Dave Odynak. "Sterilizing the 'Feeble-minded': Eugenics in Alberta, Canada, 1929–1972." *Journal of Historical Sociology* 17 (2004): 358–85.

Hodgins, Jack. "Afterword." *Sunshine Sketches of a Little Town*. Toronto: McClelland, 1989. 187–91.

Holmes, Nancy. "'In Flanders Fields'—Canada's Official Poem: Breaking Faith." *Studies in Canadian Literature* 30.1 (2005): 11–33.

Hou, Charles, and Cynthia Hou. *Great Canadian Political Cartoons: 1820–1914*. Vancouver: Moody's Lookout Press, 1997.

Indian and Northern Affairs Canada. "Residential Schools." Accessed May 2007 <http://www. ainc-inac.gc.ca/ch/rcap/sg/cg10_e.pdf>.

James, Donna. *Emily Murphy*. Markham: Fitzhenry & Whiteside, 2001.

Johnston, Hugh. "The Komagata Maru Incident." *Beyond the Komagata Maru: Race Relations Today, Conference Proceedings.* Ed. Alan Dutton. The Progressive Indo-Canadian Community Services Society, 1989. 3–8. Accessed Feb. 2007 <http://sikhpioneers.org/komagata%20maru. htm>.

Kajihara, Yuka. "An Influential Anne in Japan." Accessed Feb. 2007 <http://www.yukazine.com/lmm/e/japanne.html>.

Kerr, Kevin. *Unity (1918).* Vancouver: Talonbooks, 2002.

Keshen, Jeff. "The First World War in Print." Lamonde et al. 352–54.

Kroeker, Amy. "A 'Place' Through Language: Postcolonial Implications of Mennonite/s Writing in Western Canada." *Is Canada Postcolonial: Unsettling Canadian Literature.* Ed. Laura Moss. Waterloo: Wilfrid Laurier UP, 2003. 238–52.

Lamonde, Yvan, Patricia Lockhart Fleming, and Fiona A. Black, eds. *History of the Book in Canada: Volume II: 1840–1918.* Toronto: U of Toronto P, 2005.

Lampman, Archibald. "4 March 1893." *At the Mermaid Inn: Wilfred Campbell, Archibald Lampman, Duncan Campbell Scott in* The Globe *1892–93.* Ed. Barrie Davies. Toronto: U of Toronto P, 1979. 269–70.

Laurier, Wilfrid. *Lecture on Political Liberalism.* Quebec: *Morning Chronicle,* 1877. 1–29.

Leacock, Stephen. "Selected Poetry of Stephen Leacock (1869–1944)." Representative Poetry On-Line. Accessed February 2007 <http://rpo.library.utoronto.ca/poet/198. html>.

Legate, David M. *Stephen Leacock: A Biography.* Toronto: Doubleday, 1970.

Library and Archives of Canada. "Famous Five: The Persons Case, 1927–1929." Accessed Feb. 2007 <http://www.collectionscanada.ca/famous5/053002_e.html>.

—. "Stephen Leacock: Humorist and Educator." Accessed Feb. 2007 <http://www.collectionscanada.ca/3/5/t5-214-e.html>.

Lower, Arthur. "The Mariposa Belle." *Queen's Quarterly* 58 (Summer 1951): 220–27.

Lynch, Gerald. *Stephen Leacock: Humour and Humanity.* Montreal: McGill-Queen's UP, 1988.

MacLeod, Elizabeth. *Lucy Maud Montgomery: A Writer's Life.* Toronto: Kids Can Press, 2001.

MacMechan, Archibald. *Headwaters of Canadian Literature.* 1924. Introd. M.G. Parks. Toronto: NCL, 1974.

Macpherson, Margaret. *Nellie McClung: Voice for the Voiceless.* Montreal: XYZ Publishing, 2003.

Mander, Christine. *Emily Murphy: Rebel.* Toronto: Simon & Pierre, 1985.

Martin, Ann. "Visions of Canadian Modernism." *Canadian Literature* 191 (2004): 43–59.

—. *When Canadian Literature Moved to New York.* Toronto: U of Toronto P, 2005.

Moritz, Albert, and Theresa Moritz. *Stephen Leacock: His Remarkable Life.* Markham: Fitzhenry & Whiteside, 2002.

Morton, Desmond. *A Short History of Canada.* 3rd rev. ed. Toronto: McClelland, 1997.

Mount, Nick. "In Praise of Talking Dogs: The Study and Teaching of Early Canada's Canonless Canon." *Essays in Canadian Writing* 63 (1998): 76–98.

Nelles, H.V. *A Little History of Canada.* Don Mills: Oxford UP, 2004.

Pacey, Desmond. "The Early Twentieth Century (1897–1920)." *Creative Writing in Canada: A Short History of English-Canadian Literature.* 2nd ed. Toronto: McGraw-Hill Ryerson, 1961. 89–118.

—. "The Study of Canadian Literature." *Journal of Canadian Fiction* 2.2 (1973): 67–72.

Parker, George L. "The Evolution of Publishing in Canada." Lamonde et al. 17–32.

Parks Canada. "Dawson Historical Complex National Historical Site of Canada." Accessed Feb. 2007 <http://www.pc.gc.ca/lhn-nhs/yt/dawson/natcul/natcul5_e.asp>.

—. "Green Gables Heritage Site." Accessed Feb. 2007 <http://www.pc.gc.ca/lhn-nhs/pe/greengables/natcul/index_E.asp#PEINP>.

—. "Lucy Maud Montgomery Cavendish National Historic Site." Accessed Feb. 2007 <http://www.pc.gc.ca/lhn-nhs/pe/greengables/natcul/index_E.asp>.

Petrone, Penny. *First People, First Voices.* Toronto: U of Toronto P, 1983.

Review of *Sunshine Sketches of a Little Town.* "Literary Table." *Canadian Magazine* 40.1 (1912): 89–90.

Royal Commission on Aboriginal Peoples. *Report.* Ottawa: The Commission, 1996.

Rubio, Mary, and Elizabeth Waterston, eds. *The Selected Journals of L.M. Montgomery: Volume II: 1910–1921.* Toronto: Oxford UP, 1987.

Ruggenberg, Rob. "The Making of 'In Flanders Fields.'" Accessed Feb. 2007 <http://www.greatwar.nl/frames/default-hahn-english.html>.

Sanders, Byrone Hope. *Emily Murphy: Crusader ("Janey Canuck").* Toronto: Macmillan, 1945.

Sauerwein, Stan. *Lucy Maud Montgomery: The Incredible Life of the Creator of Anne of Green Gables.* Canmore: Altitude Publishing, 2004.

Smiley, Cal. "Novels in English: 1900 to 1920." *The Oxford Companion to Canadian Literature.* 2nd ed. Ed. Eugene Benson and William Toye. Don Mills: Oxford UP, 1997. 815–17.

Staines, David. *Selected Letters of Stephen Leacock.* Toronto: Oxford UP, 2006.

Stephen Leacock Association. "Our Mandate." Accessed Feb. 2007 <http://www.leacock.ca/ASSOCIATION.htm>.

Supreme Court of Canada. "Remarks of the Right Honourable Beverley McLachlin, P.C. Famous Five Breakfast. October 17, 2000." Accessed Feb. 2007 <http://www.scc-csc.gc.ca/aboutcourt/judges/speeches/famousfive_e.asp>.

Tector, Amy. "A Righteous War? L.M. Montgomery's Depiction of the First World War in *Rilla of Ingleside.*" *Canadian Literature* 179 (Winter 2003): 72–86.

Twigg, Alan. "Robert Service." Accessed Feb. 2007 <http://www.abcbookworld.com/?state=view_author&author_id=4285>.

Wallace, C.M., and R.M. Bray. "The Great War." *Reappraisals in Canadian History: Post Confederation.* Ed. C.M. Wallace and R.M. Bray. 3rd ed. Scarborough, ON: Prentice Hall, 1999. 236–37.

Wilson, Ian. "Creating the Future: *Canada and Its Provinces.*" Lamonde et al. 174–77.

Woo, Grace. "Canada's Forgotten Founders: The Modern Significance of the Haudenosaunee (Iroquois) Application for Membership in the League of Nations." *Law, Social Justice & Global Development Journal.* 2003. Accessed Oct. 2007 <http://elj.warwick.ac.uk/global/03-1/woo.html>.

Woodsworth, J.S. *Strangers Within Our Gates or, Coming Canadians.* Toronto: F.C. Stephenson, 1909.

index

Author names appear in **bold**; entries for figures are followed by the letter "*f*."

Grateful acknowledgement is given to the following copyright holders for permission to reproduce material in this text.

Preface

Page xii: Lionel Kearns, "Public Poem for a Manitoulin Island Canada Day," from *Two Poems for a Manitoulin Island*, Vancouver: blewointmentpress, 1976. Reprinted with permission of the author.

Introduction

Page 1: Excerpted from *Our Story: Aboriginal Voices on Canada's Past*. Copyright © 2004 by The Dominion Institute. *"Contributor's Note"* and *"The First Words"* Copyright © 2004 Brian Miracle. Reprinted by permission of Doubleday Canada.

Section I

Page 42: *The Voyages of Jacques Cartier*, ed. Ramsay Cook (University of Toronto Press, 1993). **Page 53:** *The Works of Samuel de Champlain*, Vol. II, trans. John Squair, ed. H.P. Biggar (Toronto: The Champlain Society, 1925). **Page 57:** *The Jesuit Relations and Allied Documents: A Selection*, ed. S.R. Mealing (Ottawa: Carleton University Press, 1990). **Page 59:** *The Jesuit Relations: Natives and Missionaries in Seventeenth-Century North America*, ed. Allan Greer (Boston: Bedford/St Martin's, 2000). **Page 62:** Jean de Brébeuf, "Jesus, He Is Born." Translated by John Steckley © 1984. **Page 64:** *Captain Cartwright and His Labrador Journal*, ed. Charles Wendell Townsend (London: Williams & Norgate, 1911). **Page 73:** Samuel Hearne, *A Journey from Prince of Wales's Fort in Hudson's Bay to the Northern Ocean*, ed. Richard Glover (Toronto: Macmillan, 1958). **Page 84:** *David Thompson's Narrative, 1784–1812*, ed. Richard Glover (Toronto: The Champlain Society, 1962). **Page 92:** *Narrative of a Journey to the Shores of the Polar Sea* (Edmonton: Hurtig, 1969). **Page 104:** Excerpts from *Across Arctic America: Narrative of the Fifth Thule Expedition* by Knud Rasmussen, provided by the University of Alaska Press (1999). **Pages 105, 106:** (1) Hall Collection, Fieldnotes, Book 38 in the Smithsonian Institute, Washington (notes from 1869) and (2) William Gilder, *Schwatka's Search: Sledging in the Arctic in Quest of Franklin Records* (New York: Scribner's, 1881). Excerpted from *Unravelling the Franklin Mystery: Inuit Testimony*, by David C. Woodman (Montreal: McGill-Queen's UP, 1991). **Page 107:**

Available online from Folkinfo at www.folkinfo.org/songs/displaysong.asp?SongID = 119.

Section II

Page 142: Grace Helen Mowat, *The Diverting History of a Loyalist Town*, 2nd ed. (St. Andrews, NB: Charlotte County Cottage Craft, 1937). **Page 148:** Excerpted from Ruth Holmes Whitehead and Carmelita A.M. Robertson, eds., *The Life of Boston King: Black Loyalist, Minister, and Master Carpenter*. (Nimbus Publishing and the Nova Scotia Museum, 2002). **Page 154:** Thomas McCulloch, *Letters of Mephibosheth Stepsure* (Halifax: Blackadar, 1862). **Page 162:** Oliver Goldsmith, *The Rising Village* (London: C. and C. Whittingham, 1825). **Page 176:** Anna Brownell Jameson, *Winter Studies and Summer Rambles* (London: Saunders and Otley, 1838). **Page 188:** Thomas Chandler Haliburton, *The Clockmaker*, Vol. I (London: Richard Bentley, 1839). **Page 196:** Catherine Parr Traill, *The Backwoods of Canada*, ed. Michael A. Peterman (Ottawa: Carleton University Press, 1997). **Page 211:** Susanna Moodie, *Roughing It in the Bush* (London: Richard Bentley, 1852). **Page 228:** *Blackwood's Edinburgh Magazine*, Vol LXXI, January–June 1852 (London: Blackwood, 1852). **Page 229:** Susanna Moodie, *Life in the Clearings Versus the Bush* (New York: De Witt & Davenport, n.d.). **Page 238:** From the *Atlantic Monthly* vol. 3, no. 19 (May 1859). **Page 240:** George Copway, *Life, History and Travels of Kah-ge-ga-gah-bowh* (Philadelphia: James Harmstead, 1847). **Page 246:** Mary Ann Shadd, *A Plea for Emigration Or, Notes on Canada West in its Moral, Social, and Political Aspect: Suggestions Respecting Mexico, W. Indies, and Vancouver's Island for the Information of Coloured Immigrants* (Detroit: George W. Pattison Printing, 1852).

Section III

Page 294: Available online from www.canadahistory.com/sections/documents/bna_act_1-_89.htm. **Page 299:** *The Colonial Century: English-Canadian Writing Before Confederation*, ed. A.J.M. Smith (Tecumseh Press, 1986), 229–239; and *A Book of Canadian Prose and Verse*, ed. Edmund Kemper

Broadus and Eleanor Hammond Broadus (Toronto: Macmillan, 1925), 354–355. **Page 305:** *The Search for English-Canadian Literature*, ed. Carl Ballstadt, Series: Literature of Canada, Poetry and Prose in Reprint (Toronto: University of Toronto Press, 1975), 21–24. **Page 308:** *Rose Belford's Canadian Monthly and National Review*, Vol. II (June 1878), pp. 659–675. **Page 314:** "Quebec to Ontario, A Plea for the Life of Riel, September, 1885." Available online from www.uwo.ca/english/canadianpoetry/hidden_rooms/agnes_maule_machar.htm. **Page 318:** Gerald S. Doyle, *Old-Time songs and Poetry of Newfoundland: Songs of the People from the Days of Our Forefathers*, 2nd edition (1940), p. 69. Available online from www.wtv.zone.com/phyrst/audio/nfld/01/anti.htm. **Pages 321, 324:** Available online from www.collectionscanada.ca/aboriginal/020008–3000.3-e.html. **Page 328:** *After Ypres and Other Verse* (Toronto: Musson, 1917), pp. 3–4. **Page 333:** Desmond Morton, *The Queen v. Louis Riel* (Toronto: University of Toronto Press, 1974). Also available online from www.hpl.hamilton.on.ca/history/riel/hisspeech.htm. **Page 338:** *Documenting Canada*, Dave De Brou and Bill Waiser, eds. (Saskatoon: Fifth House, 1992). **Pages 341, 343, 345:** Isabella Valancy Crawford, *Collected Poems*, Literature of Canada: Poetry and Prose in Reprint (Toronto: U of T Press, 1972). **Pages 348, 349, 350:** *The Poems of Wilfred Campbell* (Toronto: William Briggs, 1905). **Pages 354, 356, 348, 359, 360, 361:** Charles G.D. Roberts, *Selected Poetry and Critical Prose*, ed. W.J. Keith, Literature of Canada: Poetry and Prose in Reprint (Toronto: University of Toronto Press, 1974). **Page 361:** Charles G.D. Roberts, *Selected Poetry and Critical Prose*, ed. W.J. Keith, Literature of Canada: Poetry and Prose in Reprint (Toronto: University of Toronto Press, 1974), pp. 276–281. **Page 363:** Charles G.D. Roberts, *The Kindred of the Wild* (n.p., 1900). **Pages 371, 373, 374:** *The Poems of Bliss Carman*, ed. John Robert Sorfleet (Toronto: McClelland & Stewart, 1976). **Page 377:** Sara Jeannette Duncan, *Selected Journalism*, ed. Thomas E. Tausky (Ottawa: Tecumseh Press, 1978), pp. 38–40. Reprinted with permission of the publisher. **Page 380:** *The Search for English-Canadian Literature: An Anthology of Critical Articles from the Nineteenth and Early Twentieth Centuries*, ed. Carl Ballstadt, Literature of Canada: Poetry and Prose in Reprint (Toronto: University of Toronto Press, 1975), pp. 36–41. **Pages 395, 396, 398, 400, 401:** E. Pauline Johnson, *Collected Poems and Selected Prose*, ed. Carole Gerson and Veronica Strong-Boag (Toronto: University of Toronto Press, 2002). **Page 403:** *Ottawa Daily Free Press*, 21 June 1894.

Page 405: *The Moccasin Maker* (Toronto: William Briggs, 1913). **Pages 414, 416, 417, 419, 420:** *The Poems of Archibald Lampman* (Toronto: Musson, 1900). **Page 420:** *The Essay and Reviews of Archibald Lampman*, ed. D.M.R. Bentley, Post-Confederation Poetry: Texts and Contexts (London, ON: Canadian Poetry Press, 1996), pp. 92–95. **Page 427:** *A Northern Romanticism: Poets of the Confederation*, ed. Tracy Ware (Ottawa: Tecumseh Press, 2000). Reprinted with permission. **Pages 427, 431, 433, 433:** *The Poems of Duncan Campbell Scott* (Toronto: McClelland & Stewart, 1926). **Page 437:** Duncan Campbell Scott, *Addresses, Essays, and Reviews*, ed. Leslie Ritchie, Post-Confederation Poetry: Texts and contexts (London, ON: Canadian Poetry Press, 2000), pp. 82–93. **Page 440:** Duncan Campbell Scott, *The Witching of Elspie: A Book of Stories* (Toronto: McClelland & Stewart, 1923), pp. 112–120. **Page 446:** Sui Sin Far, *Mrs. Spring Fragrance and Other Writings*, ed. Amy Ling and Annette White-Parks (Urbana, IL: University of Illinois Press, 1995), pp. 192–198.

Section IV

Page 475: *Maclean's* (April 1, 1922). **Page 480:** Emily Ferguson, *Janey Canuck in the West* (Toronto: Cassell, 1910). Available online from http://digital.library.upenn.edu/women/murphy/west/west.html#IX. **Page 485:** From *Sister Woman* (1919; reprint, Ottawa: Tecumseh Press, 1992). Reprinted with permission. **Page 493:** Stephen Leacock, *Sunshine Sketches of a Little Town*, ed. Gerald Lynch (Ottawa: Tecumseh Press, 1996). **Page 507:** *University Magazine*, Vol. 6 (1907), pp. 132–141. **Page 510:** *Maclean's* (October 1915), pp. 7–9. **Page 516:** John McCrae, *In Flanders Fields and Other Poems*, ed. Sir Andrew Macphail (Toronto: William Briggs, 1919). **Page 516:** John McCrae, *In Flanders Fields and Other Poems*, ed. Sir Andrew Macphail (Toronto: William Briggs, 1919). **Page 519:** From Penny Petrone, *First People, First Voices* (Toronto: University of Toronto Press, 1983). **Page 524:** Nellie McClung, *Purple Springs* (Toronto: Thomas Allen, 1921), pp. 273–289. **Page 533:** *Maclean's* (May 1916). **Page 539:** "The Education of Betty" from *Further Chronicles of Avonlea*, by L.M. Montgomery, is reprinted with the permission of the heirs of L.M. Montgomery. *L.M. Montgomery* is a trademark of Heirs of L.M. Montgomery, Inc. **Page 552:** Robert W. Service, *The Spell of the Yukon and Other Verses* (New York: Barse & Hopkins, 1907), pp. 62–68.